Ken Jennings's Trivia Almanac

KEN JENNINGS'S
TRIVIA ALMANAC

8,888
QUESTIONS
in
365
DAYS

VILLARD BOOKS
NEW YORK

To Mindy and Wikipedia,

who are both nearly always right

———

Published in the United States by Villard Books, an imprint of The Random House Publishing Group, a division of Random House, Inc., New York.

Villard and "V" Circled Design are registered trademarks of Random House, Inc.

LIBRARY OF CONGRESS CATALOGING-IN-PUBLICATION DATA
Jennings, Ken.
Ken Jennings's trivia almanac: 8,888 questions in 365 days / Ken Jennings.
p. cm.
ISBN 978-0-345-49997-4
1. Questions and answers.   I. Title.   II. Title: Trivia almanac.
GV1507.Q50J445 2007   030—dc22   2007032197

Printed in the United States of America on acid-free paper

www.villard.com

8 9

Book design by Simon M. Sullivan

Introduction

It seemed like it was going to be so easy.

I spent most of 2005 submerged in the world of trivia nuts, writing my book *Brainiac*. I was (and still am) writing a weekly "Tuesday Trivia" e-mail quiz for visitors to my website. As a result, I was seeing trivia everywhere I looked. While driving by the Olive Garden restaurant by the mall: hmm, the Olive Garden logo is a fruit that's not an olive. While looking at a fistful of change at the grocery store: hmm, two different state quarters have George Washington on their "tails" side as well as on the "heads." While my wife was in labor: hmm, childbirth contractions are measured in units named for the capital of Uruguay. "Um, sorry, honey, my mind was elsewhere. Go ahead and push now."

I needed to get all this trivia out of my system, cleanse myself of all the clutter. The book you now hold in your hands would, I thought, be my trivia enema. (In fact, *Ken Jennings's Trivia Enema* was its original working title, before wiser heads prevailed.)

I pictured a 365-day trivia almanac, stuffed to the gills with odd historical facts from every day of the year, each tied to a related trivia quiz. What could be easier, in a world packed with exotic little factoids? It would be like gaily skipping through an alpine meadow, picking whatever wildflowers of trivia happened to catch my eye. A fact here, a question there, and pretty soon I'd have a book, right?

As it turned out, a better title for the book might have been *Ken Jennings's Trivia Aversion Therapy*. Math was never my strong suit in school, but it turns out that twenty or thirty trivia questions for each day of the calendar year runs to about nine thousand questions in total.

Nine *thousand*. That's two whole boxes of Trivial Pursuit. That's most of a season of *Jeopardy!* As far as I can tell, this is the biggest single assembly of trivia questions ever published in this country, in *any* form. And writing nine thousand trivia questions comes with challenges beyond mere volume, it turns out. In case you have professional curiosity, or just want to feel my pain (*Ken Jennings's Trivia Pity Party!*) here are a few of the difficulties inherent in writing an über-trivia book of this scale.

OVER EASY OR HARD-BOILED? My favorite trivia questions aren't simple fact retrieval. They involve a little bit of *work*—forehead furrowing, lip chewing, tossing the question around with friends and family—before the sudden flash of insight that produces the answer. "Who's the only U.S. president with a four-syllable surname?" is probably not the kind of question you can answer off the top of your head, but it's not annoyingly esoteric either. But a book of nine thousand brain-straining questions like that might be, well, a little exhausting. So I've sprinkled in some of the easy, quick-response kind of questions ("What country's national carrier is Qantas Airways?") as well as—I'll admit—a few maddeningly abstruse ones that just happen to have interesting answers ("Dolbear's Law relates air temperature to the speed of what?"). So don't flip to the answer section too quickly—given a moment's thought, you may surprise yourself with how much you actually know.

THE GENERATION GAP. A 15-year-old trivia buff and a 65-year-old trivia buff are going to have different ideas of what pop culture and what once-current events constitute fair game for quizzing. To someone of exactly the right age, the sentence "Bill Laimbeer played one of the Sleestaks on *Land of the Lost*" will elicit a smile of happy recognition. To anyone else, it will only elicit a puzzled "Bill Laim-who played one of the what-staks on *Land of the* what now?" I've tried to avoid the hopeless minutiae of *any* generation, even—as tempting as it seemed—my own Gen-X childhood. But rest assured that, no matter what your age, you'll probably feel too old for some of the questions herein and too young for others.

EQUAL TIME. Quiz show and board game questions are produced by staffs of dozens of diverse writers, but this book all poured out of one head: mine. So I'm terrified that the questions will reflect my own personal preferences and prejudices. Are there too few NASCAR questions? Too much breakfast cereal? What if there's twice as much Beatles as Elvis or more *CSI: NY* than *CSI: Miami*? What if there are two questions on the Sino-Japanese War and only one on the Russo-Japanese War? Aaaargh!

HAKUNA ERRATA. Finally, there's accuracy. I've been over this book with a fine-toothed comb, and so have many other trivia gurus of my acquaintance, but I know from experience that we couldn't have caught every possible error in a book this size. Trivia is an odd field: the very best finds are the odd and nearly unbelievable facts, and those are also the ones most likely to have been misreported or exaggerated or, sometimes, simply made up. Also, times change—this book may have been current when I finished it in the summer of 2007, but I can't vouch for all its facts if you're reading it in some remainder bin of the far-flung future of 2009 or beyond. If you spot goofs or have other comments or questions, drop me a line via Ken-Jennings.com so we can fix 'em in any future editions.

I hope you enjoy this endlessly overstuffed clown car of trivia (*Ken Jennings's Trivia Clown Car?*). Trivia, I've always thought, has the wonderful side effect of making knowledge seem fun, or even sexy. It can bring back fond memories, or spark new interests, or inspire marvel at the wonderful strangeness of the world around us. Maybe some of the facts in the nine-thousand-odd questions that follow will do something like that for you. But even if these quizzes just provide a momentary rainy day diversion—well, there's nothing trivial about that, either.

You know, I just searched the manuscript one final time for the letters "TK" (a publishing-speak placeholder abbreviation for "To Come") and immediately got back a great list of legitimate trivia answers with the letters "tk" in them: Dick Butkus, OutKast, Kamchatka, the Atkins Diet, Latka Gravas. And my first thought, even after eight grueling months of question writing, was, "Wow, what a great idea for a quiz! I wonder if I can squeeze it in somewhere."

So much for getting the trivia jones out of my system. Maybe there's still more TK.

JANUARY 1

• **1953** • J. D. SALINGER MOVES to remote Cornish, New Hampshire, and is, for the most part, never seen again. Once asked what his initials stood for, Salinger said, "Juvenile delinquent."

THE APPELLATION TRAIL
Name these famous folks, whose initials should link up into a nice chain for you.

1. What running back won the biggest landslide in Heisman voting history, beating Leroy Keyes of Purdue by 1,750 points?
2. What then-struggling English teacher did Portuguese TV journalist Jorge Arantes divorce in 1993?
3. What Canadian singer appeared on the first cover of *Entertainment Weekly*?
4. Who got his beloved New

Mexico ranch in exchange for the original manuscript of his novel *Sons and Lovers*?
5. Who set most of his most famous book in the year A.D. 802,701?
6. Who was already Gilda Radner's ex-husband when he was hired as bandleader at *Saturday Night Live* in 1985?
7. Who collaborated with James Thurber on *Is Sex Necessary?* be-

fore turning to more family-friendly books?
8. Who replaced John Paxson as Chicago Bulls point guard and was later replaced *by* him as the Bulls' general manager?
9. What playwright's friendship with Sylvia Llewelyn-Davies's family inspired a 2004 movie?
10. Who has performed marriages for both Corey Feldman and Vince Neil?

• **1993** • CZECHOSLOVAKIA IS NO MORE, dividing peacefully—and syllabically!—into the Czech Republic and Slovakia. Any other countries with long, tongue-twisting names want to help us out by doing the same? I'm looking at you, Trinidad and Tobago.

DIVISION DAY

1. What book is divided into 114 chapters called "suras"?
2. What process is divided into four parts: prophase, metaphase, anaphase, and telophase?
3. What are divided by Botts' dots?
4. What nation is divided into twenty-six cantons, each of which was an independent state until 1848?
5. What is divided into the duodenum, the jejunum, and the ileum?
6. What movie is divided into chapters bearing title cards that

include "The Gold Watch" and "The Bonnie Situation"?
7. The Carboniferous period, 300 million years ago, is divided into two epochs with the names of U.S. states. What two states?
8. What had Adams, Norris, Patrick, and Smythe divisions prior to 1993?
9. What nation is divided in two by the Cook Strait?
10. What incendiary novel is divided into three sections: "The Hearth and the Salamander," "The Sieve and the Sand," and "Burning Bright"?

11. What kind of sporting event is divided into chukkas?
12. What line of latitude was chosen as the boundary between North and South Korea after World War II?
13. What "hip-hopera" did R. Kelly divide into twenty-two serialized chapters?
14. Excepting Alaska and Louisiana, what U.S. state is divided into the fewest counties, with only three?
15. Into how many numbered sections is a dartboard divided?

Answers to the questions on this page can be found on page 35.

JANUARY 2

• **1834** • LOUIS DOBERMANN, the tax collector and dog pound owner (there's a popular guy!) for whom the pinscher will be named, is born in Germany.

BREEDER'S DIGEST

1. For his tenacity, nineteenth-century biologist Thomas Huxley was nicknamed whose "bull-dog"?
2. Ironically, German shepherds now do the rescue work at what historic Alpine hospice?
3. What detective would have made his eighth appearance in Raymond Chandler's unfinished novel *Poodle Springs*?
4. Who has coached the UConn Huskies to two national titles and an undefeated Final Four record?
5. On what PBS TV show did the Bloodhound Gang solve mysteries?
6. What two U.S. states border Mexico's largest state, Chihuahua?
7. What 1995 album did Billy Corgan describe as "*The Wall* for Generation X"?
8. What nation was forced to sign the Boxer Protocol in 1901?
9. The name of what nineteenth-century parson and avid hunter is still remembered today thanks to his beloved pet terrier Trump?
10. Where did the *Beagle 2* crash and disappear on Christmas Day 2003?

• **1928** • STUCK IN A SLOW news week and still embarrassed to have left Charles Lindbergh off their cover following his famous transatlantic flight, the editors of *Time* institute an ad hoc "Man of the Year" award, awarding the first one to Lindy.

MAJOR ISSUES

1. In 1989, what fifty-nine-year-old became *People*'s oldest Sexiest Man Alive ever?
2. Who's the only two-time *Sports Illustrated* Sportsman of the Year, so named in 1996 and 2000?
3. What magazine gives out the "Golden Calipers" to its Car of the Year winner?
4. Who beat out FDR and Gandhi (eat it, Gandhi!) to be named *Time*'s Person of the Century in 1999?
5. Who's the only *Playboy* Playmate of the Year also to make the cover of *Rolling Stone*?

• **1961** • CALTECH STUDENTS PERFORM one of history's greatest pranks, on national TV at the Rose Bowl. By infiltrating the Washington cheer squad, the pranksters sabotage a routine in which giant images were to be displayed on thousands of flip cards held by the crowd. The word "CALTECH" replaces "WASHINGTON," and UW's Husky mascot was replaced by the Caltech beaver.

DAMMED IF I KNOW
Five questions for eager beavers.

1. What city's Summer Olympics had the beaver Amik as their mascot?
2. In *Airplane!*, Barbara "June Cleaver" Billingsley proves to be fluent in what language?
3. The *Dartmouth*, the *Eleanor*, and the *Beaver* were the three ships on which what famous event from American history occurred?
4. What's the only college football team whose home stadium is larger than Penn State's Beaver Stadium?
5. The beaver is North America's largest rodent. What South American animal is the *world's* largest?

Answers to the questions on this page can be found on page 35.

• **1496** • LEONARDO DA VINCI tests a flying machine of his own invention, an "ornithopter" with flapping batlike wings, but the idea fails to get off the ground.

AVIA-TRICKS

1. Which two U.S. states salute the Wright brothers on their license plates?

2. What modern-day conglomerate built the Zero fighter planes used to bomb Pearl Harbor?

3. In what city did Charles Lindbergh take his first piloting job, flying the mail?

4. What event inspired Herbert Morrison's famous quote "Oh, the humanity!"?

5. What record-breaking pilot discovered the jet stream in his plane the *Winnie Mae*?

• **1863** • POLITICAL CARTOONIST Thomas Nast publishes his first illustration of Santa Claus in the pages of *Harper's Weekly*. Our popular image of Santa today springs directly from Nast's work.

HO HO HO

1. What branch of the Armed Forces first popularized the phrase "gung ho"?

2. HO scale is the world's most popular size of what?

3. What Devon town, named for a

Charles Kingsley novel, is the only place in Britain that ends with an exclamation point?

4. What song about a glass of wine is Don Ho's signature tune?

5. What do Mary Ann Nichols,

Annie Chapman, Liz Stride, Catherine Eddowes, and Mary Jane Kelly have in common?

• **1988** • MARGARET THATCHER becomes the longest-ruling British prime minister of the twentieth century, surpassing Herbert Asquith.

WOMAN ON TOP
What nation's only female leader has been . . .

Easy
1. Golda Meir
2. Indira Gandhi
3. Angela Merkel
4. Isabel Perón

Harder
1. Violeta Chamorro
2. Tansu Çiller
3. Kim Campbell
4. Benazir Bhutto

Yeah, Good Luck
1. Michelle Bachelet
2. Yulia Tymoshenko
3. Chandrika Kumaratunga
4. Portia Simpson-Miller

Answers to the questions on this page can be found on page 35.

JANUARY 4

• **1903** • CONEY ISLAND has decided to execute a violent elephant named Topsy, so Thomas Edison volunteers to electrocute Topsy with 6,600 volts of alternating current—part of his ongoing campaign to discredit AC in favor of his own system, direct current. This incident is the source of Edison's famous maxim "Genius is one percent inspiration, ninety-two percent perspiration, and seven percent execution of elephants."

TRUNK CALLS

1. Who called his elephant "Tantor"?

2. Which chess piece was originally called "the elephant"?

3. What late-breaking news story kicked Dumbo off the cover of *Time* magazine six weeks after the elephant cartoon's release?

4. Surus ("the Syrian"), who had a broken tusk, was the standout among whose elephants?

5. Who is worshiped by Ganapatya Hindus as the supreme god?

6. What's the only land mammal taller than the elephant?

7. What 1979 hit was the first song featuring a marching band ever to make the *Billboard* Top Ten?

8. Who produced the movie *The Elephant Man*, casting his wife in a lead role and hiring director David Lynch, but insisted on going without screen credit to avoid confusing audiences?

9. What White Stripes hit, off their album *Elephant*, is titled after singer Jack White's childhood name for a well-known religious organization?

10. Who married his own cousin Celeste in an elaborate 1931 ceremony?

11. Of the three substances that make up your teeth—enamel, dentin, and pulp—which is elephant ivory made of?

12. What word comes to us from the Greek for "thick-skinned"?

13. Which SEC college football team uses an elephant as its mascot?

14. What two Republicans are the only U.S. presidents ever to serve a full eight years as vice president as well?

15. What country's highest decoration is the Most Exalted Order of the White Elephant?

• **2004** • THE MARS ROVER *Spirit* lands on the red planet's Gusev crater and begins taking the highest-resolution pictures ever taken on any planet but this one.

THAT'S THE SPIRIT!
In what movie do these actors play ghosts?

Easy	*Harder*	*Yeah, Good Luck*
1. Bruce Willis	**1.** Rex Harrison	**1.** Jake Busey
2. Alec Baldwin	**2.** Alan Rickman	**2.** Charles Laughton
3. Nicole Kidman	**3.** Carol Kane	**3.** Paul Scofield
4. Cary Grant	**4.** Daveigh Chase	**4.** Vincent Schiavelli
5. Ray Liotta	**5.** Michelle Pfeiffer	**5.** Ian McShane

Answers to the questions on this page can be found on page 36.

• 1945 • Pepé Le Pew makes his screen debut in the short "Odor-able Kitty," in which Pepé is actually a married American skunk *pretending* to be French so he can seduce a cross-dressing male cat. ("Odor-able Kitty" is obviously ripe for rediscovery by Queer Studies majors.)

COMMON SCENTS

1. What molecule is named for the Greek word for "smell," because of the odor associated with lightning storms?

2. What band's album *Smell the Glove* was released with an all-black cover because Polymer Records and retailers balked at the misogynistic original cover?

3. What port's name comes from the Cantonese for "fragrant harbor"?

4. What TV character's trademark song was "Smelly Cat"?

5. Peanut butter, coffee, or roses—according to a Yale study, what's the number one most recognized smell among American adults?

6. Joseph Pujol, the French entertainer known as "Le Pétomane," built a whole stage act out of his virtuosity doing what?

7. What foursome—two people, an insect, and a Freudian construct—ask to be entertained in Nirvana's "Smells Like Teen Spirit"?

8. Who is Martha talking about when she tells Jesus, "Lord, by this time he stinketh," in John 11?

9. What animal's intestine secretes ambergris, a strong-smelling, waxy gunk used in making perfume?

10. Young wines are said to have "aroma." What do older wines have instead?

11. J. J. Hunsecker, Burt Lancaster's unscrupulous character in *Sweet Smell of Success*, is a thinly veiled caricature of whom?

12. As mystery fans know, cyanide is often said to have the bitter aroma of what?

13. The title tale in the best-selling children's book *The Stinky Cheese Man* is an updating of what classic story?

14. What product did Herbert Lapidus invent in 1974 by impregnating latex rubber with coconut charcoal?

15. In *Apocalypse Now*, Robert Duvall says he loves "the smell of napalm in the morning" because it smells like what?

• 1995 • America finally learns Kramer's first name, when the *Seinfeld* character's estranged mother calls him "Cosmo" for the first time.

FIRST-NAME BASIS

If its title used last names instead of first names, what movie/TV show/literary work would be called . . .

Easy
1. *Montague and Capulet*
2. *Truman & Adler*
3. *DeFazio & Feeney*
4. *Parker and Barrow*

Harder
1. *Jones 'n' Brown*
2. *Sanders & Sanders & Henderson & Henderson*
3. *Dickinson and Sawyer*
4. *Finklestein & Montgomery*

Yeah, Good Luck
1. *Shanowski & Fairfield*
2. *Hopkins and Leplastrier*
3. *Chasen and Chardin*
4. *McCardle & Lowell*

Answers to the questions on this page can be found on page 36.

• **1831** • THE NAME OF CLEAVELAND, Ohio, permanently loses the first *a* when the first issue of the *Cleveland Advertiser* shortens the city's name so it'll fit on the paper's masthead.

MISPELLINGS

1. What Margate City, New Jersey, housing area has been misspelled on the Monopoly board for almost eighty years?

2. What proper name is spelled, unusually, with a single *n* both on the Liberty Bell and in the U.S. Constitution?

3. In what 1986 film does Brian Cox portray "Hannibal Lecktor" (*sic*)?

4. Whose ~~first~~ second album was meant to be titled for the Mexican expression *Órale*, before a misspelling intervened?

5. In the Bible, whose daughter-in-law Orpah is the source for Oprah Winfrey's misspelled name?

6. What extra letter did Dan Quayle add to the word "potato" when he misspelled it in 1992?

7. Where is Jacques Plante's name misspelled five of the six times it appears?

8. What nation's dyslexic king Carl XVI Gustaf misspelled his own name on the accession document that gave him the throne?

9. What Washington Wizards All-Star still bears the misplaced *w* in his name from a birth certificate typo?

10. According to his best seller, what word inspired Chris Gardner when he saw it misspelled in a Bay Area day care center in 1981?

• **1896** • FRANCE'S PIONEERING MOVIEMAKING TEAM, the Lumière brothers, show their fifty-second silent film *Arrival of a Train at La Ciotat* to a Paris audience for the first time. According to legend, those in the audience panic and jump from their seats when they see the image of an enormous train barreling toward the camera.

SCREEN DEBUTS
Can you match up these film firsts?

1. *Pippa Passes* (1909)
2. *Inspiration* (1915)
3. *Wings* (1927)
4. *Lights of New York* (1928)
5. *It Happened One Night* (1934)
6. *Becky Sharp* (1935)
7. *Topper* (1937)
8. *Bringing Up Baby* (1938)
9. *Bwana Devil* (1952)
10. *The Robe* (1953)
11. *By Love Possessed* (1961)
12. *Ulysses* (1967)
13. *The Learning Tree* (1969)
14. *A Clockwork Orange* (1971)
15. *Sometimes a Great Notion* (1971)
16. *Westworld* (1973)
17. *Bound for Glory* (1976)
18. *Heaven's Gate* (1980)
19. *Red Dawn* (1984)
20. *Lost in Yonkers* (1993)

A. First use of Steadicam
B. First scheduled in-flight movie
C. First American film nudity
D. First all-sound film
E. First studio film with a black director
F. First film in CinemaScope
G. First "director's cut"
H. First three-strip Technicolor
I. First film shown on HBO
J. First use of the infamous "f-word"
K. First Best Picture Oscar
L. First film edited digitally, via Avid
M. First *New York Times* movie review
N. First computer graphics
O. First film with Dolby sound
P. First PG-13-rated film
Q. First film of the 3-D boom
R. First use of "gay" as slang term
S. First film to sweep the five major Oscars
T. First classic film to be "colorized"

Answers to the questions on this page can be found on page 36.

• **1797** • THE SHORT-LIVED Cispadane Republic makes the red, white, and green *Tricolore* its official flag. Today, it's the national flag of Italy. If not for the brave Cispadanes, who knows what Olive Garden restaurants would look like today?

THE ITALIAN JOB

1. What style of pants is named for an island in the Gulf of Naples?
2. What craftsman used willow, spruce, and maple woods to make the "Christian Hammer," which sold at auction for a record $3.5 million in 2006?
3. What Sergio Leone "spaghetti western" is a remake of Kurosawa's *Yojimbo*?
4. Who was the first Italian American to serve on the Supreme Court?
5. For what famous son is Genoa's airport named?

• **1927** • THE HARLEM GLOBETROTTERS play their very first game, taking on the Hinckley (Illinois) Merchants. As some Hinckley fans remember it, the Globetrotters (then the Giles Post American Legion) actually lost that first game, 43–34.

UNDERDOG DAYS

1. What 42-to-1 underdog KO'd Mike Tyson in Tokyo in 1990?
2. Who started the Colts' Super Bowl III loss to the Jets, while Johnny Unitas sat on the sidelines?
3. Whom did unknown golfer Jack Fleck beat in an 18-hole playoff to win the 1955 U.S. Open?
4. What nation did the U.S. hockey team beat in the finals of its improbable gold medal run at Lake Placid?
5. What was the first expansion team to win a World Series?
6. What was the appropriate name of the only horse ever to beat Man o' War?
7. In 1982, what tiny Hawaii Division II school somehow beat Ralph Sampson's number one Virginia Cavaliers?
8. What nation defeated mighty Brazil in the "Maracanazo" to win the 1950 World Cup?
9. What coach famously ran up and down the sidelines in disbelief after his team edged Houston in the 1983 NCAA Finals?
10. Who lost a toe to frostbite in 2002, two years after stealing a gold medal from undefeated Russian wrestler Alexander Karelin?

• **1955** • SPENCER TRACY'S CLASSIC FILM *Bad Day at Black Rock* premieres. It's the first MGM movie to be made in CinemaScope.

GOOD DAY FOR BLACK ROCK

1. In what city would you find the famous black stone called the al-Hajar-ul-Aswad?
2. What black stone is the most common volcanic rock on Earth?
3. What two words begin the title of every episode of Chris Rock's CW sitcom?
4. In what state could you visit the Black Rock Desert?
5. Anthracite and bituminous are two types of what mineral?

Answers to the questions on this page can be found on page 37.

JANUARY 8

• **1958** • JUST FOURTEEN YEARS OLD, Bobby Fischer becomes the youngest U.S. chess champion in history.

BABY GENIUSES

1. What thirteen-year-old's 1963 hit "Fingertips" was the first live recording ever to top the pop charts?

2. What Cthulhu creator was a child prodigy who recited poetry at age two and composed a verse retelling of the *Odyssey* at seven?

3. What city's famous Mozart-platz memorial was donated by Mad King Ludwig of Bavaria, a big fan of the composer?

4. *Star Trek*'s Wesley Crusher was given the name "Wesley" because it was whose real-life middle name?

5. What discoverer of quarks entered Yale at the age of fifteen?

6. What founder of Utilitarianism could read Latin and Greek at age five and went to Oxford at twelve?

7. What artist's first word as a baby was *lápiz*, meaning "pencil"?

8. Who won an Oscar for portraying musical prodigy David Helfgott?

9. What was Doogie Howser, M.D.'s real first name?

10. What thirteen-year-old became the youngest player ever to qualify for an LPGA event in 2002?

• **1982** • MA BELL BREAKS UP, as the final settlement of a Justice Department antitrust lawsuit ends AT&T's telephone monopoly.

THE NUMBER YOU HAVE DIALED

1. What was, famously, the phone number of New York City's Hotel Pennsylvania?

2. 011, 112, or 999—what's the European Union equivalent of our 911 emergency number?

3. What city requested area code 865, spelling "VOL," when it was split off from area code 423?

4. Why have owners of the phone number 776-2323 received hundreds of phone calls from people wanting to talk to God?

5. In Tommy Tutone's song, who lives at "867-5309"?

• **1999** • DISNEY ANNOUNCES A RECALL of the videotape of its kiddie cartoon *The Rescuers*, having belatedly discovered that some nameless prankster had inserted a picture of a topless woman in the background of two frames during the movie's 1977 production.

SEX CELS
In which Disney cartoon is the title character's love interest named . . .

Easy	Harder	Yeah, Good Luck
1. Jasmine	1. Prince Erik	1. Megara
2. John Smith	2. Captain Li	2. Faline
3. Esmeralda	3. Nala	3. Prince Philip

Answers to the questions on this page can be found on page 37.

• 1912 • TWO THOUSAND MARINES invade Honduras to protect "U.S. economic interests" during a local revolt. I can just picture President Taft standing on a battleship in front of a "Mission Accomplished" banner, chomping on a recently liberated banana.

IT TAKES A STEADY HAND TO PLAY OPERATION!
What countries were invaded in these carefully named U.S. operations?

1. Operation Enduring Freedom
2. Operation Just Cause
3. Operation Restore Hope
4. Operation Uphold Democracy
5. Operation Urgent Fury

A. Afghanistan
B. Grenada
C. Haiti
D. Panama
E. Somalia

• 1929 • THE SEEING EYE, America's first guide dog school, is founded in Nashville.

EYES CAPADES
Keep an eye out for the answers to these ocular questions.

1. Deuteranopia, or Daltonism, is one of the most common varieties of what condition?
2. What TV actor recorded an album of pop standards appropriately titled *Ol' Yellow Eyes Is Back*?
3. What media company's logo is a black dog whose left eye is a five-pointed star?
4. What website began with a 1989 Usenet post called "Those Eyes," listing actresses with beautiful eyes?
5. What boxer's eye injuries led to his retirements in 1982, 1984, 1987, and 1991?
6. In what Edgar Allan Poe story does an old man's oddly clouded eye lead to murder?
7. What battle in American history was the origin of the famous quote "Don't fire until you see the whites of their eyes"?
8. What part of the eye changes shape in LASIK surgery?
9. What author's Jamaican estate was called Goldeneye?
10. How many "fab" makeover artists hosted Bravo's *Queer Eye for the Straight Guy*?

• 1956 • THE FIRST "DEAR ABBY" column appears in the *San Francisco Chronicle*.

THE "DEAR" HUNTER

1. What movie is narrated by Jack Nicholson's "Dear Ndugu" letters to a Tanzanian boy he's sponsoring?
2. What nation refers to its current dictator as "Dear Leader"?
3. What well-known children's author finally won a Newbery Medal in 1984 for *Dear Mr. Henshaw*?
4. The Beatles' "Dear Prudence" is named for the sister of what actress, who didn't enjoy her stay in Rishikesh, India?
5. What ominous signature first appeared at the bottom of the "Dear Boss" letter of September 25, 1888?

Answers to the questions on this page can be found on page 37.

• **1947** • *FINIAN'S RAINBOW* opens on Broadway. Its signature tune, "How Are Things in Glocca Morra?," refers to a nonexistent village in Ireland. In fact, "Glocca Morra" isn't even real Gaelic.

A LITTLE TOWN IN THE MOUTH
Fill in the missing cities from these Broadway tunes.

1. From *42nd Street*: "Shuffle Off to _____"

2. From *Hairspray*: "Good Morning _____"

3. From *Gentlemen Prefer Blondes*: "A Little Girl from _____"

4. From *Kiss Me, Kate*: "We Open in _____"

5. From *Jesus Christ Superstar*: "Poor _____"

• **1949** • LINDA SUSAN BOREMAN is born in the Bronx. In 1972, under the name "Linda Lovelace," she will star in the hugely successful *Deep Throat;* in 1980, she'll become a leading antiporn advocate.

LOVE LACE?

1. What's the word for the small plastic tag at the end of a shoelace?

2. What president does the nutty middle brother in *Arsenic and Old Lace* believe himself to be?

3. What suburb of Paris produced the silk lace later made famous by the Big Bopper?

4. In America, the lacy plant that Europeans call wild carrot is given the name of what monarch?

5. What owner-bartender of Chicago's Lone Star Saloon was famous for his drug-laced drinks?

• **2000** • AOL ANNOUNCES a $162 billion deal to buy Time Warner, the biggest corporate merger in history. Does the A in AOL stand for "albatross"?

ORIGINAL SYNERGY
Can you match up these now-merged companies from the post-1990 acquisition mania?

1. Boeing

2. BP

3. Chevron

4. Citicorp

5. Hewlett-Packard

6. J.P. Morgan Chase

7. NBC

8. SBC

9. Verizon

10. Viacom

A. Amoco

B. AT&T

C. Bank One

D. Compaq

E. McDonnell Douglas

F. MCI

G. Paramount

H. Texaco

I. Travelers Group

J. Vivendi

Answers to the questions on this page can be found on page 38.

• **1862** • THE CITY OF WALLA WALLA, Washington, is incorporated. The local low-sulfur soil is what gives the city's namesake onions their famous sweet flavor.

TRIVIA TRIVIA
Give the doubled-up answers answers to these questions questions.

1. On what R.E.M. debut album would you find their song "Radio Free Europe"?

2. What semolina product is used to make the Moroccan dessert *seffa*?

3. What transmits African trypanosomiasis to humans and cattle?

4. What Shirley MacLaine movie did Khrushchev call "depraved" and "pornographic" when he visited the set in 1960?

5. What narrator of a 1955 novel marries Charlotte Haze for ulterior motives?

6. What 1963 song led to a thirty-one-month FBI investigation into supposed obscenities hidden in its unintelligible lyrics?

7. What 1950s Kikuyu uprising helped end British rule in Kenya?

8. What fictional foreign film often referenced on *Seinfeld* describes "a young girl's strange, erotic journey from Milan to Minsk"?

9. What name is given to the dolphin fish to make it sound more appetizing on menus?

10. Which *Flintstones* character apparently possessed superhuman strength as a toddler but never as an adult?

11. What territorial capital is located beneath Mount Alava on the island of Tutuila?

12. What is believed to have received its name from the Portuguese word for "simpleton"?

13. What band recorded the only James Bond theme song to become a *Billboard* number one?

14. For evidentiary reasons, who sued to prevent the demolition of

L.A.'s Ambassador Hotel in 2004?

15. For what film did Robert De Niro learn to play the saxophone?

16. What would you use to "Walk the Dog," "Rock the Baby," or "Pop the Clutch"?

17. What Jim Carrey movie featured the screen debut of Cheri Oteri?

18. What Black Forest town was called "Aurelia Aquensis" by the Romans?

19. What Alban Berg opera is based on the same play as the classic Louise Brooks movie *Pandora's Box*?

20. What term does rapper B.G. say he wishes he'd patented when he used it for the title of his massive 1999 hit?

• **1971** • JOURNALIST DON HOEFLER coins the phrase "Silicon Valley" in an article for *Electronic News*. Hoefler's "Valley" was the Santa Clara Valley, but today the term is used for much of the east side of the San Francisco peninsula.

NO MAN IS AN ISLAND
Name the peninsula located between . . .

1. Chesapeake Bay and the Atlantic Ocean

2. The Sea of Okhotsk and the Bering Sea

3. Lake Superior and Lake Michigan

4. The Bay of Campeche and the Caribbean Sea

5. The Sea of Azov and the Black Sea

Answers to the questions on this page can be found on page 38.

JANUARY 12

• **1963** • "Blowin' in the Wind," by a not-yet-famous Bob Dylan, is broadcast for the first time, on a BBC TV drama (*The Madhouse on Castle Street*), of all places.

JUST FOLK

1. According to "Michael, Row the Boat Ashore," where is Michael rowing?
2. Who cowrote both "Where Have All the Flowers Gone?" and "If I Had a Hammer"?

3. Who was famously named for a Joni Mitchell song covered by Judy Collins in 1969?
4. The title of the song "Kumbaya" is actually a distortion of what three-word phrase?

5. What actress is the daughter of the Scottish singer Donovan?

• **1967** • Retired doctor James Bedford becomes the first person ever to be cryonically frozen, in the hope of being revived one day when science has discovered a cure for (a) cancer and (b) being seventy-three and (c) being crudely frozen in liquid nitrogen for decades.

MANY ARE COLD, BUT FEW ARE FROZEN
Are you cool enough for this icy quiz?

1. At what chilly temperature are the Celsius and Fahrenheit scales the same?
2. What's the name of the "saber-toothed squirrel" voiced by the director in *Ice Age*?
3. What was the first food ever frozen by Clarence Birdseye, the inventor of frozen food?
4. What son of Italian immigrants received a 1953 patent for his invention, the "Model A Ice Resurfacer"?
5. With what metal band did Ice-T record the controversial "Cop Killer"?
6. What English word comes from the name of a hot spring in Iceland's Haukadalur valley?
7. What holiday is the setting for the novel and film *The Ice Storm*?
8. What is frozen to make dry ice?
9. In 1988, who became the only male figure skater ever to appear on the cover of *Sports Illustrated*?
10. What 1942–43 battle took the greatest toll in military history, with more than 1.5 million casualties due to wounds, starvation, and freezing temperatures?

• **1968** • The last episode of Patrick McGoohan's spy TV hit *Danger Man* (*Secret Agent* in the United States) airs. The show's final season lasted only two episodes, because McGoohan had resigned to create his own show: the cult hit *The Prisoner*.

THEY SPY
Match each TV operative with his or her fictional (and acronymic) employer.

1. Jack Bauer
2. Sydney Bristow
3. Jim Phelps
4. Maxwell Smart
5. Napoleon Solo

A. CONTROL
B. CTU
C. IMF
D. SD-6
E. U.N.C.L.E.

Answers to the questions on this page can be found on page 38.

• **1920** • IN A SCATHING EDITORIAL, *The New York Times* scoffs that rockets will never go to space, since they would "need to have something better than a vacuum against which to react." The day after *Apollo 11*'s 1969 launch, the *Times* will finally publish a retraction: "It is now definitely established that a rocket can function in a vacuum as well as in an atmosphere. The *Times* regrets the error."

ACTUALLY, IT *IS* ROCKET SCIENCE

1. The space shuttle's engines run on what two supercooled liquids?

2. The U.S.'s first successful ICBM was what rocket named for a Titan of Greek myth, later used to launch John Glenn into orbit?

3. Most of Robert Goddard's pioneering rocketry research took place at what western city, now associated with a different kind of spacecraft?

4. Between 1944 and 1945, almost 1,400 of what rockets fell on London?

5. What term for a rocket's propulsive force is calculated by multiplying its exhaust velocity by the burn rate of its fuel?

• **1962** • CHUBBY CHECKER'S "THE TWIST" hits number one in its second run up the charts—it had already been a number one hit in 1960. It's still the only song ever to top the Hot 100 twice.

COVER TO COVER
Nine other songs have hit number one in two different versions. Name the two-time number one sung by both . . .

1. Shocking Blue and Bananarama

2. Little Eva and Grand Funk

3. The Jackson 5 and Mariah Carey

4. Bill Withers and Club Nouveau

5. Steve Lawrence and Donny Osmond

6. LaBelle and Christina Aguilera, Lil' Kim, Mya, & Pink

7. Percy Sledge and Michael Bolton

8. The Marvelettes and the

Carpenters

9. The Supremes and Kim Wilde

10. Bonus Question: The first two times this happened, the same songwriting team was responsible. Who were they?

• **1992** • MIA FARROW DISCOVERS six nude photographs of her daughter Soon-Yi on the mantelpiece of her longtime companion, Woody Allen. Needless to say, this abruptly ends their decade-long, twelve-film collaboration.

WE ARE NOT A MUSE
Who both directed and married these actresses?

Easy
1. Linda Hamilton
2. Kate Capshaw
3. Emma Thompson
4. Judy Garland
5. Joanne Woodward

Harder
1. Frances McDormand
2. Ingrid Bergman
3. Brigitte Bardot
4. Madonna
5. Geena Davis

Yeah, Good Luck
1. Giulietta Masina
2. Arsinée Khanjian
3. Anna Karina
4. Gena Rowlands
5. Nancy Allen

Answers to the questions on this page can be found on page 39.

JANUARY 14

• **1129** • AT THE COUNCIL OF TROYES, the Catholic Church officially endorses the Knights Templar.

SURELY TEMPLES

1. Who is worshiped in the "Temple of Doom" discovered by Indiana Jones?

2. The Khmer words for "city temple" give what building its name?

3. Anciently, what was the job description of a "hierodule"?

4. Stone Temple Pilots' name was inspired by what Clorox brand's logo?

5. Who founded the "Peoples Temple" in 1955?

6. What wonder of the ancient world was destroyed by arson the same night that Alexander the Great was born?

7. What planet is home to the Jedi Temple?

8. In what city could you see the Seagull Monument at Temple Square?

9. What 1992 TV revival featured a duck wearing a Temple University sweatshirt?

10. What Islamic shrine is today built on Jerusalem's Temple Mount?

• **1939** • THE TYRONE POWER WESTERN *Jesse James* opens in New York. A scene in which a horse is forced to leap to its death from the top of a cliff leads to public outrage and eventually the American Humane Association's "No animals were harmed" disclaimer.

CREATURE FEATURES
What kind of animal is the title character of these movies?

Easy	*Harder*	*Yeah, Good Luck*
1. *Babe*	**1.** *Bringing Up Baby*	**1.** *Paulie*
2. *My Friend Flicka*	**2.** *The Yearling*	**2.** *Dunston Checks In*
3. *Finding Nemo*	**3.** *Oliver & Company*	**3.** *Andre*
4. *Mighty Joe Young*	**4.** *Ben*	**4.** *Them!*

• **1951** • THE NFL HOLDS its very first Pro Bowl, and the American Conference wins dramatically in a tight game, 28–27—probably the first and last time anyone cared about the Pro Bowl.

ALL STARSTRUCK

1. Who's the all-time leading scorer in NHL All-Star Game history, with ~~25~~ points in ~~18 eleven~~ games?

2. What team had seven of the eight starters on the 1957 National League All-Star team, thanks to ballot stuffing?

3. What Suns forward beat out Dr. J, Dominique, and Clyde Drexler to win the NBA's first Slam Dunk Contest?

4. What college football contest is fought between the Kai and Aina squads?

5. At just twenty-one, who became the youngest MVP in NBA All-Star Game history?

Answers to the questions on this page can be found on page 39.

• **1870** • THOMAS NAST CREATES a lasting symbol when he depicts the Democratic Party as a donkey in "A Live Jackass Kicking a Dead Lion" for *Harper's Weekly*.

COVERING YOUR ASS

1. In what play does a character appropriately named Bottom get an ass's head?

2. What movie ends by introducing a litter of five "dronkeys"?

3. What holy day celebrates Jesus's entry into Jerusalem on the back of a donkey?

4. What is a female donkey called?

5. In what "Kounty" were the antics on *Hee Haw* set?

• **1919** • IN BOSTON, A TWO-MILLION-GALLON TANK explodes without warning, causing the Great Molasses Flood. Buildings are leveled and twenty-one people killed by a thirty-foot wall of delicious goo.

SUGAR SUGAR
A trivia quiz that should satisfy your sweet tooth.

1. Whose unusual first name is derived from an Italian musical term for "with sweetness"?

2. What is Charlie's last name in Roald Dahl's *Charlie and the Chocolate Factory*?

3. What stadium hosted college football's Sugar Bowl from 1975 to 2005?

4. What Hershey's candy is so named because the original manufacturing process couldn't produce the perfectly round candies the company wanted?

5. At what infamous concert did the Rolling Stones first play their eventual number one hit "Brown Sugar"?

6. Strawberry, lemon, or banana—until a World War II shortage caused a change to vanilla, what was the original flavor of the cream in Twinkies?

7. What organ produces insulin and glucagon, the hormones that regulate blood sugar?

8. What is "the sweet science," according to A. J. Liebling, who popularized the term?

9. What's the name of the head elf in charge of baking Keebler cookies?

10. What classic Disney song was inspired by lyricist Robert Sherman's five-year-old son receiving the Sabin polio vaccine at school?

• **1986** • HBO AND CINEMAX begin scrambling their programming. Millions of dish owners either buy a decoder or learn to recognize nudity in doubled purply-green form.

SCRAMBLED TV
Rearrange these phrases to spell out appropriate TV show titles.

Easy
1. Slow elimination—what a bore
2. A pioneer hut: heroes till it
3. City life
4. Oho! Must jest!
5. No, a mighty bad NFL tool

Harder
1. Next-day ethics
2. Do-re-mi can ail
3. We are devious she-pets
4. Cue holy agent band
5. Plot norm: emaciated sex

Yeah, Good Luck
1. Agony mastery
2. Pathetic preen
3. My rent: so cheap
4. Sphere intro
5. Lean girls chase

Answers to the questions on this page can be found on page 39.

JANUARY 16

• **1895** • A CACHE OF BURIED WEAPONS is discovered in the gardens of Queen Liliuokalani's palace in Hawaii, and though she denies any involvement in the attempted coup, she is forced to abdicate and placed under house arrest for years. According to her own account, it is during her imprisonment that she writes the famous song "Aloha Oe."

ON HER MAJESTY'S SERVICE
Prove you're trivia royalty with this queenly quiz.

1. In 1893, who became the first woman ever to appear on a U.S. postage stamp?
2. What famous wax sculptor made the death mask of Marie Antoinette?
3. Ten of the sixteen countries of which Queen Elizabeth II is head of state are found in what continent?
4. Who are Frederick Dannay and Manfred B. Lee?
5. What is a young bee fed to ensure that it develops into a queen?
6. Who is the only Zanzibari in the Rock and Roll Hall of Fame?
7. What lagoon south of Queens, New York, is named for a local Indian tribe and has nothing to do with the Caribbean?
8. In 1973, who left her husband, producer Robert Evans, to marry her costar Steve McQueen?
9. What fictional character married his wife, Queen Aleta of the Misty Isles, during the sack of Rome in A.D. 450?
10. Currently, only the queens of Spain and Belgium and the grand duchess of Luxembourg hold the privilege of wearing white when they visit whom?

• **1938** • BENNY GOODMAN BRINGS JAZZ to Carnegie Hall, in what is now considered the most important single concert in jazz history. The performance also produces *The Famous 1938 Carnegie Hall Jazz Concert,* the music industry's first-ever double LP.

NEVER HEAR THE END OF IT
What artists were responsible for these double albums?

Easy
1. *Electric Ladyland*
2. *Exile on Main Street*
3. *Back to Basics*
4. *Bitches Brew*
5. *Sign 'o' the Times*

Harder
1. *The Fragile*
2. *Wheels of Fire*
3. *Self Portrait*
4. *In Your Honor*
5. *The Lamb Lies Down on Broadway*

Yeah, Good Luck
1. *Being There*
2. *Daydream Nation*
3. *English Settlement*
4. *Tinsel Town Rebellion*
5. *Tales from Topographic Oceans*

• **1972** • DAVID SEVILLE, creator of the Chipmunks, dies in Beverly Hills. "Seville" is really Ross Bagdasarian, an Armenian-American songwriter from Fresno.

A SHOT IN THE ARM(ENIAN)

1. What Michigan pathologist invented the Thanatron and the Mercitron?
2. What placekicker's famous "gaffe" kept Miami from shutting out the Redskins in Super Bowl VII?
3. Who spoke his native Armenian, not Kazakh, while playing Azamat in the *Borat* film?
4. What *Law & Order: CI* regular wrote and starred in the play *Talk Radio*?
5. Who defeated Tom Bradley twice in California gubernatorial elections?

Answers to the questions on this page can be found on page 40.

• **1912** • ROBERT SCOTT'S EXPEDITION reaches the South Pole, only to find that Roald Amundsen has beaten them there by more than a month. Scott's entire party dies of frostbite and hunger on its return trip.

SONGS OF THE SOUTH

1. What's the Latin name for the atmospheric glow also called the "southern lights"?
2. What's Cartman's first name on *South Park*?
3. At what nation does Panama "attach" onto South America?
4. What's the dominant fruit flavoring in Southern Comfort?
5. According to the trivia chestnut, the first foreign country you'll hit traveling due south from Detroit is . . . Canada. What Canadian city sits just across the Detroit River?
6. What TV family lived at Southfork Ranch?
7. In 2002, the NFL created the AFC and NFC South divisions. Which of their eight teams actually plays its home games to the north of two of its "North" division counterparts?
8. What style of "Dirty South" hip-hop was pioneered by Atlanta rapper Lil Jon?
9. From 1968 on, what group used the so-called Southern strategy?
10. What's the most populous city in the Southern Hemisphere?

• **1921** • DIRECTOR ROBERT FLAHERTY and Nanook, his Inuit leading man, leave Port Harrison, Quebec, to film the big bear hunt scene for Flaherty's pioneering documentary *Nanook of the North*. Flaherty actually took liberties with facts that would make Michael Moore blush—"Nanook"'s real name was Allakariallak, and he usually hunted with a gun, not the primitive spear that Flaherty insisted on.

DOC HOLLYWOOD
How much do you know about other classic documentaries?

1. What 1994 documentary focused on Chicago high school students William Gates and Arthur Agee?
2. What legendary director-to-be was one of the editors of 1970's *Woodstock*?
3. All the numbers in the titles of Michael Apted's *Up* documentary series are multiples of what number?
4. What's the only title shared by an Oscar-nominated Best Picture and an Oscar-nominated Best Documentary Feature?
5. The 1991 doc *Hearts of Darkness* follows what movie's chaotic production?

• **1950** • ELEVEN MEN VANISH with $2 million in Boston's Great Brink's Robbery, at the time the biggest robbery in U.S. history.

HEIST HEIST BABY

1. What famous 1963 heist was masterminded by Bruce Reynolds, author of *The Autobiography of a Thief*?
2. Pablo Picasso was one of the suspects questioned when what item was stolen in Paris in 1911?
3. What is the Jules Rimet Trophy, which was stolen in England in 1966?
4. What Amish country village in Pennsylvania, where *Witness* was filmed, is a frequent victim of street-sign theft?
5. What literary pickpocket's real name is Jack Dawkins?

Answers to the questions on this page can be found on page 40.

• 1788 • THE FIRST SHEEP ARRIVE in Australia, brought from South Africa with the British First Fleet. Today there are 120 million sheep in Australia, six for every human.

BY HOOK OR BY CROOK
For that many sheep you'll need a few shepherds.

1. What traditionally tops the meat in shepherd's pie?

2. What did "Kristin Shepard" do on March 21, 1980, that sealed her TV fame?

3. What are German shepherds called in Great Britain, due to lingering anti-German sentiment following World War II?

4. What actress has lived with playwright Sam Shepard for more than twenty-five years?

5. Where will I "fear no evil," according to Psalm 23, the "Shepherd Psalm"?

6. What entrepreneur did Cybill Shepherd portray in 2003 and 2005 TV movies?

7. What explorer wrote the famous reply poem to Christopher Marlowe's 1599 poem "The Passionate Shepherd to His Love"?

8. Alan Shepard was scheduled to command the ill-fated *Apollo 13* before switching missions with what astronaut?

9. *The Good Shepherd*, about the founding of the CIA, was only the second movie ever directed by what legendary actor?

10. "Shepherd moons" in the solar system, such as Prometheus and Pandora, are so called because they help shape what?

• 1943 • THE U.S. DEPARTMENT OF AGRICULTURE bans the sale of sliced bread, so that the metal in commercial bread slicers can be used in war munitions.

THE GREATEST THING SINCE . . .

1. Why did *The Greatest American Hero*'s name hurriedly change to "Ralph Hanley" in 1981?

2. In what city was Cassius Clay born in 1942?

3. Who appropriately spelled their 2005 greatest hits collection *Greatest Hitz*?

4. Max von Sydow, Donald Pleasance, and Telly Savalas—three stars of *The Greatest Story Ever Told*—all went on to play what screen role?

5. Almost since its 1961 inception, what has humbly billed itself as "The World's Greatest Comic Magazine"?

• 1952 • CURLY WILL NYUK NO MORE, dying after a series of strokes and a long illness. His brother Shemp Howard has already replaced him, reluctantly rejoining the Three Stooges.

TRIO BRAVO
Give the missing last member in these famous threesomes.

Easy
1. Emerson, Lake, and . . .
2. Athos, Porthos, and . . .
3. Executive, legislative, and . . .
4. Kukla, Fran, and . . .
5. Alvin, Simon, and . . .

Harder
1. Brahma, Vishnu, and . . .
2. Liberté, égalité, . . .
3. Cyan, magenta, and . . .
4. Wynken, Blynken, and . . .
5. Gaspar, Melchior, and . . .

Yeah, Good Luck
1. Clotho, Lachesis, and . . .
2. Luciano Pavarotti, Placido Domingo, and . . .
3. Duty, honor, and . . .
4. Triassic, Jurassic, and . . .
5. *The Bad News Bears, Breaking Training*, and . . .

Answers to the questions on this page can be found on page 40.

• **1935** • Coopers Inc. of Chicago first sells a new men's undergarment it calls the "Jockey." Tighty-whities are born.

A BRIEF QUIZ

1. What song is playing during Tom Cruise's iconic underwear dance in *Risky Business*?

2. The *Captain Underpants* books take place at Jerome Horwitz Elementary School. Jerome Horwitz is the real name of what comedian?

3. What was Bill Clinton's answer to the infamous underwear question seventeen-year-old Laetita Thompson asked him at a 1994 "Rock the Vote" event?

4. According to the 1980s slogan, what was "underwear that's fun to wear"?

5. Where is the "Naked Cowboy," an underwear-clad guitarist, famous for playing?

• **1949** • For the first time, an unnamed black-clad man leaves three red roses and a half-empty bottle of cognac on Edgar Allan Poe's grave. The mysterious annual tradition continues today.

PETAL PUSHERS
Everything's coming up roses in this quiz.

1. What actor founded the Purple Rose Theater Company in his native Michigan?

2. What year's Rose Bowl was moved from Pasadena to Durham, North Carolina?

3. What mythical Guns N' Roses album has been repeatedly delayed since 2002?

4. What real-life blind librarian was the basis for Jorge of Burgos, the blind librarian in Umberto Eco's *The Name of the Rose*?

5. What English dynasty collapsed into the Wars of the Roses?

6. The fruit of the rose plant shares its name with what part of the body?

7. After being eliminated in the last rose ceremony of ABC's first season of *The Bachelor*, who was brought back as the first *Bachelorette*?

8. What Oscar-winning Best Picture is named for a type of rose?

9. What two words appear in the original recording of "Candle in the Wind" where "England's rose" appear in the 1997 version?

10. Who receives 554 red roses on the first Saturday of every May?

• **1977** • Snow falls in Miami, for the first and only time in the city's recorded history.

SNOW WONDER

1. How many "dendrites," or arms, does a typical snowflake have?

2. Why was Ross Rebagliati temporarily stripped of his snowboarding gold at the 1998 Olympics?

3. "White Christmas" playing on Armed Forces Radio was the secret signal for what April 30, 1975, event?

4. What chain introduced "the Blizzard" in 1985?

5. What mountain pass is today named for the Illinois farmer whose family was trapped there in an 1846 snowstorm?

Answers to the questions on this page can be found on page 41.

JANUARY 20

• **1945** • LITERARY CRITIC EDMUND WILSON demolishes the Agatha Christie genre in his now-classic *New Yorker* essay "Who Cares Who Killed Roger Ackroyd?"

MURDER MOST FOUL
Do you care who killed these literary characters?

Easy	*Harder*	*Yeah, Good Luck*
1. Polonius	1. Cock Robin	1. Jay Gatsby
2. Albus Dumbledore	2. Clare Quilty	2. Fyodor Karamazov
3. Captain Ahab	3. Uncle Tom	3. Lennie Small
4. Grendel	4. Laius	4. Elizabeth Lavenza
5. Aslan	5. Richard Cory	5. Vladimir Lensky

• **1964** • BABETTE MARCH, giggling in the Cozumel surf in a demure white two-piece, becomes the first-ever *Sports Illustrated* swimsuit issue cover girl.

WATER COLORS
What color were the iconic swimsuits worn by . . .

1. Halle Berry, in *Die Another Day*	**A.** Blue
2. Borat	**B.** Green
3. Phoebe Cates, in *Fast Times at Ridgemont High*	**C.** Orange
4. The Coppertone girl, in the original ad	**D.** Pink
5. Bo Derek, in *10*	**E.** Red
6. Betty Grable, in her World War II pinup	**F.** White
7. Cheryl Tiegs, in the ubiquitous 1978 poster	**G.** Yellow

• **1982** • THINKING THAT A FAN has thrown a rubber toy bat onto the stage at a Des Moines concert, Ozzy Osbourne gamely bites off its head. Unfortunately it is (er, was) a *real* bat, and Ozzy is rushed to the hospital for rabies shots.

DO THE BATUSI

1. What publication introduced Bat Boy in June 1992?
2. Most of Transylvania is now part of what modern-day country?
3. *Anoura fistulata*, a bat recently discovered in Ecuador, is the only mammal to have what body part measuring almost twice the animal's total length?
4. What city is home to the Big Bat, a 120-foot-tall steel replica of Babe Ruth's baseball bat?
5. The Whalers, the Sabres, or the Nordiques—what team's Jim Lorentz killed a bat with his hockey stick during the infamous "Fog Game" of the 1975 Stanley Cup finals?

Answers to the questions on this page can be found on page 41.

• **1814** • Jane Austen begins work on the first chapter of *Emma*, the last novel she'll see published during her lifetime. And no wonder it ended her career—it's, like, a *total* rip-off of *Clueless*.

IN THE BEGINNING
What novels begin with these first chapters?

Easy
1. "The Three Presents of D'Artagnan the Elder"
2. "The Bite of the Raptor"
3. "Marley's Ghost"
4. "Spade & Archer"
5. "The Sound of the Shell"

Harder
1. "progris report 1 march 5, 1965"
2. "The Master of the Universe"
3. "Jonathan Harker's Journal"
4. "The Old Pyncheon Family"
5. "January: An Exceptionally Bad Start"

Yeah, Good Luck
1. "The Bertolini"
2. "Orleanna Price"
3. "The Last to See Them Alive"
4. "Not Dick Clark"
5. "In which the foot of the abbey is reached, and William demonstrates his great acumen"

• **1908** • New York City passes the Sullivan Ordinance, making it illegal for women to smoke in public.

YOU'VE COME A LONG WAY, BABY!
Answer these questions about women who died of lung cancer.

1. What 1980s icon married her second husband, contractor Roe Messner, in 1993?
2. What playwright inspired her lover Dashiell Hammett's character Nora Charles?
3. What sitcom lost both Selma Diamond and her replacement, Florence Halop, to lung cancer?
4. H. L. Mencken coined the word "ecdysiast" to describe whose famous stage act?
5. Who won two Emmys for *Lou Grant* before HBO returned her to stardom in 1999?

• **1997** • Colonel Tom Parker, Elvis Presley's longtime manager, dies in Las Vegas. "Parker" was actually the Dutch-born Andreas Cornelius van Kuijk, and he wasn't a real colonel . . .

A COLONEL OF TRUTH
. . . unlike these colonels.

1. What colonel commanded the first African-American army regiment during the Civil War?
2. What actor and former *SNL* cast member voiced the "hip" animated Colonel Sanders in recent KFC commercials?
3. What longtime world leader has retained the rank of colonel rather than promoting himself—to demonstrate, he says, the rule of the people in his country?
4. What did Colonel Potter typically call Father Mulcahy on *M*A*S*H*?
5. What 1957 film made the "Colonel Bogey March" famous?

Answers to the questions on this page can be found on page 41.

JANUARY 22

• **1253** • HENRY III GRANTS the Yorkshire town of Scarborough a charter for a yearly trading fair that will eventually become famous in song.

ARE YOU GOING TO SCARBOROUGH FAIR?

1. Parsley. What's made from beets, carrots, celery, lettuce, parsley, spinach, tomatoes, and watercress?
2. Sage. What editor of *The American Mercury* was called "the Sage of Baltimore"?
3. Rosemary. What A-list movie star was a pallbearer at his aunt Rosemary's 2002 funeral?
4. *Time.* Who's the only U.S. president since World War II never to have been named *Time*'s Man of the Year?

• **1897** • FORMER CIVIL WAR GENERAL James Shields begins his term as a Missouri senator. This is remarkable because he has already represented both Illinois and Minnesota in the Senate, making him the only senator ever to represent three states.

ACTS TO GRIND
Match these congressmen to the issue addressed by their famous namesake "Act."

1. Sonny Bono
2. Henry Dawes
3. Phil Gramm, Warren Rudman, Ernest Hollings
4. James Robert Mann
5. George Pendleton
6. Paul Sarbanes, Michael Oxley
7. John Sherman
8. Reed Smoot, W. C. Hawley
9. Robert Taft, Fred A. Hartley
10. Andrew Volstead

A. Accounting reform
B. Balanced federal budget
C. Civil service
D. Copyright extension
E. Indian land
F. Labor unions
G. Prohibition
H. Tariffs
I. Trusts
J. "White slavery"

• **2007** • CONOCOPHILLIPS TELLS *The Wall Street Journal* that, in response to a grassroots Internet campaign, it will *not* be destroying the orange "76" balls on Unocal gas stations after all but will instead donate the iconic signage to museums.

FILL 'ER UP

1. What mythological creature was the longtime mascot of Mobil gas?
2. Who opened his first restaurant in the front room of his Corbin, Kentucky, service station in 1930?
3. After his death, who was hung upside down from an Esso filling station in Milan's Piazzale Loreto?
4. What baseball team was the "Gashouse Gang"?
5. Whose estate was disputed in the "Mormon will" belonging to Utah gas station operator Melvin Dummar?
6. Whose 1957 killing spree began with the murder of Lincoln, Nebraska, gas station attendant Robert Colvert?
7. Who was Mayberry's gas station attendant until he got his own sitcom in 1964?
8. Name one of the two U.S. states in which it's illegal to pump your own gas.
9. According to the four experts on women in the movie *Say Anything*, why *are* they hanging out alone at the Gas 'n Sip on a Saturday night?
10. In 2006, 7-Eleven ended its twenty-year association with Citgo, in part, it claimed, because of the comments of what world leader?

Answers to the questions on this page can be found on page 42.

• **1960** • THE BATHYSCAPHE *Trieste* reaches the bottom of the Mariana Trench, the lowest point on the sea floor. A specially made Rolex Oyster watch, strapped to the outside of the craft, survives the descent and keeps perfect time.

WRIST-Y BUSINESS

How much time do you need for these questions about watches?

1. What Briton was honored by a 1994 50 pence coin depicting a pair of running legs and a stopwatch?
2. What does the protagonist of "The Gift of the Magi" sell to buy a watch fob?
3. 007 has been wearing a Swatch since 1995, when what upscale Swatch brand became the official wristwatch of the James Bond films?
4. What two chemical elements make up the mineral quartz?
5. What movie begins with actress Elise McKenna giving playwright Richard Collier an old pocket watch?

• **1979** • PLUTO MOVES INSIDE the orbit of planet Neptune, meaning that, for the next twenty years, Neptune and not Pluto is the outermost planet of the solar system. Of course, now that Pluto's been demoted to "trans-Neptunian loser object," the whole point is moot.

AN OUTSIDE CHANCE

This is trivia that just grazes the surface of things.

1. The "pinna" is the outer, visible part of what?
2. What former president coined the phrase "lunatic fringe" to refer to the wackos in his own reform movement?
3. What philosophical belief, from the Latin for "only the self," holds that the external world doesn't exist at all?
4. What skyscraper's exterior ornaments include radiator caps on the thirty-first floor and hood-ornament eagles on the sixty-first floor?
5. The "Mohorovicic discontinuity" divides what two outer layers of the earth?
6. What paint color was actually *un*available on the first Model Ts, though it became the only color used from 1914 to 1926?
7. Who wears an alb and a chasuble over his street clothes?
8. According to the popular 1970s ad jingle, what are "ooey, gooey, rich and chewy inside, tender flaky golden cakey outside"?
9. What is the easternmost point of the Outer Banks?
10. What would you find between the scute-covered carapace and the plastron?

• **1991** • To CELEBRATE ITS FORMAT CHANGE to classic rock, an Albuquerque FM station plays Led Zeppelin's "Stairway to Heaven" for twenty-four straight hours, leading to a deluge of listener complaints and even a police call.

STAIR MASTERY

1. In what non-Spanish-speaking world city would you find the Spanish Steps?
2. Jefferson Davis was sworn in as Confederate president on the steps of what city's state capitol?
3. A bronze statue of whom stands at the foot of the steps to the Philadelphia Art Museum?
4. What state is home to the Grand Staircase–Escalante National Monument?
5. As unveiled by the Department of Agriculture in 2005, what now has eight vertical divisions and a figure climbing stairs on the left-hand side?

Answers to the questions on this page can be found on page 42.

JANUARY 24

• **1908** • The first installment of the first Boy Scout handbook, *Scouting for Boys*, is published by Robert Baden-Powell, an ex-soldier fascinated with molding young boys into a paramilitary organization. Isn't it nice when old people have hobbies?

A SCOUT IS . . .

1. Who was known to his Meccan customers as "al-Amin," "the **trustworthy** one"?

2. Whose posthumous album *Loyal to the Game* was produced by Eminem?

3. What's the pen name of Kiah Michelle Cruse, who inherited her mother's **helpful** household hints column in 1977?

4. What "Good Little Witch" is Casper the **Friendly** Ghost's friend?

5. What city at the intersection of I-5 and I-84 is home to America's most **courteous** drivers, according to a 2007 study?

6. What food does Richard Dreyfuss use to sculpt Devils Tower, Wyoming, in *Close Encounters of the Third Kind*?

7. What were the surprisingly **obedient** subjects asked to do in Stanley Milgram's famous 1961 experiments on authority?

8. What inspirational poem of 1927 ends, "Be **cheerful.** Strive to be happy"?

9. Dollar, Budget, or Enterprise—**Thrifty** Car Rental merged with what other discount car rental agency in 1990?

10. What Hall of Famer is the only person to play as a **Brave** in Boston, Milwaukee, and Atlanta?

11. Who was president when Congress passed the first **Clean** Air Act?

12. Who complained that his most famous book had been given the "more **reverent**" title *A Cynic's Word Book* by his publisher?

• **1984** • The first Apple Macintosh goes on sale. (Justin Long, the "I'm a Mac" guy, is six years old.)

CORE SAMPLES
What fruits come in these varieties?

Easy	Harder	Yeah, Good Luck
1. Bartlett and Bosc	1. Muscat and scuppernong	1. Eureka and Meyer
2. Bing and Rainier	2. Key and kaffir	2. Redchief and Earliglow
3. Navel and blood	3. Hass and Florida	3. Redhaven and Harmony
4. Beefsteak and Roma	4. Damson and Mirabelle	4. Chubby Gray and Jubilee

• **2006** • Hilary Duff and Haylie Duff share a Worst Actress "Razzie" nomination, making them the first non-Olsen sisters to be so honored.

ANY MORE LIKE YOU AT HOME? WILL THEY STAY THERE?
Name the even less talented younger sister of these celebrities.

1. Lindsay Lohan
2. Paris Hilton
3. Britney Spears
4. Jessica Simpson
5. Kylie Minogue

Answers to the questions on this page can be found on page 42.

• **1077** • Holy Roman Emperor Henry IV travels to Canossa, Italy, hoping to persuade Pope Gregory VII to lift his excommunication. Gregory famously snubs His Highness, leaving him stewing in the snow outside the castle gates for *three full days*.

COLD SHOULDERS
Do you remember these infamous snubs?

1. Which core *Flintstones* cast member was absent from Flintstone vitamins until 1996?
2. Alfred Hitchcock famously never won a Best Director Oscar, but he did direct one Best Picture. Which movie?
3. What goddess started the Trojan War in a fit of pique, having not been invited to the wedding of Peleus and Thetis?
4. Who's the only eligible back-to-back MVP not enshrined in the Baseball Hall of Fame?
5. What novel's events are kicked off when Countess Ellen Olenska is snubbed by New York society?

• **1905** • The 3,100-carat Cullinan, the largest rough diamond ever discovered, is found in South Africa. For most of the twentieth century, *both* diamonds cut from the stone were the world's two largest, and today both are part of Britain's crown jewels.

CARAT CAKE

1. On which Hawaiian island would you find Diamond Head?
2. What, at their most difficult, are rated "Double Black Diamond" in the United States?
3. What was the last name of the two brothers who discovered diamonds on their farm, Vooruitzigt, in 1870?
4. What two Arizona Diamondbacks shared *Sports Illustrated* Sportsman of the Year honors in 2001?
5. Which Monkees number one hit was written by a young Neil Diamond?
6. What U.S. state depicts a large, round-cut diamond between the letters and numbers on its license plates?
7. What's the diamond card in a "pinochle"?
8. F. Scott Fitzgerald wrote a famous short story about "A Diamond as Big as" what New York landmark?
9. What color is the supposedly cursed Hope Diamond?
10. What's the name for the diamond-shaped "soft spots" on the skull of a newborn?

• **1954** • Dylan Thomas's radio play *Under Milk Wood* first broadcasts on the BBC. The play is set in the Welsh village of Llareggub—an in-joke by Thomas. Llareggub is "bugger all" spelled backward.

RREPEATED LLETTERS
All these answers will begin with a doubled letter, like "Llareggub."

1. Who wins the Hundred Acre Wood's first Poohsticks competition?
2. What Quechua word is also sometimes used to refer to a vicuña or guanaco?
3. What 1997 megahit asks, "When you get old and start losing your hair, can you tell me who will still care?"
4. What cloud of comets, out beyond Pluto, was named for a twentieth-century Dutch astronomer?
5. What composer's tune "Hoe-Down" is the background music for the "Beef—it's what's for dinner" TV ads?

Answers to the questions on this page can be found on page 43.

JANUARY 26

• **1848** • IN A LECTURE AT the Concord Lyceum, Henry David Thoreau first delivers his landmark essay "Civil Disobedience," which will go on to inspire both Gandhi and Martin Luther King, Jr.

PUTTING DOWN THE MAN
Question authority with trivia *questions, for a change.*

1. What was "Che" Guevara's real first name?
2. According to Bob Dylan in "Subterranean Homesick Blues," "Don't follow leaders. Watch your—" what instead?
3. What did Tommie Smith and John Carlos do to make headlines in 1968?
4. What organization's 1999 conference in Seattle led to massive street protests?
5. The famous "peace symbol" was designed to combine the semaphore positions for N and D. What do the N and D stand for?
6. What celebrated antiapartheid activist died in South African police custody in September 1977?
7. Greenwich Village's 1969 Stonewall riots took place just hours after what gay icon's funeral?
8. What country overthrew its authoritarian regime via the bloodless "Velvet Revolution"?
9. Public Enemy's "Fight the Power" first appeared on what movie's soundtrack?
10. What unknown revolutionary was, alongside "The American G.I.," one of only two nameless entries on *Time*'s list of the twentieth century's most influential people?

• **1972** • FLIGHT ATTENDANT VESNA VULOVIC free-falls a record 33,000 feet when JAT Yugoslav Flight 364 explodes over Czechoslovakia . . . and she survives.

GOING DOWN
Trivia you'll fall for.

1. How many different types of falling pieces are there in the game Tetris?
2. Who is pop band Fall Out Boy enjoying an *Evening Out with,* according to the title of their first album?
3. Albert Fall became the first U.S. cabinet officer to serve jail time for his part in what scandal?
4. The "crawlers" are the predators in what 2005 horror film?
5. What book begins "Of Man's first disobedience, and the fruit / Of that forbidden tree"?
6. Alicia Keys's hit "Fallin'" is written in E minor, but the album title suggests it *should* be sung in what other key?
7. What World Heritage Site is found along the Zambezi River, in Zambia's Mosi-oa-Tunya National Park?
8. What TV catchphrase was first uttered, in 1990, by retired nurse Edith Fore, portraying "Mrs. Fletcher"?
9. What two-word term is the top speed reached by a free-falling object?
10. What famous structure was transplanted to Lake Havasu City, Arizona, in 1971?
11. Name either of the two L.A.-area streets mentioned in the lyrics of Tom Petty's "Free Fallin'."
12. What controversial novel begins with Gibreel Farishta and Saladin Chamcha falling from an exploding jetliner?
13. Who missed out on an Olympic gold medal in 1984 after her famous collision with Zola Budd during the 3,000-meter final?
14. "Defenestration" is the act of being thrown out of what?
15. What are Butch and Etta riding during the "Raindrops Keep Fallin' on My Head" scene from *Butch Cassidy and the Sundance Kid?*

Answers to the questions on this page can be found on page 43.

JANUARY 27

• **1606** • THE TRIAL OF GUY FAWKES and his Gunpowder Plot coconspirators begins. Four days later, they'll be executed! Ah, London—the Texas of the seventeenth century.

SO GOOD YOU COULD PLOTS

1. In 1944, who was the intended assassination victim of the July 20 Plot?
2. What director's last film was 1976's *Family Plot*?
3. What novel begins "Persons attempting to find a motive in this narrative will be prosecuted . . . persons attempting to find a plot in it will be shot"?
4. What famous figure becomes an anti-Semitic U.S. president in Philip Roth's alternate-history novel *The Plot Against America*?
5. What French philosopher invented a namesake system of plotting points on two axes labeled x and y?

• **1888** • THE NATIONAL GEOGRAPHIC SOCIETY is founded at the Cosmos Club on Washington, D.C.'s, Lafayette Square.

NATIONAL GEOGRAPHY
What's the only nation that borders both *of these countries?*

Easy
1. Andorra and Portugal
2. Pakistan and Bangladesh
3. Israel and Libya
4. Uruguay and Venezuela
5. Belgium and Spain

Harder
1. Burma and Malaysia
2. Costa Rica and Honduras
3. Italy and Slovakia
4. Ecuador and Bolivia
5. Morocco and Tunisia

Yeah, Good Luck
1. Nigeria and Gabon
2. Tajikistan and Russia
3. Slovenia and Bosnia
4. Mauritania and Guinea-Bissau
5. Kazakhstan and Iran

• **1910** • THE UNFORTUNATELY NAMED PLUMBER Thomas Crapper, who helped popularize and improve the flush toilet, dies outside London.

FOUR FLUSHERS

1. What NHL team is named for a W. C. Handy standard?
2. W. C. Minor, a murderer and schizophrenic, spent the last decades of his life in a lunatic asylum writing hundreds of entries for what reference work?
3. What was the hometown of W. C. Fields, which he joked he wanted to put on his tombstone?
4. W. C. Heinz and Richard Hornberger used the pen name "Richard Hooker" to write what Korean War novel?

Answers to the questions on this page can be found on page 43.

JANUARY 28

• **1820** • THE ESTONIAN-BORN Fabian Gottlieb von Bellingshausen, exploring the south Pacific, sights ice fields and thus becomes, it is believed, the first European to discover Antarctica. In fact, if the current research is correct, he beat Britain's Edward Bransfield, often credited with the discovery, by only two days.

PIONEER AT HAND

Match these geographical features to the European explorer who discovered them—or "discovered" them, to be more PC.

1. Alaska	**A.** Vasco Nuñez de Balboa
2. Brazil	**B.** Vitus Bering
3. The Cape of Good Hope	**C.** Pedro Cabral
4. Lake Victoria	**D.** Jacques Cartier
5. The mouth of the Amazon	**E.** James Cook
6. New York Harbor	**F.** Bartolomeu Dias
7. New Zealand	**G.** Ferdinand Magellan
8. Queensland, Australia	**H.** John Speke
9. The St. Lawrence River	**I.** Abel Tasman
10. Tierra del Fuego	**J.** Giovanni de Verrazano

• **1956** • RALPH KRAMDEN IS BOUNCED from the quiz show *The $99,000 Answer* when he doesn't know who wrote "Swanee River." (Ralph's answer: "Ed Norton?")

INNER TUBE

What TV series are about these fictional shows-within-shows?

1. *The Alan Brady Show*	**3.** *Tool Time*	**5.** *When the Whistle Blows*
2. *FYI*	**4.** *The Girlie Show*	

• **1985** • FORTY-FIVE RECORDING ARTISTS gather at the A&M recording studios in Hollywood to sing "We Are the World." (The producers have cannily selected the date of the American Music Awards to ensure a big turnout.)

COUNT IT OFF

Can you put these bands in order from one to ten, based on the number of members in their most famous lineup?

1. Broken Social Scene	**5.** Iron & Wine	**9.** Toto
2. The Dave Matthews Band	**6.** Led Zeppelin	**10.** UB40
3. Eurythmics	**7.** Madness	
4. Green Day	**8.** Slipknot	

Answers to the questions on this page can be found on page 44.

• **1802** • JOHN BECKLEY IS APPOINTED the first librarian of Congress. This was a real cushy job back then, since there were only 740 books in the Library of Congress.

SHUSH LIFE

1. The first name of the inventor of the Dewey Decimal System was what famous author's last name?

2. Mohammed Khatami is both a former national librarian and a former president of what nation?

3. Rupert Giles was the librarian-mentor on what TV hit?

4. What composer of the *Symphonie Fantastique* made his living as the librarian of the Paris Conservatoire?

5. What famous fictional librarian's last name was Paroo?

• **1886** • KARL BENZ PATENTS the first gas-powered automobile, which he calls the "Motorwagen." The car was so difficult to maneuver that it repeatedly crashed into walls while Benz test-drove it, to the amusement of onlookers.

DRIVING TEST

1. What car lost 96 percent of its sales in the four years following the publication of Ralph Nader's *Unsafe at Any Speed*?

2. From 1995 almost until it was discontinued in 2004, what was the only U.S. car model to share its name with an element of the periodic table?

3. What Rolling Stones hit begins appropriately, on the album version, with the sound of car horns?

4. Whose look-alike archenemy was named KARR?

5. What company takes its name from the Japanese word for the constellation Pleiades?

6. What was the only children's story ever published by James Bond creator Ian Fleming?

7. What was the name of Henry Ford's only son?

8. In what model of SUV is Krayzie Bone "Ridin'," according to the second verse of the 2006 Chamillionaire hit?

9. With over 5.3 million sold since 1959, what's by far the most successful British car of all time?

10. In what country was the last original Volkswagen Beetle produced, in July 2003?

• **1995** • THE SAN FRANCISCO 49ERS become the first five-time Super Bowl champs.

FIVE-TIMERS CLUB

1. Who was married five times, though she had children only with her second husband and her third, Sid Luft?

2. What's being released five times a year from January 1999 to fall 2008?

3. What horror movie title character will appear if you chant his name five times in a mirror?

4. Whose album *Some Hearts* is the fastest-selling debut in country history, having gone five times platinum by 2007?

5. Whom did George Steinbrenner hire and fire five separate times?

Answers to the questions on this page can be found on page 44.

JANUARY 30

• **1958** • DALLAS'S LOVE FIELD introduces the world's first two-way moving sidewalk.

WALK THIS WAY

1. What songwriter of "A Boy Named Sue" also wrote the children's poems in *Where the Sidewalk Ends*?
2. What does a "screever" do on a sidewalk?
3. What *Three Faces of Eve* star got the first star on Hollywood's Walk of Fame?
4. What song, Status Quo's biggest hit ever, was originally intended as the B-side of the long-forgotten "Gentleman Joe's Sidewalk Café"?
5. Who was stabbed on the sidewalk outside her Queens apartment in 1964, though her neighbors didn't report the incident for half an hour?

• **1968** • THE VIETNAMESE LUNAR NEW YEAR holiday of Tet marks the beginning of the largest Viet Cong offensive of the war.

COMING AND GOING
Give these answers that are palindromes, just like "Tet."

1. In the Bible, who is the mother of the prophet Samuel?
2. What was developed thanks to Christian Hülsmeyer's 1904 invention of the "telemobiloscope"?
3. What language is spoken in the Pacific capital city of Yaren?
4. What magazine gives out the Style Awards every October?
5. In 2001, who gave the first concert in Oslo's Vallhall football arena?
6. An "umiak" is a larger version of what?
7. Who joined Alicia Keys on the 2002 hit "Gangsta Lovin'"?
8. After Toyota's Corolla, what coupe introduced in 1972 is the second oldest Japanese car model still on the market?
9. What's the name of the inflatable automatic pilot in *Airplane!*?
10. Kirk Van Houten on *The Simpsons* and Monica Geller on *Friends* have both owned a bed shaped like what?

• **1995** • A *TV GUIDE* SURVEY finds that the most trusted media personality is . . . still Walter Cronkite, more than a decade since he left the CBS anchor desk.

A MATTER OF TRUST

1. What company advises, "Trust your car to the star"?
2. What kind of trust is a REIT?
3. Kiribati, Tuvalu, or Palau—in 1994, what tiny Pacific nation became the last U.N. Trust Territory to gain independence?
4. Whose song "Clubland" begins his 1981 album *Trust*?
5. What is unusual about the "In God We Trust" motto on the U.S. Mint's recent presidential dollar coins?

Answers to the questions on this page can be found on page 44.

• **1922** • Joanne Dru, Hollywood actress (and sister of *Hollywood Squares* host Peter Marshall) is born.

IT'S UP TO U

Name these people whose names also end with the letter u.

1. Who became the chairman of the Truth and Reconciliation Commission in 1995?

2. Who has the only speaking part in Mel Brooks's *Silent Movie?*

3. In 1961, who sent in troops to eject the Portuguese from their colony of Goa?

4. Who read the poem "On the Pulse of Morning" at Bill Clinton's first inauguration?

5. What Oscar winner for *Ed Wood* turned down the role of Spock on *Star Trek?*

• **1930** • Scotch Tape, from 3M, goes on the market.

PLAID TO THE BONE

1. What 1972 comedy begins "Once upon a time there was a plaid overnight bag"?

2. What Tennessee politician always ran for office in a trademark red-and-black plaid shirt?

3. Scotland, Wales, or Northern Ireland—the Plaid Cymru party seeks independence for what country?

4. *Dead Men Don't Wear Plaid* was the last film of what legendary costume designer?

5. What company's famous plaid pattern is called "novacheck"?

• **1940** • Brattleboro, Vermont, retiree Ida May Fuller receives the U.S.'s very first Social Security check, numbered 00-000-001. Fuller had paid only three years of payroll taxes—$25—by the time she retired in 1939, but she received almost a thousandfold return on that investment, since she cannily decided to live to the age of 100, dying in 1975.

OUT TO PASTURE

Kick back and answer these retirement questions.

1. Of all the teams in the four major North American sports leagues, which team has retired more jersey numbers than any other?

2. Though he lived almost forty more years, Giaochino Rossini never composed another opera after what 1829 work, rarely performed today due to its six-hour length?

3. What word for a retired professional comes from the Latin for "having earned a discharge"?

4. Who retired from the screen after 1961's *One, Two, Three*, except for a brief return in 1981's *Ragtime*, ironically playing a police commissioner?

5. Who has been called the first victim of the "Madden curse," due to his abrupt 1999 retirement?

6. Who has had a record fourteen videos "retired" from MTV's *Total Request Live* countdown?

7. Who published his last novel, *A Passage to India*, in 1924,

though he lived 46 more years?

8. What storm name was retired and replaced by "Matthew" after the deadliest hurricane in recorded history, in 1998?

9. Despite retiring from NASA in 1997, what astronaut and physicist was the only person to serve on both the *Challenger* and *Columbia* investigation panels?

10. What 1985 movie takes place at the Sunny Shores retirement home?

Answers to the questions on this page can be found on page 45.

January Answers

JANUARY 1

THE APPELLATION TRAIL
1. O. J. Simpson
2. J. K. Rowling
3. k. d. lang
4. D. H. Lawrence
5. H. G. Wells
6. G. E. Smith
7. E. B. White
8. B. J. Armstrong
9. J. M. Barrie's (*Finding Neverland*)
10. M. C. Hammer

DIVISION DAY
1. The Qur'an
2. Cell mitosis
3. Highway lanes
4. Switzerland
5. The small intestine
6. *Pulp Fiction*
7. Pennsylvania and Mississippi
8. The NHL
9. New Zealand
10. *Fahrenheit 451*
11. A polo match
12. The Thirty-eighth Parallel
13. *Trapped in the Closet*
14. Delaware
15. Twenty

JANUARY 2

BREEDER'S DIGEST
1. Darwin's
2. The hospice of Saint Bernard
3. Philip Marlowe
4. Jim Calhoun
5. *3-2-1 Contact*
6. Texas and New Mexico
7. *Mellon Collie and the Infinite Sadness*
8. China
9. Jack Russell
10. Mars

MAJOR ISSUES
1. Sean Connery
2. Tiger Woods
3. *Motor Trend*
4. Albert Einstein
5. Jenny McCarthy

DAMMED IF I KNOW
1. Montreal's
2. Jive
3. The Boston Tea Party
4. Michigan
5. The capybara

JANUARY 3

AVIA-TRICKS
1. Ohio and North Carolina
2. Mitsubishi
3. St. Louis (hence, *Spirit of St. Louis*)
4. The *Hindenburg* explosion
5. Wiley Post

HO HO HO
1. The Marines
2. Model railroad
3. Westward Ho!
4. "Tiny Bubbles"
5. They were killed by "Jack the Ripper"

WOMAN ON TOP
Easy
1. Israel
2. India
3. Germany
4. Argentina
Harder
1. Nicaragua
2. Turkey
3. Canada
4. Pakistan
Yeah, Good Luck
1. Chile
2. Ukraine
3. Sri Lanka
4. Jamaica

January Answers

JANUARY 4

TRUNK CALLS
1. Tarzan
2. The bishop
3. Pearl Harbor
4. Hannibal
5. Ganesh
6. The giraffe
7. "Tusk," by Fleetwood Mac
8. Mel Brooks
9. "Seven Nation Army" (for the Salvation Army)
10. Babar
11. Dentin
12. Pachyderm
13. The Alabama Crimson Tide
14. Richard Nixon and George H. W. Bush
15. Thailand

THAT'S THE SPIRIT!
Easy
1. *The Sixth Sense*
2. *Beetle Juice*
3. *The Others*
4. *Topper*
5. *Field of Dreams*
Harder
1. *The Ghost and Mrs. Muir*
2. *Truly, Madly, Deeply*
3. *Scrooged*
4. *The Ring*
5. *To Gillian on Her 37th Birthday*
Yeah, Good Luck
1. *The Frighteners*
2. *The Canterville Ghost*
3. *Hamlet*
4. *Ghost*
5. *Scoop*

JANUARY 5

COMMON SCENTS
1. Ozone
2. Spinal Tap's
3. Hong Kong's
4. Phoebe Buffay's (*Friends*)
5. Coffee
6. Farting
7. A mulatto, an albino, a mosquito, a libido
8. Lazarus
9. The (sperm) whale's
10. Bouquet
11. Walter Winchell
12. Almonds
13. "The Gingerbread Man"
14. Odor Eaters
15. Victory

FIRST-NAME BASIS
Easy
1. *Romeo and Juliet*
2. *Will & Grace*
3. *Laverne & Shirley*
4. *Bonnie and Clyde*
Harder
1. *Amos 'n' Andy*
2. *Bob & Carol & Ted & Alice*
3. *Thelma and Louise*
4. *Dharma & Greg*
Yeah, Good Luck
1. *Hope & Faith*
2. *Oscar and Lucinda*
3. *Harold and Maude*
4. *Kate & Allie*

JANUARY 6

MISPELLINGS
1. Marven (Marvin) Gardens
2. Pennsylvania
3. *Manhunter*
4. Beck (*Odelay*)
5. Naomi
6. E ("potatoe")
7. The Stanley Cup
8. Sweden
9. Antawn Jamison
10. Happiness (*The Pursuit of Happyness*)

SCREEN DEBUTS
1. M
2. C
3. K
4. D
5. S
6. H
7. T
8. R
9. Q
10. F
11. B
12. J
13. E
14. O
15. I
16. N
17. A
18. G
19. P
20. L

JANUARY 7

THE ITALIAN JOB
1. Capri pants
2. Antonio Stradivarius
3. *A Fistful of Dollars*
4. Antonin Scalia
5. Christopher Columbus

UNDERDOG DAYS
1. Buster Douglas
2. Earl Morrall
3. Ben Hogan
4. Finland
5. The New York Mets
6. Upset
7. Chaminade
8. Uruguay
9. Jim Valvano
10. Rulon Gardner

GOOD DAY FOR BLACK ROCK
1. Mecca
2. Basalt
3. "Everybody Hates . . ."
4. Nevada
5. Coal

JANUARY 8

BABY GENIUSES
1. Little Stevie Wonder's
2. H. P. Lovecraft
3. Salzburg
4. Gene Roddenberry's
5. Murray Gell-Mann
6. Jeremy Bentham
7. Pablo Picasso
8. Geoffrey Rush (*Shine*)
9. Douglas
10. Michelle Wie

THE NUMBER YOU HAVE DIALED
1. (PE)6-5000
2. 112
3. Knoxville (home of the Tennessee Volunteers)
4. It was Morgan Freeman's number in *Bruce Almighty*
5. Jenny

SEX CELS
Easy
1. *Aladdin*
2. *Pocahontas*
3. *The Hunchback of Notre Dame*
Harder
1. *The Little Mermaid*
2. *Mulan*
3. *The Lion King*
Yeah, Good Luck
1. *Hercules*
2. *Bambi*
3. *Sleeping Beauty*

JANUARY 9

IT TAKES A STEADY HAND TO PLAY OPERATION!
1. A
2. D
3. E
4. C
5. B

EYES CAPADES
1. Color blindness
2. Brent Spiner (*Star Trek*'s "Data")
3. Sirius Satellite Radio's
4. The Internet Movie Database, IMDb.com
5. Sugar Ray Leonard's
6. "The Tell-tale Heart"
7. Bunker Hill
8. The cornea
9. Ian Fleming's
10. Five

THE "DEAR" HUNTER
1. *About Schmidt*
2. North Korea
3. Beverly Cleary
4. Mia Farrow
5. Jack the Ripper

January Answers

JANUARY 10

A LITTLE TOWN IN THE MOUTH
1. Buffalo
2. Baltimore
3. Little Rock
4. Venice
5. Jerusalem

LOVE LACE?
1. Aglet
2. Teddy Roosevelt
3. Chantilly
4. Queen Anne('s lace)
5. Mickey Finn

ORIGINAL SYNERGY
1. E
2. A
3. H
4. I
5. D
6. C
7. J
8. B
9. F
10. G

JANUARY 11

TRIVIA TRIVIA
1. *Murmur*
2. Couscous
3. Tsetse flies
4. *Can-Can*
5. Humbert Humbert (*Lolita*)
6. "Louie Louie"
7. The Mau Mau uprising
8. *Rochelle, Rochelle*
9. Mahimahi
10. Bamm-Bamm
11. Pago Pago, American Samoa
12. The dodo
13. Duran Duran ("A View to a Kill")
14. Sirhan Sirhan
15. *New York, New York*
16. A yo-yo
17. *Liar Liar*
18. Baden-Baden
19. *Lulu*
20. "Bling bling"

NO MAN IS AN ISLAND
1. The Delmarva Peninsula
2. The Kamchatka Peninsula
3. Michigan's Upper Peninsula
4. The Yucatán Peninsula
5. The Crimea

JANUARY 12

JUST FOLK
1. The Jordan River
2. Pete Seeger
3. Chelsea Clinton ("Chelsea Morning")
4. "Come by here"
5. Ione Skye

MANY ARE COLD, BUT FEW ARE FROZEN
1. −40°
2. Scrat
3. Fish
4. Frank Zamboni
5. Body Count
6. Geyser
7. Thanksgiving
8. Carbon dioxide
9. Brian Boitano
10. Stalingrad

THEY SPY
1. B (*24*)
2. D (*Alias*)
3. C (*Mission: Impossible*)
4. A (*Get Smart*)
5. E (*The Man from U.N.C.L.E.*)

JANUARY 13

ACTUALLY, IT *IS* ROCKET SCIENCE
1. Liquid hydrogen and liquid oxygen
2. The Atlas
3. Roswell, New Mexico
4. V-2s
5. Thrust

COVER TO COVER
1. "Venus"
2. "The Loco-Motion"
3. "I'll Be There"
4. "Lean on Me"
5. "Go Away Little Girl"
6. "Lady Marmalade"
7. "When a Man Loves a Woman"
8. "Please Mr. Postman"
9. "You Keep Me Hangin' On"
10. Gerry Goffin and Carole King ("Go Away Little Girl" and "The Loco-Motion")

WE ARE NOT A MUSE
Easy
1. James Cameron
2. Steven Spielberg
3. Kenneth Branagh
4. Vincente Minnelli
5. Paul Newman
Harder
1. Joel Coen
2. Roberto Rossellini
3. Roger Vadim
4. Guy Ritchie
5. Renny Harlin
Yeah, Good Luck
1. Federico Fellini
2. Atom Egoyan
3. Jean-Luc Godard
4. John Cassavetes
5. Brian De Palma

JANUARY 14

SURELY TEMPLES
1. Kali
2. Angkor Wat
3. Temple prostitute
4. STP Motor Oil
5. Jim Jones
6. The Temple to Artemis (or Diana) at Ephesus
7. Coruscant
8. Salt Lake City
9. *You Bet Your Life* (starring Temple grad Bill Cosby)
10. The Dome of the Rock

CREATURE FEATURES
Easy
1. Pig
2. Horse
3. Clownfish
4. Ape or gorilla
Harder
1. Leopard
2. Deer
3. Oliver was a cat
4. Rat
Yeah, Good Luck
1. Parrot (played by a conure)
2. Orangutan
3. Seal (played by a sea lion)
4. Ants

ALL STARSTRUCK
1. ~~⬛⬛⬛⬛~~ Wayne Gretzky
2. The Cincinnati Reds
3. Larry Nance
4. The Hula Bowl
5. LeBron James

JANUARY 15

COVERING YOUR ASS
1. *A Midsummer Night's Dream*
2. *Shrek 2*
3. Palm Sunday
4. A jenny
5. Kornfield Kounty

SUGAR SUGAR
1. Condoleezza (*con dolcezza*) Rice
2. Bucket
3. The Louisiana Superdome
4. Milk Duds
5. Altamont
6. Banana
7. The pancreas
8. Boxing
9. Ernie
10. "A Spoonful of Sugar"

SCRAMBLED TV
Easy
1. *Who Wants to Be a Millionaire*
2. *Little House on the Prairie*
3. *Felicity*
4. *Just Shoot Me*
5. *Monday Night Football*
Harder
1. *Sex and the City*
2. *American Idol*
3. *Desperate Housewives*
4. *Touched by an Angel*
5. *America's Next Top Model*
Yeah, Good Luck
1. *Grey's Anatomy*
2. *The Apprentice*
3. *Three's Company*
4. *The Prisoner*
5. *Charlie's Angels*

January Answers

JANUARY 16

ON HER MAJESTY'S SERVICE
1. Queen Isabella I (on a Columbus anniversary stamp)
2. Madame (Marie) Tussaud
3. North America
4. Ellery Queen
5. Royal jelly
6. Queen's Freddie Mercury
7. Jamaica Bay
8. Ali MacGraw
9. Prince Valiant
10. The pope

NEVER HEAR THE END OF IT
Easy
1. The Jimi Hendrix Experience
2. The Rolling Stones
3. Christina Aguilera
4. Miles Davis
5. Prince
Harder
1. Nine Inch Nails
2. Cream
3. Bob Dylan
4. The Foo Fighters
5. Genesis
Yeah, Good Luck
1. Wilco
2. Sonic Youth
3. XTC
4. Frank Zappa
5. Yes

A SHOT IN THE ARM(ENIAN)
1. Jack Kevorkian
2. Garo Yepremian's
3. Ken Davitian
4. Eric Bogosian
5. George Deukmejian

JANUARY 17

SONGS OF THE SOUTH
1. *Aurora australis*
2. Eric
3. Colombia
4. Peach (though it also contains orange)
5. Windsor, Ontario
6. The Ewings (*Dallas*)
7. The Indianapolis Colts
8. Crunk
9. The Republican Party
10. São Paulo

DOC HOLLYWOOD
1. *Hoop Dreams*
2. Martin Scorsese
3. Seven
4. *Spellbound*
5. *Apocalypse Now*'s

HEIST HEIST BABY
1. England's Great Train Robbery
2. The *Mona Lisa*
3. The trophy for soccer's World Cup
4. Intercourse, Pennsylvania
5. The Artful Dodger's

JANUARY 18

BY HOOK OR BY CROOK
1. Mashed potatoes
2. She shot J.R. (*Dallas*)
3. Alsatians
4. Jessica Lange
5. The valley of the shadow of death
6. Martha Stewart
7. Sir Walter Raleigh
8. Jim Lovell
9. Robert De Niro
10. Planetary rings

THE GREATEST THING SINCE . . .
1. Ralph Hinkley's name was changed when John Hinckley, Jr., shot Ronald Reagan
2. Louisville, Kentucky (the "Louisville Lip")
3. Limp Bizkit
4. Bond foe Ernst Stavro Blofeld
5. *The Fantastic Four*

TRIO BRAVO
Easy
1. Palmer
2. Aramis
3. Judicial
4. Ollie
5. Theodore
Harder
1. Shiva
2. Fraternité
3. Yellow
4. Nod
5. Belthasar
Yeah, Good Luck
1. Atropos (the Fates)
2. José Carreras
3. Country (the West Point motto)
4. Cretaceous
5. *The Bad News Bears Go to Japan*

JANUARY 19

A BRIEF QUIZ
1. "Old Time Rock & Roll"
2. Curly Howard
3. "Mostly briefs"
4. Underoos
5. Times Square

PETAL PUSHERS
1. Jeff Daniels (star of *The Purple Rose of Cairo*)
2. 1942 (after Pearl Harbor)
3. *Chinese Democracy*
4. Jorge Luis Borges
5. The Plantagenets
6. The hips
7. Trista Rehn
8. *American Beauty*
9. "Norma Jean"
10. The winner of the Kentucky Derby

SNOW WONDER
1. Six
2. He tested positive for marijuana
3. The evacuation of Saigon
4. Dairy Queen
5. Donner Pass

JANUARY 20

MURDER MOST FOUL
Easy
1. Hamlet
2. Severus Snape
3. Moby-Dick
4. Beowulf
5. The White Witch (Jadis)
Harder
1. The Sparrow
2. Humbert Humbert (*Lolita*)
3. Simon Legree (and his overseers)
4. Oedipus
5. Richard Cory (himself)
Yeah, Good Luck
1. George Wilson
2. Smerdyakov
3. George Milton (*Of Mice and Men*)
4. Frankenstein's monster
5. Eugene Onegin

WATER COLORS
1. C
2. B
3. E
4. A
5. G
6. F
7. D

DO THE BATUSI
1. The *Weekly World News*
2. Romania
3. Its tongue
4. Louisville (at the Louisville Slugger headquarters)
5. The Buffalo Sabres

JANUARY 21

IN THE BEGINNING
Easy
1. *The Three Musketeers*
2. *Jurassic Park*
3. *A Christmas Carol*
4. *The Maltese Falcon*
5. *Lord of the Flies*
Harder
1. *Flowers for Algernon*
2. *The Bonfire of the Vanities*
3. *Dracula*
4. *The House of Seven Gables*
5. *Bridget Jones's Diary*
Yeah, Good Luck
1. *A Room with a View*
2. *The Poisonwood Bible*
3. *In Cold Blood*
4. *Waiting to Exhale*
5. *The Name of the Rose*

YOU'VE COME A LONG WAY, BABY!
1. Tammy Faye Bakker
2. Lillian Hellman
3. *Night Court*
4. Gypsy Rose Lee's
5. Nancy Marchand (*The Sopranos*)

A COLONEL OF TRUTH
1. Robert Gould Shaw
2. Randy Quaid
3. Muammar Qaddafi
4. "Padre"
5. *The Bridge on the River Kwai*

JANUARY 22

ARE YOU GOING TO SCARBOR-OUGH FAIR?
1. V8 juice
2. H. L. Mencken
3. George Clooney
4. Gerald Ford

ACTS TO GRIND
1. D
2. E
3. B
4. J
5. C
6. A
7. I
8. H
9. F
10. G

FILL 'ER UP
1. Pegasus
2. Colonel Harland Sanders
3. Benito Mussolini
4. The St. Louis Cardinals
5. Howard Hughes's
6. Charles Starkweather's
7. Gomer Pyle
8. Oregon or New Jersey
9. "By choice, man!"
10. Hugo Chávez

JANUARY 23

WRIST-Y BUSINESS
1. Roger Bannister
2. Her hair
3. Omega
4. Silicon and oxygen
5. *Somewhere in Time*

AN OUTSIDE CHANCE
1. The ear
2. Theodore Roosevelt
3. Solipsism
4. The Chrysler Building's
5. The crust and the mantle
6. Black
7. A clergyman
8. Fig Newtons
9. Cape Hatteras
10. A turtle or tortoise

STAIR MASTERY
1. Rome
2. Montgomery, Alabama's
3. Rocky Balboa
4. Utah
5. The food pyramid

JANUARY 24

A SCOUT IS . . .
1. Muhammad
2. Tupac Shakur's
3. Heloise
4. Wendy
5. Portland, Oregon
6. Mashed potatoes
7. Give electric shocks to another "subject"
8. "Desiderata"
9. Dollar Rent A Car
10. Eddie Mathews
11. John F. Kennedy
12. Ambrose Bierce (*The Devil's Dictionary*)

CORE SAMPLES
Easy
1. Pears
2. Cherries
3. Oranges
4. Tomatoes
Harder
1. Grapes
2. Limes
3. Avocadoes
4. Plums
Yeah, Good Luck
1. Lemons
2. Strawberries
3. Peaches
4. Watermelon

ANY MORE LIKE YOU AT HOME? WILL THEY STAY THERE?
1. Aliana
2. Nicky
3. Jamie Lynn
4. Ashlee
5. Dannii

JANUARY 25

COLD SHOULDERS
1. Betty Rubble (bumped in favor of *the car!*)
2. *Rebecca*
3. Eris
4. Roger Maris; Dale Murphy
5. *The Age of Innocence*'s

CARAT CAKE
1. Oahu
2. Ski slopes
3. De Beers
4. Randy Johnson and Curt Schilling
5. "I'm a Believer"
6. Arkansas
7. The jack of diamonds
8. The Ritz (Hotel)
9. Blue
10. Fontanelles

RREPEATED LLETTERS
1. Eeyore
2. Llama
3. "MMMBop"
4. The Oort Cloud
5. Aaron Copland

JANUARY 26

PUTTING DOWN THE MAN
1. Ernesto
2. Parking meters
3. Gave a "Black Power" salute on the Olympic medal stand
4. The World Trade Organization
5. Nuclear disarmament
6. Steven Biko
7. Judy Garland's
8. Czechoslovakia
9. *Do the Right Thing*'s
10. Tiananmen Square's "Tank Man" or "Unknown Rebel"

GOING DOWN
1. Seven
2. *Your Girlfriend*
3. Teapot Dome
4. *The Descent*
5. *Paradise Lost*
6. A minor (*Songs in A Minor*)
7. Victoria Falls
8. "I've fallen and I can't get up."
9. Terminal velocity
10. London Bridge
11. Mulholland Drive or Ventura Boulevard
12. *The Satanic Verses*
13. Mary Decker (Slaney)
14. A window
15. A bicycle

JANUARY 27

SO GOOD YOU COULD PLOTS
1. Adolf Hitler
2. Alfred Hitchcock's
3. *The Adventures of Huckleberry Finn*
4. Charles Lindbergh
5. René Descartes (the Cartesian plane)

NATIONAL GEOGRAPHY
Easy
1. Spain
2. India
3. Egypt
4. Brazil
5. France
Harder
1. Thailand
2. Nicaragua
3. Austria
4. Peru
5. Algeria
Yeah, Good Luck
1. Cameroon
2. China
3. Croatia
4. Senegal
5. Turkmenistan

FOUR FLUSHERS
1. The St. Louis Blues
2. *The Oxford English Dictionary*
3. ("On the whole, I'd rather be in") Philadelphia
4. *M*A*S*H*

JANUARY 28

PIONEER AT HAND
1. B
2. C
3. F
4. H
5. A
6. J
7. I
8. E
9. D
10. G

INNER TUBE
1. *The Dick Van Dyke Show*
2. *Murphy Brown*
3. *Home Improvement*
4. *30 Rock*
5. *Extras*

COUNT IT OFF
1. Iron & Wine
2. Eurythmics
3. Green Day
4. Led Zeppelin
5. The Dave Matthews Band
6. Toto
7. Madness
8. UB40
9. Slipknot
10. Broken Social Scene

JANUARY 29

SHUSH LIFE
1. Melville's
2. Iran
3. *Buffy the Vampire Slayer*
4. Hector Berlioz
5. Marian the Librarian (*The Music Man*)

DRIVING TEST
1. The Chevrolet Corvair
2. The Dodge/Plymouth Neon
3. "Honky Tonk Woman" ("Country Honk")
4. KITT's (*Knight Rider*)
5. Subaru
6. *Chitty Chitty Bang Bang*
7. Edsel
8. A Ford Excursion
9. The Mini (Cooper)
10. Mexico

FIVE-TIMERS CLUB
1. Judy Garland
2. State quarters
3. Candyman
4. Carrie Underwood
5. Billy Martin

JANUARY 30

WALK THIS WAY
1. Shel Silverstein
2. Draw
3. Joanne Woodward
4. "Pictures of Matchstick Men"
5. Kitty Genovese

COMING AND GOING
1. Hannah
2. Radar
3. Nauruan
4. *Elle*
5. a-ha
6. A kayak
7. Eve
8. (Honda's) Civic
9. Otto
10. (A) racecar

A MATTER OF TRUST
1. Texaco
2. Real estate (investment)
3. Palau
4. Elvis Costello's
5. It's stamped on the *edge* of the coin

JANUARY 31

IT'S UP TO U
1. Archbishop Desmond Tutu
2. Marcel Marceau
3. Jawaharlal Nehru
4. Maya Angelou
5. Martin Landau

PLAID TO THE BONE
1. *What's Up, Doc?*
2. Lamar Alexander

3. Wales
4. Edith Head
5. Burberry's

OUT TO PASTURE
1. The Boston Celtics (21)
2. *William Tell*
3. Emeritus
4. James Cagney
5. Barry Sanders

6. Britney Spears
7. E. M. Forster
8. Mitch
9. Sally Ride
10. *Cocoon*

• **1906** • THE FIRST STEAM shovels arrive in Utah to begin excavating the Bingham Canyon copper mine near Salt Lake City. Today the 1,900-acre mine, still producing, is the world's largest man-made excavation.

COPPER TONE

1. What's added to copper to make bronze?

2. What's the only part of the Statue of Liberty's exterior that's not copper?

3. The Latin name for copper comes from what island where the ore was mined anciently?

4. Today's U.S. pennies are 2.5 percent copper. What metal is the other 97.5 percent?

5. Who was engaged to magician David Copperfield for six years in the 1990s?

• **1920** • THE "MOUNTIES" are officially formed when the North West Mounted Police merges with the Dominion Police. Look out, Snidely Whiplash.

STRAIGHT "EH?"S

Oh, Canada! How much do you know about our "Kraft dinner"–eating neighbors to the north?

1. What Canadian island was named for the father of Queen Victoria?

2. How many points are there on the maple leaf on the Canadian flag?

3. What ship sank in 1975 after passing too close to Ontario's Caribou Island when the gales of November came early?

4. What music star is named for a Soviet gymnast who won three gold medals at the 1976 Summer Olympics?

5. Prime Minister Lester Pearson won the Nobel Peace Prize for defusing what world crisis?

6. What prospector is cremated in poet Robert Service's most famous ballad?

7. What violinist-bandleader was the first inductee into the Canadian Music Hall of Fame?

8. What two Canadian provinces have capitals named for the same person?

9. What future TV western star was CBC News's "Voice of Canada" during World War II?

10. What's the name of the mainland portion of the province originally called Newfoundland?

11. What Canadian company is North America's oldest brewery?

12. What sports championship is named for a man whose great-uncle has a tea blend named for him?

13. What actor's 1999 memoir was entitled *Get a Life*?

14. What Italian army captain who settled in Toronto in 1831 lent his name to a popular teen drama?

15. What's the only one of the Great Lakes that has no Canadian waters?

Answers to the questions on this page can be found on page 79.

FEBRUARY 2

• **1602** • SHAKESPEARE'S *TWELFTH NIGHT* is probably first performed at London's Middle Temple Hall, to celebrate Candlemas, not the titular holiday. The Bard playfully labels the play "Or What You Will," making it his only work with a subtitle.

SUB POP
What famous novels use these subtitles?

Easy
1. *The Whale*
2. *And What Alice Found There*
3. *A Tale of the Christ*
4. *The Autobiography of a Horse*
5. *A Space Odyssey*

Harder
1. *From This World to That Which Is to Come*
2. *The Modern Prometheus*
3. *Life Among the Lowly*
4. *There and Back Again*
5. *The Parish Boy's Progress*

Yeah, Good Luck
1. *A Novel Without a Hero*
2. *The Sacred & Profane Memories of Captain Charles Ryder*
3. *The Children's Crusade*
4. *A Pure Woman, Faithfully Presented*
5. *The Saga of an American Family*

• **1887** • THE PUNXSUTAWNEY GROUNDHOG CLUB makes its first annual trek to Gobbler's Knob to watch a small rodent predict the weather.

TIME AFTER TIME
Celebrate your own personal Groundhog Day *with some questions about endless repeats . . . endless repeats . . . endless repeats . . .*

1. What Sanskrit word do Buddhists use to refer to the endless cycle of birth, death, and rebirth?
2. What Beatles number one hit repeats the title in the lyrics forty-one times?
3. What ad campaign gave us Sitagin hemorrhoid cream, Rottenbrau beer, Golden Grenades cereal, and Château Marmoset wine?
4. What Italian phrase for "from the beginning" is used in music notation to indicate a repeated passage?
5. What's the only team ever to appear in four consecutive Super Bowls?
6. Jack Torrence's "novel" in Kubrick's *The Shining* actually consists of what proverb, typed over and over again thousands of times?
7. What phenomenon is named for the French words for "already seen"?
8. What happens ninety-two times in a row at the beginning of Tom Stoppard's play *Rosencrantz and Guildenstern Are Dead*?
9. What word did Benoit Mandelbrot coin in 1975 for infinitely complex shapes, each tiny part of which contains the whole?
10. What movie does Turner television traditionally broadcast twelve times in a row every December 24?

• **2002** • THE NICOLE KIDMAN GHOST STORY *The Others* cleans up at Spain's Goya Awards, since it was directed by a Spaniard, Alejandro Amenábar. It's the only movie ever to win the Best Film Goya despite not having a single word of Spanish in it.

SIGNIFICANT OTHERS

1. In the title of a George Bernard Shaw play, what's *John Bull's Other Island*?
2. To counter slipping sales, what was marketed, beginning in 1987, as "the other white meat"?
3. What photographer exposed New York's squalid slum life in 1890's *How the Other Half Lives*?
4. What's the punny name of "the Other Reindeer" voiced by Drew Barrymore in a Christmas TV special?
5. What backup band was replaced with "the Other Band" for the 1992 *Human Touch/Lucky Town* tour?

Answers to the questions on this page can be found on page 79.

• **1870** • AMERICANS OF ALL RACES now have the right to vote, as long as they have a penis. Iowa votes to ratify the Fifteenth Amendment to the Constitution, giving the amendment the required three-fourths majority.

¾ TIME

1. In what lunar phase is the moon when it's three-quarters full?

2. In the "Great Upheaval," three quarters of what people were forcibly removed from Nova Scotia?
3. Three fourths of Western Australia's population lives in what city?
4. Three quarters of the cadmium mined annually is used, with nickel, to make what household items?
5. Who is credited with writing three quarters of the Federalist Papers?

• **1902** • SHEP FRIEDMAN, in the *Morning Telegraph*, coins the nickname "the Great White Way" for New York's Broadway. But Shep wasn't referring to the lights—a snowstorm that day had turned the street into, quite literally, a slippery "white way."

THOROUGH, BUT FAIR
In what city would you find the most famous street named . . .

Easy	*Harder*	*Yeah, Good Luck*
1. Rodeo Drive	**1.** Beale Street	**1.** La Rambla
2. Bourbon Street	**2.** Nevsky Prospekt	**2.** Nathan Road
3. The Champs-Élysées	**3.** Carnaby Street	**3.** Yonge Street
4. Haight Street	**4.** Biscayne Boulevard	**4.** Paseo de la Reforma
5. Peachtree Street	**5.** Lake Shore Drive	**5.** Reeperbahn

• **1956** • THE VERY FIRST MEMBERS are elected into the National Sporting Goods Hall of Fame. It's now official: there's a Hall of Fame for *everything*.

THEY'VE GOT A LOT OF BALLS
Name these proud National Sporting Goods Hall of Fame members.

1. Who went into the Hall for founding the motor company whose slogan was "Throw the oars away"?
2. What Converse salesman is the only person in both the Basketball Hall of Fame and the Sporting Goods Hall of Fame?
3. Pitching for the White Stockings in 1877, what sporting goods store owner became the first baseball star to use a glove?
4. In the nineteenth century, what Swiss-born carriagemaker switched over to making bowling balls and billiard tables?
5. In 1964, who founded Blue Ribbon Sports, which later went on to become Nike?

Answers to the questions on this page can be found on page 79.

FEBRUARY 4

• **1938** • THORNTON WILDER'S PLAY *Our Town*, set in fictional Grover's Corners, New Hampshire, opens in New York.

HOUR TOWNS
What TV shows have been set in these fictional burgs?

Easy	Harder	Yeah, Good Luck
1. Sunnydale, CA	1. Dillon, TX	1. Stuckeyville, OH
2. Bedrock	2. Quahog, RI	2. Rome, WI
3. Cabot Cove, ME	3. Capeside, MA	3. Melonville
4. Cicely, AK	4. Norwich, VT	4. Raytown
5. Orbit City	5. Mockingbird Heights	5. Collinsport, ME

• **1968** • NEAL CASSADY—the model for Dean Moriarty in Jack Kerouac's *On the Road*—dies after passing out while wandering along a Mexican railroad track.

CHEAP NOVEL TEASE
Who was the real-life model for these thinly veiled literary characters?

1. Doris Mann in *Postcards from the Edge*
2. Jack Stanton in *Primary Colors*
3. Dill in *To Kill a Mockingbird*
4. Abe Ravelstein in *Ravelstein*
5. Matthew Harrison Brady in *Inherit the Wind*

• **1991** • THE BASEBALL HALL OF FAME votes to ban Pete Rose for gambling. Rose is shocked—he had $200 on the ruling going the other way!

I'M WITH THE BANNED

1. Chicago banned the sale of what gourmet food staple in 2006?
2. Kirk Douglas helped end the Hollywood blacklist by getting writer Dalton Trumbo screen credit on what film?
3. Who was banned from *Saturday Night Live* by viewer phone vote in 1982?
4. What Asian country bans the importation and sale of chewing gum?
5. What wasn't banned in the U.S. until 1972, a full decade after Rachel Carson wrote *Silent Spring*?
6. The 2007 rule banning suspended NFL players from signing with the CFL was named for what player?
7. What appeared on the cover of the Jane's Addiction album *Ritual de lo Habitual* after retailers banned the original art?
8. Laytonville, California, parents tried to ban what Dr. Seuss book from schools for "criminaliz[ing] the forest industry"?
9. What Nicole Kidman film is banned in Zimbabwe, which resembles the movie's fictional "Republic of Matobo" a bit too much?
10. In 2005, Bhutan became the first country to entirely ban what?

Answers to the questions on this page can be found on page 80.

• **1869** • Two Cornish miners digging near Moliagul, Australia, discover a huge nugget of gold just below the surface of the soil, so big it breaks their pick when they try to unearth it. The 158-pound "Welcome Stranger" is still the largest gold nugget ever discovered.

KISS MY AUROUS
There's gold in them there questions!

1. What country was called the Gold Coast prior to its 1957 independence?
2. What Ray Charles song was the basis for Kanye West's "Gold Digger"?
3. Who gave the "Cross of Gold" speech at the 1896 Democratic National Convention?
4. In what two California cities did Neil Young say he looked for a "Heart of Gold"?
5. At the 1996 Olympics, what American tied Mark Spitz's lifetime record of nine golds?
6. What 1980s sitcoms featured sisters Missy and Tracey Gold, respectively?
7. What are Quivira and Cíbola?
8. After a 2005 visit to Katrina-ravaged New Orleans, who announced he would "never wear [his] gold again—it's an insult to God"?
9. What title character of an 1876 novel earns $12,000 when he finds the Murrel Gang's gold in McDougal's Cave?
10. As with all heavy metals, all the gold in the universe was formed by what kind of astronomical event?

• **1897** • The Indiana House of Representatives unanimously passes a measure that would square the circle and redefine pi, both mathematical impossibilities. An aghast math professor who happens to be visiting the legislature persuades the Senate to kill the bill.

GOING IN CIRCLES

1. In what city would you find the fashionable Dupont Circle neighborhood?
2. What Manhattan intersection, at the southwest corner of Central Park, was America's first traffic circle?
3. What country's founder, Father Miguel Hidalgo, is buried under the Columna de la Independencia in the middle of a busy traffic roundabout?
4. The world's first aluminum statue was the statue of Eros placed in the middle of what famed London roundabout?
5. The Place de l'Étoile is the traffic circle that surrounds what landmark?

• **1919** • Four of Hollywood's biggest draws—Charlie Chaplin, Douglas Fairbanks, Jr., D. W. Griffith, and Mary Pickford—form their own studio, which they dub United Artists.

UNITED ARTISTS
Can you match up these once-married couples from the art world?

1. Peggy Guggenheim
2. Frida Kahlo
3. Lee Krasner
4. Georgia O'Keeffe
5. Susan Weil

A. Max Ernst
B. Jackson Pollock
C. Robert Rauschenberg
D. Diego Rivera
E. Alfred Stieglitz

Answers to the questions on this page can be found on page 80.

FEBRUARY 6

• **1672** • In a letter to the Royal Society, Isaac Newton reveals his new discovery about light. White light, he has found, is actually composed of every other color of light—he calls it a "spectrum."

I GOT HUE, BABE

Some colorful trivia to brighten up your day.

1. What's the most common color of Reese's Pieces, almost two thirds again as numerous as the other shades?
2. Who's the only sportcaster who's done both play-by-play and color commentary for *Monday Night Football*?
3. What political figure is married to former *In Living Color* star Alexandra Wentworth?
4. The Apgar score is used to measure the color and condition of what?
5. What color is the one-ball in a traditional billiards set?
6. Whose paintings include *The Red Room*, *The Green Stripe*, *The Blue Nudes*, and *The Yellow Odalisque*?
7. What *Sesame Street* Muppet was bright orange during the show's first season?
8. What's the "safest" color on the Homeland Security Advisory System's color scale?
9. What genus of vines has lent its name to: a Crayola color, in 1993; a Sherlock Holmes "Lodge," in 1908; and a TV "Lane," in 2004?
10. In what city do all three of the pro sports franchises use the same two main team colors?

• **1968** • The Winter Olympics open in Grenoble, France, featuring the first unofficial Olympic mascot ever—"Schuss the Skier"—and the debut of the Games' unofficial theme song, a little trumpet piece that its composer, Leo Artaud, originally called "Bugler's Dream."

THEY'RE PLAYING OUR SONG

1. What "broke down," according to the lyrics of the *Looney Tunes* theme song?
2. What NHL team's theme music is Aram Khachaturian's most famous composition?
3. What signature tune of Glenn Miller's orchestra was originally called "Now I Lay Me Down to Weep"?
4. What musical feat has been accomplished by only four artists: Jan Hammer, the Heights, Rhythm Heritage, and John Sebastian?
5. According to his theme song, what is the *most* wonderful thing about Tiggers?
6. Who's the only character in *Peter and the Wolf* represented by a brass instrument?
7. Mets closer Billy Wagner earned jeers in New York for adopting what metal anthem as his entrance music, since it has long been used by the Yankees' Mariano Rivera?
8. What 1986 Europe hit was GOB's magic-act theme song on TV's *Arrested Development*?
9. What movie's theme is called "Gonna Fly Now"?
10. What New Age musician composed "Roundball Rock," the ubiquitous *NBA on NBC* theme of the 1990s?

Answers to the questions on this page can be found on page 80.

FEBRUARY 7

• **1960** • FRANK SINATRA INTRODUCES his paramour Judith Campbell to Senator John F. Kennedy. She will become JFK's mistress and the "close friend" with Mob ties discreetly referred to in a 1975 Senate investigation.

TRAIL TO THE CHIEF
Which U.S. president was (or is) a personal friend of these famous names?

1. John Kenneth Galbraith
2. Nathaniel Hawthorne
3. Sam Houston
4. Rock Hudson
5. Bat Masterson
6. Jim Nantz
7. Thomas Nast
8. Willie Nelson
9. Joseph Priestley
10. Kevin Spacey

• **1974** • THE SYMBIONESE LIBERATION ARMY announces that they've kidnapped heiress Patty Hearst. How come none of *today's* really annoying heiresses becomes a political prisoner?

ARMY OF DORKNESS

1. What army was founded by "General" William Booth?
2. What man, golf's first millionaire, was followed by an eponymous Army of fans?
3. A Chinese man digging a well in March 1974 discovered an 8,000-man "army" made of what?
4. What singer's "Army of Me" video was the first ever to use the "bullet-time" special effect later made famous by *The Matrix*?
5. What must be manufactured by Victorinox or Wenger to be official?

• **1984** • CHALLENGER ASTRONAUT Bruce McCandless II becomes the earth's first human satellite, as he's the first person ever to go for an untethered space walk.

CUT LOOSE

1. What CEO bounced back after being fired by Henry Ford II in 1978?
2. Lou Barlow formed Sebadoh after J Mascis booted him from what other band?
3. Why did Aaron Spelling fire actress Hunter Tylo from *Melrose Place*, leading to a multimillion-dollar lawsuit?
4. What fired general later ran against Lincoln in the 1864 election?
5. Who did the Chicago Bears fire in 1992, just four years after he was the NFL Coach of the Year?

Answers to the questions on this page can be found on page 81.

FEBRUARY 8

• **1855** • In Devon, England, a hundred-mile path of hoofprints mysteriously appears overnight in lightly fallen snow. Since the marks appear to cross obstacles like houses, rivers, and walls with no difficulty, the phenomenon becomes known as "the Devil's Footprints."

THE DEVIL'S IN THE DETAILS

1. What musical talent does the Devil display in the song "The Devil Went Down to Georgia"?
2. Before they moved to Newark, the New Jersey Devils had the same name as what current baseball team?
3. What author's version of the Devil calls himself "Memnoch"?
4. What occupation traditionally referred to its apprentices as "devils"?
5. What kind of fur coat does Cruella De Vil covet?
6. What miraculous transformation does the Devil first tempt Jesus to try in the wilderness?
7. Al Pacino's satanic character in *The Devil's Advocate* is named for what author?
8. The former penal colony of Devil's Island is located off the coast of what country?
9. What bread's name may come from German words meaning "devil's fart"?
10. What Australian city's pro basketball team was called the Devils?

• **1958** • Joseph Mankiewicz's whitewashed film version of Graham Greene's *The Quiet American* hits screens. Greene is incensed that the novel's whole point has been turned upside-down, by making Communists the villains and dedicating the film to Ngo Dinh Diem, and he angrily repudiates the movie.

ADAPTIVE PARENTS
What original literary work were these retitled movies based on?

Easy
1. *Nosferatu*
2. *Manhunter*
3. *Charly*
4. *Jackie Brown*
5. *Willy Wonka and the Chocolate Factory*

Harder
1. *The Heiress*
2. *A Place in the Sun*
3. *The Innocents*
4. *Gettysburg*
5. *Christmas with the Kranks*

Yeah, Good Luck
1. *The Door in the Floor*
2. *Eyes Wide Shut*
3. *Sabotage*
4. *Ossessione*
5. *Die Hard 2*

• **1968** • Whatchu cryin' about, Arnold? Gary Coleman is born in Zion, Illinois.

DIFF'RENT STROKES
Swimming strokes, that is.

1. Which stroke is swum first in an "medley" swimming event?
2. What hero of 1926 played herself in the 1927 film *Swim, Girl, Swim*?
3. Who's the only founding member of both the International Surfing and Swimming Halls of Fame?
4. Who outgrew a childhood chlorine allergy to become the biggest Olympic medal winner in Australian history?
5. What fictional polo player was first played on screen by swimmer Buster Crabbe?

individual

Answers to the questions on this page can be found on page 81.

• **1867** • THE "WALTZ KING," Johann Strauss, debuts his best-loved work, *The Blue Danube*, at a Vienna concert. It doesn't go over well. "The Devil take the waltz," Strauss tells his brother Josef.

WALTZ TIME

1. What Jazz Age celebrity published a single novel, *Save Me the Waltz*, before dying in a 1948 fire at a mental hospital?
2. What is the "waltzing Matilda" in the title of that traditional Australian song?

3. What brief tune was Chopin's attempt to describe a puppy chasing its tail?
4. Which Beatle and which Rolling Stone joined the Band for the jam session at the end of *The Last Waltz*?

5. Why have three bars of Francisco Tárrega's "Gran Vals" been called "the world's most heard tune"?

• **1895** • YMCA COACH WILLIAM MORGAN coins the name "Mintonette" for the new indoor sport he's created. Today we know it as "volleyball."

ATHLEXICON
What sport's vocabulary uses each of these words?

Easy
1. Mulligan
2. Buttonhook
3. Scrum
4. Peloton
5. Pickle

Harder
1. Cesta
2. Catenaccio
3. Roval
4. Googly
5. Schuss

Yeah, Good Luck
1. Oche
2. Caballerial
3. Bonspiel
4. Manchette
5. Fistmele

• **1957** • THE MOST SUCCESSFUL VERSION of "The Banana Boat Song" peaks at number four on the pop charts—and it's not by Harry Belafonte! A year before Belafonte started the calypso boom, a folk trio called the Tarriers had their own hit singing "Day-o." One third of the trio: future actor (and *Little Miss Sunshine* Oscar winner) Alan Arkin.

ONE-HIT WONDERS

1. Who released only a single album during his lifetime, the ominously named *Ready to Die*?
2. Who based her only novel on her father, a Monroeville lawyer named Amasa?
3. Who replaced Stanley Kubrick on the western film *One-Eyed Jacks*, making it the only film he ever directed?
4. What tale of the cross-dressing Leonore was Beethoven's only opera?
5. What's the name of the Giants right fielder whose one-game major-league career—two innings and no at-bats on June 29, 1905—was immortalized in the novel *Shoeless Joe* and its film adaptation, *Field of Dreams*?

Answers to the questions on this page can be found on page 81.

• **1940** • MGM RELEASES *Puss Gets the Boot,* a cartoon about a mouse-hungry tabby cat named Jasper. When the cartoon is an unexpected hit, Jasper is renamed Tom, and the Tom and Jerry series is born.

TOMMY, CAN YOU HEAR ME?

What author created these literary Toms? And can you name each work?

Easy	*Harder*	*Yeah, Good Luck*
1. Tom Joad	1. Tom Bombadil	1. Tom Brown
2. Uncle Tom	2. Tom Swift	2. Tom Tulliver
3. Tom Sawyer	3. Tom Buchanan	3. Tom Wingfield
4. Tom Marvolo Riddle	4. Tom Jones	4. Tom Gradgrind
5. Tom Robinson	5. Tom Hagen	5. Tom Snout

• **1997** • GARRY KASPAROV BECOMES the first reigning chess champion ever to lose to a computer, IBM's Deep Blue. "I can still beat it every time at Minesweeper!" an angry Kasparov snarls to reporters.

SINGIN' THE BLUES

1. The Linke Scale is used to measure the blueness of what?
2. Who did Gargamel create using ingredients like crocodile tears, the tip of an adder's tongue, and a hard stone for a heart?
3. What Blue Ridge peak in North Carolina is the highest point east of the Mississippi?
4. When do "blue laws" prohibit certain activities?
5. Having installed blue Astro-Turf in 1986, what's the only NCAA team to play football on a nongreen surface?
6. According to the last song on Joni Mitchell's *Blue,* when *was* "The Last Time [She] Saw Richard"?
7. Who was the only cast member to appear in every episode of *NYPD Blue?*
8. Ever since 1948, when Syngman Rhee moved in, the "Blue House" has been the official residence of whom?
9. What Crayola color became "midnight blue" in 1958 to remove an out-of-date geographical term?
10. What trio plays unusual instruments like the PVC, the Tubulum, the Shaker Gong, and the Piano Smasher?
11. What was studied by Project Blue Book?
12. What 2002 movie was developed under the title *Surf Girls of Maui?*
13. What St. Louis Blues wing had the highest-scoring non-Gretzky season in NHL history in 1991, with eighty-six goals?
14. At what national capital does the White Nile join the Blue Nile?
15. What branch of the U.S. armed forces do the Blue Angels belong to?

Answers to the questions on this page can be found on page 82.

• **1899** • FRANCIS BARRAUD REGISTERS his painting *Dog Looking at and Listening to a Phonograph*, a portrait of Nipper, his beloved terrier who died four years earlier. The Gramophone Company of London purchases the painting, which will become EMI's famous "His Master's Voice" logo.

PUP QUIZ
What breed is each of these famous dogs?

Easy	*Harder*	*Yeah, Good Luck*
1. Snoopy	**1.** Santa's Little Helper	**1.** Marley
2. Lassie	**2.** Toto	**2.** Fala
3. Rin Tin Tin	**3.** Checkers	**3.** Cujo
4. McGruff	**4.** Eddie (*Frasier*)	**4.** Greyfriars Bobby
5. Yukon King	**5.** Spuds MacKenzie	**5.** Asta

• **1963** • SYLVIA PLATH COMMITS SUICIDE in her flat at 23 Fitzroy Road in London—coincidentally, the former home of Irish poet W. B. Yeats.

HALF BAKED
Answer these oven-related questions that don't *involve putting your head in one.*

1. What kind of "oven" is the official state cooking pot of Utah?
2. What's the heating element in a Hasbro Easy-Bake Oven?
3. What basketball player did Danny Ainge nickname "Microwave," since he heated up so fast?
4. What kind of clay oven is used to make Indian dishes like naan and chicken tikka?
5. What 1893 opera ends with the villain being pulled from the ruins of her oven, now turned into a honey cake?

• **2002** • ORE-IDA ANNOUNCES a new potato product line: Funky Fries, to come in sweetened flavors like Cinna-Stiks and Cocoa Crispers, not to mention Technicolor varieties like Kool Blue. The public manages to suppress its gag reflex but still stays away in droves, and Funky Fries will disappear from shelves the following summer.

THE LOVE OF FLAVOR
What brand-name products come in the following varieties?

1. Man-O-Mango Berry, Great Bluedini, Rock-a-dile Red, Pink Swimmingo
2. Herb & Butter, Mexican Style, Country Cheddar, Broccoli Au Gratin
3. Yellin' Melons, Cyclone Fruits, Cotton Candy, Sour Blue Razz Berry
4. Beefy Mushroom, Old-Fashioned Vegetable, Bean with Bacon, Fiesta Chili Beef
5. Code Red, LiveWire, Blue Shock, Baja Blast
6. Loaded Baked Potato, Pizza, Chili Cheese, Ranch
7. Sizzling Cinnamon, Toasted Marshmallow, Buttered Popcorn, Juicy Pear
8. Bold & Spicy, Roasted Garlic, Thick & Hearty, Smoky Mesquite
9. Vermonty Python, Chubby Hubby, Neapolitan Dynamite, Karamel Sutra
10. Blue Raspberry, Green Apple, Fire, Fruit Punch

Answers to the questions on this page can be found on page 82.

FEBRUARY 12

• **1809** • ABRAHAM LINCOLN, who will go on to become America's first bearded president, is born (clean-shaven) in a Kentucky log cabin.

HAIR FORCE ONE
Can you match these presidents to the facial hair depicted in their White House portraits?

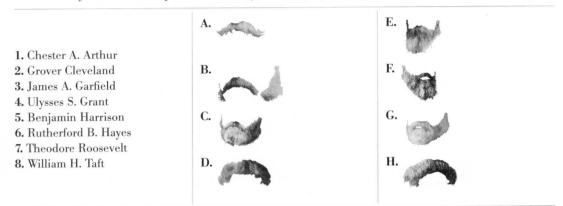

1. Chester A. Arthur
2. Grover Cleveland
3. James A. Garfield
4. Ulysses S. Grant
5. Benjamin Harrison
6. Rutherford B. Hayes
7. Theodore Roosevelt
8. William H. Taft

• **1874** • THE MOST EXPENSIVE FIRE in British history guts the London bazaar called the "Pantechnicon." Because of the furniture warehouses on the premises, and also to confuse Americans, moving vans come to be called "pantechnicons" in the U.K.

HOW THE BISCUIT CRUMBLES
Translate these words and phrases from British English to real English.

Easy	*Harder*	*Yeah, Good Luck*
1. Lorry	1. Vest	1. Spanner
2. Lift	2. Draughts	2. Tipp-ex
3. Nappy	3. Engaged tone	3. Kirby grip
4. Zebra crossing	4. Agony aunt	4. Serviette
5. Pram	5. Braces	5. Swede

• **1973** • THE STATE OF OHIO erects four signs along Interstate 71 listing distances in both miles and kilometers—the first U.S. attempt at metric road signs. They never got around to changing the speed limit signs from MPH to kilometers-per-dekaminute, though.

POWER OF TEN
What's measured in these metric units?

1. Kelvins	5. Watts	9. Newtons
2. Candelas	6. Poise	10. Becquerels
3. Hertz	7. Amperes	
4. Millibars	8. Ergs	

Answers to the questions on this page can be found on page 82.

• **1709** • A MAROONED SEAMAN named Alexander Selkirk leaves the Juan Fernández Islands aboard the privateer *Duke*, ending the lonely four-year exile that will inspire Daniel Defoe to write *Robinson Crusoe*.

ISLE BE THERE

1. Mount Suribachi is the highest point where?

2. Eunice, Henrietta, or Geraldine—what is "Lovey" Howell's real first name on *Gilligan's Island*?

3. The word "serendipity" comes to us from Serendip, the Persian name for what island?

4. Of the world's seven most populous islands, what's the only one not in Asia?

5. What island was once called Van Diemen's Land?

6. What two neighbors are the only islands ever to host Winter Olympics?

7. What iconic island, seen in movies such as *Point Blank* and *So I Married an Axe Murderer*, is named for the Spanish word for "pelican"?

8. Whose adventures take place on the fictional Island of Sodor?

9. On what island was Napoleon born?

10. What island is home to nearly all the world's lemurs?

• **1984** • THE RAINBOW COALITION is surprised at its founder's, um, colorful language, when *The Washington Post* quotes the Reverend Jesse Jackson, in a front-page story, calling New York City "Hymietown."

THE POLITICAL SPECTRUM
What do you know about these chromatically named groups?

1. What Italian patriot led the Redshirts, volunteers so named because they couldn't afford complete uniforms?

2. Who was the U.S. Green Party's first presidential candidate?

3. What five-letter word did *Time* magazine coin in 1926 to refer to left-leaners?

4. What nickname was given to the brutal Royal Irish Constabulary Reserve Force in 1920?

5. What coalition of conservative Democrats was named for the George Rodrigue paintings that hung on the walls of two Louisiana congressmen?

• **1998** • ADAM SANDLER'S *The Wedding Singer* premieres. Unfortunately for Billy Idol, that awesome deaging software from *X-Men: The Last Stand* hasn't been invented yet.

A FLOCK OF SYNONYMS
Give the 1980s New Wave band whose name might be literally redefined as . . .

1. Enoch's grandfather and the *Myrmecia*

2. The abbreviated ratios of sonic intensity

3. Our language, using post-Elizabethan phonology

4. Nostrum; panacea

5. Panamanian lightweight Panamanian lightweight

6. Symphonic and tenebrous tactics

7. Stratofortresses

8. Lacrimation for trepidation

9. Jean-Luc Godard's 1955 sci-fi noir

10. The art of harmonious bodily movements

Answers to the questions on this page can be found on page 83.

FEBRUARY 14

• **270** • SAINT VALENTINE IS MARTYRED in Rome. Wow, on Valentine's Day! I wonder if they noticed what a coincidence that was.

HEARTBEEPS

1. Nancy Wilson, of the band Heart, scores the films of what director, her husband?
2. How many chambers does the human heart have?

3. Who is pictured on a U.S. Purple Heart medal?
4. Though the rest of him lies in Westminster Abbey, what writer's heart is buried near his native Dorchester, the basis of his fictional town of Casterbridge?
5. Which Smurf has a heart tattooed on each arm?

• **1816** • COMPOSER JEAN-PAUL-EGIDE MARTINI dies in Paris. Only his vocal romance "Plaisir d'amour" is much remembered today, since its melody is the basis of the Elvis and UB40 hit "Can't Help Falling in Love."

SILLY LOVE SONGS
Who had the biggest hit singing about these kinds of love?

Easy	*Harder*	*Yeah, Good Luck*
1. Baby	**1.** California	**1.** 100% Pure
2. Higher	**2.** Radar	**2.** Fast
3. Muskrat	**3.** No Ordinary	**3.** Cool
4. Burning	**4.** Tainted	**4.** Butta
5. Endless	**5.** One	**5.** Modern

• **1994** • PRINCE MARRIES HIS GIRLFRIEND Mayte Garcia, the woman for whom he wrote "The Most Beautiful Girl in the World." Awww.

HEY, GOOD-LOOKIN'

1. The adjective "callipygian" refers to someone who has a beautiful what?
2. Who is both the youngest person ever named People's Sexiest Man Alive and, ironically, the only deceased ex–Sexiest Man?

3. What city's Mount Washington did *USA Today* determine to be the second Most Beautiful Place in America, in 2003?
4. What 1990s one-hit wonder wrote Christina Aguilera's hit "Beautiful"?

5. Whose namesake equation, $e^{i\pi} + 1 = 0$, has been called the most beautiful formula in mathematics?

Answers to the questions on this page can be found on page 83.

• **2005** • YOUTUBE.COM IS BORN, the brainchild of three former PayPal employees banking on the fact that a large search engine will one day want to pay billions of dollars for a site where people can post hilariously recut trailers to popular movies.

CINEMASHUPS

Help inspire more knee-slapping YouTube parodies—overlap two movie titles to create the fanciful mashups described in these plot summaries, like My Big Fat Greek Wedding Crashers.

1. Tallulah Bankhead and friends are stranded in the North Atlantic because Harry Bailey—killed in a sledding accident as a young boy—isn't there to shoot down their attackers.

2. When Clive Owen discovers the last pregnant women on Earth, government agents quickly show up to erase his memory.

3. Lecherous Prague doctor Daniel Day-Lewis discovers a door at his hospital workplace that leads into the brain of a popular actor.

4. An English king must relearn how to live his entire life after suffering a brain injury in the battle of Agincourt.

5. Sean Connery and Michael Caine fleece the natives of Skull Island by pretending to be a giant gorilla.

6. A redneck sheriff needs Sidney Poitier's help when zombies overrun Sparta, Mississippi.

7. Single mom Laura Linney discovers her wayward brother is a check-kiting con man on the run from the FBI.

8. Emma Thompson becomes even more protective of her flighty younger sister when it turns out she can *see the dead*!

9. A young Jedi learns that his father is actually high-diving college freshman Rodney Dangerfield.

10. Sharecropper Celie learns to express—through her music!—just what it feels like when doves cry.

11. Dog trainers Dean Jones and Suzanne Pleshette join Clint Eastwood in an epic search for buried Confederate gold.

12. Southern lawyer Matthew McConaughey defends a beautiful assassin who's been arrested for the brutal revenge she exacted against David Carradine.

13. Edie Sedgwick finds the "golden ticket" that will give her a one-day tour of Andy Warhol's magical New York studio.

14. Butler Anthony Hopkins must atone for his wasted life by preventing his evil Nazi employer from assassinating Charles de Gaulle.

15. Cop partners Judge Reinhold and Fred Savage mysteriously switch bodies while battling Cuban drug lords.

16. Cockney chimney sweep Ben Stiller goes gaga for a magical nanny who throws magical tea parties on the ceilings and uses semen as a magical hair gel.

17. Robert Mitchum marries an Irish village girl during World War I, only to see World War II kill off all their sons.

18. John Denver is enlisted by a powerful supernatural force to deliver His message: "Evacuate Tokyo before I destroy it."

19. After Mr. Freeze is defeated, Chris O'Donnell returns home only to discover that his lifelong love, Audrey Hepburn, has joined a convent.

20. Three budding actresses leave their tiny Welsh coal-mining town, hoping to make it big in the sleazy world of showbiz.

Answers to the questions on this page can be found on page 83.

• **1568** • The Catholic Church sentences the entire population of the Netherlands—three million people!—to death as heretics.

THE EXECUTION OF ALL THINGS

1. What was the better-known name of Margaretha Zelle, exotic dancer and firing squad victim?
2. In 1980, what executed man was, ironically, added to the Anglican Church's calendar of saints?
3. Retired auto worker John Demjanjuk was sentenced to death by Israel because he was believed to be the Nazi guard called by what historical nickname?

4. What two U.S. state capitals are named for people who were executed?
5. Who was the last European head of state to be executed after being removed from power?
6. According to Norman Mailer's *The Executioner's Song*, what condemned murderer may have been the illegitimate grandson of Harry Houdini?
7. For what crime was Bruno Hauptmann executed in 1936?

8. Oslo's Holocaust research center is the former home of what firing squad victim?
9. Whose execution caused the famed Spanish Armada to sail against England?
10. Plato's *Apology* consists of what man's defense against a capital charge?

• **1868** • The Benevolent and Protective Order of Elks is formed at a New York saloon.

LIVING LODGE

Every sitcom needs a goofy Elks rip-off! Match these TV shows to their fictional fraternities.

1. The Caribou Lodge
2. The Cobra Lodge
3. The Fraternal Order of Loons
4. The Kings of Queens
5. The Knights of the Scimitar

6. The Leopard Lodge
7. The Mystic Knights of the Sea
8. The Raccoons
9. The Stonecutters
10. The Water Buffaloes

A. *All in the Family*
B. *Amos 'n' Andy*
C. *Cheers*
D. *Coach*
E. *Everybody Loves Raymond*
F. *The Flintstones*

G. *Happy Days*
H. *The Honeymooners*
I. *Mama's Family*
J. *The Simpsons*

• **1950** • Developer J. C. Nichols dies. He was the brains behind Kansas City's Country Club Plaza, the U.S.'s first suburban shopping center.

PLAZA-BLE ANSWERS

1. What author hosted his famous 1966 masquerade, the "Black and White Ball," at New York's Plaza Hotel?
2. What historic plaza is named for the first publisher of the *Dal-las Morning News*?
3. What capital city is built around the famous Plaza Mayor and Puerta del Sol?
4. On what TV show would you see Kirby Plaza, named for *Fan-tastic Four* creator Jack Kirby?
5. There are currently six U.S. buildings named "Trump Plaza." In what city was the first one located?

Answers to the questions on this page can be found on page 84.

• 1801 • THE HOUSE OF REPRESENTATIVES breaks an electoral tie by electing Thomas Jefferson to the presidency over his opponent, Aaron Burr.

THE TIES THAT BIND

1. A chess game can end in a draw if no piece has been captured or pawn moved in how many moves?
2. Who kicked last-second, tiebreaking field goals to win two different Super Bowls?
3. Who was the last vice president never to cast a single tiebreaking vote in the Senate?
4. Almost twenty years later, what show tied, but couldn't surpass, *Hill Street Blues*'s record of twenty-six Emmys for a drama?
5. What's both the NBA and NHL record for number of overtime periods in a game?

• 1933 • BLONDIE BOOPADOOP marries Dagwood Bumstead, who is disinherited by his billionaire father for wedding the carefree flapper.

THE BLOND LEADING THE BLOND

1. What band's *Greatest Hits* album set a U.S. record by going twenty-nine times **platinum**?
2. Williams, Adams, or Roberts— what's the last name of the *Evil Dead* series protagonist **Ash**?
3. Who was the National League's Rookie of the Year the year after his teammate, Darryl **Strawberry**?
4. What was the one-syllable catchphrase of Little Orphan Annie's dog, **Sandy**?
5. What drink is made from fermented water, yeast, and **honey**?

• 2004 • AN ENTERPRISING CELL PHONE owner tries to auction off his phone number on eBay. Bidding tops $100,000 before Verizon yanks the sale. Why so much interest? The number was 867-5309, immortalized by Tommy Tutone in 1982.

ADD IT UP

Remember the annoying postgrunge fad of numbered band names? Finish these equations by filling in the acts' missing digits.

1. UB____ ÷ ____ Non Blondes = Mack ____
2. (Level ____ × ____ Inch Nails) − Eiffel ____ − ____Pac = _____
3. Andre ____ + (____ Mary Three × Maroon ____ × Matchbox ____ × ____ cc) = ____ Maniacs
4. (____ Cent + Sum ____) × U____ = Blink-____
5. Plus-____ + Boys ____ Men + B-____s = ____ Degrees

Answers to the questions on this page can be found on page 84.

FEBRUARY 18

• **1762** • THE MUSICAL PRODIGY Marianne Davies gives the very first performance of Benjamin Franklin's new instrument, the "glass armonica," in London's Spring Gardens. Franklin invented the instrument after hearing of a British man who could play Handel's *Water Music* on a set of tuned wineglasses.

I, GLASSES

1. Photographer Andres Serrano ignited a media firestorm in 1989 by placing what object in a glass of his own urine?
2. What did Pieter van Musschenbroek create at a namesake Dutch university in 1746 by lining a glass jar with silver foil?
3. What did Bob Hope use to hold his lemonade in *The Road to Utopia* and his milk in *Son of Paleface*?
4. What jazz legend's singing shattered the glass in the famous "Is it live or is it Memorex?" ads?
5. What whiskey cocktail lends its name to the short glass also called a "lowball"?

• **1930** • ELM FARM OLLIE, a Guernsey cow from Bismarck, Missouri, becomes the first cow ever to fly—and be milked—in an airplane. The publicity stunt was later adapted into the opera *Madame Butterfat*. No, really.

AGAINST MY BUTTER JUDGMENT

1. What four-letter clarified butter is commonly used in Indian cuisine?
2. What former I Can't Believe It's Not Butter! spokesperson was born with the last name Lanzoni?
3. Who satirized the threat of nuclear war in *The Butter Battle Book*?
4. The viceroy butterfly is so named because of its mimcry of what other species?
5. In what movie does Marlon Brando utter the infamous line "Get the butter"?
6. What was the first name of Rome's Chef di Lelio, who attracted American diners by doubling the butter in his restaurant's fettucini?
7. What novel's long-promised sequel is called *Buttercup's Baby*?
8. What synthpop instrumental was, appropriately, the biggest hit for Hot Butter?
9. Because of his butterfly tattoo, what was Henri Cherrière's nickname at Devil's Island prison?
10. Whose famous horse was named Buttermilk?

• **1952** • JUICE NEWTON is born Judy Kay Cohen in New Jersey.

JUICY THAT?
What kind of fruit juice is used to mix these cocktails?

Easy	Harder	Yeah, Good Luck
1. Mojito	**1.** Salty dog	**1.** Polish martini
2. Piña colada	**2.** Tom Collins	**2.** Lasky
3. Bloody Mary	**3.** Bronx cocktail	**3.** Cape Codder

Answers to the questions on this page can be found on page 84.

• **1913** • Cracker Jack begins including a prize in each box.

THE PRIZE IS RIGHT
Who won a Nobel Prize for discovering the following?

Easy	Harder	Yeah, Good Luck
1. DNA	**1.** Insulin	**1.** Prions
2. Radium and polonium	**2.** Inert gases	**2.** The exclusion principle
3. The neutron	**3.** Energy quanta	**3.** The citric acid cycle
4. Penicillin	**4.** The cause of tuberculosis	**4.** Nuclear fission

• **1957** • Johann Holzel, aka Falco of "Rock Me Amadeus" fame, is born in Vienna, the only surviving child of triplets.

BIRDS OF PREY

1. In its 240 mph hunting dive, what species of raptor is the fastest animal on Earth?
2. On what two near-contemporary ABC series were the crime fighters assisted by a taciturn sidekick named Hawk?
3. What could be built by the largest Lego set ever sold, a 5,195-piece monstrosity?
4. What's the only bird in the famous witches'-cauldron ingredient list from Macbeth?
5. What bird is Britain's VTOL "jump jet" named for?

• **1992** • Disney's *Beauty and the Beast* earns a Best Picture Oscar nomination, making it the only animated feature ever to be so honored.

BEAUTIES AND BEASTS
What models have been married to these, uh, beautiful-on-the-inside musicians?

1. Ric Ocasek	**5.** Seal	**9.** Marilyn Manson
2. Dave Navarro	**6.** Billy Joel	**10.** Tommy Lee
3. Tico Torres	**7.** Mick Jagger	
4. Nikki Sixx	**8.** Travis Barker	

Answers to the questions on this page can be found on page 85.

FEBRUARY 20

• **1816** • ROSSINI'S OPERA *The Barber of Seville*, now a classic, has a disastrous Rome premiere, complete with tripping actors, an audience that jeers throughout, and a cat wandering onstage during the big first-act finale. The following night, however, the second performance is a huge success.

LA TRIVIATA

1. What famous chorus from Verdi's *Il Trovatore* is sung by hammer-wielding Spanish gypsies at dawn?

2. According to Opera America, what Nagasaki-set work is the most performed opera in North America?

3. What opera ends with the line "The commedia is finished!" as Canio stabs Silvio?

4. When it reopened after World War II, what NBC orchestra conductor led the first performance at Milan's rebuilt La Scala opera house?

5. Who are "the night visitors" in Gian Carlo Menotti's opera *Amahl and the Night Visitors*?

• **1913** • KING O'MALLEY, the American-born Australian minister for home affairs, drives the ceremonial first survey peg for the nation's new capital city, to be called Canberra.

CAPITAL PUNISHMENT
What city did these nations build from the ground up to be their capitals?

Easy	*Harder*	*Yeah, Good Luck*
1. India	**1.** Pakistan	**1.** Burma
2. Russia (from 1712 to 1918)	**2.** Malta	**2.** Palau
3. Japan (from 794 to 1868)	**3.** Belize	**3.** Nigeria

• **1962** • JOHN GLENN ORBITS THE EARTH in *Friendship 7*. As he crosses the South Pacific, he sees a mysterious flock of glowing specks he calls "fireflies"—possibly vented ice crystals, but to this day, no one knows for sure.

FRIENDSHIP 7

1. Ramón Ferrer was the captain of what famous ship from American history, whose name meant "Friendship" in his native language?

2. What 2001 Green Day hymn to friendship borrows its title from a popular urban legend about Life cereal's "Mikey"?

3. In what city did eight European nations sign the "Treaty of Friendship, Co-Operation, and Mutual Assistance" in 1955?

4. Who met longtime best friend Gayle King in 1976?

5. Shelley, Browning, or Tennyson—what poet wrote the elegy *In Memoriam* for his late friend Arthur Hallam?

6. What state's motto is "Friendship," since that's supposed to have been the meaning of the state's Caddo Indian name?

7. At a 1979 wine tasting, who first began to survey his friends on their favorite New York restaurants?

Answers to the questions on this page can be found on page 85.

• **1912** • TEDDY ROOSEVELT COINS a new political phrase when, borrowing a prizefighting expression, he tells supporters in a speech, "My hat is in the ring!" He then confuses the boxing metaphor a bit by threatening to "enter the ring speaking softly and whack President Taft with a big stick."

RING THINGS

1. What two NFL quarterbacks have four Super Bowl rings?
2. What's divided by the Cassini Division?
3. According to Clarence in *It's a Wonderful Life*, what happens every time a bell rings?
4. The seismic belt called the Ring of Fire surrounds what body of water?
5. What industry did Finland's Vesa-Matti Paananen create when he wrote a free program called "Harmonium" in the late 1990s?
6. In *The Fellowship of the Ring*, what does Gandalf do to the ring to make its secret inscription visible?
7. What do a ladder, a three-legged lamb, a flaming tree, combed hair, and a centipede have in common?
8. A benzene ring is made up of atoms of what element?
9. His first name was Otto, and in 1897, he started a watch repair business in Owatonna, Minnesota. Today his namesake company boasts that it "helps people celebrate important moments." What was Otto's last name?
10. By tradition, what can you call yourself if you were born within the sound of London's Bow bells ringing?
11. According to the full title of Richard Wagner's "Ring Cycle," the fabulous ring belongs to what race of dwarves?
12. In 1986, a brittle O-ring seal was determined to be the cause of what?
13. What kind of ring is a *dohyo*?
14. What is a fairy ring made of?
15. What's the name of the metal link with two screw threads used to attach the ropes to the posts in a boxing or wrestling ring?

• **1981** • IN AN INTERVIEW WITH *Sounds* magazine, Abbo, of the punk band UK Decay, uses the term "Gothic" to describe a rising London music subculture. The "goth" scene is born.

BABY'S IN BLACK

1. Ditra Flame was the "Lady in Black" who took thirteen red roses to what actor's grave every year?
2. The singer in Johnny Cash's "Folsom Prison Blues" is, mysteriously, in a California jail for having committed a murder in what other state?
3. What's the only *Star Wars* movie in which Darth Vader uses the Force to choke someone to death?
4. What famous historical figure turns out to be the disguised Black Knight in Sir Walter Scott's *Ivanhoe*?
5. What New York country club lent its name to the kind of dinner jacket first worn there in 1886?
6. What country was policed by the Blackshirts for almost twenty-five years?
7. Who had a surprise cameo as "Agent M" in *Men in Black II*?
8. What team's rowdiest black-clad fans sit in a section called the "Black Hole"?
9. What TV persona made Cassandra Peterson a star?
10. Don Diego's secret identity, "Zorro," is the Spanish word for what animal?

Answers to the questions on this page can be found on page 85.

FEBRUARY 22

• **10,000 B.C.** • PEBBLES FLINTSTONE IS BORN at Rockville Hospital at 8 P.M., according to Hanna-Barbera. Wilma's doing fine, but that forcep-asaurus sure does leave a mark.

ROCK SOLID
Hopefully you won't find these questions too "hard."

1. Which chemical element did the ancients call brimstone?
2. What's the only non-R-rated film Oliver Stone has ever directed?
3. What kind of stone is Georgia's Stone Mountain?
4. On the strength of their second single, who made the March 29, 1973, cover of *Rolling Stone*, with the caption "What's-Their-Names Make the Cover"?
5. Whose tombstone reads, in part, "Truth and History. 21 Men. The Boy Bandit King. He Died as He Lived"?
6. What month's birthstone places highest on the Mohs scale?
7. What title character of a classic 1891 novel is arrested at Stonehenge?
8. What made-up Bible verse is the catchphrase of wrestler "Stone Cold" Steve Austin?
9. What kind of gem is El Corazón, which is "romanced" in *Romancing the Stone*?
10. In what country would you find the port of Rosetta, of Rosetta stone fame?

• **1495** • KING CHARLES VIII OF FRANCE enters Naples and is crowned king. His campaign is remembered today mostly for spreading syphilis across Europe. For years afterward, the English called syphilis "the French disease," while the French called it *la maladie anglaise*—"the English disease"!

THE FRENCH CONNECTION
Translate these "French" answers back into ze English.

1. *Pommes frites*
2. *Embrasser avec la langue*
3. *Portes-fenêtres*
4. *Cor d'harmonie*
5. *Poignet mousquetaire*

• **2006** • ALEX OSTROVSKY, of West Bloomfield, Michigan, downloads the billionth song from Apple's iTunes Web site. (Luckily for Alex, it was "Speed of Sound" by Coldplay. How'd you like your name to appear in headlines for your download of "Ice Ice Baby"?)

EYE TUNES
Questions both musicological and ophthalmological.

1. What two other actresses are name-checked in Kim Carnes's "Bette Davis Eyes"?
2. What stadium hit do we owe to a pre–Civil War folk song and the Swedish dance band Rednex?
3. The song "Suite: Judy Blue Eyes" was inspired by Stephen Stills's breakup with whom?
4. Twenty-six years before it became a pop hit, what song was originally written by Jerome Kern for the Astaire-Rogers film *Roberta*?
5. Whose first single was "I've Cried (the Blue Right Out of My Eyes)," which turned out to be an ironic reverse of her biggest hit?
6. In a 1989 film, what song finally replaced John Cusack and Cameron Crowe's earlier choices, Billy Idol's "To Be a Lover" or Fishbone's "Turn the Other Way"?
7. Who sang the theme song of the Bond film *For Your Eyes Only*, making her the only Bond vocalist to actually appear in the opening credits?
8. What song was written in 1981 when Sylvester Stallone was unable to secure the movie rights to Queen's "Another One Bites the Dust"?
9. What line is missing from some bowdlerized edits of Van Morrison's "Brown Eyed Girl"?
10. What civil rights anthem is actually a rewrite of the hymn "Keep Your Hands on the Plow, Hold On"?

Answers to the questions on this page can be found on page 86.

• **1985** • In a tight game with Purdue, Bobby Knight expresses his dissatisfaction with a referee's call by hurling a plastic chair across the basketball court.

SIT ON IT

1. In which Hitchcock movie is the protagonist confined to a wheelchair?

2. In what ominous numbered room is Winston Smith strapped to a chair at the end of *Nineteen Eighty-four*?

3. Who sits behind the "*Resolute* desk," made from the timbers of the HMS *Resolute* of the British navy?

4. What's the smallest nation with a permanent seat on the U.N. Security Council, in both population and area?

5. Today, the Smithsonian is home to the high-back wing chair used by what fictional character from 1971 to 1979?

6. Who was sent to the electric chair on the testimony of her brother David Greenglass?

7. The Siege Perilous was the name for the empty seat where?

8. What competition was dreamed up by the eccentric "Chairman Kaga"?

9. Marseille, Barcelona, or Naples—architect Ludwig Mies van der Rohe named his famous modernist lounge chair after what Mediterranean city, where it debuted?

10. What duo's biggest hits are found on 1985's *Songs from the Big Chair*?

• **2003** • ~~Mario Lemieux~~ Jarome Iginla becomes ~~the~~ the second only player in NHL history ever to complete an "ultimate hat trick" by scoring goals in all five possible ways in one game: on a power play, shorthanded, at even strength, on a penalty, and into an empty net.

TEN GALLANT HATS

Match each famous name to its owner's characteristic headwear.

1. Akbar and Jeff
2. Inspector Clouseau
3. Jacques Cousteau
4. Oliver Hardy
5. Holly Hobbie
6. Sherlock Holmes
7. Indiana Jones
8. Buster Keaton
9. Abraham Lincoln
10. Goober Pyle

A. Beanie
B. Bonnet
C. Bowler
D. Deerstalker
E. Fedora
F. Fez
G. Porkpie
H. Stovepipe
I. Trilby
J. Tuque

Answers to the questions on this page can be found on page 86.

FEBRUARY 24

• **1784** • ACCORDING TO A CHURCH REGISTER, the mysterious adventurer and alchemist called the Count of Saint Germain dies in Schleswig, Germany. But a string of rumors and sightings will have Saint Germain, "the man who does not die," popping up all over Europe well into the twentieth century.

DOWN FOR THE COUNT

1. Who killed Count Rugen?
2. What werewolf-themed cereal briefly joined Count Chocula on store shelves in 1974?
3. Whose death is a result of the souring of her relationship with her lover Count Vronsky?
4. What instrument did jazz bandleader Count Basie play?
5. What famous occultist, thrown into the Bastille for his role in "the affair of the necklace," may have actually been a Sicilian peasant named Giuseppe Balsamo?
6. Who killed Count Dooku by cutting off his head?
7. What country's kings were also counts of Holland and Flanders in the sixteenth and seventeenth centuries?
8. Who built the French country house he called the Château de Monte-Cristo?
9. The real-life Hungarian nobleman Count László Almásy was the basis for what ironically misidentified title character of literature and film?
10. What's the surname of *Sesame Street*'s The Count?

• **1969** • JOHNNY CASH'S FAMOUS performance for the inmates of San Quentin includes Shel Silverstein's novelty song "A Boy Named Sue." The live "Sue" will become the only Top Ten pop single of Cash's long career.

HE SAID, SHE SAID
Poor Sue isn't the only famous person with a gender-bending first name.

1. What novelist of westerns went by his middle name, since he was given the first name "Pearl"?
2. What actress had the word "Miss" listed before her first name in the credits of *The Waltons*?
3. According to a university tradition, whose most famous poem was inspired by a white oak on the campus of Rutgers's agriculture school?
4. Who has played a U.S. vice president on the big screen and a U.S. chief justice on the small screen?
5. What TV host's father was a longtime *Washington Post* sportswriter once erroneously listed in *Who's Who of American Women* because his given name was Shirley?
6. "Madison" is now one of the most popular baby girl names in America, thanks mostly to what actress, who sported it in a 1984 comedy?
7. *A Christmas Story* was inspired by the childhood reminiscences of what radio personality?
8. Agatha Christie's *The Mirror Crack'd* was inspired by an incident from the life of what actress, who gave birth to a severely handicapped child because an obsessed fan had given her German measles at a USO event?
9. What British satirist was briefly married, in the late 1920s, to a woman who spelled her first name the same as his?
10. Who originally sang the 1975 song that became the Dixie Chicks' biggest pop hit ever in 2002?

Answers to the questions on this page can be found on page 86.

• **1779** • JUST A WEEK AFTER Captain Cook's death, his surviving crew become the first Europeans to sight the island of Lanai. Lanai will become known as "Pineapple Island" in 1922, when the Hawaiian Pineapple Company purchases it and turns it into the world's largest plantation.

ON THE DOLE

1. What word is the actual title of the 1979 hit usually called "The Piña Colada Song"?
2. Where would you see the consumer warning "Do not use fresh or frozen pineapple, kiwi, ginger-root, papaya, figs, or guava"?
3. In what undersea city does SpongeBob SquarePants live?
4. What was the MK2 "Pineapple," later replaced by the M67 and M61?
5. What Latin American dictator was called "Carepiña"—"Pineapple Face"—because of his acne-scarred complexion?

• **1956** • NIKITA KHRUSHCHEV RENOUNCES Stalinism in the so-called secret speech, "On the Personality Cult and Its Consequences," at a closed session of the Soviet Party Congress.

PUBLIC SERVICE RENOUNCEMENT

1. In what 1863 short story does Philip Nolan renounce his U.S. citizenship?
2. If you give something up for Lent, how many days are you going without?
3. In 1969, who returned his MBE medal "against our support of America in Vietnam, and against 'Cold Turkey' slipping down the charts"?
4. Who was ordered to recant heliocentrism in 1633 by the Inquisition and spent the last decade of his life under house arrest as a result?
5. In 2004, Norodom Sihanouk renounced the throne of what Asian country?

• **2006** • ACCORDING TO U.S. CENSUS BUREAU predictions, the earth's population hits 6.5 billion—at 7:16 P.M. Eastern Time, in fact.

CENSUS WORKING OVERTIME

1. What's the most populous county in the U.S., with almost twice as many residents as the runner-up?
2. What's the EU's largest member by population?
3. What's the most populous city located north of the Arctic Circle?
4. What's the U.S. island with the largest population?
5. What's the world's most populous country whose most populous city is also its capital?
6. What state capital is the most populous American city without a team in any of the four large North American sports organizations?
7. Monaco, Andorra, or Vatican City—by a wide margin, what European nation has the world's highest population density?
8. What's the world's largest Spanish-speaking country by population?
9. What was the world's most populous city before Tokyo surpassed it in the 1960s?
10. What's the second most populated continent on Earth?

Answers to the questions on this page can be found on page 87.

FEBRUARY 26

• **1852** • JOHN HARVEY KELLOGG is born in Michigan. His invention of corn flakes really caught on—his other big idea, yogurt enemas, not so much. (Seriously. Sort of gives new meaning to "fruit on the bottom.")

TCBY
Trivia concerned by yogurt

1. In *Spaceballs*, what magic power is taught by the sage Yogurt?
2. Who is elected mayor due to the title scandal in the *Seinfeld* episode "The Non-Fat Yogurt"?

3. What brand began in 1919 with a Barcelona yogurt shop that Isaac Carasson named for his son, "little Daniel"?
4. What vegetable is most commonly added to yogurt to make

Indian *raita*?
5. According to legend, what "Magnificent" Ottoman sultan brought yogurt to France when he sent a court doctor to treat King Francis I's diarrhea?

• **1976** • SECRETARY-GENERAL U THANT proclaims the United Nations' first celebration of Earth Day.

THE GREATEST SHOWS ON EARTH
What "earthy" movie featured these costars?

Easy
1. Michael Rennie and Patricia Neal
2. David Bowie and Rip Torn
3. John Travolta and Forest Whitaker

Harder
1. Chris Rock and Regina King
2. Winona Ryder and Roberto Benigni
3. Geena Davis and Jim Carrey

Yeah, Good Luck
1. James Mason and Pat Boone
2. Chris Klein and Josh Hartnett
3. Joan Chen and Tommy Lee Jones

• **1986** • *ALL THE KING'S MEN* AUTHOR Robert Penn Warren is named the U.S.'s first official poet laureate consultant in poetry.

VERSED-CASE SCENARIO
Five more poet laureates—or is it poets laureate?

1. What Oscar-winning actor has restored the hyphen to his name that his poet laureate father, Cecil, dropped in 1927?
2. In 1968, Gwendolyn Brooks replaced what man as only the second poet laureate of Illinois?

3. Super glue, sandpaper, or X-Acto knives—what hobby essential was invented by the father of U.S. Poet Laureate Louise Glück?
4. Robert Southey became Britain's poet laureate in 1813 only because what author of *Rob*

Roy refused the honor?
5. What animated film is based on a story that future poet laureate Ted Hughes told his children to comfort them after their mother's suicide?

Answers to the questions on this page can be found on page 87.

• **1964** • THE ITALIAN GOVERNMENT requests international aid to save the Leaning Tower of Pisa, which is getting dangerously close to toppling over.

THE TOWER AND THE GLORY
What city is home to these famous towers?

Easy	Harder	Yeah, Good Luck
1. The Sears Tower	**1.** John Hancock Tower	**1.** Milad Tower
2. The CN Tower	**2.** Shukhov Tower	**2.** Rose Tower
3. Trump World Tower	**3.** Oriental Pearl Tower	**3.** JP Morgan Chase Tower
4. Westminster Clock Tower	**4.** Coit Tower	**4.** Telstra Tower

• **1973** • THE AMERICAN INDIAN MOVEMENT occupies Wounded Knee, South Dakota, beginning a seventy-one-day standoff with authorities.

WOUNDED KNEES

1. Who delivered the tackle that snapped Joe Theismann's leg below his right knee on *Monday Night Football* in 1985?
2. Who lost her world number one ranking to Kim Clijsters in 2003 when she missed two months of tennis while recuperating from knee surgery?
3. What Vikings QB became a victim of the "Madden curse" with a career-threatening knee injury in 2002?
4. Because it can be caused by too much kneeling, what's the more common name for prepatellar bursitis?
5. What NBA star made an ill-fated trip to Eagle, Colorado, in 2003 for knee surgery?

• **1974** • *PEOPLE* MAGAZINE DEBUTS. The first cover promises interviews with tabloid faves like Richard Petty, Lee Harvey Oswald's widow, and Aleksandr Solzhenitsyn (!).

UP WITH PEOPLE
Who had hits singing about these kinds of people?

Easy	Harder	Yeah, Good Luck
1. Shiny Happy	**1.** Common	**1.** Lonely
2. Everyday	**2.** The Beautiful	**2.** Voodoo
3. Short	**3.** 24 Hour Party	**3.** Sunset
4. Ordinary	**4.** Rainy Day	**4.** Happy

Answers to the questions on this page can be found on page 87.

• **1643** • One Roger Scott is tried in Boston for repeatedly sleeping in church and then striking the poor tithingman who tried to wake him. He is ordered to be "severely whipped" for the lapse.

HOUSES OF THE HOLY

1. The world's largest church is the Our Lady of Peace Basilica in Yamoussoukro, what nation's capital?
2. How do Ben and Elaine get away from the church at the end of *The Graduate*?
3. What "Best of My Love" trio started singing in church choirs as the Hutchinson Sunbeams?
4. In what city is Ebenezer Baptist Church, where Martin Luther King, Jr., and his father were pastors?
5. What Foursquare Church founder vanished mysteriously in Mexico in 1926?
6. What two characters on the original *Star Trek* have names that are also words for types of churches?
7. Christchurch is the largest city on what nation's largest island, South Island?
8. What movie classic begins at the "1st Methodist Church Kung Du" in German East Africa?
9. What Thomas Hardy novel takes its quiet title from Thomas Gray's "Elegy Written in a Country Churchyard"?
10. Who is the pipe-smoking figurehead of the Church of the SubGenius?

• **1983** • The final episode of *M*A*S*H* becomes the highest-rated program in TV history.

GOODBYE, FAREWELL, AND AMEN

1. Who divorced Neil Simon four years after starring in his film *The **Goodbye** Girl*?
2. The fiddle-and-guitar folk song "Ashokan **Farewell**" became popular in 1990 when it was used as the theme for what PBS series?
3. What title snatch of music from a Sir Arthur Sullivan song had "the sound of a great **Amen**"?
4. What silent character ended the final telecast of *Howdy Doody* by saying, "**Good-bye**, kids"?
5. Who warned against the "military-industrial complex" in his famous **farewell** address?
6. On what golf course would you find the three tricky holes called the "**Amen** Corner"?

• **2002** • The former national currencies of much of Europe cease to be legal tender, thanks to the Euro rollout. If Grandma left behind millions of francs, marks, or pesetas in a hidden stash in the attic, well, you now have a hilarious novelty gift.

YOU'RE NOT CUTE BUT EURO SO PRETTY

What countries feature (or will feature) the following on their 1-euro coin?

Easy
1. The sacred owl of Athena
2. King Juan Carlos I
3. A tree, surrounded by the words "Liberté Egalité Fraternité"
4. Mozart

Harder
1. Vitruvian Man
2. A Cláirseach harp
3. The "federal eagle"
4. Albert II (two answers)

Yeah, Good Luck
1. The Idol of Pomos
2. The Protestant reformer Primoz Trubar
3. Two swans flying
4. His Royal Highness the Grand Duke Henri

Answers to the questions on this page can be found on page 88.

• **45 B.C.** • THE JULIAN CALENDAR inserts the first Leap Day into the calendar. (Actually, the Romans made February 24 a forty-eight-hour day that year, but you know what I mean.)

LEAPER COLONY

1. Who ordered the disastrous "Great Leap Forward" in 1958?
2. What did Scott Bakula typically say after "leaping" into a new host on TV's *Quantum Leap*?
3. In 1991, who finally broke Bob Beamon's decades-old long jump record?
4. What kind of fixed-object parachute jumping takes its name from the four categories of such jumps?
5. What is a whale's leap out of the water called?
6. What video game character was originally given the name Jumpman?
7. Mark Twain's "Celebrated Jumping Frog of Calaveras County" was named for what famous orator?
8. *One Giant Leap* was the first biography ever written of whom?
9. What state motto of Virginia did John Wilkes Booth shout as he jumped from Lincoln's box to the stage of Ford's Theatre?
10. The "leap from the lion's head" is the final challenge in what 1989 movie?

• **1960** • THE LINE WINDS around the block as the world's first Playboy Club opens in Chicago.

BUNNY BUSINESS

1. At what U.S. city, its state's largest, did Bugs Bunny traditionally lament taking a left "toin"?
2. What's the Western name for the image the Japanese describe as a rabbit pounding *mochi* rice cakes?
3. Whose garden is infiltrated by Peter Rabbit?
4. What popular breed of pet rabbit was named for the Asian capital where it was first domesticated?
5. What film's title character is the only one who can see a giant demonic rabbit named Frank?

• **1968** • ON TV's *HOLLYWOOD SQUARES*, a contestant calls on Jack Palance, only to find the tough-guy actor asleep in his square. "No way was I going to wake him up!" remembered adjacent square mate Michael Landon.

DOZE WERE THE DAYS
Can you answer these drowsy questions without nodding off?

1. Under what brand name does Roche market the sedative diazepam?
2. What Native American was born Goyathlay, meaning "he who yawns"?
3. What Oscar winner gives a wordless performance as the Headless Horseman in Tim Burton's *Sleepy Hollow*?
4. Which *Friends* alum is the answer to the trivia question in the *SNL* "Lazy Sunday" sketch?
5. What 1991 hit features a recitation of the eighteenth-century children's prayer "Now I Lay Me Down to Sleep" during the bridge?

Answers to the questions on this page can be found on page 88.

February Answers

FEBRUARY 1

COPPER TONE
1. Tin
2. The torch flame is gold leaf
3. Cyprus
4. Zinc
5. Claudia Schiffer

STRAIGHT "EH?"S
1. Prince Edward Island
2. Eleven
3. The *Edmund Fitzgerald*
4. Nelly Furtado (named for Nellie Kim)
5. The Suez Crisis
6. Sam McGee
7. Guy Lombardo
8. British Columbia and Saskatchewan (Victoria and Regina)
9. Lorne Greene
10. Labrador
11. Molson
12. The CFL's Grey Cup (named for the Fourth Earl Grey)
13. William Shatner's
14. Filippo De Grassi (*Degrassi High*)
15. Lake Michigan

FEBRUARY 2

SUB POP
Easy
1. *Moby-Dick*
2. *Through the Looking-Glass*
3. *Ben-Hur*
4. *Black Beauty*
5. *2001*
Harder
1. *The Pilgrim's Progress*
2. *Frankenstein*
3. *Uncle Tom's Cabin*
4. *The Hobbit*
5. *Oliver Twist*
Yeah, Good Luck
1. *Vanity Fair*
2. *Brideshead Revisited*
3. *Slaughterhouse-Five*
4. *Tess of the D'Urbervilles*
5. *Roots*

TIME AFTER TIME
1. Samsara
2. "Let It Be"
3. Those are fake ads interrupted by the Energizer bunny
4. Da capo
5. The Buffalo Bills, who lost all four
6. "All work and no play makes Jack a dull boy"
7. Déjà vu
8. A flipped coin comes up heads
9. Fractals
10. *A Christmas Story*

SIGNIFICANT OTHERS
1. Ireland
2. Pork
3. Jacob Riis
4. Olive (the Other Reindeer, get it?)
5. The E Street Band

FEBRUARY 3

¾ TIME
1. Gibbous
2. The Acadians (today, Cajuns)
3. Perth
4. Rechargeable batteries
5. Alexander Hamilton

THOROUGH, BUT FAIR
Easy
1. Beverly Hills
2. New Orleans
3. Paris
4. San Francisco
5. Atlanta
Harder
1. Memphis
2. St. Petersburg
3. London
4. Miami
5. Chicago
Yeah, Good Luck
1. Barcelona
2. Hong Kong
3. Toronto
4. Mexico City
5. Hamburg

THEY'VE GOT A LOT OF BALLS
1. Ole Evinrude
2. Chuck Taylor
3. Albert Spalding
4. John Brunswick
5. Phil Knight

February Answers

FEBRUARY 4

HOUR TOWNS
Easy
1. *Buffy the Vampire Slayer*
2. *The Flintstones*
3. *Murder, She Wrote*
4. *Northern Exposure*
5. *The Jetsons*
Harder
1. *Friday Night Lights*
2. *The Family Guy*
3. *Dawson's Creek*
4. *Newhart*
5. *The Munsters*
Yeah, Good Luck
1. *Ed*
2. *Picket Fences*
3. *SCTV*
4. *Mama's Family*
5. *Dark Shadows*

CHEAP NOVEL TEASE
1. Debbie Reynolds
2. Bill Clinton
3. Truman Capote
4. Allan Bloom
5. William Jennings Bryan

I'M WITH THE BANNED
1. Foie gras
2. *Spartacus*
3. Andy Kaufman
4. Singapore
5. DDT
6. Ricky Williams
7. The text of the First Amendment
8. *The Lorax*
9. *The* ~~Insider~~ Interpreter
10. Tobacco

FEBRUARY 5

KISS MY AUROUS
1. Ghana
2. "I Got a Woman"
3. William Jennings Bryan
4. Hollywood and Redwood (City)
5. Carl Lewis
6. *Benson* and *Growing Pains*
7. Two of the "Seven Cities of Gold"
8. Mr. T
9. Tom Sawyer
10. Supernovas

GOING IN CIRCLES
1. Washington, D.C.
2. Columbus Circle
3. Mexico
4. Piccadilly Circus
5. The Arc de Triomphe

UNITED ARTISTS
1. A
2. D
3. B
4. E
5. C

FEBRUARY 6

I GOT HUE, BABE
1. Orange
2. Frank Gifford
3. George Stephanopoulos
4. Newborns
5. Yellow
6. Henri Matisse's
7. Oscar the Grouch
8. Green
9. Wisteria
10. Pittsburgh (black and gold)

THEY'RE PLAYING OUR SONG
1. The merry-go-round
2. The Buffalo Sabres ("Sabre Dance")
3. "Moonlight Serenade"
4. Topping the Billboard Hot 100 with a TV theme song
5. "I'm the only one"
6. The wolf (French horns)
7. "Enter Sandman"
8. "The Final Countdown"
9. *Rocky*
10. John Tesh

FEBRUARY 7

TRAIL TO THE CHIEF
1. John F. Kennedy
2. Franklin Pierce
3. Andrew Jackson
4. Ronald Reagan
5. Theodore Roosevelt
6. George H. W. Bush
7. Ulysses Grant
8. Jimmy Carter
9. Thomas Jefferson (also John Adams)
10. Bill Clinton

ARMY OF DORKNESS
1. The Salvation Army
2. Arnold Palmer ("Arnie's Army")
3. Terra-cotta
4. Björk's
5. Swiss Army knives

CUT LOOSE
1. Lee Iacocca
2. Dinosaur Jr.
3. She was pregnant
4. George McClellan
5. Mike Ditka

FEBRUARY 8

THE DEVIL'S IN THE DETAILS
1. Fiddle playing
2. The Colorado Rockies
3. Anne Rice's
4. Printers
5. Dalmatian
6. Turning stones into bread
7. John Milton
8. French Guiana
9. Pumpernickel
10. Hobart (Tasmania)

ADAPTIVE PARENTS
Easy
1. *Dracula*
2. *Red Dragon*
3. *Flowers for Algernon*
4. *Rum Punch*
5. *Charlie and the Chocolate Factory*
Harder
1. *Washington Square*
2. *An American Tragedy*
3. *The Turn of the Screw*
4. *The Killer Angels*
5. *Skipping Christmas*
Yeah, Good Luck
1. *A Widow for One Year*
2. *Traumnovelle*
3. *The Secret Agent*
4. *The Postman Always Rings Twice*
5. *58 Minutes*

DIFF'RENT STROKES
1. Butterfly
2. Gertrude Ederle
3. Duke Kahanamoku
4. Ian Thorpe
5. Flash Gordon

FEBRUARY 9

WALTZ TIME
1. Zelda Sayre Fitzgerald
2. A migrant worker's bundle or bedroll
3. The "Minute Waltz" (or Waltz in D-flat Major)
4. Ron Wood and Ringo Starr
5. It's the Nokia ring tone

ATHLEXICON
Easy
1. Golf
2. Football
3. Rugby
4. Cycling
5. Baseball
Harder
1. Jai alai
2. Soccer
3. Auto racing
4. Cricket
5. Skiing
Yeah, Good Luck
1. Darts
2. Skateboarding
3. Curling
4. Fencing
5. Archery

ONE-HIT WONDERS
1. The Notorious B.I.G.
2. Harper Lee (*To Kill a Mockingbird*)
3. Marlon Brando
4. *Fidelio*
5. Archibald "Moonlight" Graham

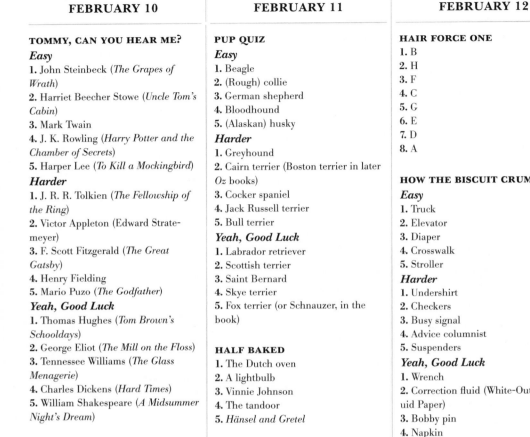

FEBRUARY 10

TOMMY, CAN YOU HEAR ME?
Easy
1. John Steinbeck (*The Grapes of Wrath*)
2. Harriet Beecher Stowe (*Uncle Tom's Cabin*)
3. Mark Twain
4. J. K. Rowling (*Harry Potter and the Chamber of Secrets*)
5. Harper Lee (*To Kill a Mockingbird*)
Harder
1. J. R. R. Tolkien (*The Fellowship of the Ring*)
2. Victor Appleton (Edward Stratemeyer)
3. F. Scott Fitzgerald (*The Great Gatsby*)
4. Henry Fielding
5. Mario Puzo (*The Godfather*)
Yeah, Good Luck
1. Thomas Hughes (*Tom Brown's Schooldays*)
2. George Eliot (*The Mill on the Floss*)
3. Tennessee Williams (*The Glass Menagerie*)
4. Charles Dickens (*Hard Times*)
5. William Shakespeare (*A Midsummer Night's Dream*)

SINGIN' THE BLUES
1. The sky
2. Smurfette
3. Mount Mitchell
4. On Sundays
5. Boise State
6. "Detroit in '68"
7. Dennis Franz
8. The president of South Korea
9. Prussian blue
10. The Blue Man Group
11. UFOs
12. *Blue Crush*
13. Brett Hull
14. Khartoum, Sudan
15. The Navy

FEBRUARY 11

PUP QUIZ
Easy
1. Beagle
2. (Rough) collie
3. German shepherd
4. Bloodhound
5. (Alaskan) husky
Harder
1. Greyhound
2. Cairn terrier (Boston terrier in later Oz books)
3. Cocker spaniel
4. Jack Russell terrier
5. Bull terrier
Yeah, Good Luck
1. Labrador retriever
2. Scottish terrier
3. Saint Bernard
4. Skye terrier
5. Fox terrier (or Schnauzer, in the book)

HALF BAKED
1. The Dutch oven
2. A lightbulb
3. Vinnie Johnson
4. The tandoor
5. *Hänsel and Gretel*

THE LOVE OF FLAVOR
1. Kool-Aid
2. Rice-a-Roni
3. Bubble Yum
4. Campbell's (Condensed) Soup
5. Mountain Dew
6. Pringles
7. Jelly Belly
8. A1
9. Ben & Jerry's
10. Jolly Ranchers

FEBRUARY 12

HAIR FORCE ONE
1. B
2. H
3. F
4. C
5. G
6. E
7. D
8. A

HOW THE BISCUIT CRUMBLES
Easy
1. Truck
2. Elevator
3. Diaper
4. Crosswalk
5. Stroller
Harder
1. Undershirt
2. Checkers
3. Busy signal
4. Advice columnist
5. Suspenders
Yeah, Good Luck
1. Wrench
2. Correction fluid (White-Out or Liquid Paper)
3. Bobby pin
4. Napkin
5. Rutabaga

POWER OF TEN
1. Temperature
2. Luminous intensity
3. Frequency
4. Pressure
5. Power
6. Viscosity
7. Electric current
8. Work
9. Force
10. Radioactivity

February Answers

FEBRUARY 13

ISLE BE THERE
1. Iwo Jima
2. Eunice
3. Sri Lanka
4. Great Britain
5. Tasmania
6. Honshu and Hokkaido
(Nagano and Sapporo)
7. Alcatraz
8. Thomas the Tank Engine's
9. Corsica
10. Madagascar

THE POLITICAL SPECTRUM
1. Giuseppe Garibaldi
2. Ralph Nader
3. Pinko
4. Black and Tans
5. The Blue Dogs

A FLOCK OF SYNONYMS
1. Adam and the Ants
2. The dBs (decibels)
3. Modern English
4. The Cure
5. Duran Duran (Roberto Durán)
6. Orchestral Manoeuvres in the
Dark
7. The B-52s
8. Tears for Fears
9. Alphaville
10. Eurythmics

FEBRUARY 14

HEARTBEEPS
1. Cameron Crowe
2. Four
3. George Washington
4. Thomas Hardy
5. Hefty Smurf

SILLY LOVE SONGS
Easy
1. The Supremes
2. Steve Winwood
3. The Captain & Tennille
4. Elvis Presley
5. Lionel Richie and Diana Ross
Harder
1. Tupac Shakur
2. Golden Earring
3. Sade
4. Soft Cell
5. Bob Marley
Yeah, Good Luck
1. Crystal Waters
2. George Michael
3. Pablo Cruise
4. Next
5. David Bowie

HEY, GOOD-LOOKIN'
1. Butt
2. John F. Kennedy, Jr.
3. Pittsburgh
4. Linda Perry (of 4 Non
Blondes)
5. Leonhard Euler

FEBRUARY 15

CINEMASHUPS
1. *It's a Wonderful Lifeboat*
2. *Children of Men in Black*
3. *The Unbearable Lightness of
Being John Malkovich*
4. *Regarding Henry V*
5. *The Man Who Would Be King
Kong*
6. *In the Heat of the Night of the
Living Dead*
7. *Catch Me If You Can Count on
Me*
8. *The Sixth Sense and Sensibility*
9. *The Empire Strikes Back to
School*
10. *The Color Purple Rain*
11. *The Good, the Bad, and the
Ugly Dachshund*
12. *A Time to Kill Bill*
13. *Charlie (or Willy Wonka) and
the Chocolate Factory Girl*
14. *The Remains of the Day of
the Jackal*
15. *Miami Vice Versa*
16. *There's Something about
Mary Poppins*
17. *Saving Private Ryan's Daughter*
18. *Oh, Godzilla!*
19. *Batman and Robin and Marian*
20. *How Green Was My Valley of
the Dolls*

FEBRUARY 16

THE EXECUTION OF ALL THINGS
1. Mata Hari
2. Sir Thomas More
3. Ivan the Terrible
4. Raleigh and St. Paul
5. Nicolae Ceausescu
6. Gary Gilmore
7. Kidnapping (and killing) the Lindbergh baby
8. Vidkun Quisling
9. Mary, Queen of Scots'
10. Socrates'

LIVING LODGE
1. E
2. I
3. D
4. A
5. C
6. G
7. B
8. H
9. J
10. F

PLAZA-BLE ANSWERS
1. Truman Capote
2. Dealey Plaza
3. Madrid
4. *Heroes*
5. Atlantic City

FEBRUARY 17

THE TIES THAT BIND
1. Fifty (by each side)
2. Adam Vinateri
3. Dan Quayle
4. *The West Wing*
5. Six

THE BLOND LEADING THE BLOND
1. The Eagles'
2. Williams
3. Dwight Gooden
4. Arf
5. Mead

ADD IT UP
1. UB40 ÷ 4 Non Blondes = Mack 10
2. (Level 42 × 9 Inch Nails) − Eiffel 65 − 2Pac = 311
3. Andre 3000 + (7 Mary Three × Maroon 5 × Matchbox 20 × 10cc) = 10,000 Maniacs
4. (50 Cent + Sum 41) × U2 = Blink-182
5. Plus-44 + Boys 2 Men + B-52s = 98 Degrees

FEBRUARY 18

I, GLASSES
1. A crucifix
2. The Leyden jar
3. "A dirty glass"
4. Ella Fitzgerald's
5. The old-fashioned

AGAINST MY BUTTER JUDGMENT
1. Ghee
2. Fabio
3. Dr. Seuss
4. The monarch butterfly
5. *Last Tango in Paris*
6. Alfredo
7. *The Princess Bride*
8. "Popcorn"
9. Papillon
10. Dale Evans's

JUICY THAT?
Easy
1. Lime
2. Pineapple
3. Tomato
Harder
1. Grapefruit
2. Lemon
3. Orange
Yeah, Good Luck
1. Apple
2. Grape
3. Cranberry

FEBRUARY 19

THE PRIZE IS RIGHT
Easy
1. James Watson and Francis Crick (with Maurice Wilkins)
2. Marie Curie
3. James Chadwick
4. Alexander Fleming (with Howard Florey and Ernst Chain)
Harder
1. Frederick Banting (with John Macleod)
2. William Ramsay
3. Max Planck
4. Robert Koch
Yeah, Good Luck
1. Stanley Prusiner
2. Wolfgang Pauli
3. Hans Krebs
4. Otto Hahn

BIRDS OF PREY
1. The peregrine falcon
2. *Spenser for Hire* and *Twin Peaks*
3. The *Millennium Falcon*
4. An owl ("howlet's wing")
5. The harrier

BEAUTIES AND BEASTS
1. Paulina Porizkova
2. Carmen Electra
3. Eva Herzegova
4. Donna D'Errico
5. Heidi Klum
6. Christie Brinkley
7. Jerry Hall (though the marriage was never official under English law)
8. Shanna Moakler
9. Dita Von Teese
10. Pamela Anderson

FEBRUARY 20

LA TRIVIATA
1. The Anvil Chorus, or "Coro di zingari"
2. *Madame Butterfly*
3. *Pagliacci (Clowns)*
4. Arturo Toscanini
5. The biblical Magi, or "three wise men"

CAPITAL PUNISHMENT
Easy
1. (New) Delhi
2. St. Petersburg
3. Kyoto
Harder
1. Islamabad
2. Valletta
3. Belmopan
Yeah, Good Luck
1. Naypyidaw
2. Melekeok
3. Abuja

FRIENDSHIP 7
1. *Amistad*
2. "Poprocks & Coke"
3. Warsaw (the Warsaw Pact)
4. Oprah Winfrey
5. Alfred, Lord Tennyson
6. Texas
7. Tim Zagat

FEBRUARY 21

RING THINGS
1. Terry Bradshaw and Joe Montana
2. Saturn's rings
3. "An angel gets its wings"
4. The Pacific Ocean
5. Ring tones
6. Heat it in a fire
7. They're among the images on the haunted videotape in *The Ring*
8. Carbon
9. Josten
10. Cockney
11. The Nibelung
12. The *Challenger* disaster
13. A sumo ring
14. Mushrooms
15. A turnbuckle

BABY'S IN BLACK
1. Rudolph Valentino's
2. Nevada ("I shot a man in Reno . . .")
3. *The Empire Strikes Back*
4. Richard the Lion-hearted
5. The Tuxedo Club
6. Italy
7. Michael Jackson
8. The Oakland Raiders'
9. Elvira, Mistress of the Dark
10. Fox

FEBRUARY 22	FEBRUARY 23	FEBRUARY 24

ROCK SOLID
1. Sulfur
2. *World Trade Center*
3. Granite
4. Dr. Hook and the Medicine Show (who sang "The Cover of *Rolling Stone*")
5. Billy the Kid's
6. April's (the diamond)
7. Tess of the D'Urbervilles
8. Austin 3:16
9. An emerald
10. Egypt

THE FRENCH CONNECTION
1. French fries
2. French-kiss
3. French door (or French window)
4. French horn
5. French cuff

EYE TUNES
1. Jean Harlow and Greta Garbo
2. "Cotton Eye Joe"
3. Judy Collins
4. "Smoke Gets in Your Eyes"
5. Crystal Gayle's (of "Don't It Make My Brown Eyes Blue" fame)
6. "In Your Eyes" (in *Say Anything*)
7. Sheena Easton
8. "Eye of the Tiger"
9. "Making love in the green grass"
10. "Keep Your Eyes on the Prize"

SIT ON IT
1. *Rear Window*
2. Room 101
3. The president of the United States
4. The United Kingdom
5. Archie Bunker
6. Ethel Rosenberg
7. The Round Table
8. Iron Chef
9. Barcelona
10. Tears for Fears

TEN GALLANT HATS
1. F
2. I
3. J
4. C
5. B
6. D
7. E
8. G
9. H
10. A

DOWN FOR THE COUNT
1. Inigo Montoya (*The Princess Bride*)
2. Fruit Brute
3. Anna Karenina's
4. Piano (also jazz organ)
5. Count di Cagliostro
6. Anakin Skywalker
7. Spain's
8. Alexandre Dumas
9. *The English Patient*
10. Von Count

HE SAID, SHE SAID
1. Zane Grey
2. Michael Learned
3. Joyce Kilmer
4. Glenn Close (*The West Wing* and *Air Force One*)
5. Maury Povich
6. Daryl Hannah (*Splash*)
7. Jean Shepherd
8. Gene Tierney
9. Evelyn Waugh
10. Stevie Nicks ("Landslide")

FEBRUARY 25

ON THE DOLE
1. "Escape"
2. On a Jell-O box
3. Bikini Bottom
4. A hand grenade
5. Manuel Noriega

PUBLIC SERVICE RENOUNCE-MENT
1. "The Man Without a Country"
2. Forty (not counting Sundays)
3. John Lennon
4. Galileo
5. Cambodia

CENSUS WORKING OVERTIME
1. Los Angeles County
2. Germany
3. Murmansk, Russia
4. Long Island
5. Indonesia
6. Austin
7. Monaco
8. Mexico
9. New York City
10. Africa

FEBRUARY 26

TCBY
1. The Schwartz
2. Rudolph Giuliani
3. Dannon
4. Cucumber
5. Suleiman the Magnificent

THE GREATEST SHOWS ON EARTH
Easy
1. *The Day the Earth Stood Still*
2. *The Man Who Fell to Earth*
3. *Battlefield Earth*
Harder
1. *Down to Earth*
2. *Night on Earth*
3. *Earth Girls Are Easy*
Yeah, Good Luck
1. *Journey to the Center of the Earth*
2. *Here on Earth*
3. *Heaven and Earth*

VERSED-CASE SCENARIO
1. Daniel Day-Lewis
2. Carl Sandburg
3. X-Acto knives
4. Sir Walter Scott
5. *The Iron Giant*

FEBRUARY 27

THE TOWER AND THE GLORY
Easy
1. Chicago
2. Toronto
3. New York City
4. London
Harder
1. Boston
2. Moscow
3. Shanghai
4. San Francisco
Yeah, Good Luck
1. Tehran
2. Dubai
3. Houston (with smaller ones in Dallas and Baton Rouge)
4. Canberra

WOUNDED KNEES
1. Lawrence Taylor
2. Serena Williams
3. Daunte Culpepper
4. Housemaid's knee
5. Kobe Bryant

UP WITH PEOPLE
Easy
1. R.E.M.
2. Sly & the Family Stone (also Arrested Development)
3. Randy Newman
4. John Legend
Harder
1. Pulp
2. Marilyn Manson
3. The Happy Mondays
4. Gordon Lightfoot
Yeah, Good Luck
1. America
2. The Prodigy
3. Donna Summer
4. R. Kelly

February Answers

FEBRUARY 28

HOUSES OF THE HOLY
1. Ivory Coast's
2. By bus
3. The Emotions
4. Atlanta
5. Aimee Semple McPherson
6. (Captain) Kirk and (Nurse) Chapel
7. New Zealand's
8. *The African Queen*
9. *Far from the Madding Crowd*
10. J. R. "Bob" Dobbs

GOODBYE, FAREWELL, AND AMEN
1. Marsha Mason
2. *The Civil War*

3. "The Lost Chord"
4. Clarabell the Clown
5. Dwight D. Eisenhower
6. Augusta National Golf Club

YOU'RE NOT CUTE BUT EURO SO PRETTY
Easy
1. Greece
2. Spain
3. France
4. Austria
Harder
1. Italy
2. Ireland
3. Germany
4. Belgium and Monaco

Yeah, Good Luck
1. Cyprus
2. Slovenia
3. Finland
4. Luxembourg

FEBRUARY 29

LEAPER COLONY
1. Mao Tse-tung
2. "Oh, boy"
3. Mike Powell
4. BASE jumping (building, antenna, span, earth)
5. Breaching or lunging
6. Mario
7. Daniel Webster
8. Neil Armstrong

9. "Sic semper tyrannis"
10. *Indiana Jones and the Last Crusade*

BUNNY BUSINESS
1. Albuquerque
2. The Man in the Moon
3. Mr. McGregor's
4. Angora (for Ankara, Turkey)
5. *Donnie Darko*

DOZE WERE THE DAYS
1. Valium
2. Geronimo
3. Christopher Walken
4. Matthew Perry ("Which *Friends* alum starred in films with Bruce Willis?")
5. "Enter Sandman"

• **1932** • THE JAPANESE INSTALL PUYI, the deposed last emperor of China, as ruler of the puppet state in Manchuria that the Japanese call "Manchukuo."

EMPIRE RECORDS

1. What medical procedure do the Germans call the *kaiser-schnitt*, or emperor's cut?

2. Who traditionally occupied the Peacock Throne?

3. Julius, Brutus, or Cassius—what's the first name of Eugene O'Neill's *The Emperor Jones*?

4. Who was the last British monarch to also be an emperor?

5. By what name was Augustus, Rome's first official *imperator*, known before he became emperor?

• **1956** • NATO'S INTERNATIONAL PHONETIC RADIO alphabet (Alfa, Bravo, Charlie, etc.) is updated to its current form, to get rid of easily confused pairs like "Nectar" and "Extra."

DID I CATCH A "NINER" IN THERE?
What's the only word in the Alfa-Bravo-Charlie alphabet that's also . . .

1. A month of the year
2. A world capital
3. A Canadian province
4. A hit network TV show

5. An alcoholic drink
6. A world nation
7. A sport
8. A comic strip

9. An airline
10. A truck model

• **1986** • MR. MISTER has the number one album in America with *Welcome to the Real World*, on the strength of the hit singles "Kyrie" and "Broken Wings." Just a few years earlier, the band's members were singing backing vocals for the Village People and Andy Gibb.

UNSOLVED MISTERS
Match these famous "Misters" with their given names.

1. Mr. Belvedere
2. Mr. Blackwell
3. Mr. Darcy
4. Mr. Dithers
5. Mr. Freeze
6. (*Dr. Jekyll and*) Mr. Hyde
7. Mr. Holland('*s Opus*)
8. Mr. Magoo
9. Mr. Miyagi
10. (*The Talented*) Mr. Ripley
11. *Mister Roberts*
12. Mr. Rogers
13. Mr. Smith (*Goes to Washington*)
14. Mr. Snuffleupagus
15. ("They Call Me") Mr. Tibbs

A. Aloysius
B. Douglas
C. Edward
D. Fitzwilliam
E. Fred
F. Glenn
G. Jefferson
H. Julius
I. Kesuke
J. Lynn
K. Quincy
L. Richard
M. Tom
N. Victor
O. Virgil

Answers to the questions on this page can be found on page 123.

MARCH 2

• **1939** • HOWARD CARTER, who led the expedition that uncovered King Tut's tomb, dies at age 64. Carter lived sixteen years after his discovery and died of natural causes—so much for the so-called Curse of the Pharaohs.

CAN YOU DIG IT?
Try to unearth the answers to these subterranean questions.

1. What city boasted the world's first subway line?
2. What novel begins in the Sandleford warren?
3. Where would you find the King's Palace, the Papoose Room, and the Witch's Finger?
4. Who is buried in Paris's Père Lachaise cemetery, except for his heart, which is sealed inside a pillar in a Warsaw chapel?
5. By a wide margin (more than three to two), what's the most abundant element in the Earth's crust?

• **1955** • BO DIDDLEY AND HIS BAND enter a Chicago studio and record two demos that will become huge R&B hits. But "I'm a Man" is dwarfed by the success of its B-side, called simply "Bo Diddley."

SINGLE DOUBLES
Can you make these unlikely cover versions make sense, by finding the single by each artist that has the same name as the artist who recorded the corresponding song?

Easy
1. Neil Diamond, "A Horse with No Name"
2. Gary Numan, "Drive"
3. Edwin Starr, "Low Rider"
4. Weezer, "Peggy Sue"
5. Bell Biv Devoe, "Unskinny Bop"

Harder
1. Aerosmith, "U + Ur Hand"
2. The Association, "Do It to It"
3. Prince, "Rocket Ride"
4. Jackson 5, "Be Near Me"
5. Herb Alpert, "Boogie Oogie Oogie"

Yeah, Good Luck
1. Keyshia Cole, "7 and 7 Is"
2. Graham Nash, "Call On Me"
3. Bobbie Gentry, "Touch Me"
4. Henry Gross, "Let the Music Play"
5. Big Audio Dynamite, "Tom Sawyer"

• **1965** • THE SOUND OF MUSIC (or "The Sound of Mucus," as Christopher Plummer called it) is released. Its enormous success will single-handedly save Twentieth Century–Fox, on the verge of bankruptcy after the 1963 failure of *Cleopatra*.

NOTES AND QUERIES

1. Baklava is usually made using what kind of paper-thin **dough**?
2. What actress is married to Taylor Hackford, the Oscar-nominated director of **Ray**?
3. Who had a best seller at age 84 with her autobiography **Me**?
4. In England, what is governed by the **FA**?
5. What country's currency, named for the sun god Inti, is the *nuevo sol*?
6. "Bad money drives out good," according to what Elizabethan financier's **law**?
7. What ingredient provides the "pearls" in bubble **tea**?
8. Before his ears were cut off in 1990 by a political rival, what nation was ruled by dictator Samuel **Doe**?

Answers to the questions on this page can be found on page 123.

• **1699** • EXPLORER SIEUR D'IBERVILLE, camping sixty miles south of New Orleans, names the site Point du Mardi Gras, in honor of the festival being celebrated that day in his French homeland.

TUESDAY TRIVIA

1. What singer-songwriter played bass in the New Wave band 'Til Tuesday?

2. Greeks consider Tuesday the unluckiest day of the week because what city fell on a Tuesday in 1453?

3. Tuesday Weld played Thalia Menninger on what TV series?

4. What disease is Mitch Albom's professor dying of in his bestseller *Tuesdays with Morrie*?

5. What movie's plot kicks off with the promise "I'm gonna blow my brains out right on this program a week from today. Tune in next Tuesday"?

• **1887** • "MIRACLE WORKER" ANNIE SULLIVAN arrives at the Alabama home of young Helen Keller. No less an authority than inventor Alexander Graham Bell helped matchmake the two strong-willed women.

DEAF JAM

1. What singer took his stage name from a Dublin hearing aid billboard?

2. What's the difference between "I love you" in American Sign Language and the "devil's horns" of heavy metal fans?

3. After a fever took his hearing, who painted his bleak "Black Paintings" in a house called Quinta del Sordo, Spanish for "House of the Deaf Man"?

4. Whose last words were actually "Pity, pity—too late!" about a gift of wine, *not* the oft-reported "I shall hear in heaven"?

5. What musical family's two oldest brothers, Virl and Tom, were born deaf?

• **1919** • IN THE SUPREME COURT RULING on ~~Schenck~~ *v. United States,* Oliver Wendell Holmes writes that "shouting fire in a crowded theater" isn't protected speech. Sadly, Justice Holmes is silent on court protection for "a ringing cell phone in a crowded theater" or "shouting 'Oh, no, you *didn't!*' at the screen in a crowded theater."

THE SATANIC "VS."

Can you match the plaintiffs in these landmark Supreme Court cases to their defendants and the issues "decided"?

1. Bowers	**A.** Arizona	**a.** Abortion
2. Griswold	**B.** Connecticut	**b.** Birth control
3. Mapp	**C.** Ferguson	**c.** Criminal rights
4. Marbury	**D.** Hardwick	**d.** Defamation
5. McCulloch	**E.** Madison	**e.** Federalism
6. Miranda	**F.** Maryland	**f.** Homosexuality
7. *The New York Times*	**G.** Ohio	**g.** Illegal searches
8. Plessy	**H.** Sandford	**h.** Role of the Court
9. Roe	**I.** Sullivan	**i.** Segregation
10. Scott	**J.** Wade	**j.** Slavery

Answers to the questions on this page can be found on page 123.

• **1845** • PRESIDENT JOHN TYLER LEAVES office and retires to his Virginia estate. Because, Tyler said, he'd been "outlawed" by the Whig Party, he renamed the plantation "Sherwood Forest." Interestingly, Sherwood Forest's owner fifty years previously had been none other than Tyler's predecessor, William Henry Harrison.

DEAR MR. RESIDENT
Name the presidents who lived in these homes.

Easy	*Harder*	*Yeah, Good Luck*
1. Monticello	1. Sagamore Hill	1. Shadow Lawn
2. Prairie Chapel Ranch	2. Rancho del Cielo	2. Peacefield
3. Mount Vernon	3. Walker's Point	3. Westland Mansion
4. The Hermitage	4. Springwood	4. The Beeches
5. La Casa Pacifica	5. Montpelier	5. Ash Lawn–Highland

• **1912** • THE GROUNDBREAKING IS HELD for the Brooklyn Dodgers' new stadium, Ebbets Field. The ballpark is named for Charles Ebbets, the Dodgers bookkeeper who went heavily into debt in 1905 to buy the team and keep it in Brooklyn.

DOUBLE-DOUBLES
"Bookkeeper" is the only English word with three consecutive double letters. Give these answers with two consecutive pairs of double letters.

1. What future cabinet officer became Stanford University's youngest provost ever in 1993?
2. What Beatles song is set "somewhere in the Black Mountain hills of Dakota"?
3. In 2004, a nine-foot-tall bronze of Bobby Bowden was dedicated in what city?
4. *Petunia, No. 2* was the first of the giant flower canvases painted by what artist?
5. What is Greenland called by its Inuit native residents?

• **1956** • A NORTH TEXAS STATE STUDENT named Roy Orbison records a song some of his classmates wrote in fifteen minutes on a frat-house roof. "Ooby Dooby" becomes his breakout hit.

LYRICIST WANTED
Match these nonsense titles to the artist who performed them.

1. "Be-Bop-a-Lula"	A. The Chords
2. "MMMBop"	B. The Crystals
3. "Doo Wop"	C. Green Day
4. "Do Wah Diddy Diddy"	D. Hanson
5. "De Do Do Do, De Da Da Da"	E. Lauryn Hill
6. "Do Da Da"	F. Manfred Mann
7. "Da Doo Ron Ron"	G. The Police
8. "Shoo-Be-Doo-Be-Doo-Da-Day"	H. Gene Vincent
9. "Shoop"	I. Salt-N-Pepa
10. "Sh-Boom"	J. Stevie Wonder

Answers to the questions on this page can be found on page 124.

• **1975** • THE HOMEBREW COMPUTER CLUB holds its first meeting in Gordon French's Palo Alto garage. Just one month later, the first "Apple I" computer will be demonstrated at one of their meetings.

RISE OF THE MACHINES

1. What failed IBM computer was advertised by a Charlie Chaplin impersonator?
2. What restaurant chain was the brainchild of Atari founder Nolan Bushnell?

3. What was the only place Tandy's popular TRS-80 computers were sold?
4. What did Coleco name its 1983 home computer in the hope that it would take a bite out of

Apple's sales?
5. What 1982 successor to the VIC-20 is still the bestselling computer model of all time?

• **1998** • THE JACK NICHOLSON–HELEN HUNT comedy *As Good As It Gets* opens in Hong Kong. Due to some vagary of Chinese wordplay that I'm not even close to understanding, its Cantonese title is *Mr. Cat Poop.*

SUB(PAR) TITLES
Can you name these English-language movies from their eccentric overseas titles?

1. *If You Leave Me, I Delete You* (2004, Italian)
2. *Monday the Whole Week* (1993, Swedish)
3. *Zero Zero Seven Dies Twice* (1967, Japanese)
4. *The Knights of the Coconut* (1975, German)

5. *Mysterious Murder in Snowy Cream* (1996, Cantonese)
6. *Going Crazy Wearing Skirts* (1959, Spanish)
7. *The Eighth Passenger of the Nostromo* (1979, Polish)
8. *Six Naked Pigs* (1997, Mandarin)

9. *Alex's Friends* (1983, Hebrew)
10. *Mom, I Missed the Plane* (1990, French)

• **2000** • A RURAL MEXICAN WOMAN named Inés Ramírez, experiencing brutal labor pains and fifty miles from the nearest midwife, performs a cesarean section *on herself* with a kitchen knife and a bottle of rubbing alcohol. Mother and son are doing fine, but I'd buy a new kitchen knife if I were her.

DO-IT-YOURSELFERS

1. Who's the only player ever to coach himself to an NBA title?
2. Who, with her husband, Leonard, founded the Hogarth Press in 1917 and used it to self-publish most of her work?
3. After losing his old one when

he lost his right hand, what color light saber did Luke Skywalker build for himself in *Return of the Jedi?*
4. Who took the crown from Pope Pius VII's hands and physically crowned himself emperor?

5. What do Steven Soderbergh's director of photography Peter Andrews and the Coen brothers' editor Roderick Jaynes have in common?

Answers to the questions on this page can be found on page 124.

MARCH 6

• **1890** • WEALTHY THEATER BUFF Eugene Schieffelin releases eighty European starlings in Central Park. (Schieffelin is on a quixotic quest to introduce into America every bird in Shakespeare, and, unfortunately, starlings are mentioned in *Henry IV, Part I*.) The 200 million starlings decimating American ecosystems today are all descended from Schieffelin's first breeding pairs.

FIVE MORE THINGS THAT ARE SHAKESPEARE'S FAULT

1. By including cannon fire in his play *Henry VIII*, Shakespeare caused the 1613 fire that destroyed what building?

2. What king probably never had the limp and hunchback Shakespeare maligned him with in a 1592 tragedy?

3. By giving Franco Zeffirelli a film career, Shakespeare is also responsible for what unwatchable 1981 teen romance film, Tom Cruise's film debut?

4. Shakespeare mentioned his wife only once in his will, making her the odd bequest of his "sec-

ond best" what?

5. In *The Merry Wives of Windsor*, Shakespeare coined what word for "passionate," cursing us with a terrible Foreigner song and thus the guitar riff from "Funky Cold Medina"?

• **1912** • OREO COOKIES GO ON SALE for the first time. Hydrox cookies, despite their reputation as a knockoff, have actually been on sale for almost four years.

IN PLAIN BLACK AND WHITE
Can you provide these monochromatic answers?

1. Who is Penelope Pussycat's would-be seducer?

2. What tinting process for black-and-white photography was named for the genus of cuttlefish that originally provided the pigment?

3. What extinct subspecies of zebra had stripes in front but a plain brown hindquarters?

4. What's the only movie principally in black and white to win a Best Picture Oscar since *The Apartment* in 1960?

5. What did Edward Teach modify by adding an hourglass and a spear?

6. In what modern-day country was Dalmatia located?

7. Who was the last white president of South Africa?

8. How many squares on a side is a daily *New York Times* crossword puzzle?

9. Francis, Benedict, or Augustine—what sixth-century saint formulated the namesake Rule listing the vows taken by most Catholic nuns?

10. What common item is usually made up of twelve pentagons and twenty hexagons?

11. What was the French film *The Emperor's March* renamed

for U.S. audiences?

12. Who plays the guitar introduction to Michael Jackson's hit "Black or White"?

13. What does a football referee signal by putting both hands high above his head with the palms together and facing upward?

14. Who is the wife in Shakespeare's only interracial married couple?

15. In chess notation, what move is indicated by "O-O"?

Answers to the questions on this page can be found on page 124.

• **1822** • ARMY CAPTAIN JOHN CLEVES SYMMES petitions Congress to mount an unusual polar expedition. Symmes has been traveling the country for years, lecturing on his pet theory: that there's a 1,400-mile-wide hole at the North Pole through which ships might enter and explore the hollow earth. Congress, sadly, turns him down.

WE ARE THE HOLLOW MEN
In what "Hollow" did these people reside?

1. Ichabod Crane	3. The *Gilmore Girls*	5. Lily, James, and Harry Potter
2. Todd Rundgren	4. Loretta Lynn	

• **1839** • EDWARD BULWER-LYTTON'S PLAY *Richelieu* opens at Covent Garden. The play is mostly forgotten today, except for one now-famous line in Act II: "The pen is mightier than the sword."

SWORD PLAY

1. What's the only NBA team to have a sword in its logo?
2. According to the Bible, what is now guarded by an angel holding a flaming sword?
3. In what movie is the Okinawan swordmaker Hattori Hanzo a character?
4. Which is the lightest of the three kinds of fencing sword?

5. Of whom did Dustin Hoffman say "He has no genitalia and he's holding a sword"?
6. Tizona, on display in a Madrid museum, was the sword belonging to what national hero?
7. What kind of sword probably takes its name from a Persian word for "lion's tail," because of its curved shape?

8. What unflattering nickname does the future King Arthur go by in T. H. White's *The Sword in the Stone*?
9. Whose "sword" is made up of a namesake nebula and the Trapezium cluster?
10. In poetry, what creature is killed with a "vorpal blade"?

• **1994** • THE SUPREME COURT RULES, in *Campbell v. Acuff-Rose Music,* that commercial parody may be allowable as "fair use"—in this case, that 2 Live Crew can use the tune to "Oh, Pretty Woman."

AND NOTHING BUT THE SPOOF
What artists' hits were parodied by "Weird Al" Yankovic as . . .

Easy	*Harder*	*Yeah, Good Luck*
1. "Like a Surgeon"	1. "Lasagna"	1. "eBay"
2. "Another One Rides the Bus"	2. "Gump"	2. "Headline News"
3. "Canadian Idiot"	3. "Couch Potato"	3. "Yoda"
4. "Living with a Hernia"	4. "My Bologna"	4. "Cavity Search"
5. "It's All About the Pentiums"	5. "Do I Creep You Out"	5. "The Brady Bunch"

Answers to the questions on this page can be found on page 125.

• **1985** • KMART ANNOUNCES that ex–Charlie's Angel Jaclyn Smith is its new TV spokeswoman and will design a clothing line for the discount retailer.

TALK ABOUT THE FASHION

Jaclyn was ahead of the curve. Match these celebrities to their personal fashion lines.

1. Bono	**A.** Apple Bottoms
2. Boy George	**B.** B-Rude
3. Hilary Duff	**C.** Edun
4. Jay-Z	**D.** House of Dereon
5. Beyoncé Knowles	**E.** L.A.M.B.
6. Jennifer Lopez	**F.** Princy
7. Nelly	**G.** Rocawear
8. Jessica Simpson	**H.** Stuff
9. Gwen Stefani	**I.** Sweetface
10. Justin Timberlake	**J.** William Rast

• **1993** • BEAVIS AND BUTT-HEAD get their own MTV series. They have appeared in occasional *Liquid Television* shorts, but this is viewers' first chance to enjoy them in half-hour units. Huh huh—you said "units."

HUH HUH—YOU SAID . . .

1. What two authors' characters are used to name the moon of Uranus?

2. What country is home to Europe's largest engineering firm, Siemens AG?

3. The adventures of what penguin filled out TV's *Woody Woodpecker Show*?

4. Who described his plucky boy heroes in formulaic novels like *Ragged Dick; or, Street Life in New York with the Bootblacks*?

5. On what namesake Asian island were the first *Homo erectus* fossils found?

6. Who talks to his own ass in Numbers 22?

7. What team lost the pennant in 1908 thanks to "Merkle's boner"?

8. The "horny toad" isn't really a toad. What kind of animal is it—a frog, a lizard, or a salamander?

9. In what TV show's titles did a guest star usually introduce himself as "the new Number Two"?

10. What islands are home to most of the world's blue-footed boobies?

Answers to the questions on this page can be found on page 125.

• **1454** • AMERIGO VESPUCCI, the Italian explorer for whom two continents will be named, is born in Florence.

MY COUNTRY, 'TIS OF THEE

1. Israel is named for the Old Testament patriarch born with what name?

2. What's the only *other* country named for an Old Testament figure?

3. What country is named for one of the New Testament apostles?

4. What country is called, in its native language, "Bharat," after its legendary founder?

5. What country is named for the founder of the "Friars Preachers" religious order?

6. What nation is named for the Hapsburg king of Spain from 1556 to 1598?

7. What's the only country named for an Italian who's *not* Amerigo Vespucci?

8. What country's name is the local pronunciation of the name of its British discoverer, Thomas Gilbert?

9. Which world nation is named for the figure who lived most recently?

10. What Pacific island chain is named for Philip IV's Austrian queen?

• **1954** • EDWARD R. MURROW AIRS his *See It Now* takedown of Joseph McCarthy.

WITCH HUNT
In what movies did these actresses portray witches?

Easy	*Harder*	*Yeah, Good Luck*
1. Billie Burke	**1.** Tilda Swinton	**1.** Veronica Lake
2. Susan Sarandon	**2.** Christina Ricci	**2.** Kim Novak
3. Neve Campbell	**3.** Bette Midler	**3.** Cassandra Gava
4. Nicole Kidman (two answers)	**4.** Ione Skye	**4.** Angela Lansbury

• **1985** • THE NATION'S FIRST ADOPT-A-HIGHWAY PROGRAM begins when the Tyler Civitan Club adopts a stretch of Highway 69 north of Tyler, Texas. The Texas Department of Transportation is beginning its "Don't Mess with Texas" antilittering campaign, which will reduce highway litter in the Lone Star State by an amazing 72 percent.

SIX QUESTIONS OVER TEXAS

1. In novels and on TV, what fictional Texas town is home to the Hat Creek Cattle Company and Livery Emporium?

2. Pre-Iraq, George W. Bush used to joke that his biggest mistake was trading what Texas Ranger away for George Bell?

3. Who was the only two-term president of the Republic of Texas?

4. How many community cards are there in a hand of Texas hold 'em?

5. What name is shared by the rivers that run through Denison, Texas, and Hanoi, Vietnam?

6. What Texas Instruments product does E.T. use to "phone home"?

Answers to the questions on this page can be found on page 125.

MARCH 10

• **1876** • Alexander Graham Bell uses his newest invention to tell his assistant, in the next room, "Mr. Watson, come here—I want to see you." Laziest . . . inventor . . . *ever.*

SECOND BANANA-RAMA
Sherlock Holmes, Alexander Graham Bell, and Frances Crick all had sidekicks named Watson. But whose sidekick was . . .

Easy	Harder	Yeah, Good Luck
1. Mini-Me	1. Baba Looey	1. Archie Goodwin
2. Sancho Panza	2. Passepartout	2. George Fenneman
3. Barney Fife	3. James Boswell	3. Sodoff Baldrick
4. Art Garfunkel	4. Pedro Sanchez	4. Willie Garvin
5. Paul Shaffer	5. Garth Algar	5. Woozy Winks

• **1926** • Sylvia Townsend Warner's *Lolly Willowes, or The Loving Huntsman* is published, the very first selection of the Book-of-the-Month Club.

BOOKS OF THE MONTH
What months complete these book titles?

Easy	Harder	Yeah, Good Luck
1. Tom Clancy's *The Hunt for Red _____*	1. Irene Hunt's *Across Five _____s*	1. Dean Koontz's *The Door to _____*
2. Ralph Ellison's *_____teenth*	2. William Faulkner's *Light in ___*	2. Ayn Rand's *The Night of _____ 16th*
3. Richard Matheson's *What Dreams _____ Come*	3. Barbara Tuchman's *The Guns of _____*	3. Nadine Gordimer's *_____'s People*
4. Ron Kovic's *Born on the Fourth of _____*	4. Saul Bellow's *The Adventures of Augie _____*	4. Geraldine Brooks's *_____*

• **2003** • The Dixie Chicks kiss country music airplay good-bye when lead singer Natalie Maines tells a London concert audience, "We're ashamed that the president of the United States is from Texas."

NATIONAL SHAME

1. What's the only country to have hosted a Summer Olympics at which it didn't win a single gold medal?
2. What's the only former Soviet republic that still calls its secret police the KGB?
3. What European nation still pledges its allegiance to a foreign monarch (the king of Spain) in its national anthem?
4. What was the last country in the Americas to abolish slavery, in 1888?
5. Until 2007, what was the only country in the world not to have registered its own Internet domain suffix, ".kp"?

Answers to the questions on this page can be found on page 126.

• **1869** • FRENCH MISSIONARY ARMAND DAVID first describes the giant panda to the West, having received a panda skin from a generous hunter. No one knows where the word "panda" comes from—it's sure not Chinese. It may come from *ponya,* a Nepali word for the ball of the foot, which would make it the only English loanword from Nepali.

YOU'LL NEVER WOK (A LOAN)
From what language did English borrow these sets of loanwords?

Easy	Harder	Yeah, Good Luck
1. Ombudsman, smorgasbord, tungsten	1. Bangle, dungarees, pundit	1. Kumquat, typhoon, wok
2. Chutzpah, glitch, schmaltz	2. Intelligentsia, mammoth, steppe	2. Caboose, cookie, yacht
3. Honcho, soy, tsunami	3. Alcohol, safari, zero	3. Lollipop, posh, pal
4. Canyon, guitar, rodeo	4. Dollar, muffin, stroll	4. Catamaran, cheroot, pariah
5. Hula, luau, ukulele	5. Amok, ketchup, orangutan	5. Aardvark, commando, trek

• **1942** • DOUGLAS MACARTHUR ABANDONS the Philippines but vows to return.

MACARTHUR 2: THE RETURN!
What movie's first sequel featured these subtitles?

Easy	Harder	Yeah, Good Luck
1. *Cruise Control*	1. *The Quickening*	1. *Lost in San Francisco*
2. *The Edge of Reason*	2. *The Sequel*	2. *Farewell to the Flesh*
3. *State of the Union*	3. *On the Move*	3. *The Colombian Connection*
4. *When Nature Calls*	4. *On the Rocks*	4. *The Adventure Home*
5. *The Road Warrior*	5. *The Other Side*	5. *The Spawning*

• **2003** • THE U.S. HOUSE OF REPRESENTATIVES, in a stirring show of patriotism, officially renames the French fries in its snack bars "freedom fries." As the anti-French fervor spreads, even the actor French Stewart begins squinting uncomfortably at passersby. Oh no, my mistake. He always looks like that.

THE UNMITIGATED GAUL
Enjoy this French quiz (or "freedom quiz," depending on your political convictions).

1. What uses the "AZERTY" layout in the French-speaking world?
2. What two African countries have capital cities whose names are synonyms—one in French, the other in English?
3. In 1853, what author founded a successful daily journal called *Le Mousquetaire?*
4. What French company is represented by a mascot named "Bibendum"?
5. What's usually the liqueur served on crêpes suzette?
6. Since one sits astride it, what invention takes its name from the French word for "pony"?
7. Whose remains were thrown into the Seine River on May 30, 1431?
8. In nineteenth-century France, what were commonly called Herschel and Leverrier?
9. The Arc de Triomphe was originally built to commemorate France's *triomphe* in what 1805 battle?
10. Who introduced her most famous formula on the appropriate date of May 5, 1921?

Answers to the questions on this page can be found on page 126.

MARCH 12

• 1924 • BELVA GAERTNER APPARENTLY MURDERS her lover Walter Law, who threatened to kill her. She will go on to be acquitted and become the basis for the "Velma" character in the musical *Chicago*.

STAGE, LEFT
Before they were household names, who originated the roles on Broadway later played on screen by . . .

1. Vivien Leigh in *A Streetcar Named Desire*
2. Timothy Dalton in *The Lion in Winter*
3. John Travolta in *Grease*

4. F. Murray Abraham in *Amadeus*
5. Gene Kelly in *Inherit the Wind*

• 1951 • *DENNIS THE MENACE* DEBUTS in newspapers. In his debut appearance, Dennis angrily taunts a cop. He's mellowed out a bit since then.

A FEW GOOD MENACE

1. What Broadway team first collaborated on *Flora the Red Menace* before going on to write *Cabaret* and *Chicago*?
2. What future star plays Natalie Portman's stand-in queen in the *Star Wars* prequel *The Phantom Menace*?

3. What gangster movie was originally titled *The Menace* and eventually subtitled *The Shame of the Nation*?
4. What newspaper editor wrote the headline "Spider-Man: Threat or Menace?"
5. Still using her unmarried

name, what actress made her film debut playing Ronnie in *Menace II Society*?

• 1967 • SUHARTO TAKES OVER from Sukarno as president of Indonesia. (No, they're not just being pretentious—*lots* of people from Java have just the one name.)

MAKING A NAME FOR THEMSELVES
What one-named musicians have these last names?

Easy
1. Ciccone
2. Sarkisian LaPiere
3. Kilcher
4. Gudmundsdottir
5. Norwood

Harder
1. Haughton
2. Quintanilla
3. Douglas
4. Armstrong
5. Forte

Yeah, Good Luck
1. Leitch
2. Safka
3. Ockerse
4. Darwish
5. DiMucci

Answers to the questions on this page can be found on page 126.

MARCH 13

• **1781** • WILLIAM HERSCHEL DISCOVERS a new planet. Disregarding the convention that planets be named for Roman gods, he calls it *Georgium Sidus* (George's Star), kissing up to King George III. Speaking of butt-kissing, his discovery is later renamed "Uranus."

WHEN IN ROME . . .
Give the Roman names of these Greek gods and goddesses.

Easy	Harder	Yeah, Good Luck
1. Ares	1. Hephaestus	1. Hestia
2. Zeus	2. Hera	2. Hypnos
3. Artemis	3. Eros	3. Eris
4. Hermes	4. Cronus	4. Persephone
5. Aphrodite	5. Athena	5. Pan

• **1954** • TINY MILAN HIGH SCHOOL, enrollment 161, beats mighty Muncie Central to win the Indiana state basketball championship. The game will inspire the movie *Hoosiers* (though in real life Milan won with a boring fourth-quarter stall, not a dramatic last-second jumper).

THE NAME OF THE GAME
What sport is the focus of each of these movies?

Easy	Harder	Yeah, Good Luck
1. *The Color of Money*	1. *Breaking Away*	1. *The Stratton Story*
2. *Tin Cup*	2. *Over the Top*	2. *Lagaan*
3. *Days of Thunder*	3. *Blue Chips*	3. *The Freshman* (1925)
4. *Bend It like Beckham*	4. *Cool Runnings*	4. *Youngblood*
5. *National Velvet*	5. *Lords of Dogtown*	5. *Fat City*

• **1994** • THE AMERICAN CHEMICAL SOCIETY stirs up controversy by announcing that element 106, a newcomer to the periodic table, will be named seaborgium, after its codiscoverer Glenn Seaborg. It marks the first time such an announcement has ever been made while the honoree is still living.

TRACE ELEMENTS
Which chemical elements' names can be spelled by the symbols for these other elements?

1. Titanium, nitrogen	4. Argon, selenium, nickel, carbon
2. Iridium, oxygen, nitrogen	5. Calcium, rubidium, oxygen, nitrogen
3. Arsenic, tantalum, titanium, neon	

Answers to the questions on this page can be found on page 127.

MARCH 14

• **1951** • AN ICONIC IMAGE IS BORN when Albert Einstein sticks out his tongue for UPI photographer Albert Sasse.

LICKER CABINET

1. What Asian dog breed is notable for its blue tongue?

2. What bloody Shakespeare play features the stage direction "Enter the empress' sons with Lavinia, her hands cut off, and her tongue cut out, and ravished"?

3. What movie was partially inspired by Jean Shepherd's unpublished story "Flick's Tongue"?

4. What comic strip introduced the metal band Billy and the Boingers, aka Deathtöngue?

5. Why do snakes flick their tongues in and out?

6. According to the popular tongue twister, what problem does the sixth sheik have?

7. What Christian feast celebrates "tongues of fire" descending on the Apostles?

8. What are the bumps on the tongue that carry the taste buds called?

9. Who wrote in his 2001 autobiography, "I was soon to find out that having a long tongue came in handy with the girls"?

10. According to the ad, how many licks does it take to get to the center of a Tootsie Pop?

• **1968** • BIFF! BAM! POW! Plagued by limp ratings that not even the addition of Yvonne Craig in a skintight Batgirl suit could help, er, elevate, TV's campy *Batman* is KO'd by ABC.

PUNCH LINES

1. WHAM! What 1984 hit was credited to George Michael in the U.K. but to "Wham! featuring George Michael" when it topped the U.S. charts?

2. BANG! What two things need to be combined to form an "interrobang"?

3. SOCK! Who made headlines in 2002 when, after scoring a touchdown in Seattle, he pulled a Sharpie pen from his sock and autographed the football?

4. CRUNCH! Cap'n Crunch's flagship is named for what fish?

5. BOOM! What name, a tribute to an Austrian physicist, is given to the speed at which airplanes produce a sonic boom?

6. CRASH! 2004's *Crash* is the only Best Picture Oscar winner to be principally set in what city?

7. ZAP! What 1970s slogan first appeared in an oft-bootlegged cartoon of a strutting man from the first issue of Robert Crumb's

Zap Comix?

8. BIFF! What's the last name of Biff, the loutish villain of the *Back to the Future* films?

9. BAM! In what country is the historic city of Bam, largely destroyed in a catastrophic 2003 earthquake?

10. POW! Hoa Lo Prison, whose name means "fiery furnace" in Vietnamese, was more commonly called what by American POWs?

Answers to the questions on this page can be found on page 127.

MARCH 15

• **1935** • ALARMED THAT THEIR PARENTS may be exhibiting and exploiting them for financial gain, the Canadian government passes the "Dionne Quintuplets' Guardianship Act," officially making the five sisters "wards of the King." Canada will, of course, spend the next few decades exhibiting and exploiting them for financial gain.

SISTERS ARE DOIN' IT FOR THEMSELVES

1. What Shakespeare play begins with a meeting of the Weird Sisters?

2. Which two actresses on TV's *Charlie's Angels* were meant to be portraying sisters?

3. Which oldest Gabor sister lied about her birth date, which made her appear to be younger than Eva and Zsa Zsa?

4. Which of the "Seven Sisters" women's colleges no longer officially exists?

5. Who was the only African-American woman to win a Grand Slam tennis singles event before the Williams sisters did?

6. Which of the Brontë sisters wrote only a single novel?

7. The world's first "sister cities" were what Spanish city and its midwestern namesake?

8. In Greek myth, what nine sisters are the daughters of Mnemosyne?

9. What Swedish pop group was anchored by sisters Jenny and Linn Berggren?

10. In 41 B.C., who ordered the death of her sister, Arsino IV?

• **1990** • NINE-YEAR-OLD CHRISTINA AGUILERA loses on *Star Search*. You're no Sinbad, Xtina!

I STILL HAVEN'T FOUND WHAT I'M LOOKING FOR
Search for these answers related to other kinds of searches.

1. What do SETI programs search for?

2. What Internet search engine runs the Babel Fish translation service?

3. Which of the *Friends* actors' fathers was a regular on the soap *Search for Tomorrow* for ten years?

4. In 1998, who was Bud Selig chosen to replace, after a six-year search?

5. After almost four hundred years of fruitless searching, what was finally navigated by Roald Amundsen in 1906?

6. In the 1956 western, what actress are *The Searchers* searching for?

7. At the age of eleven, who accidentally discovered the true identity of his baseball pitcher father while searching his mother's closet for hidden Christmas presents?

8. What classic French book has a title that's more accurately translated as *In Search of Lost Time*?

9. According to Ted Cassidy's opening narration, what TV character was "searching for a way to tap into the hidden strengths that all humans have"?

10. What future congressman cowrote the Searchers' 1964 hit "Needles and Pins"?

Answers to the questions on this page can be found on page 127.

MARCH 16

• **1867** • JOSEPH LISTER PUBLISHES "Antiseptic Principle of the Practice of Surgery," outlining his groundbreaking theory that doctors should actually *disinfect their hands and instruments*! As a result, Lister is made a baron and gets a mouthwash named after him.

LIKE A SURGEON

1. Why was Jacques Marescaux's 2001 removal of a 68-year-old woman's gallbladder called "the Lindbergh operation"?
2. What surgeon on *ER* shares his name with a "Warlord of Mars" created by Edgar Rice Burroughs?

3. In 1994, Christian Spurling confessed that the so-called Surgeon's Photo of 1934 was a fake. What was pictured in the Surgeon's Photo?
4. Who chose her new name in 1953 to honor a Danish surgeon named Christian Hamburger?
5. What operation, consisting of a laparotomy and a hysterotomy, is the most commonly performed procedure in U.S. hospitals?

• **1955** • "THE BALLAD OF DAVY CROCKETT" hits number one, making it the first and last pop hit in which a three-year-old murders an animal.

SECRET BALLAD
Who's responsible for "The Ballad of . . ."

Easy	*Harder*	*Yeah, Good Luck*
1. John and Yoko	**1.** Cable Hogue	**1.** Bilbo Baggins
2. The Green Berets	**2.** A Well-Known Gun	**2.** The Sad Café
3. Reading Gaol	**3.** Billy the Kid	**3.** A Thin Man
4. Jed Clampett	**4.** Thunder Road	**4.** Peter Pumpkinhead

• **1999** • *EVERQUEST* AND ITS FICTIONAL WORLD of Norrath go online, bringing the MMORPG (massively multiplayer online role-playing game) into the mainstream. Millions of pasty-faced young people need never go outside again.

A TRIBE CALLED QUEST

1. In Arthurian myth, what son of Lancelot led the quest that achieved the Holy Grail?
2. What *Animal House* actor made his show-biz debut as the voice of TV's *Jonny Quest*?

3. The afro-sporting ?uestlove is the drummer for what hip-hop group?
4. What mythologist helped give birth to *Star Wars* when he published his 1949 study of quest literature, *The Hero of a Thousand Faces*?
5. What quested-for treasure of Greek myth was the skin of the winged ram Chrysomallos?

Answers to the questions on this page can be found on page 128.

• **469** • ACCORDING TO TRADITION, Saint Patrick dies and is buried beside Saint Brigid and Saint Columba in the crypt below Ireland's Down Cathedral. Yup, a great holy man is dead, and you celebrate by getting smashed on cheap green beer down at Tipsy O'Shamrock's.

GREEN PIECE
Celebrate St. Paddy's Day with these green questions.

1. What actor died nine days after completing his final movie, *Soylent Green*?

2. What state's National Guard still calls itself "the Green Mountain Boys"?

3. What Green Day hit spent a record sixteen weeks atop the *Billboard* Modern Rock chart?

4. What NFL team did Vince Lombardi coach after leaving the Green Bay Packers?

5. What author wore a trademark dyed-green carnation in his lapel in 1890s London?

6. What's the name of the Jolly Green Giant's diminutive sidekick?

7. According to Norse sagas, who gave Greenland its misleading name in order to attract settlers?

8. What other TV show, besides *Green Acres*, is set in the town of Hooterville?

9. When is the optical phenomenon called a "green flash" or "green ray" visible?

10. What drink is sometimes called *la fée verte*, "the green fairy"?

• **1845** • STEPHEN PERRY PATENTS the rubber band.

BETTER LATEX THAN NEVER

1. What college football team, named for a type of rubber overshoes, plays its home games in the Rubber Bowl?

2. What chemical element is added to rubber to "vulcanize" it?

3. Tires, condoms, or erasers— the word "bungee" originally referred to what *other* common rubber object?

4. What rubber Wham-O toy inspired the name of one of the world's largest sporting events?

5. What Beatles character from a *Rubber Soul* song is given the name Jeremy Hillary Boob, Ph.D., in *Yellow Submarine*?

• **1948** • PORTLAND, OREGON, DEDICATES Mill Ends Park, an unused traffic median that a local newspaper columnist has decreed "the only leprechaun colony west of Ireland." Mill Ends Park, two feet in diameter, is still officially the world's smallest park.

PARKLIFE
In what world cities would you find these iconic parks?

Easy	*Harder*	*Yeah, Good Luck*
1. Golden Gate Park	**1.** Centennial Olympic Park	**1.** Stanley Park
2. Battery Park	**2.** Tivoli Gardens	**2.** Tiergarten
3. Hyde Park	**3.** Grant Park	**3.** Balboa Park
4. Griffith Park	**4.** Champ de Mars	**4.** Rock Creek Park
5. Gorky Park	**5.** Charles River Esplanade	**5.** Boboli Gardens

Answers to the questions on this page can be found on page 128.

MARCH 18

• **1918** • THE FIRST OCEANGOING SHIP made of cement, a $750,000 pet project of San Francisco shipbuilder Leslie Comyn, is launched. It's christened the SS *Faith*, possibly because that's what you'd need a lot of in order to board a concrete ship.

FAITH NO MORE!
Who recorded the album called Faith *that featured these songs?*

1. "Primary" (1981)
2. "Father Figure" (1987)
3. "Soon as I Get Home" (1995)
4. "This Kiss" (1998)

• **1922** • AT THE URGING OF HER RABBI FATHER, Judith Kaplan becomes the first Jewish girl ever to read from the Torah in a public Bat Mitzvah ceremony.

DAUGHTERS OF THE COVENANT

1. For whom is Hadassah, the Jewish women's organization, named?
2. What artist sang with Barbra Streisand in her Brooklyn high school choir and later sang with her again in a number one hit duet?
3. What U.S. state is represented in the Senate entirely by Jewish women?

4. What war led to Golda Meir's resignation as prime minister of Israel?
5. What director is engaged to actress Rachel Weisz?
6. Who was the first Jewish Miss America and, later, the unofficial "First Lady of New York City"?
7. Who was the last American to win an Olympic gold for figure skating?

8. Who was the only woman to hold the title office in the Book of Judges?
9. Philosopher Hannah Arendt's most famous book is named for what man "in Jerusalem"?
10. What element of the periodic table is named for a Jewish woman?

• **1931** • THE FIRST ELECTRIC SHAVER hits shelves, courtesy of Schick, Inc.

HOLLYWOOD BUZZ
What actress shaved her head for her role in these movies?

Easy	*Harder*	*Yeah, Good Luck*
1. *G. I. Jane*	**1.** *Heaven*	**1.** *The Passion of Joan of Arc*
2. *V for Vendetta*	**2.** *Empire Records*	**2.** *The Naked Kiss*
3. *Alien³*	**3.** *Dragonfly*	**3.** *Caged*
4. *Minority Report*	**4.** *Tank Girl*	**4.** *The Girl in the Kremlin*
5. *Anna and the King*	**5.** *Star Trek: The Motion Picture*	**5.** *THX 1138*

Answers to the questions on this page can be found on page 128.

• **1979** • C-SPAN GOES ON THE AIR, with live coverage of the U.S. House of Representatives. Its very first proceeding is a speech by then-congressman Al Gore—a sure sign of many gripping hours of programming to come!

CONGRESSIONAL RECORD

1. What famous diplomat represented France at the Congress of Vienna in 1814?

2. Whose personal library formed the basis of the Library of Congress after the British burned the original collection during the War of 1812?

3. What organization's flag is a black stripe for the people, a green stripe for the land, and a yellow stripe for riches?

4. In what city did the First and Second Continental Congresses meet?

5. What nation was led by the Congress Party from 1947 to 1996 almost uninterrupted?

• **1983** • AMERICA'S DRUG PROBLEM is permanently solved when First Lady Nancy Reagan guests on a very, *very* special episode of *Diff'rent Strokes* to tout her "Just Say No" campaign.

NEGATIVLAND

In fond memory of "Just Say No," here's an unusually negative quiz.

1. What negatively charged particle is the antiparticle of the positron?

2. What oddly worded catchphrase earned Whitney Houston a "Big Quote" nomination from VH-1 in 2005?

3. What vice president referred to his critics as "nattering nabobs of negativism"?

4. What is 007 enemy Dr. No's first name?

5. What Herman Melville character always answers "I would prefer not to," whenever his boss asks him to work?

6. Whose presidential campaign was targeted by the famous "Daisy Girl" negative TV ad?

7. What hip-hop artist is featured on Destiny's Child's first single, "No, No, No"?

8. What "imaginary" number is defined as the square root of −1?

9. What famous double negative is the first line in Pink Floyd's "Another Brick in the Wall (Part II)"?

10. What is absent in "negative" blood types like O negative and AB negative?

• **1994** • A RECORD-BREAKING OMELET is made in Yokohama, Japan. You know what they say—you can't make the world's largest omelet without breaking 150,000 eggs.

THE MOST IMPORTANT MEAL OF THE DAY

1. What was the first nonoriginal color of cereal pieces added to Trix, in 1980?

2. What breakfast item is the waitress serving on the cover of Supertramp's *Breakfast in America* album?

3. What's the meat in McDonald's original recipe for Egg McMuffins?

4. What American literary character's real name is Lula Mae Barnes?

5. In 1934, five years before his retirement, who became the first athlete to appear on a Wheaties box?

6. Emilio Estevez was originally cast in what other actor's role in *The Breakfast Club*?

7. In France, what's called *pain perdu*, or "lost bread"?

8. Corn Flakes, Grape Nuts, or Post Toasties—what cereal was called Elijah's Manna until 1908, when the Bible Belt branded that name as sacrilegious?

9. What nation is the world's largest exporter of coffee?

10. Who was the only *Star Wars* character honored with his own breakfast cereal?

Answers to the questions on this page can be found on page 129.

• **1602** • THE DUTCH EAST INDIA COMPANY is established and becomes the first company ever to issue stock. On CNBC, Jim Cramer is quick to pick DEIC as his *Mad Money* Pick of the Week, because, quote, "Well, there aren't any other stocks yet."

STOCK ANSWERS

1. What's the only stock from the original Dow Jones Industrial Average that's still used in computing the index?
2. What term for stable, well-established stocks comes from a $10 bet in poker?

3. What do these stocks have in common: Bluestar Airlines, Fairchild Foods, Rorker Electronics, Anacott Steel, and Teldar Paper?
4. The über-successful stock picker Warren Buffett has been

called the "Oracle of" what city, his birthplace?
5. What did the letter *Q* originally stand for in NASDAQ?

• **1980** • FORMER MESSENGER Henry Rojas signs on to be the Phoenix Suns' new mascot, the Gorilla. He'd shown up at a game in a gorilla suit earlier in the season to deliver a singing telegram, and event staff talked him into entertaining the crowd before he left.

HAIRY REASONERS
Here's some primate trivia for you to monkey with.

1. What apes are humans' closest living relatives, with 94 percent identical DNA?
2. What American company had a thirty-foot inflatable gorilla atop its Rhode Island offices for decades?
3. What's the name of King Kong's home island?
4. What ape's name is Malay for "old man of the forest"?

5. Each of the Gorillaz' first two albums has a song named in honor of what actor?
6. Whose mysterious murder ends the film *Gorillas in the Mist*?
7. What's the name of Mario's girlfriend, kidnapped by the giant ape in *Donkey Kong*?
8. What term for an adult male gorilla comes from a distinctive

patch of hair?
9. What famed TV personality wrote the screenplay for 1968's *Planet of the Apes*?
10. As a baby in 1939, who received a stuffed chimp from her father, which she named Jubilee and made into a lifelong companion?

• **1990** • FORMER PHILIPPINE FIRST LADY Imelda Marcos goes on trial in New York for corruption and racketeering.

SHOES YOUR OWN ADVENTURE

1. What South African antelope lent its name to a brand of athletic shoe?
2. Who worked as a salesman at Gary's Shoes and Accessories?

3. The shoe-obsessed Spats Colombo is the villain of what 1959 comedy?
4. What Canary Islands–born designer, famous for his stiletto-

heeled designs, opened his first store in Chelsea in 1973?
5. What song did the Drifters follow with the 1964 sequel "I've Got Sand in My Shoes"?

Answers to the questions on this page can be found on page 129.

• **1800** • POPE PIUS VII IS CROWNED at Venice. In an unusual ceremony, a *papier-mâché* tiara is used, the real one having been seized by Napoleon when he took Pius's predecessor prisoner.

AU FRANÇAIS
These are questions about English phrases borrowed from the French, like papier-mâché.

1. What can be taken "*en passant*"?
2. In 1998, who launched her signature fragrance, called *Moi*?
3. What ballet features the famous *pas de deux* between the Sugar-Plum Fairy and a cavalier?
4. George Orwell's *Animal Farm* is a *roman à clef* for what historical event?
5. What U.S. city's flag features a blue *fleur-de-lis*, representing

both its French namesake and the three rivers that converge there?
6. What domestic song from Crosby, Stills, Nash & Young's album *Déjà Vu* describes Graham Nash's brief affair with Joni Mitchell?
7. Under what *nom de plume*, a shortened form of "Moses," did Charles Dickens write his first books?

8. It's sometimes considered a fashion *faux pas* to wear white after what holiday?
9. What classic movie, in which Charlton Heston is miscast as a Mexican cop, is sometimes called the last *film noir*?
10. In British English, what's the two-initial term for a *résumé*?

• **1970** • AT A GERMAN SKI JUMP championship, Slovenian jumper Vinko Bogataj wipes out spectacularly. The crash leaves him with a mild concussion . . . and lasting fame when ABC makes him the "agony of defeat" guy in the *Wide World of Sports* opening.

GOING DOWNHILL

1. After his death in a 1998 skiing accident, what famous song title was placed on Sonny Bono's headstone?
2. What skiing legend headed the Tour de France organizing committee from 1992 to 2001?

3. Complete this analogy. Downhill : Alpine :: Cross-country : _____.
4. What U.S. state advertised "The Greatest Snow on Earth" on its license plates?
5. What German army physician

began designing his own footwear when combat boots proved too painful to wear after he injured his ankle skiing in 1945?

• **1980** • AN UNKNOWN ASSAILANT shoots J. R. Ewing on *Dallas*. Due to a SAG/AFTRA strike that summer, viewers won't find out "Who shot J.R.?" until November.

ABC-TV
Who played these television characters?

Easy	Harder	Yeah, Good Luck
1. A. C. Slater	**1.** B. J. McKay	**1.** B. J. Poteet
2. T. J. Hooker	**2.** A. J. Soprano	**2.** D. J. Conner
3. J. J. Evans	**3.** D. J. Tanner	**3.** C. J. Barnes
4. C. J. Cregg	**4.** C. J. Parker	**4.** J. J. Starbuck
5. B. J. Hunnicut	**5.** B. L. Stryker	**5.** E. L. Turner

Answers to the questions on this page can be found on page 129.

MARCH 22

• **1987** • THE GARBAGE BARGE *Mobro 4000,* having been turned away from a landfill in Islip, Long Island, begins a 6,000-mile voyage to seek a new home for the trash. Six states and three countries refuse the *Mobro*'s putrid cargo before it's finally incinerated back home in Brooklyn.

TRASH TALKING

1. At what movie's climax does Mookie throw a garbage can through the front window of Sal's Pizzeria?

2. What cartoonist of *Maus* also created the less highbrow Topps Garbage Pail Kids?

3. A fifth of what city's population lives in its infamous shantytowns, called *favelas*?

4. What Nirvana and Smashing Pumpkins record producer later became the drummer in Garbage?

5. Who was originally created from a green spring coat that Elizabeth Henson had thrown out?

6. What was the *Sanford and Son* junkyard converted to when the two stars left the show?

7. What state's bottle bill offers ten cents for used beverage containers, while other states offer only a nickel?

8. What eighteen-minute song tells the true story of its writer's arrest for illegally dumping garbage on Thanksgiving Day, 1965?

9. On what island was Fresh Kills, the world's largest landfill?

10. Who became a writer when his friend E. B. White found some of his cartoons in a trash can and submitted them to *The New Yorker*?

• **2233** • CAPTAIN KIRK WILL BE BORN, according to StarTrek.com and the tiny town of Riverside, Iowa, which has declared itself Kirk's birthplace and holds an annual festival looking forward to the great day.

I'M GETTING TOO OLD FOR THIS SHIP

Match these captains to their commands.

1. Captain Ahab
2. Jack Aubrey
3. William Bligh
4. Peter Blood
5. Captain Corcoran
6. Francis Drake
7. Jonas Grumby
8. Thor Heyerdahl
9. James Hook
10. Henry Hudson
11. John F. Kennedy
12. Lord Nelson
13. Francis Queeg
14. Edward Smith
15. Jack Sparrow

A. *Arabella*
B. *Black Pearl*
C. *Bounty*
D. *Caine*
E. *Golden Hind*
F. *Half Moon*
G. *Jolly Roger*
H. *Kon-Tiki*
I. *Minnow*
J. *Pequod*
K. *Pinafore*
L. PT-109
M. *Surprise*
N. *Titanic*
O. *Victory*

Answers to the questions on this page can be found on page 130.

• **1844** • GENERAL TOM THUMB, the famous little person in P. T. Barnum's circus, is a hit with Queen Victoria during a Buckingham Palace performance. On his way out, the two-foot-tall Thumb gets into an altercation with one of Her Majesty's poodles, who is roughly his height.

THUMB THING TO TALK ABOUT

1. Why is Oneida Lake, near Syracuse, New York, sometimes called "the thumb"?
2. What animal, which eighteenth-century settlers called a "native bear," has *two* opposable thumbs on each hand?

3. Gene Siskel owned the iconic white suit from what movie, his all-time favorite?
4. What gullible author believed that Harry Houdini had "wonderful powers" after Houdini showed him the child's trick of

pretending to remove his thumb?
5. In what 1979 novel is the "Thumb" device actually a Sub-Etha Sens-O-Matic?

• **1945** • NEW JERSEY VOTES to make Rutgers, a private college established by the Dutch Reformed Church, a state university. New Jersey is, therefore, the only U.S. state whose leading public university isn't named for the state.

COLLEGE KNOWLEDGE

What state's "University of" main campus is located in each of these cities?

Easy	*Harder*	*Yeah, Good Luck*
1. Athens	**1.** Storrs	**1.** Orono
2. Gainesville	**2.** Moscow	**2.** Durham
3. Eugene	**3.** College Park	**3.** Vermilion
4. Tuscaloosa	**4.** Charlottesville	**4.** Kingston
5. Lawrence	**5.** Norman	**5.** Columbia (two answers)

• **1952** • BILL MOSIENKO, OF THE CHICAGO BLACK HAWKS, makes NHL history when he scores the fastest hat trick in history: three goals in just twenty-one seconds elapsed.

A SEASON ON THE RINK

1. What hockey great wears number 68 to commemorate the Prague Spring of 1968?
2. What kind of animal have Detroit Red Wings fans been throwing onto their home ice before big games since 1952?

3. What hockey violation is committed when the puck travels across both the red line and the goal line without being touched?
4. What two NHL legends—a Penguin and a Canadien—were born just hours apart in Quebec

on October 5, 1965?
5. Which of the so-called original six teams was the NHL's first U.S. franchise?

Answers to the questions on this page can be found on page 130.

MARCH 24

• **1937** • Author Ernest Vincent Wright tells the AP that he's finally finished his magnum opus: a novel called *Gadsby: A Story of over 50,000 Words Without Using the Letter "E."* Wright tied down the *E* key on his typewriter to make sure he succeeded in his quixotic quest.

THIS INSPIRING, WIT-TICKLING QUIZ
Each answer uses only a single vowel, though it may be repeated many times.

1. Keren Woodward, of what 1980s band, is married to Andrew Ridgeley of Wham?
2. Who was the first female comic ever to be called over to the couch by Johnny Carson on *The Tonight Show*?
3. What two-word football nickname is thought to derive from William Corby, a former university president and chaplain to the 88th New York Volunteer Infantry at Gettysburg?
4. What 1977 novel ends with Milkman Dead learning to fly?
5. What's the Latin name for the common mouse, the world's second most abundant mammal species (after man)?
6. What's the astronomical term for three celestial bodies aligning?

• **1975** • Chuck "the Bayonne Bleeder" Wepner challenges Muhammad Ali for the world heavyweight championship. When Wepner goes the distance, even knocking Ali down in the ninth, a young actor in the crowd named Sylvester Stallone gets the idea for a movie called *Rocky*.

TITLE ROLE CALL
What actor played the title role in the original version of these first-name-basis movies?

Easy	Harder	Yeah, Good Luck
1. *Arthur*	**1.** *Oliver!*	**1.** *Edmond*
2. *Charly*	**2.** *Michael*	**2.** *Maurice*
3. *Ray*	**3.** *Jack*	**3.** *Lucas*
4. *Alfie*	**4.** *Rudy*	**4.** *Max*
5. *Alexander*	**5.** *Dave*	**5.** *Tex*

• **1984** • According to the letter read at the film's end, this is the day *The Breakfast Club* convenes for detention in the Shermer High School library.

BREAKFAST CLUB
What was the original brand of cereal pitched by these mascots?

Easy	Harder	Yeah, Good Luck
1. Dig 'Em	**1.** Sugar Bear	**1.** Wendell
2. Tony the Tiger	**2.** Crazy Craving	**2.** Chip the Wolf
3. Snap, Crackle, and Pop	**3.** Cornelius	**3.** Swerdloc
4. BuzzBee	**4.** Sonny	**4.** Sir Laffitup and Sir Cravenleigh
5. Fred Flintstone and Barney Rubble	**5.** Sunny	**5.** CinnaMon

Answers to the questions on this page can be found on page 130.

• **1199** • RICHARD THE LION-HEARTED laughs at a French boy defending a castle wall with a cross-bow and a frying pan. The boy then shoots King Richard in the neck, a wound that will kill the king two weeks later.

THE MANE ATTRACTION
Can you brave these lion-hearted questions?

1. What is called the "bark lion sentinel dog" in its native Tibet?
2. What beer-centric movie begins with the MGM lion belching rather than roaring?
3. What word did songwriter Pete Seeger inadvertently coin, misunderstanding the Zulu word "uyimbube," meaning "you're a lion"?
4. What nation's flag features a Sinhalese lion holding a sword?

5. After his 1930 coronation, whose imperial motto was "The lion of the tribe of Judah has conquered"?
6. James Earl Jones and Madge Sinclair, who play the king and queen in *The Lion King*, had also played an African king and queen in what earlier film?
7. What's the only country outside Africa where lions still live in the wild?

8. What mountain of Centre County, Pennsylvania, lent its now-famous name to the mountain lions that lived there until the 1880s?
9. What was formed by the five robot lions of the planet Arus?
10. Who began his famous penance by killing and skinning the Nemean lion?

• **1843** • THE WORLD'S FIRST UNDERWATER TUNNEL, under London's Thames River, opens to the public after an eighteen-year construction plagued by floods, fires, and toxic gas leaks.

TUNNEL VISION

1. What movie features three tunnels named Tom, Dick, and Harry?
2. What tunnel does Tony Soprano use in the *Sopranos* opening credits?

3. What nation is home to the only tunnel in the world longer than the Chunnel?
4. What bloody battle resulted when the Union set off a gunpowder-packed tunnel under

Confederate lines at the siege of Petersburg?
5. In 1900, Texas biologist Vernon Bailey discovered a network of tunnels the size of the state of Maryland. What had dug them?

• **1983** • DURING A MOTOWN TWENTY-FIFTH ANNIVERSARY TV SPECIAL, the Supremes spontaneously reunite to sing "Someday We'll Be Together." That title starts to look pretty ironic midway through the song, when Diana Ross shoves Mary Wilson toward the back of the stage.

ALL TOGETHER NOW

1. Whose song "Together Again" was the very first track ever to appear on a U.S. *Now That's What I Call Music!* collection?
2. The BBC once banned the Beatles' "Come Together" for "advertising" what product in

the lyrics?
3. What personal nickname of Mariah Carey was revealed by the title of the album that produced her comeback hit "We Belong Together"?
4. In 1967, what did *The Ed Sul-*

livan Show force the Rolling Stones to sing instead of the title of their song "Let's Spend the Night Together"?
5. In what film is Bruce Willis's first scene backed by Al Green's "Let's Stay Together"?

Answers to the questions on this page can be found on page 131.

MARCH 26

• **1935** • CLIFFORD ODETS'S FIRST PLAY, *Waiting for Lefty,* opens on Broadway (and will later be fictionalized as *Bare Ruined Choirs* in the Coen brothers' Odets-inspired film *Barton Fink*).

IF YOU'RE FEELING SINISTER
Some trivia for the left side of your brain.

1. What famed object from mythology did the Venus de Milo hold in her now-missing left hand?

2. What's the world's most populous country that drives on the left?

3. What term is used for surfers and skaters who prefer to have their left foot on the back of the board?

4. What *Top Gun* actor loses his left arm in three different movies: *Total Recall, Starship Troopers,* and *The Machinist?*

5. Polo, lacrosse, or darts—what sport officially banned left-handed play in 1975?

6. What famed Left Bank neighborhood in Paris was named for the medieval academics at the Sorbonne?

7. What Hall of Fame pitcher of the 1940s and 1950s is baseball's winningest lefty ever?

8. What replaced the left lens in the trademark glasses of the late Lisa "Left Eye" Lopes, of TLC?

9. What disease affects the protagonist of *My Left Foot?*

10. What three consecutive U.S. presidents were born left-handed?

• **1937** • CRYSTAL CITY, TEXAS, erects a statue of Popeye. Why a statue of a sailor in landlocked Crystal City? Because the town bills itself as "the Spinach Capital of the World." (Rival Spinach Capital Alma, Arkansas, not to be outdone, has a similar statue.)

SALAD DAZE
Ten questions for vegetarians.

1. What element, found in thiols, makes your pee smell funny after you eat asparagus?

2. In the United Kingdom, what's called a "courgette"?

3. What vegetable is found in dishes served "Florentine" style?

4. Which member of the Black-Eyed Peas was also the longest-running cast member of 1980s children's show *Kids Incorporated?*

5. What bulb vegetable is traditionally worn on Saint David's Day, as it's a national symbol of Wales?

6. What Grimm's fairy-tale character is named for a vegetable craved by her pregnant mother?

7. What British TV character was nearly named "Mr. Cauliflower"?

8. What vegetable did the Bush White House receive tons of in 1990 after the president, not a fan, banned it from Air Force One?

9. What comedian voiced Mr. Potato Head in the *Toy Story* movies?

10. What vegetable secretes a white, opiumlike psychotropic fluid called "lactucarium"?

Answers to the questions on this page can be found on page 131.

MARCH 27

• **1974** • Construction begins on the Trans-Alaska Pipeline, a massive construction project that will require three years, 21,000 workers, and thirty-one accidental deaths before it's completed.

OILY EDITION

1. What ABC TV star is the great-grandson of a billionaire oilman?
2. The American Heart Association recommends that heart patients take one gram of fish oil a day, since it contains what kind of fatty acids?
3. What two slang terms for oil are used in the *Beverly Hillbillies* theme song?
4. What kind of oil, a product of the flax plant, is used to make most oil paints?
5. What's the only New World member of OPEC?

• **1990** • Lucasfilm files a $300 million trademark infringement lawsuit against 2 Live Crew rapper Luther Campbell, who's been using the stage name Luke Skyywalker.

CLONE WARS
Give these answers, which sound like—but aren't, Lucasfilm!—Star Wars characters.

1. What sandwich bread, because of its shape, takes its name from the Italian for "carpet slipper"?
2. Bhakti, hatha, and kriya are all varieties of what?
3. What computer language uses as its logo a blue mug with red steam rising from it?
4. What Bleecker Street music club became famous for its punk shows, not the bluegrass, blues, and country it was named for?
5. What film's theme song is "Nothing's Gonna Stop Us Now," by Starship?

• **1998** • The FDA approves Viagra, the United States' first male impotence drug.

ARTIFICIAL ERECTIONS
Answer these questions about statues erected to fictional characters.

1. What two characters are sculpted on Hannibal, Missouri's, Main Street?
2. What Copenhagen tourist attraction had a burqa draped over it in 2004 by vandals protesting Turkey's bid to join the EU?
3. What sitcom character is depicted in the bronze statue that TV Land erected in downtown Salem, Massachusetts, in 2005?
4. What German city is home to a statue called *The Town Musicians*?
5. What character, who led a gang of children who were lost in Kensington Gardens, today stands in bronze in that London park?

Answers to the questions on this page can be found on page 131.

MARCH 28

• **1939** • Generalissimo Francisco Franco conquers Madrid, ending the Spanish Civil War.

FROM BEYOND THE GRAVE

Francisco Franco is still dead, as Saturday Night Live used to remind us. Answer these questions about posthumous achievements.

1. What future cabinet member lost a 2000 Senate election to the late Mel Carnahan, the first deceased person ever elected to the Senate?

2. Whose posthumous albums include *R U Still Down?*, *Still I Rise*, and *Until the End of Time*?

3. In 1999, who became the only actor inducted into the Motorcycle Hall of Fame?

4. What artist sold only one painting, *The Red Vineyard*, during his lifetime?

5. What closeted author wrote "Publishable, but worth it?" on the manuscript to his posthumously published *Maurice*, about a gay love affair?

6. What screen legend's last film, sadly, was *Transformers: The Movie*, in which he posthumously played the planet-robot Unicron?

7. *Songbird* is a book about what jazz singer's remarkable posthumous career?

8. Who's the only person ever to have the Baseball Hall of Fame's five-year waiting period waived before his induction?

9. What tongue-in-cheek Internet awards are *always* given posthumously, unless the recipient is sterile?

10. In 2000, on the fortieth anniversary of his name making headlines, who was posthumously awarded a Distinguished Flying Cross and a Prisoner of War Medal?

• **1979** • Three Mile Island melts down, alarming locals but doing wonders for the box office of *The China Syndrome*, which was released less than two weeks earlier.

THREE-MILE ISLANDS

1. What three-mile-wide New Brunswick island was FDR's summer home?

2. What "island," the southernmost tip of Brooklyn, has three miles of famous boardwalk?

3. One of the Midwest's "Quad Cities" is named for what three-mile-long island in the Mississippi?

4. About half of the population of what Pacific island has the surname Christian?

5. What time-travel film was shot on Michigan's three-mile-long Mackinac Island?

• **2001** • Sean "Puffy" Combs tells MTV News that in the wake of his acquittal on weapons charges, he's changing his name from "Puff Daddy" to "P. Diddy."

KEEPING IT REAL

Can you spot these hip-hop performers from their real names?

Easy	*Harder*	*Yeah, Good Luck*
1. Christopher Wallace	**1.** O'Shea Jackson	**1.** Robert Diggs
2. Marshall Mathers	**2.** Aliaune Thiam	**2.** Shad Moss
3. Calvin Broadus	**3.** James Smith	**3.** Clifford Harris
4. Chris Bridges	**4.** Earl Simmons	**4.** Artis Ivey
5. Shawn Carter	**5.** Robert Van Winkle	**5.** Dennis Coles

Answers to the questions on this page can be found on page 132.

• **1925** • THE U.S. GOVERNMENT DENIES John F. Edmiston's trademark on "salt water taffy." Edmiston had claimed to be the inventor of the term and used his claim to demand millions in royalties from America's taffy-pulling giants.

BACK TO THE SALT MINES

1. Utah's Great Salt Lake is the largest remnant of what enormous prehistoric lake?

2. What chemical element has been added to table salt since 1924, to help prevent goiter?

3. Whose name was said to be Melusade or, in Jewish tradition, Edith?

4. In the famous logo, what is the Morton Salt girl holding in her right hand?

5. What company originally owned the name "Saltine," before losing it to trademark dilution?

6. According to Pliny the Elder, what word do we get from the Roman practice of paying soldiers in salt?

7. In *Charlie and the Chocolate Factory*, what animals dispose of Veruca Salt?

8. What TV character had great success with his recipe for Chocolate Salty Balls?

9. The world's least salty seawater is found in the Gulf of Bothnia, between what two countries?

10. What is halite more commonly called?

11. Despite its name, the hip-hop act Salt-N-Pepa was a trio, not a duo. What was the name of Salt-N-Pepa's DJ?

12. At what university was Gatorade invented, in 1965?

13. Who was the only world leader to sign both SALT arms control treaties?

14. What kind of animal is *Artemia salina*, the "sea monkey" of novelty pet ad fame?

15. What salty Procter & Gamble potato snack brand was named by picking a street at random from a Cincinnati phone book?

• **1975** • JOHN WOODEN ANNOUNCES his retirement from basketball coaching. Three days later, he will win the final game of his career, his unmatched tenth NCAA championship.

RECORD PLAYERS
What athletes are famous for these career marks?

Easy	Harder	Yeah, Good Luck
1. 22,895 receiving yards	**1.** 11 NBA titles	**1.** 44.2 points per game
2. .366	**2.** 49-0	**2.** 2,295 runs
3. 7 no-hitters	**3.** 200 races won	**3.** 18 Olympic medals
4. 18 majors	**4.** 2,857 points	**4.** 4,211 turnovers

Answers to the questions on this page can be found on page 132.

MARCH 30

• **1880** • Wabash, Indiana, becomes the world's first town to replace all its gas streetlights with that newfangled electricity.

CURRENT EVENTS

1. What metal item on the end of a kite string gave off the sparks in Benjamin Franklin's famous 1752 experiment?

2. What's the official title of the chief electrician on a movie set?

3. Electrical resistance is measured in ohms. Before the 1971 adoption of the "siemens" unit, what was electrical conductance, the *opposite* of resistance, measured in?

4. Who was the only U.S. presidential assassin to die in the electric chair?

5. What university's fans signal their sports nickname with the semiobscene gesture called the "shocker"?

6. What's the common name for batteries that contain zinc and manganese dioxide?

7. When Bob Dylan "went electric" to loud booing at the 1965 Newport Folk Festival, what agricultural song opened his set?

8. Which flavor of Life Savers can produce sparks when crushed?

9. What Italian scientist discovered methane and invented the first battery?

10. What movie is loosely based on Philip K. Dick's novel *Do Androids Dream of Electric Sheep?*

11. The electric eel is native only to what continent?

12. What Kiss song did Ace Frehley write after an ungrounded railing nearly electrocuted him during a 1976 Florida concert?

13. What Bruins and Rangers legend founded the Tampa Bay Lightning in 1991?

14. What's the name for the chemical and electrical connections formed at the gaps between nerve cells?

15. How much electricity is needed to power the flux capacitor in the *Back to the Future* films?

• **1975** • To celebrate Easter, Uruguayan conductor José Serebrier agrees to host a concert of sacred music in Mexico City. Unused to conducting with a baton, Serebrier manages to stab himself through the hand with it but stanches the blood flow with his handkerchief and makes it through the last twenty minutes of the piece.

CONCERT MASTERY

1. What longtime London Symphony Orchestra conductor is also Woody Allen's father-in-law?

2. What city's orchestra did Eugene Ormandy conduct for forty-four years?

3. The Black Panther benefit lampooned in Tom Wolfe's "Radical Chic" took place in what celebrity conductor's duplex?

4. What director of the New York Philharmonic was the first American to conduct at the famous Bayreuth Festival?

5. In what country was Zubin Mehta born?

Answers to the questions on this page can be found on page 132.

MARCH 31

• **1889** • THE EIFFEL TOWER IS INAUGURATED in Paris, as city VIPs are invited to climb the 1,792 steps to the tower's top. (The elevators won't open for months.)

CITY OF LIGHT

1. In Europe, but not the U.S., what are measured in "Paris Points"?

2. Whose 1863 novel *Paris in the Twentieth Century* was discovered in a trunk and published in 1994?

3. What two July events close the Champs-Élysées every year?

4. In *Casablanca*'s Paris flashbacks, "the Germans wore gray," but what color did Ilsa wear?

5. What Paris-born actress returned to her hometown for 2004's *Before Sunset*?

6. Who's the only member of the Rock and Roll Hall of Fame buried in Paris?

7. What composer brought Parisian taxi horns home to New York to use as instruments in the 1928 premiere of one of his most famous works?

8. What Parisian hill is home to the Moulin Rouge and the Sacré-Coeur Basilica?

9. On what saint's day in 1572 did Catherine de Medicis have 3,000 Protestants killed in Paris?

10. What gardens on the Seine are named for the palace that burned down there during the Paris Commune?

• **1933** • MGM's *GABRIEL OVER THE WHITE HOUSE* premieres. William Randolph Hearst bankrolled this bizarre fantasy, in which a hackish president, played by Walter Huston, "finds religion" after a near-death experiment—and proceeds to become a heroic fascist dictator!

OVAL OFFICE BOX OFFICE
Who played the chief executive in these movies?

Easy	Harder	Yeah, Good Luck
1. *Air Force One*	**1.** *Mars Attacks!*	**1.** *The Pelican Brief*
2. *The American President*	**2.** *Deep Impact*	**2.** *Being There*
3. *Dr. Strangelove*	**3.** *Absolute Power*	**3.** *Superman II*
4. *Dave*	**4.** *Head of State*	**4.** *Seven Days in May*
5. *Independence Day*	**5.** *Canadian Bacon*	**5.** *Fail-Safe*

• **1997** • THE ARIZONA WILDCATS FACE the Kentucky Wildcats in the NCAA basketball championship game. Who wins? The Wildcats!

EN MASSE-COTS
What's the only team name shared between these two leagues?

1. The NFL and the CFL

2. The SEC East and the SEC West

3. The NHL and Major League Baseball

4. The NBA and the WNBA

(though one is pluralized)

5. The NASL and MLS

Answers to the questions on this page can be found on page 133.

March Answers

MARCH 1

EMPIRE RECORDS
1. A cesarean section
2. The shah of Iran
3. Brutus
4. George VI
5. Octavian (Gaius Julius Caesar Octavianus)

DID I CATCH A "NINER" IN THERE?
1. November
2. Lima
3. Quebec
4. Hotel
5. Whiskey
6. India
7. Golf
8. Foxtrot
9. Delta
10. Sierra

UNSOLVED MISTERS
1. J
2. L
3. D
4. H
5. N
6. C
7. F
8. K
9. I
10. M
11. B
12. E
13. G
14. A
15. O

MARCH 2

CAN YOU DIG IT?
1. London
2. *Watership Down*
3. Carlsbad Caverns
4. Frédéric Chopin
5. Oxygen

SINGLE DOUBLES
Easy
1. America
2. Cars
3. War
4. Buddy Holly
5. Poison
Harder
1. Pink
2. Cherish
3. Kiss
4. ABC
5. A Taste of Honey
Yeah, Good Luck
1. Love
2. Chicago
3. Fancy
4. Shannon
5. Rush

NOTES AND QUERIES
1. Phyllo
2. Helen Mirren
3. Katharine Hepburn
4. Soccer (the Football Association)
5. Peru
6. Sir Thomas Gresham
7. Tapioca
8. Liberia

MARCH 3

TUESDAY TRIVIA
1. Aimee Mann
2. Constantinople
3. *The Many Loves of Dobie Gillis*
4. Lou Gehrig's disease, or ALS
5. *Network*

DEAF JAM
1. Bono (Bonovox brand hearing aids)
2. The extended thumb in "I love you"
3. Francisco Goya
4. Ludwig van Beethoven
5. The Osmonds

THE SATANIC "VS."
1. D, f
2. B, b
3. G, g
4. E, h
5. F, e
6. A, c
7. I, d
8. C, i
9. J, a
10. H, j

March Answers

MARCH 4

DEAR MR. RESIDENT

Easy
1. Thomas Jefferson
2. George W. Bush
3. George Washington
4. Andrew Jackson
5. Richard Nixon

Harder
1. Theodore Roosevelt
2. Ronald Reagan
3. George H. W. Bush
4. Franklin Roosevelt
5. James Madison

Yeah, Good Luck
1. Woodrow Wilson
2. John Adams
3. Grover Cleveland
4. Calvin Coolidge
5. James Monroe

DOUBLE-DOUBLES
1. Condoleezza Rice
2. "Rocky Raccoon"
3. Tallahassee
4. Georgia O'Keeffe
5. Kaallalit Nunaat

LYRICIST WANTED
1. H
2. D
3. E
4. F
5. G
6. C
7. B
8. J
9. I
10. A

MARCH 5

RISE OF THE MACHINES
1. The PCjr
2. Chuck E. Cheese's
3. RadioShack
4. Adam
5. The Commodore 64

SUB(PAR) TITLES
1. *Eternal Sunshine of the Spotless Mind*
2. *Groundhog Day*
3. *You Only Live Twice*
4. *Monty Python and the Holy Grail*
5. *Fargo*
6. *Some Like It Hot*
7. *Alien*
8. *The Full Monty*
9. *The Big Chill*
10. *Home Alone*

DO-IT-YOURSELFERS
1. Bill Russell
2. Virginia Woolf
3. Green
4. Napoleon
5. They don't exist; they're just pseudonyms for the director

MARCH 6

FIVE MORE THINGS THAT ARE SHAKESPEARE'S FAULT
1. The Globe Theatre
2. Richard III
3. *Endless Love*
4. Bed
5. Hot-blooded

IN PLAIN BLACK AND WHITE
1. Pepe Le Pew
2. Sepia
3. The quagga
4. *Schindler's List*
5. The Jolly Roger (Teach was Blackbeard)
6. Croatia
7. F. W. de Klerk
8. Fifteen
9. Saint Augustine
10. A soccer ball
11. *March of the Penguins*
12. Slash
13. A safety
14. Desdemona (in *Othello*)
15. Castling (kingside)

MARCH 7

WE ARE THE HOLLOW MEN
1. Sleepy Hollow
2. Mink Hollow
3. Stars Hollow
4. Butcher Hollow
5. Godric's Hollow

SWORD PLAY
1. The Cleveland Cavaliers
2. The Garden of Eden
3. *Kill Bill*
4. The foil
5. The Oscar
6. El Cid
7. The scimitar
8. Wart
9. Orion's
10. The Jabberwock

AND NOTHING BUT THE SPOOF
Easy
1. Madonna
2. Queen
3. Green Day
4. James Brown
5. Puff Daddy
Harder
1. Ritchie Valens
2. Presidents of the United States of America
3. Eminem
4. The Knack
5. Taylor Hicks
Yeah, Good Luck
1. Backstreet Boys
2. Crash Test Dummies
3. The Kinks
4. U2
5. Men Without Hats

MARCH 8

TALK ABOUT THE FASHION
1. C
2. B
3. H
4. G
5. D
6. I
7. A
8. F
9. E
10. J

HUH HUH—YOU SAID . . .
1. William Shakespeare and Alexander Pope
2. Germany
3. Chilly Willy
4. Horatio Alger
5. Java
6. Balaam
7. The New York Giants
8. A lizard
9. *The Prisoner*
10. The Galápagos Islands

MARCH 9

MY COUNTRY, 'TIS OF THEE
1. Jacob
2. The Solomon Islands
3. São Tomé and Príncipe (for Saint Thomas)
4. India
5. The Dominican Republic (but not Dominica)
6. The Philippines (for Philip II)
7. Colombia
8. Kiribati
9. Bolivia (Simón Bolívar, 1783–1830)
10. The Marianas (Marie-Anne of Austria)

WITCH HUNT
Easy
1. *The Wizard of Oz*
2. *The Witches of Eastwick*
3. *The Craft*
4. *Practical Magic, Bewitched*
Harder
1. *The Lion, the Witch, and the Wardrobe*
2. *Sleepy Hollow*
3. *Hocus Pocus*
4. *Four Rooms*
Yeah, Good Luck
1. *I Married a Witch*
2. *Bell, Book and Candle*
3. *Conan the Barbarian*
4. *Bedknobs and Broomsticks*

SIX QUESTIONS OVER TEXAS
1. Lonesome Dove
2. Sammy Sosa
3. Sam Houston
4. Five
5. Red River
6. The Speak & Spell

MARCH 10

SECOND BANANA-RAMA
Easy
1. Dr. Evil
2. Don Quixote
3. Sheriff Andy Taylor
4. Paul Simon
5. David Letterman
Harder
1. Quick Draw McGraw
2. Phileas Fogg
3. Dr. Samuel Johnson
4. Napoleon Dynamite
5. Wayne Campbell
Yeah, Good Luck
1. Nero Wolfe
2. Groucho Marx
3. Edmund Blackadder
4. Modesty Blaise
5. Plastic Man

BOOKS OF THE MONTH
Easy
1. *October*
2. *June*
3. *May*
4. *July*
Harder
1. *April*
2. *August*
3. *August*
4. *March*
Yeah, Good Luck
1. *December*
2. *January*
3. *July*
4. *March*

NATIONAL SHAME
1. Canada
2. Belarus
3. The Netherlands
4. Brazil
5. North Korea

MARCH 11

YOU'LL NEVER WOK (A LOAN)
Easy
1. Swedish
2. Yiddish
3. Japanese
4. Spanish
5. Hawaiian
Harder
1. Hindi
2. Russian
3. Arabic
4. German
5. Malay
Yeah, Good Luck
1. Cantonese
2. Dutch
3. Romany
4. Tamil
5. Afrikaans

MACARTHUR 2: THE RETURN!
Easy
1. *Speed*
2. *Bridget Jones's Diary*
3. *xXx*
4. *Ace Ventura, Pet Detective*
5. *Mad Max*
Harder
1. *Highlander*
2. *Airplane!*
3. *Mannequin*
4. *Arthur*
5. *Poltergeist*
Yeah, Good Luck
1. *Homeward Bound*
2. *Candyman*
3. *Delta Force*
4. *Free Willy*
5. *Piranha*

THE UNMITIGATED GAUL
1. A typewriter or computer keyboard
2. Gabon (Libreville) and Sierra Leone (Freetown)
3. Alexandre Dumas
4. Michelin
5. Grand Marnier
6. The bidet
7. Joan of Arc's
8. Uranus and Neptune
9. Austerlitz
10. Coco Chanel

MARCH 12

STAGE, LEFT
1. Jessica Tandy
2. Christopher Walken
3. Barry Bostwick
4. Ian McKellen
5. Tony Randall

A FEW GOOD MENACE
1. (John) Kander and (Fred) Ebb
2. Keira Knightley
3. *Scarface*
4. J. Jonah Jameson
5. Jada Pinkett

MAKING A NAME FOR THEM-SELVES
Easy
1. Madonna
2. Cher
3. Jewel
4. Björk
5. Brandy
Harder
1. Aaliyah
2. Selena
3. Ashanti
4. Dido
5. Fabian
Yeah, Good Luck
1. Donovan
2. Melanie
3. Taco
4. Tiffany
5. Dion

MARCH 13

WHEN IN ROME . . .

Easy

1. Mars
2. Jupiter (or Jove)
3. Diana
4. Mercury
5. Venus

Harder

1. Vulcan
2. Juno
3. Cupid
4. Saturn
5. Minerva

Yeah, Good Luck

1. Vesta
2. Somnus
3. Discordia
4. Proserpine
5. Faunus

THE NAME OF THE GAME

Easy

1. Pool
2. Golf
3. (Stock) car racing
4. Soccer
5. Horse racing (steeplechase)

Harder

1. Bicycle racing
2. Arm wrestling
3. Basketball
4. (Four-man) bobsled
5. Skateboarding

Yeah, Good Luck

1. Baseball
2. Cricket
3. Football
4. Ice hockey
5. Boxing

TRACE ELEMENTS

1. Tin
2. Iron
3. Astatine
4. Arsenic
5. Carbon

MARCH 14

LICKER CABINET

1. The Chow Chow
2. *Titus Andronicus*
3. *A Christmas Story*
4. *Bloom County*
5. To smell
6. His sixth sheep's sick
7. Pentecost (or Whitsunday)
8. Papillae
9. Gene Simmons
10. Three

PUNCH LINES

1. "Careless Whisper"
2. A question mark and an exclamation point
3. Terrell Owens
4. The guppy
5. Mach 1
6. Los Angeles
7. "Keep on truckin'"
8. Tannen
9. Iran
10. The Hanoi Hilton

MARCH 15

SISTERS ARE DOIN' IT FOR THEMSELVES

1. *Macbeth*
2. Farrah Fawcett-Majors and Cheryl Ladd
3. Magda
4. Radcliffe (now part of Harvard)
5. Althea Gibson
6. Emily Brontë (*Wuthering Heights*)
7. Toledo
8. The Muses
9. Ace of Base
10. Cleopatra

I STILL HAVEN'T FOUND WHAT I'M LOOKING FOR

1. Extraterrestrial intelligence (aliens)
2. AltaVista
3. Jennifer Aniston's
4. Faye Vincent (as baseball commisioner)
5. The Northwest Passage
6. Natalie Wood
7. Tim McGraw
8. *Remembrance of Things Past*
9. Dr. David Banner (*The Incredible Hulk*)
10. Sonny Bono

MARCH 16

LIKE A SURGEON
1. It was transatlantic: the surgeons were in New York, operating a robot on the patient in France
2. John Carter
3. The Loch Ness Monster
4. Christine Jorgensen
5. A cesarean section

SECRET BALLAD
Easy
1. The Beatles
2. Barry Sadler
3. Oscar Wilde
4. Flatt and Scruggs
Harder
1. Sam Peckinpah
2. Elton John
3. Billy Joel
4. Robert Mitchum
Yeah, Good Luck
1. Leonard Nimoy
2. Carson McCullers
3. Bob Dylan
4. XTC

A TRIBE CALLED QUEST
1. Galahad
2. Tim Matheson
3. The Roots
4. Joseph Campbell
5. The Golden Fleece

MARCH 17

GREEN PIECE
1. Edward G. Robinson
2. Vermont
3. "Boulevard of Broken Dreams"
4. The Washington Redskins
5. Oscar Wilde
6. Little Green Sprout
7. Eric the Red
8. *Petticoat Junction*
9. Sunrise or sunset
10. Absinthe

BETTER LATEX THAN NEVER
1. The University of Akron Zips
2. Sulfur
3. An eraser
4. The Super Bowl was named after Superballs
5. "Nowhere Man"

PARKLIFE
Easy
1. San Francisco
2. New York City
3. London
4. Los Angeles
5. Moscow
Harder
1. Atlanta
2. Copenhagen
3. Chicago
4. Paris
5. Boston
Yeah, Good Luck
1. Vancouver
2. Berlin
3. San Diego
4. Washington, D.C.
5. Florence

MARCH 18

FAITH NO MORE!
1. The Cure
2. George Michael
3. Faith Evans
4. Faith Hill

DAUGHTERS OF THE COVENANT
1. Esther
2. Neil Diamond ("You Don't Bring Me Flowers")
3. California
4. The Yom Kippur War
5. Darren Aronofsky
6. Bess Myerson
7. Sarah Hughes
8. Deborah
9. (Adolf) Eichmann
10. Meitnerium (for Lise Meitner)

HOLLYWOOD BUZZ
Easy
1. Demi Moore
2. Natalie Portman
3. Sigourney Weaver
4. Samantha Morton
5. Bai Ling
Harder
1. Cate Blanchett
2. Robin Tunney
3. Alison Lohman
4. Lori Petty
5. Persis Khambatta
Yeah, Good Luck
1. Renée Maria Falconetti
2. Constance Towers
3. Eleanor Parker
4. Natalie Darryl
5. Maggie McOmie

MARCH 19

CONGRESSIONAL RECORD
1. Talleyrand
2. Thomas Jefferson's
3. The African National Congress's
4. Philadelphia
5. India

NEGATIVLAND
1. The electron
2. "Hell to the no!"
3. Spiro Agnew
4. Julius
5. Bartleby the Scrivener
6. Barry Goldwater's
7. Wyclef Jean
8. *i*
9. "We don't need no education"
10. Rhesus antigens (Rh or RhD)

THE MOST IMPORTANT MEAL OF THE DAY
1. Purple
2. Orange juice
3. Canadian bacon
4. Holly Golightly (*Breakfast at Tiffany's*)
5. Lou Gehrig
6. Judd Nelson's
7. French toast
8. Post Toasties
9. Brazil
10. C-3PO

MARCH 20

STOCK ANSWERS
1. General Electric
2. Blue chips
3. They're fictional stocks in Oliver Stone's *Wall Street*
4. Omaha
5. Quotations

HAIRY REASONERS
1. Chimpanzees
2. Samsonite
3. Skull Island
4. The orangutan's
5. Clint Eastwood ("Clint Eastwood" and "Dirty Harry")
6. Dian Fossey's
7. Pauline
8. Silverback
9. Rod Serling
10. Jane Goodall

SHOES YOUR OWN ADVENTURE
1. The rhebok
2. Al Bundy (*Married . . . with Children*)
3. *Some Like It Hot*
4. Manolo Blahnik
5. "Under the Boardwalk"

MARCH 21

AU FRANÇAIS
1. Pawns, in chess
2. Miss Piggy
3. *The Nutcracker*
4. The Russian Revolution
5. St. Louis
6. "Our House"
7. "Boz"
8. Labor Day
9. *Touch of Evil*
10. C.V. (curriculum vitae)

GOING DOWNHILL
1. "The Beat Goes On"
2. Jean-Claude Killy
3. Nordic
4. Utah
5. Dr. (Klaus) Martens

ABC-TV
Easy
1. Mario Lopez
2. William Shatner
3. Jimmie Walker
4. Allison Janney
5. Mike Farrell
Harder
1. Greg Evigan
2. Robert Iler
3. Candace Cameron
4. Pamela Anderson
5. Burt Reynolds
Yeah, Good Luck
1. Judith Ivey
2. Michael Fishman
3. David Spade
4. Dale Robertson
5. Ben Vereen

MARCH 22

TRASH TALKING
1. *Do the Right Thing*'s
2. Art Spiegelman
3. Rio de Janeiro's
4. Butch Vig
5. Kermit the Frog
6. A residential hotel (the Sanford Arms)
7. Michigan's
8. "Alice's Restaurant (Massacree)"
9. Staten Island
10. James Thurber

I'M GETTING TOO OLD FOR THIS SHIP
1. J
2. M
3. C
4. A
5. K
6. E
7. I (*Gilligan's Island*'s "Skipper")
8. H
9. G
10. F
11. L
12. O
13. D
14. N
15. B

MARCH 23

THUMB THING TO TALK ABOUT
1. It sits beside the Finger Lakes
2. The koala
3. *Saturday Night Fever*
4. Arthur Conan Doyle
5. *The Hitchhiker's Guide to the Galaxy*

COLLEGE KNOWLEDGE
Easy
1. Georgia
2. Florida
3. Oregon
4. Alabama
5. Kansas
Harder
1. Connecticut
2. Idaho
3. Maryland
4. Virginia
5. Oklahoma
Yeah, Good Luck
1. Maine
2. New Hampshire
3. South Dakota
4. Rhode Island
5. South Carolina and Missouri

A SEASON ON THE RINK
1. Jaromir Jagr
2. An octopus
3. Icing
4. Mario Lemieux and Patrick Roy
5. The Boston Bruins

MARCH 24

THIS INSPIRING, WIT-TICKLING QUIZ
1. Bananarama
2. Ellen DeGeneres
3. Fighting Irish
4. *Song of Solomon*
5. *Mus musculus*
6. Syzygy

TITLE ROLE CALL
Easy
1. Dudley Moore
2. Cliff Robertson
3. Jamie Foxx
4. Michael Caine
5. Colin Farrell
Harder
1. Mark Lester
2. John Travolta
3. Robin Williams
4. Sean Astin
5. Kevin Kline
Yeah, Good Luck
1. William H. Macy
2. James Wilby
3. Corey Haim
4. John Cusack
5. Matt Dillon

BREAKFAST CLUB
Easy
1. (Sugar or Honey) Smacks
2. (Sugar) Frosted Flakes
3. Rice Krispies
4. Honey Nut Cheerios
5. Fruity (or Cocoa) Pebbles
Harder
1. Super Sugar Crisp (or Golden Crisp)
2. Honeycomb
3. Kellogg's Corn Flakes
4. Cocoa Puffs
5. Kellogg's Raisin Bran
Yeah, Good Luck
1. Cinnamon Toast Crunch
2. Cookie Crisp
3. Kix
4. King Vitaman
5. Apple Jacks

MARCH 25

THE MANE ATTRACTION
1. The Lhasa apso
2. *Strange Brew*
3. "Wimoweh" ("The Lion Sleeps Tonight")
4. Sri Lanka
5. Haile Selassie's
6. *Coming to America*
7. India
8. Mount Nittany (hence, the Penn State Nittany Lions)
9. Voltron
10. Hercules

TUNNEL VISION
1. *The Great Escape*
2. The Lincoln Tunnel
3. Japan (the 33-mile tunnel between Honshu and Hokkaido)
4. The Battle of the Crater
5. Prairie dogs

ALL TOGETHER NOW
1. Janet Jackson
2. Coca-Cola
3. (*The Emancipation of*) Mimi
4. "Let's spend some time together"
5. *Pulp Fiction*

MARCH 26

IF YOU'RE FEELING SINISTER
1. The golden apple of Paris
2. ~~Japan~~ India
3. Goofy
4. Michael Ironside
5. Polo
6. The Latin Quarter
7. Warren Spahn
8. A condom
9. Cerebral palsy
10. Reagan, Bush, and Clinton (though Reagan learned to favor his right)

SALAD DAZE
1. Sulfur
2. A zucchini
3. Spinach
4. Fergie
5. The leek
6. Rapunzel
7. Mr. Bean
8. Broccoli
9. Don Rickles
10. Lettuce

MARCH 27

OILY EDITION
1. Balthazar Getty (great-grandson of J. Paul Getty)
2. Omega-3 fatty acids
3. "Black gold" and "Texas tea"
4. Linseed oil
5. Venezuela

CLONE WARS
1. Ciabatta
2. Yoga
3. Java
4. CBGB
5. *Mannequin*

ARTIFICIAL ERECTIONS
1. Tom Sawyer and Huckleberry Finn
2. The Little Mermaid
3. Samantha Stephens (*Bewitched*)
4. Bremen
5. Peter Pan

MARCH 28	MARCH 29	MARCH 30

FROM BEYOND THE GRAVE
1. John Ashcroft
2. Tupac Shakur
3. Steve McQueen
4. Vincent van Gogh
5. E. M. Forster
6. Orson Welles
7. Eva Cassidy
8. Roberto Clemente
9. The Darwin Awards
10. Francis Gary Powers

THREE-MILE ISLANDS
1. Campobello
2. Coney Island
3. Rock Island
4. Pitcairn Island
5. *Somewhere in Time*

KEEPING IT REAL
Easy
1. The Notorious B.I.G.
2. Eminem
3. Snoop Dogg
4. Ludacris
5. Jay-Z
Harder
1. Ice Cube
2. Akon
3. LL Cool J
4. DMX
5. Vanilla Ice
Yeah, Good Luck
1. RZA
2. Bow Wow
3. T.I.
4. Coolio
5. Ghostface Killah

BACK TO THE SALT MINES
1. Lake Bonneville
2. Iodine
3. Lot's wife
4. An umbrella
5. Nabisco
6. Salary
7. Squirrels
8. Chef (*South Park*)
9. Sweden and Finland
10. Rock salt
11. Spinderella
12. The University of Florida (hence, Gators)
13. Leonid Brezhnev
14. Brine shrimp
15. Pringles

RECORD PLAYERS
Easy
1. Jerry Rice
2. Ty Cobb
3. Nolan Ryan
4. Jack Nicklaus
Harder
1. Bill Russell
2. Rocky Marciano
3. Richard Petty
4. Wayne Gretzky
Yeah, Good Luck
1. Pete Maravich
2. Rickey Henderson
3. Larissa Latynina
4. Karl Malone

CURRENT EVENTS
1. A key
2. Gaffer
3. Mhos ("ohm" spelled backward)
4. Leon Czolgosz
5. Wichita State's
6. Alkaline batteries
7. "Maggie's Farm"
8. Wintergreen (Wint-O-Green)
9. Alessandro Volta
10. *Blade Runner*
11. South America
12. "Shock Me"
13. Phil Esposito
14. Synapses
15. 1.21 gigawatts

CONCERT MASTERY
1. André Previn
2. Philadelphia's
3. Leonard Bernstein's
4. Lorin Maazel
5. India

MARCH 31

CITY OF LIGHT
1. Shoe sizes
2. Jules Verne's
3. Bastille Day and the end of the Tour de France
4. Blue
5. Julie Delpy
6. Jim Morrison
7. George Gershwin (*An American in Paris*)
8. Montmartre
9. St. Bartholomew's Day
10. The Tuileries

OVAL OFFICE BOX OFFICE
Easy
1. Harrison Ford
2. Michael Douglas
3. Peter Sellers
4. Kevin Kline
5. Bill Pullman
Harder
1. Jack Nicholson
2. Morgan Freeman
3. Gene Hackman
4. Chris Rock
5. Alan Alda
Yeah, Good Luck
1. Robert Culp
2. Jack Warden

3. E. G. Marshall
4. Fredric March
5. Henry Fonda

EN MASSE-COTS
1. The Lions (Detroit and B.C.)
2. The Bulldogs (Georgia and Mississippi State)
3. The Rangers (New York and Texas)
4. The Sun(s) (Phoenix and Connecticut)
5. The Dynamo (Denver and Houston)

• **1931** • A TEXAS TRANSPORTATION and energy law firm is so impressed with the young attorney who beat them in court that they hire him, which is how future Watergate prosecutor Leon Jaworski comes to join Fulbright and Jaworski.

BAR SCENE
Match these law firms to their fictional origins.

1. Bendini, Lambert & Locke	**A.** *Ally McBeal*
2. Cage, Fish and Associates	**B.** *Angel*
3. Crane, Poole & Schmidt	**C.** *Boston Legal*
4. Dewey, Cheatem & Howe	**D.** *Daredevil*
5. Flywheel, Shyster & Flywheel	**E.** *The Devil's Advocate*
6. McKenzie Brackman	**F.** *The Firm*
7. Milton, Chadwick & Waters	**G.** *Harvey Birdman, Attorney-at-Law*
8. Nelson & Murdock	**H.** *L.A. Law*
9. Sebben & Sebben	**I.** The Marx Brothers
10. Wolfram and Hart	**J.** The Three Stooges

• **1950** • A BIRMINGHAM SOLICITOR'S CLERK named Anthony Pratt is granted a patent for his new board game Cluedo (later shortened to Clue in the United States). Pratt's original application specifies nine weapons, many of which (the Ax, the Shillelagh, the Syringe) would be unfamiliar to today's players.

A LEAD PIPE CINCH
One question apiece for Clue's six weapons.

1. What common English word derives from the Latin for "lead," for the Roman practice of making water **pipe**s out of lead?
2. Which **Revolver** track is the only Beatles song on which no Beatle plays an instrument?

3. What Hartford manufacturing company began making hex-head **wrench**es during World War II?
4. What actor—half of a fifty-two-year Hollywood marriage—also adapted the screenplay for Hitchcock's movie **Rope**?

5. On October 17, 1989, what happened twenty-six minutes before game three of the World Series was about to begin at **Candlestick** Park?
6. What is the surgical **knife** called an *izmel* used for?

• **1957** • THE BBC AIRS a deadpan April Fools' Day report on a bumper spaghetti harvest in Switzerland. The next day, hundreds of gullible Britons phone the BBC to ask how they can grow spaghetti trees at home.

GROWING PAINS

1. According to Chairman Mao, "political power grows out of" what?
2. Who fretted over exponential population growth in his *An

Essay on the Principles of Population?*
3. In what gland is HGH, human growth hormone, produced?
4. What flower name completes

the title of the state song of Colorado, "Where the ____ Grow"?
5. What 1904 play was subtitled "The Boy Who Wouldn't Grow Up"?

Answers to the questions on this page can be found on page 167.

APRIL 2

• **1513** • Juan Ponce de León lands on a coast he calls "Florida," for its flowery vegetation. In 1535, a Spanish historian will claim that Ponce de León was looking for a legendary land called "Bimini," whose waters could cure his sexual impotence.

FOUNTAIN OF YOUTH

1. What founder of PCs Limited went on to become the youngest Fortune 500 CEO in history?
2. Mel Harris and Timothy Busfield were still in their twenties when they were cast in what TV series in 1987?
3. What are infant marsupials called?
4. What TV host is the youngest of eleven children, many of whom pronounce their last name differently from his?
5. Who played his first game for D.C. United in 2003 at the tender age of 14?
6. The six youngest Nobel laureates ever all won in what field?
7. What did Benjamin Britten write the "Young Person's Guide to" in 1945?
8. Who opened her first school, Rome's Casa dei Bambini, in 1907?
9. What Internet portal was sued for copyright infringement in 2000 by the star of *Young Einstein?*
10. What skateboarding actor-to-be plays the main character in Sonic Youth's video for "100%"?

• **1951** • Jack Kerouac begins a Benzedrine-fueled twenty-one-day writing marathon, taping together his paper into a 119-foot, 8-inch scroll so he can type continuously. The result on April 22: the finished manuscript of *On the Road.*

"BEAT" GENERATION

1. In what state were "My Governor Can Beat Up Your Governor" bumper stickers popular beginning in 1998?
2. What hitmaker produced the 2009 PlayStation music mixer game *Beaterator?*
3. In what sport are the Beaters in charge of batting away the Bludgers?
4. In 2007, what school beat the Ohio State Buckeyes for the national championships in both football and basketball?
5. What dessert consists of beaten egg whites, sugar, and cream of tartar?
6. What bassist's romance with Astrid Kirchherr is the subject of the film *Backbeat?*
7. Bartender, cabdriver, or convenience store clerk—what was Rodney King's occupation at the time of his infamous 1991 arrest and beating?
8. In 2007, the inventors of the computer program Chinook proved that their program cannot be beaten at what game?
9. What kind of beat can be divided into S_1, caused by the AV valves, and S_2, caused by the semilunar valves?
10. Who performs the guest guitar solo on Michael Jackson's "Beat It"?

Answers to the questions on this page can be found on page 167.

• **1862** • IN A MASSIVE INTERNATIONAL LAUNCH, the first part of Victor Hugo's *Les Misérables* is published, and crowds line up in front of bookshops. According to one popular legend, Hugo sends the world's shortest telegram to his publisher, asking, "?" The reply: "!"

COMMA SUTRA

Answer these impeccably punctuated questions about punctuation.

1. What late American's son, Rich, said in 2005, "My father's name is synonymous with the word 'asterisk' "?

2. What world capital was the birthplace of Victor Borge, the comic pianist of "Phonetic Punctuation" fame?

3. What's the only Best Picture Oscar winner whose title ends with an exclamation point?

4. What did Kurt Vonnegut describe by saying, "They are transvestite hermaphrodites, standing for absolutely nothing. All they do is show you've been to college"?

5. In 2004, for the Internet age, what new character was added to the Morse code alphabet, the first official addition since World War I?

6. What's the name for the little squiggle above the Spanish *ñ*, without which a sentence like "Tengo veinte años" ("I'm twenty years old") would instead read "Tengo veinte anos" ("I have twenty anuses")?

7. What band's lone hit was originally called "69 Tears" before receiving a more radio-friendly title?

8. What punctuation mark do mathematicians use to express a number's factorial?

9. What kind of animal is referenced in the title of Lynne Truss's punctuation guide *Eats, Shoots & Leaves*?

10. What began as a ligature of the letters "e" and "t"?

• **1941** • EL RANCHO VEGAS OPENS, the first Las Vegas hotel on what will become known as "the Strip."

STRIP SEARCH

1. What 1883 novel's most memorable character was based on William Henley, the one-legged poet of "Invictus"?

2. What company bought naming rights to the Florida Suncoast Dome in 1996?

3. According to Thomas Malory, Sir Bedivere's last knightly act is to return what to a lake?

4. What desert is home to the Ahaggar and Tibesti mountains?

5. What Kander-Ebb song did Philadelphia cream cheese, confusingly, use in 1980s TV commercials?

6. A causeway lined with hundreds of sphinxes once connected Karnak to what other great Egyptian temple?

7. What original animal mascot for Trix cereal was replaced by a rabbit in 1967?

8. In what 2006 film did Sebastian Foucan, the inventor of "free running," show off his sport?

9. What's the more common word for a fata morgana?

10. In what layer of the Earth's atmosphere is Antarctica's famed "ozone hole"?

Answers to the questions on this page can be found on page 167.

APRIL 4

• 1851 • AFTER THE COMPROMISE of 1850 creates the Utah territory, the provisional government votes to dissolve Deseret, a proposed state covering most of modern-day Utah, Nevada, and Arizona. The name "Deseret" is a word in the Book of Mormon meaning "honeybee."

PLAN BEE

1. What large U.S. city calls its newspaper the *Bee*?

2. Bee yellow, bee orange, or bee purple—what invisible "color" can bees see on flower petals?

3. In 2007, who jumped from the roof of Cannes's Carlton Hotel wearing a giant bee costume?

4. What are male honeybees called?

5. What sports term is the short-est word ever to decide the National Spelling Bee?

6. Whose tombstone, in Siler City, North Carolina, bears the inscription "Aunt Bee"?

7. Whose opera *The Tale of Tsar Saltan* contains "The Flight of the Bumblebee"?

8. Who was the only one of the Astros' "Killer Bs" ever to win an MVP award?

9. In what movie does Walter Brennan annoy people with the question "Was you ever bit by a dead bee?"

10. Which member of the Bee Gees played no instruments on-stage?

• 1984 • WINSTON SMITH BEGINS keeping his diary of life in "Oceania" (a dystopian future nation consisting of Britain, the Americas, the South Pacific, and southern Africa) in George Orwell's *Nineteen Eighty-four*.

MAPS AND LEGENDS
Match these fictional nations to their locations and the books that take place there.

1. Brobdingnag	**A.** Africa	**a.** *Cat's Cradle*
2. Costaguana	**B.** The Alps	**b.** *Gulliver's Travels*
3. Florin	**C.** The Caribbean	**c.** *Lord Jim*
4. Genovia	**D.** Central Europe	**d.** *The Mouse That Roared*
5. Grand Fenwick	**E.** The East Indies	**e.** *Nostromo*
6. Ishmaelia	**F.** Indochina	**f.** *The Princess Bride*
7. Patusan	**G.** The Mediterranean	**g.** *The Princess Diaries*
8. Ruritania	**H.** Near Alaska	**h.** *The Prisoner of Zenda*
9. San Lorenzo	**I.** Scandinavia	**i.** *Scoop*
10. Sarkhan	**J.** South America	**j.** *The Ugly American*

Answers to the questions on this page can be found on page 168.

• **1734** • HENRY FIELDING'S PLAY *Don Quixote in England* premieres at the Haymarket Theatre, including the first known use of the exclamation "Odds bodkins!" "Odds bodkins" is actually a "minced oath" for the more profane "God's body!"

GOD'S BODY

1. Who scored the famous "Hand of God" goal in the 1986 World Cup?

2. What was the unusual hit single from the Crash Test Dummies' 1993 album *God Shuffled His Feet*?

3. Which of his ten fingers is God using to give Adam life on the ceiling of the Sistine Chapel?

4. Mexico, India, or Egypt—in what nation did the woven-yarn craft of "God's eyes" originate?

5. What's the correct name of the famous John Gillespie Magee sonnet that ends "Put out my hand and touch the face of God"?

• **1984** • WITH A TWELVE-FOOT SKYHOOK from the right baseline, Kareem Abdul-Jabbar surpasses Wilt Chamberlain's 31,419-point record to become the highest scorer in NBA history.

PLAYING HOOKY

1. What trade name comes from combining the French words for velvet and hook?

2. Whose number one 1990 album *To the Extreme* simply repackaged the songs from his indie-label debut, *Hooked*?

3. What poker hand are you holding if you have "two fish-hooks"?

4. How does the hook-handed Woody Harrelson lose his right hand in the film *Kingpin*?

5. What Reds and Tigers manager was nicknamed "Captain Hook" for his tendency to pull pitchers early?

6. What U.S. president was born in Kinderhook, New York?

7. Until their 2007 breakup, Peter Hook spent almost three decades as the bassist for what Manchester band?

8. In 1990s ads, what was the memorable 800 number of Hooked on Phonics?

9. On *The Simpsons*, what character's wife is voiced by *SNL*'s Jan Hooks?

10. Scientist Robert Hooke was chosen to assist what man in rebuilding London following the Great Fire?

• **2004** • THE TOWN OF HASLACH, in Upper Austria, revokes the honorary citizenship it awarded Adolf Hitler in 1938. Haslach, the last town to so honor Hitler, apparently took sixty-six years to notice the Führer's civic shortcomings.

MR. NATURAL(IZED)

Only seven foreigners have ever been made honorary citizens of the United States. Which of them hailed from . . .

1. France	**3.** Albania	**5.** England (a married couple)
2. United Kingdom	**4.** Poland	**6.** Sweden

Answers to the questions on this page can be found on page 168.

APRIL 6

• **1644** • THOSE PURITAN KILLJOYS in England's "Long Parliament" ban the Maypole, calling it "a heathenish vanity, generally abused to superstition and wickedness."

POLE POSITION

1. For whom is the left-field foul pole at Boston's Fenway Park officially named?
2. What has two poles as a result of Amperian currents?
3. The point on land closest to the North Pole belongs to what nation?
4. What were the first modern Olympic pole vaulters' poles made of?
5. What holiday is celebrated with an aluminum pole, the Airing of Grievances, and Feats of Strength?
6. What common object is designed to recall the bloodstained bandages of medieval times?
7. What former sitcom costars play the two lead boys in 2004's *The Polar Express*?
8. Who renamed the Antarctic Plateau "King Haakon VII's Plateau" in 1911?
9. What kind of pole hosts "See You at the Pole" gatherings?
10. Who has been the pole sitter at a record six Indy 500s, from 1979 to 1991?

• **1963** • THE PORTLAND GARAGE BAND The Kingsmen lays down a sloppy version of a Richard Berry song during a one-hour recording session. A Boston DJ plays the raucous song as his "Worst Record of the Week" and it catches on with listeners, surprising the Kingsmen by becoming a huge national hit.

HEY HEY, MY MY
What double-word song title was a hit single for these artists?

Easy	*Harder*	*Yeah, Good Luck*
1. The Archies	**1.** The Thompson Twins	**1.** The Castaways
2. Billy Idol	**2.** Neil Diamond	**2.** Naked Eyes
3. Paula Abdul	**3.** Santana	**3.** The New Christy Minstrels
4. The Mamas and the Papas	**4.** Elvis Costello	**4.** Run-D.M.C.
5. Amy Grant	**5.** David Bowie	**5.** The Beau Brummels

• **1966** • RIOTS ERUPT ON THE STREETS of Kowloon after the colonial government approves a five-cent hike in the fare on Hong Kong's famous Star Ferry.

FERRY TALES

1. Who ferries the dead across the river Acheron in Greek myth?
2. What state is *today* home to Harpers Ferry, but is not the state in which it was located at the time of John Brown's raid?
3. What color is New York's Staten Island Ferry?
4. What British pop group did Bryan Ferry lead after Brian Eno's 1973 departure?
5. What late actor was named in tribute to the lessons taught by the ferryman Vasudeva in Hermann Hesse's novel *Siddhartha*?

Answers to the questions on this page can be found on page 168.

• **1859** • IN HIS STORE, the English chemist John Walker sells the first "friction lights," which he invented accidentally last year by mixing potassium chlorate and antimony sulfide. Today we call them "matches."

MATCH POINT
"Match" wits with these five questions.

1. What musical was based on Thornton Wilder's play *The Matchmaker*?
2. What two *Rocky III* costars won the final match of the very first WrestleMania?
3. What future game show host was the first regular panelist on *Match Game '73*?
4. What match play event, similar to the Ryder Cup, pits a U.S. team against a *non*-European international team?
5. In 1996, who became the first U.S. presidential hopeful ever to opt out of accepting federal matching funds for his campaign?

• **1926** • VIOLET GIBSON, the mentally deranged sister of Irish peer Baron Ashbourne, shoots Italian dictator Benito Mussolini in the streets of Rome. The bullet passes through both of Il Duce's nostrils, and one bandage later, the parade continues as planned.

I SHOT THE SHERIFF
Who was assassinated by each of these people?

Easy	Harder	Yeah, Good Luck
1. James Earl Ray	1. Dan White	1. Yigal Amir
2. Leon Czolgosz	2. Ramón Mercader	2. Talmadge Hayer
3. Charlotte Corday	3. Nathuram Godse	3. Giuseppe Zangara
4. Gavrilo Princip	4. Carl Weiss	4. Khalid Islambouli

• **1969** • THE FAMILIAR SILHOUETTE Major League Baseball logo makes its debut, as players wear it on their uniforms for the first time. Though popular legend says the player in the logo was modeled on Harmon Killebrew, the league refuses to name names.

CLUB SCENE
What's the only Major League Baseball team whose official logo features . . .

Easy	Harder	Yeah, Good Luck
1. A bell	1. A compass	1. Home plate
2. An earring	2. A hat	2. A bridge
3. A crown	3. Barley	3. A weapon

Answers to the questions on this page can be found on page 169.

APRIL 8

• **1630** • JOHN WINTHROP IS ELECTED governor of the Massachusetts Bay Colony. Today, he's best remembered for his sermon "A Model of Christian Charity," in which he compared America to a "city upon a hill."

A CITY ON A HILL

1. What Notting Hill road is home to London's most famous antique market?
2. Until 1790, what was known as Jenkins Hill?

3. What island, whose name means "island of many hills," is home to Murray Hill, Lenox Hill, Marble Hill, and Rose Hill?
4. What San Francisco hill is

home to a famous colony of wild parrots?
5. According to legend, what city was founded on Palatine Hill?

• **1966** • "IS GOD DEAD?" asks *Time* magazine on a surprisingly goth all-black cover.

PUTTING THE "MORTAL" BACK IN "IMMORTAL"
Answer these questions about dead gods.

1. What Egyptian god was dismembered by his brother Set and then rebuilt by his wife, Isis—except for his penis, which, sadly, had been eaten by a fish?
2. In Norse mythology, at what apocalyptic final battle will Odin be devoured by the wolf Fenrir

and Thor be poisoned by the Midgard serpent?
3. "Calvary" and "Golgotha," the two names for the hill where Christ was crucified, are both words meaning what?
4. What handsome Greek god, killed by a wild boar, inspired

Percy Shelley's elegy for his friend Keats?
5. Before he took ill, who was booked to play the London Palladium on January 20, 1996, to honor his one hundredth birthday?

• **1990** • LAURA PALMER IS FOUND DEAD, wrapped in plastic, on the first *Twin Peaks*.

TWIN PEEKS

1. What comedian has real-life twin sons named Matthew and Gregory?
2. Who are the Glimmer Twins?
3. What Hall of Famer played his entire major-league career for the Minnesota Twins?
4. What kind of twins are also called "dizygotic"?

5. What kind of animal suckled Romulus and Remus?
6. The New Wave band Thompson Twins were named for characters in what comics series?
7. What did Ross and Norris McWhirter compile as a promotional giveaway in 1955?
8. What city is home to the

eighty-eight-story Petronas Twin Towers?
9. What future star appeared uncredited as Arnold Schwarzenegger and Danny DeVito's mom in *Twins*?
10. What EU nation is led by a president and a prime minister who are identical twins?

Answers to the questions on this page can be found on page 169.

• **1682** • FRENCH EXPLORER Robert de La Salle discovers the mouth of the Mississippi River and names the basin "La Louisiane," to honor King Louis XIV.

ORAL FIXATION

In what country would you find the mouths of these rivers?

Easy	Harder	Yeah, Good Luck
1. Yangtze	1. Colorado	1. Dnieper
2. Amazon	2. Murray	2. Salween
3. Volga	3. Ganges	3. Orinoco
4. Nile	4. Yukon	4. Limpopo
5. Mekong	5. Rhine	5. Volta

• **1932** • FUTURE *TARZAN* STAR CHEETA is born in Liberia. Cheeta is still alive and well in a Palm Springs animal sanctuary, making him the world's oldest (nonhuman) primate on record.

SEE MONKEYS

Match these hairy screen stars to their species.

1. Bonzo, *Bedtime for Bonzo*	A. Capuchin monkey
2. Buddy, *Buddy*	B. Chimpanzee
3. Clyde, *Any Which Way You Can*	C. Gorilla
4. Marcel, *Friends*	D. Human
5. Rafiki, *The Lion King*	E. Mandrill
6. Robin Williams, *Awakenings*	F. Orangutan

• **1945** • IN A NEW RULE, the NFL requires all players to wear socks as part of the official uniform.

THE JOY OF SOCKS

1. What Labrador retriever supplanted Socks the cat as the Clintons' favorite pet in 1997?

2. At age 17, who played the title schoolgirl in *The Bachelor and the Bobby-Soxer?*

3. Whose "Play-Along" included fellow socks Charley Horse and Hush Puppy?

4. Who donated the only sock displayed on its own in the Baseball Hall of Fame?

5. On the cover of their first EP, the Red Hot Chili Peppers duplicated what album cover, wearing only a single sock apiece?

6. Who said, "Sock it to *me?*" on the September 16, 1968, episode of *Laugh-In?*

7. What movie's title character is given a new name when he's seen playing with Two Socks?

8. What colors are the Rock 'Em Sock 'Em Robots?

9. Which of the infamous "Black Sox" was banned from baseball despite never having agreed to the fix?

10. What common sock pattern is named for the westernmost region of Scotland?

Answers to the questions on this page can be found on page 169.

APRIL 10

• **1896** • GREEK WATER CARRIER SPIRIDON LOUIS becomes a hero in Athens when he wins the first track and field Olympic gold for his homeland by winning the marathon, a race designed to commemorate the Athenian victory of the 490 B.C. Battle of Marathon.

MY BIG FAT GREEK ALPHABET

1. Who played the title character in the film *The Omega Man*?
2. What film introduced the fraternity Lambda Lambda Lambda?

3. Horse, tiger, or wolf—what kind of animal is Pi Patel's lifeboat companion for seven months in the novel *Life of Pi*?
4. At the delta of the Danube

River, what body of water does it flow into?
5. What short-lived 1970s TV series was set on Moonbase Alpha?

• **1921** • COUNTRY SINGER AND CHARACTER ACTOR Sheb Wooley is born in Oklahoma. Wooley's biggest hit was his novelty number "Purple People Eater," but movie buffs know him as the screamer behind the "Wilhelm scream," a ubiquitous Hollywood sound effect that's been heard in everything from *A Star Is Born* to *Star Wars*.

IN A MANNER OF SHRIEKING

1. What working title for the movie *Scream* later named a hit 2000 film?
2. Whose campaign was hurt by the so-called I Have a Scream speech he gave after the 2004 Iowa caucus?

3. On January 22, 1892, what artist wrote in his diary that while out walking with friends, he "sensed an infinite scream passing through nature"?
4. The U.S. Army's elite 101st Airborne Division is known as

the "Screaming" what?
5. What Screamin' Jay Hawkins hit was banned by many radio stations, which called its grunts and groans "cannibalistic"?

• **1939** • EDUCATOR FRANK W. CYR holds a conference at Columbia University's Teachers College with the aim of improving school bus safety. The result of the conference: a glossy yellow color called "National Chrome" is chosen as the American school bus standard. For the rest of his life, Cyr will be known as the "Father of the Yellow School Bus."

THEY WERE ALL YELLOW

1. What army is invading Pepperland in the Beatles film *Yellow Submarine*?
2. The 3,400-mile Yellow River is what country's second longest?
3. Why was paradise paved over, according to Joni Mitchell's "Big Yellow Taxi"?
4. Health problems in 2006 led Greg Page to quit as the "Yellow"

member of what Australian group?
5. Which Yellowstone geyser, with eruptions 100 feet taller than Old Faithful's, is the world's tallest?
6. In soccer, how many yellow cards lead to a player's disqualification?
7. Which chemical element is a

bright yellow solid at room temperature?
8. What Hungarian-born newspaperman's *New York World* was in the vanguard of "yellow journalism" during the 1890s?
9. Which Scandinavian nation has a yellow cross on its flag?
10. Who appears on the cover of the *Pokémon Yellow* video game?

Answers to the questions on this page can be found on page 170.

• **1849** • WALTER HUNT RECEIVES a patent for a single piece of wire, which he's twisted cleverly into the first modern safety pin.

SAFETY DANCE

1. By U.S. law, exit signs in buildings must be one of what two colors?

2. Sodium azide, a highly toxic chemical, is best-known for being used to develop what life-saving devices?

3. What actor campaigned against helmet laws until he was almost killed in a helmetless 1988 motorcycle accident?

4. Because her name became a slang term for a life preserver, who is the only actress whose name is an entry in Merriam-Webster's dictionary?

5. What L.A. Ram and future TV cop is the only player in NFL history ever to record two safeties in a single game?

• **2003** • IN A WEIRD CASE of NBA Stockholm Syndrome, the Miami Heat retire Michael Jordan's number 23 jersey, even though he never played for the team—and, in fact, booted them from the playoffs three times in the 1990s.

JERSEY CITY

Can you match up the athletes who memorably wore the same number and name that number? (Hint: the athletes at left are listed in ascending order.)

1. Secretariat	**A.** Dizzy Dean
2. Babe Ruth	**B.** Dale Earnhardt
3. Brett Favre	**C.** Lou Gehrig
4. Mia Hamm	**D.** Gordie Howe
5. Guy Lafleur	**E.** Derek Jeter
6. Wilt Chamberlain	**F.** Magic Johnson
7. John Havlicek	**G.** Dan Marino
8. Jim Brown	**H.** Walter Payton
9. Nolan Ryan	**I.** Pelé
10. Hank Aaron	**J.** Jerry West

• **2007** • THE U.S. POST OFFICE sells its first "forever stamps," which will always be good no matter how much stamp prices rise.

FOREVER AND A DAY

1. Who played the Dark Knight for the only time in *Batman Forever*?

2. Fans of what first-person shooter video game franchise have been waiting more than a decade for its fourth installment, ironically subtitled *Forever*?

3. What Hobbity actor has "Living is easy with eyes closed," from "Strawberry Fields Forever," tattooed on his left arm?

4. What company coined the influential ad slogan "A diamond is forever"?

5. 1975's *Forever...* was billed as what author's first novel for adults?

Answers to the questions on this page can be found on page 170.

APRIL 12

• **1902** • Dr. George Still publishes an article on an "abnormal defect on moral control" he has discovered in children. Not until 1996 will Dr. Still's discovery get its modern name: attention-deficit/hyperactivity disorder, or ADHD.

SHORT ATTENTION SPAN THEATER

I'm not sure if these people have ADHD, or if they just need to make up their mind already.

1. What "Saturday Night Massacre" figure is the only person to have served in four different U.S. cabinet positions during his career?

2. What play was written under a host of working titles, including *The Moth, Blanche's Chair in the Moon,* and *The Poker Night*?

3. Who's the only coach to have led seven different teams to the NBA playoffs?

4. On what kiddie film franchise does director Robert Rodriguez also have credits as writer, producer, composer, editor, cinematographer, production designer, sound mixer, camera operator, and visual effects supervisor?

5. Who's the only person ever to host shows on ABC, CBS, and NBC simultaneously, doing triple duty from 1984 to 1987?

• **1961** • Richard Rodgers wins a Grammy Award for *The Sound of Music*'s cast album, making him the first person to win all four top showbiz awards: an Oscar, an Emmy, a Tony, and a Grammy. (There are now eight others, including Mel Brooks, John Gielgud, Helen Hayes, Audrey Hepburn, Rita Moreno, and Mike Nichols.)

I'D LIKE TO THANK THE ACADEMY

Match these less famous awards with the fields in which they're given.

1. Caldecott Medal
2. Clio Award
3. Darwin Award
4. Edgar Award
5. Eisner Award
6. Fields Medal
7. Hugo Award
8. Juno Award
9. Naismith Award
10. Obie Award
11. Patsy Award
12. Peabody Award
13. Pritzker Prize
14. Turing Award
15. Vezina Trophy

A. Advertising
B. Animal acting
C. Architecture
D. Canadian music
E. Children's book illustration
F. College basketball
G. Comic books
H. Computer science
I. Death
J. Hockey goaltending
K. Mathematics
L. Mystery writing
M. Off-Broadway theater
N. Radio and television
O. Science fiction

Answers to the questions on this page can be found on page 170.

APRIL 13

• **1663** • EXAMINING A SAMPLE of cork under an early microscope, Robert Hooke of the British Royal Society notes that the plant material seems to be made up of boxy compartments that remind him of monks' quarters, so he coins the word "cells" for them.

"CELL"ING OUT

1. What Irish author's last published poem was released under the pseudonym "C.3.3," his prison cell number?
2. What grapefruit-sized object has been reckoned to be the largest single cell on earth?
3. Whose breakthrough 2001 album could have been synonymously titled *Leukocytes*?
4. Marc Bolan's wife, Gloria Jones, first released what song, later a much bigger hit for Soft Cell?
5. What single company accounts for fully half the market capitalization of the Helsinki stock exchange?

• **1843** • CHANG AND ENG, Barnum's famed "Siamese twins," marry sisters Adelaide and Sarah Anne Yates. They adopt the last name "Bunker," buy land and slaves, and settle down in rural North Carolina. Sadly, the Yates sisters don't get along, and Chang and Eng have to split their week between two separate households.

THAI ME UP, THAI ME DOWN

1. What popular tourist destination is Thailand's largest island?
2. What tropical fruit is the main ingredient in Thai *som tam* salad?
3. What two musicals, one Broadway hit and one West End hit, opened thirty-five years apart and were both set in Bangkok?
4. What popular aquarium fish is known as *pla-kad* in its native Thailand?
5. What modern sport grew out of the ancient Thai sport Muay Thai?

• **1970** • RICKY SCHRODER IS BORN in Staten Island. When he grows up, Ricky will drop the *y* and become one of TV's great fill-in men, replacing Jimmy Smits on *NYPD Blue* and Roger Cross on *24*.

CAST AWAY
Who played the new addition replacing these TV regulars?

Easy
1. Phil Hartman, *NewsRadio*
2. Norman Fell, *Three's Company*
3. Michael J. Fox, *Spin City*
4. Valerie Harper, *Valerie*
5. Nicholas Colasanto, *Cheers*

Harder
1. Polly Holliday, *Alice*
2. Charlotte Rae, *The Facts of Life*
3. William Frawley, *My Three Sons*
4. George Dzundza, *Law & Order*
5. Rob Lowe, *The West Wing*

Yeah, Good Luck
1. Freddie Prinze, *Chico and the Man*
2. Rob Morrow, *Northern Exposure*
3. Larry Wilcox, *CHiPs*
4. Terry Farrell, *Deep Space Nine*
5. Terry Farrell, *Becker*

Answers to the questions on this page can be found on page 171.

APRIL 14

• 1881 • EL PASO MARSHAL DALLAS STOUDENMIRE becomes a legend when he kills three men in the famous "Four Dead in Five Seconds" gunfight.

CRIME SCENES
In what city were these famous people killed?

Easy	Harder	Yeah, Good Luck
1. Archduke Ferdinand	**1.** Billy Clanton	**1.** Bob Crane
2. Wild Bill Hickok	**2.** Rasputin	**2.** Veronica Guerin
3. Martin Luther King, Jr.	**3.** William McKinley	**3.** Medger Evers
4. Indira Gandhi	**4.** JonBenét Ramsey	**4.** Elizabeth Short
5. Tupac Shakur	**5.** Rafael Trujillo	**5.** Anton Cermak

• 1966 • THE BEATLES RECORD "RAIN," the B-side of "Paperback Writer" and the first rock song ever to feature "hidden messages" via back-masked vocals.

WHAT LIES BENEATH
Can you reveal these hidden answers?

1. Who reveals "the man behind the curtain" in *The Wizard of Oz*?
2. What hides the face of the bowler-hatted title figure in René Magritte's painting *The Son of Man*?
3. Who devised the Trojan Horse and led the men hidden inside it?
4. In the *Harry Potter* books, the entrance to Gryffindor Tower is hidden behind a painting of whom?
5. Whittaker Chambers hid Alger Hiss's purloined State Department documents in a hollowed-out what?

• 2003 • RESEARCHERS ANNOUNCE THE COMPLETION of the Human Genome Project, a thirteen-year effort to decode the billions of nucleotides in the human genome.

GENE-HACK MEN

1. How many pairs of chromosomes are there in each human cell?
2. Housefly, horsefly, or fruit fly—what kind of insect is *Drosophila melanogaster*, the most studied organism in genetics?
3. DNA was discovered in Cambridge in 1953. What famous person with the initials "D.N.A." had been born in Cambridge in 1952?
4. What scientist was also the sixth abbot of Brno's Abbey of Saint Thomas?
5. Which of the four bases of DNA *isn't* found in RNA?

Answers to the questions on this page can be found on page 171.

• **1955** • INCOME TAX DAY in the United States falls on its current date for the first time. (It was originally March 1, after the passage of the Sixteenth Amendment, and was later bumped back to March 15.)

TAXING TRIVIA

1. Gandhi's famous march to Dandi in 1930 was an act of protest against Great Britain's tax on what?

2. What two British politicians of the 1960s are mentioned by George Harrison in "Taxman"?

3. Which of the four biblical Gospels was written by an ex-tax collector?

4. Where did Al Capone spend the majority of his 1931 sentence for tax evasion?

5. What did the 1980s bands the Go-Gos, R.E.M., Black Sabbath, and Fine Young Cannibals have in common?

6. What August 18, 1988, sound bite was later called "the six most destructive words in the history of presidential politics"?

7. Thoreau's "Civil Disobedience" was inspired by the jail time he did for refusing to pay a poll tax supporting what war?

8. Whose 1990 double album

Who'll Buy My Memories? is also called *The IRS Tapes*, since that's where all the proceeds went?

9. With his famous "Taxpayer" character of the 1930s, *New York World* cartoonist Will B. Johnstone invented the famous image of a man wearing what?

10. Which section of the Internal Revenue Code was created in 1978, intended by Congress as a way for executives to defer their salary tax-free?

• **1971** • GEORGE C. SCOTT WINS a Best Actor Oscar for playing *Patton* but isn't there to receive the award. He had earlier telegrammed the Academy asking that his name be withdrawn. "The whole thing is a goddamn meat parade," he says.

MEAT ON PARADE

1. What's the traditional meat on a Reuben sandwich?

2. In an annual "index," what item does *The Economist* use to express currency rates and buying power between countries?

3. What cut of beef, often used for hamburger, is also called the "seven-bone steak"?

4. In Britain, what kind of meat

comes in rashers?

5. What job, once held by James Garner and Robert Mitchum, is now filled by Sam Elliott?

6. The "-am" in "Spam" is obviously for "ham." What's the "sp-" for?

7. In the nursery rhyme "This Little Piggy," what meat did the third little piggy eat?

8. What snack did Teressa Bellissimo invent at the Anchor Bar, in upstate New York, on October 3, 1964?

9. What kind of sausage would more authentically be called "mortadella" in its namesake city?

10. What delicacy comes from ▮▮▮▮ cattle?
Wagyu

Answers to the questions on this page can be found on page 171.

APRIL 16

• **1850** • MARIE TUSSAUD DIES IN LONDON, fifteen years after opening her popular wax museum on Baker Street.

WAX ON, WAX OFF

1. Who starred in more 3-D movies than any other actor, beginning with 1953's *House of Wax*?
2. What was first made by suspending paraffin in a solution of water and antifreeze?
3. In Greek myth, whose death in the Aegean Sea, near Samos, was caused by melting wax?
4. What would you wax with "Mr. Zog's Sex Wax—the Best for Your Stick"?
5. What Indonesian word names the art of successively waxing and dyeing fabric?

• **1936** • DAGWOOD BUMSTEAD WHIPS UP the first of his namesake sandwiches, using tongue, onion, mustard, sardines, beans, and horseradish.

A BREAD IN THE HAND
Are you the earl of sandwich trivia?

1. In what state are submarine sandwiches traditionally called "po' boys"?
2. Who christened Hawaii "the Sandwich Islands" in 1778?
3. What play begins with Algernon Moncrieff eating all of Lady Bracknell's cucumber sandwiches?
4. What's sometimes called a "licking stick" or a "tin sandwich"?
5. Who insisted on calling Iraqi WMDs "BLTs" when he interviewed Pat Buchanan in 2003?

• **1977** • DAVID "HUTCH" SOUL BECOMES David "One-Hit Wonder" Soul when "Don't Give Up on Us" tops the charts. After that, we gave up on him.

A SENSE OF WONDER
Name the only Top Forty hit that—believe it or not—these music legends ever enjoyed.

Easy	*Harder*	*Yeah, Good Luck*
1. Lou Reed	**1.** Jimi Hendrix	**1.** Iggy Pop
2. Devo	**2.** Randy Newman	**2.** Rush
3. Janis Joplin	**3.** The Grateful Dead	**3.** Bo Diddley
4. Carl Perkins	**4.** Frank Zappa	**4.** Nina Simone
5. Radiohead	**5.** T. Rex	**5.** Warren Zevon

Answers to the questions on this page can be found on page 172.

• **1852** • A young New Mexico bartender, arrested for wounding a rival in a duel, escapes from jail and flees the territory. Ironically, this fugitive will grow up to become Judge Roy Bean, "the Law west of the Pecos."

THE MUSICAL FRUIT

Five questions on the unbearable lightness of beans.

1. What kind of bean produces the Asian-style bean sprouts in the produce section of supermarkets?
2. How many times are traditional Mexican refried beans fried?
3. What Indianapolis grocer made his name by selling canned pork and beans to U.S. troops during the Civil War?
4. What kind of wine accompanies Hannibal Lecter's liver and fava bean dinner?
5. What optical component is named for the bean whose shape it resembles?

• **1952** • Harry Truman proclaims the first "National Day of Prayer." Hey, I don't see *you* praying! Get on it! What are you, some kind of Communist?

PRAY IT FORWARD

1. What German artist made this famous brush drawing?

2. What prayer is said ten times during each sequence of a Catholic rosary?
3. What former musician, now a famous TV personality, played bass on Madonna's "Like a Prayer"?

4. On what Jewish holiday is the "Kol Nidre" prayer recited?
5. According to the 1940s jingle, after what two men pitched did Boston Braves fans "pray for rain"?

• **1961** • Fifteen hundred Cuban exiles land in the Bahia de Cochinos on the southern coast of Cuba, beginning the ill-fated Bay of Pigs invasion. (The bay's "cochinos" are actually Caribbean triggerfish, not Latino pigs.)

PIG LATIN

Each answer in this quiz will be the Pig Latin translation of a common English word, clued in parentheses after each question.

1. What brainchild of Wisconsin senator Gaylord Nelson was first celebrated on April 22, 1970? (Shortage)
2. Who was married to her radio comedy partner Phil Harris from 1941 to 1995? (Erect genitalia)
3. What California region includes Alameda and Contra Costa counties? (Robby Benson's Disney character)
4. Wilhelm Roentgen won the first Nobel Prize in Physics for discovering what kind of radiation? (Reagan's dog)
5. What company is now known as Quixtar in the U.S. and Canada? (*Make It Big* band)

Answers to the questions on this page can be found on page 172.

• **1924** • THE VERY FIRST BOOK of crosswords appears, from a brand-new publishing house. *The Cross Word Puzzle Book,* sold with a pencil attached, becomes a huge hit, sparking a national fad and ensuring the future success of Richard Simon and Max Schuster.

TRUE GRID
Match these familiar words of "crosswordese"
to their definitions.

1. Adit	**A.** Ancient Greek portico
2. Anoa	**B.** Anglo-Saxon laborer
3. Ecru	**C.** Beige
4. Esker	**D.** Glacial ridge
5. Esne	**E.** Hawaiian goose
6. Etui	**F.** Layer of the eye
7. Nene	**G.** Mine shaft passage
8. Osier	**H.** Needle case
9. Stoa	**I.** Willow twig
10. Uvea	**J.** Wild Celebes ox

• **1948** • CLIFTON HILLEGASS, THE CREATOR OF the eponymous *CliffsNotes,* is born in Nebraska. His parents send out a bullet-pointed summary to friends who couldn't be bothered to read the whole birth announcement.

FOR THOSE WHO DIDN'T DO THE ASSIGNED READING
Can you name these children's classics from the title of their first chapter?

Easy
1. "Down the Rabbit-Hole"
2. "The Boy Who Lived"
3. "The Cyclone"
4. "Mowgli's Brothers"

Harder
1. "Up the Mountain to Alm-Uncle"
2. "Mrs. Whatsit"
3. "The Old Sea-dog at the Admiral Benbow"
4. "Mrs. Rachel Lynde Is Surprised"

Yeah, Good Luck
1. "Into the Primitive"
2. "The Shifting Reef"
3. "In the Drain"
4. "The River Bank"

• **1980** • CANAAN BANANA BECOMES the first president of the new nation of Zimbabwe—largely a ceremonial office, since Prime Minister Robert Mugabe holds the real power.

MASS A-PEEL
Name these other famous people with fruity names.

1. Whose second album is usually just called *When the Pawn . . . ,* since the full title is ninety words long?
2. What famous philanthropist was the only Treasury secretary ever to serve under three presidents?

3. What *Desperate Housewives* creator broke into TV as a personal assistant to actress Dixie Carter?
4. What basketball player sang a cover of "Sweet Georgia Brown," appropriately enough, on his 1998 album *Welcome to My World?*

5. In 1641, who married Mary Stuart, the daughter of England's King ~~Charles I~~ James II ?

Answers to the questions on this page can be found on page 172.

• **1948** • ABC, THE TELEVISION NETWORK, goes on the air. The very first program is *On the Corner,* a variety show featuring second-rate nightclub acts and hosted by radio wit Henry Morgan.

EASY AS ABC
Each letter of the alphabet will be used once below.

1. James Bond works for M, but what single initial is used for the real-life director of Britain's MI6?

2. In a departing prank, what letter did Clinton staffers remove from computer keyboards when they vacated their White House offices in 2001?

3. For what movie did director Fritz Lang himself dub the whistling for star Peter Lorre?

4. In photography, what kind of "number" is used to measure lens speed?

5. What's the only letter that doesn't appear in the periodic table of elements?

6. What's the most common blood type in the U.S. today?

7. On *Twin Peaks,* what letter was found under Laura Palmer's fingernail?

8. In what key is Johann Pachelbel's famous *Canon?*

9. Thanks to *Sesame Street,* which letter is *E.T.: The Extra-Terrestrial*'s first word of English?

10. A deficiency of which vitamin can lead to night blindness?

11. What's the only consonant sound that can end a word in Japanese?

12. Which Washington, D.C., street is often used as shorthand for the lobbying industry?

13. What spectral class does our sun belong to?

14. What code name does Linda Fiorentino receive at the end of *Men in Black?*

15. What letter of the alphabet do IATA airport codes for Canada begin with?

16. On *The Today Show* in August 2005, what did Sean Combs say "was getting between me and my fans"?

17. When actress Peg Entwistle committed suicide at the Hollywood sign in 1932, which letter did she jump from?

18. Archie Andrews wears the letter *R* on his sweater, for Riverdale. What letter traditionally appeared on Jughead's turtlenecks?

19. What mysterious title character is Herbert Stencil hunting for in Thomas Pynchon's first novel?

20. What letter begins the three most kid-friendly video game ratings?

21. What seminal L.A. punk band was discovered by Ray Manzarek of the Doors?

22. What was the first letter ever turned by Vanna White on *Wheel of Fortune?*

23. What's the first letter of the alphabet that's skipped in each year's tropical storm naming?

24. What is the Burmese word for "Mr."?

25. What did PAX TV change its name to on July 1, 2005?

26. What's the only letter to also name a Best Picture Oscar–nominated film?

Answers to the questions on this page can be found on page 173.

• **1862** • SCIENTISTS LOUIS PASTEUR and Claude Bernard first test heating liquids to kill bacteria and prevent fermentation. If Louis hadn't been on such an ego trip, we might be drinking "bernardized" milk today.

DEAR DAIRY

1. The most traditional Greek feta cheese is made from what animal's milk?
2. What thin cotton fabric used in summer suits takes its name from Persian words for "milk and sugar"?
3. What 1971 film was partially set in the Korova Milk Bar?
4. What is the nearest spiral galaxy to our own Milky Way?
5. What was the answer to the trivia question in the very first "Got Milk?" ad, in 1993?
6. What 1964 Broadway hit centered on a milkman and his five daughters?
7. Who invented condensed milk in 1856?
8. What classic novel ends with Rose of Sharon breast-feeding a starving hobo?
9. Who ended his Carnegie Hall concert by loading the audience into thirty-five buses and taking them out for milk and cookies?
10. You've seen 1% and 2%, but—to the nearest quarter of a percent—what percentage butterfat is "whole" milk?

• **1999** • SPANISH-BORN VENTRILOQUIST Señor Wences dies in New York City at the age of 103. Do you think anyone did the "S'all right!" gag with the casket? Because that would have been ~~awesome~~ *totally* disrespectful.

READ NY LIKS!
Match these ventriloquists to their dummies.

1. Edgar Bergen
2. Wayland Flowers
3. Jimmy Nelson
4. Willie Tyler
5. Paul Winchell

A. Farfel
B. Lester
C. Jerry Mahoney
D. Madame
E. Mortimer Snerd

• **2004** • PRINCE'S COMEBACK ALBUM *Musicology* drops. It will soon go double platinum, partially thanks to Prince's clever notion to "sell" every concert attendee a copy of the album.

YOU CAN HAVE IT -OLOGY

1. If semiology is the study of signs, what is sinology the study of?
2. What organization grew out of the Hubbard Dianetic Research Foundation?

3. What pseudoscience is being illustrated in the following drawing?

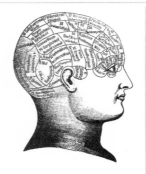

4. What branch of philosophy deals with the end of the world?
5. What of yours would a graphologist analyze?

Answers to the questions on this page can be found on page 173.

APRIL 21

• **1618** • A SPANISH JESUIT MISSIONARY named Pedro Paéz becomes, as far as we know, the first European to discover the source of the Blue Nile, above Ethiopia's Lake Tana.

NOT JUST A RIVER IN EGYPT
Answer these questions about serious cases of denial.

1. Who died of AIDS in 1987, insisting to the end that he wasn't gay and his obvious weight loss was the result of a "watermelon diet"?
2. What were the famous last words of General John Sedgwick, the highest-ranking Union officer

killed in the Civil War?
3. What was the only government ever to recognize the "nations" of Bophuthatswana, Transkei, and Venda?
4. What unorthodox scientific belief was championed by the Universal Zetetic Society?

5. Who died still believing that his wife, Lynn Fontane, was five years his junior, despite many news reports that she was really a full decade older?

• **1959** • AUSTRALIA'S ALFRED DEAN reels in a 2,600-pound whale shark, the largest fish ever caught.

ANGLER OF REPOSE

1. Who did fisherman Donato Dalrymple rescue from the water on Thanksgiving Day, 1999?
2. What bestseller tells the story of the fishing boat *Andrea Gail*?
3. To what office is Kiril Lakota elected in *The Shoes of the Fisherman*?
4. Who charms the crabs at Fisherman's Wharf right out of their

shells?
5. What catch do Ennis and Jack pretend to be after during their "fishing trips" in *Brokeback Mountain*?
6. What are trammels and seines?
7. What TV show's theme song was called "The Fishin' Hole"?
8. What were the last names of fishermen David and Ezra, who

opened their first sporting goods store in New York?
9. *A River Runs Through It* concerns fly-fishing in what U.S. state?
10. What kind of animal attacked Jimmy Carter during an April 1979 fishing trip?

• **1976** • THE U.S. GOVERNMENT BEGINS administering swine flu shots, in anticipation of a possible pandemic. The vaccination program will end by December, following reports that the vaccine is killing more patients than the flu would have.

TWIST AND SNOUT

1. What's the name of Porky Pig's girlfriend?
2. What element must be burned out of pig iron to make steel?
3. What northernmost state capi-

tal on the Mississippi River was founded under the name of Pig's Eye Landing?
4. What two-word phrase is the first writing to appear in *Char-*

lotte's Web?
5. What part of a pig is eaten as "chitterlings"?

Answers to the questions on this page can be found on page 173.

APRIL 22

• **1878** • CONGRESS'S 1876 TURF PROTECTION ACT, keeping kids off the Capitol lawn, leaves Washington's annual Easter egg roll homeless, so Rutherford B. Hayes offers to host it at the White House. An annual tradition is born.

A MAD SCRAMBLE
How many of these egg questions can you answer egg-zactly?

1. What fictional island is constantly at war with Blefuscu over the correct way to eat a boiled egg?
2. What comedian played the son of Mork and Mindy, hatched during the show's final season?
3. Besides the platypus (and Mork), what's the only egg-laying mammal?
4. What kind of sauce is served on eggs Benedict?
5. What was the home country of famed jeweler Peter Carl Fabergé?
6. What was John Woo's last Hong Kong film, *God of Guns*, renamed for U.S. release?
7. If they are the eggmen, what am I?
8. What 1925 novel was originally titled *Trimalchio in West Egg*?
9. What open-faced Italian omelette is, despite its name, more often baked than fried?
10. What screen duo first appeared in the supporting cast of 1949's *The Egg and I*?
11. What 1960 classic originated when Bennett Cerf bet one of his authors that he couldn't write a book using only fifty words?
12. What 1990 dance craze gave the Digital Underground their biggest hit?
13. What Italian physician was the first to describe the way the ovaries connect to the uterus in humans?
14. What's the better-known word for "aubergine"?
15. What movie resulted when Woody Allen redubbed the Japanese film *Key of Keys* with a new plot about a top secret egg salad recipe?

• **1978** • STEVE MARTIN PERFORMS "King Tut" on *Saturday Night Live*. The song will propel his album *A Wild and Crazy Guy* to the number two spot on the *Billboard* album chart, the last comedy album to chart so high.

WILD AND CRAZY GUYS

1. What dog is the hero of Jack London's *The Call of the Wild*?
2. Gnarls Barkley's megahit "Crazy" is on what 2006 debut album, named for an NBC TV series?
3. What word do we derive from the Salish Indian word for "wild man"?
4. What did Ignatz Mouse enjoy throwing at Krazy Kat's head?
5. Who, per her dying wish, is buried next to Wild Bill Hickok?
6. What object falls onto a Kalahari Desert village at the beginning of the movie *The Gods Must Be Crazy*?
7. What's the name of the little boy who discovers *Where the Wild Things Are*?
8. What would perform a Crazy Ivan?
9. What major-league team has won two World Series as a wild card?
10. What movie's theme was remixed in 2005 into Crazy Frog's biggest hit?

Answers to the questions on this page can be found on page 174.

• **1374** • EDWARD III OF ENGLAND grants a favorite poet, Geoffrey Chaucer, "a gallon of wine daily for the rest of his life." A gallon a day?!

BOTTLED UP

1. What kind of wine takes its name from the Spanish town of Jerez, where it's made?
2. What's the French name for a restaurant wine steward?
3. UB40's first number one hit, "Red Red Wine," was a cover of whose song?
4. In what state is Sherwood Anderson's fictional town of Wines-burg?
5. What red wine does Paul Giamatti refuse to drink in the movie *Sideways*?
6. Who's the first person to plant a vineyard in the Bible?
7. What grape, used to make a popular California wine, is called Primitivo in Europe?
8. Susie Amy's character on *Foot-ballers' Wives*, who killed a man with a wine bottle, also shares her name with what wine?
9. Who is the Roman equivalent of Dionysus, the Greek god of wine?
10. Chablis is the northernmost district of what French wine region?

• **1982** • JULIO FRANCO MAKES his major-league debut for the Philadelphia Phillies. Twenty-five years later, he'll still be playing, making him the oldest position player in baseball history.

GOING LONG
This quiz on amazing longevity shouldn't take you long.

1. Who filibustered for a record twenty-four hours and eighteen minutes—with a urine pail standing at the ready—in the hope of preventing the Civil Rights Act of 1957?
2. What kind of animal was Harriet, who died at the Queensland Zoo in 2006 and was claimed to have belonged to Charles Darwin?
3. What album spent a record 741 weeks on *Billboard*'s Top 200 Albums chart?
4. According to the Bible, who died at the ripe old age of 930?
5. What is the subject of Claude Lanzmann's award-winning nine-hour film *Shoah*?
6. Having first aired on September 27, 1954, what's the longest-running show on American nighttime TV?
7. In office since 1959, who is the world's longest-serving political leader?
8. The Tibetan county of Zhongdian has officially renamed itself what, after the valley of long life from the novel *Lost Horizon*?
9. Though an eleven-year cease-fire held from 1972 to 1983, what African country has been embroiled in a civil war since 1955?
10. The seventy-four-minute maximum length of a CD was chosen, according to Philips Electronics, to accommodate what famous symphony?

Answers to the questions on this page can be found on page 174.

APRIL 24

• 387 • TWO FAMOUS CHURCH FATHERS meet for a quick dip: the night before Easter, Augustine of Hippo is baptized by Ambrose of Milan.

CHURCH FATHERS
Name the dads who begat these biblical folks.

Easy	Harder	Yeah, Good Luck
1. Solomon	1. Seth	1. Samson
2. Joseph	2. David	2. Moses
3. John the Baptist	3. James and John	3. Methuselah
4. Isaac	4. Jonathan	4. Peter and Andrew
5. Ham, Shem, and Japheth	5. Maher-shalal-hash-baz	5. Joshua

• 1903 • IN A MASONIC CEREMONY, Teddy Roosevelt lays the cornerstone for the north gate of Yellowstone National Park, today called Roosevelt Arch. A Masonic ceremony?! Wow, maybe *National Treasure* was right.

STATE OF THE ARCH

1. What come in three basic patterns: arches, loops, and whorls?
2. St. Louis's Gateway Arch is officially named for what U.S. president?
3. What company lost more than $300 million on the failed Arch Deluxe?
4. What state depicts Delicate Arch on its license plates?
5. What would a doctor call *pes planus*?

• 1915 • AT THE SECOND BATTLE OF YPRES, the Germans bombard the Canadian troops with poison gas. The Canadians bravely hold their positions, having discovered that they can make gas masks by peeing into their hankies! (The ammonia in the urine neutralizes the chlorine.) I hope each and every one of those brave men received the Purple Bladder.

PRECIOUS BODILY FLUIDS
In what part of the body would you find these secretions?

1. Chyme
2. Amniotic fluid
3. Sebum
4. Cowper's fluid
5. Aqueous humor

Answers to the questions on this page can be found on page 174.

APRIL 25

• **1792** • CLAUDE ROUGET DE LISLE composes a marching song for the Army of the Rhine. When soldiers from Marseille first introduce it to Paris during the French Revolution, it becomes known as "La Marseillaise."

GALLIC SYMBOLS

1. A magician, a figure skater, or a pickpocket—who would use the French drop, the double lift, and the DeManche change?
2. What spice is named for the capital of French Guiana?
3. Which Beatles song has a French horn solo?
4. What do most tourists call the Vieux Carré?
5. What pioneering fighter pilot of World War I is remembered today mostly by tennis fans at the French Open?
6. What do the British call a "French letter"?
7. What athlete was born in ~~Sandersville~~ *West Baden* ~~Springs~~, Indiana, in December 1956? (raised in French Lick)
8. Gene Hackman's *French Connection* cop is nicknamed for what cartoon character?
9. What Daniel French sculpture is seen by 3.4 million visitors every year?
10. Sarah Woodruff is the title character of what 1969 novel?

• **1940** • A MONUMENT IS ERECTED two miles northwest of Lebanon, Kansas, pinpointing the exact geographic center of the United States. The U.S. Coast and Geodetic Survey's math may be a little off, however, since its methodology involved—no lie—cutting a map of the United States out of cardboard and then balancing it on a pin.

WHAT'S THE MATTER WITH KANSAS?

1. What famous name is the only Kansas basketball coach to have a losing record during his tenure?
2. "Project Kansas" was the name for the top secret 1985 attempt to revamp what product?
3. What forms the only part of the Kansas border, a seventy-five-mile stretch, that's not drawn with a straight-edge?
4. What Kansas song does Keanu Reeves use to wow Socrates in *Bill & Ted's Excellent Adventure*?
5. Charles Dawes, Charles Curtis, or Charles Evans Hughes—what Kansan was the only Native American ever to serve as U.S. vice president?

• **1972** • ACTOR GEORGE SANDERS (Addison DeWitt in *All About Eve* and Mr. Freeze on *Batman*) kills himself in Spain. The suicide note begins, "Dear world, I am leaving because I am bored."

SUICIDE IS PAINLESS
What regular on each of these shows ended up taking his or her own life?

Easy
1. *Fantasy Island*
2. *The Adventures of Superman*
3. *Chico and the Man*
4. *Family Feud*

Harder
1. *St. Elsewhere*
2. *Suddenly Susan*
3. *The Today Show*
4. *Family Affair*

Yeah, Good Luck
1. *Saturday Night Live*
2. *The Farmer's Daughter*
3. *Make Room for Daddy*
4. *Gibbsville*

Answers to the questions on this page can be found on page 175.

APRIL 26

• **1819** • THE INDEPENDENT ORDER OF ODD FELLOWS is formed in Baltimore.

ODD FELLOWS

1. What eccentric artist based his famous mustache on that worn by painter Diego Velázquez?
2. With what team did Dennis Rodman win his first NBA title?
3. What inventor of the Difference Engine once baked himself in an oven for five minutes, "to see what would happen"?
4. What doctor, whose life was fictionalized in a 1998 film, founded the Gesundheit! Institute and named his oldest son "Atomic Zagnut"?
5. After his trial, Michael Jackson fled Neverland Ranch for what island nation?

• **1910** • TOMOYUKI TANAKA, the Toho film producer who gave the world Godzilla, is born in Japan.

DESTINATION TOKYO
Sure, Mothra's a moth. But what are these Japanese monsters?

1. Ebirah	**A.** Beetle
2. Gamera	**B.** Cuttlefish
3. Gezora	**C.** Praying mantis
4. Gigan	**D.** Pterosaur
5. Kamacuras	**E.** Robot
6. King Ghidorah	**F.** Sea serpent
7. Kumonga	**G.** Shrimp
8. Manda	**H.** Spider
9. Megalon	**I.** Three-headed dragon
10. Rodan	**J.** Turtle

• **2000** • NATIONAL SECRETARIES DAY, observed since the Commerce Department created it in 1952, is officially renamed "Administrative Professionals' Day" for the new millennium. Washington's powerful greeting card and flower lobbies chortle with glee.

PERFORMANCE REVIEW
Yeah, we're gonna need you to go ahead and have this workplace trivia done by the end of the day . . .

1. What did Ray Tomlinson send in Cambridge, Massachusetts, in late 1971?
2. What is distinctive about the hair of *Dilbert*'s unnamed boss?
3. May Day, as an international workers' celebration, dates back to what 1886 event?
4. "Gem" is the trade name for the most common, three-loop design of what?
5. Complete this analogy: BBC : Slough :: NBC : _____.
6. What kind of animal dangles from a tree branch in the famous 1970s motivational poster captioned "Hang in there, baby!"?
7. Tellurium, selenium, or germanium—what chemical element provides the photoconductive surface covering the drum in most photocopiers?
8. What item didn't exist in the Swingline catalog until its appearance in the 1999 film *Office Space* created a popular demand for it?
9. Liquid Paper was invented by Bette Graham, the mother of which of the Monkees?
10. What federal agency, which targets workplace discrimination, was chaired by Clarence Thomas for most of the 1980s?

Answers to the questions on this page can be found on page 175.

• **1667** • JOHN MILTON SELLS the copyright for his upcoming epic *Paradise Lost*, essentially a retelling of the Book of Genesis from the much more interesting point of view of Lucifer. Milton's book deal is the oldest author's contract known to exist.

SECOND PERSON SINGULAR

What literary works have been retold from a different character's viewpoint as . . .

Easy	Harder	Yeah, Good Luck
1. *Ahab's Wife*	**1.** *Lo's Diary*	**1.** *March*
2. *Rosencrantz and Guildenstern Are Dead*	**2.** *The Wind Done Gone*	**2.** *Wide Sargasso Sea*
3. *Grendel*	**3.** *Wicked*	**3.** *An Assembly Such as This*
4. *Finn*	**4.** *The Penelopiad*	**4.** *Mary Reilly*

• **1897** • GRANT'S TOMB IS DEDICATED. Who's buried in it? Well, nobody. Have you seen it? It's *above ground.* Duh.

NOTES FROM THE UNDERGROUND

Name these famous corpses from their excerpted epitaphs.

1. LOVE WILL TEAR US APART
2. EVERY HOUSEWIFE'S FRIEND. -30-
3. THE CELEBRATED NAVIGATOR WHO FIRST TRANSPLANTED THE BREAD-FRUIT TREE FROM OTAHETTE TO THE WEST INDIES
4. HERE LIES ONE WHOSE NAME WAS WRIT IN WATER
5. THAT'S ALL FOLKS
6. HIS SPIRIT IS IN VERMONT NOW
7. THE LAST STOOGE
8. FAITHFUL TO THE CAUSE OF PROHIBITION—SHE HATH DONE WHAT SHE COULD
9. EVERYBODY LOVES SOMEBODY SOMETIME
10. QUOTH THE RAVEN, "NEVER-MORE"

• **1964** • JOHN LENNON'S POETRY COLLECTION *In His Own Write* is released in the United States. It is the first solo Beatles project of any kind.

EVERY DAY I WRITE THE BOOK

What literary work inspired each of these pop songs?

Easy	Harder	Yeah, Good Luck
1. "White Rabbit," Jefferson Airplane	**1.** "Patrick Bateman," the Manic Street Preachers	**1.** "Love and Destroy," Franz Ferdinand
2. "Big Brother," David Bowie	**2.** "Killing an Arab," the Cure	**2.** "Pull Me Under," Dream Theater
3. "The Ghost of Tom Joad," Bruce Springsteen	**3.** "Don't Stand So Close to Me," the Police	**3.** "Chapter 24," Pink Floyd
4. "Who Wrote Holden Caulfield," Green Day	**4.** "Scentless Apprentice," Nirvana	**4.** "Moon Over Bourbon Street," Sting
5. "The Battle of Evermore," Led Zeppelin	**5.** "Holland 1945," Neutral Milk Hotel	**5.** "Tomorrow Never Knows," the Beatles

Answers to the questions on this page can be found on page 175.

APRIL 28

• **1926** • A GIANT SEQUOIA named "General Grant," the world's second largest organism, is officially proclaimed "The Nation's Christmas Tree" by President Calvin Coolidge.

VOCAL QUINTETS

Each answer will, just like "sequoia" and "vocal quintet," have only five vowels: a, e, i, o, and u, once apiece.

1. What song was the Beach Boys' first *Billboard* number one hit?

2. What Lamborghini model, whose name is Spanish for "bat," does Bruce Wayne very appropriately drive in *Batman Begins*?

3. Harry Truman was the first U.S. president of what religious persuasion?

4. According to the poem, how many spectators saw Mighty Casey strike out?

5. What occupation is shared by TV protagonists Sean McNamara and Christian Troy?

6. What noisy word comes from the capital of Hell in Milton's *Paradise Lost*?

7. Whose production company is Red Om Films, named for her husband?

8. What does Ringo Starr play rather than drums on the Beatles' first single, "Love Me Do"?

9. David Schmidt won the 2001 Ig Nobel Prize in Physics for discovering the horizontal vortex that makes what household item blow inward?

10. What word for a wimp comes from the title character of Harold Webster's comic strip *The Timid Soul*?

11. Until *Ben-Hur* broke its record, what was the bestselling novel of the nineteenth century?

12. What ingredient appears alongside potatoes in the Indian dish aloo gobi?

13. Who revealed he was HIV-positive in his 1995 autobiography *Breaking the Surface*?

14. World champion sky surfer Rob Harris was killed in 1995 while filming a TV commercial for what product?

15. Who moved in 1994 to Wyoming, the setting of her most famous short story?

16. The father of Austin Powers's nemesis, Dr. Evil, would drunkenly claim to have invented what?

17. What musical did *Cats* surpass as the longest running in Broadway history?

18. What African country is the only member of the Commonwealth of Nations that was never part of the British Empire?

19. What cabinet department has recently been led by the appropriately named Rod Paige and Margaret Spellings?

20. What city is home to the University of Haiti?

• **1950** • RAMA IX, KING OF THAILAND, marries his wife, Queen Sirikit, at Bangkok's Pathumwan Palace. He fell for his fifteen-year-old cousin (yikes!) when both were studying in Europe.

WITH THIS KING I THEE WED

Name the royal spouses who married . . .

Easy
1. Grace Kelly
2. Anne Boleyn
3. Sarah Ferguson
4. Prince Albert (of piercing fame)
5. Marie Antoinette

Harder
1. Peter III of Russia
2. Amenhotep IV
3. Wallis Simpson
4. Rita Hayworth
5. William III of England

Yeah, Good Luck
1. Lisa Halaby
2. Princess Sophia of Greece
3. Timothy Laurence
4. Anne of Austria
5. Farah Diba

Answers to the questions on this page can be found on page 176.

• **1852** • PETER MARK ROGET, the founder of the University of Manchester School of Medicine and inventor of the log-log slide rule, performs his most lasting accomplishment: publishing a book of 15,000 synonyms he calls a "thesaurus."

FOR FUTURE REFERENCE

1. What reference classic is still named for the defunct New York newspaper that first published it in 1868?
2. What was the last name of George and Charles, two brothers who revised Noah Webster's dictionary after his 1843 death?
3. What kind of information resource takes its name from a Hawaiian word for "quick"?
4. What Cambridge bookstore manager wrote "What is familiar to one class of readers may be quite new to another" in the introduction to his famous work?
5. When subjects of *Who's Who* pass away, what companion volume do they move to?

• **1856** • THE USS *SUPPLY* ARRIVES at Indianola, Texas, with a cargo of thirty-four Egyptian camels for the U.S. Camel Corps, a pet project of Secretary of War Jefferson Davis. But the smelly, bad-tempered camels aren't popular with the men, and the corps is soon disbanded, leaving the camels to wander the American Southwest.

CAMELCASE

Give these "CamelCase" words—that is, words with an intermediate capital letter, like "MasterCard" or "PlayStation."

1. What did Teleworld, Inc., rename itself in 1999, after its flagship product?
2. Who was sued in 1999 by Rosa Parks after they used her name to title a hit song?
3. What was originally sold in 1965 under the name "Chemgrass"?
4. Hitwise announced in 2006 that, for the first time, what site had passed Yahoo! to become America's most popular website?
5. What show debuted on September 7, 1979, with George Grande anchoring?

• **1939** • "MARYLAND, MY MARYLAND" is officially adopted as Maryland's state song. This despite the fact that the 1861 ditty is a plea for Marylanders to join the Confederacy and begins by dissing Abraham Lincoln: "The despot's heel is on thy shore!"

ALL GONE TO LOOK FOR AMERICA

Can you pick out the musical acts that sang these stately songs?

1. Arrested Development
2. The Beach Boys
3. The Bee Gees
4. Crosby, Stills, Nash & Young
5. Phantom Planet
6. Chris Rea
7. Sonic Youth
8. Bruce Springsteen
9. U2
10. Neil Young

A. "Alabama"
B. "California"
C. "Hawaii"
D. "Massachusetts"
E. "Nebraska"
F. "New Hampshire"
G. "New York"
H. "Ohio"
I. "Tennessee"
J. "Texas"

Answers to the questions on this page can be found on page 176.

APRIL 30

• **1494** • Christopher Columbus sails into a Caribbean bay he calls "Puerto Grande." Today, it's called Guantánamo Bay, aka "Human Rights Violation Grande."

ACE OF BAYS

1. James Bay forms the southern end of what larger bay?

2. What bay is Otis Redding serenading in "(Sittin' on) the Dock of the Bay"?

3. Who was the first coach of the Green Bay Packers?

4. Who lived in Seattle's fictional Elliott Bay Towers?

5. What Pacific inlet was called "Stingray Bay" until Captain Cook renamed it for "the great quantity of plants" his scientists had discovered?

6. What island in Manila Bay was the site of a famous 1942 siege?

7. Who solves crimes in Bayport, located on Barmet Bay?

8. In what bay would you find the Andaman and Nicobar islands?

9. What ship's destination is the sunny beach of Peppermint Bay?

10. What bay is actually the United States's largest tidal estuary?

• **1894** • "Coxey's Army" of unemployed workers arrives in Washington, D.C., to protest the joblessness caused by the Panic of 1893 . . . and its leaders are immediately arrested, for ignoring the "Keep Off the Grass" signs on the U.S. Capitol lawn.

OUT OF POSITION
Commemorate Coxey's Army with this quiz on unemployment.

1. What city, Pennsylvania's third largest, was the subject of a 1982 Billy Joel song about layoffs?

2. What Japanese word for "wave person" refers to a masterless samurai?

3. Whose first book was *Down* and *Out in Paris and London*, about his year among the poverty-stricken underclass of those cities?

4. What 1993 movie's title character is actually out-of-work voice actor Daniel Hillard?

5. What term derived from Seattle's down-at-the-heels Yesler Avenue, used by the lumber industry to slide felled trees toward Puget Sound?

• **1907** • British mathematician Charles Howard Hinton dies in the middle of an after-dinner toast. Hinton's accomplishments include inventing the first baseball pitching machine and coining the word "tesseract" to refer to a four-dimensional hypercube.

SMALL PACKAGES
Fiction is full of apparent tesseracts—that is, spaces that must extend into the fourth dimension, since they seem to be bigger on the inside than they are on the outside.

1. What does Doctor Who's vast spacecraft, the TARDIS, look like from the outside?

2. Whose doghouse apparently contains a basement, a pool table, an Andrew Wyeth painting, and a Jacuzzi?

3. What object on the *Sesame Street* set somehow contains a swimming pool and an elephant named Fluffy?

4. What event does Harry Potter attend while staying in a three-room apartment that looks, from the outside, like a tiny camping tent?

5. Who pulls a potted plant and hat stand out of her bottomless carpetbag?

Answers to the questions on this page can be found on page 176.

April Answers

APRIL 1	APRIL 2	APRIL 3

BAR SCENE
1. F
2. A
3. C
4. J
5. I
6. H
7. E
8. D
9. G
10. B

A LEAD PIPE CINCH
1. Plumbing (*plumbum* is lead)
2. "Eleanor Rigby"
3. The Allen Manufacturing Company (inventors of the Allen wrench)
4. Hume Cronyn
5. An earthquake
6. The circumcision at a bris

GROWING PAINS
1. The barrel of a gun
2. Thomas Malthus
3. The pituitary
4. Columbines
5. *Peter Pan*

FOUNTAIN OF YOUTH
1. Michael Dell
2. *thirtysomething*
3. Joeys
4. Stephen Colbert
5. Freddy Adu
6. Physics
7. The Orchestra
8. Maria Montessori
9. Yahoo! (by Yahoo Serious)
10. Jason Lee

"BEAT" GENERATION
1. Minnesota
2. Timbaland
3. Quidditch
4. Florida
5. Meringue
6. Stu Sutcliffe
7. Cabdriver
8. Checkers
9. A heartbeat
10. Eddie Van Halen

COMMA SUTRA
1. Roger Maris's
2. Copenhagen
3. *Oliver!*
4. Semicolons
5. @
6. The tilde
7. ? and the Mysterians' ("96 Tears")
8. !
9. A panda
10. The ampersand, & (*et* means "and" in French)

STRIP SEARCH
1. *Treasure Island*
2. Tropicana
3. Excalibur
4. Sahara
5. "New York, New York" (because of its opening line: "Start spreading the news")
6. Luxor
7. Flamingo
8. *Casino Royale*
9. Mirage
10. Stratosphere

April Answers

APRIL 4

PLAN BEE
1. Sacramento
2. Bee purple
3. Jerry Seinfield (promoting *Bee Movie*)
4. Drones
5. Luge
6. Frances Bavier
7. Nikolai Rimsky-Korsakov's
8. Jeff Bagwell
9. *To Have and Have Not*
10. Robin Gibb

MAPS AND LEGENDS
1. H, b
2. J, e
3. I, f
4. G, g
5. B, d
6. A, i
7. E, c
8. D, h
9. C, a
10. F, j

APRIL 5

GOD'S BODY
1. Diego Maradona
2. "Mmmm Mmmm Mmmm Mmmm"
3. His right index finger
4. Mexico
5. "High Flight"

PLAYING HOOKY
1. Velcro (***vel**ours* and ***cro**chet*)
2. Vanilla Ice
3. A pair of jacks
4. In a bowling ball return
5. Sparky Anderson
6. Martin Van Buren
7. New Order
8. 1-800-ABC-DEFG
9. Apu's
10. Christopher Wren

MR. NATURAL(IZED)
1. The Marquis de Lafayette
2. Winston Churchill
3. Mother Teresa
4. Casimir Pulaski
5. William and Hannah Penn
6. Raoul Wallenberg

APRIL 6

POLE POSITION
1. Carlton Fisk
2. A magnet
3. Denmark (it's Greenland)
4. Bamboo
5. Festivus (*Seinfeld*)
6. A barber pole
7. Tom Hanks and Peter Scolari (*Bosom Buddies*)
8. Roald Amundsen
9. Flagpoles (for school prayer)
10. Rick Mears

HEY HEY, MY MY
Easy
1. "Sugar, Sugar"
2. "Mony Mony"
3. "Rush Rush"
4. "Monday, Monday"
5. "Baby Baby"
Harder
1. "Doctor! Doctor!"
2. "Cherry, Cherry"
3. "Maria Maria"
4. "Radio Radio"
5. "Rebel Rebel"
Yeah, Good Luck
1. "Liar Liar"
2. "Promises, Promises"
3. "Green, Green"
4. "Mary, Mary"
5. "Laugh Laugh"

FERRY TALES
1. Charon
2. West Virginia
3. Orange
4. Roxy Music
5. River Phoenix

APRIL 7

MATCH POINT
1. *Hello, Dolly!*
2. Mr. T and Hulk Hogan
3. Richard Dawson
4. The Presidents Cup
5. Steve Forbes

I SHOT THE SHERIFF
Easy
1. Martin Luther King, Jr.
2. William McKinley
3. Jean-Paul Marat
4. Archduke Ferdinand
Harder
1. Harvey Milk and George Moscone
2. Leon Trotsky
3. Mahatma Gandhi
4. Huey Long
Yeah, Good Luck
1. Yitzhak Rabin
2. Malcolm X
3. Anton Cermak
4. Anwar Sadat

CLUB SCENE
Easy
1. Philadelphia Phillies
2. Pittsburgh Pirates
3. Kansas City Royals
Harder
1. Seattle Mariners
2. New York Yankees
3. Milwaukee Brewers
Yeah, Good Luck
1. Baltimore Orioles
2. New York Mets
3. Atlanta Braves (a tomahawk)

APRIL 8

A CITY ON A HILL
1. Portobello Road
2. Capitol Hill
3. Manhattan
4. Telegraph Hill
5. Rome

PUTTING THE "MORTAL" BACK IN "IMMORTAL"
1. Osiris
2. Ragnarok
3. Skull
4. Adonis ("Adonais")
5. George Burns

TWIN PEEKS
1. Ray Romano
2. Mick Jagger and Keith Richards
3. Kirby Puckett
4. Fraternal twins
5. A wolf
6. *The Adventures of Tintin*
7. *The Guinness Book of World Records*
8. Kuala Lumpur
9. Heather Graham
10. Poland

APRIL 9

ORAL FIXATION
Easy
1. China
2. Brazil
3. Russia
4. Egypt
5. Vietnam
Harder
1. Mexico
2. Australia
3. Bangladesh
4. The United States
5. The Netherlands
Yeah, Good Luck
1. Ukraine
2. Myanmar
3. Venezuela
4. Mozambique
5. Ghana

SEE MONKEYS
1. B
2. C
3. F
4. A
5. E
6. D

THE JOY OF SOCKS
1. Buddy
2. Shirley Temple
3. Lamb Chop's
4. Curt Schilling
5. *Abbey Road*
6. Richard Nixon
7. *Dances with Wolves*'s
8. Blue and red
9. Buck Weaver
10. Argyle

April Answers

APRIL 10

IN A MANNER OF SHRIEKING
1. *Scary Movie*
2. Howard Dean's
3. Edvard Munch
4. Eagles
5. "I Put a Spell on You"

MY BIG FAT GREEK ALPHABET
1. Charlton Heston
2. *Revenge of the Nerds*
3. A tiger
4. The Black Sea
5. *Space: 1999*

THEY WERE ALL YELLOW
1. The Blue Meanies
2. China's
3. To put up a parking lot
4. The Wiggles
5. Steamboat Geyser
6. Two
7. Sulfur
8. Joseph Pulitzer's
9. Sweden
10. Pikachu

APRIL 11

SAFETY DANCE
1. Red or green
2. Air bags
3. Gary Busey
4. Mae West
5. Fred Dryer (*Hunter*)

JERSEY CITY
1. E, 2
2. B, 3
3. C, 4
4. D, 9
5. I, 10
6. G, 13
7. A, 17
8. F, 32
9. H, 34
10. J, 44

FOREVER AND A DAY
1. Val Kilmer
2. *Duke Nukem*
3. Dominic Monaghan
4. De Beers
5. Judy Blume's

APRIL 12

SHORT ATTENTION SPAN THEATER
1. Elliot Richardson (Commerce; Attorney General; Defense; and Health, Education, and Welfare)
2. *A Streetcar Named Desire*
3. Larry Brown
4. *Spy Kids*
5. Dick Clark (*American Bandstand, The $25,000 Pyramid, TV's Bloopers & Practical Jokes*)

I'D LIKE TO THANK THE ACADEMY
1. E
2. A
3. I
4. L
5. G
6. K
7. O
8. D
9. F
10. M
11. B
12. N
13. C
14. H
15. J

APRIL 13

"CELL"ING OUT
1. Oscar Wilde's
2. An ostrich egg yolk
3. The White Stripes (*White Blood Cells*)
4. "Tainted Love"
5. Nokia

THAI ME UP, THAI ME DOWN
1. Phuket
2. Papaya
3. *The King and I* and *Chess*
4. The Siamese fighting fish
5. Kickboxing

CAST AWAY
Easy
1. Jon Lovitz
2. Don Knotts
3. Charlie Sheen
4. Sandy Duncan
5. Woody Harrelson
Harder
1. Diane Ladd
2. Cloris Leachman
3. William Demarest
4. Paul Sorvino
5. Joshua Malina
Yeah, Good Luck
1. Gabriel Melgar
2. Paul Provenza
3. Tom Reilly
4. Nicole de Boer
5. Nancy Travis

APRIL 14

CRIME SCENES
Easy
1. Sarajevo
2. Deadwood
3. Memphis
4. New Delhi
5. Las Vegas
Harder
1. Tombstone
2. St. Petersburg
3. Buffalo
4. Boulder, Colorado
5. Santo Domingo
Yeah, Good Luck
1. Scottsdale, Arizona
2. Dublin
3. Jackson, Mississippi
4. Los Angeles (the "Black Dahlia")
5. Miami

WHAT LIES BENEATH
1. Toto
2. An apple
3. Odysseus
4. The Fat Lady
5. Pumpkin

GENE-HACK MEN
1. Twenty-three
2. The fruit fly
3. Douglas (Noel) Adams
4. Gregor Mendel
5. Thymine

APRIL 15

TAXING TRIVIA
1. Salt
2. Harold Wilson and Edward Heath
3. Matthew
4. Alcatraz
5. They were signed to I.R.S. records
6. Bush's "Read my lips: no new taxes"
7. The Mexican-American War
8. Willie Nelson's
9. A barrel
10. 401(k)

MEAT ON PARADE
1. Corned beef
2. A Big Mac
3. Chuck steak
4. Bacon
5. Voicing the "Beef: it's what's for dinner" ads
6. "Spiced"
7. Roast beef
8. Buffalo wings
9. Bologna
10. Kobe beef

April Answers

APRIL 16

WAX ON, WAX OFF
1. Vincent Price
2. The lava lamp
3. Icarus's
4. A surfboard
5. Batik

A BREAD IN THE HAND
1. Louisiana
2. Captain Cook
3. *The Importance of Being Earnest*
4. A harmonica
5. Ali G (Sacha Baron Cohen)

A SENSE OF WONDER
Easy
1. "Walk on the Wild Side"
2. "Whip It"
3. "Me and Bobby McGee"
4. "Blue Suede Shoes"
5. "Creep"
Harder
1. "All Along the Watchtower"
2. "Short People"
3. "Touch of Grey"
4. "Valley Girl"
5. "Bang a Gong (Get It On)"
Yeah, Good Luck
1. "Candy"
2. "New World Man"
3. "Say Man"
4. "I Loves You Porgy"
5. "Werewolves of London"

APRIL 17

THE MUSICAL FRUIT
1. Mung beans
2. Just once
3. Gilbert Van Camp
4. Chianti
5. Lens (for lentils)

PRAY IT FORWARD
1. Albrecht Dürer
2. Hail Mary
3. Randy Jackson
4. Yom Kippur
5. (Warren) Spahn and (Johnny) Sain

PIG LATIN
1. Earth Day (dearth)
2. Alice Faye (phallus)
3. East Bay (Beast)
4. X-ray (Rex)
5. Amway (Wham!)

APRIL 18

TRUE GRID
1. G
2. J
3. C
4. D
5. B
6. H
7. E
8. I
9. A
10. F

FOR THOSE WHO DIDN'T DO THE ASSIGNED READING
Easy
1. *Alice in Wonderland*
2. *Harry Potter and the Sorcerer's Stone*
3. *The Wonderful Wizard of Oz*
4. *The Jungle Book*
Harder
1. *Heidi*
2. *A Wrinkle in Time*
3. *Treasure Island*
4. *Anne of Green Gables*
Yeah, Good Luck
1. *The Call of the Wild*
2. *20,000 Leagues Under the Sea*
3. *Stuart Little*
4. *The Wind in the Willows*

MASS A-PEEL
1. Fiona Apple's
2. Andrew Mellon
3. Marc Cherry
4. Meadowlark Lemon
5. William of Orange

APRIL 19

EASY AS ABC
1. C
2. W
3. *M*
4. F
5. J
6. O
7. R
8. D
9. B
10. A
11. N
12. K
13. G
14. L
15. Y
16. P (in "P. Diddy")
17. H
18. S
19. V
20. E
21. X
22. T
23. Q
24. U
25. i
26. Z
(This spells out a passable twenty-six-letter "pangram" sentence: "Cwm fjord bank glyphs vext quiz.")

APRIL 20

DEAR DAIRY
1. Sheep's milk
2. Seersucker
3. *A Clockwork Orange*
4. The Andromeda Galaxy
5. Aaron Burr
6. *Fiddler on the Roof*
7. Gail Borden, Jr.
8. *The Grapes of Wrath*
9. Andy Kaufman
10. 3¼%

READ NY LIKS!
1. E
2. D
3. A
4. B
5. C

YOU CAN HAVE IT -OLOGY
1. China
2. The Church of Scientology
3. Phrenology
4. Eschatology
5. Your handwriting

APRIL 21

NOT JUST A RIVER IN EGYPT
1. Liberace
2. "They couldn't hit an elephant at this distance."
3. South Africa
4. A flat earth
5. Alfred Lunt

ANGLER OF REPOSE
1. Elián González
2. *The Perfect Storm*
3. Pope
4. "Phyllis . . . it sure isn't you!" (from the theme song to TV's *Phyllis*)
5. Trout
6. Fishing nets
7. *The Andy Griffith Show*
8. Abercrombie and Fitch
9. Montana
10. A rabbit

TWIST AND SNOUT
1. Petunia
2. Carbon
3. St. Paul, Minnesota
4. "Some pig"
5. The intestines

April Answers

APRIL 22

A MAD SCRAMBLE
1. Lilliput
2. Jonathan Winters
3. The echidna
4. Hollandaise sauce
5. Russia
6. *Hard-Boiled*
7. "I am the walrus"
8. *The Great Gatsby*
9. Frittata
10. Ma and Pa Kettle
11. *Green Eggs and Ham*
12. "The Humpty Hump"
13. Gabriele Falloppio (or Fallopius)
14. Eggplant
15. *What's Up, Tiger Lily?*

WILD AND CRAZY GUYS
1. Buck
2. *St. Elsewhere*
3. Sasquatch
4. A brick
5. Calamity Jane
6. A Coke bottle
7. Max
8. A (Russian) submarine
9. The Florida Marlins
10. *Beverly Hills Cop*

APRIL 23

BOTTLED UP
1. Sherry
2. A sommelier
3. Neil Diamond's
4. Ohio
5. Merlot
6. Noah
7. Zinfandel
8. Chardonnay
9. Bacchus
10. Burgundy

GOING LONG
1. Strom Thurmond
2. A (Galápagos giant) tortoise
3. *Dark Side of the Moon*
4. Adam
5. The Holocaust
6. *The Tonight Show*
7. Fidel Castro
8. Shangri-La
9. Sudan
10. Beethoven's Ninth

APRIL 24

CHURCH FATHERS
Easy
1. David
2. Jacob
3. Zechariah
4. Abraham
5. Noah
Harder
1. Adam
2. Jesse
3. Zebedee
4. Saul
5. Isaiah
Yeah, Good Luck
1. Manoah
2. Amram
3. Enoch
4. Jonah
5. Nun

STATE OF THE ARCH
1. Fingerprints
2. Thomas Jefferson
3. McDonald's
4. Utah
5. Fallen arches (or flat feet)

PRECIOUS BODILY FLUIDS
1. The stomach
2. The uterus
3. The skin
4. The penis (or urethra)
5. The eye

APRIL 25

GALLIC SYMBOLS
1. A magician
2. Cayenne pepper
3. "For No One"
4. The French Quarter (of New Orleans)
5. Roland Garros
6. A condom
7. Larry Bird
8. Popeye ("Popeye" Doyle)
9. The Lincoln Memorial
10. *The French Lieutenant's Woman*

WHAT'S THE MATTER WITH KANSAS?
1. James Naismith
2. Coca-Cola
3. The Missouri River
4. "Dust in the Wind"
5. Charles Curtis

SUICIDE IS PAINLESS
Easy
1. Hervé Villechaize
2. George Reeves
3. Freddie Prinze
4. Ray Combs
Harder
1. Ed Flanders
2. David Strickland
3. Dave Garroway
4. Brian Keith
Yeah, Good Luck
1. Charles Rocket
2. Inger Stevens
3. Rusty Hamer
4. Gig Young

APRIL 26

ODD FELLOWS
1. Salvador Dalí
2. The Detroit Pistons
3. Charles Babbage
4. Patch Adams
5. Bahrain

DESTINATION TOKYO
1. G
2. J
3. B
4. E
5. C
6. I
7. H
8. F
9. A
10. D

PERFORMANCE REVIEW
1. The first e-mail
2. It's pointy
3. The Haymarket labor riot
4. The paper clip
5. Scranton (*The Office*)
6. A cat
7. Selenium
8. A red stapler
9. Mike Nesmith
10. The EEOC (Equal Employment Opportunity Commission)

APRIL 27

SECOND PERSON SINGULAR
Easy
1. *Moby-Dick*
2. *Hamlet*
3. *Beowulf*
4. *The Adventures of Huckleberry Finn*

Harder
1. *Lolita*
2. *Gone with the Wind*
3. *The Wonderful Wizard of Oz*
4. *The Odyssey*
Yeah, Good Luck
1. *Little Women*
2. *Jane Eyre*
3. *Pride and Prejudice*
4. *Dr. Jekyll and Mr. Hyde*

NOTES FROM THE UNDERGROUND
1. Ian Curtis
2. Heloise
3. William Bligh
4. John Keats
5. Mel Blanc
6. Ethan Allen
7. Curly Joe DeRita
8. Carry Nation
9. Dean Martin
10. Edgar Allan Poe

EVERY DAY I WRITE THE BOOK
Easy
1. *Alice in Wonderland*
2. *1984*
3. *The Grapes of Wrath*
4. *The Catcher in the Rye*
5. *The Lord of the Rings*
Harder
1. *American Psycho*
2. *The Stranger*
3. *Lolita*
4. *Perfume*
5. *The Diary of Anne Frank*
Yeah, Good Luck
1. *The Master and Margarita*
2. *Hamlet*
3. The *I Ching*
4. *Interview with a Vampire*
5. The Tibetan *Book of the Dead*

April Answers

APRIL 28

VOCAL QUINTETS
1. "I Get Around"
2. Murciélago
3. Southern Baptist
4. Five thousand
5. Plastic surgeon (*Nip/Tuck*)
6. Pandemonium
7. Julia Roberts (Red Om is "Moder" backwards)
8. The tambourine
9. The shower curtain
10. Milquetoast
11. *Uncle Tom's Cabin*
12. Cauliflower
13. Greg Louganis
14. Mountain Dew
15. Annie Proulx ("Brokeback Mountain")
16. The question mark
17. *A Chorus Line*
18. Mozambique
19. Education
20. Port-au-Prince

WITH THIS KING I THEE WED
Easy
1. Rainier III of Monaco
2. Henry VIII
3. Prince Andrew
4. Queen Victoria
5. Louis XVI
Harder
1. Catherine the Great
2. Nefertiti
3. Edward VIII
4. Aly Khan
5. Mary II
Yeah, Good Luck
1. King Hussein of Jordan
2. Juan Carlos I of Spain
3. Princess Anne
4. Louis XIII
5. The shah of Iran

APRIL 29

FOR FUTURE REFERENCE
1. *The World Almanac and Book of Facts*
2. Merriam
3. A wiki
4. John Bartlett (*Bartlett's Familiar Quotations*)
5. *Who Was Who*

CAMELCASE
1. TiVo
2. OutKast
3. AstroTurf
4. MySpace
5. SportsCenter

ALL GONE TO LOOK FOR AMERICA
1. I
2. C
3. D
4. H
5. B
6. J
7. F
8. E
9. G
10. A

APRIL 30

ACE OF BAYS
1. Hudson Bay
2. San Francisco Bay
3. Curly Lambeau
4. Frasier Crane (and Martin and Daphne and Eddie)
5. Botany Bay
6. Corregidor
7. The Hardy Boys
8. The Bay of Bengal
9. The good ship *Lollipop*
10. Chesapeake Bay

OUT OF POSITION
1. Allentown
2. Ronin
3. George Orwell
4. *Mrs. Doubtfire*
5. Skid Row

SMALL PACKAGES
1. A police box
2. Snoopy's
3. Oscar the Grouch's trash can
4. The Quidditch World Cup
5. Mary Poppins

• 1006 • SURPRISED CHINESE AND EGYPTIAN astronomers spot a new star in the constellation Lupus, which we now know to be the brightest supernova in recorded history.

STAR-SPANGLED

1. What New York banker did bridezilla Star Jones marry in a 2004 extravaganza?

2. James I, Charles I, or George I— what king was executed, in part, for the excesses of his inquisitional "Star Chamber"?

3. Many Bothan spies died to ensure the destruction of what?

4. What 1984 hit repeatedly asks, "Come on, shine your heavenly body tonight"?

5. What future secretary of state became America's first five-star general in December 1944?

6. The United States has more stars on its flag than any other country, with fifty. What nation is in second place, with twenty-seven?

7. In 3000 B.C., it was Thuban. In 12,000 years, it will be Vega. What is it today?

8. Starfish belong to what animal phylum, whose name means "spiny skin"?

9. Who merged with the struggling Cleveland Barons in 1978?

10. The Don McLean song that begins "Starry starry night" is actually named for what painter?

11. According to the prologue to *Romeo and Juliet*, in what city do the "pair of star-cross'd lovers take their life"?

12. What other late-night veteran succeeded Ed McMahon as the host of *Star Search* in a 2003 revival?

13. Bart Starr was, of course, the winning quarterback of the famous 1967 "Ice Bowl" NFL championship. Who was the losing quarterback?

14. What kind of enormous, cool star will our own sun become in five billion years?

15. Complete this analogy: Judy Garland : James Mason :: Barbra Streisand : _____.

• 1966 • A GRADUATION BARBECUE in the backyard of Berkeley history major Diana Paxson becomes a full-fledged medieval costume party, and the "Society for Creative Anachronism," now boasting 30,000 codpiece-wearing members, is born.

LET'S DO THE TIME WARP AGAIN
Answer these trapped-in-the-past questions.

1. Not until 2002 did Sony end production of its recorders using what doomed video standard?

2. What hit 2004 film, though set in the present day, features a high school dance where Alphaville's "Forever Young" and a cover of Cyndi Lauper's "Time After Time" play?

3. A California Chumash Indian woman, who appears to have been killed by a blow to the head 9,000 years ago, is the only human ever to be found where?

4. The time-traveling scientist in TV's *Quantum Leap* shares his name with what absurdist playwright?

5. Because it's been retired to honor Jackie Robinson, what New York Yankee is the last baseball player allowed to wear uniform number 42?

6. What does Miss Havisham constantly wear in Dickens's *Great Expectations*?

7. Thimpu, the world's only capital city with no traffic lights, is the capital of what tiny kingdom?

8. What shell-shaped French cake leads the narrator into his 1.5-million-word flashback in Proust's *Remembrance of Things Past*?

9. Who shocked Pittsburgh fans in the summer of 1999 when he returned home from Italy finally shorn of his trademark mullet?

10. What was the first decade revisited by VH-1's *I Love the . . .* series?

Answers to the questions on this page can be found on page 211.

• **1899** • BEFORE ENTERING AN INSANE ASYLUM, Vincent van Gogh sends his painting *Sunflowers* to his brother Theo. This is the painting that a Japanese bidder will buy for a record $40 million in 1987.

POSING POSIES
Who painted these famous flowery works?

1. *Carnation, Lily, Lily, Rose*
2. *The Hibiscus Tree*
3. *Irises*
4. *Jack-in-the-Pulpit, Nos. I–IV*
5. *Water Lilies*

A. Paul Gauguin
B. Claude Monet
C. Georgia O'Keefe
D. John Singer Sargent
E. Vincent van Gogh

• **1972** • J. EDGAR HOOVER is found dead of heart disease at his Washington home.

WHAT A DRAG!
Let's take a quiet moment to remember Hoover the way he would have wanted: with some transvestite trivia.

1. Who draft-dodged the Trojan War by dressing as a woman in the court of King Lycomedes?
2. What 1993 film's title character has the first name Euphegenia?
3. Who often performed as falsetto-voiced middle-aged housewives called "pepperpots" in their sketches?
4. The United States' first law school for women was named for what cross-dressing Shakespearean character?
5. The protagonists of *Some Like It Hot* dress as women because they're in hiding, having witnessed what real-life event?
6. What was the pseudonym of famous cross-dresser Amandine-Aurore-Lucile Dupin?
7. What British comedian refers to himself as an "executive transvestite"?
8. Who won an Oscar for playing a cross-dresser going by the name of "Thomas Kent"?
9. The injunction against cross-dressing in Deuteronomy 22:5 was the reason given for whose execution?
10. Heinrich, Hermann, or Hansel—in *Hedwig and the Angry Inch*, what was Hedwig's (male) birth name?

• **1999** • AFTER THREE BOTTLES OF RUM and a bout of arm wrestling with Royal Navy sailors, hard-partying actor Oliver Reed suffers a fatal heart attack in Malta during the filming of *Gladiator*. Today the tavern where he died has been renamed "Ollie's Last Pub."

PUB QUIZ

1. What kind of dark beer comes in "dry," "Irish," and "Imperial Russian" varieties?
2. What's the claim to fame of Beacon Hill's Bull & Finch Pub?
3. How many points is the red inner circle on a dartboard bull's-eye worth?
4. What kind of "lunch" is the common British pub meal of a piece of Cheddar, crusty bread, and a pickle?
5. On what island is Paddy's Pub, the site of a 2002 terrorist bombing?

Answers to the questions on this page can be found on page 211.

• **1968** • THE FIRST PROTESTS at the Sorbonne begin the Paris student uprising of May 1968, which will inspire John Lennon's song "Revolution."

REVOLUTION 9

1. What current world leader began his plan to take power after the 1989 Caracazo riots?

2. Who took the throne in the "Glorious Revolution" of 1688?

3. What kind of poison disfigured Ukrainian reformer Viktor Yushchenko, leading to the Orange Revolution of 2004?

4. Shirley Temple Black was the U.S. ambassador to what nation at the time of its 1989 revolution?

5. What Morris Day–led band faces off against Prince and the Revolution in the film *Purple Rain*?

6. The Bolshevik Revolution is sometimes known by the name of what month in which it began?

7. What kind of "revolution" comes in 2ndMIX, EXTREME, and SuperNOVA variations?

8. Whom did the Daughters of the American Revolution bar from singing at Constitution Hall in 1936?

9. What were renamed Brumaire, Germinal, and Thermidor, among other names, during the French Revolution?

• **2003** • JUST THREE YEARS AFTER appearing on New Hampshire's state quarter, the famous "Old Man of the Mountain," the product of thousands of years of glaciation and erosion, collapses overnight. Easy come, easy go.

A FIT OF PEAK

1. What European country is named for the dark-looking Dinaric Alps?

2. What two U.S. states have the word "Mountain" in their official nicknames?

3. What fictional village sits in the shadow of Mount Crumpit?

4. What was known as "Bolshaya Gora" when it was part of Russia?

5. Sir Edmund Hillary appears on the currency of what nation, his native country?

6. What was first marketed with hillbilly-themed advertising, since its name is a euphemism for moonshine?

7. What distinction is usually claimed to belong to Gangkhar Puensum, a 24,000-foot peak in Bhutan?

8. What three Disneyland attractions have the word "Mountain" in the name?

9. What harbor is overlooked by Victoria Peak?

10. Who covered Marvin Gaye and Tammi Terrell's "Ain't No Mountain High Enough" and made it into a number one hit?

11. Where would you find the 89,000-foot peak Olympus Mons?

12. What Moroccan mountain range is named for the Titan that, in Greek myth, Perseus turned to stone there?

13. What New England peak famous for its bad weather was the site of a record 231-mph wind gust in 1934?

14. What two members of the *Brokeback Mountain* cast have siblings who are also award-winning actors?

15. What range contains the world's highest mountains not located in Asia?

Answers to the questions on this page can be found on page 211.

MAY 4

• **1895** • Completed more than three years earlier, the Memorial Arch in Greenwich Village's Washington Square is finally dedicated. The first arch on the site was a flimsy wooden job, erected in 1889 to celebrate the centennial of George Washington's inauguration.

SQUARE DANCE

1. What Kellogg's product was introduced to compete with Post's unsuccessful Country Squares?
2. What 1980 film is named for the legendary square-shaped capital of Kublai Khan?
3. What color is the square that's the logo for H&R Block?
4. What former Broadway *Annie* and future Emmy winner was the star of TV's *Square Pegs*?

5. What country borders both of the world's only two nations with square flags?
6. Who would use a Punnett square—an architect, a geneticist, or a sailor?
7. What organization's symbols are the square and compasses?
8. What's the name of the flat, square prison that holds the Kryptonian criminals in the *Su-*

perman movies?
9. What European capital's two largest plazas—Charles Square and Wenceslas Square—are named for beloved kings?
10. Complete this analogy. New Deal : Franklin Roosevelt :: Square Deal : _____.

• **1942** • The first "code talker" recruits—Navajos speaking in a secret code based on their tribal language—join the U.S. Marines. Their spoken code will never be cracked by the Japanese and will be used well into the Vietnam era.

CODE TALKERS

Decode these questions about five famous people with codes named after them.

1. What U.S. state's civil law is most closely based on the Napoleonic Code?
2. What scriptural phrase, spoken by Balaam in Numbers 23:23, is now more closely associated with

Samuel Morse?
3. What civilization lived by the Code of Hammurabi?
4. At the end of *The Da Vinci Code*, the Holy Grail is revealed to be buried at what popular

spot?
5. The Hollywood "Production Code" of the 1930s was named for what former postmaster general and chairman of the Republican National Committee?

• **1971** • A tiny Canadian environmental group, the Don't Make a Wave Committee, officially changes its name to the Greenpeace Foundation.

CATCH A WAVE

1. What is the Japanese word for "harbor wave"?
2. What military contractor, famous for making the Patriot missile system, also invented the first microwave ovens?

3. What French New Wave director plays the UFO expert in *Close Encounters of the Third Kind*?
4. What famed Motown songwriting trio had their first Top Ten hit with "Heat Wave"?

5. What are the "ten" referred to when a surfer "hangs ten" on a wave?

Answers to the questions on this page can be found on page 212.

• **1862** • THE MEXICAN ARMY faces the invading troops of Napoleon III in the Battle of Puebla. Though Puebla *was* finally taken by the French, the moral victory is still celebrated in Mexico and by Mexican Americans as "Cinco de Mayo."

HISPANIC ROOM

1. Of the U.S. states that border Mexico, which shares the shortest border?

2. In 1988, César Chávez conducted a thirty-six-day fast to encourage Americans to boycott what fruit?

3. What last name is shared by Clinton cabinet member Henry and *The House on Mango Street* author Sandra?

4. Because of their 200-pound difference in weight, what leading couple of the art world were sometimes called "the Elephant and the Dove"?

5. ABC's hit *Ugly Betty* is based on the telenovela *Yo soy Betty la fea*, from what Latin American country?

6. Because his father was from Minorca, in Spain, what Civil War hero was the U.S. Navy's first Hispanic admiral?

7. What four-word catchphrase of the 1990s was popularized by "Gidget," a three-year-old actor who went on to appear in *Legally Blonde 2*?

8. Who hit his 3,000th and final hit in the last regular-season at-bat of his prematurely curtailed major-league career?

9. The first Latino members of the Rock and Roll Hall of Fame were three members of what band, inducted in 1998?

10. What Mexican general who governed California for four months in 1835 would probably be surprised by how he's remembered in San Francisco today?

• **1966** • WILLIE MAYS HITS home run number 512, passing Mel Ott to become the National League's all-time leader.

SAY HEY

1. What's the real name of the Gary Glitter track often called "The Hey Song"?

2. What TV show's announcer was Hank "Hey Now!" Kingsley?

3. What's the last name of *A Streetcar Named Desire*'s Stella, of "Hey, Stella!" fame?

4. Whose 2000 death from cancer led to the E! headline " 'Hey, Vern!' Guy Dies"?

5. Besides "Hey Jude," what other Beatles song title begins with the word "Hey"?

• **1984** • AT A TINY COMIC BOOK CONVENTION in Portsmouth, New Hampshire, Kevin Eastman and Peter Laird try to hawk the first issue of their self-published comic, which they call *Teenage Mutant Ninja Turtles*.

THE BRAVE AND THE BOLD

Name these comic book superteams from their founding lineups.

1. Superman, Batman, Wonder Woman, Flash, Green Lantern, Aquaman, Martian Manhunter

2. Angel, Beast, Cyclops, Iceman, Marvel Girl

3. Thor, Iron Man, the Hulk, Ant-Man, the Wasp

4. Robin, Kid Flash, Aqualad, Wonder Girl

5. Cosmic Boy, Saturn Girl, Lightning Boy

Answers to the questions on this page can be found on page 212.

MAY 6

• **1913** • F. NEPHI GRIGG is born in Nampa, Idaho. In 1953, looking for a way to use the leftover potato shavings from Ore-Ida's new frozen French fries, Grigg will change history forever when he invents . . . the Tater Tot.

LEFTOVERS

1. Arno Penzias and Robert Wilson shared a Nobel Prize for accidentally discovering "CMB," leftover radiation from what?
2. Which two castaways were the "and the rest" in the first version of the *Gilligan's Island* theme?

3. What Australian snack is made from the yeast extract left over from making beer?
4. The last two surviving jurors from the film *12 Angry Men* were actors who shared what first name?

5. What popular destination was built on the land left over when Metropolitan Stadium, where the Twins and Vikings played, was torn down?

• **1954** • ROGER BANNISTER BREAKS the "four-minute-mile" barrier in a race at Oxford. *Sports Illustrated* names him its first Sportsman of the Year, even though his record lasts only forty-six days before his Australian rival John Landy breaks it by a second and a half.

ATHLETIC SUPPORTERS
What former Sportsmen of the Year does Sports Illustrated *describe with these citations?*

1. "The NBA's first black head coach"
2. "The prime mover and also the heart of the Cincinnati Reds' 'Big Red Machine' "
3. "The 1975 Wimbledon champion . . . fought diligently for human rights"
4. "The 27-year-old 'Hammer' sent Patterson to the canvas with

a vicious right"
5. "In 1972 . . . she became the first female player to win more than $100,000 in a year"
6. "Suspending and fining star players Paul Hornung and Alex Karras"
7. "Went on to win the Tour by seven minutes and 17 seconds, the second-biggest winning mar-

gin of his career"
8. "Won 27 Grand Prix races during his career and popularized Formula One racing"
9. "Most decorated female Olympian in U.S. history"
10. "Radically redefined the role of the NHL defenseman"

• **1974** • THE PULITZER PRIZE FOR FICTION is left out of the annual awards. The angry fiction jury reveals that it had recommended Thomas Pynchon's World War II epic *Gravity's Rainbow*, only to have the Pulitzer board dismiss it as "unreadable," "turgid," and "obscene."

THEM'S FIGHTIN' WORDS
During what war were these literary works set?

Easy
1. The *Iliad*
2. *Cold Mountain*
3. *Catch-22*
4. *M*A*S*H*

Harder
1. *The African Queen*
2. *For Whom the Bell Tolls*
3. *War and Peace*
4. *The Last of the Mohicans*

Yeah, Good Luck
1. *Simplicissimus*
2. *The Short-Timers*
3. *Richard III*
4. *The Hornet's Nest*

Answers to the questions on this page can be found on page 212.

• **1429** • AT THE BATTLES OF LES TOURELLES, Joan of Arc takes an arrow in the shoulder, as she predicted. "The witch is dead!" crow the English archers, but Joan returns dramatically to lead the final charge.

AN ARROW ESCAPE

1. What group's honor society is the Order of the Arrow?
2. For an *SNL* monologue, who once played the banjo with an arrow through his head?
3. What are the arrowlike projectiles fired by a crossbow called?
4. What company's world-famous logo has, since 1994, contained a subliminal "white arrow" hidden between the last two letters?

5. What slot on the back of an arrow's shaft keeps it on the bowstring?

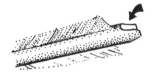

6. In what fictional midwestern city did Sinclair Lewis set *Babbitt* and *Arrowsmith*?

7. What popular movie website took its name from a John Travolta line in *Broken Arrow*?
8. What third-century martyr was ordered shot full of arrows by Diocletian?
9. Whose emblem, a white arrowhead, came from a sketch Lamar Hunt drew on a napkin in 1963?
10. The constellation Sagittarius is usually depicted as aiming its arrow at what fierce neighbor?

• **1925** • FOOTBALL COACH AND SUBSTITUTE TEACHER John Scopes is arrested for having taught evolution to high schoolers. The arrest has been cooked up by the ACLU, looking for a case to test Tennessee's antievolution "Butler Act," and by the town of Dayton, which is looking for some free publicity.

A BARREL OF MONKEYS

1. Who first appeared in the 1939 children's book *Cecily G and the Nine Monkeys*?
2. What team's fans were inspired by the Rally Monkey?
3. Europe's only free-range monkeys are the Barbary apes, which live where?
4. Which character is most seriously injured by the winged monkeys in the film *The Wizard of Oz*?

5. What did Pipsqueak the marmoset captivate America by doing on November 2, 1979?
6. What two people appear in the famous photo taken aboard the yacht *Monkey Business* in May 1987?
7. What brightly colored monkey is the world's largest?
8. What power does "The Monkey's Paw" possess in the 1902 short story?

9. What South American monkey took its name from the order of Catholic friars its fur was thought to resemble?
10. What apparatus do monkeys use in the "infinite monkey theorem" thought experiment?

Answers to the questions on this page can be found on page 213.

• **1877** • The first Westminster Kennel Club dog show is held in New York's Gilmore Gardens, making it the second oldest continuously held American sporting event, after the Kentucky Derby.

UNLEASHED
Take good care of these questions about pets.

1. What kind of "pet sounds" are actually heard at the end of the Beach Boys album of that name?
2. Who's the most famous resident of Mr. Peebles' pet shop?
3. What pet bird takes its name from Australian Aborigine words for "good eating"?
4. What baseball team plays its home games at Petco Park?
5. What common aquarium fish is named for the naturalist who discovered it in Trinidad in 1876?
6. According to the American Kennel Club, the United States' two most popular dog breeds for most of the last decade both had

what word in their breed name?
7. The Clintons' White House cat, Socks, now lives with what woman, Clinton's personal secretary, who became famous during the Monica Lewinsky hearings?
8. Nepetalactone is the active ingredient in what pet product?
9. What kind of dinosaur is the Flintstones' Dino?
10. What imports from a Baja California beach made Gary Drahl a millionaire in late 1975?
11. The title character of what 2000 film is a Norwich terrier named Winky?
12. Los Angeles, Berlin, or

Paris—what city is home to the world's very first pet cemetery, in which Rin Tin Tin is buried?
13. Paris Hilton's chihuahua is named for what character from a 1928 play?
14. In what country did the domesticated "potbellied pig" originate?
15. What physical condition, with which Dan Aykroyd, Alexander the Great, and Kate Bosworth were all born, is much more common in dogs and cats than humans?

• **1914** • W. W. Hodkinson creates the modern movie industry when he founds Paramount Pictures. The mountain logo he doodles on a napkin is based on Ben Lomond, near his hometown of Ogden, Utah.

MEN OF LETTERS
Give these other famous names with a doubled first initial like W. W. Hodkinson's.

1. What author set his most famous works near his Ashdown Forest home in Sussex, the same home where Brian Jones of the Rolling Stones drowned in 1969?
2. Who shares lead vocals with

Bono on the U2 song "When Loves Comes to Town"?
3. Who invented a waterproof boot that he began selling to his fellow Maine hunters in 1912?
4. After a locomotive struck his

parents' car in 1926, who eulogized his father in "my father moved through dooms of love"?
5. Who based his hit comic book character "Dyno Woman" on his own sister Thelma?

Answers to the questions on this page can be found on page 213.

• 1902 • OHIO OFFICIALLY ADOPTS its unusually shaped state flag—not a rectangle but a "burgee." The double triangles, says the flag's designer, represent the state's hills and valleys. Not until 2005 will the state figure out an official way to fold the damned thing.

RECTANGLE TANGLE

1. What Shakespeare play features a "love rectangle" between Lysander, Demetrius, Hermia, and Helena?

2. In the NBA, the free-throw lane is a 12-by-15-foot rectangle. What shape is it in international play?

3. What's the only Canadian province whose borders (using the proper map projection) form a rectangle?

4. What can be produced by taking a rectangle of paper, giving it a half twist on its long axis, and then joining two opposite sides?

5. Whose painting *Homage to Matisse*, showing two of his characteristic colored rectangles (blue and orange this time) sold at auction for a record $22 million in 2005?

• 1914 • WOODROW WILSON DECLARES the first national "Mother's Day" in the U.S. This will be the most touching sign of maternal devotion from the Oval Office until the 1980s, when President Reagan will insist on calling Nancy "Mommy" for eight years.

STAGE MOTHERS
Name the famous mothers of these stars.

Easy	Harder	Yeah, Good Luck
1. Liza Minnelli	1. Gwyneth Paltrow	1. Miguel Ferrer
2. Kate Hudson	2. Ben Stiller	2. Joely Richardson
3. Carrie Fisher	3. Melanie Griffith	3. Mia Farrow
4. Larry Hagman	4. Sean Astin	4. Rashida Jones
5. Jamie Lee Curtis	5. Jason Schwartzman	5. Campbell Scott

• 1961 • *AMAZING ADVENTURES* NO. 3, the first comic book printed under the Marvel Comics label, comes off the presses. Stan Lee, famous for his alliterative prose, claims he gave alliterative names to many of his characters simply to help him remember their names.

SUPER SECRETS
Can you spot these superheroes from their sonorous secret identities?

Easy	Harder	Yeah, Good Luck
1. Peter Parker	1. Scott Summers	1. Warren Worthington
2. Clark Kent	2. Reed Richards	2. Richard Rider
3. Bruce Banner	3. Stephen Strange	3. Dinah Drake
4. Matt Murdock	4. J'onn J'onzz	4. Brian Braddock
5. Billy Batson	5. Susan Storm	5. Wally West

Answers to the questions on this page can be found on page 213.

• **1775** • ACCORDING TO SPRINGFIELD TRADITION, the citizens of the Simpsons' hometown hold their first "Whacking Day," a celebration of snake clubbing.

(SPRING)FIELD GUIDE
Give the little-heard other names of these Simpsons *characters.*

FIRST NAMES

Easy	*Harder*	*Yeah, Good Luck*
1. Grandpa Simpson	1. Chief Wiggum	1. Professor Frink
2. Principal Skinner	2. Mayor Quimby	2. Mrs. Hoover
3. Mr. Burns	3. Reverend Lovejoy	3. Dr. Hibbert
4. Mr. Smithers	4. Mrs. Krabappel	4. Superintendent Chalmers

LAST NAMES

Easy	*Harder*	*Yeah, Good Luck*
1. Barney	1. Apu	1. Lenny and Carl
2. Krusty the Klown	2. The Sea Captain	2. Otto
3. Dr. Nick	3. Nelson	3. Cletus the Slackjawed Yokel
4. Jimbo	4. Martin	4. Fat Tony

• **1977** • BRAVES MANAGER DAVE BRISTOL heads home to North Carolina for a ten-day vacation—after a sixteen-game losing streak, owner Ted Turner wants to try managing the team himself. After just one game in the dugout (loss number seventeen), the league will inform Turner that there are rules against a baseball manager having a financial stake in his team, and Bristol will return early.

FRONT OFFICE SPACE
What sports team is owned or co-owned by . . .

Easy	*Harder*	*Yeah, Good Luck*
1. George Steinbrenner	1. Dan Rooney	1. Pat Bowlen
2. Mario Lemieux	2. Wayne Gretzky	2. Mike Ilitch (two teams)
3. Mark Cuban	3. Jerry Buss	3. Robert L. Johnson
4. Al Davis	4. Paul Allen (two teams)	4. John Mara
5. Jerry Jones	5. Senator Herb Kohl	5. Peter Angelos

Answers to the questions on this page can be found on page 214.

• **1897** • *NAPOLEON DYNAMITE* FANS rejoice: naturalist Carl Hagenbeck successfully breeds "a rare alliance between those two great and formidable felidae, the lion and the tiger." Eye of the liger, baby!

ALL-TIME HYBRID
What different animals are mingled to produce these mythical creatures?

Easy	Harder	Yeah, Good Luck
1. Mermaid	1. Sphinx	1. Hippocamp
2. Centaur	2. Harpy	2. Lamia
3. Faun	3. Griffin	3. Chimera
4. Minotaur	4. Cockatrice	4. Manticore

• **1963** • EIGHT THOUSAND REVELERS get up off their sackbuts and attend the Renaissance Pleasure Faire in North Hollywood, marking the beginning of the Renaissance festival fad in America. Huzzah!

AL FRESCO
Some questions on the real *Renaissance.*

1. Venetian painter Jacopo Robusti was better known by what name, because he was the son of a cloth dyer?
2. In Botticelli's *The Birth of Venus*, what is Venus standing on as she rides to shore?
3. What was named for Pope Sixtus IV when it was consecrated in a 1483 Mass?
4. What's the center of the inscribed circle in which Leonardo da Vinci's "Vitruvian Man" stands?
5. What is the only signed work of Michelangelo?

• **1991** • THE NATIONAL STUTTERING PROJECT pickets Warner Bros., demanding that Porky Pig lose his offensive stutter. (His stutter? Where's the League of Decency demanding that he finally put on some damn pants?)

TH-TH-TH-THAT'S ALL, FOLKS!

1. Which *Alice in Wonderland* character is a reference to its author, Lewis Carroll, who used to stutter when saying his own name?
2. The stutter on the chorus of what 1974 hit was a joke aimed at the singer's stuttering brother, George Bachman?
3. What British actor, fittingly, founded the London Centre for Stammering Children?
4. Because of her stammer, whose wife, Annie, shunned the spotlight following her husband's sudden 1962 fame?
5. What rapper, currently prisoner 00469659 at Louisiana's Elayn Hunt Correctional Center, raps on the hit 2001 remix of Joe's song "Stutter"?

Answers to the questions on this page can be found on page 214.

MAY 12

• **1593** • PLAYWRIGHT THOMAS KYD, whose *Spanish Tragedy* inspired Shakespeare's *Hamlet,* is arrested by the Crown when a "heretical" pamphlet is found in his lodgings. Kyd protests that the tract actually belongs to his famous roommate, fellow playwright Christopher Marlowe.

CHRONIC ROOMMATE-ISM

1. What director was the college roommate of J. Geils Band frontman Peter Wolf, until, ironically, he kicked Wolf out for being "too weird"?
2. What Canadian rocker was, briefly, Rick James's roommate, while they were playing together in a band called the Mynah Birds?
3. Erich Segal has said that he based Oliver Barrett IV, the protagonist of his novel *Love Story*, on what Harvard roommates of his acquaintance, a future actor and a future politician?
4. Mousy actor Wally Cox once formed a real-life *Odd Couple*

with what manly actor, though Cox hated his pet raccoon so much he finally moved out?
5. What Big Ten coach with four Final Fours under his belt was the college roommate, at Northern Michigan, of future NFL coach Steve Mariucci?
6. What comedian, Christopher Reeve's Juilliard roommate, was, Reeve said, the first person to make him laugh following his 1995 accident?
7. Some Washington eyebrows raised when U.S. vice president William R. King and what future president lived together in the capital for sixteen years?

8. What actor got his unusual nickname from his college roommate Stanley Tucci, who didn't like calling him "Irving"?
9. Notre Dame coach Charlie Weis used to play pranks on what Hall of Fame quarterback while they bunked together in college?
10. What two acting legends, Pasadena Playhouse friends and New York roomies back in the day, never worked on screen together until 2002's *Runaway Jury*?

• **1974** • THE CINCINNATI CITY COUNCIL accepts the resignation of the city's mayor-elect after he admitted patronizing a prostitute. The disgraced pol is no less than future talk-show host Jerry Springer.

HOSTS WITH THE MOST

1. Except during World War II, what team has hosted an NFL game every Thanksgiving Day since 1934?
2. What game show host took his stage name from the college in his West Virginia hometown?
3. What detective novel begins with a dinner hosted by the mysteriously absent "Mr. U. N. Owen"?
4. The Egyptian plover is a bird best known for its symbiotic relationship with what host animal?

5. Who hosted the "Mad Tea-Party" in *Alice in Wonderland*?
6. What are the only two ingredients allowed in the "host," the Catholic Communion wafer?
7. What food item shares its name with Brad and Janet's hospitable host in *The Rocky Horror Picture Show*?
8. The host country's flag typically arrives last in the Parade of Nations that opens each Olympic Games. What was the only Games where this didn't happen?

9. What actor has guest-hosted *Saturday Night Live* thirteen times, more than anyone but Steve Martin?
10. What Ukrainian city hosted the last World War II summit of the "Big Three"?

Answers to the questions on this page can be found on page 214.

• **1917** • THREE PORTUGUESE CHILDREN report seeing the Blessed Virgin outside Fátima, Portugal, leading to mass pilgrimages.

THERE'S SOMETHING ABOUT MARY
Name these people whose mothers were named Mary.

1. Who made his West End debut playing alongside his mother in *South Pacific*?
2. Who plays drums on the Beatles track "Back in the U.S.S.R"?

3. Who commissioned a new translation of the Bible at the Hampton Court Conference he called in 1604?
4. Who was the only person to be

nearby at three different presidential assassinations?
5. What famed paleontologist was also the first head of the Kenyan Wildlife Service?

• **1940** • WINSTON CHURCHILL GIVES his famous first speech as prime minister, about "blood, toil, tears, and sweat."

I'VE GOTTA SECRETE
How much do you know about your own bodily fluids?

1. What is the liquid component of blood called?
2. What video game was originally called *Snots and Boogers* and then *@!#?@!?*
3. What substance makes feces brown and jaundice sufferers yellow?
4. In the shortest verse in the Bible, "Jesus wept" (John 11:35), who is Jesus weeping for?

5. What thin yellow fluid do the mammary glands secrete before lactation begins?
6. In what film is General Jack Ripper obsessed with America's "precious bodily fluids"?
7. Of the world's snakes with the most potent venom, nine of the ten are natives of what country?
8. Two of the "four humors" the ancients believed controlled tem-

perament consist of what bodily fluid?
9. What *Harry Potter* snacks come in flavors including earwax, booger, and vomit?
10. What element did alchemist Hennig Brand discover in 1669 when, boiling his own urine in the hopes of making gold, he observed glowing fumes?

• **1950** • A VERY LITTLE STEVIE WONDER is born prematurely in Saginaw, Michigan. Too much oxygen during his hospital incubator stay probably causes his lifelong blindness.

SONGS IN THE KEY OF LIFE
Name the artists behind these life-affirming hits.

Easy
1. "You Light Up My Life" (1977)
2. "(I've Had) the Time of My Life" (1987)
3. "Got to Get You into My Life" (1967)

Harder
1. "All My Life" (1998)
2. "Love of My Life" (1975)
3. "Last Night a DJ Saved My Life" (1982)

Yeah, Good Luck
1. "Story of My Life" (1990)
2. "It's My Life" (1965)
3. "Welcome to My Life" (2004)

Answers to the questions on this page can be found on page 215.

MAY 14

• **~~1938~~** • A FIVE-YEAR-OLD PERUVIAN GIRL named Lina Medina gives birth to a son, making her the youngest mother on record.

1939

MOM'S THE WORD

1. According to Fountains of Wayne, whose mom "has got it goin' on"?
2. Which of TV's *Golden Girls* plays the title character in *Stop! Or My Mom Will Shoot?*

3. Whose first book was the 2006 memoir *Peace Mom?*
4. On what TV show is Momcorp the world's largest megacorporation?
5. Who played Janine, aka "Sti-

fler's mom," in the *American Pie* movies?

• **1949** • AT A FUND-RAISING TOUR of homes in New Canaan, Connecticut, neighbors get their first look at Philip Johnson's "Glass House," a transparent 56-by-32-foot rectangle that the architect has built as his residence. The sensational house catapults Johnson to fame—at the time of his 2005 death (still in the Glass House), he will be called America's greatest living architect.

A SORT OF HOMECOMING
Who or what lives in . . .

1. Gracie Mansion
2. An aerie
3. A log cabin with chicken legs
4. A Florida estate called Xanadu

5. A pineapple under the sea
6. An apiary
7. The tippy-top floor of the Plaza Hotel
8. A holt

9. A hogan
10. A deluxe apartment in the sky

• **1983** • TATTOO YELLS "De plane! De plane!" on *Fantasy Island* for the final time. After demanding the same salary as Ricardo Montalban, Hervé Villechaize is dropped from the show in favor of Lawrence, a proto-*Belvedere* butler played by Christopher Hewett.

SWITCHING CHANNELS
Name the TV characters that have been played by these multiple actors.

Easy
1. Julie Newmar, Eartha Kitt, Lee Meriwether
2. Dick York, Dick Sargent
3. Eve Plumb, Geri Reischl
4. Phyllis Coates, Noel Neill
5. Richard Thomas, Robert Wightman

Harder
1. Barbara Bel Geddes, Donna Reed
2. Lecy Goranson, Sarah Chalke
3. Mike Evans, Damon Evans
4. Tom Baker, David Tennant, et al.
5. Philip Bruns, Barney Martin

Yeah, Good Luck
1. Janet Hubert-Whitten, Daphne Maxwell Reid
2. Pamela Sue Martin, Emma Samms
3. Dixie Carter, Mary Ann Mobley
4. Beverley Owen, Pat Priest
5. Lisa Robin Kelly, Christina Moore

Answers to the questions on this page can be found on page 215.

MAY 15

• **1970** • JOHN SIMON, OF *NEW YORK* MAGAZINE, runs his infamous review of Diana Rigg's nude scene in *Abelard and Heloise:* "Diana Rigg is built like a brick mausoleum with insufficient flying buttresses."

MORTAR, SHE WROTE
Are you an expert on brick bric-a-brac?

1. Gold, ice cream, or heroin—what is the title object of the 2006 film *Brick* a brick of?
2. What word for mud bricks comes to us from the ancient Egyptian word "dbt"?
3. What teenage trauma did Ben Folds commemorate in his 1997 hit "Brick"?
4. "The Brick Testament" is a website that re-creates the Bible in what form?

5. What Tennessee Williams title character is married to Brick Pollitt?
6. Why did PETA buy a brick at San Diego's new ballpark that reads "Break open your cold ones—Toast the Padres—Enjoy this champion organization"?
7. What port, its state's largest city, is nicknamed the Brick City?
8. Saluting a 1977 hit, what soul band was inducted into the Na-

tional Brick Distributors' Hall of Fame in 1991?
9. What TV show's eateries include The Brick tavern and Roslyn's Café?
10. What redbrick complex lies between the Alexander Garden and Red Square?

• **1997** • THE WASHINGTON BULLETS are officially renamed "Wizards," beating out the other finalists: the Dragons, Express, Stallions, and Sea Dogs.

I'M A MAGIC MAN
Can you conjure up these answers about ten different wizards?

1. What was the real name of TV's *Mr. Wizard*?
2. Who did sports fans know as "the Wizard of Westwood"?
3. Who sings "Pinball Wizard" in the film *Tommy*?
4. What former KKK imperial wizard used the pen name "Dorothy Vanderbilt" to pen a 1976 book of sex tips for women?

5. What baseball player titled his memoir *Wizard*?
6. What wizard is seduced and left powerless by the evil Nimue?
7. Who met her first husband, Victor Willis of the Village People, while understudying the role of Glinda in *The Wiz* on Broadway?
8. What name is given, in the

Harry Potter books, to someone who can't do magic, despite having wizard heritage?
9. Thomas Edison was "the Wizard of Menlo Park" in what U.S. state?
10. Who's the only actor ever to be Oscar-nominated for playing a wizard?

Answers to the questions on this page can be found on page 215.

MAY 16

• **1866** • ACCORDING TO CADBURY-SCHWEPPES, pharmacist Charles Elmer Hires brews up the first batch of his eponymous root beer on this date, inspired by an herbal tea he'd been served on his honeymoon in New Jersey.

ROOTS ROCK
Get to the bottom of this quiz about roots.

1. What kind of dental specialist performs root canals?
2. What slave name does Kunta Kinte's owner force him to adopt in Alex Haley's *Roots*?
3. What plant's roots are used to make tapioca?
4. Ten is, of course, a square root of 100. What other number is as well?

5. In First Timothy, what does Paul say is "the root of all evil"?
6. The Roots' album *Things Fall Apart* begins with a snatch of dialogue between Denzel Washington and Wesley Snipes, taken from what movie?
7. The Bitterroot Range of the Rockies is located on the border between what two states?

8. What plant takes its name for the Chinese words for "man root"?
9. What trademark is used in public relations to refer to phony grassroots campaigns?
10. What country is home to Roots, the company that outfits the U.S. Olympic team?

• **1929** • *WINGS* WINS the Best Production award at the first Oscar ceremony. It's often remembered as the first Best Picture, though the more prestigious award that night was called "Best Quality of Production" and was won by F. W. Murnau's (much better) film *Sunrise*.

A MATTER OF A PINION
Questions about wings, avian and otherwise.

1. What novelist's most famous character is the aptly named Isadora Wing?
2. The Detroit Red Wings are one of only two NHL teams with a monochromatic (white and just one other color) logo. What's the other one?
3. Whose young neighbor Stewart always wears a Winger T-shirt?

4. On what island is the TV series *Wings* set?
5. What American TV actor plays himself as a fallen angel in Wim Wenders's *Wings of Desire*?
6. What hinged surfaces on a plane's wingtips allow the aircraft to roll?
7. Before he formed Wings, what's the only song Paul McCartney ever composed with the

word "wings" in the lyrics?
8. The "Wandering" species of what bird has the longest wingspan in nature?
9. Where would you find the countries of Qumar and Equatorial Kundu?
10. What Greek goddess is depicted in the famous Winged Victory of Samothrace?

Answers to the questions on this page can be found on page 216.

• **1991** • BRIAN BOSWORTH *IS* . . . *Stone Cold.* Sadly, he will lose to Vanilla Ice in the year's unusually competitive Razzie race for Worst New Star.

HAM-DUNK
What athlete tried his hand at acting in these movies?

Easy
1. *Airplane!*
2. *The Scorpion King*
3. *There's Something About Mary*
4. *The Naked Gun*
5. *The Dirty Dozen*

Harder
1. *Action Jackson*
2. *Lock, Stock, and Two Smoking Barrels*
3. *Blazing Saddles*
4. *Steel*
5. *Dumb and Dumber*

Yeah, Good Luck
1. *Amazing Grace and Chuck*
2. *Black Caesar*
3. *Mitchell*
4. *Old Yeller*
5. *Harvard Man*

• **1997** • THE IDENTICAL HANSEN QUADRUPLETS make history when they all graduate from Baylor University on the same day.

FOUR BETTER OR WORSE
Give the missing last member in these famous quartets.

Easy
1. Matthew, Mark, Luke, and . . .
2. Mr. Fantastic, Invisible Girl, Human Torch, and . . .
3. Strings, woodwinds, brass, and . . .
4. Leonardo, Donatello, Michelangelo, and . . .
5. Earth, air, fire, and . . .

Harder
1. Agnetha, Björn, Benny, and . . .
2. Solid, liquid, gas, and . . .
3. Reading, Short Line, B&O, and . . .
4. Carats, clarity, color, and . . .
5. Swords, wands, coins, and . . .

Yeah, Good Luck
1. Of speech, of worship, from want, and . . .
2. Pison, Gihon, Hiddekel, and . . .
3. Adenine, thymine, guanine, and . . .
4. "Burnt Norton," "East Coker," "The Dry Salvages," and . . .
5. Joe Greene, L. C. Greenwood, Ernie Holmes, and . . .

• **2005** • FLEET STREET, whose name was once synonymous with the British press, loses its last news office, as Reuters begins its relocation to new offices in Canary Wharf.

STREET SMARTS

1. What famous street follows the line of a twelve-foot stockade begun in 1653 by Peter Stuyvesant?
2. What thoroughfare was the site of Hollywood scandals like River Phoenix's death and Hugh Grant's arrest?
3. The city of Liverpool recently stalled plans to rename streets historically linked to the slave trade when it realized that what famous street was on the list?
4. What road, which names a 2002 film, divides Wayne County from affluent Oakland and ~~Macomb~~ Counties? Macomb
5. New York's Tribeca neighborhood is so named because it's the triangle south of what major street?
6. Spartacus and his fellow slaves were crucified alongside what Roman highway, the "queen of the long roads"?
7. What London street is home to a famous theater and, in a children's song, to "the Muffin Man"?
8. What is the official name of New York's Sixth Avenue, though it's used only by clueless out-of-towners?
9. What runs from the Stratosphere in the north to McCarran Airport in the south?
10. What American street is best known for its eight switchbacks between Hyde and Leavenworth?

Answers to the questions on this page can be found on page 216.

MAY 18

• **1917** • The Selective Service Act introduces the modern draft, requiring men aged 21 to 30 to register for military service in World War I.

DRAFTY IN HERE

What team drafted these number one picks from the world of professional sports?

Easy	*Harder*	*Yeah, Good Luck*
1. Terry Bradshaw	**1.** John Elway	**1.** Chris Webber
2. Ken Griffey, Jr.	**2.** Chipper Jones	**2.** Ben McDonald
3. Mario Lemieux	**3.** Rick DiPietro	**3.** Aundray Bruce
4. Peyton Manning	**4.** Lew Alcindor	**4.** Matt Bush
5. LeBron James	**5.** Larry Johnson	**5.** Dale McCourt

• **1964** • Eric Burdon and the Animals record their now-classic cover of "The House of the Rising Sun," nailing it in one take. It becomes the first four-minute song ever to top the pop charts.

THE DAWN PATROL

1. Who gave Impressionism its name with his 1873 painting *Impression, Sunrise*?

2. What European city do Ethan Hawke and Julie Delpy wander in *Before Sunrise*?

3. What provides the red color in a Tequila Sunrise?

4. The Hurricanes, the Panthers, or the Thrashers—what NHL team plays its home games in a suburb called Sunrise?

5. In the Northern Hemisphere, the day with the earliest sunrise falls in what month?

• **1998** • The New Republic publishes Stephen Glass's story "Hack Heaven," about teenage computer hackers. Unfortunately, Glass has invented every person and company in the story, even creating dummy websites and voice mail accounts when editors began checking his sources, and he's soon fired.

THE FIVE *W*S (AND ONE *H*)

1. Whose crime was witnessed only by Cindy Lou **Who**?

2. What Big East school took the cryptic name for its sports teams from the Greek word for "**what**"?

3. What Dublin, Ohio–based company trades under the ticker symbol **WEN**?

4. After the 1990 NFL draft, who found himself teammates with his Heisman Trophy successor, Andre **Ware**?

5. Who had the last number one hit of the 1950s with his song "**Why**"?

6. What Steinbeck novel takes its title from a poem by Julia Ward **Howe**?

Answers to the questions on this page can be found on page 216.

• 1664 • A STRONOMER R OBERT H OOKE records seeing a dark spot in the southern hemisphere of Jupiter. This may be the first discovery of Jupiter's "Great Red Spot," a giant storm twice the diameter of the earth.

SPOT CHECK

1. What painter used his trademark Benday dots in canvases like *Drowning Girl* and *Whaam!*?
2. How many pips are on the two sides of the domino in the Domino's Pizza logo?
3. Of what famous family are Pongo and Perdita the parents?
4. What's the more common name for the retinal scotoma caused by the optic nerve?
5. In the nursery rhyme "Ladybird, Ladybird," why is the bug told to "fly away home"?
6. Each Pac-Man maze features 240 regular dots and how many larger "power pellets"?

7. What officially replaced "CQD" on July 1, 1908?
8. What are the "spots" in the British dessert Spotted Dick?
9. What world nation has three consecutive dotted characters in its name when written in mixed-case letters?
10. What is counted by the Wolf Number, named for Swiss mathematician Rudolf Wolf, who helped discover their influence on geomagnetism?
11. What singer of "Itsy Bitsy Teenie Weenie Yellow Polka Dot Bikini" was in Dallas on November 22, 1963, waving at the mo-

torcade just blocks before Kennedy was shot?
12. What painter's masterpiece contains—in addition to its human subjects—three dogs, a horse, a monkey, and a butterfly?
13. What is the *Pale Blue Dot* in the title of Carl Sagan's 1994 book?
14. How many dot positions are there in each letter of the Braille alphabet?
15. What word for a series of dots is a top secret code word in the Bond film *Casino Royale*?

• 1993 • T HE *90210* GANG GRADUATES from Beverly Hills High, most preparing to enter fictional "California University." Oddly, they never run into the *Saved by the Bell* cast, also attending good old California U the same year, but on a different network.

ACA-DUMMY-A
What do dumb teen comedies and dumb sitcoms have in common? Phony universities!

1. Adams College
2. Coolidge College
3. Faber College
4. Grand Lakes University
5. Harrison University
6. Hillman College
7. Langley College
8. Leland College
9. Pacific Tech
10. Worthington University

A. *Animal House*
B. *Back to School*
C. *Dawson's Creek*
D. *A Different World*
E. *The Facts of Life*
F. *Family Ties*
G. *Old School*
H. *Real Genius*
I. *Revenge of the Nerds*
J. *Van Wilder*

Answers to the questions on this page can be found on page 217.

MAY 20

• 1902 • Cuba adopts its "Estrella Solitaria" flag design—"the Lone Star." Even though it was inspired by the U.S. Stars and Stripes, the flag is still used today by Castro's Cuba.

STAR SEARCH
What national flags use these unusual stars?

1.

2.

3.

4.

5.

6.

• 1916 • *Boy with Baby Carriage,* painted by a young Norman Rockwell, appears on the cover of *The Saturday Evening Post*—the first of more than three hundred Rockwell paintings to make the cover.

SUBSCRIPTION APTITUDE TEST
Complete these magazine analogies. Make sure to fill in all the bubbles on your answer sheet completely. You may begin now.

1. *O* : Oprah Winfrey :: *Living* : _____

2. *The Devil Wears Prada* : *Runway* :: *Ugly Betty* : _____

3. Alfred E. Neuman : *Mad* :: Sylvester P. Smythe : _____

4. *Time* : the U.S. :: *Maclean's* : _____

5. *Playboy* : Playmate :: *Penthouse* : _____

6. *George* : Cindy Crawford :: *People* : _____

7. *YM* : "Your" :: *FHM* : _____

8. *Vogue* : *Teen Vogue* :: *Cosmopolitan* : _____

9. *Shattered Glass* : *The New Republic* :: *Almost Famous* : _____

10. 500 top-grossing companies : *Fortune* :: 500 fastest-growing companies : _____

• 2002 • A British government survey finds that Brussels sprouts are the most-hated vegetable in the United Kingdom.

BIG-CITY DINING
Answer these questions about other foods named for world capitals.

1. What tuber, also called the sunroot or topinambur, is actually native to North America, not the Middle East?

2. What dish is prepared by frying a breaded, buttered chicken breast?

3. What chili pepper was believed the hottest in the world until the Naga Jolokia pepper was discovered in India in 2000?

4. Besides corn, what's the other principal ingredient in succotash?

5. In much of Europe, the sausages we call "hot dogs" are named for what city?

Answers to the questions on this page can be found on page 217.

• **1898** • THE CAR BUMPER IS INVENTED, when one is mounted onto the front of a prototype Präsident, a Czech car being built in Moravia. Unfortunately, the bumper falls off ten miles into the car's test run to Vienna, and the design feature is abandoned.

CAR-PE DIEM
Match up these automotive firsts.

1. First air bags	**A.** 1895 Peugeot L'Eclair
2. First antilock brakes	**B.** 1901 Oldsmobile
3. First battery ignition	**C.** 1910 Cadillac Model Thirty
4. First GPS navigation	**D.** 1914 Scripps-Booth
5. First pneumatic tires	**E.** 1928 Studebaker
6. First power locks	**F.** 1939 Buick
7. First speedometer	**G.** 1959 Volvo Amazon
8. First three-point seatbelts	**H.** 1966 Jensen FF
9. First turn signals	**I.** 1974 Oldsmobile Toronado
10. First windshield defroster	**J.** 1990 Mazda Cosmo

• **1921** • CARL WICKMAN BEGINS a bus service transporting iron ore miners around Hibbing, Minnesota. His new company will become Greyhound bus lines.

BUS TA MOVE

1. In the movie *Speed*, dropping below what speed will blow up the bus?
2. A statue of what TV character stands outside the Eighth Avenue entrance of New York's Port Authority Bus Terminal?
3. In what city did Rosa Parks refuse to move to the back of the bus?
4. What has coast-to-coast commuter John Madden dubbed his famous luxury bus?
5. What Ken Kesey–led group toured America in a psychedelic school bus called "Furthur"?

• **1954** • THE SENATE VOTES down a proposed constitutional amendment lowering the voting age to eighteen. It will take the Vietnam War to eventually ratify the amendment, in 1971.

THE AMEND CORNER
Which numbered amendment to the Constitution deals with . . .

Easy	*Harder*	*Yeah, Good Luck*
1. Self-incrimination	**1.** The income tax	**1.** Poll taxes
2. Freedom of speech	**2.** Instituting Prohibition	**2.** Washington, D.C.
3. Searches and seizures	**3.** Abolishing slavery	**3.** How senators are elected
4. The right to bear arms	**4.** Women's suffrage	**4.** Presidential succession

Answers to the questions on this page can be found on page 217.

MAY 22

• **1849** • A PATENT FOR LIFTING BOATS over shoals is issued to a mechanically minded U.S. congressman. Though the device is never built, it makes Abraham Lincoln the only president ever to hold a patent.

PATENTLY RIDICULOUS
Match these celebrity inventors to their unlikely brainstorms.

1. Marlon Brando	**A.** Accordion-shaped ashtray
2. Gary Burghoff	**B.** Stretchy spiral toy egg
3. Harry Connick, Jr.	**C.** Diaper with outer pocket for "wipes"
4. Charles Fleischer	**D.** Guitarlike keyboard instrument design
5. Michael Jackson	**E.** Three-blowout party noisemaker horn
6. Penn Jillette	**F.** Unjammable torpedo guidance system
7. Danny Kaye	**G.** Hot tub with naughtily angled water jets
8. Hedy Lamarr	**H.** Leg-plate guitar support
9. Jamie Lee Curtis	**I.** Ultrasnug butt-flattering pantyhose
10. Zeppo Marx	**J.** Artificial heart
11. Julie Newmar	**K.** 45-degree-leaning "antigravity" illusion
12. Prince	**L.** Bongo-drumskin tightening device
13. Eddie Van Halen	**M.** Pulse rate monitor
14. Lawrence Welk	**N.** Electronic sheet music display
15. Paul Winchell	**O.** Noisemaking, chum-dispensing fish attractor

• **1995** • IN A NOTORIOUS CLIFFHANGER, the nutty Kimberly blows up the titular apartment building on TV's *Melrose Place*. Semirecurring character Tiffany Hart turns out to be the only fatality—even Marcia Cross's career eventually recovers.

RENT CONTROL
Not every apartment building is as explosive as Melrose Place.

1. Coincidentally, in what apartment complex was Rose Mary Woods living in the early 1970s?
2. Since 1961, where have Margo Magee, Tommie Thompson, and Lu Ann Powers lived?
3. *The Apartment* and *Annie Hall* are the only two Oscar-winning Best Pictures to each mention *another* Best Picture winner within the film. What are the two films referenced?
4. In the 1996 movie, what kind of animal shares *Joe's Apartment* with him?
5. What two music stars died in the same London flat, then owned by Harry Nilsson, in 1974 and 1978, respectively?
6. Orange, green, or purple—what color were the walls in Monica's apartment, on TV's *Friends*?
7. The Broadway hit *Rent* translates what opera to a Greenwich Village apartment?
8. In 1966, Johnny Cash briefly shared a Nashville apartment with what other country legend?
9. What 1967 film classic was filmed at the Dakota, the same apartment building where John Lennon was later shot?
10. According to the title of a 1947 play, how does one get from the New Orleans train station to the apartment at 632 Elysian Fields?

Answers to the questions on this page can be found on page 218.

• **1928** • MICKEY MOUSE SPEAKS for the first time in *The Karnival Kid*. Walt Disney himself provides the voice for that fateful first line: "Hot dogs, hot dogs!"

CARRYING A TOON
Who provided the original voice for these animated characters?

Easy	Harder	Yeah, Good Luck
1. Buzz Lightyear	1. Stewie Griffin	1. Inspector Gadget
2. Marge Simpson	2. The Iron Giant	2. SpongeBob SquarePants
3. Daffy Duck	3. Hank (*King of the*) Hill	3. Garfield
4. Aladdin's Genie	4. The Lion King (as an adult)	4. Winnie-the-Pooh
5. Shrek	5. Mr. Magoo	5. Yogi Bear

• **1974** • KEN JENNINGS, OF *JEOPARDY!* streak fame, is born in Washington, while Ray Stevens's novelty hit "The Streak," appropriately enough, sits atop the *Billboard* charts.

IRON HORSES
Answer these questions about much *more impressive streaks.*

1. Who had a 2,495-game winning streak ended by the New Jersey Reds on January 5, 1971?

2. What author wrote America's bestselling novel every year from 1993 to 2000, with a *different* novel every year?

3. Pitchers for what major league baseball team have owned the record for "most consecutive scoreless innings" since 1968?

4. What Mariah Carey and Boyz II Men collaboration topped the Hot 100 chart for a record sixteen weeks in 1995?

5. What's the only name ever used by four British kings in a row?

6. After his famous hitting streak ended, Joe DiMaggio said he'd been one game away from an endorsement by what company?

7. What William Hurt movie is the box-office Nancy Zerg that ended *Titanic*'s fifteen-week earnings streak?

8. Who began forty-five straight lines of his poem *Howl* with the word "who"?

9. What did the Federal Reserve System do a record seventeen consecutive times between 2004 and 2006?

10. What event was won by the same team the first twenty-five times it was held, from 1851 to 1983?

11. What's the only TV show to top the Nielsen ratings five seasons in a row, from 1972 to 1976?

12. Whose thirty-year-old record did Roger Federer break in 2007 with 161 straight weeks atop the men's tennis rankings?

13. In 2004, what replaced *The Adventures of Ozzie and Harriet* as the longest-running sitcom in American history?

14. What NFL quarterback shattered Ron Jaworski's old record for most consecutive starts?

15. Who has won more Senate elections—nine straight—than any other politician in history?

Answers to the questions on this page can be found on page 218.

MAY 24

• **1626** • Peter Minuit "buys" the island of Manhattan from the local Canarsie tribe (who don't even live there) for 60 guilders'—about $24—worth of cloth and buttons.

INDIGENOUS INDIGNATION

1. What legendary chief's death on December 15, 1890, led directly to the famous massacre at Wounded Knee?
2. What U.S. state has the slogan "Native America" on its license plates?

3. What great Onondaga orator persuaded five Indian nations to form the Iroquois Confederacy?
4. According to General Philip Sheridan's famous quote, "The only good Indians I ever saw were" what?

5. What Wampanoag chief saved the Plymouth colony from starvation and attended their 1621 harvest festival—the "first Thanksgiving"?

• **1941** • British actor Esmond Knight is left totally blind by a German shell during the Battle of Denmark Strait. Remarkably, he returns to acting, convincingly playing the (sighted) Nazi villain in 1943's *The Silver Fleet*. Despite never regaining most of his sight, Knight will go on to have a forty-five-year screen acting career.

MUST-SEES
Who played the blind character in each of these movies?

Easy
1. *Wait Until Dark*
2. *Ray*
3. *Scent of a Woman*
4. *Daredevil*
5. *The Miracle Worker*

Harder
1. *Red Dragon*
2. *Tommy*
3. *Jennifer Eight*
4. *The Village*
5. *Butterflies Are Free*

Yeah, Good Luck
1. *Sneakers*
2. *City Lights*
3. *A Patch of Blue*
4. *The Hotel New Hampshire*
5. *Places in the Heart*

• **1969** • At a San Diego concert, backed by the original members of the Experience for one of the last times, Jimi Hendrix playfully misquotes his famously misheard lyric to "Purple Haze" by clearly singing, "'Scuse me while I kiss that guy."

MONDEGREEN DAY
From what songs do these other famous "mondegreens"—commonly misunderstood lyrics—come?
(Bonus points for naming the artist and correct lyric.)

1. "There's a bathroom on the right."
2. "We split up on the docks at night."
3. "The girl with colitis goes by."
4. "Last night I dreamt of some bagels."
5. "Wrapped up like a douche"
6. "Hold me closer, Tony Danza"
7. "Here we are now, in

containers"
8. "Round John Virgin, mother and child"
9. "You and me and Leslie"
10. "Lock the cashbox"

Answers to the questions on this page can be found on page 218.

• **1862** • STONEWALL JACKSON WINS the first Battle of Winchester, Virginia. All told, the Shenandoah Valley town will change hands seventy-two times during the Civil War.

SWITCHING TEAMS

1. Though his seat had been held by a Republican for a record 144 years, who reshaped the Senate by becoming an independent in 2001?
2. What was pioneering transsexual Christine Jorgensen's first name be-fore her surgery?
3. The last major league team to switch from the AL to the NL, and the last NFL team to switch from the AFC to the NFC, both origi-nated in what city?
4. What nation switched sides in World War II on September 8, 1943?
5. Seafloor spreading at midoceanic ridges is how scientists first discov-ered the periodic reversal of what?

• **1961** • PRESIDENT KENNEDY GIVES his famous speech to Congress, vowing to land a man on the moon within nine years. In a less-quoted addendum, he vows that "a man will play golf on the moon" within eleven years and "man will become, frankly, pretty bored with the moon" within fifteen.

SPACE RACE

1. What proper noun was the first word spoken to the world from the surface of the moon?
2. For whom is the Cosmonauts Training Center in Star City, Russia, named?
3. The only two sitting U.S. senators ever to go into space shared what pair of initials?
4. Which space shuttle is named for the ship on which Robert Scott first sailed to Antarctica?
5. What does *Mir*, the name of the Russian space station, mean in Russian?
6. Before the 2004 launch of Space-Ship One, who was the last Ameri-can ever to go into space alone?
7. Who did the American media nickname "Muttnik"?
8. Who's the only character to have a speaking role in both *The Right Stuff* and *Apollo 13*?
9. Did Neil Armstrong first set foot on the moon with his left or right foot?
10. Why did the Shire of Esperance, in Western Australia, issue the United States a $400 fine for litter-ing in 1979?

• **1980** • "SUICIDE IS PAINLESS," better known as "that theme from *M*A*S*H*," belatedly tops the British pop charts. Robert Altman's fourteen-year-old son had written the lyrics to the song, earning him much more in royalties than his father ever got for directing the film.

SAME OLD SONG
What TV shows have used these pop songs as their themes?

Easy
1. "Who Are You," the Who
2. "Cleveland Rocks," the Presi-dents of the United States of America
3. "Love and Marriage," Frank Sinatra
4. "Bad Boys," Inner Circle
5. "With a Little Help from My Friends," Joe Cocker

Harder
1. "How Soon Is Now?," Love Spit Love
2. "Woke Up This Morning," A3
3. "Reflections," Diana Ross and the Supremes
4. "Save Me," Remy Zero
5. "A Little Less Conversation," Elvis Presley

Yeah, Good Luck
1. "Stand," R.E.M.
2. "Even a Dog Can Shake Hands," Warren Zevon
3. "Here with Me," Dido
4. "Bad Reputation," Joan Jett
5. "Yakety Sax," Boots Randolph

Answers to the questions on this page can be found on page 219.

MAY 26

• **1896** • THE DOW JONES Industrial Average is first published.

KEEPING UP WITH THE JONESES

1. What is Indiana Jones's real first name?
2. What famed musician is the father of singer Norah Jones?
3. What empress gave John Paul Jones a navy job after his American military career ended?
4. What was the nickname of 6-foot, 9-inch Cowboys defensive end Ed Jones?
5. On what "Special" Illinois Central route was Casey Jones the engineer?

• **1959** • CHARLIE BROWN PASSES OUT chocolate cigars as his sister is born in the panels of *Peanuts*. The precocious Sally ages faster than her castmates—she will begin kindergarten in August 1962, having barely turned three.

BROTHER FROM ANOTHER PANEL
In what newspaper comic strip would you find these siblings?

Easy
1. Billy, Dolly, Jeffy, PJ
2. Alexander, Cookie
3. Michael, Elizabeth, April
4. Peter, Paige, Jason
5. Honi, Hamlet

Harder
1. Arn, Karen, Valeta, Galan, Nathan
2. Zoe, Hammy, Wren
3. Huey, Riley
4. Chip, Dot, Ditto, Trixie
5. Hans, Fritz

Yeah, Good Luck
1. Clayton, Katy, Nick
2. Skeezix, Corky, Judy
3. Jughaid, Tater
4. Norman, Patrick, Penny
5. Chad, Jeremy

Bonus Question: Which set of "siblings" above is actually made up of first cousins?

• **1968** • DRIVERS IN ICELAND switch from driving on the left to driving on the right—the only casualty is one cyclist's broken leg. Austria, Czechoslovakia, Hungary, Portugal, and Sweden also switched in the twentieth century, leaving the British Isles the only place in Europe that still drives on the left.

BLOC PARTY
What unusual distinction is shared by these countries and no others?

1. Brazil, Colombia, Congo, Ecuador, Gabon, Indonesia, Kenya, São Tomé and Príncipe, Somalia, Uganda
2. Argentina, Australia, China, Nepal, Russia, Tanzania, the U.S.
3. Finland, Greece, Honduras, Israel, Micronesia, Somalia
4. Austria, Burma, Egypt, Ghana, Norway, Peru, South Korea, Sweden
5. Austria, Bosnia, Canada, France, Germany, Italy, Japan, Norway, Switzerland, the U.S.
6. Chad, Finland, Iran, Ireland, Oman, Spain
7. Afghanistan, Australia, Burma, Canada, French Polynesia, India, Iran, Nepal, New Zealand, Sri Lanka
8. Benin, Bolivia, Chile, Ivory Coast, Malaysia, Montenegro, Netherlands, Philippines, South Africa, Sri Lanka, Swaziland, Tanzania
9. Cyprus, Egypt, Lebanon, the Sudan, Syria, the U.K.
10. Argentina, Brazil, France, Italy, Germany, the U.K., Uruguay

Answers to the questions on this page can be found on page 219.

• **1935** • THE FIRST NATIONAL minimum wage—a whopping twenty-five cents an hour—is abolished by the Supreme Court, which finds FDR's National Industrial Recovery Act unconstitutional.

SPARE ANY CHANGE?
Answer these questions about small sums.

1. Whose trademark hat always had a $1.98 price tag hanging off one side?
2. What organization has never cashed the $3.76 check it got from the NFL after "winning" a 1985 antitrust lawsuit?

3. What short story begins, "$1.87. That was all. And sixty cents of it was in pennies"?
4. Whose life savings had dwindled down to $1.73 by the time he decided to shoot George Wallace in

1972?
5. On July 12, 1979, the White Sox let fans into a double-header for just 98 cents if they brought with them what item, to be blown up at second base between games?

• **1962** • THE FIRE DEPARTMENT of Centralia, Pennsylvania, starts a fire in the town's garbage dump. Unfortunately, the fire spreads to an abandoned coal mine and proves impossible to extinguish. Today the town is almost abandoned, and surveys predict that the underground fire will burn for another century.

I ME MINE

1. What animal was used in British coal mines until being phased out in 1986?
2. Bauxite ore is mined so it can be processed into what metal?

3. As fans of her 2004 comeback album might know, in what town did Loretta Lynn grow up a "Coal Miner's Daughter"?
4. What metal was found in

Nevada's famed Comstock Lode?
5. What John Sayles coal-mining movie was filmed in Thurmond, West Virginia, not in the title town?

• **1988** • THE TINY TOWN of Hay-on-Wye, on the Welsh-English border, celebrates its first annual literary festival. It's since grown into one of the world's largest bookfests—Bill Clinton called it a "Woodstock of the mind"—and turned Hay-on-Wye into a mecca for book lovers, now boasting forty-odd used bookstores for only 1,900 residents.

STACKED

1. What Arab political party is named for a bookstore that Zaki al-Arsuzi opened in Damascus, Syria, in the 1940s?
2. What British author wrote *Keep the Aspidistra Flying* about his years working as an assistant at a used bookshop in Hampstead?
3. In what city would you find Powell's City of Books, the largest independent bookstore in the United States?
4. Who ran Dartmouth, England's, successful Harbour Bookshop from

1951 to 1972 and spent his days avoiding Winnie-the-Pooh fans who came into the store?
5. What rock anthem includes the immortal lyric "Put me to work in the school bookstore / Check-out counter and I got bored"?
6. What historic San Francisco bookstore was also America's first all-paperback bookstore when it set up shop in 1953?
7. What famous couple—both Romantic authors—first met at William Godwin's London children's

bookshop in 1812?
8. Presto, Cadabra, or Kazam—what was the magical original name of the online bookstore that changed its name in 1995 to Amazon.com?
9. Who carried hundreds of imported books in his Philadelphia shop in the 1730s, the same decade in which he started America's first lending library?
10. What poet slammed unscrupulous bookseller Edmund Curll in his 1728 poem "The Dunciad"?

Answers to the questions on this page can be found on page 219.

MAY 28

• **1897** • CARPENTER AND SOMETIME cough syrup maker Pearle Wait tries selling a new product made of fruit syrup and gelatin. Dubbed "Jell-O" by his wife, the snack comes in four flavors: strawberry, raspberry, orange, and lemon. All sell poorly.

FRUIT COCKTAIL
What's traditionally the chief fruit ingredient in . . .

1. Tapenade	**3.** A rickey	**5.** Tarte tatin
2. Black forest cake	**4.** Guacamole	

• **1982** • MR. T PITIES his first fool, as that catchphrase debuts in the blockbuster sequel *Rocky III*.

THE III DEGREE
All these people have a big, fat, patrician "III" after their full names.

1. Who was the first black actor to play Shakespeare's Othello on film?
2. What onetime NBA Finals MVP was the last owner of the CBA before its 2001 bankruptcy?
3. Bono shared *Time* Man of the Year honors with what other man and his wife?
4. What former governor currently heads the Democratic National Committee?
5. What future radio star had a number one hit with his novelty number "Disco Duck"?
6. Who took Barry Goldwater's seat when the longtime senator retired in 1986?
7. What regular character did Larry David always voice on *Seinfeld*, even after he left the show?
8. What rapper's younger cousin Michael Francis raps under the stage name "Two Five"?
9. What actor took his name off his directorial debut, 2006's *Shortcut to Happiness*, which sat on the shelf for a record six years before being released?
10. Who won Pulitzers for his plays *A Delicate Balance*, *Seascape*, and *Three Tall Women*?

• **1998** • GERI HALLIWELL MISSES a Spice Girls concert in Oslo. At first the band claims that Ginger Spice is ill, but two days later, Halliwell announces that she has fallen out with the girls and left the band. Mourning preteen girls hold candlelight vigils worldwide.

SPICEWORLD

1. How many herbs and spices are in the Colonel's secret recipe, according to KFC ads?
2. Ninety percent of the world's true cinnamon comes from what island nation?
3. What's the traditional herb in pesto sauce?
4. Oregano, cloves, or nutmeg—what slightly hallucinogenic spice did Malcolm X use to get high while in prison?
5. What kind of flower does saffron come from?

Answers to the questions on this page can be found on page 220.

• **1660** • CHARLES II REENTERS London on his birthday, completing the English Restoration. The occasion was long celebrated in Britain as "Oak Apple Day," in memory of the oak tree that saved His Majesty's life by hiding him after the battle of Worcester.

RESTORED EDITIONS

In honor of the English Restoration, here are five other restorations.

1. What building was a dilapidated ruin in 1831 when a best-selling novel that year prompted architect Eugène Emmanuel Viollet-le-Duc to lead a restoration effort?
2. What is the primary ingredient in the silvery amalgam still used in dental restoration?
3. A four-hour restoration of what 1927 epic restored the reputation of forgotten silent film director Abel Gance shortly before his 1981 death?
4. What country's Meiji Restoration began in 1866?
5. What Leonardo da Vinci masterpiece, now restored, was so unrecognizable by 1652 that an arched doorway was cut right through the bottom of it?

• **1839** • HIRAM ULYSSES GRANT arrives at West Point, only to find he's been misregistered as "Ulysses Simpson Grant." Hiram, who didn't think his "H.U.G." initials would go over well in the military anyway, happily adopts the new name.

SHORT AND SWEET

Answer these questions about abbreviations, acronyms, and initialisms.

1. Other than poor Hiram Ulysses, who's the only U.S. president whose three initials spell a word?
2. What brand is known as PFK in French-speaking Quebec and Spanish-speaking Puerto Rico?
3. Whose children's books involve a mysterious secret organization known only as "V.F.D."?
4. Where did the abbreviation "INRI" traditionally appear?
5. Which of these agencies—the FCC, the FDIC, the FTC, and the ICC—is not a commission? What is it instead?
6. Citigroup jumped on the one-letter stock ticker abbreviation C after what company dropped it in a 1998 merger?
7. What's the only U.S. state whose two-letter postal code is two vowels?
8. What do these abbreviations have in common: ESPN, the AARP, DVD, AT&T, NASDAQ, and SAT?
9. Why has Sioux Falls Regional Airport in South Dakota been trying to change its three-letter airport designation for years?
10. What two things are "TO" used to represent in basketball?

• **1997** • AN EXCITABLE REBECCA SEALFON wins the National Spelling Bee by shrieking the word "euonym" (Webster's: "a good or appropriate name").

LET'S EUONYM FIGHT

Name—and spell!—the onetime National Spelling Bee–winning word that means . . .

1. The white of an egg
2. A Japanese aircraft loaded with explosives
3. The shorter arm of a cruciform church
4. A trapezoidal stringed instrument played with hammers
5. Before the Great Flood

Answers to the questions on this page can be found on page 220.

• **1946** • THE BRAVES' BAMA ROWELL hits a home run into the right field clock at Ebbets Field, sending up a shower of sparks and inspiring a young aspiring novelist in the stands, one Bernard Malamud, to write *The Natural*.

100% ALL NATURAL

1. What kind of natural disaster destroyed three of the Seven Wonders of the Ancient World?
2. What irrational number is the base of a natural logarithm?
3. What famous director asked that his name be removed from the screenplay credit to Oliver Stone's *Natural Born Killers*?
4. What Chicago natural history museum features Sue, the world's largest *Tyrannosaurus rex* skeleton?
5. What future game show host had a Top Forty hit with 1968's "Naturally Stoned"?
6. What cartoonist created the bearded guru named Mr. Natural?
7. What French obstetrician revolutionized natural childbirth with his 1956 book *Painless Childbirth*?
8. What state has adopted the new official nickname of "The Natural State"?
9. What gas is the main component in natural gas?
10. What philosopher argued for natural rights in his 1651 *Leviathan*?

• **1969** • FORMER CHILD STAR Natalie Wood, on a break between her two marriages to Robert Wagner, marries producer Richard Gregson.

MINOR FAME
What future celeb made a child-actor appearance as . . .

Easy
1. Kate in *Mermaids*
2. Velvet in *National Velvet*
3. Gertie in *E.T.*
4. Opie on *Andy Griffith*
5. Iris in *Taxi Driver*

Harder
1. Kyra in *The Sixth Sense*
2. Luke on *Growing Pains*
3. Huw in *How Green Was My Valley*
4. Lauren in *Heat*
5. Danny in *City Slickers*

Yeah, Good Luck
1. Joe in *Radio Days*
2. Derek on *Silver Spoons*
3. Molly in *Home Alone 3*
4. Mickey in *Our Gang*
5. Lauren in *A Little Romance*

• **1995** • NASA ENGINEERS COME BACK from Memorial Day weekend only to discover seventy small holes in the space shuttle's fuel tank insulation, delaying launch by more than a month. Northern flicker woodpeckers are determined to be the culprits, and today NASA employs woodpecker decoys and spotters full-time.

ORBITERS OF TASTE
Which NASA space shuttle shares its name with . . .

1. The most-subscribed-to cable network in America
2. The deepest point of the Mariana Trench
3. The ship that carried Captain Cook to Australia
4. The company that introduced the first LP record albums
5. The largest resort on Paradise Island, in the Bahamas

Answers to the questions on this page can be found on page 220.

• **1578** • KING HENRI III lays the first stone for Paris's Pont Neuf, the oldest of the city's many bridges over the Seine River. Ironically, Pont Neuf means "new bridge" in French.

WE BUILT THIS CITY

What's the major river running through these world cities?

Easy	Harder	Yeah, Good Luck
1. London	1. Boston	1. Seoul
2. Washington, D.C.	2. Baghdad	2. Dublin
3. Vienna	3. St. Petersburg	3. Amsterdam
4. Cairo	4. Cleveland	4. Melbourne
5. Rome	5. Florence	5. Buenos Aires

• **1929** • ATLANTIC CITY CONVENTION HALL is dedicated. The mammoth organ in Boardwalk Hall Auditorium boasts 33,114 pipes, making it the largest pipe organ ever constructed.

THE ORGAN TRAIL

In what organ of the human body would you find . . .

1. Nephrons, loops of Henle, Bowman's capsules
2. The islets of Langerhans, the duct of Wirsung
3. The medulla, the pons, the amygdala
4. The sclera, the fovea, the cornea
5. The seminiferous tubules, the Sertoli cells, the efferent ducts
6. The caudate lobe, the common bile duct, hepatocytes
7. The malleus, the Eustachian tube, the cochlea
8. The pleurae, the bronchi, the alveoli
9. The endometrium, the cervix
10. The pyloris, the esophageal sphincter, parietal cells

• **2000** • A STUMBLE BY UKULELE-STRUMMING senior citizen Sonja Christopher costs her tribe a box of waterproof matches, and so she becomes the first castaway ever "voted off the island" on the American *Survivor.*

IMMUNITY CHALLENGE

1. What letter of the alphabet identifies the "helper" and "killer" white blood cells that play a role in human immune response?
2. Whose wife, Adrienne, claimed in a 1988 DUI trial that she should enjoy diplomatic immunity, for having married the "Ambassador of Soul"?
3. What Colorado congresswoman called Ronald Reagan the "Teflon president," for his seeming immunity to criticism?
4. The word "vaccine" comes from the Latin for "cow," because of early observations that dairymaids seemed to be immune to what deadly disease?
5. In 1991, who received immunity from nineteen counts of murder after he agreed to testify against Mob boss John Gotti?

Answers to the questions on this page can be found on page 221.

May Answers

MAY 1	MAY 2	MAY 3

STAR-SPANGLED
1. Al Reynolds
2. Charles I
3. The second Death Star
4. "Lucky Star"
5. George Marshall
6. Brazil
7. Polaris (the North Star)
8. Echinoderms
9. The Minnesota North Stars
10. Vincent van Gogh ("Vincent")
11. Verona
12. Arsenio Hall
13. Don Meredith
14. A red giant
15. Kris Kristofferson (*A Star Is Born* costars)

LET'S DO THE TIME WARP AGAIN
1. Betamax
2. *Napoleon Dynamite*
3. The La Brea tar pits
4. Samuel Beckett
5. Mariano Rivera
6. Her wedding dress
7. Bhutan
8. A madeleine
9. Jaromir Jagr
10. The 1980s

POSING POSIES
1. D
2. A
3. E
4. C
5. B

WHAT A DRAG!
1. Achilles
2. *Mrs. Doubtfire*'s
3. Monty Python
4. Portia (*The Merchant of Venice*)
5. The Saint Valentine's Day Massacre
6. George Sand
7. Eddie Izzard
8. Gwyneth Paltrow (*Shakespeare in Love*)
9. Joan of Arc's
10. Hansel

PUB QUIZ
1. Stout
2. Its exterior was used for the bar in *Cheers*
3. Fifty
4. Ploughman's
5. Bali

REVOLUTION 9
1. Hugo Chávez
2. William and Mary
3. Dioxin
4. Czechoslovakia
5. The Time
6. October
7. *Dance Dance Revolution*
8. Marian Anderson
9. The months of the year

A FIT OF PEAK
1. Montenegro
2. West Virginia (The Mountain State) and Vermont (The Green Mountain State)
3. Whoville (*How the Grinch Stole Christmas*)
4. Mount McKinley (or Denali)
5. New Zealand
6. Mountain Dew
7. The highest unclimbed mountain in the world
8. Space Mountain, Splash Mountain, Big Thunder Mountain Railroad
9. Hong Kong
10. Diana Ross
11. Mars
12. The Atlas Mountains
13. Mount Washington
14. Jake Gyllenhaal (Maggie) and Randy Quaid (Dennis)
15. The Andes

May Answers

MAY 4	MAY 5	MAY 6

SQUARE DANCE
1. Pop-Tarts
2. *Xanadu*
3. Green
4. Sarah Jessica Parker
5. Italy (Switzerland and the Vatican)
6. A geneticist
7. Freemasonry
8. The Phantom Zone
9. Prague's
10. Theodore Roosevelt

CODE TALKERS
1. Louisiana's
2. "What hath God wrought?"
3. The Babylonians
4. The Louvre Museum
5. Will Hays

CATCH A WAVE
1. Tsunami
2. Raytheon
3. François Truffaut
4. Holland-Dozier-Holland
5. His ten toes

HISPANIC ROOM
1. California
2. Grapes
3. Cisneros
4. Diego Rivera and Frida Kahlo
5. ~~Venezuela~~ Colombia
6. David Farragut
7. "Yo quiero *Taco Bell*"
8. Roberto Clemente
9. Santana
10. José Castro (for whom the Castro district was named)

SAY HEY
1. "Rock and Roll (Part Two)"
2. *The Larry Sanders Show's*
3. Kowalski
4. Jim Varney's
5. "Hey Bulldog"

THE BRAVE AND THE BOLD
1. The Justice League of America
2. The X-Men
3. The Avengers
4. The Teen Titans
5. The Legion of Super-Heroes

LEFTOVERS
1. The Big Bang
2. The Professor and Mary Ann
3. Vegemite
4. Jack (Warden and Klugman)
5. The Mall of America

ATHLETIC SUPPORTERS
1. Bill Russell
2. Pete Rose
3. Arthur Ashe
4. Ingemar Johansson
5. Billie Jean King
6. Pete Rozelle
7. Lance Armstrong
8. Jackie Stewart
9. Bonnie Blair
10. Bobby Orr

THEM'S FIGHTIN' WORDS
Easy
1. Trojan War
2. U.S. Civil War
3. World War II
4. Korean War
Harder
1. World War I
2. Spanish Civil War
3. Napoleonic Wars
4. French and Indian War (Seven Years' War)
Yeah, Good Luck
1. Thirty Years' War
2. Vietnam War
3. Wars of the Roses
4. American Revolution

MAY 7

AN ARROW ESCAPE
1. The Boy Scouts of America
2. Steve Martin
3. Bolts
4. FedEx
5. The nock
6. Zenith
7. Ain't It Cool News
8. Saint Sebastian
9. The Kansas City Chiefs
10. Scorpio

A BARREL OF MONKEYS
1. Curious George
2. The Anaheim Angels'
3. Gibraltar
4. The Scarecrow
5. Peeing on Johnny Carson
6. Gary Hart and Donna Rice
7. The mandrill
8. It grants three wishes
9. The capuchin
10. Typewriters

MAY 8

UNLEASHED
1. Dogs barking
2. Magilla Gorilla
3. The budgerigar
4. The San Diego Padres
5. The guppy
6. Retriever (Labrador and golden)
7. Betty Currie
8. Catnip
9. A snorkasaurus
10. Pet Rocks
11. *Best in Show*
12. Paris
13. Tinkerbell
14. Vietnam
15. Heterochromia—two different-colored eyes

MEN OF LETTERS
1. A. A. Milne
2. B. B. King
3. L. L. Bean
4. E. E. Cummings
5. J. J. Evans (*Good Times*)

MAY 9

RECTANGLE TANGLE
1. *A Midsummer Night's Dream*
2. A trapezoid
3. Saskatchewan
4. A Möbius strip
5. Mark Rothko's

STAGE MOTHERS
Easy
1. Judy Garland
2. Goldie Hawn
3. Debbie Reynolds
4. Mary Martin
5. Janet Leigh
Harder
1. Blythe Danner
2. Anne Meara
3. Tippi Hedren
4. Patty Duke
5. Talia Shire
Yeah, Good Luck
1. Rosemary Clooney
2. Vanessa Redgrave
3. Maureen O'Sullivan
4. Peggy Lipton
5. Colleen Dewhurst

SUPER SECRETS
Easy
1. Spider-Man
2. Superman
3. The Hulk
4. Daredevil
5. Captain Marvel

Harder
1. Cyclops
2. Mr. Fantastic
3. Doctor Strange
4. The Martian Manhunter
5. Invisible Girl/Woman
Yeah, Good Luck
1. Angel (or Archangel)
2. Nova
3. Black Canary
4. Captain Britain
5. The Flash (or Kid Flash)

May Answers

MAY 10

(SPRING)FIELD GUIDE

FIRST NAMES
Easy
1. Abraham
2. (W.) Seymour (really Armin)
3. C(harles) Montgomery
4. Waylon
Harder
1. Clancy
2. Joe
3. Timothy
4. Edna
Yeah, Good Luck
1. John
2. Elizabeth
3. Julius
4. Gary

LAST NAMES
Easy
1. Gumbel
2. Krustofski
3. Riviera
4. Jones
Harder
1. Nahasapeemapetilon
2. McCallister
3. Muntz
4. Prince
Yeah, Good Luck
1. Leonard and Carlson
2. Mann
3. Spuckler
4. D'Amico

FRONT OFFICE SPACE
Easy
1. New York Yankees
2. Pittsburgh Penguins
3. Dallas Mavericks
4. Oakland Raiders
5. Dallas Cowboys
Harder
1. Pittsburgh Steelers
2. Phoenix Coyotes
3. Los Angeles Lakers
4. Seattle Seahawks and Portland Trail Blazers
5. Milwaukee Bucks

Yeah, Good Luck
1. Denver Broncos
2. Detroit Red Wings and Detroit Tigers
3. Charlotte Bobcats
4. New York Giants
5. Baltimore Orioles

MAY 11

ALL-TIME HYBRID
Easy
1. Woman and fish
2. Human and horse
3. Human and goat
4. Human and bull
Harder
1. Woman and lion
2. Woman and bird
3. Eagle and lion
4. Rooster and serpent
Yeah, Good Luck
1. Horse and fish
2. Woman and serpent
3. Lion, goat, and serpent
4. Human, lion, and dragon or scorpion

AL FRESCO
1. Tintoretto
2. A seashell
3. The Sistine Chapel
4. His navel
5. The *Pietá*

TH-TH-TH-THAT'S ALL, FOLKS!
1. The Dodo (from "Do-Do-Dodgson")
2. "You Ain't Seen Nothing Yet"
3. Michael Palin (who stuttered in *A Fish Called Wanda*)
4. John Glenn
5. Mystikal

MAY 12

CHRONIC ROOMMATE-ISM
1. David Lynch
2. Neil Young
3. Tommy Lee Jones and Al Gore
4. Marlon Brando
5. Tom Izzo
6. Robin Williams
7. James Buchanan
8. Ving Rhames
9. Joe Montana
10. Gene Hackman and Dustin Hoffman

HOSTS WITH THE MOST
1. The Detroit Lions
2. Peter Marshall
3. *Ten Little Indians* or *And Then There Were None*
4. The crocodile (whose teeth it picks)
5. The March Hare
6. Wheat flour and water
7. A frankfurter (Frank N. Furter)
8. Athens 2004 (since Greece always enters *first*)
9. Alec Baldwin
10. Yalta

MAY 13	MAY 14	MAY 15

THERE'S SOMETHING ABOUT MARY
1. Larry Hagman (Mary Martin's son)
2. Paul McCartney
3. James I (the "King James Version")
4. Robert Lincoln
5. Richard Leakey

I'VE GOTTA SECRETE
1. Plasma
2. *Q*Bert*
3. Bilirubin
4. Lazarus
5. Colostrum
6. *Dr. Strangelove or: How I Learned to Stop Worrying and Love the Bomb*
7. Australia
8. Bile (yellow bile and black bile)
9. Bertie Bott's Every Flavor Beans
10. Phosphorous

SONGS IN THE KEY OF LIFE
Easy
1. Debby Boone
2. Bill Medley and Jennifer Warnes
3. The Beatles
Harder
1. K-Ci and JoJo
2. Queen
3. Indeep
Yeah, Good Luck
1. Social Distortion
2. The Animals
3. Simple Plan

MOM'S THE WORD
1. Stacy's
2. Estelle Getty
3. Cindy Sheehan's
4. *Futurama*
5. Jennifer Coolidge

A SORT OF HOMECOMING
1. The mayor of New York
2. An eagle (or other large raptor)
3. Baba Yaga
4. Charles Foster Kane (*Citizen Kane*)
5. SpongeBob SquarePants
6. Bees
7. Eloise
8. Otters
9. Navajos
10. *The Jeffersons*

SWITCHING CHANNELS
Easy
1. Catwoman
2. Darrin Stephens
3. Jan Brady
4. Lois Lane
5. John-Boy Walton
Harder
1. "Miss Ellie" Ewing
2. Becky Conner (*Roseanne*)
3. Lionel Jefferson
4. Doctor Who
5. Morty Seinfeld
Yeah, Good Luck
1. Aunt Vivian Banks (*Fresh Prince*)
2. Fallon Carrington Colby (*Dynasty*)
3. Maggie McKinney (*Diff'rent Strokes*)
4. Marilyn Munster
5. Laurie Forman (*That '70s Show*)

MORTAR, SHE WROTE
1. Heroin
2. Adobe
3. His girlfriend's abortion
4. Lego
5. Maggie the Cat (*Cat on a Hot Tin Roof*)
6. Its acronym is "Boycott Petco," the park's sponsor
7. Newark, New Jersey
8. The Commodores ("Brick House")
9. *Northern Exposure*
10. The Kremlin

I'M A MAGIC MAN
1. Don Herbert
2. John Wooden
3. Elton John
4. David Duke
5. Ozzie Smith
6. Merlin
7. Phylicia Ayers-Allen (now Rashad)
8. A squib
9. New Jersey
10. Ian McKellen (*The Fellowship of the Ring*)

MAY 16

ROOTS ROCK
1. An endodontist
2. Toby
3. The cassava's
4. −10
5. The love of money
6. *Mo' Better Blues*
7. Idaho and Montana
8. Ginseng
9. AstroTurf
10. Canada

A MATTER OF A PINION
1. Erica Jong's (*Fear of Flying*)
2. The Toronto Maple Leafs
3. Beavis and Butt-Head's
4. Nantucket
5. Peter Falk
6. Ailerons
7. "Blackbird"
8. Albatross
9. On TV's *The West Wing*
10. Nike

MAY 17

HAM-DUNK
Easy
1. Kareem Abdul-Jabbar
2. The Rock
3. Brett Favre
4. O. J. Simpson
5. Jim Brown
Harder
1. Carl Weathers
2. Vinnie Jones
3. Alex Karras
4. Shaquille O'Neal
5. Cam Neely
Yeah, Good Luck
1. Alex English
2. Fred Williamson
3. Merlin Olsen
4. Chuck Connors
5. Ray Allen

FOUR BETTER OR WORSE
Easy
1. John
2. The Thing
3. Percussion
4. Raphael
5. Water
Harder
1. Anni-Frid (ABBA)
2. Plasma
3. Pennsylvania (Monopoly railroads)
4. Cut
5. Cups (tarot suits)
Yeah, Good Luck
1. From fear (FDR's Four Freedoms)
2. Euphrates (Garden of Eden rivers)
3. Cytosine (DNA bases)
4. "Little Gidding" (T. S. Eliot's *Four Quartets*)
5. Dwight White (the "Steel Curtain")

STREET SMARTS
1. Wall Street
2. Sunset Strip
3. Penny Lane
4. 8 Mile Road
5. Canal Street ("**Tri**angle **Be**low **Cana**l")
6. The Appian Way
7. Drury Lane
8. Avenue of the Americas
9. The Las Vegas Strip
10. Lombard Street (in San Francisco)

MAY 18

DRAFTY IN HERE
Easy
1. Pittsburgh Steelers
2. Seattle Mariners
3. Pittsburgh Penguins
4. Indianapolis Colts
5. Cleveland Cavaliers

Harder
1. Baltimore Colts
2. Atlanta Braves
3. New York Islanders
4. Milwaukee Bucks
5. Charlotte Hornets
Yeah, Good Luck
1. Orlando Magic
2. Baltimore Orioles
3. Atlanta Falcons
4. San Diego Padres
5. Detroit Red Wings

THE DAWN PATROL
1. Claude Monet
2. Vienna
3. Grenadine
4. The Florida Panthers
5. July (*not* June, surprisingly)

THE FIVE *W*S (AND ONE *H*)
1. The Grinch's
2. Georgetown ("Hoya")
3. Wendy's
4. Barry Sanders
5. Frankie Avalon
6. *The Grapes of Wrath* ("Battle Hymn of the Republic")

MAY 19

SPOT CHECK
1. Roy Lichtenstein
2. Two and one, respectively
3. The 101 Dalmatians
4. Your blind spot
5. Her house is on fire and her children are gone
6. Four
7. SOS
8. Currants
9. Fiji
10. Sunspots
11. Brian Hyland
12. Georges Seurat's (*Sunday Afternoon on the Island of La Grande Jatte*)
13. Earth, as seen from space
14. Six
15. Ellipsis

ACA-DUMMY-A
1. I
2. J
3. A
4. B
5. G
6. D
7. E
8. F
9. H
10. C

MAY 20

STAR SEARCH
1. Australia
2. North Korea
3. The Marshall Islands
4. Israel
5. Ethiopia
6. Zimbabwe

SUBSCRIPTION APTITUDE TEST
1. Martha Stewart
2. *Mode*
3. *Cracked*
4. Canada
5. Pet
6. Mia Farrow (first cover girl)
7. "For Him"
8. *Cosmo Girl*
9. *Rolling Stone*
10. *Inc.*

BIG-CITY DINING
1. The Jerusalem artichoke
2. Chicken Kiev
3. Habanero (named for Havana)
4. Lima beans
5. Vienna

MAY 21

CAR-PE DIEM
1. I
2. H
3. C
4. J
5. A
6. D
7. B
8. G
9. F
10. E

BUS TA MOVE
1. 50 mph
2. Ralph Kramden
3. Montgomery, Alabama
4. The Maddencruiser
5. The Merry Pranksters

THE AMEND CORNER
Easy
1. Fifth
2. First
3. Fourth
4. Second
Harder
1. Sixteenth
2. Eighteenth
3. Thirteenth
4. Nineteenth
Yeah, Good Luck
1. Twenty-fourth
2. Twenty-third
3. Seventeenth
4. Twenty-fifth

MAY 22

PATENTLY RIDICULOUS
1. L
2. O
3. N
4. B
5. K
6. G
7. E
8. F
9. C
10. M
11. I
12. D
13. H
14. A
15. J

RENT CONTROL
1. The Watergate (Woods was Nixon's secretary)
2. Apartment 3-G
3. *Grand Hotel* and *The Godfather*
4. Cockroaches
5. Mama Cass and Keith Moon
6. Purple
7. *La Bohème*
8. Waylon Jennings
9. *Rosemary's Baby*
10. On *A Streetcar Named Desire*

MAY 23

CARRYING A TOON
Easy
1. Tim Allen
2. Julie Kavner
3. Mel Blanc
4. Robin Williams
5. Mike Myers
Harder
1. Seth MacFarlane
2. Vin Diesel
3. Mike Judge
4. Matthew Broderick
5. Jim Backus

Yeah, Good Luck
1. Don Adams
2. Tom Kenny
3. Lorenzo Music
4. Sterling Holloway
5. Daws Butler

IRON HORSES
1. The Harlem Globetrotters
2. John Grisham
3. The Los Angeles Dodgers (Don Drysdale and Orel Hershiser)
4. "One Sweet Day"
5. George
6. Heinz (57 games)
7. *Lost in Space*
8. Allen Ginsberg
9. Raise interest rates
10. The America's Cup
11. *All in the Family*
12. Jimmy Connors
13. *The Simpsons*
14. Brett Favre
15. Robert Byrd

MAY 24

INDIGENOUS INDIGNATION
1. Sitting Bull's
2. Oklahoma
3. Hiawatha (Ayonwentah)
4. "Dead"
5. Massasoit

MUST-SEES
Easy
1. Audrey Hepburn
2. Jamie Foxx
3. Al Pacino
4. Ben Affleck
5. Patty Duke
Harder
1. Emily Watson
2. Roger Daltrey
3. Uma Thurman
4. Bryce Dallas Howard
5. Edward Albert

Yeah, Good Luck
1. David Strathairn
2. Virginia Cherrill
3. Elizabeth Hartman
4. Wallace Shawn (and, later, Beau Bridges)
5. John Malkovich

MONDEGREEN DAY
1. "There's a bad moon on the rise" ("Bad Moon Rising," Creedence Clearwater Revival)
2. "We split up on a dark, sad night" ("Tangled Up in Blue," Bob Dylan)
3. "The girl with kaleidoscope eyes" ("Lucy in the Sky with Diamonds," the Beatles)
4. "Last night I dreamt of San Pedro" ("La Isla Bonita," Madonna)
5. "Revved up like a deuce" ("Blinded by the Light," Manfred Mann's Earth Band)
6. "Hold me closer, tiny dancer" ("Tiny Dancer," Elton John)
7. "Here we are now, entertain us" ("Smells Like Teen Spirit," Nirvana)
8. "Round yon virgin mother and child" ("Silent Night")
9. "You and me endlessly" ("Groovin'," the Rascals)
10. "Rock the Casbah" ("Rock the Casbah," the Clash)

MAY 25

SWITCHING TEAMS
1. James Jeffords
2. George
3. Seattle (the Brewers and the Seahawks)
4. Italy
5. The earth's magnetic field

SPACE RACE
1. Houston
2. Yuri Gagarin
3. J. G. (Jake Garn and John Glenn)
4. The *Discovery*
5. Peace
6. Gordon Cooper
7. Laika
8. Deke Slayton
9. Left
10. Pieces of Skylab fell there

SAME OLD SONG
Easy
1. *CSI*
2. *The Drew Carey Show*
3. *Married . . . with Children*
4. *Cops*
5. *The Wonder Years*
Harder
1. *Charmed*
2. *The Sopranos*
3. *China Beach*
4. *Smallville*
5. *Las Vegas*
Yeah, Good Luck
1. *Get a Life*
2. *Action*
3. *Roswell*
4. *Freaks and Geeks*
5. *The Benny Hill Show*

MAY 26

KEEPING UP WITH THE JONESES
1. Henry
2. Ravi Shankar
3. Catherine the Great
4. "Too Tall"
5. The Cannonball Special

BROTHER FROM ANOTHER PANEL
Easy
1. *The Family Circus*
2. *Blondie*
3. *For Better or For Worse*
4. *FoxTrot*
5. *Hagar the Horrible*
Harder
1. *Prince Valiant*
2. *Baby Blues*
3. *The Boondocks*
4. *Hi and Lois*
5. *The Katzenjammer Kids*
Yeah, Good Luck
1. *Adam*
2. *Gasoline Alley*
3. *Barney Google and Snuffy Smith*
4. *Drabble*
5. *Zits*
Bonus Question: Tater and Jughaid are cousins, not brothers.

BLOC PARTY
1. The Equator passes through them
2. They're home to the highest peaks on their respective continents
3. Their flags are only blue and white
4. Home countries of U.N. secretaries-general
5. They've hosted Winter Olympics
6. They form a common word if you remove their first letter

7. All have unusual time zones (offset by 15, 30, or 45 minutes, not an even number of hours)
8. They have more than one capital city
9. Their currency is the pound
10. They've won World Cups

MAY 27

SPARE ANY CHANGE?
1. Minnie Pearl's
2. The USFL
3. "The Gift of the Magi"
4. Arthur Bremer
5. A disco record (the infamous "Disco Demolition Night")

I ME MINE
1. Canaries
2. Aluminum
3. Van Lear, Kentucky (*Van Lear Rose*)
4. Silver
5. *Matewan*

STACKED
1. The Ba'ath Party
2. George Orwell
3. Portland, Oregon
4. Christopher Robin Milne
5. "Smokin' in the Boys' Room"
6. City Lights Bookstore
7. Percy and Mary Shelley
8. Cadabra.com
9. Benjamin Franklin
10. Alexander Pope

May Answers

MAY 28

FRUIT COCKTAIL
1. Olives
2. Cherries
3. Limes
4. Avocadoes
5. Apples

THE III DEGREE
1. Laurence Fishburne III
2. Isiah Thomas III
3. William Gates III
4. Howard Dean III
5. Rick Dees III
6. John McCain III
7. George Steinbrenner III
8. 50 Cent (Curtis Johnson III)
9. Alec Baldwin III
10. Edward Albee III

SPICEWORLD
1. Eleven
2. Sri Lanka
3. Basil
4. Nutmeg
5. A crocus

MAY 29

RESTORED EDITIONS
1. Notre Dame de Paris
2. Mercury
3. *Napoleon*
4. Japan
5. *The Last Supper*

SHORT AND SWEET
1. James A. Garfield
2. KFC
3. Lemony Snicket's
4. On Christ's crucifix
5. The FDIC is a "corporation"
6. Chrysler
7. Iowa (IA)
8. They now officially stand for nothing
9. I₅code is "SUX"
10. Turnover and time out

LET'S EUONYM FIGHT
1. Albumen
2. Kamikaze
3. Transept
4. Dulcimer
5. Antediluvian

MAY 30

100% ALL NATURAL
1. Earthquakes
2. *e*
3. Quentin Tarantino
4. The Field Museum
5. Chuck Woolery
6. R. Crumb
7. Dr. Fernand Lamaze
8. Arkansas
9. Methane
10. Thomas Hobbes

MINOR FAME
Easy
1. Christina Ricci
2. Elizabeth Taylor
3. Drew Barrymore
4. Ron Howard
5. Jodie Foster
Harder
1. Mischa Barton
2. Leonardo DiCaprio
3. Roddy McDowall
4. Natalie Portman
5. Jake Gyllenhaal
Yeah, Good Luck
1. Seth Green
2. Jason Bateman
3. Scarlett Johansson
4. Robert Blake
5. Diane Lane

ORBITERS OF TASTE
1. *Discovery*
2. *Challenger*
3. *Endeavour*
4. *Columbia*
5. *Atlantis*

MAY 31

WE BUILT THIS CITY
Easy
1. Thames
2. Potomac
3. Danube
4. Nile
5. Tiber
Harder
1. Charles
2. Tigris
3. Neva
4. Cuyahoga
5. Arno

Yeah, Good Luck
1. Han
2. Liffey
3. Amstel
4. Yarra
5. Río de la Plata

THE ORGAN TRAIL
1. The kidneys
2. The pancreas
3. The brain
4. The eye
5. The testes

6. The liver
7. The ear
8. The lungs
9. The uterus
10. The stomach

IMMUNITY CHALLENGE
1. T
2. James Brown's
3. Pat Schroeder
4. Smallpox
5. Sammy "the Bull" Gravano

JUNE 1

• **1896** • AMERICAN MOTORCYCLE RACING is born when 73-year-old Sylvester Roper brings a steam-powered two-wheeler he has invented to a Boston bicycle race. The cyclists jeer the old man, until they discover his machine can run circles around them. Tragically, Roper then tries to set some speed records and is killed in the resulting crash.

SEASON CYCLE

1. What 1971 novel arose from the author's *Sports Illustrated* assignment to cover the Mint 400 desert motocross?
2. What make of motorcycle, once America's largest, did New Zealander Burt Munro use to set land-speed records, in life as in

the Anthony Hopkins film?
3. What off-road endurance race is named after the African capital where it usually ends?
4. The first Harley-Davidson appeared at a 1904 race in what city, still home to Harley headquarters?

5. The Grand Prix in what city, the first European colony in Asia, is the only street-circuit road race in which both car and motorcycle events are held?

• **2001** • FAUX-METAL BAND Spinal Tap begins its "Back from the Dead" tour at Hollywood's Greek Theater. Some fans won't catch on until the 2003 release of *A Mighty Wind* that Tap's opening act, a clean-cut trio called the Folksmen, is in fact composed of Christopher Guest, Michael McKean, and Harry Shearer—the same musicians who play Spinal Tap, only in different wigs.

COME TOGETHER
What do these sets of bands have in common?

1. The Bee Gees, the Breeders, Nelson, the Proclaimers
2. Alphaville, Bad Company, Fine Young Cannibals, 10,000 Maniacs
3. a-ha, Duran Duran, Garbage, Paul McCartney and Wings
4. Badfinger, the Band, Joy Division, Nirvana
5. Blind Faith, Cream, Derek and the Dominoes, the Yardbirds
6. The Carpenters, Gary Lewis and the Playboys, Genesis, Rare

Earth
7. Belle and Sebastian, Franz Ferdinand, Simple Minds, Travis
8. Bad Company, Iron Maiden, Kool and the Gang, New Kids on the Block, Train
9. The Charlatans, Dinosaur Jr., Green Jelly, Suede
10. Air Supply, Steely Dan, T-Rex, the White Stripes
11. The Byrds, Destiny's Child, 'N Sync, the Ohio Express

12. Death Cab for Cutie, Judas Priest, Radiohead, Shakespear's Sister
13. Five for Fighting, the Flaming Lips, the Kinks, R.E.M.
14. Frankie Goes to Hollywood, It's a Beautiful Day, They Might Be Giants, Yo La Tengo
15. INXS, Jethro Tull, Magnetic Fields, My Morning Jacket

Answers to the questions on this page can be found on page 255.

JUNE 2

• **1763** • Ojibway and Sauk Indians take Michigan's Fort Michilimackinac in inventive fashion—they stage a game of lacrosse just outside the gates of the fort, and when the ball "accidentally" flies over the wall, they ambush the troops inside.

ALL YOUR BASE ARE BELONG TO US
In what U.S. states would you find these historic forts?

Easy	Harder	Yeah, Good Luck
1. Sumter	1. Ticonderoga	1. Point
2. Knox	2. Hood	2. Sill
3. Leavenworth	3. Dix	3. Donelson
4. Wayne	4. Bragg	4. Shafter
5. McHenry	5. Benning	5. Eustis

• **1989** • Rolling Stones bassist Bill Wyman marries the nineteen-year-old Mandy Smith, whom he's been dating since she was thirteen. In 1993, Wyman's son Stephen will be engaged to Mandy's *mother*, Patsy, nearly making Wyman his own ex-wife's step-grandfather.

ALL YOUR BASS ARE BELONG TO US
Name these bands from their bassists.

Easy	Harder	Yeah, Good Luck
1. Flea	1. Stefan Lessard	1. Dave "Phoenix" Farrell
2. John Paul Jones	2. Andy Rourke	2. Cait O'Riordan
3. Sting	3. Geddy Lee	3. Hub
4. John Entwistle	4. Les Claypool	4. Eric Judy
5. Krist Novoselic	5. Peter Cetera	5. Pete Quaife

• **1999** • The Bhutan Broadcasting Service begins transmitting, bringing television to the world's last TV-free country.

WHAT'S ON FIRST?
Answer these questions about non-Bhutanese TV firsts.

1. What puppet show aired the first U.S. network television broadcast using today's color TV system?
2. In 1972, who became the first TV title character to get an abortion?
3. What was the first cable series to win an Emmy for Best Drama?
4. What William Boyd character headlined TV's first western?
5. What was Fox's first series to win a TV season's Nielsen ratings?

Answers to the questions on this page can be found on page 255.

• **1974** • GOLDA MEIR RESIGNS as prime minister of Israel. She was only the world's third elected female head of state, after Sri Lanka's Sirimavo Bandaranaike and India's Indira Gandhi.

WHO'S ON THIRD?

A bronze medal for every one of these third-place questions you can answer.

1. Danville, Virginia, was the third and last city to have what distinction?

2. What center was both the third Milwaukee Buck and the third Detroit Piston to make the Basketball Hall of Fame?

3. After Elvis and the Beatles, who became the third artist to replace themselves at number one, with "I'll Make Love to You" and "On Bended Knee"?

4. What passes the U.S. to become the world's third largest country in area, if you count its disputed territory?

5. Who was the third African American to make the cover of *Vogue* and the third to win a Best Supporting Actress Oscar?

6. In what city is the al-Aqsa Mosque, Islam's third holiest site, located?

7. In 2003, who became the third

Englishman ever to sign with Spain's Real Madrid?

8. Tim Drake is the third and current person to serve as what famous sidekick?

9. What city's Bank of America Plaza is America's tallest building outside of New York and Chicago?

10. What current head of state is only the third woman ever to serve on the G8?

• **1975** • BOB FOSSE'S *CHICAGO* opens on Broadway, with future *Law & Order* star Jerry Orbach in the part later played onscreen by Richard Gere.

(AIN'T GONNA PLAY) SUNG CITY

What Broadway musicals featured these municipal songs?

Easy	*Harder*	*Yeah, Good Luck*
1. "New York, New York"	**1.** "Manchester England"	**1.** "Salzburg"
2. "Anatevka"	**2.** "Santa Fe"	**2.** "Rumson"
3. "Kansas City"	**3.** "Hooverville"	**3.** "Solla Sollew"
4. "Buenos Aires"	**4.** "Gary, Indiana"	**4.** "Chicago"

• **2003** • THE AMERICAN FILM INSTITUTE chooses the fifty greatest heroes and the fifty greatest villains in movie history. Arnold Schwarzenegger hosts the broadcast, since his "Terminator" protagonist is the only character on both lists.

SIN-EMATIC

In what movie did these top villains, according to the AFI, appear?

Easy	*Harder*	*Yeah, Good Luck*
1. HAL 9000	**1.** Amon Goeth	**1.** Dr. Szell
2. Norman Bates	**2.** Annie Wilkes	**2.** Harry Powell
3. Joan Crawford	**3.** Noah Cross	**3.** Hans Gruber
4. Verbal Kint	**4.** Mrs. Danvers	**4.** Alonzo Harris
5. Travis Bickle	**5.** Henry F. Potter	**5.** Regina Giddens

Answers to the questions on this page can be found on pages 255–256.

JUNE 4

• **278 B.C.** • ACCORDING TO LEGEND, Chinese poet Qu Yuan, banished by his king, writes a very sad poem about political corruption and then kills himself by wading into the Miluo River holding a heavy rock. His neighbors try unsuccessfully to rescue him in fishing boats, which is said to be the origin of the modern Chinese "Dragon Boat Festival."

HERE BE DRAGONS

1. What was the name of Puff the Magic Dragon's homeland?

2. What future star's neck is broken by Bruce Lee in the cave fight in *Enter the Dragon*?

3. What is Gary Gygax's claim to fame?

4. What southern general, the hero of Shiloh and Murfreesboro, went on to become the first Grand Dragon of the Ku Klux Klan?

5. What nation is home to the Komodo dragon?

6. What hero of Wagner's *Ring* opera cycle slays the dragon Fafner?

7. What city's Dragons lost the World League of American Football's very first World Bowl?

8. Where did this dragon appear?

9. What part of Britain has Cadwalader's red dragon on its flag?

10. What kind of tea takes its name from the Chinese for "black dragon"?

• **1944** • INTELLIGENCE AGENTS SHOW UP at the Surrey home of crossword constructor Leonard Dawe, wondering why the top secret D-Day code words UTAH, OMAHA, OVERLORD, and NEPTUNE had all appeared in his *Telegraph* crosswords the previous month. A confused Dawe insists that the whole thing was merely a coincidence, and the agents "decided not to shoot us after all," as he will later say.

BONDS . . . COMMON BONDS
What are these sets of four words all types of?

1. Chinook, mistral, simoom, sirocco

2. C, Java, Lisp, Python

3. Braeburn, Cameo, Fuji, Gala

4. Bezique, Bourré, rumino, slapjack

5. Flemish, honda, Klemheist, sheepshank

6. Buccinator, sartorius, soleus, trapezius

7. Arial, Garamond, Palatino, Verdana

8. Akita, Corgi, Samoyed, Viszla

9. Bouzouki, psaltery, rebec, shamisen

10. Charlotte, choctaw, lutz, twizzle

11. Farfalle, gigli, mafaldine, orzo

12. Bongo, duiker, kudu, lechwe

13. Accio, Alohomora, Crucio, Expelliarmus

14. Breve, crotchet, minim, quaver

15. Fourchée, Lorraine, Maltese, Moline

16. Gaff, gennaker, lateen, Marconi

17. Bilbo, claymore, katana, spadroon

18. Baht, dirham, forint, real

19. Baldachin, percale, tricotine, tulle

20. Do-si-dos, Samoas, Tagalongs, Trefoils

Answers to the questions on this page can be found on page 256.

• 1783 • THE MONTGOLFIER BROTHERS first demonstrate their *globe aérostatique,* which they successfully fly a mile up in the air. It's the first hot-air balloon.

THE NAME OF THE BRO'S
Show a little brotherly love for these famous brothers.

1. Which was the oldest Marx brother?

2. What was the last name of the seven Italian brothers whose company, in 1955, found a new household use for the agricultural pumps it was producing?

3. What star small forward is the father of NBA brothers Scooter, Drew, Jon, and Brent?

4. Where did Susie fall asleep in the Everly Brothers song "Wake Up Little Susie"?

5. Which two disciples of Jesus were called the *Boanerges,* or "Sons of Thunder"?

6. In what city was the Wright brothers' bicycle shop?

7. What's the day job of the Mario Brothers of video-game fame?

8. What youngest brother of the music world was a former host of *Solid Gold*?

9. Whose girlfriends are named Callie Shaw and Iola Morton?

10. What three brothers have more home runs than any other trio of brothers in baseball history?

• 1947 • IN A HARVARD GRADUATION ADDRESS, Secretary of State George Marshall offers American aid to rebuild Europe, a proposal that comes to be called the Marshall Plan.

ALL ACCORDING TO PLAN
What famous plans are outlined here?

1. • Create collective farms called *kolkhoz*
• Set up Machine Tractor Stations
• Stimulate heavy industry
• Bring about massive famine

2. • Arrive on Earth in flying saucers
• Stimulate the pituitary and pineal glands of the recently deceased
• Create zombie army
• Raise hell

3. • Disregard neutrality of the Low Countries
• Sweep rapidly through northern France, bypass Paris
• Force French army to surrender or flee into Switzerland
• Next up: Russia!

4. • Find $4.4 million in crashed plane
• Suffocate snoopy local barber on snowmobile
• Shoot hunting buddies

• Burn money

5. • Blockade southern ports to stop cotton exports
• Prevent importation of war supplies
• Sail gunboats down the Mississippi
• Divide the Confederacy

Answers to the questions on this page can be found on page 256.

JUNE 6

• **1916** • THOMAS DIXON TRIES to cash in on the success of 1915's *The Birth of a Nation*, based on his Klan-glorifying novel *The Clansman,* by producing a follow-up called *The Fall of a Nation*. Though the film is lost today, it's considered the first sequel in movie history.

ON-SCREEN SEX(TETS)
What do these sets of movies have in common?

1. *Blowup, The Bridges of Madison County, Funny Face, Rear Window, Salvador, Spider-Man*
2. *The Adventures of Priscilla Queen of the Desert, Forrest Gump, Lolita, Match Point, A Matter of Life and Death, Two for the Road*
3. *Flash Gordon, From Hell, Ghost World, A History of Violence, Nausicaa and the Valley of the Wind, Road to Perdition*
4. *Donnie Darko, Fatal Attraction, Monty Python and the Holy Grail, Roger and Me, The Rules of the Game, Song of the South*
5. *Good Night and Good Luck, Grand Hotel, The Man Who Shot Liberty Valance, My Little Chickadee, The Red Shoes, Spider-Man*
6. *Airplane, I Want to Live, Moulin Rouge, Oklahoma!, Safety Last, That Thing You Do*
7. *Die Hard, Edward Scissorhands, Eyes Wide Shut, The Lion in Winter, Moonstruck, The Thin Man*
8. *Beauty and the Beast* (1991), *King Kong* (1933), *Little Miss Sunshine, The Matrix, Mister Roberts, Singin' in the Rain*
9. *Far from Heaven, The Great Gatsby, The Music Man, Panic Room, Some Like It Hot, Sullivan's Travels*
10. *Chasing Amy, Harvey, House of Frankenstein, Rebecca, Rosemary's Baby, Waiting for Guffman*
11. *The Hours, The Hustler, "One Froggy Evening," Raiders of the Lost Ark, Scarface* (1983), *A Star Is Born*
12. *Casino Royale* (2006), *Don't Look Now, Everyone Says I Love You, Indiana Jones and the Last Crusade, Top Hat, Trouble in Paradise*
13. *Brighton Rock, Chinatown, A Civil Action, Five Graves to Cairo, Stalag 17, The Third Man*
14. *Arthur, G.I. Jane, Hannibal, Live and Let Die, Ordinary People, A Walk to Remember*
15. *The Big Sleep, Far and Away, Gattaca, The Great Dictator, Shanghai Surprise, Who's Afraid of Virginia Woolf?*
16. *Apocalypse Now, Fantasia, Gangs of New York, Last Action Hero, Punch-Drunk Love, The Ring*
17. *Andrei Rublev, Pleasantville, Schindler's List, Wings of Desire, The Wizard of Oz, The Women*
18. *The Godfather Part II, On the Town, Planet of the Apes, Saboteur, Splash, X-Men*
19. *Before Sunset, Cleo from 5 to 7, High Noon, Rope, The Set-Up, Timecode*
20. *Batman Begins, Dead Again, Dr. Strangelove, Gone With the Wind, Quiz Show, Who Framed Roger Rabbit*

Answers to the questions on this page can be found on page 256.

• **1926** • ANTONIO GAUDI IS RUN OVER by a Barcelona tram. Cab drivers think the impoverished architect looks like a bum and refuse to pick him up, so he is finally taken, unrecognized, to a pauper's hospital, where he dies. He is buried in the crypt of his still-unfinished masterpiece, the famous Sagrada Familia cathedral.

MASTER BUILDERS

1. Architect Walter Gropius founded what famous German art school in Weimar in 1919?
2. What toy was invented by the son of Frank Lloyd Wright, who said he was inspired by his father's earthquake-proof foundation for Tokyo's Imperial Hotel?
3. The title of Morris Lapidus's memoir *Too Much Is Never Enough* is a stab at what famous aphorism of Ludwig Mies van der Rohe?
4. The architect known as "Le Corbusier" took that pseudonym in part because, in French, it suggests what animal, which he believed he resembled in profile?
5. *The Da Vinci Code* repeats the untrue myth that the glass pyramid in front of the Louvre consists of how many panes?
6. The Oscar-nominated film *My Architect* was made by the son of what Estonian-born architect, who died in a Penn Station bathroom in 1974?
7. Whose design for Seattle's Experience Music rock museum is meant to recall smashed electric guitars, though some locals call it "the Hemorrhoids"?
8. What country was the birthplace of architects Alvar Aalto and Eero Saarinen?
9. Architect Daniel Libeskind became famous overnight in 2003 when he won the commission to design what?
10. What Chinese-born architect designed the Rock and Roll Hall of Fame?

• **1989** • DON THE BEACHCOMBER, the "tiki" restaurateur who introduced America to the cocktail umbrella, dies in Honolulu.

LET A SMILE BE YOUR UMBRELLA

1. What animal's head appears on the handle of Mary Poppins's umbrella?
2. In 1991, who erected three thousand blue and yellow umbrellas on the coasts of California and Japan?
3. What city's umbrella pines inspired the most famous work of composer Ottorino Respighi?
4. Farnsworth Bentley became famous for holding whose umbrellas?
5. Why were the earliest English umbrellas nicknamed "Robinsons"?

• **1993** • PRINCE ANNOUNCES HE WILL B changing his name 2 an unpronounceable symbol. The word "glyph," previously just a very good Scrabble play, begins to appear in *People* and *Parade* magazines for the very first time.

THE ATHLETES FORMERLY KNOWN AS
What are the current names of the sports teams with these onetime names?

Easy	*Harder*	*Yeah, Good Luck*
1. Montreal Expos	**1.** Winnipeg Jets	**1.** Seattle Pilots
2. Houston Oilers	**2.** Washington Senators (two answers)	**2.** Syracuse Nationals
3. Quebec Nordiques	**3.** Minnesota North Stars	**3.** Decatur Staleys
4. Baltimore Bullets	**4.** Hartford Whalers	**4.** Portsmouth Spartans
5. Cleveland Browns	**5.** Baltimore Orioles	**5.** Cincinnati Royals

Answers to the questions on this page can be found on page 257.

JUNE 8

• **1970** • The Wham-O Manufacturing Company files for a patent on its new "Foamable Resinous Composition." Today we call it Silly String.

STRING THEORY

1. What was piloted by Vietnam veteran Stringfellow Hawke?

2. What did the Electro String Instrument Corporation change its name to, to capitalize on a distant relationship between its founders and a World War I hero?

3. What kind of cheese is most commonly sold in the U.S. as processed "string cheese"?

4. What two future Hall of Famers were backed up by third-string quarterback Steve Bono for five full seasons?

5. What TV series about International Rescue pilots was filmed in "supermarionation"?

• **1978** • Though Bruce Lee has been dead for five years, that doesn't stop old martial arts footage from being repackaged into a new release, *Game of Death*. And the ghoulish Bruceploitation will continue with 1981's *Game of Death II*.

THE LAST PICTURE SHOW
What screen legends made their final appearance in these movies?

Easy
1. *Giant*
2. *The Shootist*
3. *The Misfits* (two answers)
4. *Guess Who's Coming to Dinner*
5. *On Golden Pond*

Harder
1. *The Harder They Fall*
2. *High Society*
3. *Always*
4. *Walk, Don't Run*
5. *The Score*

Yeah, Good Luck
1. *Ship of Fools*
2. *Witness for the Prosecution*
3. *Autumn Sonata*
4. *Silent Tongue*
5. *To Be or Not to Be*

• **1982** • At a Rolling Stones concert in Berlin, Carlo Karges is struck by the weird beauty of a mass balloon release. He's inspired to write the protest song that becomes a worldwide hit for Nena: "99 Red Balloons."

THINGS ARE LOOKING UP
A quiz whose answers can be found overhead.

1. What household device uses the rare synthetic element americium?

2. What slogan is painted on the nose of Robert Duvall's Wagner-blasting helicopter in *Apocalypse Now*?

3. What zone of radiation was first detected by *Explorer*, the first U.S. satellite?

4. What brightly colored species is the state bird of a record seven different states?

5. What college football team's fight song is "Down the Field," *not* the more popular "Rocky Top"?

6. What did "Glamorous Glennis" do on October 19, 1947?

7. *Freedom, Truth,* or *Justice*—what's the name of the bronze figure that stands atop the U.S. Capitol dome?

8. What violinist performed the title character's solos in the film *Fiddler on the Roof*?

9. What does a howdah sit atop?

10. What name is given to the full moon closest to the autumn equinox?

Answers to the questions on this page can be found on page 257.

JUNE 9

• **1967** • Author Dorothy Parker is cremated in New York. Unfortunately, she left no instructions for the ashes' disposal, so they will sit in her lawyer's filing cabinet for fifteen years. She donated her literary estate to civil rights causes, so the NAACP finally has her buried at its Baltimore headquarters in 1988, under the epitaph Parker chose for herself: "Excuse my dust."

ASHES TO ASHES

1. What Filipino volcano's 1991 eruption produced ten times more ash than Mount Saint Helens had?
2. Ash Wednesday marks the first day of what?
3. What sport's most famous series is played for the Ashes urn?
4. What rock star caused a stir in 2007 when he said that he'd snorted his late father's cremains?
5. In what Irish city did Frank McCourt set his memoir *Angela's Ashes*?

• **1973** • Secretariat wins the Belmont Stakes by an amazing thirty-one lengths. His time of 2:24 is still the fastest mile and a half ever on a dirt track.

DUST TO DUST

1. What's the last name of Clint Eastwood's character "Dirty" Harry?
2. What made-up expletive is *Battlestar Galactica*'s dirty word of choice?
3. What nation saw thousands of forced disappearances during its "Dirty War" of 1976 to 1983?
4. Who wrote and sang "She's Like the Wind," which became a hit off the *Dirty Dancing* sound track?
5. What ingredient gives Cajun "dirty rice" its dark color?

• **2004** • The village I'll delicately spell "F***ing," near Salzburg, Austria, votes not to change its unusual name. The town came by the name perfectly respectably, saluting a sixth-century nobleman called Focko, but, frankly, the townsfolk are getting a little tired of their street signs being stolen.

FOUR-LETTER NAMES

What less eyebrow-raising four-letter words name these famous people?

Easy
1. *4′33″* composer John and *Adaptation* star Nicolas
2. Gary Hart pal Donna and wide receiver Jerry
3. Singer Lesley and Parents Music Resource Center founder Tipper
4. Gucci designer Tom and pitcher Whitey
5. Poker player Annie and Klansman David

Harder
1. Secretary of State Elihu and *NewsRadio*'s Stephen
2. Nobel laureate Pearl and big-game hunter Frank
3. Grateful Dead drummer Mickey and lyricist Lorenz
4. Bush chief of staff Andrew and *Ender's Game* author Orson Scott
5. NBA great Bernard and Canadian prime minister William Lyon Mackenzie

Yeah, Good Luck
1. Alt-country singer Neko and AOL cofounder Steve
2. Polaroid inventor Edwin and saxophonist Harold
3. Football coach Walter and *Police Academy* actress Colleen
4. Cinematographer Conrad and physicist Edwin
5. Murderer Harry K. and *Inspector Morse* star John

Answers to the questions on this page can be found on page 257.

JUNE 10

• 1898 • DALMATIAN GOES EXTINCT—not the firehouse dog but the ancient Balkan language. The last native speaker was a deaf, toothless old man named Tuone Adaina, who tried to teach it to Italian linguists but was blown up by a land mine before he could conclude the lessons.

A CIVIL TONGUE

1. In what country is Magyar, unrelated to any of its neighbors' languages, spoken?
2. What's the world's most common second language?
3. What language has official status in more Asian countries than any other—twelve?
4. King Sejong appears on the 10,000-won bill for having created *hangul*, the written alphabet of what language?
5. What children's game takes its name from the Swahili word for "build"?
6. In which EU country is the first national language spoken fluently by fewer than a tenth of its people?
7. What fruit's name comes from the Nahuatl word for "testicle," because of its shape?
8. Which of the U.N.'s six languages is an official language of the fewest of its member countries, only two?
9. What's the only common English loanword from Finnish?
10. In what novel is the language Nadsat spoken?

• 1935 • ALCOHOLICS ANONYMOUS IS FOUNDED when stockbroker "Bill W." gives cofounder "Dr. Bob" a bottle of beer—his last ever—to steady his hand during surgery. Wait, A.A. celebrates two buddies having a beer as its founding date?

12-STEP PROGRAM
Answer these questions about other "A.A."s.

1. What city is threatened by the effects of acqua alta?
2. What punk band's last album was 1995's *¡Adios Amigos!*?
3. What's the common household name for diluted acetic acid?
4. Besides Arthur Ashe, who's the only other black man ever to win a Grand Slam tennis event?
5. What foreign army occupied Addis Ababa in May 1936?
6. What was the home state of Alan Alda's characters in both *M*A*S*H* and *The Aviator*?
7. In slang, what's "Adam's ale"?
8. What nation's flag has the phrase "Allahu Akbar" written between the green stars?
9. What amino acid is popularly linked to turkey's drowsiness-inducing properties?
10. Who did the Anaheim Angels defeat in their only World Series win ever?
11. Who left his Air America radio show in 2007 to run for the U.S. Senate?
12. What's the only movie remake (not just a second adaptation of a literary work) to win a Best Picture Academy Award?

Answers to the questions on this page can be found on page 258.

• **1938** • Johnny Vander Meer no-hits the Boston Braves at Cincinnati's Crosley Field. Four days later in Brooklyn, he will no-hit the Dodgers, despite walking the bases loaded in the bottom of the ninth, for the only consecutive no-hitters in major league history.

BACK TO BACK

1. What two covers of Tommy James and the Shondells songs hit number one in consecutive weeks of November 1987?
2. What two consecutive signs of the Zodiac begin with the same letter?
3. What happens to Neo twice in a row that clues Trinity in to a glitch in *The Matrix*?
4. What are the only two consecutive prime numbers?
5. What's the only team ever to repeat as NCAA basketball champions with the same five starters?
6. Who's the last artist to win two consecutive Album of the Year Grammys, for *Innervisions* and *Fulfillingness' First Finale*?
7. In 1983, Francis Ford Coppola filmed back-to-back adaptations of two books by what Oklahoma novelist?
8. What person was specifically exempted from the Twenty-second Amendment to the Constitution, limiting U.S. presidents to two terms?
9. Yawning, sneezing, or hiccuping—according to Japanese superstition, doing what twice in a row is a sign that someone's gossiping about you?
10. What's the only stadium ever to host two consecutive Super Bowls?

• **1966** • *Melody Maker* reports the secret rehearsals of a new band composed of the Yardbirds' Eric Clapton, Manfred Mann's Jack Bruce, and the Graham Bond Organisation's Ginger Baker. The trio's current bands aren't happy about the bombshell, but when Cream first performs a month later, it becomes rock's first "supergroup."

SUPER TROUPERS
What supergroups were composed of members of . . .

1. The Byrds, Buffalo Springfield, the Hollies
2. Free, Mott the Hoople, King Crimson
3. Santana, the Steve Miller Band, the Tubes
4. The Beatles, Electric Light Orchestra, the Heartbreakers
5. Cream, Traffic, Family
6. Stone Temple Pilots, Guns N' Roses, Wasted Youth
7. Soundgarden, Rage Against the Machine
8. The Nice, King Crimson, Atomic Rooster
9. New Order, the Smiths, Pet Shop Boys
10. Yes, the Buggles, King Crimson

Answers to the questions on this page can be found on page 258.

JUNE 12

• **1827** • BOTANIST ROBERT BROWN, looking at pollen grains under a microscope in his London home, is annoyed by their erratic jittering. He doesn't know it, but he's just discovered the random movement of liquids that's today called Brownian motion, in his honor.

RANDOM HOUSE
Try these nonrandom questions about random events.

1. What West Coast city would have been named for a *different* New England city if an 1845 coin toss had gone the other way?
2. What Georgetown star was the first player to be chosen by an NBA draft lottery winner?

3. What Scottish band is named for a Michigan port that its members picked out by randomly sticking a pin into a U.S. map?
4. What's the shortest standard reply on a Magic 8-Ball?
5. According to mathematician

Persi Diaconis's famous paper, how many times must a deck of cards be shuffled in order to be truly random?

• **1939** • THE BASEBALL HALL OF FAME is dedicated in Cooperstown, New York. Locals hope for an influx of tourists to a region whose chief industry—hops—was crippled by Prohibition.

KIDS IN THE HALL
Match these sports' Halls of Fame with their respective cities.

1. Basketball
2. Bowling
3. Boxing
4. Golf
5. Horse racing
6. Pro football
7. Swimming
8. Tennis
9. Track and field
10. Volleyball

A. Canastota, New York
B. Canton, Ohio
C. Fort Lauderdale, Florida
D. Holyoke, Massachusetts
E. Indianapolis, Indiana
F. Newport, Rhode Island
G. Saratoga Springs, New York
H. Springfield, Massachusetts
I. St. Augustine, Florida
J. St. Louis, Missouri

• **1942** • FOR HER THIRTEENTH BIRTHDAY, a young Amsterdam girl named Anne Frank receives a red and white autograph book that she decides to use for a diary.

IT'S A GIFT

1. In 1995, whom did Drew Barrymore flash on air as a forty-eighth birthday present?
2. Who received a twelve-foot scrub python for his sixth birthday, because his parents ran a Queensland animal park?
3. What puppy was, ironically,

the runt of the litter when Emily Elizabeth chose him as a birthday present in a 1962 book?
4. In *Toy Story*, who receives Buzz Lightyear for his seventh birthday and a puppy for ~~his~~ Christmas?
5. What play did Agatha Christie

write as an eightieth birthday present for Queen Elizabeth's grandmother, Queen Mary?

Answers to the questions on this page can be found on page 258.

• 1978 • COHOSTS HAROLD HAYES AND ROBERT HUGHES have tanked so badly on the first telecast of ABC newsmagazine *20/20* that Hugh Downs is quickly brought out of retirement to host the second show, soon to be joined by Barbara Walters.

VANITY PAIR

Can you match these TV presenters and name the show they cohosted?

1. Tom Bergeron	**A.** David Brinkley
2. Tom Braden	**B.** Pat Buchanan
3. Roy Clark	**C.** Adam Carolla
4. Mary Hart	**D.** Frank Gifford
5. Chet Huntley	**E.** Samantha Harris
6. Jimmy Kimmel	**F.** Stacy Hayes
7. Marilyn McCoo	**G.** Jamie Hyneman
8. Al Michaels	**H.** Buck Owens
9. Adam Savage	**I.** Rex Smith
10. Chuck Woolery	**J.** John Tesh

• 1986 • MARY-KATE AND ASHLEY OLSEN are born in Sherman Oaks, California . . . on Friday the thirteenth. (Cue ominous chords.)

UNLUCKY STRIKES

Thirteen questions about the number thirteen.

1. What morbid structure traditionally has thirteen steps?

2. What Hall of Fame quarterback, jersey number 13, threw a touchdown pass in each of his first thirteen playoff games?

3. What disease grounded astronaut Ken Mattingly from *Apollo 13*?

4. What novel begins, "It was a bright cold day in April, and the clocks were striking thirteen"?

5. John Carpenter's *Assault on Precinct 13* is an homage to what classic Howard Hawks western?

6. How many stripes were there on the American flag that inspired Francis Scott Key to write "The Star-Spangled Banner"?

7. What floor number is often skipped in Chinese buildings, as the thirteenth is in the West?

8. What two border states were the twelfth and thirteenth states admitted to the Confederacy, though the South never controlled them?

9. Ophiuchus, the thirteenth constellation of the Zodiac, is depicted as a man holding up what—a sword, a snake, or a severed head?

10. What's the subject of the 1969 memoir *Thirteen Days*?

11. A Jewish Bar Mitzvah ceremony is held when a boy turns 13. At what age is a girl's Bat Mitzvah celebrated?

12. What sport has thirteen players per team in "league" rules but fifteen in "union" play?

13. Whose series of thirteen children's books of thirteen chapters each ended in 2006 with *The End*?

Answers to the questions on this page can be found on page 259.

JUNE 14

• **1777** • THE CONTINENTAL CONGRESS adopts the Stars and Stripes as the flag of the United States.

FLAG DAY

1. How many soldiers are shown raising the flag over Iwo Jima in the famous photograph and statue?

2. What does Bruce Springsteen have tucked in his back pocket on the cover of *Born in the U.S.A.?*

3. According to Betsy Ross's family, what was the first American flag made from?

4. What's the only place on U.S. soil where another flag is allowed to be hung above the Stars and Stripes?

5. During one of his famous freedom-of-speech cases, who wore an American flag to court as a diaper?

• **1798** • COTTON GIN INVENTOR Eli Whitney contracts with the U.S. government to produce ten thousand muskets. This sparks his interest in the new idea of machinery with interchangeable parts, and Whitney will become an evangelist for interchangeability for the rest of his life.

THE SOME OF ITS PARTS
What has these parts?

1. Barbican, bailey, bastion, bulwark

2. Cytoplasm, lysosomes, centriole, Golgi body

3. Fetlock, pastern, flank, muzzle

4. Bowsprit, spreader, shroud, taffrail

5. Newel, riser, tread, baluster

6. Foible, forte, pommel, ricasso

7. Serif, beak, descender, counter

8. Dado, echinus, fluting, scotia

9. Scend, spindrift, trough, curl

10. Peduncle, tepal, perianth, pistil

• **1937** • THE MARIHUANA TAX ACT of 1937 regulates legal marijuana use out of existence.

CHRONIC TOWN
A quiz that may give you the munchies.

1. What political party was led until 1985 by the brutal Pol Pot?

2. In the video for Tom Petty and the Heartbreakers' "Mary Jane's Last Dance," who plays Mary Jane?

3. Who was fired from the Interior Department in 1865 for having written *Leaves of Grass?*

4. What African region has been ravaged by a militia called the Janjaweed?

5. Who invented the method he called "rope-a-dope"?

Answers to the questions on this page can be found on page 259.

• **1667** • King Louis XIV's personal physician, Jean-Baptiste Denys, administers medicine's first documented blood transfusion when he gives a 15-year-old boy an infusion of sheep's blood. Do not try this at home.

IN A LIGHTER VEIN
A bloody hard quiz.

1. The "K" in vitamin K stands for the Danish spelling of what eleven-letter word?

2. What country's civil war is the setting for the film *Blood Diamond*?

3. Who used hypnotism to treat the hemophilia of Tsarevich Alexei?

4. What's the stage name of rapper Jayceon Taylor, a onetime member of L.A. gang the Bloods?

5. In Shaw's *Pygmalion*, Eliza Doolittle offends the society types by saying the word "bloody." What word serves the same purpose in *My Fair Lady*?

6. Shechita is the method of producing meat that is what?

7. Who was hunted by Dutch physician Abraham van Helsing?

8. What's the largest artery in the human body?

9. What kind of blood is dumped on Stephen King's *Carrie*?

10. What Burlingame, California, company was founded in 1984 to provide blood and urine analysis to athletes?

11. What Sam Peckinpah western did Roger Ebert describe as "200 simultaneous blood transfusions with no recipients"?

12. What was misspelled in blood on Leno and Rosemary LaBianca's refrigerator on August 10, 1969?

13. A cake, a steak, or a shake—what edible item is depicted on the cover of the Rolling Stones' *Let It Bleed*?

14. What two kinds of pressure are represented by the two figures in a blood pressure measurement?

15. What state was "Bleeding" in the 1850s, in the words of Horace Greeley?

• **1859** • A U.S.-Canada border skirmish erupts on San Juan Island, between Washington state and British Columbia. Today the crisis is called the Pig War, since the only casualty was a black Canadian boar that was shot while eating an American farmer's potatoes.

RUN FOR THE BORDER
What's the only nation that shares a land border with these countries (like Canada vis-à-vis the United States)?

Easy	*Harder*	*Yeah, Good Luck*
1. United Kingdom	**1.** Denmark	**1.** East Timor
2. Haiti	**2.** Qatar	**2.** The Gambia
3. Vatican City	**3.** Monaco	**3.** Brunei
4. Portugal	**4.** San Marino	**4.** Lesotho

Answers to the questions on this page can be found on page 259.

JUNE 16

• **1939** • MR. E. ETTLES, who runs the swimming pool in Trowbridge, Wiltshire, is shocked to see that what he took to be falling hailstones is actually hundreds of tiny frogs. "Frog rains" are enormously rare (unless you're in a Paul Thomas Anderson movie), but they can happen.

LIKE THE WEATHER

1. What's the better-known nickname of the "Halloween Nor'easter" of 1991?
2. What was the first Major League Baseball team to play in a stadium with a fully retractable roof?
3. What classic Frank Loesser winter song is a duet between two characters called "The Mouse" and "The Wolf"?
4. It was Bernard Vonnegut, the brother of novelist Kurt, who discovered what commercial use for silver iodide?
5. The U.S. isn't the only large English-speaking nation that hasn't ratified the Kyoto Protocol against global warming. What's the other?
6. Who began his long TV career in 1969 as the weekend weatherman on WLWI in Indianapolis?
7. What winds bring warm, dry, smog-free weather to southern California every autumn?
8. Sufficiently powerful tropical storms in the Atlantic are called hurricanes. What are they called in the western Pacific?
9. What does a hygrometer measure?
10. What do a German physicist named Gabriel and a Swedish astronomer named Anders have in common with Irish engineer William Thomson?

• **1943** • CHARLIE CHAPLIN IS MARRIED for the fourth time, to 17-year-old Oona O'Neill. His new father-in-law, playwright Eugene O'Neill, is so outraged that he never speaks to Oona again.

FATHER OF THE BRIDE
Match these famous people to their equally famous (current or former) fathers-in-law.

1. Jason Bateman
2. George Clooney
3. Kenneth Cole
4. Daniel Day-Lewis
5. Danny Elfman
6. Christopher Guest
7. Diane Lane
8. Sheryl Lee
9. Virginia Madsen
10. John McEnroe
11. P. J. O'Rourke
12. Geraldo Rivera
13. Chris Sarandon
14. Jane Seymour
15. Catherine Zeta-Jones

A. Paul Anka
B. Richard Attenborough
C. Martin Balsam
D. James Brolin
E. Mario Cuomo
F. Tony Curtis
G. Neil Diamond
H. Kirk Douglas
I. Peter Fonda
J. Monty Hall
K. John Huston
L. Sidney Lumet
M. Arthur Miller
N. Ryan O'Neal
O. Kurt Vonnegut

Answers to the questions on this page can be found on page 260.

• **1964** • AFTER THE MARVELETTES reject the song as too childish, the Supremes release "Where Did Our Love Go," their breakout hit. The Marvelettes' sinking career never recovers from the goof.

"WHERE" HOUSE

1. Before his U.S. renaming, what was Waldo originally called when the *Where's Waldo?* books were released in the U.K.?

2. The Coen brothers' movie *O Brother, Where Art Thou?* was loosely based on what work of literature?

3. Who co-opted the Wendy's slogan "Where's the beef?" in a 1984 debate?

4. What five-man vocal group provided the music for TV's *Where in the World Is Carmen Sandiego?*

5. What common item is tracked by the website Where's George?

6. Who voiced Shaggy on *Scooby Doo, Where Are You?*

7. The Fermi paradox, in science, is often called the "Where are they?" paradox. Who's the "they"?

8. Audi, Renault, or Volvo—what European make is the missing vehicle in *Dude, Where's My Car?*

9. What artist considered his masterpiece to be the Tahitian tableau *Where Do We Come From? What Are We? Where Are We Going?*

10. What two future Munsters costarred in *Car 54, Where Are You?*

• **1974** • JOHN LE CARRÉ PUBLISHES the first book of his "Karla trilogy": *Tinker, Tailor, Soldier, Spy,* named for an old children's counting rhyme.

TINKER, TAILOR, SOLDIER, SAILOR . . .

1. For what team did the famed double-play combo "**Tinker** to Evers to Chance" play?

2. In what band did Roger, Andy, and John **Taylor** (no relation) all play?

3. In what church was the twentieth century's first "Unknown **Soldier**" buried?

4. What port, in modern-day Iraq, was home to the legendary Sinbad the **Sailor**?

5. What **rich man** is the only real-life American ever to have two actors Oscar-nominated for portraying him?

6. What word for a wandering Asian ascetic comes from the Arabic for "**poor man**"?

7. Despite being disguised as an old **beggar man,** who was quickly recognized at home by his faithful dog Argos?

8. Susan Orlean wrote a 1998 bestseller about Florida's John Laroche, the titular "**thief**" of what?

9. What German lab assistant is remembered today only because, in an 1877 experiment with **Dr.** Robert Koch, he devised a new way to grow bacteria in gelatin?

10. What Baltimore **lawyer** was held prisoner by the British fleet on September 14, 1814, after having dined aboard the HMS *Tonnant*?

11. What Oglala **Indian chief** is the subject of the unfinished Black Hills memorial, begun in 1948, that will dwarf Mount Rushmore if ever completed?

Answers to the questions on this page can be found on page 260.

JUNE 18

• **1746** • Over breakfast at a London tavern, Dr. Samuel Johnson signs a contract to produce his groundbreaking *A Dictionary of the English Language*, which will occupy him for the next ten years.

FROM A TO Z
All these answers have their letters in alphabetical order, like the words "billowy" and "chintz."

1. What Sonic Youth LP did *Entertainment Weekly* call the best album of 1992?
2. Before "hello" was common, what word did Alexander Graham Bell suggest for answering the phone?
3. What French word for "jewel" became a common name for American movie houses?
4. What animal is also called a wildebeest?

5. What kind of tissue sample does a pathologist take to tell whether or not a tumor is malignant?
6. In 1990, what movie won the first acting Oscar for a black woman since 1939?
7. The rock band Seven Mary Three took their name from a police call sign on what TV series?
8. The name of what shield of

Zeus from Greek myth has come to mean "protection" or "auspices"?
9. The ruby anniversary celebrates how many years of marriage?
10. What kind of khaki cotton pants are so named because U.S. soldiers first bought them in Asia during the Spanish-American War?

• **2006** • Paul McCartney turns 64, as predicted by a song he recorded forty years ago. But with a personal fortune now estimated at $1.5 billion, he probably doesn't care much if we'll still need him, if we'll still feed him.

YE OLDE TRIVIA

1. In what war did the oak-sided USS *Constitution* gain its nickname, "Old Ironsides"?
2. What baseball player is Santiago's hero in *The Old Man and the Sea*?
3. Who's the oldest singer ever to win a season of *American Idol*?
4. What's the alcohol in an old-fashioned?
5. What do ventriloquist Señor Wences, first woman governor Nellie Tayloe Ross, football coach Amos Alonzo Stagg, director Leni Riefenstahl, and composer Irving Berlin have in common?
6. What Oscar-winning actor is

also the artistic director of London's Old Vic theater?
7. Three days before dying, who passed George III as the oldest monarch ever to hold the British throne?
8. Bear, wolf, or cougar—what kind of animal's bite forces Travis Coates to put down his dog, Old Yeller?
9. What Bavarian physician presented a 1906 paper called "On a Peculiar Disease of the Cerebral Cortex"?
10. What rapper performs at the "Mitch-a-palooza" in the movie *Old School*?
11. Exodus, Leviticus, or

Deuteronomy—which book of the Old Testament also names one of the felines in T. S. Eliot's *Old Possum's Book of Practical Cats*?
12. Who hosted *This Old House* for its first ten seasons?
13. The insult "You sockdologizing old man-trap!" were the last words ever heard by whom?
14. Who's the oldest major-league pitcher ever to throw a no-hitter?
15. By what name was the world's largest-circulation magazine, *AARP: The Magazine*, known for its first forty-five years?

Answers to the questions on this page can be found on page 260.

• 1910 • To HONOR CIVIL WAR VETERAN William Jackson Smart, his daughter Sonora Dodd organizes the first June Father's Day festivities, in Spokane, Washington.

DAD TO THE BONE

Match each person to the field they're sometimes called the "Father of."

1. Tim Berners-Lee	**A.** Baseball
2. Henry Chadwick	**B.** Country music
3. Philo Farnsworth	**C.** History
4. Hugo Gernsback	**D.** Microbiology
5. Herodotus	**E.** Photography
6. Theodor Herzl	**F.** Science fiction
7. Hipparchus	**G.** Television
8. Anton von Leeuwenhoek	**H.** Trigonometry
9. Nicéphore Niepce	**I.** The World Wide Web
10. Jimmie Rodgers	**J.** Zionism

• 1943 • WITH SO MANY MEN overseas fighting World War II, the NFL downsizes. The Steelers and Eagles are combined into one Pennsylvania team commonly called the "Steagles."

BLEND AMBITION

Give these "portmanteau" (combined-word) answers.

1. What hometown of Scott Joplin and Ross Perot is named for the three states whose border it sits near?

2. What genre of film gave us *Dolemite*, *Superfly*, and *Cleopatra Jones*?

3. Where did England's Graham Fagg and France's Philippe Cozette historically shake hands on December 1, 1990?

4. What's the technical term for Internet "smileys" like this one :)?

5. What fitness program did Judi Sheppard Missett create in 1969 in Carlsbad, California?

6. What rare economic condition results when rising prices and recession occur at once?

7. What Adam Sandler movie's tagline billed it as "a comedy with a language all its own"?

8. What is the Red Hot Chili Peppers' biggest-selling album ever?

9. What "ethnolect" did the Oakland School Board make famous in 1996?

10. What word has Beyoncé Knowles defined as "beautiful, bountiful, and bounce-able"?

• 1949 • THE FLEDGLING NASCAR ORGANIZATION holds its first "strictly stock" race in Charlotte, North Carolina. Unlike today's high-tech racers, these early cars actually were "stock" cars—practically unmodified factory models.

STRICTLY STOCK

1. What two things are being compared in a stock's "P/E ratio"?

2. What single event shut down the New York Stock Exchange for more than four months, longer than all its other unscheduled closures combined?

3. Who was president when the Dow Jones Industrial Average finally regained its pre-1929 peak?

4. What Missouri-based company uses "BUD" as its ticker symbol?

5. Complete this analogy. New York : Dow Jones :: Tokyo : _____.

Answers to the questions on this page can be found on page 261.

• **1942** • BRIAN WILSON IS BORN in Hawthorne, California. His father (and future Beach Boys manager) is Murry Wilson, a machinist whose part-time songwriting career led to one minor hit, "Two-Step Side-Step," which Lawrence Welk played on his radio show.

I KNOW THERE'S AN ANSWER
Answer these questions with the titles of Beach Boys songs.

1. What takes exactly eight minutes and twenty seconds to reach the earth?
2. What was the nickname of Ohio restaurateur Dave Thomas's second daughter, red-headed Melinda Lou Thomas?
3. According to the name of the short story that inspired Steven Spielberg's *A.I.: Artificial Intelligence*, how long do

"Super-Toys Last"?
4. What Clorox "Formula" was named in honor of its inventor's birthday, April 9?
5. What Indiana city is named for a legendary Indian chief whose name is Miami for "Black Walnut"?
6. What sitcom was almost titled "Six of One" or "Across the Hall"?

7. What animated film begins in Shiverpool, Antarctica?
8. John the Baptist survived in the wilderness by eating locusts and what other food?
9. Before he turned to acting, what was Marky Mark's only number one song?
10. If not for Marseille, what would be the largest French city on the Mediterranean?

• **1963** • THE RED-TELEPHONE "HOTLINE" between the White House and the Kremlin is established.

HOT STUFF

1. What reality show gave America the beloved catchphrase "That's hot"?
2. What American spot hit a world-record 134° F in July 1913?
3. What was the subtitle of the 1993 sequel to *Hot Shots!*?
4. What U.S. president was raised in a spa town called Hot Springs?

5. What company now owns both the Hot Wheels *and* Matchbox brands?
6. What jazzman's first recording band was the Hot Five?
7. What are made hot by capsaicin?
8. What *SNL* cast member voiced "Waldo" in Van Halen's "Hot for

Teacher" video?
9. What talk show opens with the "Hot Topics" rundown?
10. What natural phenomenon can reach a temperature of 50,000° F, five times hotter than the surface of the sun?

• **2006** • JON HEIN SELLS his website, jumptheshark.com, to *TV Guide* for more than $1 million. You now have one minute to feel bad about every half-stoned conversation you had with your college roommates that *didn't* make you a million dollars. Go.

SHARK WEEK
According to Hein, who or what "jumped the shark" at these precise moments?

1. "The birth of Mearth"
2. "Terry Kath dies and the band forgets about the numbers"
3. "The tank"
4. "He became Yusuf Islam"

5. "At the Oscars—channeling to Tibet"
6. "Junior sings at Jackie Jr.'s wake"
7. "Scott Norwood hooks it wide

right in Tampa"
8. *"One from the Heart"*
9. "Tawana Brawley"
10. "Riley and the Initiative"

• 1947 • ACTOR MICHAEL GROSS is born in Chicago. By an astounding coincidence, Gross's *Family Ties* wife-to-be, Meredith Baxter, is born on the very same day, in Pasadena.

NON-FAMILY TIES

They don't share a birthday, but what do these odd groups of people have in common?

1. Kofi Annan, John Elway, Linda Hamilton, Elvis Presley, Kiefer Sutherland
2. Lewis Carroll, Sonny Liston, Karl Marx, Tom Mix, Mae West
3. Matthew Broderick, Laura Bush, William Holden, Barbara Mandrell, Craig MacTavish
4. Lucille Ball, Joseph G. Cannon, John Lennon, Eddie Mathews, Marilyn Monroe

5. David Bowie, Albert Brooks, Ray Charles, Stewart Granger, Michael Keaton
6. James Arness, Michael Crichton, John Kenneth Galbraith, Krist Novoselic, Peter the Great
7. Jose Canseco, Patrick Ewing, Kelsey Grammer, Alexander Hamilton, Empress Josephine
8. Art Buchwald, Ella Fitzgerald, Frida Kahlo, Cole Porter, Santa Anna

9. Otto von Bismarck, Kit Carson, Christopher Columbus, James Madison, the Apostle Paul
10. Lauren Ambrose, Erskine Caldwell, Georgia O'Keeffe, Paul McCartney, Kurt Vonnegut

---

• 2005 • CROATIAN TENNIS STAR Ivo Karlovic uses his 6-foot, 10-inch height to serve a record 51 aces in a Wimbledon match against Daniele Bracciali—but still loses the match.

ACE IN THE HOLE

Here are ten more aces to consider.

1. Besides aces, what was the other pair in Wild Bill Hickok's famous "dead man's hand"?
2. Ironically, who played an inexperienced young physician named Ace on the 1984 sitcom *E/R*?
3. Who fights crime alongside a German shepherd named Ace?
4. How many enemy planes must a pilot shoot down to be called an ace?
5. Chess, backgammon, or cribbage—what game's equipment is used to play acey-deucey?
6. What kind of animal's kidnapping is solved by *Ace Ventura: Pet Detective*?
7. What ace of the 1961 Yankees team won twenty-five games and the Cy Young Award, but was overshadowed by the Mantle-

Maris home run chase?
8. According to the Ace of Base song "All That She Wants," what *is* all she wants?
9. What is the lowest-ranking ace in bridge?
10. What other singer's death inspired Paul Simon to write "The Late Great Johnny Ace"?

Answers to the questions on this page can be found on page 261.

JUNE 22

• **1808** • AFTER FIGHTING OVER A WOMAN, M. de Grandpré and M. le Pique agree to settle the matter like gentlemen . . . in hot-air balloons, above Paris. Le Pique and his second are killed when de Grandpré's shot puts a hole in their balloon.

RAMPANT INFLATION

1. Whose famous balloon says "State Fair Omaha" on the outside?

2. What billionaire piloted the first hot-air balloon ever to cross the Atlantic?

3. What feline was the first-ever character balloon in the Macy's Thanksgiving Day Parade?

4. What color balloons were added to Lucky Charms in 1989?

5. Who produced a sixty-inch balloon for the "bubble dance" she first performed at the 1934 World's Fair?

• **1882** • WILLIAM MATTHIAS SCHOLL—still twenty-two years from being foot care guru "Dr. Scholl"—is born in Chicago.

THE AGONY OF DE FEET

1. What's the more common name for the foot ailment also called verrucas?

2. The cartoon *Happy Feet* is dedicated to what man, who plays an Australian elephant seal in the film?

3. What two Olympic team sports are played barefoot? (These are genuine *team* sports, with multiple teammates and both teams in the game at the same time.)

4. Achilles' vulnerable heel was the result of his being dipped, as an infant, in what mythical river?

5. From left to right, what are the *una corda*, *sostenuto*, and damper?

• **1975** • "I'M NOT IN LOVE" hits number one in the UK, becoming the biggest hit ever for British band 10cc. Producer Jonathan King always claimed the band's name came to him in a dream, despite the popular rumor that it's meant to refer to a prodigious volume of, er, precious bodily fluids.

COLLECTED CONUNDRA

In honor of the band, can you name these 10 "C.C.."s?

1. What's another name for a "numismatist"?

2. In a famous line from *The Third Man*, what Bavarian invention does Harry Lime mistakenly attribute to five hundred years of peace in Switzerland?

3. Hearing of whose death led Dorothy Parker to quip, "How can they tell?"

4. When I-580 is finally completed, it will mean that what city is no longer one of the five U.S. state capitals not served by the interstate highway system?

5. What's the largest land bird in North America?

6. In 1999, at age 13, who became the youngest solo artist ever to have a record go platinum?

7. Which Kurt Vonnegut novel is named for the game that physicist Felix Hoenikker was playing when the bomb was dropped on Hiroshima?

8. What usually has cream in its "New England" version and tomatoes in its "Manhattan" version?

9. What did presidential candidate Estes Kefauver ill-advisedly wear on the cover of the March 24, 1952, issue of *Time* magazine?

10. Unless you're a marsupial, what band of white fibers in your cerebrum connects your left brain with your right brain?

Answers to the questions on this page can be found on page 262.

• **1894** • PIERRE DE COUBERTIN convenes the congress in Paris that begins the modern Olympic movement. However, since the first IOC constitution specified that the president should represent the Games' host country, de Coubertin was *not* the first IOC president. Instead, a Greek businessman named Demetrius Vikelas was elected.

I'M IN CHARGE HERE!

What office or position was first held by . . .

Easy	Harder	Yeah, Good Luck
1. David Ben-Gurion	1. Kenesaw Mountain Landis	1. George Clinton
2. Steve Allen	2. Trygve Lie	2. Douglas Fairbanks
3. Tom Landry	3. James Forrestal	3. Muhammad Naguib
4. Caesar Augustus	4. John Dryden	4. Margaret Gorman
5. John Adams	5. John A. McDonald	5. Margaret Farrar

• **1917** • WHEN RED SOX PITCHER Babe Ruth slugs an umpire and is ejected with nobody out in the first, Ernie Shore is tossed into the game with almost no warm-up. Ruth's only base runner is caught stealing, and Shore retires the next twenty-six Washington Senators, for one of the oddest no-hitters in baseball history.

PITCHER PERFECT

1. Who made Baseball Hall of Fame history by marrying a *Basketball* Hall of Famer, Ann Meyers, in 1986?
2. What pitcher lent his name to UCL (ulnar collateral ligament) reconstruction?
3. Since 1976, what product has sponsored the annual award to baseball's best relief pitcher?
4. In 1928, for the A's, who became the only pitcher ever to throw two immaculate innings (nine pitches, three strikeouts) in the same season?
5. What pitcher, named for one president, was portrayed by another onscreen?

• **1960** • THE FDA APPROVES "the Pill" for contraceptive use in the United States. Not every nation is so quick to hop on the birth control bandwagon—Japan won't approve the Pill until 1999!

INCONCEIVABLE

1. What family-planning pioneer coined the phrase "birth control" in 1914?
2. What brand of contraceptive did Elaine Benes hoard on *Seinfeld*?
3. What town in southwestern France is home, appropriately enough, to a museum of birth control devices?
4. What "mocktail" can be mixed from cranberry and grapefruit juice and peach nectar?
5. Who is killed by God in Genesis 38:10 for using coitus interruptus with his wife, Tamar?

Answers to the questions on this page can be found on page 262.

JUNE 24

• **1880** • "O Canada" is first performed at a Saint-Jean-Baptiste Day banquet in Quebec.

TYPE "OH"

1. Whose first big hit, "Oh, Carol," was about his ex-girlfriend Carole King?

2. What future *Grey's Anatomy* costar played Sandra Oh's lover in *Under the Tuscan Sun*?

3. What state is home to the singer of Stephen Foster's "Oh! Susanna"?

4. Whose last book was *Oh, the Places You'll Go*?

5. What did Sadaharu Oh do 868 times, a professional world record?

• **1902** • American polar explorer Evelyn Baldwin writes an urgent note and throws it into the Arctic Ocean: "Five ponies and 150 dogs remain. Desire hay, fish, and 30 sledges." The bottle will be found by a Russian fisherman . . . but in 1948, far too late to send for help. (Baldwin returned safe and sound and died in his bed in 1933.)

BOTTLED UP

1. What hit sitcom was based on the 1964 Tony Randall film *The Brass Bottle*?

2. What German mathematician devised an impossible one-sided bottle in 1882?

3. How many bottles unexpectedly appear in the last verse of the Police song "Message in a Bottle"?

4. What comes in the "hobble-skirt" bottle designed in 1915 by Earl Dean, who based it on an encyclopedia picture of a cocoa pod?

5. Balk, dunk, or punt—what sports term is also the name of the dimple at the bottom of a wine bottle?

6. On what planet did the bottle city of Kandor originate?

7. Molotov cocktails were first used by what country after the Soviets invaded it in 1939?

8. Frank Sinatra was buried with a bottle of what whiskey, his favorite drink?

9. What did Antarctic explorers Paul Siple and Charles Passel first calculate in 1945 by leaving water bottles outside until they froze?

10. What playwright, whose real given names were Thomas Lanier, died in 1983 when he choked on the cap from a bottle of eyedrops?

• **1973** • In Twin Falls, Idaho, Evel Knievel fails to make it across the Snake River Canyon in his second and final test of the X-2 Skycycle.

A DESCENT PLACE TO LIVE
Match these fictional characters to their hometowns.

1. Bullwinkle J. Moose
2. George Bailey
3. *Hope & Faith*
4. Miles Roby
5. Mr. Deeds

A. Bedford Falls
B. Empire Falls
C. Frostbite Falls
D. Glen Falls
E. Mandrake Falls

Answers to the questions on this page can be found on page 262.

• **1977** • Virginia forest ranger Roy Sullivan is hit by lightning while fishing, the record-setting *seventh* time he has been hit over the course of his lifetime. Seven—that's good luck!

ZAPPED!

1. Which of Santa's reindeer have names that mean "thunder" and "lightning" in German?
2. What movie's protagonist is named Lightning McQueen?
3. Who invented the lightning rod, though he refused to patent it, claiming to be uninterested in profit?
4. Actor Jim Caviezel was struck by lightning during the filming of what film?
5. What NFL team replaced its AFL-era horse logo with a bolt of lightning?
6. Whose 1984 album *Ride the Lightning* features an electric chair on the sleeve?
7. Who were Arges, Brontes, and Steropes, who forged Zeus's thunderbolts in Greek myth?
8. What happened to police scientist Barry Allen after lightning struck the chemicals in his lab?
9. What's the name of the baseball bat that *The Natural* makes from a lightning-felled tree?
10. What's the name of this mad-scientist device, a reference to Genesis 28?

• **1984** • On the orders of nutball dictator Nicolae Ceausescu, construction work begins on "the House of the People," a giant government building in Bucharest, Romania. With its tons of steel, crystal, and Transylvanian marble, the giant boondoggle still stands today as the heaviest building on Earth.

WEIGHTY MATTERS

1. According to its first line, in what city is the Band's song "The Weight" set?
2. What Italian wrote, in 1643, "We live submerged at the bottom of an ocean of elementary air, which is known by incontestable experiments to have weight"?
3. According to Modest Mouse, "even if things get too heavy," what will we all do?
4. What's the heaviest chemical element on the periodic table that has a one-letter abbreviation?
5. After losing 60 pounds to play the lead role in *The Machinist*, who then had to gain 100 pounds in six months to play a superhero?
6. What word, from the French for "goods of weight," names our old-fashioned pounds-and-ounces system?
7. In 1997, what Oscar winner was replaced by Sarah Ferguson as Weight Watchers' spokesperson?
8. What's the heaviest internal organ in the human body?
9. In what 1952 play is Giles Corey "pressed" to death, his last words being "More weight"?
10. What's the significance of the four-centimeter-tall platinum-iridium block sitting in a high-security vault just outside Paris?
11. What tree's edible seeds were once used to weigh diamonds?
12. Who's the heaviest football player ever to score a Super Bowl touchdown?
13. What 1968 hit was the first song to use the phrase "heavy metal"?
14. Which two boxing weight classifications are named for animals?
15. What 1979 movie's title character uses, as his carnival spiel, "For one dollar I'll guess your weight, your height, or your sex"?

Answers to the questions on this page can be found on page 263.

JUNE 26

• 1284 • ACCORDING TO THE BROTHERS GRIMM tale, the Pied Piper rids the city of Hamelin of all its pesky rats, and then of all its pesky children.

THE RAT PATROL

1. What TV title character has a rat named Steve McQueen?

2. What is the more common name for benzoic sulfinide, linked in 1977 to bladder cancer in lab rats?

3. Which member of "the Rat Pack" was married to a Kennedy?

4. What kind of American desert rat can survive indefinitely without drinking water?

5. Fusilli, Macaroni, or Linguini—what's the name of the hapless chef in the film *Ratatouille*?

6. What 1984 Ratt hit featured a cross-dressing Milton Berle in its video?

7. What disease, caused by the bacteria *Y. pestis*, is spread by fleas and rats?

8. What horror movie was based on the novel *Ratman's Notebooks*?

9. Whose sensei is a rat named Master Splinter?

10. The first attested use of the word "scuzzy" was in reference to "Ratso" Rizzo, in what film?

• 1974 • THE FIRST GROCERY UPC code is scanned at a Marsh Supermarket checkout in Troy, Ohio. The first item purchased? A ten-pack of Juicy Fruit gum.

JUICY FRUITS

1. The word "grenade" derives from the name of what fruit?

2. What are the two fruit juices in a cosmopolitan?

3. According to Langston Hughes, what might "dry up, like a raisin in the sun"?

4. What's Mick Jagger's favorite flavor of soda, according to "You Can't Always Get What You Want"?

5. Mexican laetrile, once thought to be an anticancer drug, is extracted from the seeds of what fruit?

6. What fruit appears in the Olive Garden logo? (Hint: not olives.)

7. Whose print of a banana is the cover of the 1967 album *The Velvet Underground and Nico*?

8. In the *Godfather* films, what fruit's appearance foreshadows death?

9. What corporate logo consists of an apple, two bunches of grapes, some gooseberries, and three leaves?

10. Grape, cherry, or fruit punch—what flavor of "Kool-Aid" (actually Flavor Aid) was used at Jonestown?

11. The phrase "banana republic" was first coined by O. Henry in reference to what country?

12. What fruit is a hybrid of the mandarin orange and the grapefruit?

13. Darryl Strawberry is one of only two players to have won a World Series with both the Mets and the Yankees. Who's the other?

14. The journey in Roald Dahl's *James and the Giant Peach* ends with the peach impaled on what?

15. Enzymes from the papaya fruit are used to make what kitchen staple?

16. In Greek myth, Hippomenes scattered distracting golden apples during a footrace in his attempt to win whose hand in marriage?

17. What pieces of fruit contain three princesses in Sergei Prokofiev's most famous opera?

18. Why was Mary Mallon famous in the early 1900s for her signature dessert of peaches and ice cream?

19. What's a Chinese gooseberry?

20. Which one of Strawberry Shortcake's four original toy "friends" was a boy?

Answers to the questions on this page can be found on page 263.

• 1967 • THE WORLD'S FIRST electronic ATM is installed in North London. As a publicity stunt, British TV star Reg Varney makes the first withdrawal.

MATCHING FUNDS
Can you match up the images on the front and back of a piece of U.S. paper currency and give the denomination in question?

1. Benjamin Franklin	**A.** Declaration of Independence delegates
2. Ulysses S. Grant	**B.** Independence Hall
3. Alexander Hamilton	**C.** The Treasury Building
4. Andrew Jackson	**D.** The U.S. Capitol
5. Thomas Jefferson	**E.** The White House

• 1979 • JOHN CLEESE'S AMNESTY INTERNATIONAL benefit *The Secret Policeman's Ball* begins in London. U2's Bono will later credit the show with sparking his interest in social activism.

SO I CAN, SO I CAN
Answer these questions about people who, like Bono, are famed for wearing sunglasses indoors.

1. Fashion guru Anna Wintour is the editor of what magazine?
2. Who won a 1991 best male vocalist Grammy despite having died in 1988?
3. Who edited books like *The Cartoon History of the Universe* and Dorothy West's *The Wedding* while working at Doubleday?
4. What Jack Nicholson title refers to the one Bach, two Chopin, and two Mozart compositions played in the movie?
5. What Canadian-born TV star was the Blues Brothers' first arranger and is the musical director at the Rock and Roll Hall of Fame?

• 2003 • THE NATIONAL DO NOT CALL registry is opened for telemarketer-harried Americans, enrolling seven million numbers the very first day.

FORBID AND FORGET
Don't let these ten "don't"s trip you up.

1. What company's informal corporate motto is "Don't be evil"?
2. What movie is available in the "Don't Call Me Shirley!" DVD edition?
3. What TV show opened with a "control voice" saying, "Do not attempt to adjust the picture"?
4. What briefly made Journey's twenty-five-year-old hit "Don't Stop Believing" the most-downloaded song on iTunes in June 2007?
5. When going directly to jail, a Monopoly player is commanded not to do what two things?
6. What specific animal appeared above the "Don't Tread on Me" motto on early American flags?
7. A sestina, a rondeau, or a villanelle—what kind of nineteen-line poem is Dylan Thomas's "Do Not Go Gentle into That Good Night"?
8. What movie's tagline was "Don't get him wet, keep him out of bright light, and never feed him after midnight"?
9. What does a DNR order at a hospital stand for?
10. What 1977 hit was the theme of Bill Clinton's 1992 presidential campaign?

Answers to the questions on this page can be found on page 263.

• **1846** • BELGIAN FLAUTIST Adolphe Sax is granted a patent for his new single-reed woodwind, which he calls the saxophone.

BLOW ME

1. What's the first instrument that listeners hear at a performance of George Gershwin's "Rhapsody in Blue"?
2. What is this instrument, called *il fagotto* in Italian?

3. What trumpetlike horn is jazzman Chuck Mangione's instrument?
4. What instrument do Australian Aborigines traditionally make from termite-hollowed eucalyptus trees?
5. What brand of cough drops uses an alphorn in its commercials?
6. The sousaphone is a marching-band version of what symphony instrument?
7. What's the most common "singing membranophone"?
8. Because of an unfortunate incident in Exodus, what animal's horns are expressly forbidden from being used to make a Jewish shofar?
9. Which modern instrument was called the sackbut until the nineteenth century?
10. What instrument, familiar to *Legend of Zelda* players, is used to play the famous theme from *The Good, the Bad, and the Ugly*?

• **1876** • TWO DAYS AFTER the Battle of Little Bighorn, a burial party finds Captain Myles Keogh's horse Comanche in a thicket, wounded by seven arrows but still alive. Comanche becomes famous as the only survivor of "Custer's Last Stand."

MY LITTLE PONY
Name the famous horse that belonged to . . .

Easy
1. The Lone Ranger
2. Gumby
3. Wilbur Post
4. Roy Rogers
5. Dudley Do-Right

Harder
1. Robert E. Lee
2. Don Quixote
3. Tom Mix
4. Alexander the Great
5. Tonto

Yeah, Good Luck
1. Caligula
2. Ichabod Crane
3. Napoleon
4. Gandalf
5. Zorro

• **1935** • WAIKIKI MERCHANT ELLERY CHUN first advertises his new "Aloha shirts," which he's created to use up leftover kimono fabric he couldn't get rid of. They're a smash with tourists.

LEI LADY LEI

1. What's the second largest of the Hawaiian Islands?
2. What iconic Hawaiian object was based on the Portuguese *braguinha*?
3. What Olympic champ was sheriff of Honolulu from 1932 to 1961?
4. The name of what other U.S. state titles a national memorial in Hawaii?
5. What word did the University of Hawaii Warriors drop from their team name in 2001?

Answers to the questions on this page can be found on page 264.

• **1888** • THE FIRST KNOWN RECORDING of classical music is made in London's Crystal Palace, when George Gouraud performs Handel's *Israel in Egypt* for Edison's wax cylinder.

HOOKED ON CLASSICS

1. Whose Adagio for Strings is best known as the theme from the movie *Platoon*?

2. Who wrote sonnets called "La primavera," "L'estate," "L'autunno," and "L'inverno," to be read with the movements of his most famous work?

3. What river provided the water for which Handel wrote *Water Music?*

4. What famous name in opera was the son-in-law of composer Franz Liszt?

5. What's the name of the mystery woman "Für" whom Beethoven wrote his well-known Bagatelle in A Minor?

• **1956** • PRESIDENT EISENHOWER CREATES the Interstate Highway System, arguing that better roads between American cities are needed for civil defense.

ROADS SCHOLARS

In what state are state highways marked with these symbols?

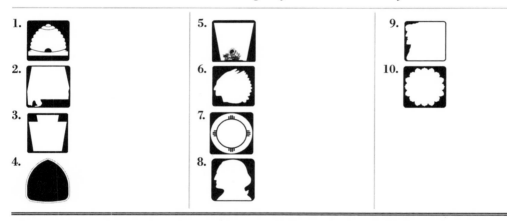

1.

2.

3.

4.

5.

6.

7.

8.

9.

10.

• **1995** • DIANE WHITE, WRITING in the *Boston Globe,* coins the word "bridezilla."

ALTAR EGOS

1. Of whom did Oscar Levant quip "Always a bride, never a bridesmaid"?

2. What bloodbath followed Henry of Navarre's 1572 wedding to Marguerite of Valois?

3. In what film is the real name of "the Bride" revealed to be Beatrix Kiddo?

4. What literary title character's wedding is interrupted at the altar by a lawyer's revelation that the groom is already married to Bertha Mason?

5. Who was the last bride to marry in the White House?

Answers to the questions on this page can be found on page 264.

• **1859** • CHARLES BLONDIN BECOMES an instant celebrity for his tightrope walk across Niagara Falls. This nineteenth-century David Blaine crosses blindfolded, on stilts, with a wheelbarrow, and even cooks and eats an omelette en route.

DON'T GO CHASING WATERFALLS

1. In what 1986 movie does Jeremy Irons scale South America's Iguazu Falls?
2. The island in the middle of Victoria Falls is named for what famous man, the first European to see the falls?
3. What country is home to Angel Falls, the world's tallest waterfall?
4. What literary villain died during a struggle at Reichenbach Falls?
5. What river's waterfalls led to the naming of the Cascade Range?

• **1987** • MADONNA RELEASES "Who's That Girl?," the theme song to her new film, which had originally been titled *Slammer*.

WHO'S THAT GIRL?

Name the number one hit from each of these artists with "girl" in the title.

Easy	*Harder*	*Yeah, Good Luck*
1. Rick Springfield	**1.** Pet Shop Boys	**1.** The Chi-Lites
2. Gwen Stefani	**2.** The Four Seasons	**2.** Steve Lawrence
3. The Temptations	**3.** Hall & Oates	**3.** Milli Vanilli
4. Avril Lavigne	**4.** Paula Abdul	**4.** Elton John
5. Christina Aguilera	**5.** Donna Summer	**5.** Charlie Rich

• **1987** • CANADA INTRODUCES ITS NEW bronze-plated dollar coin. Because of the waterbird pictured on the reverse, the coin is quickly nicknamed "the Loonie."

THE THING WITH FEATHERS

What bird was used as an alias by each of these people?

1. CIA agent Joe Turner, in a Robert Redford film
2. Costumed criminal Oswald Chesterfield Cobblepot
3. The new leader of the title gang in *The Warriors*
4. Tom Clancy's CIA agent in the Kremlin
5. Michael Arlen's detective rip-off of *The Saint*, played on-screen by George Sanders

Answers to the questions on this page can be found on page 264.

June Answers

JUNE 1

SEASON CYCLE
1. *Fear and Loathing in Las Vegas*
2. Indian (*The World's Fastest Indian*)
3. The Dakar Rally
4. Milwaukee
5. Macau

COME TOGETHER
1. Have a pair of twins
2. Names inspired by movie titles
3. Sang James Bond themes
4. Band member committed suicide
5. Eric Clapton
6. Drummer sang lead
7. Hailed from Glasgow
8. Had an eponymous song on an eponymous album
9. Changed their name for legal reasons
10. Duos
11. Had a hit with a repeated three-word title ("Turn! Turn! Turn!," "Bills, Bills, Bills," "Bye Bye Bye," "Yummy Yummy Yummy")
12. Named for a song by another artist
13. Had hits about Superman
14. Complete-sentence band names
15. One-letter album titles (*X*, *A*, *i*, *Z*)

JUNE 2

ALL YOUR BASE ARE BELONG TO US
Easy
1. South Carolina
2. Kentucky
3. Kansas
4. Indiana
5. Maryland

Harder
1. New York
2. Texas
3. New Jersey
4. North Carolina
5. Georgia

Yeah, Good Luck
1. California
2. Oklahoma
3. Tennessee
4. Hawaii
5. Virginia

ALL YOUR BASS ARE BELONG TO US
Easy
1. Red Hot Chili Peppers (and Fear)
2. Led Zeppelin
3. The Police
4. The Who
5. Nirvana

Harder
1. The Dave Matthews Band
2. The Smiths
3. Rush
4. Primus
5. Chicago

Yeah, Good Luck
1. Linkin Park
2. The Pogues
3. The Roots
4. Modest Mouse
5. The Kinks

WHAT'S ON FIRST?
1. *Kukla, Fran and Ollie*
2. Maude Findlay
3. *The Sopranos*
4. Hopalong Cassidy
5. *American Idol*

JUNE 3

WHO'S ON THIRD?
1. Capital of the Confederacy
2. Bob Lanier
3. Boyz II Men
4. China (if you include two areas also claimed by India)
5. Jennifer Hudson
6. Jerusalem
7. David Beckham
8. Robin
9. Atlanta's
10. Angela Merkel

(AIN'T GONNA PLAY) SUNG CITY
Easy
1. *On the Town*
2. *Fiddler on the Roof*
3. *Oklahoma!*
4. *Evita*

Harder
1. *Hair*
2. *Rent*
3. *Annie*
4. *The Music Man*

Yeah, Good Luck
1. *Bells Are Ringing*
2. *Paint Your Wagon*
3. *Seussical*
4. *Pal Joey*

SIN-EMATIC
Easy
1. *2001: A Space Odyssey*
2. *Psycho*
3. *Mommie Dearest*
4. *The Usual Suspects*
5. *Taxi Driver*

JUNE 3 (cont'd)

Harder
1. *Schindler's List*
2. *Misery*
3. *Chinatown*
4. *Rebecca*
5. *It's a Wonderful Life*
Yeah, Good Luck
1. *Marathon Man*
2. *The Night of the Hunter*
3. *Die Hard*
4. *Training Day*
5. *The Little Foxes*

JUNE 4

HERE BE DRAGONS
1. Honah Lee
2. Jackie Chan
3. He created Dungeons & Dragons
4. Nathan Bedford Forrest
5. Indonesia
6. Siegfried
7. Barcelona
8. Adventure, for the Atari 2600
9. Wales
10. Oolong

BONDS . . . COMMON BONDS
1. Winds
2. Computer languages
3. Apples
4. Card games
5. Knots
6. Muscles
7. Fonts
8. Dog breeds
9. Stringed instruments
10. Figure-skating maneuvers
11. Pasta
12. Antelopes

13. Spells in *Harry Potter*
14. Musical notes
15. Crosses
16. Sails
17. Swords
18. Currencies
19. Fabrics
20. Girl Scout cookies

JUNE 5

THE NAME OF THE BRO'S
1. Chico (although an older brother, Manfred, died in infancy)
2. Jacuzzi
3. Rick Barry
4. At the movies
5. James and John
6. Dayton, Ohio
7. Plumbers
8. Andy Gibb
9. The Hardy Boys
10. The DiMaggios

ALL ACCORDING TO PLAN
1. The first Five-Year Plan
2. *Plan 9 from Outer Space*
3. The Schlieffen Plan
4. *A Simple Plan*
5. The Anaconda Plan

JUNE 6

ON-SCREEN SEX(TETS)
1. Photographer protagonists
2. Memorable scenes involving Ping-Pong
3. Adapted from comics
4. Feature rabbits
5. Last line is the movie's title
6. Titles have exclamation marks
7. Set at Christmastime
8. Two codirectors
9. Shot while the lead actress was pregnant
10. Title character never appears
11. Main character shares name with a state (Virginia Woolf, Minnesota Fats, Michigan J. Frog, Indiana Jones, Tony Montana, Norman Maine)
12. Partially set in Venice
13. Great director plays a villain (Richard Attenborough, John Huston, Sydney Pollack, Otto Preminger, Erich von Stroheim, Orson Welles)
14. Star named Moore (Dudley, Demi, Julianne, Roger, Mary Tyler, Mandy)
15. Stars were married
16. No opening title card
17. Part color, part black and white
18. Feature the Statue of Liberty
19. Play out in real time
20. British lead actor plays American

JUNE 7	JUNE 8	JUNE 9

MASTER BUILDERS
1. The Bauhaus
2. Lincoln Logs
3. "Less is more"
4. A crow
5. 666
6. Louis Kahn
7. Frank Gehry
8. Finland
9. The rebuilt World Trade Center site
10. I. M. Pei

LET A SMILE BE YOUR UMBRELLA
1. A parrot
2. Christo
3. Rome's (*The Pines of Rome*)
4. Puff Daddy's
5. For Robinson Crusoe (who proudly carried a homemade goatskin umbrella around his island)

THE ATHLETES FORMERLY KNOWN AS
Easy
1. Washington Nationals
2. Tennessee Titans
3. Colorado Avalanche
4. Washington Wizards
5. Baltimore Ravens
Harder
1. Phoenix Coyotes
2. Minnesota Twins, Texas Rangers
3. Dallas Stars
4. Carolina Hurricanes
5. New York Yankees
Yeah, Good Luck
1. Milwaukee Brewers
2. Philadelphia 76ers
3. Chicago Bears
4. Detroit Lions
5. Sacramento Kings

STRING THEORY
1. Airwolf
2. Rickenbacker
3. Mozzarella
4. Joe Montana and Steve Young
5. *Thunderbirds*

THE LAST PICTURE SHOW
Easy
1. James Dean
2. John Wayne
3. Clark Gable, Marilyn Monroe
4. Spencer Tracy
5. Henry Fonda
Harder
1. Humphrey Bogart
2. Grace Kelly
3. Audrey Hepburn
4. Cary Grant
5. Marlon Brando
Yeah, Good Luck
1. Vivien Leigh
2. Tyrone Power
3. Ingrid Bergman
4. River Phoenix
5. Carole Lombard

THINGS ARE LOOKING UP
1. Smoke detectors
2. "Death from above"
3. The Van Allen belt
4. The cardinal
5. Tennessee's
6. Broke the sound barrier for the first time (Chuck Yeager's plane)
7. *Freedom*
8. Isaac Stern
9. An elephant
10. Harvest moon

ASHES TO ASHES
1. Mount Pinatubo's
2. Lent
3. Cricket's
4. Keith Richards
5. Limerick

DUST TO DUST
1. Callahan
2. Frak
3. Argentina
4. Patrick Swayze
5. Chicken liver or giblets

FOUR-LETTER NAMES
Easy
1. Cage
2. Rice
3. Gore
4. Ford
5. Duke
Harder
1. Root
2. Buck
3. Hart
4. Card
5. King
Yeah, Good Luck
1. Case
2. Land
3. Camp
4. Hall
5. Thaw

JUNE 10

A CIVIL TONGUE
1. Hungary
2. English
3. Arabic
4. Korean
5. Jenga
6. Ireland (Gaelic)
7. The avocado's
8. Chinese (China and Singapore)
9. Sauna
10. *A Clockwork Orange*

12-STEP PROGRAM
1. Venice
2. The Ramones
3. Vinegar
4. Yannick Noah
5. Italy's
6. Maine
7. Water
8. Iraq
9. Tryptophan
10. The San Francisco Giants
11. Al Franken
12. *The Departed*

JUNE 11

BACK TO BACK
1. Tiffany's "I Think We're Alone Now" and Billy Idol's "Mony Mony"
2. Scorpio and Sagittarius
3. A black cat passes him
4. 2 and 3
5. Florida
6. Stevie Wonder
7. S. E. Hinton (*The Outsiders* and *Rumble Fish*)
8. Harry Truman (who was already in office)
9. Sneezing
10. The Orange Bowl

SUPER TROUPERS
1. Crosby, Stills, Nash & Young
2. Bad Company
3. Journey
4. The Traveling Wilburys
5. Blind Faith
6. Velvet Revolver
7. Audioslave
8. Emerson, Lake & Palmer
9. Electronic
10. Asia

JUNE 12

RANDOM HOUSE
1. Portland, Oregon (nearly named Boston)
2. Patrick Ewing
3. The Bay City Rollers
4. "Yes"
5. Seven

KIDS IN THE HALL
1. H
2. J
3. A
4. I
5. G
6. B
7. C
8. F
9. E
10. D

IT'S A GIFT
1. David Letterman
2. Steve Irwin
3. Clifford the Big Red Dog
4. Andy
5. *The Mousetrap*

JUNE 13

VANITY PAIR
1. E, *Dancing with the Stars*
2. B, *Crossfire*
3. H, *Hee Haw*
4. J, *Entertainment Tonight*
5. A, NBC's nightly news, *The Huntley-Brinkley Report*
6. C, *The Man Show*
7. I, *Solid Gold*
8. D, *Monday Night Football*
9. G, *MythBusters*
10. F, *Lingo*

UNLUCKY STRIKES
1. A gallows
2. Dan Marino
3. The measles
4. *Nineteen Eighty-four*
5. *Rio Bravo*
6. Fifteen
7. Four
8. Missouri and Kentucky
9. A snake
10. The Cuban Missile Crisis
11. 12
12. Rugby
13. Lemony Snicket's

JUNE 14

FLAG DAY
1. Six
2. A baseball cap
3. Hemp
4. At the United Nations
5. Larry Flynt

THE SOME OF ITS PARTS
1. A castle
2. A cell
3. A horse (or other equine)
4. A sailboat
5. A staircase
6. A fencing blade
7. A letter
8. A column
9. A wave
10. A flower

CHRONIC TOWN
1. The Khmer Rouge
2. Kim Basinger
3. Walt Whitman
4. Darfur
5. Muhammad Ali

JUNE 15

IN A LIGHTER VEIN
1. Coagulation
2. Sierra Leone's
3. Rasputin
4. The Game
5. "Arse"
6. Kosher
7. Count Dracula
8. The aorta
9. Pig's blood
10. BALCO
11. *The Wild Bunch*
12. "Helter Skelter" (by the Manson Family)
13. A cake
14. Systolic and diastolic
15. Kansas

RUN FOR THE BORDER
Easy
1. Ireland
2. The Dominican Republic
3. Italy
4. Spain
Harder
1. Germany
2. Saudi Arabia
3. France
4. Italy
Yeah, Good Luck
1. Indonesia
2. Senegal
3. Malaysia
4. South Africa

JUNE 16

LIKE THE WEATHER
1. The "perfect storm"
2. The Toronto Blue Jays
3. "Baby, It's Cold Outside"
4. Seeding clouds (rainmaking)
5. Australia
6. David Letterman
7. The Santa Ana winds
8. Typhoons
9. Humidity
10. They have temperature scales named for them (Fahrenheit, Celsius, Lord Kelvin)

FATHER OF THE BRIDE
1. A
2. C
3. E
4. M
5. I
6. F
7. D
8. G
9. K
10. N
11. L
12. O
13. J
14. B
15. H

JUNE 17

"WHERE" HOUSE
1. Wally
2. Homer's *Odyssey*
3. Walter Mondale
4. Rockapella
5. Dollar bills (and other paper currency)
6. Casey Kasem
7. Extraterrestrials
8. Renault
9. Paul Gauguin
10. Fred Gwynne and Al Lewis

TINKER, TAILOR, SOLDIER, SAILOR . . .
1. The Chicago Cubs
2. Duran Duran
3. Westminster Abbey
4. Basra
5. Howard Hughes (in *Melvin and Howard* and *The Aviator*)
6. Fakir
7. Odysseus
8. Orchids
9. Julius Petri (the Petri dish)
10. Francis Scott Key
11. Crazy Horse

JUNE 18

FROM A TO Z
1. *Dirty*
2. "Ahoy"
3. Bijou
4. Gnu
5. Biopsy
6. *Ghost*
7. *CHiPs*
8. Aegis
9. Forty
10. Chinos

YE OLDE TRIVIA
1. The War of 1812
2. Joe DiMaggio
3. Taylor Hicks
4. Whiskey
5. All lived to be over 100 years old
6. Kevin Spacey
7. Queen Victoria
8. A wolf's
9. Alois Alzheimer
10. Snoop Dogg
11. Deuteronomy
12. Bob Vila
13. Abraham Lincoln
14. Nolan Ryan
15. *Modern Maturity*

JUNE 19	JUNE 20	JUNE 21

DAD TO THE BONE
1. I
2. A
3. G
4. F
5. C
6. J
7. H
8. D
9. E
10. B

BLEND AMBITION
1. Texarkana (Texas, Arkansas, Louisiana)
2. Blaxploitation
3. The Chunnel
4. Emoticons
5. Jazzercise
6. Stagflation
7. *Spanglish*'s
8. *Californication*
9. Ebonics
10. "Bootylicious"

STRICTLY STOCK
1. Share price and earnings
2. World War I
3. Eisenhower (1954)
4. Anheuser-Busch
5. Nikkei (the Nikkei 225 index)

I KNOW THERE'S AN ANSWER
1. "The Warmth of the Sun"
2. "Wendy"
3. "All Summer Long"
4. "409"
5. "Kokomo"
6. "Friends"
7. "Surf's Up"
8. "Wild Honey"
9. "Good Vibrations"
10. "Wouldn't It Be Nice"

HOT STUFF
1. *The Simple Life*
2. Death Valley
3. *Part Deux*
4. Bill Clinton
5. Mattel
6. Louis Armstrong
7. Chili peppers
8. Phil Hartman
9. *The View*
10. Lightning

SHARK WEEK
1. *Mork and Mindy*
2. Chicago
3. Michael Dukakis
4. Cat Stevens
5. Richard Gere
6. *The Sopranos*
7. The Buffalo Bills
8. Francis Ford Coppola
9. Al Sharpton
10. *Buffy the Vampire Slayer*

NON-FAMILY TIES
1. Were born a twin
2. Appear on the cover of *Sgt. Pepper's Lonely Hearts Club Band*
3. Killed another driver in a car accident
4. Appeared on the first cover of a magazine (*TV Guide, Time, Rolling Stone, Sports Illustrated, Playboy*)
5. Changed their name because another celebrity was already using their real name (Davy Jones, Albert Einstein, Sugar Ray Robinson, James Stewart, Michael Douglas)
6. Are very tall (6 feet, 7 inches or taller)
7. Were born in the West Indies
8. Had a leg amputated
9. Have a U.S. state capital named for them
10. Married a photographer

ACE IN THE HOLE
1. Eights
2. George Clooney
3. Batman
4. Five
5. Backgammon
6. A dolphin's
7. Whitey Ford
8. Another baby
9. Clubs
10. John Lennon's

June Answers

JUNE 22

RAMPANT INFLATION
1. The Wizard of Oz's
2. Richard Branson
3. Felix the Cat
4. Red
5. Sally Rand

THE AGONY OF DE FEET
1. Plantar warts
2. Steve Irwin
3. Water polo and beach volleyball
4. The Styx
5. The pedals on a piano

COLLECTED CONUNDRA
1. Coin collector
2. Cuckoo clocks
3. Calvin Coolidge
4. Carson City
5. California condor
6. Charlotte Church
7. *Cat's Cradle*
8. Clam chowder
9. Coonskin cap
10. Corpus callosum

JUNE 23

I'M IN CHARGE HERE!
Easy
1. Prime minister of Israel
2. *Tonight Show* host
3. Dallas Cowboys coach
4. Emperor of Rome
5. Vice president
Harder
1. Baseball commissioner
2. U.N. secretary-general
3. Secretary of defense
4. British poet laureate
5. Prime minister of Canada
Yeah, Good Luck
1. Governor of New York
2. President of the Motion Picture Academy
3. President of Egypt
4. Miss America
5. *New York Times* crossword editor

PITCHER PERFECT
1. Don Drysdale
2. Tommy John
3. Rolaids
4. Lefty Grove
5. Grover Cleveland Alexander (played by Ronald Reagan)

INCONCEIVABLE
1. Margaret Sanger
2. The Today sponge
3. Condom
4. Safe sex on the beach
5. Onan

JUNE 24

TYPE "OH"
1. Neil Sedaka's
2. Kate Walsh
3. Alabama
4. Dr. Seuss's
5. Hit a home run

BOTTLED UP
1. *I Dream of Jeannie*
2. Felix Klein
3. A hundred billion
4. Coca-Cola
5. Punt
6. Krypton
7. Finland
8. Jack Daniel's
9. Windchill factor
10. Tennessee Williams

A DESCENT PLACE TO LIVE
1. C
2. A
3. D
4. B
5. E

JUNE 25	JUNE 26	JUNE 27

ZAPPED!
1. Donner and Blitzen
2. *Cars*
3. Benjamin Franklin
4. *The Passion of the Christ*
5. The San Diego Chargers
6. Metallica's
7. The Cyclops
8. He turned into the Flash
9. Wonderboy
10. A Jacob's ladder

WEIGHTY MATTERS
1. Nazareth
2. Evangelista Torricelli (inventor of the barometer)
3. "Float On"
4. Uranium
5. Christian Bale (*Batman Begins*)
6. Avoirdupois
7. Lynn Redgrave
8. The liver
9. *The Crucible*
10. It's the official prototype kilogram
11. The carob tree's (hence, carats)
12. William "Refrigerator" Perry (350 pounds)
13. "Born to Be Wild"
14. Bantamweight and flyweight
15. *The Jerk*

THE RAT PATROL
1. Dr. Gregory House
2. Saccharin
3. Peter Lawford
4. The kangaroo rat
5. Linguini
6. "Round and Round"
7. Bubonic plague
8. *Willard*
9. The Teenage Mutant Ninja Turtles'
10. *Midnight Cowboy*

JUICY FRUITS
1. Pomegranate
2. Cranberry and lime
3. A dream deferred
4. Cherry red
5. Apricots
6. Grapes
7. Andy Warhol's
8. Oranges
9. Fruit of the Loom
10. Grape
11. Honduras
12. The tangelo
13. Dwight Gooden
14. The Empire State Building
15. Meat tenderizer
16. Atalanta's
17. Oranges (*The Love for Three Oranges*)
18. It gave people typhus (she was "Typhoid Mary")
19. A kiwifruit
20. Huckleberry Pie

MATCHING FUNDS
1. B, $100
2. D, $50
3. C, $10
4. E, $20
5. A, $2

SO I CAN, SO I CAN
1. *Vogue*
2. Roy Orbison ("Oh, Pretty Woman")
3. Jacqueline Kennedy Onassis
4. *Five Easy Pieces*
5. Paul Shaffer

FORBID AND FORGET
1. Google's
2. *Airplane!*
3. *The Outer Limits*
4. Its use in the last scene of *The Sopranos'* finale
5. Do not pass Go. Do not collect $200.
6. A rattlesnake
7. A villanelle
8. *Gremlins*
9. Do Not Resuscitate
10. "Don't Stop" by Fleetwood Mac

JUNE 28	JUNE 29	JUNE 30

JUNE 28

BLOW ME
1. A clarinet
2. The bassoon
3. The flugelhorn
4. The didgeridoo
5. Ricola
6. The tuba
7. The kazoo
8. Cattle's (because of Aaron's golden calf)
9. The trombone
10. The ocarina

MY LITTLE PONY
Easy
1. Silver
2. Pokey
3. Mister Ed
4. Trigger
5. Horse
Harder
1. Traveller
2. Rocinante
3. Tony
4. Bucephalus
5. Scout
Yeah, Good Luck
1. Incitatus
2. Gunpowder
3. Marengo
4. Shadowfax
5. Tornado

LEI LADY LEI
1. Maui
2. The ukulele
3. Duke Kahanamoku
4. Arizona (the USS *Arizona*)
5. Rainbow

JUNE 29

HOOKED ON CLASSICS
1. Samuel Barber's
2. Antonio Vivaldi (*The Four Seasons*)
3. The Thames
4. Richard Wagner
5. Elise

ROADS SCHOLARS
1. Utah
2. Alabama
3. Pennsylvania (a keystone)
4. California (a 49ers mining spade)
5. Nebraska
6. North Dakota
7. New Mexico
8. Washington
9. New Hampshire
10. Kansas (a sunflower)

ALTAR EGOS
1. Elizabeth Taylor
2. The Saint Bartholomew's Day Massacre
3. *Kill Bill* (*Volume 2*, to be specific)
4. Jane Eyre's
5. Tricia Nixon

JUNE 30

DON'T GO CHASING WATER-FALLS
1. *The Mission*
2. David Livingstone
3. Venezuela
4. Professor Moriarty
5. The Columbia's

WHO'S THAT GIRL?
Easy
1. "Jessie's Girl"
2. "Hollaback Girl"
3. "My Girl"
4. "Girlfriend"
5. "What a Girl Wants"
Harder
1. "West End Girls"
2. "Big Girls Don't Cry"
3. "Rich Girl"
4. "Forever Your Girl"
5. "Bad Girls"
Yeah, Good Luck
1. "Oh Girl"
2. "Go Away Little Girl"
3. "Girl I'm Gonna Miss You"
4. "Island Girl"
5. "The Most Beautiful Girl"

THE THING WITH FEATHERS
1. (*Three Days of*) The Condor
2. The Penguin
3. Swan
4. The Cardinal
5. The Falcon

• **1862** • AFTER THE COSTLY LOSSES of the Seven Days' Battles, George McLellan's "Peninsula Campaign" ends in failure, just miles from the Confederate capital of Richmond. McLellan's larger army could have won the war if he'd pressed on to Richmond; instead, three years of bloodshed lie ahead.

PENINSULA CAMPAIGN

1. What peninsula is held together, at its narrowest point, by the Isthmus of Kra?

2. At what Seward Peninsula city does the Iditarod end?

3. "Al-Jazeera," which means "the peninsula" in Arabic, is a reference to what peninsular nation, where it's headquartered?

4. What does "lo Stivale," the local name for the Italian peninsula, mean in Italian?

5. What U.S. peninsula is home to a namesake national park, whose Quinault Rain Forest is the wettest spot in the continental U.S.?

6. What triangular peninsula's highest point is actually Mount St. Catherine and not its namesake peak?

7. Anzac Day, in Australia and New Zealand, commemorates the date of the bloody 1915 landing

on what Turkish peninsula?

8. What name is given to the mainland peninsula that's part of Hong Kong?

9. Where do "Yoopers" live?

10. In what country is the Bataan Peninsula, home to a famous 1942 "Death March"?

• **2007** • NEW YORK CITY RESTAURANTS are now strictly limited in what they fry or spread thanks to America's strictest ban on trans fats.

"TRANS-" FACTS

1. What nation removed the prefix "Trans" from before its name in June 1949?

2. What TV series has produced episodes called ". . . And Found" and ". . . In Translation"?

3. What gets changed by the process of transubstantiation?

4. What city is the eastern terminus of the Trans-Siberian Railway?

5. Who bought Trans World Airlines in 1939?

6. A poster for what band's album *Transatlanticism* hung in Seth Cohen's bedroom on *The O.C.*?

7. What movie character is a "sweet transvestite from Transsexual, Transylvania"?

8. What kind of transplant was first performed in France in

2005, on a woman who'd been attacked by her dog?

9. What is the home planet of Hasbro's Transformers toys?

10. What novelist's father, Bronson, was one of the founders of the Transcendentalist movement?

Answers to the questions on this page can be found on page 299.

• **1942** • CARY GRANT STARS as Cole Porter in the lavish Warner musical *Night and Day*. The title might as well describe the movie's differences from Porter's real life, since Grant plays the gay Porter as deeply, heterosexually in love with his "beard" wife, Linda.

BIO-PICKS
Who's been played, in the movies, by both these actors?

Easy	Harder	Yeah, Good Luck
1. Cate Blanchett, Judi Dench	1. Kirk Douglas, Tim Roth	1. John Cusack, Edward Norton
2. Willem Defoe, James Caviezel	2. Raymond Massey, Henry Fonda	2. Robert Duvall, Colin Farrell
3. Denzel Washington, Mario Van Peebles	3. Catherine O'Hara, Sandra Bullock	3. Laurence Olivier, Gregory Peck
4. Robert Downey, Eddie Izzard	4. John Gavin, Rex Harrison	4. Rosemary Murphy, Jennifer Jason Leigh
5. Ray Liotta, D. B. Sweeney	5. Norma Shearer, Kirsten Dunst	5. Gailard Sartain, Stephen Lee

• **1957** • THE CARY GRANT–DEBORAH KERR tearjerker *An Affair to Remember* premieres, for which we can blame *Sleepless in Seattle*.

AFFAIRS TO REMEMBER
Name these "affairs" from a few of their principals.

1. Marie-Georges Picquart, Émile Zola, Auguste Mercier	3. Christine Keeler, Dr. Stephen Ward, Yevgeny Ivanov	5. Buffy, Jody, Cissy
2. John Poindexter, Robert Mc-Farlane, Oliver North	4. John Marshall, Elbridge Gerry, Charles Maurice de Talleyrand	

• **2000** • VICENTE FOX IS ELECTED president of Mexico, ending the PRI party's uninterrupted sixty-year rule.

CRAZY LIKE A FOX

1. What TV series closes with a logo for "30th Century Fox"?
2. What phrase for false disdain comes from one of Aesop's fables, about a fox unable to leap up to a hanging vine?
3. What was comedian Redd Foxx's real last name?
4. What actor did Michael J. Fox replace as Marty McFly in *Back to the Future*?
5. Which of Santa's reindeer is named for a female fox?
6. George Fox is traditionally called the founder of what religious group?
7. Flying foxes aren't foxes at all—they're the largest type of what kind of animal?
8. Jimi Hendrix's "Foxy Lady" was a tribute to Heather Taylor, the model who later married what rock front man?
9. In what country was actor and former NBAer Rick Fox born?
10. What famous event happened in the parking lot of the Machus Red Fox restaurant outside Detroit on July 30, 1975?

Answers to the questions on this page can be found on page 299.

• **1844** • THE LAST NESTING PAIR of great auks is shot by sailors on the Icelandic island of Eldey. They also crush the pair's egg.

WELL, THAT'S JUST GREAT

1. What two "Great" lakes are the largest two lakes entirely within Canada?

2. Who's the palindromic protagonist of Dickens's *Great Expectations*?

3. What comedy hit was produced under the working title *East Great Falls High*?

4. What president proposed the Great Society?

5. Radio's first spin-off, *The Great Gildersleeve*, originated from what other comedy series?

6. *The Great Rock 'n' Roll Swindle* is a mockumentary about what band?

7. What phrase from Virgil, meaning "Providence has favored our undertakings," appears on the back of the Great Seal of the United States?

8. The Great Barrier Reef sits off the coast of what Australian state?

9. *The Great White Hope* is a fictionalized account of what first black heavyweight boxing champ?

10. What day of the week was the initial October 24, 1929, crash that kicked off the Great Depression?

• **1863** • THE DISASTROUS BLOODBATH of Pickett's Charge marks the end of the battle of Gettysburg and the "high-water mark of the Confederacy." It will be seen as the turning point of the Civil War.

NORTH AND SOUTH

The Union and Confederacy couldn't even agree on what to call their battlegrounds. Can you match up these northern and southern names for the same engagement?

1. Antietam	**A.** Elkhorn Tavern
2. Bull Run	**B.** Manassas
3. Pea Ridge	**C.** Murfreesboro
4. Shiloh	**D.** Pittsburg Landing
5. Stones River	**E.** Sharpsburg

• **1971** • This is the end, beautiful friend: JIM MORRISON'S BODY is found in a Paris bathtub dead of a heroin overdose.

BEFORE I GET OLD

Given a musical group, name the band member who OD'd young.

Easy	*Harder*	*Yeah, Good Luck*
1. Big Brother and the Holding Company	**1.** Blind Melon	**1.** Mother Love Bone
2. The Sex Pistols	**2.** The Wu-Tang Clan	**2.** Red Hot Chili Peppers
3. The Byrds	**3.** Milli Vanilli	**3.** Hole
4. The Blues Brothers	**4.** Thin Lizzy	**4.** The Germs
5. The Who	**5.** Alice in Chains	**5.** Sublime

Answers to the questions on this page can be found on page 299.

JULY 4

• **1826** • ON THE FIFTIETH ANNIVERSARY of the signing of the Declaration of Independence, two of the three surviving signers die within hours of each other: John Adams and Thomas Jefferson.

FOUNDING FATHERS

1. Washington's famous crossing of the Delaware was en route to what Revolutionary War battle?
2. Who said "Is life so dear, or peace so sweet, as to be purchased at the price of chains and slavery? Forbid it, Almighty God!"?
3. Under what Roman pseudonym were the Federalist Papers written?
4. Who was the oldest signer of the Declaration of Independence?
5. Who was the only slave ever known to have stayed in John Adams's household?

• **1924** • AN INDEPENDENCE DAY CUSTOMER RUSH depletes Tijuana chef Caesar Cardini's supply of salad ingredients, so he whips up a new concoction tableside. The Caesar salad is born.

HAIL CAESAR

1. Julius Caesar was killed on the fifteenth day of March, but during most months, the Roman ides actually fell on a different date. Which?
2. What politician, a U.S. congressman until 2003, was named for Julius Caesar?
3. What's the protagonist's name—and the last word of the film—in 1931's *Little Caesar*?
4. What Shakespearean title character is killed, as prophesied, by an enemy who was born via cesarean section?
5. In what movie does Sid Caesar cameo as football coach Calhoun?

• **1991** • MINNEAPOLIS ALT-ROCK BAND The Replacements officially breaks up, after their famous "It Ain't Over 'Til the Fat Roadie Plays" farewell performance at Chicago's Grant Park. One by one, the band members hand off their equipment to their road crew toward the end of the concert, so the show ends with the roadies "replacing" the Replacements.

THE REPLACEMENTS

1. What color M&M was retired to make way for blue M&Ms in 1995?
2. At the start of what movie does the star deadpan to the camera, "This never happened to the other fellow"?
3. In the Bible, who did Matthias replace?
4. What is Ryan Minor's claim to (very limited) sports fame?
5. What were the names of the "scab" Duke cousins who took over *The Dukes of Hazzard* during John Schneider and Tom Wopat's 1982 contract dispute?
6. When the Eiffel Tower was completed, it replaced what American building as the world's tallest structure?
7. In 2001, what surpassed tuna as America's most eaten seafood?
8. What bird did Ben Franklin suggest replace the bald eagle as a national emblem?
9. Steven Hill was replaced as TD Waterhouse's TV pitchman by which of his *Law & Order* cast mates?
10. What was the capital of Brazil until Brasilia was completed?

Answers to the questions on this page can be found on page 300.

• **1687** • NEWTON'S FIRST, SECOND, and Third Laws of Motion are published for the first time, when Sir Isaac revolutionizes math and science in his *Philosophiae naturalis principia mathematica.*

ORDINAL SINS
Can you put these answers back in the right order?

1. What's another name for a quaver?
2. What world's currency is the Linden dollar?
3. What position was only ever held by Louisiana-born Varina Howell?
4. Loma Linda, California, is the largest U.S. city where mail is delivered on Sundays, because of what organization's strong presence there?

5. What baseball position has produced fewer Hall of Famers than any other?
6. What's the name of Ron Kovic's bestselling autobiography?
7. What mythical title has been given to poets from Sappho to Anne Bradstreet?
8. What retailer was Claire Danes's employer in *Shopgirl* and the site of Winona Ryder's

shoplifting arrest?
9. What body controversially found the Pledge of Allegiance unconstitutional in the 2002 *Newdow* case?
10. What was the last horror film to earn a Best Picture Oscar nomination?

• **1937** • THE CANNED-"MEAT" PRODUCT Spam first hits grocery store shelves.

NO ACCOUNTING FOR TASTE
In honor of Spam, a quiz on other matters of questionable taste.

1. What U.S. president loved Fresca so much he had a soda tap installed for the Oval Office?
2. What was the first rap single to hit number one on *Billboard's* Hot 100?

3. At the 2001 Oscars, what animal did Björk dress as?
4. What Sacramento-born "Painter of Light" calls himself "America's most-collected living artist"?

5. In 1983, the Minnesota North Stars passed up Cam Neely, Steve Yzerman, and Pat Lafontaine to draft what American, the only high school player ever to go number one in the NHL?

• **1994** • WHEN UMPIRES CONFISCATE Albert Belle's bat on suspicion of being corked, the Cleveland Indians go into full *Mission: Impossible* mode, sending pitcher Jason Grimsley wriggling into an overhead crawl space to switch bats. But Grimsley's subterfuge is easily detected: he accidentally replaces Belle's bat with one labeled as Paul Sorrento's.

YOUR CHEATIN' HEART

1. What sports event did Rosie Ruiz win by cheating in 1980?
2. What January 6, 1994, act got Shane Shant a four-year prison sentence?
3. What did "Black Sox" pitcher Eddie Cicotte do in the first at-

bat of the 1919 World Series to signal that the fix was in?
4. What future NBA head coach hit the free throws that seemingly won the U.S. the gold medal at the disputed 1972 Olympic basketball finals?

5. According to 2001 revelations, what famous event in sports history was made possible by a Polo Grounds telescope?

Answers to the questions on this page can be found on page 300.

JULY 6

• **1885** • NINE-YEAR-OLD JOSEPH MEISTER, having been bitten by a rabid dog, becomes the first recipient of Louis Pasteur's rabies vaccine. Later in life, he will serve as caretaker at the Pasteur Institute in Paris.

A SHOT IN THE ARM

1. An ongoing parents' lawsuit blames the vaccine additive thiomersal for causing what syndrome?

2. The MMR vaccine immunizes against what three illnesses?

3. What nickname for the antipolio National Foundation for Infantile Paralysis was coined by entertainer Eddie Cantor?

4. What rock group's name is a homophone for a Sinclair Lewis novel about a vaccination pioneer?

5. What disease does the "tine test" detect?

• **1916** • A JAMES MONTGOMERY FLAGG painting of Uncle Sam debuts in *Leslie's Weekly* magazine with a caption reading "What are you doing for preparedness?" Seven months later, paired with a new caption ("I want YOU for U.S. Army!"), it will become one of the most famous images in American history.

SAY UNCLE

1. In the song "Zip-a-Dee-Doo-Dah," what kind of animal sits on Uncle Remus's shoulder?

2. *Dallas*'s Patrick Duffy is the uncle of what Cy Young winner who now pitches for the Giants?

3. Worst . . . uncle . . . ever. What Shakespeare title character orders the murder of two of his own nephews?

4. What two long-running 1980s TV shows featured characters called "Uncle Jesse"?

5. What familiar product is Rich Uncle Pennybags the mascot for?

6. What two American leading men can call director Francis Ford Coppola "Uncle Francis"?

7. In *Uncle Tom's Cabin*, Eliza's famous flight across the ice floes takes place on what frozen river?

8. What's the avian name of the acronymic evil organization on *The Man from U.N.C.L.E.*?

9. In U.S. Army history, who was "Uncle Billy"?

10. The Oscar for humanitarian work is named for what actor, Leslie Nielsen's uncle?

• **1979** • AFTER SPENDING FIFTEEN MONTHS in a Seattle hospital, Jon Brower Minnoch, the heaviest man ever, announces that he's lost 924 pounds—he's down to a svelte 476.

MISTER BIG

1. What acoustic track was the only number one hit for 1990s hard-rock band Mr. Big?

2. Mr. Big is the largest chocolate bar produced by what British confectioner?

3. Drug lord Mr. Big is the villain of what James Bond novel and film?

4. Boris and Natasha's sometime superior Mr. Big works for the government of what fictional nation?

5. What was Big's real first name revealed to be in the last episode of *Sex and the City*?

Answers to the questions on this page can be found on page 300.

• **1591** • THE PAMPLONA RUNNING of the bulls is held in the summer for the first time—prior to this year, it was a late September event.

TORO! TORO! TORO!

1. What household product is named for the bull that was designed as the "husband" of Borden's Elsie the Cow?

2. What song is, appropriately, attributed to a seventeenth-century composer, Dr. John Bull?

3. Who told reporters "I'm as fit as a bull moose!" when he founded the Progressive Party in 1912?

4. What future *Cheers* star plays Mob boss Tommy Como in *Raging Bull*?

5. The Chicago Bulls take the court to "Sirius," an instrumental track by what prog-rock band?

6. In what country did Red Bull originate as *Krating Daeng*?

7. What island was home to the Minotaur's Labyrinth?

8. In 1520, who burned his copy of *Decet romanum pontificem*, the papal bull excommunicating him?

9. What Sioux tribe did Sitting Bull belong to?

10. Nostradamus, Machiavelli, or Magellan—what famous sixteenth-century name is also "Bull" Shannon's first name on *Night Court*?

• **1912** • THE FIRST MODERN PENTATHLON begins, at the Stockholm Olympics. The fifth-place finisher is no less than the young George S. Patton, who would have medaled if not for his poor performance in—ironically—the shooting event.

GENERAL KNOWLEDGE

1. After the Civil War, which Union general became the first president of the NRA?

2. Despite an earlier military failure, who was appointed governor-general of India in 1786 and 1805?

3. Which general's father led the investigation of the Lindbergh baby kidnapping?

4. Who was made a general in 1935, when he was selected to create the Nazi Luftwaffe?

5. Garfield, Harrison, or McKinley—before Eisenhower, who was the last general elected U.S. president?

6. Roman general Scipio Africanus gained his African surname from his famous defeat of whom?

7. Which *My Three Sons* star grew up to play the scared soldier that George C. Scott pimp-slaps in *Patton*?

8. What South American general had an Ecuadorian currency and a Bolivian city named for him, even though he was Venezuelan-born?

9. What dish, named for a famous general, is coated in foie gras, mushrooms, and puff pastry?

10. Whom did Gerald Ford promote to General of the Armies of the United States in 1975, a position held previously only by "Black Jack" Pershing?

Answers to the questions on this page can be found on page 301.

JULY 8

• **1663** • CHARLES II GRANTS a charter to the rather wordily named "Colony of Rhode Island and Providence Plantations." As a result, Rhode Island still has the longest formal name of any state: it's officially "The State of Rhode Island and Providence Plantations."

STATE DEPARTMENT
What's the only U.S. state name . . .

1. With only one syllable	**3.** That ends with the state's own postal abbreviation	nants (uninterrupted by spaces)
2. That has no letters in common with its state capital's name	**4.** With four consecutive conso-	**5.** That honors a non-English king

• **1950** • A YOUNG COMEDIAN named Jackie Gleason replaces Jerry Lester as the host of DuMont's *Cavalcade of Stars.*

THE GREAT ONE
What nations were led by these rulers?

Easy	*Harder*	*Yeah, Good Luck*
1. Peter the Great	**1.** Cyrus the Great	**1.** Simeon the Great
2. Alexander the Great	**2.** Akbar the Great	**2.** Theodoric the Great
3. Kamehameha the Great	**3.** Pompey the Great	**3.** Casimir the Great
4. Rameses the Great	**4.** Frederick the Great	**4.** Sargon the Great

• **1963** • SENSITIVE LINEMAN ROSEY GRIER is traded to the Los Angeles Rams, joining Lamar Lundy, Deacon Jones, and Merlin Olsen to form a defensive line that soon becomes known as "the Fearsome Foursome."

QUAD SQUADS
What does each of these fearsome foursomes of sports have in common?

1. Alex Delvecchio, Darrell Green, John Stockton, Carl Yastrzemski	**4.** Lyle Alzado, Larry Brown, Sandy Koufax, Kerri Strug	Howe, Robert Parish, Pete Rose
2. Danny Ainge, Dave DeBusschere, Drew Henson, Brian Jordan	**5.** Ronnie Lott, Jackie Robinson, Paul Warfield, James Worthy	**9.** Rick Barry, Bobby Hull, Ken Norton, Dick Weber
3. Muhammad Ali, Alex Karras, Denny McLain, Kermit Washington	**6.** Daryl Johnston, Mark Messier, Mike Mussina, Harry Watson	**10.** Rocky Marciano, Thurman Munson, Knute Rockne, Payne Stewart
	7. Ron Hextall, Chuck Howley, Bobby Richardson, Jerry West	
	8. Morten Andersen, Gordie	

Answers to the questions on this page can be found on page 301.

JULY 9

• **1846** • CONGRESS RETURNS TO VIRGINIA the portion of the District of Columbia that lies south of the Potomac River.

GIVE THAT BACK!

1. What object was returned to Edinburgh Castle in 1996, though Westminster Abbey is still allowed to borrow it for coronations?
2. What president returned the U.S.-controlled Panama Canal Zone to Panama?
3. What painting was recovered by Norwegian police three months after it was stolen, the same day the Lillehammer Olympics opened?
4. To whom did Brian Leetch hand over the team captaincy of the New York Rangers when he returned to the team in 2000?
5. *Pee-Wee's Big Adventure* is to recover what beloved stolen item?

• **1927** • THE TERRITORY OF ALASKA first flies its official flag. Designed by 13-year-old Benny Benson of Seward, it depicts the Big Dipper and the North Star.

A-LIST STARS
Can you identify these constellations with the naked eye?

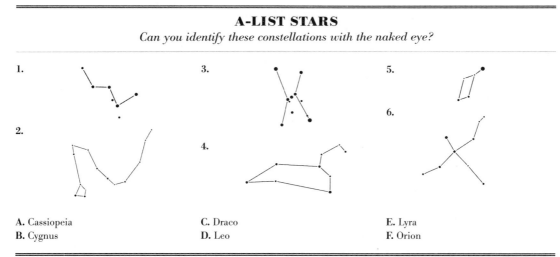

1.

2.

3.

4.

5.

6.

A. Cassiopeia
B. Cygnus
C. Draco
D. Leo
E. Lyra
F. Orion

• **2002** • WITH BOTH TEAMS OUT of pitchers in the eleventh inning, Major League Baseball calls the 73rd All-Star Game a 7–7 tie. "Let them play! Let them play!" the unhappy Milwaukee crowd chants, throwing garbage onto the field.

SPORTFOLIO
How many players to a side in each of these sports? (Not counting the bench, where appropriate.)

Easy	*Harder*	*Yeah, Good Luck*
1. Basketball	**1.** Volleyball	**1.** Team handball
2. Beach volleyball	**2.** Curling	**2.** Ultimate Frisbee
3. Ice hockey	**3.** Water polo	**3.** Polo
4. Baseball	**4.** Soccer	**4.** Australian rules football
5. American football	**5.** Men's field lacrosse	**5.** Quidditch

Answers to the questions on this page can be found on page 301.

JULY 10

• **1066** • THE SPANISH NATIONAL HERO Rodrigo Díaz de Vivar, aka El Cid, dies in Valencia.

RAISING "EL"

1. What Mexican *ciudad* sits across the Rio Grande from El Paso, Texas?

2. What sheriff's alter ego was the masked "El Kabong"?

3. What 1995 film was Robert Rodriguez's big-budget follow-up to the $7,000 hit *El Mariachi*?

4. What pitcher with four World Series rings is nicknamed "El Duque"?

5. El Greco painted a famous *View of* what Spanish city, his adoptive hometown?

• **1882** • FORMER TEXAS GOVERNOR James "Big Jim" Hogg officially becomes the worst father in world history when he names his newborn daughter "Ima."

THY NAME IS WOMAN

1. What's the first book of the Bible named for a woman?

2. Jennifer's sudden 1970 leap to become America's most popular name for baby girls, a title it held until 1984, is often attributed to what novel and movie?

3. What tiny Idaho town of 128 residents leaped to fame in 1994 thanks to its namesake's Olympic performance?

4. Up until the 1980s, the vast majority of Japanese girls were given names that ended with what syllable?

5. Mabel, Maisie, or Mary—what's the real first name of Tyler Perry's most famous creation, Madea?

6. What two late-1950s Broadway musicals featured songs titled "Maria"?

7. What woman's name has one *l* according to Elvis Costello but two according to the Pixies?

8. Both of TV's *Gilmore Girls* have what first name?

9. What given name appears in the title of the debut novels of both Stephen King and Theodore Dreiser?

10. What city—America's twentieth largest—is the most populous U.S. city named for a woman?

• **1967** • THE "KIWI" DOLLAR REPLACES the New Zealand pound, as the Southern Hemisphere nation decimalizes its currency.

OLD MONEY
Which European countries replaced, or will replace, these currencies with the euro?

Easy	*Harder*	*Yeah, Good Luck*
1. Escudo	**1.** Schilling	**1.** Lev (2010)
2. Deutsche mark	**2.** Markka	**2.** Forint (2010)
3. Drachma	**3.** Zloty (2011)	**3.** Tolar
4. Pound	**4.** Guilder	**4.** Kroon (2010)

Answers to the questions on this page can be found on page 302.

• **1754** • PHYSICIAN AND PRUDE Thomas Bowdler is born near Bath, England. Bowdler will give us the word "bowdlerize" with his expurgated 1807 version of Shakespeare, in which Lady Macbeth says "Out, crimson spot!" instead of "Out, damned spot!" and Ophelia didn't really *mean* to kill herself—she just slipped!

DEAR PRUDE HENS
Five family-friendly questions about good old-fashioned puritanism.

1. What food is named for a nineteenth-century Connecticut minister who believed that eating whole-wheat-flour biscuits would curb sexual urges?
2. What's the only NC-17-rated movie ever to open in wide U.S. release?

3. What state, ironically, cast the thirty-sixth and deciding vote to repeal Prohibition in 1933?
4. In 1970, psychologist Linnda Caporael claimed that a crop of fungus-infested rye was responsible for what historical event?
5. Though Little Ricky's birth on

I Love Lucy was the highest-rated show in TV history at the time, what word did CBS forbid the show from using that season?

• **1989** • THEIR NEW ALBUM *Mind Bomb* introduces the newest member of English pop band The The: Johnny Marr of the Smiths.

THE THE

1. What long-running soap opera dropped the "The" in its title in 1975?
2. What tiny West African nation added a "The" to its name when it gained independence on ~~April 30, 1960~~ February 18, 1965?

3. What H. G. Wells title would become a Ralph Ellison novel without the initial "the"?
4. What famous goof occurs in the credits of the 1965 B-movie *Attack of the Eye Creatures*?
5. "The" is the most common

word in spoken English. What other three-letter word comes in second?

• **1997** • GRIGORIO FUENTES TURNS 100. Fuentes, a Cuban fisherman and first mate to Ernest Hemingway, spent the last decades of his life claiming to have been the model for Santiago in *The Old Man and the Sea,* even though he was only 52 when the book was released.

TITLE WAVE
Name these literary works from their title characters.

Easy	*Harder*	*Yeah, Good Luck*
1. Willy Loman	**1.** Bigger Thomas	**1.** Offred
2. Edmond Dantès	**2.** Chingachgook	**2.** Prince Myshkin
3. Bilbo Baggins	**3.** Oliver Mellors	**3.** Michael Henchard
4. Quasimodo	**4.** Roy Hobbs	**4.** Frankie Addams
5. Henry Higgins	**5.** Isabel Archer	**5.** Meursault

Answers to the questions on this page can be found on page 302.

JULY 12

• **1794** • CANNON FIRE AT THE SIEGE of Calvi causes Horatio Nelson, the English admiral, to lose the sight in his right eye. More seriously, historians have since discovered, it also deprived him of his right eyebrow. A museum waxwork of Nelson was plucked accordingly in 2005.

BILL OF RIGHTS
Do you have the "right" stuff for this one-sided quiz?

1. What's the only currently minted U.S. coin whose "heads" side shows a profile facing right, not left?

2. Which NFL team wears its logo only on the right side of its helmets?

3. The heart's right ventricle pumps directly into what blood vessel, the body's only artery that carries deoxygenated blood?

4. What rock guitarist lost most of his right middle finger to his brother Clifford's ax during a wood-chopping accident at age four?

5. All of the countries in the mainland Americas drive on the right side of the road—except for what two neighbors?

6. What actor is the subject of R.E.M.'s "Monty Got a Raw Deal" and the Clash's "The Right Profile"?

7. Whose right-hand man—quite literally—is Mr. Smee?

8. A right-handed pitcher's curveball breaks from right to left. What pitch breaks the opposite way, from left to right?

9. What artist painted himself sketching on the far right edge of his painting "The Gross Clinic"?

10. On what TV show did Hillary Clinton describe "a vast right-wing conspiracy" in 1998?

• **1916** • TWO MEN ARE KILLED by a shark in Matawan Creek, New Jersey, ending the spate of shark attacks that would inspire the novel *Jaws*.

JUST FOR FIN

1. An episode of what sitcom spawned the phrase "jumped the shark"?

2. What largest lake of Central America is home to unusual freshwater sharks?

3. Which *Saturday Night Live* cast member played the Land Shark?

4. What rock group was behind the infamous "Mudshark Incident" at Seattle's Edgewater Inn in 1969?

5. What's the world's largest predatory fish?

6. The San Jose Sharks were the Bay Area's first NHL team since what expansion team left in 1976?

7. What network has aired "Shark Week" every summer since 1988?

8. What street gang rumbles with the Sharks in *West Side Story*?

9. What Hyundai coupe gets its name from the Spanish word for "shark"?

10. In what ship's 1945 sinking were as many as eighty sailors eaten by whitetip sharks?

Answers to the questions on this page can be found on page 302.

• **1872** • CHARLES GOUNOD COMPOSES a little piano ditty he calls "Funeral March of a Marionette." No one really cares for eighty years, but then the tune becomes the famous theme of *Alfred Hitchcock Presents.*

SHOW TUNES
What TV shows had each of these themes?

Easy
1. "Believe It or Not"
2. "Making Our Dreams Come True"
3. "Where Everybody Knows Your Name"
4. "I'll Be There for You"
5. "The Ballad of Jed Clampett"

Harder
1. "Thank You for Being a Friend"
2. "Boss of Me"
3. "The Streetbeater"
4. "Good Ol' Boys"
5. "Final Frontier"

Yeah, Good Luck
1. "Then Came You"
2. "The Toy Parade"
3. "There's a New Girl in Town"
4. "There's No Place like Home"
5. "Falling"

• **1935** • TEDDY WILSON AND GENE KRUPA join the "King of Swing" for the first recording session of the Benny Goodman Trio. The presence of Wilson, a black man, was particularly historic, since the trio became the first major integrated combo in jazz history.

KINGS OF SWING

1. What sports team used the Swinging Friar as its team emblem until 1984?
2. What Reagan appointee is currently the only "swing vote" on the Supreme Court?
3. What's the name of the rhythm guitarist who knows "all the chords" in Dire Straits' "Sultans of Swing"?
4. What noun is used as a slangy adjective for "good" or "cool" thirty-four times in the 1996 movie *Swingers*?
5. What swing state is the U.S.'s most reliable political bellwether, having voted for the winning candidate in twenty-five of the last twenty-six presidential elections?

• **2002** • A REMIX OF ELVIS PRESLEY'S "A Little Less Conversation" ends its chart-topping run in Britain, having broken the long-standing tie between Elvis and the Beatles for most number ones.

A LITTLE MORE CONVERSATION
What songs begin with these exchanges of dialogue?

1. "Oh, my, God. Becky, look at her butt. It is so big."
2. "Betty, is that Jimmy's ring you're wearing?" "Mm-hmm."
3. "Hey, I can't find nothing on the radio." "Uh, yo, turn to that station."
4. "Hey Jack, what's happenin'?" "Oh, I don't know." "Well, uh, rumor around town says you think you might be heading down to the shore."
5. "Wendy?" "Yes, Lisa?" "Is the water warm enough?" "Yes, Lisa."
6. "Hey bra', how we doin', man?" "All right." "It's been a while, man, life's so rad!"
7. "Are you ready, Theodore?" "Ready, Dave!"
8. "What you gonna play now?" "Bobby, I don't know, but whatever I play, it's got to be funky."
9. "Got to get this airplane off." "Naw, leave it, yeah."
10. "Whaddya think the teacher's gonna look like this year?" "My butt, man!"

Answers to the questions on this page can be found on page 303.

• **1531** • FEARING THAT SHE'LL NEVER be able to give him a son, Henry VIII separates from Catherine of Aragon, abandoning her at Windsor Castle on the pretext of leaving for a hunting trip. One down, five to go.

ALL I NEED IS THE HEIR THAT I BREED
Which of Henry VIII's six wives . . .

1. May never have slept with him	**5.** Was the daughter of Columbus's patrons, Ferdinand and Isabella	**10.** Is rumored to have had six fingers on her left hand
2. Was the mother of Queen Elizabeth I	**6.** Died of cancer	
3. Is buried beside him	**7.** Was Anne Boleyn's cousin	
4. Doesn't share her first name with any of the other five	**8.** Was German	
	9. Was married four times herself	

• **1957** • WITH BOTH MEN in the legal doghouse due to tax troubles, Abbott and Costello split up amicably. They even agree to joint custody of Stinky.

BREAKING UP IS HARD TO DO
A quiz on other historic splits.

1. What movie was split into two parts, *Death Proof* and *Planet Terror*, for overseas release?
2. What rival faction split from the Bolsheviks at the Communist Party Congress of 1903?
3. Name either of the two U.S. states that can split their presidential electoral vote by congressional district.
4. The first atomic bomb test split an atom of what fissionable element?
5. What two pins are left standing in bowling's hardest split to pick up?
6. What kind of animal was Snorky, the only one of the Banana Splits who didn't talk?
7. What split up into Gondwanaland and Laurasia?
8. Who split up with the 2001 Oscar host in 1997 and with the 2007 Oscar host in 2000?
9. What Omaha company has the New York Stock Exchange's highest-priced stock, as it never allows stock splits?
10. What band's 2005 split led to the creation of Plus-44 and Angels and Airwaves?

Answers to the questions on this page can be found on page 303.

• 971 • THE BODY OF A Winchester bishop named Swithin is moved indoors for his canonization, leading—so the legend goes—to a torrential rainstorm. According to tradition, if it rains in Britain on Saint Swithin's Day, it will continue to rain for forty days straight.

HIT THE SHOWERS
Into every question, a little rain must fall.

1. What supermodel plays the bride in Guns N' Roses' "November Rain" video?
2. According to Dustin Hoffman in *Rain Man*, what's the only airline that has never had a crash?
3. What two Top Ten Creedence Clearwater Revival hits ask about the rain?
4. Parts of what Chilean desert have gone four hundred years without rainfall?
5. What baseball team has only ever had one home rainout, on June 15, 1976?
6. What actor blogs at "Schrute-Space" at NBC.com?
7. The Arabic word for "season" gave us what name for South Asia's rainy season?
8. Whose halftime set at Super Bowl XLI was, appropriately enough, performed during a downpour?
9. Gene Kelly sings "Singin' in the Rain" over the end credits of what 1971 film?
10. What precedes "The rain fell in torrents" as the first line of Edward Bulwer-Lytton's novel *Paul Clifford*?

• 1792 • TODAY IS THE DEADLINE for a contest to design the U.S. Capitol, still called the "Congress House." None of the submissions sparks George Washington's interest, so he chooses a late-arriving design from an amateur architect named William Thornton instead.

UNDA THE ROTUNDA
What U.S. state is represented by these figures in the Capitol's Statuary Hall?

Easy
1. George Washington and Robert E. Lee
2. Stephen Austin and Sam Houston
3. Father Damien and Kamehameha I
4. Philo T. Farnsworth and Brigham Young

Harder
1. Will Rogers and Sequoyah
2. Jefferson Davis and James Zachariah George
3. John Stark and Daniel Webster
4. Andrew Jackson and John Sevier

Yeah, Good Luck
1. Oliver Morton and Lew Wallace
2. Robert Fulton and John Muhlenberg
3. Patrick McCarran and Sarah Winnemucca
4. Jeanette Rankin and Charles Marion Russell

• 1978 • COMICS-PAGE NEWCOMER Garfield eats his very first lasagna. Heh heh, lasagna. Classic. And he hates Mondays!

GREED, FOR LACK OF A BETTER WORD, IS GOOD
Get your fill of questions on Garfield-style gluttony.

1. What animal, a U.S. state symbol, is sometimes also called the "glutton"?
2. What "wafer-thin" food makes the morbidly obese Mr. Creosote explode in *Monty Python's The Meaning of Life*?
3. Who popularized the "turducken," by offering one to the winner of Thanksgiving Day NFL games?
4. In 2005, what product reintroduced its catchphrase "I can't believe I ate the whole thing"?
5. What restaurant has hosted the famous Hot Dog Eating Contest at Coney Island every Fourth of July since 1916?

Answers to the questions on this page can be found on page 303.

JULY 16

• **1868** • WILKIE COLLINS'S *THE MOONSTONE,* about Sergeant Cuff's search for the missing title diamond, is published in London. Today's it's called the first English-language detective novel.

WATCHING THE DETECTIVES
What author created these sleuths?

Easy	*Harder*	*Yeah, Good Luck*
1. Miss Marple	**1.** Nero Wolfe	**1.** James Qwilleran
2. Perry Mason	**2.** Father Brown	**2.** Roderick Alleyn
3. Mike Hammer	**3.** Dr. Kay Scarpetta	**3.** Adam Dalgliesh
4. Sherlock Holmes	**4.** Travis McGee	**4.** Lord Peter Wimsey
5. Philip Marlowe	**5.** The Continental Op	**5.** Dr. Gideon Fell

• **1916** • PICASSO'S CUBIST MASTERPIECE *Les demoiselles d'Avignon* ignites a furor when it's first exhibited in Paris. (Today it hangs in the Museum of Modern Art in New York—it *didn't* go down on the *Titanic,* no matter what James Cameron may tell you.)

AVENUE CUBE
A different kind of Cubist quiz.

1. Who was the lead singer of the Sugarcubes?
2. What was the brand name of the 4 × 4 sequel to the 3 × 3 Rubik's Cube?
3. What pastime is the subject of the Christian Slater movie *Gleaming the Cube?*
4. What's the smallest number, other than 0 and 1, that's both a perfect square and a perfect cube?
5. What replaced the GameCube on November 19, 2006?

• **1995** • A SCIENCE TEXTBOOK becomes the first item ever sold on a newly opened website called Amazon.com.

NO MORE PENCILS, NO MORE BOOKS
Five questions on textbooks. Please write your answers on a separate worksheet.

1. Who first formulated the periodic table while writing the landmark 1870 chemistry textbook *Principles of Chemistry?*
2. In 1936, Dick and Jane's dog Spot ("See Spot run!") was changed from a terrier into what newly popular breed?
3. Whose military textbook *Infantry Attacks* was read, famously, by George Patton?
4. What hit TV show has a title pronounced the same as—but spelled differently from—an 1858 book now in its thirty-ninth edition?
5. What state's board of education voted in November 2005 to teach intelligent design alongside biology textbooks?

Answers to the questions on this page can be found on page 304.

• **1955** • WHEN DISNEYLAND OPENS, it's the Unfinished-est Place on Earth. A plumbers' strike means that the sweltering park has almost no drinking fountains, and the landscaping is still incomplete, so Walt tells gardeners to put fancy Latin labels on all the weeds.

FANTASY LANDS
Name the author who created . . .

Easy	*Harder*	*Yeah, Good Luck*
1. Oz	1. Neverland	1. Pellucidar
2. Narnia	2. Gormenghast	2. Poictesme
3. Middle-Earth	3. Earthsea	3. Alagaësia
4. Wonderland	4. Utopia	4. Fantastica
5. Lilliput	5. Prydain	5. Discworld

• **2006** • A MICROPHONE PICKS UP George W. Bush greeting Prime Minister Tony Blair with a hearty "Yo, Blair!" at a G-8 conference in St. Petersburg.

TRANSATLANTICISM
Answers these questions about Anglo-American relations.

1. What's the only U.S. state with a Union Jack on its flag?
2. In 2006, what omnipresent song became the first British single to top the U.S. charts in almost a decade?
3. What movie depicts Harold Abrahams's victory over heavily favored Americans Charlie Paddock and Jackson Scholz?
4. Winston Churchill is believed to have invented the term "special relationship" for America's ties to Britain, in the same Fulton, Missouri, speech more famous for coining what other phrase?
5. What album track, never a Top Forty hit, was the first song the Beatles ever performed on their *Ed Sullivan Show* debut?
6. Who's the only American-born member of Monty Python?
7. What U.S. state was named for the future James II of England?
8. What U.S. TV hit was a transplant of the British sitcom *Till Death Us Do Part*, about Alf Garnett and his long-suffering wife, Else?
9. What chemical element has an extra syllable in its more correct British pronunciation?
10. What famous Briton with an American wife was the governor of the Bahamas during World War II?
11. What Major League Soccer team signed David Beckham to a $50 million contract in 2007?
12. Who's the last British movie star ever to top the annual Quigley Poll of top U.S. box-office draws, in 1966 and 1967?
13. What famous battle of the War of 1812 took place two weeks *after* the Treaty of Ghent had been signed, ending the war?
14. What East Coast port is the largest U.S. city to share its name with a British county?
15. What comic author, the epitome of Britishness, was accused of collaboration with the Nazis after World War II and so spent the last twenty years of his life a U.S. citizen?

Answers to the questions on this page can be found on page 304.

JULY 18

• **1936** • THE FIRST OSCAR MAYER Wienermobile, a thirteen-foot-long hot dog, rolls out of a General Motors factory in Chicago.

WHEEL PEOPLE
What distinctive vehicles were driven by . . .

Easy	*Harder*	*Yeah, Good Luck*
1. Michael Knight	1. Fred Jones	1. Jim Douglas
2. Speed Racer	2. Arnie Cunningham	2. Humbert Humbert
3. Bo and Luke Duke	3. The Green Hornet	3. Caractacus Potts

• **1941** • MARTHA REEVES, STILL twenty years away from fronting the Vandellas, is born in Alabama.

SEND BACKUP!
Name these backing bands from their lead singers.

Easy	*Harder*	*Yeah, Good Luck*
1. Smokey Robinson	1. Marky Mark	1. Bobby "Boris" Pickett
2. Joan Jett	2. Jonathan Richman	2. Bo Donaldson
3. Tom Petty	3. George Thorogood	3. Robyn Hitchcock
4. Gladys Knight	4. Edie Brickell	4. Billy J. Kramer
5. Buddy Holly	5. Bruce Hornsby	5. Little Joe Cook

• **1976** • NADIA COMANECI SCORES the first perfect 10 in women's Olympic gymnastics history. The scoreboard, unequipped to handle the extra digit, displays her mark as a "1.00."

PERFECTIONISM
Can you score a perfect 5.0 on these questions?

1. What was Balki's home island on TV's *Perfect Strangers*?
2. What New Wave band used to say, with some truth, that their name was Chinese for "perfect pitch"?
3. Who's the oldest man ever to pitch a major-league perfect game?
4. The Michael Douglas/Gwyneth Paltrow film *A Perfect Murder* is a remake of what 1950s thriller?
5. Perfecto, torpedo, and parejo are all shapes of what?

Answers to the questions on this page can be found on page 304.

• **1946** • Marilyn Monroe takes her first screen test and is subsequently signed by Twentieth Century–Fox. Her big debut: she's visible for a few seconds on the church steps in 1948's unforgettable *Scudda Hoo! Scudda Hay!*

NOD AT FIRST

What actress earned an Oscar nomination for these very first screen appearances?

Easy	Harder	Yeah, Good Luck
1. *Mary Poppins*	1. *Maria Full of Grace*	1. *Gaslight*
2. *Children of a Lesser God*	2. *On the Waterfront*	2. *The Heart Is a Lonely Hunter*
3. *Dreamgirls*	3. *Breaking the Waves*	3. *The Turning Point*
4. *The Piano*	4. *Goodbye, Mr. Chips*	4. *Alfie*
5. *Funny Girl*	5. *Raging Bull*	5. *Sayonara*

• **1966** • After the home team spends three months playing on an outfield of green-painted dirt, enough artificial grass is finally produced to complete the field at the Houston Astrodome. The Monsanto product is soon renamed "AstroTurf."

DOME SWEET DOME

1. Who built the world's first free-standing geodesic dome in 1949?

2. Who called their signature red hats "Flowerpots" or "Energy Domes"?

3. What California peak, which erupted in 1915, is the world's largest lava dome?

4. Who plays their home games in the so-called Dean Dome?

5. Who was, appropriately enough, the first person buried in the crypt beneath the dome of Saint Paul's Cathedral?

• **1984** • Geraldine Ferraro wins the vice presidential nomination at the Democratic National Convention, making her the first woman ever to appear on a major-party presidential ticket.

IT'S A MAN'S WORLD

Match these women with their electoral firsts. Bonus points for naming the specific state/city/office involved.

1. Rebecca Latimer Felton	A. First woman governor
2. Bertha Landes	B. First woman mayor of a major U.S. city
3. Frances Perkins	C. First woman in the cabinet
4. Jeanette Rankin	D. First woman in the House of Representatives
5. Nellie Tayloe Ross	E. First woman in the Senate

Answers to the questions on this page can be found on page 305.

JULY 20

• **1802** • A BAPTIST CONGREGATION in Cheshire, Massachusetts, gathers to make Thomas Jefferson a giant wheel of cheese, in gratitude for his commitment to religious tolerance. The thirteen-foot cheese wheel, weighing more than 1,200 pounds, will be delivered that winter as a holiday gift to the White House, where it will pungently remain for more than two years.

IDLE CHEDDAR
Say "cheese"!

1. Who described his most famous painting as "the Camembert of time"?

2. Britain's Wensleydale cheese dairies were facing bankruptcy when they were saved in 1995 by what fictional character declaring it his favorite cheese?

3. What common lasagna ingredient is actually a by-product of making another lasagna ingredient, mozzarella?

4. What 6-foot, 5-inch-tall comedian came from a family surnamed "Cheese" before his father changed it?

5. What do Americans commonly call Emmental cheese?

6. Milwaukee's Ralph Bruno carved up his family's sofa in 1987 to make the first what?

7. What is traditionally served in a *caquelon* heated above a *rechaud*?

8. What kind of animal is Chuck E. Cheese?

9. The title of Robert Cormier's novel *I Am the Cheese* is a reference to the last line of what song?

10. Gouda and Edam are cities in what country?

• **1976** • THE U.S. ISSUES one Richard McFee the first patent ever for a "lightweight compact unit which simulates the exercise obtained while climbing stairs." The StairMaster is born!

MASTERS OF THE UNIVERSE
Can you master these ten questions?

1. In a symphony orchestra, what instrument is played by the concertmaster?

2. Sigourney Weaver plays the Gatekeeper in *Ghostbusters*, but who plays the Keymaster?

3. What rock band brought suit in 1994 claiming that Ticketmaster was an illegal monopoly?

4. Who was the U.S.'s first postmaster general?

5. Which Old Master signed his paintings with his full Cretan name, Doménicos Theotokópoulos?

6. Sir Frances Walsingham was what English monarch's "spymaster"?

7. What Transfiguration teacher succeeded Armando Dippet as headmaster of his alma mater?

8. Oldest son Al was the first ringmaster of what famous circus?

9. What group, fronted by Grandmaster Flash, was the first hip-hop act ever inducted into the Rock and Roll Hall of Fame?

10. In July 1999, what chess grand master achieved an "Elo rating" of 2851, the highest in history?

Answers to the questions on this page can be found on page 305.

• **1861** • GENERAL BARNARD BEE, during the first battle of Bull Run, gives Thomas Jackson his famous nickname when he notes that Jackson is "standing like a stone wall." Bee died minutes later, so we can't ask him, but some witnesses believe that he was expressing annoyance, not admiration, at Jackson—that he was saying, in effect, "Little help here?!"

BATTLEFIELD MIRTH

Name these military legends from their affectionate nicknames.

Easy	*Harder*	*Yeah, Good Luck*
1. The Little Corporal	**1.** The Swamp Fox	**1.** Old Fuss and Feathers
2. Stormin' Norman	**2.** Cump	**2.** The Marble Man
3. Unconditional Surrender	**3.** Mad Anthony	**3.** Light Horse Harry
4. Ol' Blood and Guts	**4.** The G.I. General	**4.** The Fighting Quaker
5. The Red Baron	**5.** The Desert Fox	**5.** Gentleman Johnny

• **1972** • GEORGE CARLIN IS ARRESTED at Milwaukee's annual Summerfest for delivering his famous "Seven Words You Can Never Say on Television" routine.

FOUR-LETTER WORDS

1. What four letters were removed from the end of Los Angeles's Hollywood sign in 1949?

2. What's the only four-letter movie title to win a Best Picture Oscar?

3. What four colors in a box of sixty-four Crayola crayons have four-letter names?

4. In the King James Bible, all but three books of the New Testament end with what word?

5. There are seven *adjacent* world countries whose names end with the same four letters. What are the four letters?

6. By a wide margin, what Internet term was the most-looked-up word on Merriam-Webster's dictionary website in 2004?

7. What's the only four-letter TV show ever to win a Best Drama Emmy?

8. What's the only Asian country whose common name is only one syllable? How about Africa?

9. What two words are tattooed on Robert Mitchum's knuckles in *The Night of the Hunter*?

10. What's the only U.S. city to boast a radio station whose call letters are the exact name of the city?

11. According to the latest *Oxford English Dictionary*, what's the most common noun in the English language?

12. What song, written as a birthday present for Suzanne DeYoung in 1978, is the only four-letter song by a four-letter band ever to top the *Billboard* charts?

13. Besides being topics of concern for farmers, what do the words clay, root, hull, and rice have in common?

14. What are the only two four-letter cities to host a Summer and a Winter Olympics, respectively?

15. What masculine first name is also the zoological term for "fish semen"?

Answers to the questions on this page can be found on page 305.

• **1994** • ROGER EBERT REVIEWS Rob Reiner's flop *North*, awarding it zero stars. Ebert's 2000 book *I Hated, Hated, Hated This Movie* will draw its title from this review.

TRIVIA BOREALIS
Ten questions with northern exposure.

1. What's the northernmost city ever to host a Summer Olympics?
2. What woman, who rose to fame as Oliver North's secretary in 1987, later married ex–Doors manager Danny Sugerman?
3. What Inuit word for "our land" names Canada's newest territory, split off from the Northwest Territories in 1999?
4. Despite his death in 1994, who is still "Eternal President" of North Korea, according to its constitution?
5. What film's climax came from the director's desire to shoot a movie called *The Man Who Sneezed in Lincoln's Nose*?
6. In what country is Africa's northernmost point?
7. What North American Soccer League team signed Pelé in 1975?
8. In the TV holiday favorite *Rudolph the Red-nosed Reindeer*, what would the North Pole's misfit elf, Hermey, rather be than a toymaker?
9. What TV title role did Jay North play for four seasons?
10. What country was called Northern Rhodesia until 1984?

• **2002** • MATTEL LOSES ITS COURT CASE against Scandinavian pop group Aqua, the one-hit wonders of "Barbie Girl" fame. The judge's much-quoted decision ends, "The parties are advised to chill."

DRESS ME UP, TAKE YOUR TIME, I'M YOUR DOLLIE
What character from a pop song wears . . .

1. Electric boots and a mohair suit
2. A face that she keeps in a jar by the door
3. A hat strategically dipped below one eye and an apricot scarf
4. Baggy clothes that made her friends stick up their nose
5. A screwed-down hairdo and snow-white tan
6. Heavy boots of lead
7. Her vest, while Jack's in his corset
8. Fancy gloves, so there's never, never a trace of red
9. Clothes ripped like the Incredible Hulk
10. Fancy clothes, diamond rings, a 32 gun in his pocket for fun, and a razor in his shoe

Answers to the questions on this page can be found on page 306.

JULY 23

• **1973** • At the height of the Watergate scandal, President Nixon refuses to turn over presidential tape recordings to the special prosecutor.

GATED COMMUNITY
Match these more recent "-gate" scandals with the targeted official.

1. Gropegate
2. Macacagate
3. Nannygate
4. Plamegate
5. Troopergate

A. George Allen
B. Zoe Baird
C. Bill Clinton
D. "Scooter" Libby
E. Arnold Schwarzenegger

• **1982** • The members of the International Whaling Commission vote to begin a moratorium on commercial whaling beginning in 1985.

TRAFFIC CETACEANS

1. What whale took its name from the milky-white liquid eighteenth-century whalers harvested from its head?
2. Who played in his twenty-third and final NHL All-Star Game as a Hartford Whaler?
3. Whalebone corsets weren't made from bone at all but from what part of the whale?
4. The residents of what Danish islands kill almost a thousand pilot whales in their controversial annual hunt?
5. What's the appropriate stage name of musician Richard Melville Hall?

• **2000** • Carlton Fisk is inducted into the Baseball Hall of Fame, making him the answer to the trivia question "Who's the only Baseball Hall of Fame player whose first name is the last name of another Hall of Famer"? (Okay, I never said it was a *good* trivia question.)

SPORTMANTEAU
What superathlete can be created, à la "Steve Carlton Fisk," by overlapping the names of . . .

1. The 1982 NFL Rookie of the Year and the 1997 NBA Rookie of the Year
2. The one-year leader of the "Gashouse Gang" and the thirty-six-year leader of the Tar Heels
3. The first recipient of the Jesse Owens Award and the first high school basketball player to go straight to the pros
4. The gymnast who starred in *American Anthem* and the pitcher who wrote *Me and the Spitter*
5. The oldest major leaguer ever to hit a home run and the first African-American Super Bowl MVP
6. The Laker who coined the word "three-peat" and the winner of a 1981–84 "four-peat" at the World Figure Skating Championships
7. The executive who broke baseball's color barrier and the player who broke Lou Brock's steals record
8. The orchestrator of the "Miracle on Ice" and the "Human Vacuum Cleaner"
9. A career .900 free-throw shooter (second place) and a career hitter of 700-something homers (first place)
10. The 1995 Heisman Trophy winner, the 1980 AL MVP winner, and the 1991 Hart Memorial Trophy winner

Answers to the questions on this page can be found on page 306.

JULY 24

• **1190** • WILLIAM DE FORCE arrives at Lisbon, where he takes over the British navy for the Third Crusade. William delivers to the fleet King Richard's rules of conduct for the voyage, which include "boyling pitch . . . and feathers or downe" to be poured on thieves. It's history's first recorded mention of tarring and feathering.

WHERE THERE'S A QUILL
These questions of a feather flock together.

1. What did Yankee Doodle call the feather in his hat?
2. Avian flu in China led to 2006 price hikes in what piece of sporting equipment?
3. Who wore "yellow feathers in her hair and a dress cut down to there"?
4. What Halle Berry movie is named for the password in the Marx Brothers' *Horse Feathers*?
5. What dinosaur contemporary has a name meaning "ancient feather"?
6. According to Emily Dickinson, what's "the thing with feathers"?
7. What kind of bird is Wallace and Gromit's nemesis, Feathers McGraw?
8. What civilization worshiped a feathered serpent called Quetzalcoatl?
9. What kind of bird is an eider, from which true eiderdown comes?
10. What movie begins with a feather coming to rest in front of a Savannah, Georgia, bus stop?

• **1901** • WILLIAM SYDNEY PORTER is released from a Texas jail, having served three years for embezzlement. While in prison, he has written and sold his first magazine short stories, beginning a new career as "O. Henry."

CON TRACTS
Who wrote the following while behind bars?

Easy	Harder	Yeah, Good Luck
1. *Mein Kampf*	**1.** *The Pisan Cantos*	**1.** *Our Lady of the Flowers*
2. *The Pilgrim's Progress*	**2.** *De Profundis*	**2.** *Il Milione*
3. *120 Days of Sodom*	**3.** *Le Morte Darthur*	**3.** *The Consolation of Philosophy*

• **1908** • ITALIAN RUNNER DORANDO PIETRI becomes dehydrated and disoriented during the Olympic marathon in London. Near the end of the race, Pietri, in the lead, falls five times and is helped up each time by race officials. Though he still "wins" the race, his runners-up protest the assisted finish, and Pietri is disqualified.

HEAVY MEDAL
In what city did each of these athletes earn their greatest summer Olympic glory?

Easy	Harder	Yeah, Good Luck
1. Mary Lou Retton	**1.** Bob Beamon	**1.** Michelle Smith
2. Jesse Owens	**2.** Jim Thorpe	**2.** Kristin Otto
3. Mark Spitz	**3.** Paavo Nurmi	**3.** Bobby Joe Morrow
4. Nadia Comaneci	**4.** Babe Didrikson	**4.** Vitaly Scherbo
5. Michael Phelps	**5.** Cathy Freeman	**5.** Billy Mills

Answers to the questions on this page can be found on page 306.

JULY 25

• **1831** • CYRUS MCCORMICK DOESN'T fear the reaper, demonstrating his revolutionary new invention on a field of oats near Steele's Tavern, Virginia.

AGRICULTURE CLUB

1. What literary locale is called "Manor Farm" at the start of the novel?

2. Crop rotation farmers often alternate their grains with soybeans to help "fix" what element in the soil?

3. What U.S. city is named for a Roman general famed for leaving his troops and retiring to his farm?

4. What general signed Special Field Orders, No. 15, the so-called 40 acres and a mule grant to freed slaves?

5. What signature color of paint are John Deere tractors?

6. What CCR front man made his solo concert debut at the first Farm Aid, in 1985?

7. What kind of farm is a formicarium?

8. What TV show's cops operate out of a converted church they call "the Barn"?

9. Of the four "H" words in the pledge of the 4-H club, what's the only one that's not part of the body?

10. According to a 2006 study by Jon Gettman, what's the U.S.'s biggest cash crop?

• **1946** • JERRY LEWIS AND DEAN MARTIN take the stage together for the first time at Atlantic City's Club 500.

SCHTICKING UP FOR EACH OTHER
Give the other member of these comedy pairings.

Easy
1. Dan Rowan and . . .
2. Penn Jillette and . . .
3. George Burns and . . .
4. Mike Nichols and . . .
5. Stan Laurel and . . .

Harder
1. Johnny Wayne and . . .
2. Jerry Stiller and . . .
3. Bob Elliott and . . .
4. Bob Odenkirk and . . .
5. Jack Burns and . . .

Yeah, Good Luck
1. Ole Olsen and . . .
2. Ronnie Barker and . . .
3. Bert Wheeler and . . .
4. Marty Allen and . . .
5. Bob Hudson and . . .

• **1986** • AT CHICAGO'S GREEN MILL tavern, construction worker Marc Smith adds a new competitive wrinkle to the weekly Chicago Poetry Ensemble show, and the "poetry slam" is born. Harold Bloom will later call this moment "the death of art."

SLAMMIN'

1. Who are the only women ever to slam-dunk the ball in a WNBA game?

2. What rock epic begins "The screen door slams, Mary's dress sways"?

3. Though Manny Ramirez is closing in, who still holds the major-league career record with twenty-three grand slams?

4. What do the Plastics call their "slam book" in the 2004 comedy

Mean Girls?
5. Who resigned in 2004, eighteen months after telling President Bush that the evidence for Iraqi WMDs was "a slam-dunk case"?

Answers to the questions on this page can be found on page 307.

JULY 26

• **1775** • THE UNITED STATES POSTAL SERVICE is founded. Until 1971, the postmaster general will be a cabinet-level position, dead last in the presidential line of succession.

ADD AGENCY
Which cabinet-level department administers each of these?

Easy	Harder	Yeah, Good Luck
1. The FDA	1. The Coast Guard	1. The National Weather Service
2. The FAA	2. The Bureau of Indian Affairs	2. The Forest Service
3. The National Park Service	3. OSHA	3. The NNSA
4. The FBI	4. The CDC	4. The Bureau of the Census
5. The U.S. Mint	5. Fannie Mae	5. The Office for Civil Rights

• **1990** • THE AMERICANS WITH DISABILITIES ACT BECOMES LAW.

MISS CONGENITALITY
Match each physical oddity to the celebrity who can boast it.

1. Tom Brokaw	A. Cleft palate
2. Gary Burghoff	B. Double row of eyelashes
3. Donny Osmond	C. Four deformed fingers
4. Elizabeth Taylor	D. Internal organs misplaced
5. Mark Wahlberg	E. Supernumerary (third) nipple

• **69,163** • IT'S ONLY SIXTY-SEVEN THOUSAND years away: the next time a transit of Mercury and a transit of Venus will occur simultaneously. In other words, from Earth, both planets will be seen crossing the sun at the same time! Plan to take the day off work.

SOL MUSIC
Here comes the sun trivia.

1. What's the highest-circulation U.S. newspaper that calls itself the *Sun*?

2. What's the name for the sun's outer "atmosphere," visible only during a total solar eclipse?

3. What thirty-five-year-old sports event did Arizona's Sun Devil Stadium lose in 2006?

4. Before the dialogue was cut down, what album originally ended with Abbey Road Studios doorman Gerry Driscoll saying "The only thing that makes it look light is the sun"?

5. In myth, who defeated the serpent Apep every night in his solar barge?

6. What was the better-known *nom de crime* of Harry Longabaugh?

7. What "Sun King"'s seventy-two-year reign makes him the longest-ruling European monarch of all time?

8. What team did NBA star Steve Nash play for between his two stints with the Phoenix Suns?

9. What is the infirmity of Jake Barnes, the protagonist of *The Sun Also Rises*?

10. What future comedy megastar had a small role in *Empire of the Sun* as the POW called "Dainty"?

Answers to the questions on this page can be found on page 307.

• 1972 • THE F-15 "EAGLE" fighter jet makes its maiden flight at Edwards Air Force Base. Kenny Loggins singing "Danger Zone" is, sadly, still fourteen years away.

EAGLE-EYED

1. Who was the only U.S. president ever to be an Eagle Scout?
2. What's the more common name for a "double-eagle," or three under par, on a golf hole?
3. Who received a chalet called "the Eagle's Nest" for his fiftieth birthday in 1939?
4. What phrase appears on the ribbon in the bald eagle's beak on a one-dollar bill?
5. What future coaching and broadcasting great was drafted by the Philadelphia Eagles in 1958 but never played a single NFL game, due to a training camp knee injury?
6. What nation, the world's newest, has a gold double-headed eagle on its flag?
7. What mysterious word from the Eagles' hit "Hotel California" translates in English to "little marijuana buds"?
8. What was the chosen sport of Eddie "the Eagle" Edwards, whose hapless performance at the 1988 Olympics made him a star?
9. Other than the bald eagle, what's the only species of eagle found in the U.S.?
10. The eagles are one of the five armies in the "Battle of the Five Armies" that ends what 1937 novel?

• 1984 • PETE ROSE HITS career single number 3,053 against the Phillies, surpassing Ty Cobb's fifty-five-year-old record.

SINGLED OUT

1. What faddish word comes from the Japanese for "single number"?
2. Bing Crosby's "White Christmas" is the biggest-selling single of all time, but what 1990s hit is currently in second place?
3. What 1970s bachelor prime minister was the last single P.M. of Britain?
4. z.com, one of only three active single-letter .com domains, belongs to what car company?
5. Of the four men's tennis players with the most singles tournament wins in the open era, who's the only one not born in the U.S.?

• 2003 • FOLLOWING A MERGER, Philadelphia's First Union Center officially changes its name to the Wachovia Center. Thousands of Sixers and Flyers fans, who can no longer refer to the building as the "F.U. Center," mourn.

FIELD TESTING
Name these sports spots from their nicknames

Easy	Harder	Yeah, Good Luck
1. The House That Ruth Built	1. The Igloo	1. The Pit
2. The Frozen Tundra	2. The Dawg Pound	2. The Tank
3. The Brickyard	3. The Thunderdome	3. The Grand Old Lady
4. Chavez Ravine	4. The Juice Box	4. The Track Too Tough to Tame
5. The Horseshoe	5. The Big House	5. The Woodshed

Answers to the questions on this page can be found on page 307.

JULY 28

• **1933** • A FAN SENDS singer Rudy Vallee the very first singing telegram.

THE WAY WE WIRE

1. The Zimmermann Telegram resulted in U.S. entry into what war?

2. What French novel begins with the narrator receiving this telegram: "Your mother died today. Funeral tomorrow. Deep sympathy"?

3. What did Cary Grant famously reply to a magazine editor's telegram asking, "How old Cary Grant"?

4. Who sent the 1884 cable that said, "I will not accept if nominated and will not serve if elected"?

5. Who was Oscar-nominated for playing a telegraph boy in *The Human Comedy*?

• **1973** • LEE MAJORS MARRIES Farrah Fawcett. A decade later, when divorce ends the marriage, she'll lose the hyphen and alimony payments will make him *The Three Million Dollar Man*.

DASH BOARD
Give these famous-and-hyphenated names.

1. John Larroquette and what other sitcom actor are the only two people ever to win four Supporting Actor Emmys?

2. What Greek director of *Missing* and *Z* is the first cousin of *Wayne's World* director Penelope Spheeris?

3. In 1998, a fisherman fishing off Marseille reeled in a bracelet belonging to what French author, whose plane vanished in 1944?

4. What photojournalist's work made the first cover of *Life* magazine?

5. Who were the winners of the James E. Sullivan Award for amateur athletics in 1986 and 1988, respectively?

6. Whose paintings include *At the Moulin de la Galette* and *At the Moulin Rouge*?

7. What French anthropologist dropped the prehyphen part of his name when he taught at Barnard College, so as not to be confused with a maker of blue jeans?

8. Who was the only U.N. secretary-general not elected to a second term?

9. What actress's production company is Milkwood Films, named in honor of fellow Wales native Dylan Thomas?

10. Whose real-life half sister, Lauren Bowles, played her sister on *Watching Ellie*?

• **1976** • THE DEADLIEST EARTHQUAKE of the twentieth century hits Tangshan, China, killing more than a quarter-million people. Though the quake strikes unusually suddenly, local animals weren't fooled—locals report dogs barking wildly, geese eating one another, and goldfish jumping out of bowls.

NOT STIRRED
Five questions to shake things up.

1. What NBA star was known for his signature spin move, the Dream Shake?

2. What animated trio is made up of Master Shake, Frylock, and Meatwad?

3. What two leaders shook hands—for the first time ever, in public—on the White House lawn on September 13, 1994?

4. Frank Zappa's 1979 album *Sheik Yerbouti* was a salute to what band's 1976 hit?

5. What event is the subject of John Reed's book *Ten Days That Shook the World*?

Answers to the questions on this page can be found on page 308.

• **1947** • ENIAC, THE FIRST PROGRAMMABLE digital computer, is switched on at the army's Aberdeen Proving Ground in Maryland, where it begins eight years of continuous operation.

GET WITH THE PROGRAM!

What popular computer language shares its name with . . .

1. The most populous island in the world
2. The serpent Apollo slew at Delphi

3. John Travolta's *second* movie with Samuel L. Jackson
4. The vitamin formerly known as ascorbic acid

5. The SI unit of pressure

• **1998** • PUFF DADDY ANNOUNCES his upcoming fashion line, to be called "Sean John" after the mogul's two given names.

RHYME AND REASON

Give these answers made up of two rhyming words, like "Sean John."

1. Who was introduced to his future partner, Kyle Gass, by actor Tim Robbins?
2. Who titled his 1989 autobiography *Holy Cow!*?
3. Which character in *Through the Looking-Glass* is a self-portrait of author Lewis Carroll himself?
4. The Empire State Building went dark for fifteen minutes to mark the August 2004 death of what actress?
5. What did Malcolm X describe as "a killer-diller coat with a drape shape, reet pleats and shoulders padded like a lunatic's cell"?

6. What famed London street is home to gentlemen's clubs like the Athenaeum and the Reform Club?
7. Who were Pete Cochran, Linc Hayes, and Julie Barnes?
8. What metal band usually depicts a man wearing a Hannibal Lecter mask and a straitjacket on its album covers?
9. What peace activist was the emcee at Woodstock?
10. What White Mountains cave complex was one of the last Taliban strongholds in Afghanistan?
11. What TV title character lived at 485 Mapleton Drive, Mayfield?
12. What song did U2 introduce

by saying, "This is a song Charles Manson stole from the Beatles. We're stealing it back"?
13. What movie's title mission is completed using the Five-Point-Palm Exploding Heart Technique?
14. What nickname is shared by Charles Russell, Harold Reese, and Paul Reubens?
15. What massive database of legal documents and news articles sued Toyota for trademark infringement in 1987?

Answers to the questions on this page can be found on page 308.

• **1619** • THE FIRST ELECTED LEGISLATURE in the New World meets for the first time when the Virginia House of Burgesses convenes in Jamestown.

ASSEMBLY LANGUAGE
What nations are governed by these legislatures?

Easy	Harder	Yeah, Good Luck
1. The Diet	1. The States-General	1. The Eduskunta
2. The House of Lords	2. The Althing	2. The Great Khural
3. The Knesset	3. The Dáil Éireann	3. The Kuvendi
4. The Bundestag	4. The Rajya Sabha	4. The Storting
5. The Duma	5. The Riksdag	5. The Jatiyo Sangshad

• **1916** • GERMAN SABOTEURS SET OFF bombs on Black Tom Island in New York Harbor. The resulting blasts are felt as far away as Philadelphia and do $100,000 in damage to the Statue of Liberty, popping bolts right out of her right arm. The arm has been closed to tourists ever since.

ARMED AND DANGEROUS

1. What do you do to put your arms "akimbo"?

2. What epic poem begins "*Arma virumque cano*" ("Of arms and the man I sing")?

3. What does an NFL referee signal by stretching his arms out at his sides with his palms down?

4. How many arms does a squid have?

5. How many arms does the U.S. Senate have?

• **1932** • THREE-STRIP TECHNICOLOR debuts in Walt Disney's Silly Symphony *Flowers and Trees,* which will go on to win the first Oscar for animated shorts.

TINT POLE MOVIES
What color has described these things in movie titles?

Easy	Harder	Yeah, Good Luck
1. Haze, Noon, Rain	1. Bears, State, Streak	1. Fire, Ice, Mansions
2. Heat, Chicks, Oleander	2. Narcissus, Rain, Sunday	2. Corner, Scorpion, Sorghum
3. Cadillac, Flamingos, Motel	3. Chips, Collar, Thunder	3. Earth, Sky, Jack

Answers to the questions on this page can be found on page 308.

JULY 31

• **1853** • POLISH PHARMACIST IGNACY LUKASIEWICZ gives a new invention he's been tinkering with—a kerosene lamp—to a local hospital for an emergency surgery. Thanks to kerosene, the whale oil industry will collapse within just a few years. Lukasiewicz has probably inadvertently saved every whale on Earth from extinction.

THE LIGHT STUFF

1. What's the shade of a Tiffany lamp made of?
2. In *The Arabian Nights*, the tale of Aladdin and his lamp is actually set in what non-Arabian country?
3. What type of lamp is named for the kind of gas—usually iodine or bromine—in which the filament is suspended?
4. Whose most famous poem ends "I lift my lamp beside the golden door"?

5. What musical instrument shares its name with the bracket on which a lampshade hangs?

6. Where did two lanterns historically hang on the night of April 18, 1775?
7. What "Lady of the Lamp" was named for the Italian city where she was born?
8. Green Lantern's ring is powerless against objects of what color?
9. What film company's logo uses a lamp called Luxo, Jr., as the letter *I*?
10. What was the Greek philosopher Diogenes looking for when he wandered through Athens holding a lantern?

• **1931** • AUSTIN PATTERSON, THE CHEMISTRY guy at Merriam-Webster, submits an index card to his dictionary editor stating that density can be abbreviated as "D or d." Unfortunately, someone misreads Patterson's note and, for the next decade, the word "dord" is defined as "density" in Webster's, one of the most famous errors in lexicographical history.

"D" COMPOSITION

1. Comedy band Tenacious D took its name from what sportscaster's catchphrase for good defense?
2. Where are U.S. coins with a "D" mark minted?

3. What was the Allies' code name for the "D-Day" invasion of Normandy?
4. Whom did rapper Chuck D "fire" from Public Enemy in 1989 for making anti-Semitic

comments?
5. Deuterium is sometimes abbreviated "D" by chemists even though it's not an element. It's actually an isotope of what other element?

• **1987** • THE VAMPIRE HIT *The Lost Boys* is released, featuring the first of seven collaborations between "the two Coreys"—*The Goonies* star Corey Feldman and *Lucas* star Corey Haim.

SAY MY NAME

1. Which two Spice Girls shared the same first name?
2. Sorry, Kerry-Edwards voters: what's still the only U.S. president–vice president ticket ever to

use the same first name in office?
3. What company was founded in 1976 by "the two Steves"?
4. What's the only first name shared by two members of Monty

Python?
5. What U.S. state is currently represented by two senators who share exactly the same first name?

Answers to the questions on this page can be found on page 309.

July Answers

JULY 1

PENINSULA CAMPAIGN
1. The Malay Peninsula
2. Nome, Alaska
3. Qatar
4. "The boot"
5. The Olympic Peninsula
6. The Sinai Peninsula
7. Gallipoli
8. Kowloon
9. Michigan's Upper Peninsula
10. The Philippines

"TRANS-" FACTS
1. Jordan
2. *Lost*
3. The Catholic Eucharist wafer and wine
4. Vladivostok
5. Howard Hughes
6. Death Cab for Cutie
7. Frank N. Furter (*The Rocky Horror Picture Show*)
8. A face transplant
9. Cybertron
10. Louisa May Alcott's

JULY 2

BIO-PICKS
Easy
1. Queen Elizabeth I
2. Jesus Christ
3. Malcolm X
4. Charlie Chaplin
5. "Shoeless Joe" Jackson

Harder
1. Vincent van Gogh
2. Abraham Lincoln
3. Harper Lee
4. Julius Caesar
5. Marie Antoinette
Yeah, Good Luck
1. Nelson Rockefeller
2. Jesse James
3. Douglas MacArthur
4. Dorothy Parker
5. The Big Bopper

AFFAIRS TO REMEMBER
1. The Dreyfus Affair
2. The Iran-Contra Affair
3. The Profumo Affair
4. The XYZ Affair
5. *Family Affair*

CRAZY LIKE A FOX
1. *Futurama*
2. "Sour grapes"
3. Sanford
4. Eric Stolz
5. Vixen
6. The Quakers (or Society of Friends)
7. Bats (fruit bats)
8. Roger Daltrey
9. Canada
10. Jimmy Hoffa disappeared

JULY 3

WELL, THAT'S JUST GREAT
1. Great Bear and Great Slave Lakes
2. Pip

3. *American Pie and Wallace and Gromit: The Curse of the Were-Rabbit*
4. Lyndon Johnson
5. *Fibber McGee and Molly*
6. The Sex Pistols
7. "*Annuit coeptis*"
8. Queensland
9. Jack Johnson
10. Thursday (Black Thursday)

NORTH AND SOUTH
1. E
2. B
3. A
4. D
5. C

BEFORE I GET OLD
Easy
1. Janis Joplin
2. Sid Vicious
3. Gram Parsons
4. John Belushi
5. Keith Moon
Harder
1. Shannon Hoon
2. Ol' Dirty Bastard
3. Rob Pilatus
4. Phil Lynott
5. Layne Staley
Yeah, Good Luck
1. Andrew Wood
2. Hillel Slovak
3. Kristen Pfaff
4. Darby Crash
5. Bradley Nowell

JULY 4	JULY 5	JULY 6

FOUNDING FATHERS
1. The Battle of Trenton
2. Patrick Henry (the next sentence ends "Give me liberty or give me death!")
3. Publius
4. Benjamin Franklin
5. Sally Hemings

HAIL CAESAR
1. The thirteenth
2. J. C. Watts
3. Rico
4. Macbeth
5. *Grease*

THE REPLACEMENTS
1. Tan
2. *On Her Majesty's Secret Service*
3. Judas Iscariot
4. Replaced Cal Ripken, Jr., at third base to end Ripken's streak
5. Coy and Vance
6. The Washington Monument
7. Shrimp
8. The wild turkey
9. Sam Waterston
10. Rio de Janeiro

ORDINAL SINS
1. An eighth note
2. Second Life
3. First Lady of the Confederacy
4. The Seventh-Day Adventist Church
5. Third base
6. *Born on the Fourth of July*
7. "The Tenth Muse"
8. Saks Fifth Avenue
9. The Ninth Circuit Court of Appeals
10. *The Sixth Sense*
(so the correct order is 3-2-5-6-8-10-4-1-9-7)

NO ACCOUNTING FOR TASTE
1. Lyndon Johnson
2. "Ice Ice Baby"
3. A swan
4. Thomas Kincaid
5. Brian Lawton

YOUR CHEATIN' HEART
1. The Boston Marathon
2. Kneecapping Nancy Kerrigan
3. Hit the batter with a pitch
4. Doug Collins
5. Bobby Thomson's "Shot Heard 'Round the World" home run (the Giants were stealing signs)

A SHOT IN THE ARM
1. Autism
2. Measles, mumps, rubella (German measles)
3. The March of Dimes
4. Aerosmith (*Arrowsmith*)
5. Tuberculosis

SAY UNCLE
1. A bluebird
2. Barry Zito
3. Richard III
4. *The Dukes of Hazzard* and *Full House*
5. Monopoly
6. Nicolas Cage and Jason Schwartzman
7. The Ohio
8. THRUSH
9. William Tecumseh Sherman
10. Jean Hersholt

MISTER BIG
1. "To Be with You"
2. Cadbury's
3. *Live and Let Die*
4. Pottsylvania
5. John

JULY 7

TORO! TORO! TORO!
1. Elmer's glue
2. "God Save the King/Queen"
3. Theodore Roosevelt
4. Nicholas "Coach" Colasanto
5. The Alan Parsons Project
6. Thailand
7. Crete
8. Martin Luther
9. The (Hunkpapa) Lakota
10. Nostradamus

GENERAL KNOWLEDGE
1. Ambrose Burnside
2. Charles Cornwallis
3. Norman Schwarzkopf
4. Hermann Goering
5. Benjamin Harrison
6. Hannibal
7. Tim Considine
8. Antonio José de Sucre
9. Beef Wellington
10. George Washington, posthumously

JULY 8

STATE DEPARTMENT
1. Maine
2. South Dakota
3. Kentucky
4. New Hampshire
5. Louisiana

THE GREAT ONE
Easy
1. Russia
2. Macedon
3. Hawaii
4. Egypt
Harder
1. Persia
2. India
3. Rome
4. Prussia
Yeah, Good Luck
1. Bulgaria
2. The Ostrogoths
3. Poland
4. Akkad

QUAD SQUADS
1. Longest careers for one team in their respective sports
2. Played baseball and one other pro sport
3. Controversial suspensions
4. Jewish-American athletes
5. Wore number 42
6. Nicknamed "Moose"
7. Won a championship MVP award even though their team lost
8. Most games played in their respective sports
9. Sons followed in their footsteps
10. Died in plane crashes

JULY 9

GIVE THAT BACK!
1. The Stone of Scone
2. Jimmy Carter
3. *The Scream*
4. Mark Messier
5. His bike

A-LIST STARS
1. A
2. C
3. F
4. D
5. E
6. B

SPORTFOLIO
Easy
1. Five
2. Two
3. Six
4. Nine
5. Eleven
Harder
1. Six
2. Four
3. Seven
4. Eleven
5. Ten
Yeah, Good Luck
1. Seven
2. Seven
3. Four (Eight including horses!)
4. Eighteen
5. Seven

July Answers

JULY 10

RAISING "EL"
1. Ciudad Juárez
2. Quick Draw McGraw's
3. *Desperado*
4. Orlando Hernández
5. Toledo

THY NAME IS WOMAN
1. Ruth
2. *Love Story*
3. Picabo (Picabo Street)
4. -ko
5. Mabel
6. *West Side Story* and *The Sound of Music*
7. "Al(l)ison"
8. Lorelei
9. Carrie (*Sister Carrie* and *Carrie*)
10. Charlotte

OLD MONEY
Easy
1. Portugal
2. Germany
3. Greece
4. Ireland
Harder
1. Austria
2. Finland
3. Poland
4. The Netherlands
Yeah, Good Luck
1. Bulgaria
2. Hungary
3. Slovenia
4. Estonia

JULY 11

DEAR PRUDE HENS
1. Graham crackers (for Reverend Sylvester Graham)
2. *Showgirls*
3. Utah
4. The Salem witch trials
5. Pregnant

THE THE
1. *Guiding Light*
2. The Gambia
3. *The Invisible Man*
4. The word "the" appears twice
5. And

TITLE WAVE
Easy
1. *Death of a Salesman*
2. *The Count of Monte Cristo*
3. *The Hobbit*
4. *The Hunchback of Notre Dame*
5. *Pygmalion*
Harder
1. *Native Son*
2. *The Last of the Mohicans*
3. *Lady Chatterley's Lover*
4. *The Natural*
5. *The Portrait of a Lady*
Yeah, Good Luck
1. *The Handmaid's Tale*
2. *The Idiot*
3. *The Mayor of Casterbridge*
4. *The Member of the Wedding*
5. *The Stranger*

JULY 12

BILL OF RIGHTS
1. The penny
2. The Pittsburgh Steelers
3. The pulmonary artery
4. Jerry Garcia
5. Guyana and Suriname
6. Montgomery Clift
7. Captain Hook
8. A screwball
9. Thomas Eakins
10. *The Today Show*

JUST FOR FIN
1. *Happy Days*
2. Lake Nicaragua
3. Chevy Chase
4. Led Zeppelin
5. The great white shark
6. The Oakland Seals
7. The Discovery Channel
8. The Jets
9. The Tiburon
10. The USS *Indianapolis*

JULY 13

SHOW TUNES
Easy
1. *The Greatest American Hero*
2. *Laverne & Shirley*
3. *Cheers*
4. *Friends*
5. *The Beverly Hillbillies*
Harder
1. *The Golden Girls*
2. *Malcolm in the Middle*
3. *Sanford and Son*
4. *The Dukes of Hazzard*
5. *Mad About You*
Yeah, Good Luck
1. *Webster*
2. *Leave It to Beaver*
3. *Alice*
4. *227*
5. *Twin Peaks*

KINGS OF SWING
1. The San Diego Padres
2. Anthony Kennedy
3. Guitar George
4. Money
5. Missouri

A LITTLE MORE CONVERSA-TION
1. "Baby Got Back" (Sir Mix-a-Lot)
2. "Leader of the Pack" (the Shangri-Las)
3. "Radio Song" (R.E.M.)
4. "Bitchin' Camaro" (Dead ~~Kennedys~~ Milkmen)
5. "Computer Blue" (Prince and the Revolution)
6. "Undone (The Sweater Song)" (Weezer)
7. "The Chipmunk Song (Christmas Don't Be Late)" (the Chipmunks)
8. "Make It Funky (Part 1)" (James Brown)

9. "Black Country Woman" (Led Zeppelin)
10. "Hot for Teacher" (Van Halen)

JULY 14

ALL I NEED IS THE HEIR THAT I BREED
1. Anne of Cleves
2. Anne Boleyn
3. Jane Seymour
4. Jane Seymour
5. Catherine of Aragon
6. Catherine of Aragon
7. Catherine Howard
8. Anne of Cleves
9. Catherine Parr
10. Anne Boleyn

BREAKING UP IS HARD TO DO
1. *Grindhouse*
2. The Mensheviks
3. Maine or Nebraska
4. Plutonium
5. The 7 and 10
6. An elephant
7. Pangaea
8. Anne Heche (Steve Martin and Ellen DeGeneres)
9. Berkshire Hathaway
10. Blink-182

JULY 15

HIT THE SHOWERS
1. Stephanie Seymour
2. Qantas
3. "Have You Ever Seen the Rain?" and "Who'll Stop the Rain"
4. The Atacama
5. The Houston Astros
6. Rainn Wilson
7. Monsoon
8. Prince's (he ended with "Purple Rain")
9. *A Clockwork Orange*
10. "It was a dark and stormy night"

UNDA THE ROTUNDA
Easy
1. Virginia
2. Texas
3. Hawaii
4. Utah
Harder
1. Oklahoma
2. Mississippi
3. New Hampshire
4. Tennessee
Yeah, Good Luck
1. Indiana
2. Pennsylvania
3. Nevada
4. Montana

GREED, FOR LACK OF A BET-TER WORD, IS GOOD
1. The wolverine
2. A mint
3. John Madden
4. Alka-Seltzer
5. Nathan's Famous

July Answers

JULY 16

WATCHING THE DETECTIVES
Easy
1. Agatha Christie
2. Erle Stanley Gardner
3. Mickey Spillane
4. Arthur Conan Doyle
5. Raymond Chandler
Harder
1. Rex Stout
2. G. K. Chesterton
3. Patricia Cornwell
4. John D. MacDonald
5. Dashiell Hammett
Yeah, Good Luck
1. Lilian Jackson Braun
2. Ngaio Marsh
3. P. D. James
4. Dorothy Sayers
5. John Dickson Carr

AVENUE CUBE
1. Björk
2. Rubik's Revenge
3. Skateboarding
4. 64 (4^3 and 8^2)
5. The Wii

NO MORE PENCILS, NO MORE BOOKS
1. Dmitri Mendeleev
2. A cocker spaniel
3. Erwin Rommel's ("Rommel, you magnificent bastard—I read your book!")
4. *Grey's Anatomy*
5. Kansas's

JULY 17

FANTASY LANDS
Easy
1. L. Frank Baum
2. C. S. Lewis
3. J. R. R. Tolkien
4. Lewis Carroll
5. Jonathan Swift
Harder
1. J. M. Barrie
2. Mervyn Peake
3. Ursula K. Le Guin
4. Thomas More
5. Lloyd Alexander
Yeah, Good Luck
1. Edgar Rice Burroughs
2. James Branch Cabell
3. Christopher Paolini
4. Michael Ende
5. Terry Pratchett

TRANSATLANTICISM
1. Hawaii
2. "You're Beautiful" (James Blunt)
3. *Chariots of Fire*
4. "Iron Curtain"
5. "All My Loving"
6. Terry Gilliam
7. New York
8. *All in the Family*
9. Alumin(i)um
10. King Edward VIII
11. The Los Angeles Galaxy
12. Julie Andrews
13. The Battle of New Orleans
14. Norfolk, Virginia
15. P. G. Wodehouse

JULY 18

WHEEL PEOPLE
Easy
1. KITT
2. The Mach Five
3. The General Lee
Harder
1. The Mystery Machine
2. Christine
3. Black Beauty
Yeah, Good Luck
1. Herbie, the Love Bug
2. Melmoth
3. Chitty Chitty Bang Bang

SEND BACKUP!
Easy
1. The Miracles
2. The Blackhearts
3. The Heartbreakers
4. The Pips
5. The Crickets
Harder
1. The Funky Bunch
2. The Modern Lovers
3. The Destroyers
4. The New Bohemians
5. The Range
Yeah, Good Luck
1. The Crypt-Kickers
2. The Heywoods
3. The Egyptians
4. The Dakotas
5. The Thrillers

PERFECTIONISM
1. Mypos
2. Wang Chung
3. Randy Johnson (40)
4. *Dial M for Murder*
5. Cigars (figurados)

JULY 19

NOD AT FIRST
Easy
1. Julie Andrews
2. Marlee Matlin
3. Jennifer Hudson
4. Anna Paquin
5. Barbra Streisand
Harder
1. Catalina Sandino Moreno
2. Eva Marie Saint
3. Emily Watson
4. Greer Garson
5. Cathy Moriarty
Yeah, Good Luck
1. Angela Lansbury
2. Sondra Locke
3. Leslie Browne
4. Vivien Merchant
5. Miyoshi Umeki

DOME SWEET DOME
1. Buckminster Fuller
2. Devo
3. Lassen Peak
4. The North Carolina Tar Heels (formerly coached by Dean Smith)
5. Christopher Wren

IT'S A MAN'S WORLD
1. E (Georgia)
2. B (Seattle)
3. C (secretary of labor)
4. D (Montana)
5. A (Wyoming)

JULY 20

IDLE CHEDDAR
1. Salvador Dalí (*The Persistence of Memory*)
2. Wallace (of "and Gromit" fame)
3. Ricotta
4. John Cleese
5. Swiss cheese
6. Green Bay Packers "cheesehead" hat
7. Fondue
8. A mouse
9. "Farmer in the Dell" ("the cheese stands alone")
10. The Netherlands

"MASTERS" OF THE UNIVERSE
1. (First) violin
2. Rick Moranis
3. Pearl Jam
4. Benjamin Franklin
5. El Greco
6. Elizabeth I's
7. Albus Dumbledore (*Harry Potter*)
8. Ringling Brothers
9. The Furious Five
10. Garry Kasparov

JULY 21

BATTLEFIELD MIRTH
Easy
1. Napoleon Bonaparte
2. Norman Schwarzkopf
3. Ulysses S. Grant
4. George Patton
5. Manfred von Richtofen
Harder
1. Francis Marion
2. William Tecumseh Sherman
3. Anthony Wayne
4. Omar Bradley
5. Erwin Rommel
Yeah, Good Luck
1. Winfield Scott
2. Robert E. Lee
3. Henry Lee
4. Smedley Butler
5. John Burgoyne

FOUR-LETTER WORDS
1. "Land"
2. *Gigi*
3. Blue, gray, gold, plum
4. Amen
5. -stan
6. Blog
7. *Lost*
8. Laos and Chad
9. LOVE and HATE
10. Waco
11. Time
12. "Babe" by Styx
13. They're surnames of U.S. secretaries of state
14. Rome and Oslo
15. Milt

JULY 22

TRIVIA BOREALIS
1. Helsinki beats Stockholm by a nose
2. Fawn Hall
3. Nunavut
4. Kim Il-Sung
5. *North by Northwest*'s
6. Tunisia
7. The New York Cosmos
8. A dentist
9. Dennis the Menace
10. Zambia

DRESS ME UP, TAKE YOUR TIME, I'M YOUR DOLLIE
1. Bennie ("and the Jets")
2. Eleanor Rigby
3. You ("You're So Vain")
4. Sk8er Boi
5. Ziggy Stardust
6. Iron Man
7. Sweet Jane
8. Mack the Knife
9. Slim Shady ("My Name Is")
10. Bad, Bad Leroy Brown

JULY 23

GATED COMMUNITY
1. E
2. A
3. B
4. D
5. C

TRAFFIC CETACEANS
1. The sperm whale
2. Gordie Howe
3. Baleen
4. The Faroe Islands
5. Moby

SPORTMANTEAU
1. Marcus Allen Iverson
2. Dizzy Dean Smith
3. Edwin Moses Malone
4. Mitch Gaylord Perry
5. Julio Franco Harris
6. Byron Scott Hamilton
7. Branch Rickey Henderson
8. Herb Brooks Robinson
9. Rick Barry Bonds
10. Eddie George Brett Hull

JULY 24

WHERE THERE'S A QUILL
1. "Macaroni"
2. Badminton birdies (shuttlecocks)
3. Lola ("Copacabana")
4. *Swordfish*
5. Archaeopteryx
6. Hope
7. A penguin (disguised as a chicken)
8. The Aztecs
9. A duck
10. *Forrest Gump*

CON TRACTS
Easy
1. Adolf Hitler
2. John Bunyan
3. The Marquis de Sade
Harder
1. Ezra Pound
2. Oscar Wilde
3. Thomas Malory
Yeah, Good Luck
1. Jean Genet
2. Marco Polo
3. Boethius

HEAVY MEDAL
Easy
1. Los Angeles
2. Berlin
3. Munich
4. Montreal
5. Athens
Harder
1. Mexico City
2. Stockholm
3. Paris
4. Los Angeles
5. Sydney
Yeah, Good Luck
1. Atlanta
2. Seoul
3. Melbourne
4. Barcelona
5. Tokyo

JULY 25

AGRICULTURE CLUB
1. Animal Farm
2. Nitrogen
3. Cincinnati (Lucius Quintus Cincinnatus)
4. William Tecumseh Sherman
5. Green
6. John Fogerty
7. An ant farm
8. *The Shield*
9. Health (Head, Heart, and Hands are the other three)
10. Marijuana

SCHTICKING UP FOR EACH OTHER
Easy
1. Dick Martin
2. Teller
3. Gracie Allen
4. Elaine May
5. Oliver Hardy
Harder
1. Frank Shuster
2. Anne Meara
3. Ray Goulding
4. David Cross
5. Avery Schreiber
Yeah, Good Luck
1. Chic Johnson
2. Ronnie Corbett
3. Robert Woolsey
4. Steve Rossi
5. Ron Landry

SLAMMIN'
1. Lisa Leslie ✝ Candace Parker
2. "Thunder Road" (Bruce Springsteen)
3. Lou Gehrig
4. "The Burn Book"
5. George Tenet

JULY 26

ADD AGENCY
Easy
1. Health and Human Services
2. Transportation
3. Interior
4. Justice
5. The Treasury
Harder
1. Homeland Security
2. Interior
3. Labor
4. Health and Human Services
5. Housing and Urban Development
Yeah, Good Luck
1. Commerce
2. Agriculture
3. Energy
4. Commerce
5. Education

MISS CONGENITALITY
1. A
2. C
3. D
4. B
5. E

SOL MUSIC
1. The Baltimore *Sun*
2. The corona
3. The Fiesta Bowl
4. *The Dark Side of the Moon*
5. Ra
6. The Sundance Kid
7. Louis XIV
8. The Dallas Mavericks
9. He's impotent from a war wound
10. Ben Stiller

JULY 27

EAGLE-EYED
1. Gerald Ford
2. An "albatross"
3. Adolf Hitler
4. "E Pluribus Unum"
5. John Madden
6. Montenegro
7. "Colitas"
8. Ski jumping
9. The golden eagle
10. *The Hobbit*

SINGLED OUT
1. Sudoku
2. "Candle in the Wind 1997"
3. Edward Heath
4. Nissan
5. Ivan Lendl

FIELD TESTING
Easy
1. Yankee Stadium
2. Lambeau Field
3. Indianapolis Speedway
4. Dodger Stadium
5. Ohio Stadium
Harder
1. Mellon Arena
2. Cleveland Browns Stadium
3. The Hubert H. Humphrey Metrodome
4. Minute Maid Park
5. Michigan Stadium
Yeah, Good Luck
1. University Arena (New Mexico)
2. HP Pavilion
3. Los Angeles Memorial Coliseum
4. Darlington Raceway
5. LP Field

JULY 28

THE WAY WE WIRE
1. World War I
2. *The Stranger*
3. "Old Cary Grant fine. How you?"
4. William Tecumseh Sherman
5. Mickey Rooney

DASH BOARD
1. David Hyde-Pierce
2. Constantin Costa-Gavras
3. Antoine de Saint-Exupéry
4. Margaret Bourke-White
5. Jackie Joyner-Kersee and Florence Griffith-Joyner
6. Henri de Toulouse-Lautrec
7. Claude Lévi-Strauss
8. Boutros Boutros-Ghali
9. Catherine Zeta-Jones
10. Julia Louis-Dreyfus

NOT STIRRED
1. Hakeem Olajuwon
2. Aqua Teen Hunger Force
3. Yitzhak Rabin and Yasser Arafat
4. KC and the Sunshine Band ("Shake Your Booty")
5. The Russian Revolution

JULY 29

GET WITH THE PROGRAM!
1. Java
2. Python
3. BASIC
4. C
5. Pascal

RHYME AND REASON
1. Jack Black (of Tenacious D)
2. Harry Caray
3. The White Knight
4. Fay Wray
5. A zoot suit
6. Pall Mall
7. The Mod Squad
8. Quiet Riot
9. Wavy Gravy
10. Tora Bora
11. Beaver Cleaver
12. "Helter Skelter"
13. *Kill Bill*
14. "Pee-Wee"
15. Lexis Nexis

JULY 30

ASSEMBLY LANGUAGE
Easy
1. Japan
2. The United Kingdom
3. Israel
4. Germany
5. Russia
Harder
1. The Netherlands
2. Iceland
3. Ireland
4. India
5. Sweden
Yeah, Good Luck
1. Finland
2. Mongolia
3. Albania
4. Norway
5. Bangladesh

ARMED AND DANGEROUS
1. Put your hands on your hips with your elbows out
2. The *Aeneid*
3. Unsportsmanlike conduct
4. Ten
5. 199 (Daniel Inouye lost an arm in Italy during World War II)

TINT POLE MOVIES
Easy
1. Purple
2. White
3. Pink
Harder
1. Silver
2. Black
3. Blue
Yeah, Good Luck
1. Green
2. Red
3. Yellow

JULY 31

THE LIGHT STUFF
1. (Stained) glass
2. China
3. A halogen lamp
4. Emma Lazarus's ("The New Colossus")
5. The harp
6. Boston's Old North Church (for Paul Revere)
7. Florence Nightingale
8. Yellow
9. Pixar's
10. An honest man

"D" COMPOSITION
1. Marv Albert's
2. Denver
3. Operation Overlord
4. Professor Griff
5. Hydrogen

SAY MY NAME
1. Scary and Sporty (Melanie Brown and Melanie Chisholm)
2. John Quincy Adams and John C. Calhoun
3. Apple Computer
4. Terry (Jones and Gilliam)
5. Hawaii (Daniel Inouye and Daniel Akaka)

• 1825 • ARMY SURGEON WILLIAM BEAUMONT begins his experiments with fur trader Alexis St. Martin, who has a hole in his abdomen from an oddly healed 1822 musket wound. By dipping food on strings directly into St. Martin's stomach, Beaumont uncovers the secrets of digestion, becoming known as the "Father of Gastric Physiology."

BELLY WILDER

Can you stomach this quiz?

1. What slang term for the stomach is the highest-scoring ailment in Operation?
2. Rennet, an enzyme-filled juice from animal stomachs, is used in the making of what?
3. In his Snake Plissken movies, what kind of snake is Kurt Russell's stomach tattoo?
4. Chemically, what kind of acid is stomach acid?
5. What comedy show parodied soap operas with *As the Stomach Turns*?

• 1978 • NEW YORK CITY PASSES Section 161.03 of its health code, the famous "poop scoop" law, and pet owners reluctantly begin cleaning up after their dogs—at least when cops are watching.

THE SCOOP-Y GANG

1. What scoop out cirques, coombs, and corries?
2. What magazine scooped *The Washington Post* to the 2005 revelation that Mark Felt was "Deep Throat"?
3. If you're scooping up spicy doro wat with big hunks of injera, what country's cuisine are you enjoying?
4. What 1969 bestseller begins with a satellite called SCOOP crashing in Arizona?
5. What two former Seahawks QBs are the NFL's career leaders in fumble recoveries, scooping up 56 and 47 respectively?

• 1981 • MTV LAUNCHES, playing "Video Killed the Radio Star," by the Buggles, its first video ever. Twenty minutes later, MTV plays "Rockin' the Paradise" by Styx, which turns out to be its last video ever, as the channel then launches into a twenty-four-hour *Road Rules* marathon.

STRAIGHT TO VIDEOS

1. California's Venice High School, which became Rydell High in the film *Grease*, was also the setting for what career-making 1998 video?
2. What legendary director shot the Michael Jackson video "Bad"?
3. What video made stars of the overall-clad "Sal" and "Harv"?
4. What musician, killed on February 3, 1959, is believed to have coined the term "music video" when he made short films for three of his songs in 1958?
5. Who are Nathan Wind, Vic Colfari, and Sir Stewart Wallace?
6. What Oscar winner also won an MTV Video Music Award in 2001 for Fatboy Slim's "Weapon of Choice" video?
7. In what 1992 video do words like "numb," "problem," and "harmless" flash on the screen, in chalk, mirroring the lyric "Try to erase this from the blackboard"?
8. What smash video features a vintage performance by the fictional band The Love Below?
9. Aardman Animations, of *Wallace and Gromit* fame, is also responsible for what most-played video in MTV history?
10. What video's literary images include the martyred Saint Sebastian and Gabriel García Márquez's "Very Old Man with Enormous Wings"?

Answers to the questions on this page can be found on page 345.

AUGUST 2

• **1798** • HORATIO NELSON ROUTS the French at the battle of the Nile. This inspires one Dr. Burney to coin history's most famous anagram, transposing "Horatio Nelson" into *"Honor est a Nilo,"* Latin for "Honor is from the Nile."

"ERIC CLAPTON" IS A "NARCOLEPTIC"

Whose famous name can be anagrammed into the capitalized word in each question?

1. Who still ENDEARS himself to audiences, in reruns, as the city editor of the *Los Angeles Tribune*?

2. Who appeared in his LEANEST-budget film when he narrated Troma's fourth *Toxic Avenger* movie under the pseudonym "Peter Parker"?

3. Who sings lead vocals on the 1965 song that inspired They Might Be Giants' RETROGRADELY titled "I Hope I Get Old Before I Die"?

4. Who played the Solveig Dommartin role in the 1987 reimagining of *Wings of Desire*, which moved the setting from Berlin, GERMANY, to Los Angeles?

5. Who DELIBERATED before turning down the lead roles in *Mr. Ed* and *My Three Sons* and then went on to 1960s sitcom stardom on a different show?

6. Whose GENERAL conversion from soul music to gospel was a result of his girlfriend, Mary Woodson, scalding him with boiling grits and then killing herself in 1974?

7. On TV's MORDANTLY funny *King of the Hill*, Bobby attends a Texas middle school named for whom?

8. Sales of Ray-Ban Wayfarers exploded after what actor's COSTUMIER fitted him with a pair for the 1983 film in which he portrayed Joel Goodson?

9. Jacques Cousteau's grandson Philippe has described, in INTERVIEWS, how he was present at the death of what man?

10. Whose 1969 hit "Make Your Own Kind of Music" OSCILLATES wildly in speed and volume when used to creepy effect on TV's *Lost*?

11. Who played the HOMINAL robot, Ash, in *Alien*?

12. Whose UNSUPERABLE children's show gave early roles to actors like Laurence Fishburne, Natasha Lyonne, and S. Epatha Merkerson?

13. After Vince Clarke left Depeche Mode, who became the main GERMINATOR of the band's songs?

14. What professional politician-MISTRUSTER has hosted TV's longest-running program since 1991?

15. Who claims that a contact lens allergy is what prevents her from being ISOLABLE from her signature tortoiseshell glasses?

• **1956** • ALBERT HENRY WOOLSON dies in Duluth at the age, it is believed, of 109. Since he was the drummer boy for a Minnesota army regiment in 1864, Woolson is the last veteran of the Civil War.

SOLE SURVIVOR

1. Who was Martha, found dead in Cincinnati on the afternoon of September 1, 1914?

2. What actor, a TV veteran, is also the last living member of *The Magnificent Seven*?

3. In 2006, what quarterback became the last USFL veteran to play in an NFL game?

4. What does the U.N. call the last remaining colony on mainland Africa?

5. What poem takes place "on the eighteenth of April, in Seventy-Five: hardly a man is now alive who remembers that famous day and year"?

Answers to the questions on this page can be found on page 345.

• **1857** • SAM HOUSTON IS DEFEATED in his first bid for the governorship of Texas, but he'll win that office in 1859, making him the only governor in U.S. history ever to lead two different U.S. states (he was previously governor of Tennessee).

GOOBER(NATORIAL) PILE
What states have been led by these governors?

Easy
1. Harold Stassen and Jesse Ventura
2. Woodrow Wilson and Jim McGreevey
3. Earl Warren and Jerry Brown
4. Patrick Henry and Douglas Wilder
5. Theodore and Franklin Roosevelt

Harder
1. Hannibal Hamlin and Edmund Muskie
2. Zell Miller and Alexander Stephens
3. Orval Faubus and Jim Guy Tucker
4. William McKinley and Salmon P. Chase
5. John Connally and Ann Richards

Yeah, Good Luck
1. James Polk and Austin Peay
2. Philip La Follette and Tommy Thompson
3. Evan Mecham and Bruce Babbitt
4. Benjamin Butler and Edward Everett
5. Gifford Pinchot and Milton Shapp

• **1943** • GENERAL GEORGE PATTON slaps a shell-shocked soldier in hospital and is nearly court-martialed, though Eisenhower hushes up the affair. The incident later becomes one of the most memorable scenes in George C. Scott's 1970 portrayal of him in *Patton*.

TONY DANZA SYNDROME
What actors shared the same first names as the characters they played in these movies?

Easy
1. *The Shining*
2. *The Elephant Man*
3. *The Big Lebowski*
4. *The King of Comedy*

Harder
1. *The Devil Wears Prada*
2. *While You Were Sleeping*
3. *I Never Sang for My Father*
4. *The Shootist*

Yeah, Good Luck
1. *Georgy Girl*
2. *Goodfellas*
3. *Blackboard Jungle*
4. *Brewster's Millions*

• **1979** • AT THE HEIGHT of the energy crisis, America reels as gas prices top $1 a gallon for the first time. Ah, the good old days.

IT'S A GAS

1. What snooty nickname is applied to gases like neon, argon, krypton, and xenon that refuse to interact with other elements?
2. Ronald Reagan made headlines in 1980 for claiming that 80 percent of air pollution comes from what?
3. Name one of the two non-metals on the periodic table that end with the "-ium" suffix normally reserved for metals.
4. What's the chemical name for a dentist's "laughing gas"?
5. What gas makes up 96 percent of the atmosphere of Venus but just .04 percent of our atmosphere?

Answers to the questions on this page can be found on page 345.

AUGUST 4

• **1834** • MATHEMATICIAN JOHN VENN is born in Yorkshire. He will invent Venn diagrams, the overlapping circles used in set theory.

REMEMBER VENN

What's the only item that could belong in the overlapping area in these Venn diagrams?

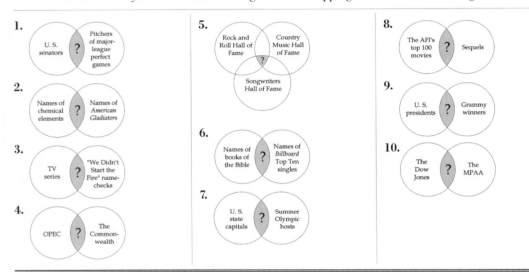

1. U.S. senators **?** Pitchers of major-league perfect games

2. Names of chemical elements **?** Names of *American Gladiators*

3. TV series **?** "We Didn't Start the Fire" name-checks

4. OPEC **?** The Commonwealth

5. Rock and Roll Hall of Fame **?** Country Music Hall of Fame **?** Songwriters Hall of Fame

6. Names of books of the Bible **?** Names of *Billboard* Top Ten singles

7. U.S. state capitals **?** Summer Olympic hosts

8. The AFI's top 100 movies **?** Sequels

9. U.S. presidents **?** Grammy winners

10. The Dow Jones **?** The MPAA

• **1952** • THE FIRST KENTUCKY FRIED CHICKEN restaurant opens—not in Kentucky but in Salt Lake City, Utah.

FINGER-LICKIN' GOOD

Match these fast-food chains to their interchangeable-sounding slogans.

1. "Eat up"	**A.** Arby's
2. "What you crave"	**B.** A & W
3. "Different is good"	**C.** Burger King
4. "Do what tastes right"	**D.** Dairy Queen
5. "Gather 'round the good stuff"	**E.** Pizza Hut
6. "Think outside the bun"	**F.** Quiznos
7. "The fire's ready"	**G.** Subway
8. "We treat you right"	**H.** Taco Bell
9. "All American food"	**I.** Wendy's
10. "Eat fresh"	**J.** White Castle

Answers to the questions on this page can be found on page 346.

AUGUST 5

• 1903 • EDUCATOR RENSIS LIKERT is born in Wyoming. You don't know Likert, but you've probably seen his namesake "scale." The Likert scale is a question followed by some range of answers, such as Strongly Disagree, Disagree, Agree, and Strongly Agree.

DRAWN TO SCALES
Can you match these scales to the things they measure?

1. The Bark scale	A. Chili pepper hotness
2. The Binet-Simon scale	B. Earthquake magnitude
3. The Holmes and Rahe scale	C. Energy available to alien civilizations
4. The Kardashev scale	D. Hurricane strength
5. The Kelvin scale	E. Intelligence
6. The Mohs scale	F. Mineral hardness
7. The Richter scale	G. Pain of insect stings
8. The Saffir-Simpson scale	H. Perceived loudness of sounds
9. The Schmidt index	I. Stress caused by life events
10. The Scoville scale	J. Temperature

• 1912 • INDIANA SENATOR ALBERT BEVERIDGE coins a new political term when he tells the "Bull Moose" Party, at its Chicago convention, "This party has come from the grass roots."

LAWN TERM MEMORY
Ten grass-roots questions—no mower, no less.

1. What's the only Grand Slam tennis event still played on grass?
2. What plant is the largest member of the Poaceae family, the true grasses?
3. Who was given a gift of a hat pin and a copy of *Leaves of Grass* on February 28, 1997?
4. The critical clue in what movie turns out to be a Japanese gardener complaining that salt water is "bad for glass"?
5. Tifgreen and Tifway, the best golf course grasses, are varieties of what kind of grass named for a British territory?
6. Who shocked the public with his 1863 painting *Luncheon on the Grass*?
7. What raconteur and *Topkapi* star joked that he wanted his tombstone to read "Keep off the grass?"
8. What TV show is produced by Honolulu's Grass Skirt Productions?
9. According to Erma Bombeck's best seller, where is the grass always greener?
10. What Hollywood legend made his screen debut in 1961's *Splendor in the Grass*?

Answers to the questions on this page can be found on page 346.

AUGUST 6

• **1930** • NEW YORK JUDGE Robert Crater enjoys a quiet dinner with his showgirl mistress and a lawyer friend, then hops into a taxi and is never heard from again.

VANISHING ACTS

1. What union did Jimmy Hoffa head until his 1975 disappearance?

2. What hero of the War of 1812 established his own "kingdom," called Campeche, at Galveston, Texas, until disappearing overnight in 1821?

3. What instrument did vanished bandleader Glenn Miller play?

4. On what Caribbean island did Natalee Holloway disappear in 2005?

5. What author of *The Devil's Dictionary* disappeared while accompanying Pancho Villa's army through Mexico in 1913?

6. For what mysterious figure is the latch on the inside of some Boeing passenger jet doors named?

7. In what South American country were Butch Cassidy and the Sundance Kid rumored killed in 1908?

8. What explorer disappeared in 1928 while on a rescue mission for survivors of the crashed airship *Italia*?

9. Over what ocean did Amelia Earhart disappear?

10. Who saved thousands of Hungarian Jews from the Holocaust before vanishing into a Soviet prison in 1945?

• **1964** • THE WORLD'S OLDEST TREE, a Great Basin bristlecone pine called Prometheus, is cut down by researchers and the U.S. Forest Service so that—get this—its age can be determined.

TREE-VENGE!
Sometimes trees get people back. Match these famous names to the kind of tree that killed them.

1. Marc Bolan (of T-Rex)	**A.** Oak
2. Sonny Bono	**B.** Pecan
3. Albert Camus	**C.** Pine
4. Jim Croce	**D.** Plane tree
5. Jackson Pollock	**E.** Sycamore

• **1971** • PRINCIPAL PHOTOGRAPHY on *The Godfather* ends. Paramount is queasy about the results—director Francis Ford Coppola insisted on an unknown stage actor, Al Pacino, in the lead, though the studio wanted Warren Beatty or Robert Redford.

THANK YOU, GODFATHER
What genre are each of these musicians said to be "godfathers" of?

1. Neil Young	**3.** Afrika Bambaataa	**5.** The Cure
2. James Brown	**4.** Iggy Pop	

Answers to the questions on this page can be found on page 346.

• **1854** • JAPAN ESTABLISHES the *Hinomaru*, the familiar "Rising Sun" design, as the official flag to be flown from its ships.

FAVORITE SUN
What countries display these less familiar suns on their flags?

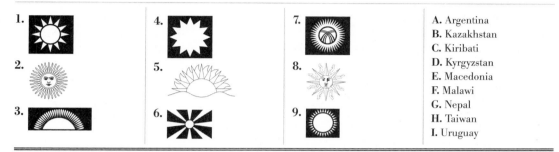

1.

2.

3.

4.

5.

6.

7.

8.

9.

A. Argentina
B. Kazakhstan
C. Kiribati
D. Kyrgyzstan
E. Macedonia
F. Malawi
G. Nepal
H. Taiwan
I. Uruguay

• **1881** • BUFFALO DENTIST ALFRED SOUTHWICK watches a drunk man die by accidentally touching an electrical generator. Southwick becomes fascinated with the idea of using electrocution to execute criminals (wow, dentists really *are* sadists!) and helps pass laws in twenty states to make the electric chair a reality.

BRUSHES WITH GREATNESS
Five dentists who changed history. Four of them recommend Trident!

1. What jazz legend was named after his father, an East Saint Louis dentist who once ran for the Illinois state legislature?
2. What did retired Seattle dentist Barney Clark make headlines for receiving on December 2, 1982?
3. What did George Harrison's dentist, John Riley, do in April 1965 that changed the face of rock?
4. Ex-dentist Gurbanguly Berdimuhammedow is now the dictator of what Caspian Sea nation?
5. In her only book, who gave the unflattering nickname "Dr. Dussel," meaning "nitwit," to Amsterdam dentist Fritz Pfeffer?

• **1988** • NIKE UNVEILS A $20 MILLION, one-month campaign for its shoes. The tagline, tossed off by adman Dan Wieder in a meeting, is the simple "Just do it," which he borrowed from the last words of serial killer Gary Gilmore. It becomes Nike's corporate slogan for decades, and *Advertising Age* named it the fourth best advertising campaign of the century.

PERFECT PITCH
What brands were hawked by these other slogans from Advertising Age's *"Top 100"?*

Easy
#**1:** "Think small"
#**2:** "The pause that refreshes"
#**5:** "You deserve a break today"
#**10:** "We try harder"
#**15:** "Good to the last drop"

Harder
#**35:** "When it rains it pours"
#**38:** "Look, Ma! No cavities!"
#**40:** "Takes a licking and keeps on ticking"
#**44:** "Tastes good—like a cigarette should"
#**48:** "Always a bridesmaid, but never a bride"

Yeah, Good Luck
#**49:** "The penalty of leadership"
#**56:** "It's so simple"
#**69:** "A buck well spent"
#**71:** "The instrument of the immortals"
#**87:** "It's a miracle"

Answers to the questions on this page can be found on page 347.

• **1890** • An anonymous article in the *Chicago Tribune* documents the "Indian rope trick" for the first time. A century later, the article will be revealed as a hoax perpetrated by reporter John Elbert Wilkie, who went on to head the U.S. Secret Service for fourteen years.

ON THE ROPES

1. What Best Picture–winning film was adapted from the short story collection *Rope Burns*?

2. Who began his career as "the Cherokee Kid," the trick roper in Texas Jack's Wild West Circus?

3. What measurement was derived from the rope to which a boat's "chip log" was tied?

4. What's the American term for the rope maneuver called "abseiling" in Europe?

5. In a famous short story, on what bridge was Peyton Farquhar condemned to be hanged before the rope broke?

6. Where did tightrope artist Philippe Petit illegally walk on August 7, 1974?

7. What famous murders inspired Alfred Hitchcock's film *Rope*?

8. Who provoked controversy with the phone-sex conversation on her 1997 album *The Velvet Rope*?

9. Who was knocked out in 1974 by the "rope-a-dope" method?

10. According to legend, who cut the tree-bark rope tied into a "Gordian knot"?

• **1991** • The Gabin-Konstantynow radio mast near Warsaw collapses, meaning that the title of "world's tallest structure" once again belongs to the KVLY-TV antenna near tiny Blanchard, North Dakota.

SUCH GREAT HEIGHTS
Get high on these lofty questions.

1. What's the highest-pitched instrument in the orchestra?

2. Mount Sunflower is what state's highest point?

3. Who has held the world record in the pole vault—6.14 meters—for more than twenty years?

4. Where did the world's tallest bird, the giant moa, live until it went extinct around 1500?

5. What musical instrument does Jack steal from the beanstalk giant?

6. Which of the main categories of cloud, with a name meaning "curl of hair," forms at the highest altitudes?

7. What soft drink line was named after a competitor's unusually tall bottles?

8. Before being surpassed, what was the world's tallest building for just a few months in 1930?

9. Which player has the all-time highest *career* salary (not adjusted for inflation) in Major League Baseball?

10. What number from drug-culture slang probably originated in 1971, from the time of day when a group of San Rafael High potheads would meet up to get high?

Answers to the questions on this page can be found on page 347.

• **1944** • SMOKEY BEAR (NO "THE"!) first appears on Forest Service posters.

A CHILD'S GARDEN OF URSUS
Only you *can name the creators of these famous bears.*

Easy	*Harder*	*Yeah, Good Luck*
1. Winnie-the-Pooh	**1.** Paddington	**1.** Rupert Bear
2. Yogi Bear	**2.** Corduroy	**2.** Old Ben
3. Fozzie Bear	**3.** Br'er Bear	**3.** Gentle Ben
4. Baloo	**4.** Papa, Mama, Brother, Sister, and Honey Bear	**4.** P. T. Bridgeport

• **1974** • IN AN EAST ROOM CEREMONY, Gerald Ford, by all accounts a very nice guy, somehow becomes leader of the free world.

IT'S RAINING MEH
Answer these questions about mediocrity. Or don't. Whatever.

1. Who hit .202 with three homers while playing outfield for the Birmingham Barons in 1994?
2. What Canadian-born educator became famous for noting that "Every employee tends to rise to his level of incompetence"?
3. What do the initials stand for in PGP digital encryption?
4. What eighteenth-century opera composer, actually a hit musician in his day, was converted into a symbol of spiteful mediocrity by Peter Shaffer's *Amadeus?*
5. IQ tests are designed to produce what number as an average score?

• **1983** • IN MBABANE, QUEEN DZELIWE is replaced by Ntombi as queen regent of Swaziland.

MPROBABLE SPELLINGS
These answers, like many Swazi words, all begin with an unusual pair of consonants.

1. What company opened its first Italian eatery at Brooklyn's Kings Plaza Shopping Center in 1967?
2. What bird's "Willow" species is the state bird of Alaska, while its "Rock" species represents Canada's Nunavut province?
3. What African country calls itself the "Land of a Thousand Hills"?
4. What murder mystery novelist got her unusual first name from a Maori word meaning "reflections on the water"?
5. What alternate to the QWERTY keyboard layout puts all the vowels under the home fingers of the left hand?
6. What band based its hit "China in Your Hand" on Mary Shelley's *Frankenstein?*
7. What translucent, multilayer painting technique gives the *Mona Lisa*'s smile its famously enigmatic appearance?
8. What imp would return to his native fifth dimension only when Superman tricked him into saying his name backward?
9. What ethnic group began a wave of immigration to the U.S.—specifically the Minneapolis and Fresno areas—after the 1975 Communist takeover of Laos?
10. What Toyota sports car model had to be renamed the "Celica Sports Package" in January 2005, for PR reasons?

Answers to the questions on this page can be found on page 347.

AUGUST 10

• **1967** • CHRIS GAINES, GARTH BROOKS'S fictional rock alter ego, is born in Brisbane, Australia, to an Olympic swimmer and her coach husband.

EVEN BETTER THAN THE REAL THING

Match these fictional bands to their big hits.

1. The Be Sharps	**A.** "Baby on Board"
2. Drive Shaft	**B.** "Big Bottom"
3. Eddie and the Cruisers	**C.** "Cheese and Onions"
4. Jesse and the Rippers	**D.** "Every Beat of My Heart"
5. Josie and the Pussycats	**E.** "Forever"
6. The Rutles	**F.** "Man of Constant Sorrow"
7. The Soggy Bottom Boys	**G.** "On the Dark Side"
8. 2ge+her	**H.** "Say It (Don't Spray It)"
9. Spinal Tap	**I.** "That Thing You Do"
10. The Wonders	**J.** "You All Everybody"

• **1988** • THE LAST SHOT OF THE last episode of TV's *St. Elsewhere* seems to reveal that the whole series took place in the imagination of an autistic boy with a snow globe. Fans note that, through a complicated web of spin-offs and crossovers, a huge percentage of recent American TV has apparently taken place inside the magical snow globe.

SPIN CITY

From what "parent" TV show did each of these series spin off?

Easy	*Harder*	*Yeah, Good Luck*
1. *Trapper John, M.D.*	**1.** *Mork and Mindy*	**1.** *Diagnosis Murder*
2. *Lou Grant*	**2.** *The Facts of Life*	**2.** *Empty Nest*
3. *Private Practice*	**3.** *Melrose Place*	**3.** *Young Americans*
4. *A Different World*	**4.** *Family Matters*	**4.** *Top of the Heap*
5. *Frasier*	**5.** *The Andy Griffith Show*	**5.** *The Law and Harry McGraw*

• **2004** • THE CINCINNATI REDS' Adam Dunn hits baseball's longest home run in years when he clears the upper deck at Great American Ball Park and lands his ball in the Ohio River. It's been called the first major-league home run ever to cross a state line in flight.

HEAVY HITTERS

1. Who was nicknamed "Mr. November" after hitting Major League Baseball's first ever November homer?

2. What two Hall of Famers had the given names "Henry Louis"?

3. What slugger wrote the 1994 *Sports Illustrated* article "Time in a Bottle"?

4. How many home runs did Sammy Sosa hit the year of Mark McGwire's record-breaking 70?

5. What Murderer's Row second baseman was the first person in baseball history ever to hit two grand slams in the same game?

Answers to the questions on this page can be found on page 348.

AUGUST 11

• **1779** • THE AMERICAN NAVY loses all forty-three of its warships in the disastrous Penobscot Expedition, the worst naval defeat in U.S. history until Pearl Harbor. The campaign went so badly that even Paul Revere was court-martialed for his part in it.

NAVAL-GAZING

1. Nine of the last twelve U.S. aircraft carriers commissioned have been named for what?
2. What naval hobbyist produced the landmark book *All the World's Fighting Ships* in 1898?
3. What Danish peninsula lent its name to the largest naval battle of World War I?
4. Which U.S. state is home to the world's largest naval base?

5. What writer was called *el manco de Lepanto*, the cripple of Lepanto, for his injury from that 1571 battle?
6. What famous three-word order did Winston Churchill give following the loss of the British battlecruiser *Hood*?
7. What does "PT" stand for in the names of Navy PT boats?
8. John Paul Jones's frigate was

named *Bonhomme Richard*, after whose pen name?
9. What London square is, appropriately, home to Nelson's Column?
10. What rank is the U.S. Navy equivalent of the army's five-star general?

• **1953** • TERRENCE BOLLEA IS BORN in Georgia—but not until 1979 will he adopt the name we know him by today, Hulk Hogan.

THE SQUARED CIRCLE

1. The family on *Married . . . with Children* was named in honor of what wrestler?
2. What Edward Elgar composition did Gorgeous George use as his theme, making him the first wrestler ever to use entrance music?

3. What pro wrestler grew up next door to playwright Samuel Beckett?
4. Miami, Nebraska, or Alabama—Dwayne "The Rock" Johnson won an NCAA championship playing football for what school?

5. The WWF changed its acronym after a 2000 lawsuit from what conservationist NGO?

• **1958** • THE FIRST MR. CLEAN commercials make their TV debut. Procter & Gamble says that Mr. Clean is a sailor. Wow! For a sailor, his bald, muscular, earring-wearing look predates the Village People's "In the Navy" by twenty years!

"CLEAN" LIVING

1. In what Olympic sport is the "clean and jerk" event held?
2. Who was the only clean-shaven U.S. president in the fifty years between Grant and Taft?

3. Who washes his hands in Matthew 27:24?
4. What TV veteran originated the role of neat freak Felix Unger in *The Odd Couple* on Broadway?

5. What bathroom cleaner was originally advertised by the Scrubbing Bubbles?

Answers to the questions on this page can be found on page 348.

AUGUST 12

• 1801 • GROCER-TO-BE JOHN CADBURY is born in Birmingham, England. A strong believer in the temperance movement, Cadbury will begin manufacturing his own brand of chocolate in the hope of tempting drinkers away from the demon alcohol.

CHOCOLATE THUNDER

1. In 2006, what surpassed *Like Water for Chocolate* to become the top-grossing Spanish-language movie in U.S. history?
2. What animal shape are the chocolate pieces in Ben & Jerry's flavor "Vermonty Python"?

3. What famous event in sports history happened in Hershey, Pennsylvania, of all places, on March 2, 1962?
4. What top-selling candy bar in the world was named for a beloved horse of the Mars

family?
5. Chocolate's addictive properties are due to what alkaloid, whose name means "food of the gods"?

• 1958 • PHOTOGRAPHER ART KANE, for his first photo shoot, crowds fifty-seven jazz legends in front of a New York brownstone and takes the famous shot now called *A Great Day in Harlem.*

JAZZ HANDS

1. What musician had a first name from Roman myth and the even more unusual middle name "Sphere"?
2. What jazz innovator claimed that his cosmic philosophy was born in 1936 when aliens ab-

ducted him and took him to Saturn?
3. What 1959 Dave Brubeck Quartet piece borrows its name from its unusual time signature?
4. What instrument did Lionel Hampton introduce to jazz in

1930?
5. What 1959 album, in which the sidemen include John Coltrane on tenor sax, is the bestselling jazz LP of all time?

• 1969 • IN CHICAGO, THE GUESS WHO record "American Woman," which will become the first song ever to top the American and Canadian singles charts at the same time.

NORTH AMERICAN IDOL
Name these U.S. bands from their lone Canadian member.

1. Denny Doherty
2. James LaBrie

3. Neil Young
4. Melissa Auf der Maur

5. Zal Yanovsky

Answers to the questions on this page can be found on page 348.

• **1902** • ACCORDING TO HOTEL LORE, Singapore's last wild tiger is shot to death under the Bar and Billiard Room of the luxurious Raffles Hotel.

INN-TERNATIONAL
Answer these questions about world hotels.

1. What chocolate cake is named for the Vienna hotel that keeps its recipe secret?
2. What city's Hotel Adlon was the site of Michael Jackson's 2002 baby dangling?
3. What fashion icon died in 1971 at the suite at Paris's Hotel Ritz, now named for her, where she'd lived for decades?
4. What's now the more common nickname for Africa's Belgian-owned resort Hotel des Mille Collines?
5. What are the hotel-inspired names of the two old men who heckle *The Muppet Show*?
6. Kuala Lumpur, Taipei, or Dubai—where will the Asia-Asia Hotel, the world's largest, be completed by 2016?
7. According to graffiti in room 652 of Edinburgh's Balmoral Hotel, what literary milestone was reached there on January 11, 2007?
8. What city is home to the Ryugyong Hotel, an unfinished 105-story pyramid abandoned in 1992?
9. At what New York hotel was Sid Vicious accused of killing Nancy Spungen?
10. In what city is the Schloss Cecilienhof, site of a historic 1945 conference?

• **1976** • TWO YEARS BEFORE HITTING it big on *Taxi*, a starry-eyed young boxer named "Dangerous" Tony Danza, in his first fight, scores a knockout over Earl "Shotgun" Harris.

DANZA IN THE DARK
As an actor, Tony Danza appears to have a hard time answering to any other first name than his own.
Match the last name of each fictional "Tony" to the show in which he appeared.

1. Banta	A. *Taxi*	**Bonus Danza!** In what Best Pic-
2. Canetti	B. *Who's the Boss?*	ture Oscar–winning film does Tony
3. Danza	C. *Hudson Street*	Danza appear?
4. DiMeo	D. *The Tony Danza Show* (1997)	
5. Micelli	E. *The Tony Danza Show* (2004)	

• **2004** • *ALIEN VS. PREDATOR* HITS THEATERS! No matter who wins, whoever pays $10.50 to see this crap loses!

SMASHED HITS
Make new movie titles by combining two others. For example, the answer to "Arnold Schwarzenegger +
The Monkees = David Lynch" would be "Eraser + Head = Eraserhead."

1. Irene Jacob + Al Pacino = Jim Belushi
2. Warren Beatty + Burt Reynolds = Scott Baio
3. Demi Moore + Jack Lemmon = Bill Cosby
4. Tom Cruise + Jeremy Irons = Arnold Schwarzenegger
5. Cary Grant + Samantha Morton = Sergio Leone
6. Bette Midler + Bruce Dern = Anna Magnani
7. Bob Hoskins + Bruce Dern = Julia Roberts
8. Abel Gance + Cecil B. DeMille = Jon Heder ← Charlize Theron
9. ~~Halle Berry~~ + William Katt = Sony Pictures Animation
10. Peter Lorre + Woody Allen = Alec Baldwin

Answers to the questions on this page can be found on page 349.

AUGUST 14

• **1849** • CHARLES EDWARD GORDON CRAWFORD is born. While serving as district judge in India, he will found the world's first "naturist" club—which has only two other members, both missionary's sons. Maybe it's just me, but three naked guys just hanging out in Bombay doesn't really sound like a very good nudist colony.

BARELY THERE
Can you get to the naked truth behind these questions?

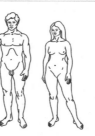

1. What magazine ran the famous cover of a very pregnant Demi Moore in the buff?
2. According to the TV series, how many stories are there in *The Naked City*?
3. Where would you see this couple?

4. What attorney general spent $8,000 on blue drapes to cover up the nude statues in the Great Hall of the Department of Justice?
5. Who was onstage when Robert Opel streaked the 1974 Academy Awards?

• **1956** • BRITISH NOVELISTS IRIS MURDOCH and John Bayley marry at Oxford. Their marriage inspires the movie *Iris*, in which—for the only time in movie history—*two* stars (Kate Winslet and Judi Dench) are Oscar-nominated for playing the title character.

WOMAN OF THE YEAR
What actress played the title role in these first-name-basis movies?

Easy	*Harder*	*Yeah, Good Luck*
1. *Frida*	1. *Julia*	1. *Gloria* (1980)
2. *Heidi* (1929)	2. *Tess*	2. *Angie*
3. *Amélie*	3. *Marnie*	3. *Lolita* (1962)
4. *Gilda*	4. *Laura*	4. *Annie*
5. *Nell*	5. *Eddie*	5. *Lili*

• **2006** • A WELSH HIGHWAY COUNCIL COPS to a little translation goof in a road construction sign near Cardiff. The English on the sign says "Cyclists dismount," but the Welsh translation below apparently reads, "Bladder disease has returned."

TONGUE TWISTERS
Trivia that was lost in translation.

1. What biblical object may be a King James Version mistranslation of "a robe with long sleeves"?
2. Julius Nyerere, who did the first Swahili translations of Shakespeare, later became the first president of what nation?

3. Mikhail Gorbachev, Tony Blair, or Jimmy Carter—on a state visit, whose statement that he "loved" the Polish people was rendered as "I sexually desire the Polish people" by a translator error?

4. What 1997 epic was retitled *His Powerful Device Makes Him Famous* for Hong Kong release?
5. What Latin phrase, well known to Americans, actually comes from a poem, attributed to Virgil, about a salad recipe?

Answers to the questions on this page can be found on page 349.

AUGUST 15

• **1281** • THE MONGOLS' INVASION of Japan fails when, for a second time, a typhoon destroys their fleet. The Japanese will come to call these fortuitous storms "divine wind," or *kamikaze*.

TURNING JAPANESE

1. How many *morae*, Or "syllables," are there in Japanese haiku?

2. Who are Kambei, Katsuhiro, Gorobei, Shichiroji, Kyuzo, Heihachi, and Kikuchiyo?

3. Which island of Japan is just twenty-six miles from Russia at its closest point?

4. Gwen Stefani has named her backup dancers after what fashionable shopping district of Tokyo?

5. Japan's World War II surrender was signed aboard what vessel, the last battleship ever built by the U.S. Navy?

6. Who got his name by combining the Japanese words for "gorilla" and "whale"?

7. What do sumo wrestlers throw into the ring to purify it before each bout?

8. What takes its name from the Japanese for "whimsical pictures"?

9. What children's hobby uses the Yoshizawa-Randlett diagramming system?

10. What brand of whiskey does a nonplussed Bill Murray advertise in the film *Lost in Translation*?

11. What flower symbolizes the throne of the Japanese emperor?

12. What famous quartet was originally named Oikake ("Chaser"), Machibuse ("Ambusher"), Kimagure ("Fickle"), and Otoboke ("Stupid")?

13. What popular *koan* may be answered by thrusting the palm toward the teacher?

14. What's the Japanese name for a potentially poisonous delicacy made from puffer fish meat?

15. What is Takeru Kobayashi famous for?

• **1857** • A NOTE IN THE LIVERPOOL, Nova Scotia, *Transcript* provides the first published evidence of the Oak Island "Money Pit," which has stymied treasure hunters for 150 years.

X MARKS THE SPOT
Can you dig up these treasured answers?

1. What children's TV character lived in the Treasure House?

2. What legendary Arizona gold mine is named in honor of prospector Jacob Waltz?

3. The cipher that leads to the treasure in the movie *National Treasure* is hidden on the back side of what?

4. Besides his other treasure, who also carries a leather pouch that will always hold a single silver shilling?

5. Who directed his own father to Oscar gold in *The Treasure of the Sierra Madre*?

6. What was the first name of the pirate Captain Kidd?

7. In German myth, what river hides the treasure of the Nibelung?

8. Who did Brazil name an official national treasure in 1962, so he wouldn't emigrate to Italy?

9. What movie concerns the search for One-Eyed Willie's pirate treasure?

10. Atocha, which shares its name with a famous sunken treasure ship, is the largest railway station in what city?

Answers to the questions on this page can be found on page 349.

AUGUST 16

• **1954** • THE FIRST ISSUE OF *Sports Illustrated* hits newsstands.

SPORTS, ILLUSTRATED
Name these sports, given a bird's-eye view of their playing surfaces.

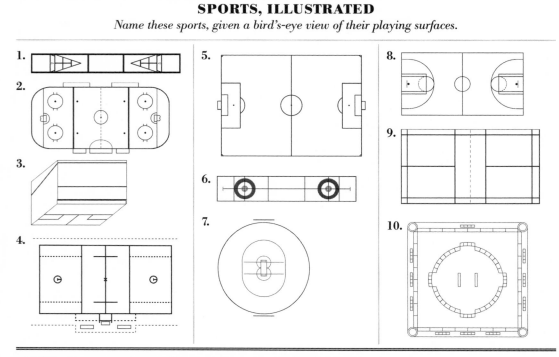

• **1962** • COMEDIAN STEVE CARELL is born, a 0-year-old virgin, in Massachusetts.

VIRGIN RECORDS
Whose celebrity celibacy allowed them to accomplish the following feats?

1. Defeating Rutherford B. Hayes in the 1876 popular vote
2. Playing in a record 1,192 con-secutive NBA games
3. Becoming Britain's youngest-ever prime minister
4. Inventing calculus
5. Founding the nursing school at London's St. Thomas' Hospital

• **1969** • CHARLES MANSON IS ARRESTED, along with twenty-five followers, in a police raid at "The Family"'s mountain ranch.

TALL IN THE FAMILY
Match up the first names of the fathers of these famous families.

1. *The Addams Family*
2. The Carter Family
3. *The Family Circus*
4. *The Hogan Family*
5. The Jackson family

A. Alvin
B. Bill
C. Gomez
D. Joseph
E. Michael

Answers to the questions on this page can be found on page 350.

• **1986** • A YEAR AND A HALF after losing his left arm in a street-racing accident, Def Leppard drummer Rick Allen rejoins the band live for the first time, seated behind a specially customized drum kit at the "Monsters of Rock" festival.

RE-PERCUSSIONS

1. Queen and Duran Duran both had drummers with what name?
2. According to a famous *SNL* catchphrase, what's the only prescription for Christopher Walken's fever?
3. Who published his Civil War poetry in *Drum-Taps*?
4. What cousin of the glockenspiel was named for its ethereal, "heavenly" sound?

5. On what TV show did Gene Gene the Dancing Machine perform?
6. Who composed the song "Peace on Earth" to accompany Bing Crosby's rendition of "The Little Drummer Boy"?
7. In what Caribbean country did steel drums originate?
8. The Strokes, the Hives, or the Killers—what band took its

name from the fictional band name on the drum in the New Order video "Crystal"?
9. What drummer died after accompanying Paul McCartney to a screening of *The Buddy Holly Story*?
10. Who performed an over-the-top spoken-word version of "Mr. Tambourine Man" on his album *The Transformed Man*?

• **1987** • MANILA INTERNATIONAL AIRPORT is renamed Ninoy Aquino International Airport, after the exiled Filipino leader assassinated there in 1983. Naming an airport after someone who died there? It's certainly an honor, but . . . sort of a macabre one, right?

FLIGHT CLUB
What city named its airport after these luminaries?

Easy
1. John Lennon
2. Charles de Gaulle
3. Louis Armstrong
4. John Foster Dulles
5. Ayatollah Khomeini

Harder
1. Leonardo da Vinci
2. Frédéric Chopin
3. Jomo Kenyatta
4. Marco Polo
5. Benito Juárez

Yeah, Good Luck
1. Lester Pearson
2. Toussaint Louverture
3. Ted Stevens
4. Galileo Galilei
5. Lech Walesa

• **1998** • BILL CLINTON TESTIFIES, for the first time, to having had an "improper physical relationship" with intern Monica Lewinsky.

AFFAIRS OF STATE
Match the chief executives to their reported flings.

1. George H. W. Bush
2. Grover Cleveland
3. Bill Clinton
4. Dwight Eisenhower
5. James Garfield

6. Warren Harding
7. Thomas Jefferson
8. John Kennedy
9. Lyndon Johnson
10. Franklin Roosevelt

A. Lucia Calhoun
B. Angie Dickinson
C. Jennifer Fitzgerald
D. Gennifer Flowers
E. Alice Glass

F. Maria Halpin
G. Sally Hemings
H. Lucy Page Mercer
I. Carrie Phillips
J. Kay Summersby

Answers to the questions on this page can be found on page 350.

AUGUST 18

• **1785** • THE COUNTESS DE LAMOTTE, a con artist, is arrested for her part in the notorious scandal called "the affair of the necklace," which implicated Marie Antoinette herself.

JEWELRY BOX

1. Who got his signature left-ear piercing in 1986, after interviewee Liza Minnelli encouraged him to do it?

2. What cartoon character is named for Princess Dala's diamond in a 1963 film?

3. What piece of jewelry—which turns out to be fake—does Madame Loisel lose in the title of Guy de Maupassant's most famous short story?

4. Tiffany and Co. has a registered trademark on its signature shade of what color?

5. "Tennis bracelets" are so named because of a 1987 incident involving what athlete?

6. What film coined the term "cameo appearance" for a brief star turn in a movie?

7. Who blinded himself with Jocasta's brooch?

8. What shape was the nipple shield that Janet Jackson sported during her 2004 Super Bowl "wardrobe malfunction"?

9. *Girl with a Pearl Earring* is one of only thirty-five extant works of what Dutch painter?

10. Who wears the "Pescatorio," or Ring of the Fisherman?

• **1868** • FRENCH ASTRONOMER PIERRE JANSSEN discovers helium—not on Earth, which has plenty of the stuff, but on the sun! Scientists scoff at the idea of detecting an element in space before it's found on Earth, but Janssen's findings are soon confirmed.

ELEMENTARY, MY DEAR WATSON
Which element of the periodic table was named for . . .

Easy	*Harder*	*Yeah, Good Luck*
1. The inventor of dynamite	1. The moon	1. Paris
2. The Norse god of thunder	2. The sun	2. The inventor of the cyclotron
3. A U.S. state	3. An Italian	3. The father of Pelops
4. A married couple	4. A Titan of Greek myth	4. A New Zealander
5. The seventh planet from the sun	5. The formulator of the periodic table	5. A Scottish village

• **1961** • THOUSANDS OF SEABIRDS suddenly and mysteriously pummel coastal homes in Santa Cruz, California. Alfred Hitchcock requests a local newspaper report of the incident, which will inspire scenes in his upcoming thriller *The Birds*.

BIRD IS THE WORD
A major character in these movies uses what bird name as a surname?

Easy	*Harder*	*Yeah, Good Luck*
1. *To Kill a Mockingbird*	1. *My Favorite Year*	1. *Sexy Beast*
2. *Clue*	2. *Psycho*	2. *Dead End*
3. *The Silence of the Lambs*	3. *The Jazz Singer*	3. *This Gun for Hire*

Answers to the questions on this page can be found on page 350.

AUGUST 19

• 1839 • THE FRENCH GOVERNMENT, having bought the patent to Louis Daguerre's namesake photographic process, announces that it will make the daguerreotype a "free gift to the world."

IN CAMERA
Answer these questions on great photographers.

1. In what mountain range is the 12,000-foot Mount Ansel Adams?
2. Who died a penniless alcoholic in a New York charity ward just blocks from the gallery where his "The Dead of Antietam" exhibition opened in 1862?

3. Fred Astaire's character in *Funny Face* was based on what fashion photographer?
4. Eadward Muybridge took his famous pictures of bodies in motion in order to answer what unsettled nineteenth-century

question?
5. What photographer had a twenty-year relationship with late author Susan Sontag?

• 1913 • CLARENCE CRANE TRADEMARKS his new invention: Life Savers candy. The trademark Life Savers shape wasn't in the original design—it was added by the pill manufacturer Crane hired to make the candies. His malfunctioning machine couldn't press them without a hole in the middle.

THE HOLE TRUTH

1. Who sang lead vocals for the rock band Hole?
2. Who is Dinah, whom Alice thinks about nostalgically as she falls down the rabbit hole to Wonderland?
3. What world leader, according to state-run media, hit eleven holes in one in his very first round of golf?
4. What kind of object is smaller than its own Schwarzschild radius?
5. What was the name of Bilbo and Frodo Baggins' hobbit hole?
6. What movie star founded the

Hole in the Wall summer camps for ill children?
7. How many hole cards is each player dealt in Texas hold 'em?
8. The "goddess of peace" sits atop what Berlin landmark, which was, ironically, restored in 2002 to remove World War II–era bullet holes?
9. What's the "toad" in traditional English toad-in-the-hole?
10. Who said, "Except . . . I thrust my hand into his side, I will not believe"?
11. What 1968 film takes place partially in the Sea of Holes?

12. Montreal, Buenos Aires, or Kyoto—what city names the 1987 accord designed to shrink Antarctica's "ozone hole" by banning CFCs?
13. What river, America's thirteenth longest, flows through Jackson Hole, Wyoming?
14. In *The Shawshank Redemption*, Andy initially hides his escape hole behind a poster of what actress?
15. Trepanation is the practice of drilling holes where?

Answers to the questions on this page can be found on page 351.

AUGUST 20

• **1896** • THREE KANSAS INVENTORS apply for a patent on the dial telephone.

TEXTONYMS

Textonyms are words that map to the same number sequence on a telephone keypad, like BARMAID and CARNAGE (2276243). Can you figure out these pairs of textonyms?

1. What song won Johnny Cash his last Country Music Award? / What title was given to Nanak, the founder of Sikhism?
2. How did Ponce de León, Claudius, and Tycho Brahe all die? / What is the world's best-selling vodka?
3. What did Keats call a "season of mists and mellow fruitfulness"? / What item would a tailor measure in lignes?
4. What company owns Gatorade, Quaker Oats, and Frito-Lay? / What language do natives call Farsi?

5. What kind of cuisine gave us kimchi and bulgogi? / What river is formed by the merging of the Hasbani, the Banias, the Dan, and the Ayoun?
6. What is Johnny Chase's nickname on *Entourage*? / What currency is used by twenty different African nations?
7. On what island is King Arthur buried? / What kind of bird is the mascot for Cocoa Puffs?
8. What name for military battle dress is derived from the tiring manual work performed by soldiers? / What relation was psy-

chiatrist Anna Freud to Sigmund?
9. What kind of "Girls" are Haylie and Hilary Duff, in the title of their first film together? / On what TV show did Roger Moore replace James Garner?
10. In what month does Hispanic Heritage Month begin? / In math, what lists can be summed into series?

• **1999** • FRENCH "URBAN CLIMBER" Alain Robert, aka "Spiderman," climbs Chicago's Sears Tower at dawn, using no tools but his bare hands and climbing shoes. He is arrested when he reaches the roof and booked for trespassing.

WORLD WIDE WEBS

Can your spider-sense handle these arachnid questions?

1. What whirling Italian folk dance was said to cure the bite of the large local wolf spider?
2. What's the only U.S. university to currently name its athletic teams after spiders?
3. How did black widow spiders—or, more specifically, their silk—help win World War II?
4. Who plays the title character in the 1955 musical *Daddy Long Legs*?

5. Complete this analogy: Clark Kent : *The Daily Planet* :: Peter Parker : _____.
6. What two singers, who have forty-five number one country songs between them, were both born with the last name Webb?
7. Who received a speeding ticket while driving his Porsche Spyder on September 30, 1955?
8. What poisonous American spider is sometimes called the "vio-

lin" or "fiddleback" spider, for its distinctive markings?
9. Who was found in a "spider hole" on December 13, 2003?
10. "Spiders," from the *Scream 3* sound track, was the second single ever from what Armenian-American metal band?

Answers to the questions on this page can be found on page 351.

AUGUST 21

• 1858 • THE FIRST LINCOLN-DOUGLAS DEBATE is held, in Ottawa, Illinois. Jim Lehrer not having been invented yet, the leisurely format allows each candidate to speak for an hour uninterrupted.

WALL OF SOUND BITES
Who gave these famous quotes from twentieth-century debates?

---

1. "Senator, you are no Jack Kennedy."
2. "There you go again."

3. "I think you know that I've opposed the death penalty during all my life."

4. "There is no Soviet domination of Eastern Europe."
5. "Who am I? Why am I here?"

• 1986 • IN A RARE "LIMNIC ERUPTION," the volcanic Lake Nyos in Cameroon suddenly releases 1.5 million tons of carbon dioxide into the surrounding valley, suffocating thousands.

THE HOT SPOT
In what countries would you find, or try not to find, these active volcanoes?

Easy
1. Etna
2. Lassen Peak
3. Krakatoa
4. Fuji

Harder
1. Pelée
2. Santorini
3. Popocatépetl
4. Erebus

Yeah, Good Luck
1. Nevado del Ruiz
2. Lamington
3. Nyiragongo
4. Taal

• 1997 • OLDSMOBILE BECOMES THE FIRST American car brand to celebrate its one hundredth anniversary. Suggested new ad slogan: "This is not your great-grandfather's Oldsmobile!"

CENTURY CITY

---

1. The NAACP dates its founding to February 12, 1909, to honor the hundredth anniversary of what event?
2. Which U.S. state is called the "Centennial State"?

3. What privately funded spacecraft made its first powered flight on December 17, 2003, one hundred years to the day after the Wright brothers' first flight?
4. What team won the hundredth

anniversary Stanley Cup—its twenty-fourth Cup—in 1993?
5. On his hundredth birthday, the intersection of Hollywood and Vine was officially renamed for whom?

Answers to the questions on this page can be found on page 351.

AUGUST 22

• **1485** • THE BATTLE OF BOSWORTH FIELD marks the end of the Plantagenet dynasty—but it also marks the first outbreak of a strange, virulent epidemic called the "English sweat," which kills thousands, often within hours of the first symptoms. The cause of the mysterious plague is still unknown.

PARTS UNKNOWN
And, speaking of unknown . . .

1. What war saw the first soldier buried at Arlington's Tomb of the Unknowns?
2. What unusual item was worn by *The Gong Show*'s Unknown Comic, Murray Langston?

3. What ominous phrase, used to mark *terra incognita* on old maps, derives from the sixteenth-century Hunt-Lenox globe?
4. What was poured on anyone who said "I don't know" on *You*

Can't Do That on Television?
5. In what movie is $200,000 of Confederate gold buried in the grave marked "Unknown" next to Arch Stanton?

• **1932** • THE BBC BEGINS experimental television broadcasts from its Broadcasting House in London.

LITTLE BRITAIN
What British TV series featured these characters?

1. Mr. Steed and Emma Peel
2. James Hacker, MP, and Sir Humphrey Appleby
3. Basil and Sybil
4. Saffron and Bubble
5. Eddie "Fitz" Fitzgerald and Jane "Panhandle" Penhaligon

6. Tinky Winky, Dipsy, Laa-Laa, and Po
7. The "It's" Man, Mr. Eric Praline, the Spanish Inquisition
8. Dave Lister and Frankenstein
9. David Brent and Gareth Keenan

10. Jeff Tracy and Lady Penelope Creighton-Ward

• **1978** • PRESIDENT JOMO KENYATTA, the founding father of Kenya, dies in Mombasa.

PATER PATRIAE
Name these countries from their national heroes, considered "founding fathers."

Easy	*Harder*	*Yeah, Good Luck*
1. Sun Yat-sen	1. Muhammad Ali Jinnah	1. Bernardo O'Higgins
2. Peter the Great	2. José de San Martín	2. Stefan Stambolov
3. Giuseppe Garibaldi	3. Mustafa Kemal Atatürk	3. Patrice Lumumba
4. Mahatma Gandhi	4. Eamon de Valera	4. Afonso I
5. Otto von Bismarck	5. José Martí	5. Obafemi Awolowo

Answers to the questions on this page can be found on page 352.

• **1928** • EXPLORER RICHARD HALLIBURTON completes his much-publicized swim through the Panama Canal. His 36-cent toll is still the lowest ever paid for a Panama Canal transit.

CANAL ZONE

1. In what film is Bill Murray the author of the play *Return to Love Canal?*

2. Which middle layer of a tooth contains the root canals?

3. What nation is home to the ancient Grand Canal, still the longest artificial waterway in the world?

4. The Italian Giovanni Schiapa-relli is best known today for naming most of the canals where?

5. What river was connected to Lake Erie by the Erie Canal?

6. What canals in the human ear serve as the body's balance organ?

7. What two-time presidential hopeful was born in the Panama Canal Zone?

8. Venice's Grand Canal ends at what huge square, the city's only piazza?

9. The Suez Crisis of 1956 was precipitated by Egypt's plans to build what?

10. What is *Le Bureau,* a hit on France's pay-TV channel Canal Plus?

• **1973** • FOUR BANK EMPLOYEES are held hostage for almost a week in a botched attempt at robbing the Norrmalmstorg branch of Sweden's Kreditbanken. After their release, all the hostages actually *defend* their captor to the police, and the term "Stockholm syndrome" is coined.

DAS KAPITAL
Other stuff named for world capitals.

1. What movie kills off a racehorse named Khartoum?

2. In 1977, Gerald Ford pardoned Iva Toguri D'Aquino, convicted of treason in 1949 under suspicion of being whom?

3. What city's music scene gave us R.E.M., Danger Mouse, and the B-52s?

4. The strongest earthquake ever to hit the continental U.S. hap-pened not along the San Andreas Fault but along what southeast Missouri fault line?

5. What kind of dog is Pluto's girlfriend, Fifi?

6. What ornately woven fabric was originally known as "diaper" in the West, before it borrowed a new name from a Middle Eastern capital city?

7. What James Joyce story collec-tion begins with "The Sisters" and ends with "The Dead"?

8. Who rode his horse Copen-hagen at the Battle of Waterloo?

9. What common office supply item is named for the Asian *abaca* fiber used to make them?

10. Who founded Heiress Records in 2004?

Answers to the questions on this page can be found on page 352.

AUGUST 24

• **79** • AUTHOR PLINY THE ELDER heads to Mount Vesuvius, the scientist in him eager to investigate the ongoing volcanic eruption. He is killed in the attempt.

DOWN BY LAVA

1. In one myth, what dance was first performed by Hi'iaka to appease the volcano goddess, Pele?
2. The 83-year-old man killed by Mount St. Helens when he refused to evacuate his cabin

shared his name with what U.S. president?
3. The red Oslo sky in what 1893 painting has been explained as a result of the eruption of Krakatoa?

4. What was created, almost seven thousand years ago, by the eruption of Mount Mazama?
5. What volcano is the world's tallest mountain, when measured base to summit?

• **1853** • SARATOGA SPRINGS DINER chef George Crum gets fed up with a customer who keeps sending his fried potatoes back, wanting them crispier and crispier. He stir-fries superthin potato slices into what he thinks will be an inedible concoction—only to find the customer enthusiastic about the innovation. The "Saratoga chip," the first potato chip, is born.

CHIPS OFF THE OLD BLOCK

1. The easiest way to tell Chip 'n' Dale apart is by their nose color. What colors are Chip 'n' Dale's noses?
2. What microchip company is one of only two NASDAQ stocks in the Dow Jones Industrial Average?
3. Chips worth $2.50 are used, typically, only in what casino game?
4. Who beat out Clark Gable in *Gone With the Wind*, Jimmy

Stewart in *Mr. Smith Goes to Washington*, and Laurence Olivier in *Wuthering Heights* when he won his only Oscar for playing Mr. Chips?
5. What snack chip comes in Original, Harvest Cheddar, French Onion, and Garden Salsa flavors?
6. Vince, Frank or Joe—what was "Ponch"'s real first name on *CHiPs*?
7. What ratings-based blocker

has been built into all U.S. TVs sold since 2000?
8. What Merrilee Rush hit was written by Chip Taylor, the brother of actor Jon Voight?
9. What two Orlando Magic teammates made their screen debuts in *Blue Chips*?
10. What actor, "Chip" on *My Three Sons*, has a name that suggests both the principals in a famous 1871 meeting?

• **1938** • A MILLION BAD PIANO DUETS are made possible when Hoagy Carmichael copyrights "Heart and Soul."

SOUL PROPRIETORS

1. What was the name of the devil to whom Faust sold his soul?
2. What two actresses with the same name have both starred in *Soul Food*, one in the 1997 film and the other in the subsequent

Showtime TV series?
3. What was the real first name of David Soul's "Hutch" on *Starsky and Hutch*?
4. Whose Atlantic recordings are collected in a set called *Queen of Soul*?

5. What is the Buddhist equivalent of the Hindu *moksha*—liberating the soul from its endless cycle of birth and rebirth?

Answers to the questions on this page can be found on page 352.

• **1835** • THE *NEW YORK SUN* BEGINS a six-article series describing the fantastic new animals (unicorns, flying bat people, etc.) that English astronomer John Herschel has discovered on the moon. Thousands of readers fall for the hoax.

SATELLITE ENTERTAINMENT

These moons orbit what planet (or, in one case, "planet") of the solar system?

Easy	Harder	Yeah, Good Luck
1. Deimos	1. Miranda	1. Mimas
2. Io	2. Titan	2. Leda
3. Luna	3. Charon	3. Proteus

• **1916** • CONGRESS CREATES THE NATIONAL PARK SERVICE, to "conserve the scenery and the natural and historic objects and the wild life and pic-a-nic baskets therein." Okay, just kidding about the pic-a-nic baskets.

LONE RANGERS

What's the only national park in these U.S. states?

Easy	Harder	Yeah, Good Luck
1. Kentucky	1. Idaho	1. North Dakota
2. Oregon	2. Arkansas	2. South Carolina
3. Tennessee	3. Virginia	3. Maine
4. New Mexico	4. Michigan	4. Nevada

• **1927** • THE FRENCH TENNIS TEAM takes on Japan in Davis Cup play. René Lacoste and his team captain have seen an alligator-skin suitcase in a Boston shop window and made it the prize in a little side wager on the match. This bet is the origin of Lacoste's nickname "*le crocodile*" and, later, the alligator logo on his namesake shirts.

TOP FIVE

How much do you know about these shirts?

1. What two metal bands are honored on Beavis and Butt-Head's usual T-shirts?
2. What famous clipper ship took its name from Scots words for "short shirt" in a Robert Burns poem?
3. What TV show's famed "puffy shirt" is in the Smithsonian today?
4. In 1999, what redshirt freshman became the first Division I football player ever named his league's Player of the Year and Rookie of the Year in the same year?
5. What Thames River town lent its name to the collarless polo shirts first worn by its rowing team?

Answers to the questions on this page can be found on page 353.

• **1862** • WILLIAM BANTING BEGINS the fad diet that will lose him fifty pounds and, after he publishes his pamphlet "A Letter on Corpulence," will make him history's first weight loss celebrity. "Banting" becomes the English word for "dieting" for a time, and even today, dieting is called *bantning* in Sweden.

NOW AND THIN

1. What's the last name of svelte Subway spokesman "Jared"?
2. What's the more common name for "vertical banded gastroplasty," or VBG?

3. What New York cardiologist published his bestselling *Diet Revolution* in 1972?
4. Who lost forty-three pounds for his one-scene role in *The Sixth Sense?*

5. The South Beach Diet is named for a section of what city?

• **1910** • STRUGGLING WITH SEXUAL IMPOTENCE and suicidal impulses after learning that his wife has been having an affair with architect Walter Gropius, composer Gustav Mahler travels to Holland for a consultation with no less an authority than Sigmund Freud. Mahler will write that his four-hour chat with Freud worked wonders.

SHRINK RAP

1. What's the first of Elizabeth Kübler-Ross's Five Stages of Grief?
2. Whose "Analyst" was James Coburn in a 1967 film?

3. What word did Carl Jung coin to mean "temporally coincident occurrences of acausal events"?
4. What director plays a psychiatrist's psychiatrist—Dr. Melfi's

shrink—on *The Sopranos?*
5. What did Freud call the female counterpart of the Oedipus complex?

• **1940** • DON LaFONTAINE IS BORN in Duluth, Minnesota. Even if you've never heard Don's name, you know his distinctive voice. His deep, booming tones have narrated more than 5,000 movie trailers and ads, earning him the nicknames "Thunder Throat" and "Mr. Voice."

IN A WORLD . . . !
Match these movies with their (mostly) offscreen narrators.

1. *The Age of Innocence*
2. *A.I.: Artificial Intelligence*
3. *Alive*
4. *Charlotte's Web*
5. *The Hitchhiker's Guide to the Galaxy*
6. *How the Grinch Stole Christmas*
7. *Lemony Snicket's A Series of Unfortunate Events*
8. *The Right Stuff*
9. *The Royal Tenenbaums*
10. *Simon Birch*
11. *Stand by Me*
12. *The Texas Chain Saw Massacre*
13. *To Kill a Mockingbird*
14. *War of the Worlds*
15. *Zulu*

A. Alec Baldwin
B. Richard Burton
C. Jim Carrey
D. Richard Dreyfuss
E. Morgan Freeman
F. Stephen Fry
G. Levon Helm
H. Anthony Hopkins
I. Ben Kingsley
J. John Larroquette
K. Jude Law
L. John Malkovich
M. Sam Shepard
N. Kim Stanley
O. Joanne Woodward

Answers to the questions on this page can be found on page 353.

• **1820** • THE FIRST HARDY MOUNTAINEERS reach the top of the Zugspitze, Germany's highest point . . . or so they think. In 2006, a newly discovered map will show that local hunters and shepherds had been scaling the peak at least fifty years before.

SUMMIT MEETING

What mountain is the tallest point of these nations?

Easy	*Harder*	*Yeah, Good Luck*
1. Greece	1. Australia	1. Pakistan
2. Nepal	2. Tanzania	2. Ecuador
3. The United States	3. Russia	3. Great Britain
4. France	4. Canada	4. Turkey
5. Japan	5. Argentina	5. San Marino

• **1943** • TUESDAY WELD IS BORN in New York City. On a Friday.

WEEK-MINDED

1. What Broadway great's daughter wrote the book *Freaky Friday*?

2. What day of the week do the Bangles *wish* it was in "Manic Monday"?

3. Three of four assassinated U.S. presidents—Lincoln, McKinley, and Kennedy—were fatally shot on what day of the week?

4. In 1982, what seven-year-old became *Saturday Night Live*'s youngest host ever?

5. What day of the week is Mardi Gras?

6. What is Gabriel Syme's code name, according to the title of G. K. Chesterton's most famous novel?

7. Who was (eventually) fired in the "Saturday Night Massacre" of October 1973?

8. Which of the two leads of 1995's *Friday* didn't appear in either of the sequels?

9. What did Wednesday Addams call her headless doll on *The Addams Family*?

10. What badge number was retired by the LAPD when Jack "Joe Friday" Webb died in 1982?

• **1997** • THE INTERNATIONAL FEDERATION OF ANATOMISTS decrees that the body part popularly known as "cleavage" will now be officially called the "intermammary sulcus."

GRAZE ANATOMY

What's the more colloquial term for these parts of the body?

Easy	*Harder*	*Yeah, Good Luck*
1. Clavicle	1. Axilla	1. Naris
2. Tympanum	2. Scapula	2. Metacarpophalangeal joints
3. Umbilicus	3. Laryngeal prominence	3. Hallux
4. Epidermis	4. Nates	4. Eponychium

Answers to the questions on this page can be found on page 353.

AUGUST 28

• **1207** • KING JOHN SIGNS the royal charter officially creating the city of Liverpool. The jokey adjective form "Liverpudlian," however, won't be coined for another six hundred years. ("Pool" to "puddle," get it?)

HOMETOWN BUFFET
What city do you hail from if you're a . . .

Easy	Harder	Yeah, Good Luck
1. Cairene	1. Varsovian	1. Haligonian
2. Münchner	2. Muscovite	2. Porteño
3. Angeleno	3. Yerushalmi	3. Capitalino
4. Madrilenian	4. Capetonian	4. Mancunian
5. Neapolitan	5. Novocastrian	5. Carioca

• **1963** • DR. MARTIN LUTHER KING, JR., gives his famous "I Have a Dream" speech.

DREAM ACADEMY
Other great thinkers have been inspired by dreams as well.

1. What song, whose melody was born in a 1965 dream in Jane Asher's London flat, went by the working title "Scrambled Eggs" until the final lyrics were written?

2. A dream about a snake eating its own tail helped scientist Friedrich Kekulé discover the ring structure of what organic compound?

3. According to Samuel Taylor Coleridge, what classic dream-inspired poem would have been much longer if a mysterious "person from Porlock" hadn't interrupted his reverie?

4. Whose life work was inspired by a dream in which a man named Victoricus appeared, holding a letter titled "The Voice of the Irish"?

5. Despite resemblances to two Harlan Ellison *Outer Limits* episodes, what movie does James Cameron claim originated in a fever dream he had in a Rome hotel in 1981?

6. What was the first neurotransmitter ever discovered, thanks to notes that scientist Otto Loewi scribbled to himself after waking from the same dream two nights running?

7. In 1954, artist Jasper Johns's career was changed forever when he dreamed that he was painting a large version of what?

8. An 1816 lecture on evolution inspired young Mary Godwin to dream about a scientist and a "hideous phantasm," which led her to write what novel?

9. Who claimed that an 1853 dream of drowning, during an afternoon nap in La Spezia, Italy, inspired the prelude to *Das Rheingold*?

10. What did Elias Howe invent in 1845 after dreaming of a tribe of cannibals pounding spears that had holes drilled in their tips?

• **1964** • AT NEW YORK'S DELMONICO HOTEL, Bob Dylan turns the Beatles on to marijuana.

COMFORTABLY NUMB
Who sang these paeans to their drugs of choice?

1. "Heroin," 1967	**3.** "Caffeine," 1992	**5.** "Alcohol," 2005
2. "Cocaine," 1977	**4.** "Amphetamine," 1997	

Answers to the questions on this page can be found on page 354.

AUGUST 29

• **1885** • GOTTLIEB DAIMLER PATENTS the first motorcycle—just his pioneering gasoline engine mounted onto a wooden bicycle frame. Top speed for the bike: seven miles per hour!

START SEEING MOTORCYCLES

1. What is the appropriate three-letter stock ticker symbol for Harley-Davidson?

2. A "thumper" is a motorcycle with how many cylinders in its engine?

3. Who got his nickname from a Butte, Montana, city jailer after he crashed his motorcycle in a 1956 police chase?

4. Who played the non-Estrada motorcycle cop in the first five seasons of *CHiPs*?

5. What NBA coach calls *Zen and the Art of Motorcycle Maintenance* his favorite book?

6. What bike company makes the Ninja, Vulcan, and Eliminator motorcycles?

7. On what 1979 song about a motorcycle crash were the cycle sound effects actually played by Todd Rundgren on a guitar?

8. Peter Fonda's leather-clad biker in *Easy Rider* adopts the name of what comic book hero?

9. Who wrote *The Motorcycle Diaries* about his 22,000-mile trip on a 1939 Norton?

10. What Oscar-winning Best Picture *begins* with the title character's death in a motorcycle crash?

• **1995** • ALBERT CAMUS' NOVEL *The First Man* is published, thirty-four years after his death. The manuscript was found in the wreckage of the car crash that killed Camus in 1960.

GHOST STORIES

Name the late authors behind these posthumously published works.

Easy
1. *Persuasion*
2. *The Silmarillion*
3. *The Diary of a Young Girl*
4. *Faust Part Two*
5. *The Man with the Golden Gun*

Harder
1. *A Confederacy of Dunces*
2. *The Mystery of Edwin Drood*
3. *The Last Tycoon*
4. *The Prince*
5. *Forward the Foundation*

Yeah, Good Luck
1. *The Master and Margarita*
2. *The Way of All Flesh*
3. *Radio Free Albemuth*
4. *Bouvard et Pécuchet*
5. *A Long Fatal Love Chase*

• **1997** • ACCORDING TO THE *TERMINATOR* FILMS, the "Skynet" defense system becomes sentient and wipes out humanity with a series of nuclear strikes.

SKY NET

1. *October Sky* is an anagram for the title of what book, upon which the film was based?

2. What movie ends with the line "Keep watching the skies"?

3. Who plays the same part in *Abre los ojos* and its American remake, *Vanilla Sky*?

4. What rapper was married to actress Ione Skye for eight years?

5. What late actor was resurrected to play the villain in *Sky Captain and the World of Tomorrow*?

Answers to the questions on this page can be found on page 354.

• **1990** • KEN GRIFFEY, JR., and his veteran father become the first father-son combo ever to play for the same major league team. Both hit singles in the very first inning.

"JR." SAMPLES

1. Whom did wordplay-minded sports fans know by the nickname "Mario, Jr."?
2. Who was the first actor nominated for a Best Actor Oscar for portraying another Best Actor nominee?
3. From what historically black Atlanta college did Martin Luther King, Jr., graduate?
4. Who celebrated his favorite fetish by writing magazine stories under the pseudonym "Ann Gora"?
5. Who played Dr. Leo Markus, Grace Adler's husband on *Will & Grace*?
6. When John Hinckley, Jr., shot Ronald Reagan, he had five photos of whom in his wallet?
7. What two future Hall of Famers started at third base in the longest professional baseball game in history, a thirty-three-inning marathon between the Rochester Red Wings and the Pawtucket Red Sox?
8. Freddie Prinze, Jr., met his wife, Sarah Michelle Gellar, on the set of what film?
9. Describing his most difficult songwriting challenge, Ray Parker, Jr., lamented that "there aren't many words that rhyme with" what?
10. As *Monday Night Football* fans know, what is Hank Williams, Jr.'s, real first name?

• **2000** • THE LIBRARY HOTEL OPENS in New York. In this book-lined boutique hotel, every floor has its own library classification (the third floor is 300s for Social Sciences, the eighth floor is the 800s for Literature, etc.). In 2003, the owners of the Dewey Decimal System will—no joke—sue the hotel for trademark infringement.

THE INN CROWD

1. What city can claim seventeen of the U.S.'s twenty largest hotels?
2. What two athletes—an Olympic gold medalist and an NFL All-Pro—wrestled the gun away from Sirhan Sirhan after Bobby Kennedy's 1968 assassination in the pantry of a Los Angeles hotel?
3. The B-sides of what debut White Stripes single were actually recorded in room 286 of the title establishment?
4. What Swiss entrepreneur was called "the king of hoteliers and hotelier to kings"?
5. Burl Ives, Hoyt Axton, or Sheb Wooley—what actor-singer's mother, Mae, cowrote the song "Heartbreak Hotel"?
6. What animal is Susie always dressed as in John Irving's *The Hotel New Hampshire*?
7. How many Oscar nominations did 1932 Best Picture winner *Grand Hotel* receive?
8. At what Whitman, Massachusetts, inn was the chocolate chip cookie invented in 1933?
9. At what fictional hotel and casino is TV's *Las Vegas* set?
10. Concierges claim that the name of their profession derives from the medieval position *comte de cierges*, the keeper of what?

Answers to the questions on this page can be found on page 354.

• **12** • CALIGULA IS BORN. Well, Gaius Julius Caesar Germanicus is born, anyway. As a two-year-old, his mom will dress him in armor and soldier's boots, and the troops will begin to call him "Caligula"—Latin for "little boots."

THESE BOOTS AREN'T MADE FOR WALKING

1. The "boot" used to clamp the wheels of illegally parked cars is named for what U.S. city where they were first used in 1953?
2. What's referred to in the title of the film *Das Boot*?
3. What do we call the part of a car that the British call the "boot"?
4. What technique did IBM engineer David Bradley invent for rebooting a PC?
5. What squarish gulf makes up the "arch" in Italy's boot?

• ~~1965~~ 1967 • A NATION MOURNS as *F Troop* goes off the air.

PARTY OF FIVE
Provide the missing initials (like the F in F Troop) that begin the names of these TV series. Each set of five will spell the name of a sixth TV series, reading down.

Easy
1. ____SI: Miami
2. ____.R. Pufnstuf
3. ____Dream of Jeannie
4. ____M Magazine
5. ____.W.A.T.

Harder
1. ____.A. Doctors
2. ____.K.A. Pablo
3. ____V Nation
4. ____! True Hollywood Story
5. ____ U the Girl

Yeah, Good Luck
1. ____ Squad
2. ____.E.S. Hudson Street
3. ____C: Undercover
4. ____.C. Follies
5. ____Z Streets

• **1976** • GEORGE HARRISON IS FOUND GUILTY of "subconsciously plagiarizing" the melody to his hit "My Sweet Lord" from the Chiffons' "He's So Fine." He will end up paying more than half a million dollars to the estate of that song's late composer.

THEMED SONGS
It's not a plagiarized melody, but what do these sets of songs all have in common?

1. The Cure's "Just Like Heaven," Peter Gabriel's "Lead a Normal Life," George Michael's "One More Try," U2's "Running to Stand Still"
2. The Beastie Boys' "Hey Ladies," Beyoncé's "Deja Vu," Adam Sandler's "The Chanukah Song," Simon and Garfunkel's "Mrs. Robinson"
3. Procol Harum's "A Whiter Shade of Pale," Santana's "Love of My Life," Eric Carmen's "All By Myself," the Toys' "A Lover's Concerto"
4. Eminem's "Without Me," Public Enemy's "Fight the Power," R.E.M.'s "Man on the Moon," Shania Twain's "That Don't Impress Me Much"
5. Gloria Gaynor's "I Will Survive," Oasis's "Acquiesce," Rod Stewart's "Maggie May," Gene Vincent's "Be-Bop-a-Lula"
6. Chamillionaire's "Ridin'," Coolio's "Gangsta's Paradise," Michael Jackson's "Beat It," Nirvana's "Smells Like Teen Spirit"
7. Elvis Costello's "Radio Radio," Bob Marley's "War," the Replacements' "Bastards of Young," Ashlee Simpson's "Autobiography"
8. Badfinger's "Day After Day," David Bowie's "Fame," Harry Nilsson's "Spaceman," the Rolling Stones' "We Love You"
9. Beck's "Loser," Def Leppard's "Rocket," Pink Floyd's "Empty Spaces," Prince's "Darling Nikki"
10. Golden Earring's "Radar Love," Tom Petty's "Runnin' Down a Dream," Johnny Rivers' "Summer Rain," Bruce Springsteen's "Thunder Road"

Answers to the questions on this page can be found on page 355.

August Answers

AUGUST 1

BELLY WILDER
1. The "Breadbasket"
2. Cheese
3. Cobra
4. Hydrochloric acid (HCl)
5. *The Carol Burnett Show*

THE SCOOP-Y GANG
1. Glaciers
2. *Vanity Fair*
3. Ethopia's (or Eritrea's)
4. *The Andromeda Strain*
5. Warren Moon and Dave Krieg

STRAIGHT TO VIDEOS
1. ". . . Baby One More Time" (Britney Spears)
2. Martin Scorsese
3. "Money for Nothing" (Dire Straits)
4. "The Big Bopper," J. P. Richardson
5. Characters in the Beastie Boys' cop-show spoof "Sabotage"
6. Christopher Walken
7. "Jeremy" (Pearl Jam)
8. "Hey Ya!" (OutKast)
9. "Sledgehammer" (Peter Gabriel)
10. "Losing My Religion" (R.E.M.)

AUGUST 2

"ERIC CLAPTON" IS A "NAR-COLEPTIC"
1. Ed Asner
2. Stan Lee
3. Roger Daltrey
4. Meg Ryan (*City of Angels*)
5. Eddie Albert
6. Al Green
7. Tom Landry
8. Tom Cruise (in *Risky Business*)
9. Steve Irwin
10. Cass Elliot
11. Ian Holm
12. Paul Reubens
13. Martin Gore
14. Tim Russert (*Meet the Press*)
15. Lisa Loeb

SOLE SURVIVOR
1. The world's last passenger pigeon
2. Robert Vaughn
3. Doug Flutie
4. Western Sahara
5. "Paul Revere's Ride"

AUGUST 3

GOOBER(NATORIAL) PILE
Easy
1. Minnesota
2. New Jersey
3. California
4. Virginia
5. New York

Harder
1. Maine
2. Georgia
3. Arkansas
4. Ohio
5. Texas

Yeah, Good Luck
1. Tennessee
2. Wisconsin
3. Arizona
4. Massachusetts
5. Pennsylvania

TONY DANZA SYNDROME
Easy
1. Jack Nicholson/Torrence
2. John Hurt/Merrick
3. Jeff Bridges/Lebowski
4. Jerry Lewis/Langford
Harder
1. Emily Blunt/Charlton
2. Peter Gallagher/Callaghan
3. Gene Hackman/Garrison
4. John Wayne/Books
Yeah, Good Luck
1. James Mason/Leamington
2. Paul Sorvino/Cicero
3. Anne Francis/Dadier
4. Jack Buchanan/Brewster

IT'S A GAS
1. Noble (or inert) gases
2. Trees
3. Helium or selenium
4. Nitrous oxide
5. Carbon dioxide

August Answers

AUGUST 4

REMEMBER VENN
1. Jim Bunning
2. Gold
3. *Wheel of Fortune*
4. Nigeria
5. Johnny Cash (Jimmie Rodgers and Hank Williams are in the Rock and Roll Hall of Fame as well, though not as performers)
6. Daniel (Elton John)
7. Atlanta
8. *The Godfather Part II*
9. Bill Clinton
10. The Walt Disney Company

FINGER-LICKIN' GOOD
1. F
2. J
3. A
4. I
5. E
6. H
7. C
8. D
9. B
10. G

AUGUST 5

DRAWN TO SCALES
1. H
2. E
3. I
4. C
5. J
6. F
7. B
8. D
9. G
10. A

LAWN TERM MEMORY
1. Wimbledon
2. Bamboo
3. Monica Lewinsky
4. *Chinatown*
5. Bermuda grass
6. Édouard Manet
7. Peter Ustinov
8. *Lost*
9. Over the septic tank
10. Warren Beatty

AUGUST 6

VANISHING ACTS
1. The Teamsters
2. Jean Lafitte
3. Trombone
4. Aruba
5. Ambrose Bierce
6. "D. B." (Dan) Cooper
7. Bolivia
8. Roald Amundsen
9. The Pacific
10. Raoul Wallenberg

TREE-VENGE!
1. E
2. C
3. D
4. B
5. A

THANK YOU, GODFATHER
1. Grunge
2. Soul
3. Hip-hop
4. Punk
5. Goth

AUGUST 7

FAVORITE SUN
1. H
2. A
3. F
4. G
5. C
6. E
7. D
8. I
9. B

BRUSHES WITH GREATNESS
1. Miles Davis
2. An artificial heart
3. Gave the Beatles LSD
4. Turkmenistan
5. Anne Frank

PERFECT PITCH
Easy
#1: Volkswagen
#2: Coca-Cola
#5: McDonald's
#10: Avis
#15: Maxwell House
Harder
#35: Morton Salt
#38: Crest
#40: Timex
#44: Winston
#48: Listerine
Yeah, Good Luck
#49: Cadillac
#56: Polaroid
#69: Springmaid
#71: Steinway & Sons
#87: Xerox

AUGUST 8

ON THE ROPES
1. *Million Dollar Baby*
2. Will Rogers
3. The knot
4. Rappeling
5. ("An Occurrence at") Owl Creek Bridge
6. Between the World Trade Center towers
7. The Leopold and Loeb killings
8. Janet Jackson
9. George Foreman
10. Alexander the Great

SUCH GREAT HEIGHTS
1. The piccolo
2. Kansas
3. Sergei Bubka
4. New Zealand
5. A harp
6. Cirrus
7. Nehi ("knee-high")
8. The Chrysler Building
9. Barry Bonds
10. 420

AUGUST 9

A CHILD'S GARDEN OF URSUS
Easy
1. A. A. Milne
2. William Hanna and Joseph Barbera
3. Jim Henson (voice by Frank Oz)
4. Rudyard Kipling
Harder
1. Michael Bond
2. Don Freeman
3. Joel Chandler Harris
4. Stan and Jan Berenstain
Yeah, Good Luck
1. Mary Tourtel
2. William Faulkner
3. Walt Morey
4. Walt Kelly

IT'S RAINING MEH
1. Michael Jordan
2. Dr. Laurence J. Peter (The "Peter Principle")
3. Pretty Good Privacy
4. Antonio Salieri
5. 100

MPROBABLE SPELLINGS
1. Sbarro
2. The ptarmigan's
3. Rwanda
4. Ngaio Marsh
5. Dvořák
6. T'Pau
7. Sfumato
8. Mr. Mxyzptlk
9. Hmong
10. Tsunami (due to the catastrophic tsunami in South Asia)

August Answers

AUGUST 10

EVEN BETTER THAN THE REAL THING
1. A (*The Simpsons*)
2. J (*Lost*)
3. G
4. E (*Full House*)
5. D
6. C
7. F (*O Brother, Where Art Thou?*)
8. H
9. B
10. I

SPIN CITY
Easy
1. *M*A*S*H*
2. *The Mary Tyler Moore Show*
3. *Grey's Anatomy*
4. *The Cosby Show*
5. *Cheers*
Harder
1. *Happy Days*
2. *Diff'rent Strokes*
3. *Beverly Hills 90210*
4. *Perfect Strangers*
5. *The Danny Thomas Show*
Yeah, Good Luck
1. *Jake and the Fatman*
2. *The Golden Girls*
3. *Dawson's Creek*
4. *Married . . . with Children*
5. *Murder, She Wrote*

HEAVY HITTERS
1. Derek Jeter
2. Lou Gehrig and Hank Aaron
3. Mickey Mantle
4. 66
5. Tony Lazzeri

AUGUST 11

NAVAL-GAZING
1. U.S. presidents
2. Fred T. Jane (*Jane's*)
3. Jutland
4. Virginia (Norfolk)
5. Miguel de Cervantes
6. "Sink the *Bismarck*"
7. Patrol Torpedo
8. Benjamin Franklin's ("Poor Richard")
9. Trafalgar Square
10. Fleet Admiral

THE SQUARED CIRCLE
1. King Kong Bundy
2. "Pomp and Circumstance"
3. Andre the Giant
4. Miami
5. The World Wildlife Fund

"CLEAN" LIVING
1. Weightlifting
2. William McKinley
3. Pontius Pilate
4. Art Carney
5. Dow bathroom cleaner

AUGUST 12

CHOCOLATE THUNDER
1. *Pan's Labyrinth*
2. Cows (for the catapulted ones in *Monty Python and the Holy Grail*)
3. Wilt Chamberlain's 100-point game
4. Snickers
5. Theobromine

JAZZ HANDS
1. Thelonious Monk
2. Sun Ra
3. "Take Five"
4. The vibraphone
5. *Kind of Blue* (Miles Davis)

NORTH AMERICAN IDOL
1. The Mamas and the Papas
2. Dream Theater
3. Crosby, Stills, Nash & Young or Buffalo Springfield
4. Hole or Smashing Pumpkins
5. The Lovin' Spoonful

AUGUST 13

INN-TERNATIONAL
1. Sachertorte (the Hotel Sacher)
2. Berlin's
3. Coco Chanel
4. "Hotel Rwanda"
5. Statler and Waldorf
6. Dubai
7. The *Harry Potter* series was completed
8. Pyongyang, North Korea
9. The Chelsea Hotel
10. Potsdam

DANZA IN THE DARK
1. A
2. C
3. E
4. D
5. B
Bonus Danza! *Crash*

SMASHED HITS
1. *Red + Heat*
2. *Bugsy + Malone*
3. *Ghost + Dad*
4. *Collateral + Damage*
5. *Once Upon a Time + In America*
6. *The Rose + Tattoo*
7. *Mona Lisa + Smile*
8. *Napoleon + Dynamite*
9. *Monster + House*
10. *M + Alice*

AUGUST 14

BARELY THERE
1. *Vanity Fair*
2. Eight million
3. In outer space, on a plaque on the *Pioneer 10* and *11* spacecraft
4. John Ashcroft
5. David Niven

WOMAN OF THE YEAR
Easy
1. Salma Hayek
2. Shirley Temple
3. Audrey Tautou
4. Rita Hayworth
5. Jodie Foster
Harder
1. Vanessa Redgrave
2. Nastassja Kinski
3. Tippi Hedren
4. Gene Tierney
5. Whoopi Goldberg
Yeah, Good Luck
1. Gena Rowlands
2. Geena Davis
3. Sue Lyon
4. Aileen Quinn
5. Leslie Caron

TONGUE TWISTERS
1. Joseph's "coat of many colors"
2. Tanzania
3. Jimmy Carter
4. *Boogie Nights*
5. *E pluribus unum*

AUGUST 15

TURNING JAPANESE
1. Seventeen
2. *The Seven Samurai*
3. Hokkaido
4. Harajuku
5. The USS *Missouri*
6. Godzilla (*gorira + kujira =* Gojira)
7. Salt
8. Manga
9. Origami
10. Suntory
11. The chrysanthemum
12. The ghosts in Pac-Man
13. "What is the sound of one hand clapping?"
14. Fugu
15. Competitive eating

X MARKS THE SPOT
1. Captain Kangaroo
2. The Lost Dutchman mine
3. The Declaration of Independence
4. A leprechaun
5. John Huston
6. William
7. The Rhine ("Das Rheingold")
8. Pelé
9. *The Goonies*
10. Madrid

AUGUST 16

SPORTS, ILLUSTRATED
1. Shuffleboard
2. Ice hockey
3. Squash
4. Lacrosse
5. Soccer
6. Curling
7. Cricket
8. Basketball
9. Badminton
10. Sumo

VIRGIN RECORDS
1. Samuel Tilden
2. A. C. Green
3. William Pitt (the Younger)
4. Isaac Newton
5. Florence Nightingale

TALL IN THE FAMILY
1. C
2. A
3. B
4. E
5. D

AUGUST 17

RE-PERCUSSIONS
1. Roger Taylor
2. "More cowbell!"
3. Walt Whitman
4. The celesta
5. *The Gong Show*
6. David Bowie
7. Trinidad and Tobago
8. The Killers
9. ~~Buddy Rich~~ Keith Moon
10. William Shatner

FLIGHT CLUB
Easy
1. Liverpool
2. Paris
3. New Orleans
4. Washington, D.C.
5. Teheran
Harder
1. Rome
2. Warsaw
3. Nairobi
4. Venice
5. Mexico City
Yeah, Good Luck
1. Toronto
2. Port-au-Prince
3. Anchorage
4. Pisa
5. Gdansk

AFFAIRS OF STATE
1. C
2. F
3. D
4. J
5. A
6. I
7. G
8. B
9. E
10. H

AUGUST 18

JEWELRY BOX
1. Ed Bradley
2. The Pink Panther
3. "The Necklace"
4. Blue
5. Chris Evert
6. *Around the World in Eighty Days*

7. Oedipus
8. A sun
9. Jan Vermeer
10. The pope

ELEMENTARY, MY DEAR WATSON
Easy
1. Nobelium
2. Thorium
3. Californium
4. Curium
5. Uranium
Harder
1. Selenium
2. Helium
3. Fermium
4. Promethium
5. Mendelevium
Yeah, Good Luck
1. Lutetium
2. Lawrencium
3. Tantalum
4. Rutherfordium
5. Strontium

BIRD IS THE WORD
Easy
1. (Atticus) Finch
2. (Mrs.) Peacock
3. (Clarice) Starling
Harder
1. (Alan) Swann
2. (Marion) Crane
3. (Jack) Robin
Yeah, Good Luck
1. (Gary) Dove
2. (Baby Face) Martin
3. (Philip) Raven

AUGUST 19

IN CAMERA
1. The Sierra Nevada
2. Mathew Brady
3. Richard Avedon
4. Does a horse ever have all four hooves off the ground at once as it gallops?
5. Annie Leibovitz

THE HOLE TRUTH
1. Courtney Love
2. Her cat
3. Kim Jong-Il
4. A black hole
5. Bag End
6. Paul Newman (for Butch Cassidy's Hole in the Wall Gang)
7. Two
8. The Brandenburg Gate
9. Sausage
10. Thomas
11. *Yellow Submarine*
12. Montreal
13. The Snake River
14. Rita Hayworth
15. In the skull

AUGUST 20

TEXTONYMS
1. "Hurt" / Guru (4878)
2. Poisoned / Smirnoff (76476633)
3. Autumn / Button (288866)
4. PepsiCo / Persian (7377426)
5. Korean / Jordan (567326)
6. Drama / Franc (37262)
7. Avalon / Cuckoo (282566)
8. Fatigues / Daughter (32844837)
9. Material / *Maverick* (62837425)
10. September / Sequences (737836237)

WORLD WIDE WEBS
1. The tarantella
2. Richmond
3. It was used to make gun sights
4. Fred Astaire
5. *The Daily Bugle*
6. Loretta Lynn and Crystal Gale
7. James Dean
8. The brown recluse
9. Saddam Hussein
10. System of a Down

AUGUST 21

WALL OF SOUND BITES
1. Lloyd Bentsen
2. Ronald Reagan
3. Michael Dukakis
4. Gerald Ford
5. James Stockdale

THE HOT SPOT
Easy
1. Italy
2. The United States
3. Indonesia
4. Japan
Harder
1. Martinique
2. Greece
3. Mexico
4. No country—Antarctica
Yeah, Good Luck
1. Colombia
2. Papua New Guinea
3. The Congo
4. The Philippines

CENTURY CITY
1. Abraham Lincoln's birth
2. Colorado
3. SpaceShipOne
4. The Montreal Canadiens
5. Bob Hope

AUGUST 22	**AUGUST 23**	**AUGUST 24**

AUGUST 22

PARTS UNKNOWN
1. World War I
2. A paper bag (over his head)
3. "Here be dragons"
4. Green slime
5. *The Good, the Bad, and the Ugly*

LITTLE BRITAIN
1. *The Avengers*
2. *Yes, Minister* (or *Yes, Prime Minister*)
3. *Fawlty Towers*
4. *Absolutely Fabulous*
5. *Cracker*
6. *Teletubbies*
7. *Monty Python's Flying Circus*
8. *Red Dwarf*
9. *The Office*
10. *Thunderbirds*

PATER PATRIAE
Easy
1. Taiwan
2. Russia
3. Italy
4. India
5. Germany
Harder
1. Pakistan
2. Argentina
3. Turkey
4. Ireland
5. Cuba
Yeah, Good Luck
1. Chile
2. Bulgaria
3. Congo
4. Portugal
5. Nigeria

AUGUST 23

CANAL ZONE
1. *Tootsie*
2. The dentin
3. China
4. Mars
5. The Hudson River
6. The semicircular canals
7. John McCain
8. Piazza San Marco (St. Mark's Square)
9. The Aswan Dam
10. France's version of *The Office*

DAS KAPITAL
1. *The Godfather*
2. "Tokyo Rose"
3. Athens, Georgia
4. New Madrid
5. Pekingese
6. Damask (from Damascus)
7. *Dubliners*
8. The Duke of Wellington
9. Manila envelopes
10. Paris Hilton

AUGUST 24

DOWN BY LAVA
1. The hula
2. Harry Truman
3. *The Scream*
4. Crater Lake
5. Mauna Kea

CHIPS OFF THE OLD BLOCK
1. Black and red, respectively
2. Intel (Microsoft is the other)
3. Blackjack
4. Robert Donat
5. Sun Chips
6. Frank
7. The V-chip
8. "Angel of the Morning"
9. Shaquille O'Neal and Anfernee Hardaway
10. Stanley Livingston

SOUL PROPRIETORS
1. Mephistopheles
2. Vanessa A. Williams and Vanessa L. Williams
3. Ken
4. Aretha Franklin
5. Nirvana

AUGUST 25

SATELLITE ENTERTAINMENT
Easy
1. Mars
2. Jupiter
3. Earth
Harder
1. Uranus
2. Saturn
3. Pluto
Yeah, Good Luck
1. Saturn
2. Jupiter
3. Neptune

LONE RANGERS
Easy
1. Mammoth Cave
2. Crater Lake
3. Great Smoky Mountains
4. Carlsbad Caverns
Harder
1. Yellowstone
2. Hot Springs
3. Shenandoah
4. Isle Royale
Yeah, Good Luck
1. Theodore Roosevelt
2. Congaree
3. Acadia
4. Great Basin

TOP FIVE
1. AC/DC and Metallica
2. The *Cutty Sark*
3. *Seinfeld*'s
4. Michael Vick
5. Henley(-on-Thames)

AUGUST 26

NOW AND THIN
1. Fogle
2. Stomach stapling
3. Robert Atkins
4. Donnie Wahlberg
5. Miami Beach

SHRINK RAP
1. Denial
2. The president's
3. Synchronicity
4. Peter Bogdanovich
5. The Elektra complex

IN A WORLD . . . !
1. O
2. I
3. L
4. M
5. F
6. H
7. K
8. G
9. A
10. C
11. D
12. J
13. N
14. E
15. B

AUGUST 27

SUMMIT MEETING
Easy
1. Olympus
2. Everest
3. McKinley (Denali)
4. Blanc
5. Fuji

Harder
1. Kosciusko
2. Kilimanjaro
3. Elbrus
4. Logan
5. Aconcagua
Yeah, Good Luck
1. K2
2. Chimborazo
3. Ben Nevis
4. Ararat
5. Titano

WEEK-MINDED
1. Richard Rodgers's (Mary Rodgers)
2. Sunday
3. Friday
4. Drew Barrymore
5. Tuesday
6. Thursday (*The Man Who Was Thursday*)
7. Archibald Cox
8. Chris Tucker
9. Marie Antoinette
10. 714

GRAZE ANATOMY
Easy
1. Collarbone
2. Eardrum
3. Belly button or navel
4. Skin
Harder
1. Armpit
2. Shoulder blade
3. Adam's apple
4. Buttocks
Yeah, Good Luck
1. Nostril
2. Knuckles
3. Big toe
4. Cuticle

August Answers

AUGUST 28

HOMETOWN BUFFET
Easy
1. Cairo
2. Munich
3. Los Angeles
4. Madrid
5. Naples
Harder
1. Warsaw
2. Moscow
3. Jerusaleum
4. Cape Town
5. Newcastle(-upon-Tyne)
Yeah, Good Luck
1. Halifax
2. Buenos Aires
3. Mexico City
4. Manchester
5. Rio de Janeiro

DREAM ACADEMY
1. "Yesterday"
2. Benzene
3. "Kubla Khan"
4. St. Patrick
5. *The Terminator*
6. Acetylcholine
7. The American flag
8. *Frankenstein*
9. Richard Wagner
10. The sewing machine

COMFORTABLY NUMB
1. The Velvet Underground
2. Eric Clapton
3. Faith No More
4. Everclear
5. Brad Paisley

AUGUST 29

START SEEING MOTORCYCLES
1. HOG
2. Two
3. "Evel" Knievel
4. Larry Wilcox
5. Phil Jackson
6. Kawasaki
7. "Bat Out of Hell" (Meat Loaf)
8. Captain America
9. Che Guevara
10. *Lawrence of Arabia*

GHOST STORIES
Easy
1. Jane Austen
2. J. R. R. Tolkien
3. Anne Frank
4. Johann Wilhelm von Goethe
5. Ian Fleming
Harder
1. John Kennedy Toole
2. Charles Dickens
3. F. Scott Fitzgerald
4. Niccolò Machiavelli
5. Isaac Asimov
Yeah, Good Luck
1. Mikhail Bulgakov
2. Samuel Butler
3. Philip K. Dick
4. Gustave Flaubert
5. Louisa May Alcott

SKY NET
1. *Rocket Boys*
2. *The Thing (from Another World)*
3. Penélope Cruz
4. Adam Horovitz (the Beastie Boys)
5. Laurence Olivier

AUGUST 30

"JR." SAMPLES
1. Jaromir Jagr ("Jaromir" is an anagram of "Mario, Jr.")
2. Robert Downey, Jr. (*Chaplin*)
3. Morehouse
4. Ed Wood, Jr.
5. Harry Connick, Jr.
6. Jodie Foster
7. Wade Boggs and Cal Ripken, Jr.
8. *I Know What You Did Last Summer*
9. "Ghostbusters"
10. Randall

THE INN CROWD
1. Las Vegas
2. Rafer Johnson and Rosey Grier
3. "Hotel Yorba"
4. César Ritz
5. Hoyt Axton's
6. A bear
7. Just one: Best Picture
8. The Toll House Inn
9. The Montecito
10. Candles

AUGUST 31

THESE BOOTS AREN'T MADE FOR WALKING
1. Denver
2. A German U-boat
3. The trunk
4. Control-Alt-Delete
5. The Gulf of Taranto

PARTY OF FIVE

Easy	Harder	Yeah, Good Luck
1. C	1. L	1. M
2. H	2. A	2. A
3. I	3. T	3. U
4. P	4. E	4. D
5. S	5. R	5. E

THEMED SONGS
1. The title isn't sung until the last line
2. Name-check baseball players (Sadaharu Oh, Juan Pierre, Rod Carew, Joe DiMaggio)
3. Based on classical compositions
4. Mention Elvis
5. B-sides that became hits
6. Spoofed by "Weird Al" Yankovic
7. Controversial *Saturday Night Live* performances
8. Beatles guest on each (George, John, Ringo, and Paul, respectively)
9. Backward-masked vocals
10. About listening to other songs ("Coming On Strong," "Runaway," "Sgt. Pepper's Lonely Hearts Club Band," "Only the Lonely")

• **1271** • THE ELECTION OF Gregory X ends the longest interregnum, or pope-free gap, in Catholic history. The intrigue-filled three-year vacancy ends only when the mayor of Viterbo locks the College of Cardinals in a palace with a bare minimum of food, saying they can't come out until they elect a pope. And clean their rooms.

HELP WANTED

1. What position was filled using this 1860 want ad? "Wanted. Young, skinny, wiry fellows. Not over 18. Must be expert riders. Willing to risk death daily. Orphans preferred."
2. What movie begins with front man Dewey Finn being kicked out of his band, leaving a vacancy in No Vacancy?
3. What president oversaw the longest vice presidential vacancy in America's history?
4. Why did a September 8, 1965,

Variety ad seek "4 insane boys, ages 17–21"?
5. Who, following his 1951 firing, was replaced by Matthew B. Ridgway?

• **1903** • MASSACHUSETTS ISSUES the country's first license plates. A car enthusiast named Frederick Tudor gets the coveted plate number 1.

BETTER PLATE THAN NEVER
What state's plates have used these slogans?

Easy
1. 10,000 Lakes
2. America's Dairyland
3. Famous Potatoes
4. The First State
5. Big Sky Country

Harder
1. You've Got a Friend in
2. 400th Anniversary
3. Amber Waves of Grain
4. Sportsman's Paradise
5. Live Free or Die

Yeah, Good Luck
1. Wild, Wonderful
2. Smiling Faces, Beautiful Places
3. Vacationland
4. The Hospitality State
5. Discover the Spirit

• **1977** • RENEE RICHARDS LOSES in straight sets in her women's singles debut to Virginia Wade at the U.S. Open. The match makes history because Renee is the former Dr. Richard Raskind, *men's* singles player in the 1960 U.S. Open.

NET GAIN
Tennis trivia, anyone?

1. Who was the first living person to appear on a Swiss postage stamp?
2. What Elton John hit was a tribute to Billie Jean King?
3. What number one–ranked tennis player of the 1990s was named for a number one–ranked player of the 1980s?
4. The U.S. Open's main tennis court is named for whom?
5. Whose $20-million-plus annual income makes her the highest-paid female athlete of all time?
6. Who's the only player ever to win tennis's singles Grand Slam twice?
7. What tennis player called her occasional lapses of concentration "going walkabout"?
8. What's the term for a tennis serve that touches the net on its way into the service box?
9. What tennis champ of the 1920s was jailed twice, later in life, for picking up teenage boys?
10. What city is home to the Australian Open?

Answers to the questions on this page can be found on page 389.

SEPTEMBER 2

• **1752** • THE BRITISH EMPIRE FINALLY SWITCHES over to the Gregorian calendar, going straight from Wednesday, September 2, to Thursday, September 14. This is the only eleven-day gap in British history that *can't* be explained away with alcohol.

DAYS OF OUR LIVES
Answer these questions inspired by the calendar.

1. What's the only sign of the Zodiac that starts with the same letter as one of the months during which it falls?

2. What is more correctly called a Chanukiah when it has nine branches instead of seven?

3. What are the only two days of the year that never have any scheduled games in the four major North American professional sports associations?

4. What company's slogan comes from a 1953 ad campaign that offered a different product "for every day of the month"?

5. To what nation does Easter Island belong?

6. The biblical Book of Esther explains the origins of which Jewish feast day?

7. What post went unfilled for the only time ever in March 1955, due to a missed publishing deadline?

8. What are Unity, Self-Determination, Collective Work and Responsibility, Cooperative Economics, Purpose, Creativity, and Faith?

9. What's the only month whose birthstone isn't a mineral?

10. What two U.S. states don't observe Daylight Saving Time?

11. Years in the Islamic calendar are numbered "A.H." rather than

"A.D." What does the *H* stand for?

12. According to AT&T, on what day of the year are the most collect calls placed?

13. Of the eleven U.S. federal holidays, which is observed only by D.C.-area federal employees?

14. What are known as "Nochebuena" and "Nochevieja," or "Good Night" and "Old Night," in the Spanish-speaking world?

15. What's the only day of the week still given a Latinate name in English?

• **1990** • THE GOLDEN GATE PARK POLICE having cracked down on the annual burning of a giant wooden effigy every summer at San Francisco's Baker Beach, the bonfire takes place in the Black Rock Desert for the first time. The Burning Man festival has found its permanent home.

JUST DESERTS

1. By a strict definition of desert, what's the earth's largest, half again the size of the Sahara?

2. What's the more common name for the desert planet of Arrakis?

3. On TV's *Vega$*, Tony Curtis played the owner of Las Vegas's Desert Inn, who shared his name with what novelist?

4. What Chinese desert is said to

have a name meaning "If you go in, you won't come out"?

5. What late world leader met his second wife, British secretary Antoinette Gardiner, during the shooting of *Lawrence of Arabia*?

6. Complete this numerical analogy. Two : Bactrian :: one : _____.

7. Where would you find the Gibson and Simpson Deserts?

8. What California national park (not Joshua Tree!) is pictured on the cover of U2's album *The Joshua Tree*?

9. In what desert do Africa's Bushmen people live?

10. What U.S. city's second largest paper is the *Deseret Morning News*?

Answers to the questions on this page can be found on page 389.

• **590** • GREGORY I BECOMES POPE. Among his other papal achievements, Gregory is responsible for the first formulation of the so-called Seven Deadly Sins.

ACCESS OF EVIL

1. The U2 song "**Pride** (In the Name of Love)" mistakenly places what 6 P.M. event in the "early morning"?

2. In a 1908 article, who coined the term "penis **envy**"?

3. From what state does the Joad family begin its journey west in *The Grapes of **Wrath***?

4. What animals make up the suborder Vermilingua, the closest living cousins to the **sloths**?

5. What **gluttony** poster boy is the first child to find a Golden Ticket in *Charlie and the Chocolate Factory?*

6. What artist is the subject of Irving Stone's novel ***Lust** for*

Life?

7. What Wall Street figure helped inspire the movie *Wall Street* when he told a Berkeley audience, "I think **greed** is healthy. You can be greedy and still feel good about yourself"?

• **1979** • THE COWBOYS BEAT St. Louis 22–21 in their home opener. The announcer of this nationally televised game calls the Cowboys "America's Team," the title of their recently released NFL Films highlights package, and the nickname sticks.

CLUBLAND

Which sports team was home to the lineup nicknamed . . .

Easy
1. Monsters of the Midway
2. Phi Slamma Jamma
3. The Steel Curtain
4. The Bronx Bombers
5. Showtime

Harder
1. Run TMC
2. Orange Crush
3. The No-Name Defense
4. Broad Street Bullies
5. The Fab Five

Yeah, Good Luck
1. The Electric Company
2. Harvey's Wallbangers
3. The Hitless Wonders
4. The Over the Hill Gang
5. The French Connection

• **1997** • IN THE HOPE OF sexing up *Star Trek: Voyager* a new cast member, Jeri Ryan, is introduced. Her character, "Seven of Nine," brings a whole new meaning to the phrase "Borg implants."

NINE OF SEVEN

1. Which member of the so-called Chicago Seven had the same last name as the judge in the case?

2. What athlete's name is slang for a score of 7 on a golf hole?

3. Which of George Carlin's famous "seven dirty words" is now commonplace on network TV?

4. How many of *The Seven Samurai* survive the film?

5. Who has done seven times what Bernard Hinault and Eddy Merckx, among others, have each done five times?

6. According to Judges 16, whose hair was worn in seven braids?

7. Who self-medicated with a "seven-per-cent solution" of cocaine and water?

8. What scientific genius is responsible for the "ROY G BIV"

seven-color spectrum still commonly used today?

9. After "You Give Good Love" peaked at number three, who passed the Beatles' and Bee Gees' record by hitting number one with seven consecutive singles?

Answers to the questions on this page can be found on page 389.

SEPTEMBER 4

• **1908** • GERMANY SCHAEFER, THE CLOWNISH Detroit Tigers second baseman, tries out an unusual baseball strategy. After stealing second in a failed attempt at a double steal, Schaefer wants to try the double steal again, so he steals first *from second*. In 1920, baseball will finally pass a rule forbidding players to run the bases backward.

REVERSE ENGINEERING
A few forward questions on backward things.

1. The sorcerer in what movie is the cleverly named "Yen Sid"?
2. Who revolutionized the high jump at the 1968 Summer Olympics by clearing the bar back first?
3. What nationality lends its name to the reverse notation used in some calculators?
4. What nicknames did the backward-dressing Chris Kelly and Chris Smith use as members of the early-1990s tween-rap fad Kris Kross?
5. The last letter of the Cyrillic alphabet is a backward version of what Latin letter?

• **1957** • FORD DECLARES "E DAY" for the proud rollout of its new brand, the Edsel. The Edsel, of course, fails spectacularly and will be voted the "Ugliest Car Ever Made" in a 2003 survey. Sorry, Pontiac Aztek! Maybe next time.

SO UNPRETTY

1. What was widely considered an eyesore when completed in 1887, with Guy de Maupassant calling it an "ungracious skeleton"?
2. Who's the only person to land atop Mr. Blackwell's "Worst Dressed" list three times, in 2001, 2006, and 2007?
3. What fruit was bred with a tangerine to create the Ugli fruit?
4. What singer/guitarist, now famous in another field, fronted the band Ugly Rumours in 1974?
5. Who was called "that long-armed gorilla" by Edwin Stanton and "a well-meaning baboon" by George ~~McClellan~~ McClellan? [handwritten]
6. What unattractive toy did Danish woodcutter Thomas Dam first carve in 1959?
7. What Oscar-nominated movie star is a producer of TV's *Ugly Betty*?
8. What was Joseph Merrick better known as?
9. Which of his wives did Henry VIII call "the Flanders mare" for her ugliness?
10. What kind of bird is the ugly duckling, really?

• **2006** • TWO MISSOURI PROFESSORS discover the (currently) largest known prime number: $2^{32,582,657} - 1$. That number has just over 9 million digits—a shame for its finders, who would have won a $100,000 prize if they'd found the first 10-million-digit prime.

"PRIME" DIRECTIVE

1. What's the name of the police detective played by Helen Mirren on British TV's *Prime Suspect*?
2. Who was president when the U.S. prime rate hit its all-time high of 21½%?
3. Complete this analogy: Autobots : Optimus Prime :: Decepticons : _____.
4. What singing group was known as the Primettes until 1961?
5. What are the only two countries of continental Europe that the prime meridian passes through?
6. Of the six mysterious "numbers" on TV's *Lost*, what's the only prime number?
7. In his *Metaphysics*, what philosopher first made the "prime mover" argument for the existence of God?
8. Who won an Oscar for depicting *The Prime of Miss Jean Brodie*?
9. Choice, Select, or Preferred—what's the second best USDA grade for beef, immediately following "Prime"?
10. What unusual prime-time distinction did the 1960s' *Batman* and *Peyton Place* share with *American Idol* today?

Answers to the questions on this page can be found on page 390.

SEPTEMBER 5

• 1607 • SAILORS ABOARD THE HMS *Dragon* put on an amateur production of *Hamlet*. Since the ship is anchored off Sierra Leone at the time, this is regarded as the first-ever performance of Shakespeare outside Europe.

ALL THE MEN AND WOMEN MERELY PLAYERS

1. Which Shakespeare play's two protagonists both have names meaning "blessed"?

2. What Shakespearean character also goes by the name of Robin Goodfellow?

3. What name did the Bard give to a record five of his characters, including the title character of one of his comedies?

4. Which Shakespeare play was once adapted into an opera by the appropriately named Rolando Miranda?

5. What Shakespearean villain has more lines than any other nontitle character in one of his plays?

• 1900 • LIONEL, THE TOY TRAIN GIANT, incorporates in New York. Its products are designed for a 2⅛-inch scale that Lionel trademarks as "Standard Gauge," though it matches no other toy train on the market—a brilliant anticompatibility maneuver worthy of modern-day Microsoft execs.

SIZE MATTERS
What comes in these arrays of sizes?

1. Small, medium, large, extra large, jumbo, colossal, super colossal

2. Baby, boudoir, conservatory, concert

3. Magnum, Jeroboam, Rehoboam, Melchizedek

4. Pea, marble, dime, penny, nickel, quarter, half-dollar, walnut, golf ball, hen egg, tennis ball, baseball, grapefruit, softball

5. Short, tall, grande, venti

• 2640 • JOHN CAGE'S 1987 PIECE *Organ²/ASLSP* is scheduled to end at the Saint Burchardi church in Halberstadt, Germany. The performance began in 2001; the first chord lasted more than two years. The organist is taking very literally Cage's instruction that the piece be played "as slow as possible."

FUTURE SHOCK

1. March 22, 2285, will be the first time in almost five hundred years that what holiday will fall on its earliest possible date?

2. The first "time capsule" to bear that name is due to be unearthed from Flushing Meadows in the year 6939, the 5,000th anniversary of what?

3. February of what year will see the odd-looking Super Bowl L?

4. The NASA spacecraft set to replace the space shuttle in 2012 will bear the name of what constellation?

5. What will be the first year since 1961 that looks the same right side up and upside down?

6. What novel is set in the year 2540, or A.F. (After Ford) 632?

7. According to the official divisions between constellations, what will begin around 2600 A.D., not back in 1967?

8. In 2084, the Pitjantjatjara Aborigines' lease of Uluru to the government will expire. What is Uluru called in English?

9. What is due to become the first city to host the modern Olympics three times?

10. What twentieth-century pilot first appeared in the novella *Armageddon 2419 A.D.*?

Answers to the questions on this page can be found on page 390.

• **1952** • CANADA'S FIRST TELEVISION STATION, CBFT in Montreal, goes on the air.

NORTHERN EXPOSURE
Name the Canadian regular on these American TV shows.

Easy	Harder	Yeah, Good Luck (two answers each)
1. *Family Ties*	1. *Alias*	1. *NewsRadio*
2. *Lost*	2. *Sex and the City*	2. *Party of Five*
3. *In Living Color*	3. *Bonanza*	3. *Star Trek*
4. *Perry Mason*	4. *Law & Order*	4. *St. Elsewhere*
5. *Primetime Glick*	5. *Grey's Anatomy*	5. *Beverly Hills 90210*

• **1953** • AT THE ELEVENTH World Science Fiction Convention in Philadelphia, sci-fi author Theodore Sturgeon gives a speech in which he formulates the now-famous Sturgeon's Law: "Ninety percent of everything is crud."

SOMETHING'S FISHY
Answer these questions about other folks with ichthyological names.

1. What vocal range did Lance Bass sing in 'N Sync?
2. What TV host served as Edmund Hillary's zoologist during his 1960 Yeti-hunting expedition in the Himalayas?
3. What *Mulholland Drive* actress is titled Countess von Bismarck-Schönhausen?
4. What Treasury secretary in Lincoln's cabinet appeared on the $10,000 bill?
5. What reporter traveled the world accompanied by Captain Archibald Haddock?
6. What author's alter ego is a pulp science fiction author named Kilgore Trout?
7. What explorer discovered the mountain that inspired Katharine Lee Bates to write "America the Beautiful"?
8. What did FCC Chairman Newton Minow famously compare television to, in a 1961 speech?
9. What four-letter initialism has been added to the Oxford American College Dictionary, thanks to Rachael Ray?
10. Whose painting *No. 5, 1948* became the world's most expensive when David Geffen sold it in 2006?

• **1991** • LENINGRAD IS RENAMED St. Petersburg, after almost seven decades with its Communist name. Hey, Ontario had a township named after Stalin until 1986.

ISTANBUL, NOT CONSTANTINOPLE
What's the current name of the city formerly known as . . .

Easy	Harder	Yeah, Good Luck
1. Saigon	1. Batavia	1. Salisbury
2. New Amsterdam	2. Danzig	2. North Tarrytown, New York
3. Edo	3. York	3. Gorky
4. Bombay	4. Leopoldville	4. Lourenço Marques
5. Peking	5. Christiania	5. Jesselton

Answers to the questions on this page can be found on page 390.

• 1775 • HISTORY'S FIRST SUBMARINE attack takes place off what is now called Liberty Island, as the American *Turtle* takes on HMS *Eagle*. As the little one-man contraption fails in both its attempts to sink the *Eagle*, this is also history's first *completely unsuccessful* submarine attack.

TURTLE POWER

1. Which two of the four artists with Teenage Mutant Ninja Turtles named for them are famous for sculptures of David?

2. What kind of nut is traditionally found in "turtle" candy?

3. What Mike Myers character had a black turtleneck and a monkey named Klaus?

4. In 1968, whom did the Turtles regale with the vaguely flattering line "You're my pride and joy, et cetera"?

5. As a culinary in-joke, what kind of animal's head does the "Mock Turtle" have in the original illustrations to *Alice in Wonderland*?

6. What TV show's character Turtle is based on Mark Wahlberg's real-life personal assistant, Donkey?

7. The world's largest tortoises are natives of what archipelago?

8. What movie hero's two pet turtles, Cuff and Link, reappeared for the first time in decades in a 2006 sequel?

9. Lisp, Delphi, or Logo—what language, often used to educate kids about computer programming, used a graphical cursor called a "turtle"?

10. What was first called Liquid Plastone when it was invented in 1941 by Ben Hirsch, also the in-

ventor of the chocolate-covered banana?

11. What are you doing if you are performing spinning floats like the Turtle, the Cricket, or the Jackhammer?

12. Who created Yertle the Turtle in 1958 as a metaphor for fascism?

13. Where would you find the turtlelike creatures called Koopa Troopas?

14. What state's official state reptile is the diamondback terrapin?

15. When the Bible says "the voice of the turtle is heard in our land," what nonreptilian animal is actually meant?

• 1985 • ZAK STARKEY'S WIFE, Sarah, gives birth to little Tatia Jayne Starkey, making Ringo Starr the first Beatle grandfather.

GRANDCHILDREN OF MEN

1. What mystery novelist has a granddaughter named Kinsey, named for her most famous creation?

2. Which two-time presidential also-ran was the grandson, and namesake, of Grover Cleveland's second vice president?

3. What propitious distinction is shared by Perry Como and Black Sabbath bassist Geezer Butler?

4. Max Planck, Max Born, or Max Factor—Olivia Newton-John is the granddaughter of what Nobel Prize–winning German physicist?

5. Who chose his grandson Gary, an attorney, to start accompanying him in TV ads in 1983?

Answers to the questions on this page can be found on page 391.

SEPTEMBER 8

• 1973 • NONE OTHER THAN *The Mary Tyler Moore Show*'s Ted Knight is the narrator ("Meanwhile, at the Hall of Justice . . .") when *Super Friends* makes its TV debut.

B.F.F.!!!
Buddy up to these super-friendly questions.

1. What is an *amicus curiae* a friend of?
2. What ballpark is sometimes called "The Friendly Confines"?
3. Which U.S. state was specifically founded as a haven for members of the Society of Friends?
4. What computer company sold the Amiga from 1985 to 1996?
5. Who had a sister named Minga, a dog named Nopey, and friends named Prickle and Goo?
6. At what Civil War battle was "Stonewall" Jackson killed by friendly fire?
7. According to Norman Bates in *Psycho*, who is a boy's best friend?
8. What's the minimum age to open an account on MySpace.com?
9. What's the better-known title for best friends Valentine and Proteus?
10. What are the first two words of every *Friends* episode title but the first and last ones?

• 2001 • VENUS WILLIAMS DEFEATS her sister Serena in the U.S. Open finals, the first all-sister Grand Slam final match since the very first Wimbledon ladies' final 117 years earlier.

SIBLING RIVALRY

1. What were the professions of Cain and Abel, respectively?
2. What rock band faced a near breakup after a 2000 fistfight in a Barcelona bar?
3. For what 1941 movie did Joan Fontaine win a Best Actress Oscar, kicking off her feud with fellow nominee and older sister Olivia de Havilland?
4. According to legend, who took the throne in 445 A.D. after killing his brother Bleda on a hunting trip?
5. Who were Pauline Esther Friedman and Esther Pauline Friedman?
6. In *The Godfather Part II*, Michael Corleone has Fredo killed during a fishing trip on what lake?
7. What two teams faced off in the first NFL game between two brothers as starting quarter-backs?
8. What band, which never contained any actual siblings, reunited for the 2000 album *Sibling Rivalry*?
9. Who invented a fictional boyfriend named "George Glass" to keep up with her older sister?
10. In literature, what two traits are famously represented by Elinor and Marianne Dashwood?

Answers to the questions on this page can be found on page 391.

• **1836** • ABRAHAM LINCOLN RECEIVES his license to practice law from the Illinois Supreme Court.

PRE-OCCUPATIONS
What U.S. presidents had these former jobs on their résumés?

Easy	*Harder*	*Yeah, Good Luck*
1. President of Princeton	1. Haberdasher	1. Ordained minister
2. Sports team executive	2. Police commissioner	2. Male model
3. Peanut farmer	3. Engineer	3. Tailor
4. Architect	4. President of Columbia	4. Law school dean
5. B-movie actor	5. Sheriff and hangman	5. Newspaper editor

• **1947** • HARVARD RESEARCHERS TRACE a problem with the Mark II, an early electromechanical computer, to a live moth trapped in a relay. It's the first computer bug ever to be caused by an *actual* bug.

BUGGY RIDE

1. Enterprise, Alabama, erected a statue to what beetle, for helping spur it on to plant more diversified crops?
2. What members of family Odonata are also called darning needles?
3. What kind of insect was Master Po's nickname for Caine on *Kung Fu?*
4. Dolbear's Law states the relationship between air temperature and what?
5. In the four major North American sports leagues, what's the only team whose name is that of an insect?
6. The scarab beetle was sacred to what civilization?
7. What social insects are so numerous that they make up about a fifth of the earth's total biomass?
8. What do insects use their spiracles for?
9. One third of all U.S. states that have official state insects have chosen what insect?
10. What kind of insect made *Jurassic Park* possible?

• **2002** • BUZZ ALDRIN, THE SECOND MAN on the moon, punches Bart Sibrel in the jaw. Sibrel is a conspiracy theorist who stalks former astronauts, hoping they'll admit that the Apollo missions were a massive hoax.

BORN TO RUNNER-UP
When you care enough to send the second best.

1. After the U.S., what island nation was the second New World colony to declare independence from Europe?
2. What's the second most abundant element in the earth's atmosphere?
3. Robert Byrd is currently the longest-serving U.S. senator, but who's runner-up?
4. The Jets were, of course, the first AFL team to win a Super Bowl. Who was the second?
5. What Alaskan river is the U.S.'s second longest, after the Mississippi-Missouri?

Answers to the questions on this page can be found on page 391.

• **1955** • Gunsmoke makes its TV debut and will go on to run a record twenty seasons in prime time, not counting the years that CBS will air reruns under the name *Marshal Dillon*.

OLD SITCOMS NEVER DIE
What TV series used these new titles for reruns or syndication?

Easy	Harder	Yeah, Good Luck
1. *Ponderosa*	1. *Love That Bob*	1. *Federal Men*
2. *Jeff's Collie*	2. *The Ted Knight Show*	2. *Brave Stallion*
3. *Andy of Mayberry*	3. *Badge 714*	3. *Call Mr. D*
4. *Sergeant Bilko*	4. *Major Adams, Trailmaster*	4. *San Francisco Beat*
5. *Robert Young, Family Doctor*	5. *The Raymond Burr Show*	5. *Jet Jackson, Flying Commando*

• **1977** • Tunisian immigrant Hamida Djandoubi becomes the last victim of the guillotine, which has been the only legal method of execution in France since 1792.

DEAD HEADS

1. What Spanish explorer, beheaded in 1519 for treason, was the first European to see the Pacific Ocean from the Americas?

2. In a 1967 movie, who is sent to prison for cutting the heads off parking meters?

3. What *Alice in Wonderland* character is constantly shouting "Off with their heads!"?

4. Which letter in the word *Seven* is replaced, in that film's onscreen title, by the number 7?

5. How many of his wives did Henry VIII behead?

6. What was unusual about the decapitations of Oliver Cromwell and Goliath?

7. What modern-day insult originally referred to a performer who bit the heads off chickens?

8. What character is called Jokanaan in the Richard Strauss opera *Salomé*?

9. According to the *New York Post*'s famed April 15, 1983, headline, where was a "headless body" found?

10. What 1819 short story protagonist was based on Tarrytown, New York, schoolteacher Jesse Merwin?

• **2004** • Karen Finley's play *George and Martha*—imagining a perverse, abusive love affair between George W. Bush and Martha Stewart—opens off-off-Broadway.

GEORGE AND MARTHA

1. How many children did George "Father of His Country" Washington have with his wife, Martha?

2. Who lives next door to George and Martha Wilson?

3. What kind of animal are George and Martha, the best friends in James Marshall's beloved series of children's books?

4. What 1966 film had the tagline "You are cordially invited to George and Martha's for an evening of fun and games" on its poster?

5. What comic character is the daughter of George and Martha Moppet?

Answers to the questions on this page can be found on page 392.

• **1974** • THE WORLD GOLF HALL OF FAME opens in North Carolina, with thirteen charter members including Sam Snead, Ben Hogan, Bobby Jones, and Arnold Palmer.

ONE BRIEF ENSHRINING MOMENT

What Hall of Fame counts these people among their founding class?

Easy
1. Fats Domino, Sam Cooke
2. Honus Wagner, Christy Mathewson
3. Jimmie Rodgers, Hank Williams
4. Johnny Weissmuller, Gertrude Ederle
5. Robert Goddard, Neil Armstrong

Harder
1. Emmett Kelly, Otto Griebling
2. José Capablanca, Emanuel Lasker
3. George Mikan, Chuck Hyatt
4. David Sarnoff, Paddy Chayefsky
5. Dick Weber, Don Carter

Yeah, Good Luck
1. Jack Williams, Yakima Canutt
2. Dorothea Dix, Margaret Sanger
3. James Dwight, Robert Wrenn
4. George Wagner, Bruno Sammartino
5. Mel Hein, Dutch Kelly

• **1978** • BULGARIAN JOURNALIST GEORGI MARKOV, a critic of his country's Communist government, dies in London in bizarre Cold War fashion: while he was crossing Waterloo Bridge, the KGB used a tricked-up umbrella to inject a ricin pellet into his thigh.

SPY VS. SPY

What nations have or had police/intelligence agencies called . . .

1. Stasi
2. Mossad
3. SAVAK
4. MI6
5. Cheka

• **1993** • THE WORLD'S FIRST CORNFIELD maze opens in Annville, Pennsylvania, a fund-raiser for midwestern flood relief. The attraction's name, "The Amazing Maize Maze," is a suggestion from composer Stephen Sondheim.

MAYBE I'M A MAZE

1. What's the first fruit to appear in the Pac-Man maze?
2. Where in your body is the vestibular labyrinth, which can cause labyrinth disease?
3. *Pan's Labyrinth* is set in the aftermath of what war?
4. What movie's protagonist freezes to death in the hedge maze of the Overlook Hotel?
5. What famous inventor from Greek myth invented the Minotaur's Labyrinth?

Answers to the questions on this page can be found on page 392.

SEPTEMBER 12

• **1953** • An expert "jury" appointed by the mayor of Los Angeles gives "Los Angeles" its current pronunciation, deciding against the then-common "an-gull-eez"

ANY WAY YOU SAY IT

1. What concert staple is the last song on 1973's *Pronounced 'lĕh-nērd 'skin-nērd?*
2. Because of an unusual local pronunciation, what's the only U.S. state capital with a one-syllable name?
3. What athlete changed the pronunciation of his name in 1970 to rhyme with an award he hoped to win?
4. What's the first word whose pronunciation is disputed in Gershwin's "Let's Call the Whole Thing Off"?
5. What's the only state to mandate an official pronunciation of its name?

• **1976** • The mummy of Rameses II, pharaoh of Egypt, is sent to Paris so scientists can study a fungal infection. Rameses is issued a passport that lists his occupation as "King (deceased)," and France treats the arrival with all the pomp of a state visit.

ME, A PHARAOH?

1. What Egyptian queen was the stepmother of King Tutankhamen?
2. What Egyptian mathematician shared his name with all the kings of Egypt's last dynasty of pharaohs?
3. In Exodus, what final plague convinces Pharaoh to let Moses's people go?
4. Who was assassinated by a man who yelled "Death to pharaoh!" before he fired?
5. What did Cleopatra hide in a basket of figs on November 30, 30 B.C.?

• **1985** • A long-standing scientific controversy is resolved: pandas are bears after all, not raccoons. The taxonomic battle was ended by genetic testing showing a close relationship between giant pandas and the other bears of the Ursidae family.

DIRECT ORDERS
What kind of animal would you find in these taxonomic orders?

Easy
1. Primate
2. Lagomorpha
3. Cetacea
4. Proboscidae

Harder
1. Chiroptera
2. Sirenia
3. Lepidoptera
4. Testudines

Yeah, Good Luck
1. Blattodea
2. Psittaciformes
3. Tubulidentata
4. Anura

Answers to the questions on this page can be found on page 392.

• **1276** • PORTUGAL'S PEDRO JULIÃO becomes pope, choosing the name John XXI. The only problem: there was never any John XX! A numbering screwup led to the goof.

TIMES NEW ROMAN

Catholic trivia—but hopefully with Mass appeal.

1. What *SNL* cast member was arrested at the Vatican in 1981 for impersonating a priest?

2. What Catholic nation is the world's only country literally named for Jesus?

3. In 1995, the Vatican compiled a list of the greatest movies of all time, specifically citing fifteen for their treatment of religion. Name either of the two Oscar-winning Best Pictures on that list.

4. Which of the seven sacraments does a Catholic typically receive first?

5. Decades before JFK, what electoral runner-up was the first Catholic major-party candidate for U.S. president?

• **1959** • THE FIRST FLAG IS PLACED on the moon's surface—and it's not the Stars and Stripes. The Soviet probe *Luna 2* launches, carrying an explosive chamber full of tiny stainless-steel "pennants" that, presumably, scatter when the craft crashes into the moon.

THE CRATER GOOD

1. What's the technical term for the lava flows on the moon sometimes called "seas"?

2. What kind of animal is being put to bed in *Goodnight, Moon*?

3. What worldwide news organization is today owned by Reverend Sun Myung Moon's Unification Church?

4. What political scandal stole headlines while *Apollo 11* was on its way to the moon?

5. Where on your body would you find a "lunula"?

6. In what state is Craters of the Moon National Monument, the largest lava field in the lower forty-eight states?

7. What was the name of the detective agency on TV's *Moonlighting*?

8. Where were the moons Nyx and Hydra discovered in 2005?

9. Who are Luna, Artemis, and Diana, who advise *Sailor Moon*?

10. Despite the rule against it, which state did put a living person on its state quarter?

11. Warren Moon was one of two starting quarterbacks in the Canadian Football League's 1981 Grey Cup. What future politician was the other?

12. What two planets are mentioned in the Sinatra classic "Fly Me to the Moon"?

13. What hit movie comedy was originally titled *The Bride and the Wolf*?

14. What novel's success earned Charles Frazier a whopping $8 million advance for his follow-up, *Thirteen Moons*?

15. What title of a well-known sci-fi novel and movie was also the first word ever spoken from the surface of the moon?

Answers to the questions on this page can be found on page 393.

SEPTEMBER 14

• **1898** • Two TRAVELING SALESMAN meet by chance at the Central House hotel in Boscobel, Wisconsin, and decide to begin an organization for Christian business travelers. The result of their encounter is the Gideons, the group responsible for countless hotel room Bibles.

PAST BIBLE HEROES
Who performed these biblical miracles? (Hint: we will not accept "God.")

Easy	*Harder*	*Yeah, Good Luck*
1. Parting the Red Sea	1. Destroying Dagon's temple	1. Healing Naaman
2. Surviving the lions' den	2. Interpreting Pharaoh's dream	2. The raising of Tabitha
3. Feeding the 5,000	3. Killing the priests of Baal	3. Keeping his wool dry
4. Conquering Jericho	4. Surviving the fiery furnace	4. Surviving a snakebite

• **1954** • The VICTIM OF INDUSTRY pressure and government censorship, EC Comics announces that it's folding its flagship horror and sci-fi magazines, a line that produced such classics as *Weird Science* and *Tales from the Crypt*.

TALES FROM THE CRYPT
How much do you know about stories told from . . . ?

1. What's the name of the dead narrator on ABC's *Desperate Housewives*?
2. What novel begins, in the past tense, "My name was Salmon, like the fish; first name, Susie"?
3. From what unusual location does the late Joe Gillis narrate *Sunset Boulevard*?
4. Who won a $50 prize for his 1833 story "MS. Found in a Bottle," narrated by the victim of a shipwreck?
5. What movie ends with narrator Lester Burnham learning that the moment of his death "isn't a second at all—it stretches on forever, like an ocean of time"?

• **1977** • CONTESTANT YOLANDA BOWSLEY, called to "come on down!" on *The Price Is Right*, becomes the victim of an infamous "wardrobe malfunction" when her tube top slips a crucial four inches.

BREAST IN SHOW

1. Who designed the famous conical bra Madonna wore during her 1990 tour?
2. What color ribbon is worn to promote breast cancer awareness?
3. Because of an oft-cited resemblance to mermaids, what word do we derive from the Carib Indian word for "breast"?
4. What bare-breasted figure is "Leading the People" in Delacroix's painting of the 1830 July Revolution?
5. Jennifer Love Hewitt said that she named her breasts after what film's two title characters?

Answers to the questions on this page can be found on page 393.

• 1938 • LÉON THEREMIN, INVENTOR of the eerie-sounding namesake electronic instrument, leaves New York for Russia at the height of his fame . . . and isn't seen again in the U.S. for fifty-three years. He was imprisoned by Stalin and spent the intervening decades designing bugs for the KGB.

CAN'T STOP THE MUSIC

1. What small instrument has a name that means, in its native language, "jumping flea"?

2. *As You Like It, Much Ado About Nothing,* or *Twelfth Night*—what Shakespeare comedy begins, "If music be the food of love, play on!"

3. For what musical instrument was the capo invented?

4. What are the only two states with musical instruments pictured on their state quarters?

5. What two compositions do Tom Hanks and Robert Loggia play on the giant piano keyboard in *Big*?

6. What top secret 2001 product was code-named "Dulcimer" prior to its launch?

7. What kind of instrument did Laurens Hammond invent in 1934?

8. Piano, violin, or clarinet— what instrument was the Suzuki method first invented to teach?

9. What Australian actress named her first child Banjo?

10. What instrument was played by Big Walter Horton, Sonny Boy Williamson, and Sugar Blue?

• 1973 • ARCHIE GRIFFIN OF OHIO STATE begins his amazing thirty-one-game streak of 100-yard rushing games. He will win Heisman Trophies in *both* of his next two seasons, making him the only repeat winner in the award's history.

TWO-TIMERS

1. Who's the only chief executive who will appear on two of the U.S. Mint's new series of presidential $1 coins?

2. What's the only city that has twice been home to MTV's *The Real World*?

3. What literary prize are J. M. Coetzee and Peter Carey the only people to win twice?

4. Who was the last person to lose two straight U.S. presidential elections as a major-party candidate?

5. Before Tiger Woods, who was the only golfer to complete a career Grand Slam twice?

6. Who was the first two-time *People* Sexiest Man Alive, though he shared the first award, in 1993, with his then-wife?

7. Who's the only person to win the Indy 500 in both front- and rear-engined cars?

8. What real-life figure did actor Gael García Bernal portray twice on film, once in a 2002 miniseries and once in a 2004 film?

9. Who won the NL Comeback Player of the Year award twice, in 1993 and 2000?

10. Three songs made *Rolling Stone*'s list of the 500 Greatest Songs of All Time in two different versions. Name the Carl Perkins, Bob Dylan, and Aerosmith songs in question.

Answers to the questions on this page can be found on page 393.

• **1918** • WITH TWELVE MODEL T Fords, twenty-year-old Chicagoan Walter Jacobs opens America's first car rental company.

AUTO MOTIVE

1. What scientific unit of frequency is named for the German physicist who invented the world's first radio antenna?
2. What chapel, built in 1744, takes its now-famous name from the Spanish word for "cottonwood"?

3. At current rates, Zimbabwe has the world's least valuable, and the Cayman Islands the world's most valuable, what?
4. In tennis scoring, what word describes the situation of a player winning a point from deuce and therefore being just

one point away from winning a game?
5. The first space shuttle, OV-101, was set to be named *Constitution*, but, after NASA received 100,000 letters from sci-fi fans, its name was changed to what?

• **1956** • PLAY-DOH HITS SHELVES, originally invented as a wallpaper cleaner but now retooled as a children's toy.

GREECE IS THE WORD

In honor of Play-Doh, answer these questions on Greek philosophy.

1. In Plato's *Symposium*, Aristophanes' speech is interrupted by what medical condition, which is eventually cured by sneezing?
2. "The blood of Socrates" is a nickname for the red spots found on the stems of what plant, also called "spotted parsley"?

3. What Canadian actor has played Rudyard Kipling, Mike Wallace, Sherlock Holmes, and Aristotle on screen?
4. The paradoxes of Zeno, which featured Achilles, a tortoise, and an arrow, were designed to show that what is illusory or even

impossible?
5. What philosopher-mathematician led a cultlike secret society where divulging secrets was punishable by death and eating beans was forbidden?

• **1975** • PAPUA NEW GUINEA achieves independence from Australia.

I WANNA BE FREE

From what country did these nations declare independence?

Easy
1. Brazil, 1822
2. Vatican City, 1929
3. Korea, 1945
4. The Philippines, 1946
5. India, 1947

Harder
1. Finland, 1917
2. Iceland, 1944
3. Kuwait, 1961
4. Bangladesh, 1971
5. East Timor, 2002

Yeah, Good Luck
1. The Dominican Republic, 1844
2. Madagascar, 1960
3. Rwanda, 1962
4. Suriname, 1975
5. Eritrea, 1993

Answers to the questions on this page can be found on page 394.

• **1771** • Scottish comic novelist Tobias Smollett, the creator of alliterative, picaresque protagonists like Ferdinand Fathom, Roderick Random, and Peregrine Pickle, dies at his Italian villa.

ALLITERATURE

Name these literary classics from tongue-twisting plot summaries.

1. Puritan preacher provokes parishioner Prynne's peccadillos, producing pregnancy, penitence, and Pearl.

2. Tyke trades tattered togs with twin Tom, triggering troubles transferring Tudor title.

3. Local landowner's loftiness looks loathsome to Lizzy; little Lydia leaves with lieutenant lothario.

4. Suspicious surgeon sees sickness spread in Saharan seaport. Serum solves squat; spouse succumbs in sanatorium.

5. Limey Lemuel's log lampoons London's ludicrousness, limning landings at Lilliput, Laputa, and Luggnagg.

6. Depressed Danish dauphin, disturbed by dad's death, dethrones depraved dastard, despite doubt, delay, and darling's drowning.

7. Emasculated expatriate emptily esteems elegant Englishwoman, enters España, enjoys extreme entertainment.

8. Paradoxical policy punishes patrols of pilots posted in Pianosa, producing paranoia.

9. Alabama attorney Atticus attempts to absolve African American accused of assault.

10. Separated from society, schoolkids solemnly sanctify seashell, skewer sow skull on stake, steal sissy's spectacles, slay Simon.

11. Bitter bureaucrat and beautiful brunette are beguiled by bogus "Brotherhood," brainwashed by Big Brother.

12. Man, maltreated when Mom marries Mr. Murdstone, moves in with money-mismanaging Mr. Micawber.

13. Sensitive Starkfield serf, suicidally saddened by suspicious spouse, suffers sled smashup.

14. Close-mouthed cripple clings to crystalline critters, crushes on clever clerk.

15. Dick Diver diagnoses depressed dame, deflowers dewy debutante, drinks, divorces.

16. Wicked waif warns woodcarver of his whoppers when his wooden whiffer widens, wins wisdom when wolfed by whale.

17. Flames of futuristic fireman's fondness for fiction are fanned by former faculty fellow Faber.

18. Beautiful Bathsheba brushes off Boldwood but bonds with benevolent bailiff.

19. Kompany kaptain kruises up Kongo to kollect karismatic konverted kolonialist Kurtz.

20. Pumblechook presents Pip to presumed patroness, preoccupied with past. Petrifying prisoner proves to be Pip's promoter.

Answers to the questions on this page can be found on page 394.

SEPTEMBER 18

• **1844** • PAINTER C. M. COOLIDGE IS BORN. You've probably never heard of Coolidge, but just ponder how much less kitschy life would be without him: he invented those boardwalk standees with head-shaped holes cut out, and—even better!—painted the *Dogs Playing Poker* series for a Minnesota ad agency in 1903.

HANDS ACROSS AMERICA
People play poker too.

1. What TV series featured poker buddies named Murray, Vinnie, Speed, and Roy?

2. What casino hosted the annual World Series of Poker from 1970 to 2005?

3. What poker hand is worth more than a flush but less than four of a kind?

4. According to Kenny Rogers's "The Gambler," what's the best that you can hope for?

5. What literary detective lived on a houseboat called the *Busted Flush?*

• **1990** • A 500-POUND REPLICA of a Hershey's Kiss is dropped from the flagpole at One Times Square in New York City to announce the debut of Hershey's Kisses with almonds.

ORAL EXAM
Kisses of the non-chocolate variety.

1. What's the only Best Picture Oscar winner also to take home the coveted "Best Kiss" MTV Movie Award?

2. What practice comes from the Inuit and Pacific Islander custom of mutually sniffing the sweat glands of the cheeks?

3. Elizabeth Hickey's appropriately titled novel *The Painted Kiss* is about Émilie Floge, the mistress of what painter?

4. What two characters did NBC insist not touch lips when they kissed in the 1968 *Star Trek* episode "Plato's Stepchildren"?

5. Two thirds of all people tilt their heads which way to kiss?

6. What Kiss guitarist designed the rock band's iconic logo?

7. The story of Paolo and Francesca da Rimini in what famous literary work inspired Rodin's famous sculpture *The Kiss?*

8. Why have twenty-odd men, over the years, claimed to have kissed New York nurse Edith Cullen Shain?

9. A mention of what 1980s TV show in the lyrics helps date the Prince hit "Kiss"?

10. What's the better-known name of the "pygmy chimpanzee," the only animal other than humans that enjoys tongue kissing?

11. The first kiss in the Bible is between what father and son?

12. What 1989 Italian film ends with a montage of screen kisses, including smooches from *His Girl Friday*, *The Gold Rush*, and *The Adventures of Robin Hood?*

13. In Norse mythology, the invincible god Balder is killed by an arrow of what plant, the only plant that didn't swear never to harm him?

14. What, besides a crick in your neck and possibly herpes simplex, is the traditional reward for kissing Ireland's Blarney Stone?

15. What fictional rocker had a big 1958 hit with "One Last Kiss"?

Answers to the questions on this page can be found on page 394.

• **1982** • CARNEGIE MELLON COMPUTER SCIENTIST Scott Fahlman suggests, in a historic message board posting to his department, that a colon, hyphen, and close parenthesis be used to represent a sideways smiley face online. :-)

TURN TURN TURN
Answer these sideways questions.

1. What ocean liner rolled over on its side and sank after colliding with the SS *Stockholm* in 1956?
2. What title action of a 1939 movie occurs when Governor Hubert "Happy" Hopper flips a coin that lands on its edge?
3. Venus, Uranus, or Neptune—what planet spins "on its side" relative to its orbit around the sun?
4. What animal's name is given to the kind of camera dolly that can move sideways as well as back and forth?
5. In 1917, Marcel Duchamp turned what object sideways and tried to enter it in art shows under the title *Fountain?*

• **1988** • ACTOR ROY KINNEAR is thrown from a horse while filming *The Return of the Three Musketeers* and later dies from the injuries. The film's distraught director, Richard Lester, vows never to make another movie.

THE LATE SHOW
What actor appeared posthumously in each of these movies?

Easy
1. *Rebel Without a Cause*
2. *The Crow*
3. *Canadian Bacon*
4. *Enter the Dragon*

Harder
1. *Queen of the Damned*
2. *Bad Santa*
3. *Plan 9 from Outer Space*
4. *Twilight Zone: The Movie*

Yeah, Good Luck
1. *Brainstorm*
2. *Atlantis: The Lost Empire*
3. *Dirty Work*
4. *UHF*

• **1995** • JOHN BAUR AND MARK SUMMERS celebrate the first Talk Like a Pirate Day, an idea they hit upon the previous June after spicing up a racquetball game with some eighteenth-century nautical slang. After Dave Barry plugs it in a 2002 column, the made-up holiday really starts to catch on.

SHIVER ME TIMBERS

1. Jim Hawkins and Long John Silver's ship in *Treasure Island* is named for a different island. Which?
2. What hero of the wars with the Barbary pirates is also famous for his toast "Right or wrong, our country"?
3. The only two world nations with an *x* in their English name were also home to the world's most influential "pirate radio" stations. What are they?
4. What future leader was kidnapped by pirates in 78 B.C. and, insulted by their low ransom demand, returned to crucify them after his release?
5. In *The Pirates of Penzance,* the hero's pirate troubles are the result of his birthday falling on what day?
6. According to the famous sea shanty, how many men were there "on a dead man's chest"?
7. Johnny Depp's and Keira Knightley's *Pirates of the Caribbean* characters are both named for birds. Which two birds?
8. Which of the five founding members of the Baseball Hall of Fame was a longtime Pittsburgh Pirate?
9. What film centers around the writing of *Romeo and Ethel the Pirate's Daughter?*
10. In a 1992 Beastie Boys song, who is asked, "What's another word for pirate treasure?"

Answers to the questions on this page can be found on page 395.

SEPTEMBER 20

• **1899** • HERBERT BEERBOHM TREE begins his acclaimed run of *King John* in London. A filmed version of the play, the same year, is the oldest known movie adaptation of Shakespeare.

PLAY-GIARISM

Can you match these movies to the Shakespeare plays that, uh, "inspired" them?

1. *A Double Life*	A. *Hamlet*
2. *Forbidden Planet*	B. *Henry IV, Part 1*
3. *Get Over It*	C. *King Lear*
4. *My Own Private Idaho*	D. *Macbeth*
5. *She's the Man*	E. *A Midsummer Night's Dream*
6. *Strange Brew*	F. *Othello*
7. *10 Things I Hate About You*	G. *Romeo and Juliet*
8. *A Thousand Acres*	H. *The Taming of the Shrew*
9. *Throne of Blood*	I. *The Tempest*
10. *West Side Story*	J. *Twelfth Night*

• **1999** • RICHARD BELZER REPRISES his *Homicide: Life on the Street* character Detective John Munch in the first episode of *Law & Order: Special Victims Unit*. Besides regular gigs on those two long-running shows, Belzer has since played Munch on series from *The X-Files* to *Arrested Development* to *Sesame Street*. That guy gets around.

SIX IS COMPANY

What common bond is shared by each of these lists of TV shows?

1. *Cheers, Frasier, Magnum P.I., The Mary Tyler Moore Show, The Prisoner, Will & Grace*
2. *Checking In, CSI: New York, Gomer Pyle U.S.M.C., Good Times, Models Inc., Mork and Mindy*
3. *Due South, E/R, Good Times, Kolchak: The Night Stalker, Married . . . with Children, Webster*
4. *The Beverly Hillbillies, Bewitched, I Dream of Jeannie, Lost in Space, My Three Sons, The Wild Wild West*
5. *Alice, The Brady Bunch, Eight Is Enough, The Fall Guy, Mystery Science Theater 3000, 21 Jump Street*
6. *Dynasty, Happy Days, Hope & Faith, The Love Boat, Married . . . with Children, Sports Night*
7. *The Bionic Woman, Buffy the Vampire Slayer, Get Smart, In the Heat of the Night, Leave It to Beaver, Taxi*
8. *Family Affair, Full House, The Hogan Family, Please Don't Eat the Daisies, Rugrats, 7th Heaven*
9. *Arrested Development, The Bob Newhart Show, Cheers, Growing Pains, Monk, The Sopranos*
10. *All in the Family, Antiques Roadshow, Three's Company, Queer as Folk, Sanford and Son, Too Close for Comfort*

Answers to the questions on this page can be found on page 395.

• **1780** • BENEDICT ARNOLD, THE HERO OF Saratoga, sells out! British major John André rows up the Hudson by night so that Arnold can hand over the plans to West Point.

QUIZ-LING
Name these people convicted of treason.

1. Who is commemorated in the nursery rhyme that begins "Remember, remember the fifth of November"?
2. Who also killed Countess Sophie on June 28, 1914?

3. What Hungarian prime minister was secretly executed in 1958?
4. A tune about what man's "Body" was later used for "The Battle Hymn of the Republic"?

5. Who was nicknamed "Madame Deficit" by the press in 1786?

• **1823** • ACCORDING TO JOSEPH SMITH, an angel called Moroni first visits him to tell him about the "golden plates" that will be translated as the Book of Mormon.

HALO, I LOVE YOU

1. Who was the only *Charlie's Angels* actress to last for the show's entire run?
2. What final book of the Old Testament is named for the Hebrew word for "my angel"?

3. What movie cowboy was the original owner of the California Angels?
4. Who does Christine Daaé believe is her "Angel of Music"?
5. Who ended his first inaugural

address by appealing to "the better angels of our nature"?

• **1979** • PAUL SIMONON OF THE CLASH smashes his bass against the stage during a concert at New York's Palladium. Photographer Pennie Smith captures the moment, which becomes the cover of *London Calling* and one of the most famous images in rock history.

AX NICELY
Name the guitarist who played the solo on these songs, from Guitar World *magazine's list of the 100 greatest solos ever.*

Easy	*Harder*	*Yeah, Good Luck*
#1: "Stairway to Heaven"	#20: "Bohemian Rhapsody"	#57: "Walk"
#5: "All Along the Watchtower"	#24: "Fade to Black"	#73: "Stash"
#6: "November Rain"	#29: "For the Love of God"	#83: "Scuttle Buttin' "
#10: "Crossroads"	#44: "Alive"	#87: "Cult of Personality"
#12: "Johnny B. Goode"	#45: "Light My Fire"	#98: "Under a Glass Moon"

Answers to the questions on this page can be found on page 395.

SEPTEMBER 22

• **1735** • ROBERT WALPOLE MOVES into 10 Downing Street, becoming the first British prime minister to live at the famous address.

PUBLIC ADDRESS SYSTEM

Can you find these famous addresses *without a map?*

1. What *77 Sunset Strip* regular actually played a vicious killer in the show's pilot?

2. What's the street address of the TV brownstone where Bert, Ernie, Oscar the Grouch, et al., live?

3. Who was the landlady at 221B Baker Street?

4. As fans of *The Blues Brothers* know, 1060 West Addison Street is the address of what?

5. What veterinarian's address is Oxenthorpe Road, Puddleby-on-the-Marsh, Slopshire?

6. The White House is 1600 Pennsylvania Avenue, of course. But what cabinet department occupies the massive building at *1500* Pennsylvania Avenue?

7. What comedian had two sons star on TV's *21 Jump Street*?

8. What NFL team plays its home games at 100 Art Rooney

Avenue?

9. What number is shared by the Munsters' Mockingbird Lane address and Disneyland's Harbor Boulevard address?

10. The song "Love Street" is actually about whose house at 1812 Rothdell Trail?

• **1927** • GENE TUNNEY HOLDS OFF former champ Jack Dempsey to retain his heavyweight boxing title, thanks to the famous "Long Count." Referee Dave Barry (no relation), takes thirteen seconds to count Tunney out in the seventh, giving him time to recover.

BAD CALLS

1. Who won the 1990 AP national championship thanks in part to the notorious "fifth down" win over Missouri?

2. What unusual overtime goof did referee Phil Luckett make in

a Thanksgiving 1998 Steelers-Lions game?

3. What Olympic sport is the subject of the HBO documentary *:03 from Gold*?

4. Who lost a World Cup quarter-

final due to the "Hand of God" goal?

5. What stadium's right-field wall now has a railing thanks to the uncalled spectator interference of Jeffrey Maier in 1996?

• **1972** • *THE BRADY BUNCH* GOES to Hawaii! Don Ho! Vincent Price!

TV NATION

In what states were these TV title locales?

Easy	*Harder*	*Yeah, Good Luck*
1. Mayberry	**1.** Hazzard County	**1.** Fernwood
2. Twin Peaks	**2.** Tree Hill	**2.** Eureka
3. South Park	**3.** Eerie	**3.** Port Charles
4. Everwood	**4.** Jericho	**4.** Push

Answers to the questions on this page can be found on page 396.

• 1845 • ENGINEER ALEXANDER CARTWRIGHT formalizes the Knickerbocker Rules, twenty guidelines for his "ball game" club, the New York Knickerbockers. These rules will become the basis of modern baseball.

THE RULING CLASS

What lists of regulations are being excerpted here?

1. One: please don't operate the grinder or the press if you've been drinking. Two: please don't smoke in bed or use candles.
2. Three: what precedes debate on a question. Four: what motions to be in writing, and how they shall be divided.

3. Five: don't call him and rarely return his calls. Six: always end phone calls first.
4. Seven: if your pants hang off your hips, I'll gladly secure them with my staple gun. Eight: dates must be in crowded public places. You want romance? Read

a book.
5. Nine: should a glove burst, or come off, it must be replaced to the referee's satisfaction. Ten: a man on one knee is considered down and if struck is entitled to the stakes.

• 1952 • VICE PRESIDENT RICHARD NIXON, facing the possibility of being dropped from Eisenhower's ticket, gives the "Checkers speech," insisting that his kids will keep their new cocker spaniel. Checkers will eventually die on September 8, 1964, after which Julie and Tricia won't have him to kick around anymore.

VEEP VEEP

Name these U.S. presidents given a pair of their vice presidents.

Easy
1. Hannibal Hamlin and Andrew Johnson
2. Spiro Agnew and Gerald Ford
3. Henry Wallace and Harry Truman

Harder
1. Aaron Burr and George Clinton
2. Garret Hobart and Theodore Roosevelt
3. John C. Calhoun and Martin Van Buren

Yeah, Good Luck
1. Henry Wilson and Schuyler Colfax
2. George Clinton and Elbridge Gerry
3. Thomas Hendricks and Adlai Stevenson

• 2004 • ESTÉE LAUDER ANNOUNCES the release of Donald Trump: The Fragrance. America announces the final stage of Donald Trump: The Backlash.

BUSINESS SCENTS

Match these celebrities to their signature fragrances.

1. Ashanti
2. Antonio Banderas
3. Cher
4. Derek Jeter
5. Beyoncé Knowles
6. Jennifer Lopez
7. Mary-Kate and

Ashley Olsen
8. Sarah Jessica Parker
9. Britney Spears
10. Elizabeth Taylor

A. Coast to Coast
B. Driven
C. Fantasy
D. Glow
E. Lovely
F. Passion
G. Precious Jewel

H. Spirit
I. True Star
J. Uninhibited

Answers to the questions on this page can be found on page 396.

SEPTEMBER 24

• **1848** • BRANWELL BRONTË, the only brother of literature's famous Brontë sisters, dies of tuberculosis. Branwell was a hard-partying alcoholic and probably a drug addict—as you could no doubt tell from the bad-ass heavy-metal umlaut over the "e" in his name.

PUNK-TUATION

Correctly place the unnecessary umlauts in each of these bands' names.

1. Blue Oyster Cult
2. Husker Du
3. Motley Crue
4. Motorhead
5. Queensryche
6. Spinal Tap

• **1906** • THEODORE ROOSEVELT MAKES Devils Tower, Wyoming, the first National Monument, possibly because aliens have been giving him visions of the spot for months.

MONUMENT VALLEY

1. What part of New York's Statue of Liberty National Monument is actually in New Jersey?
2. For whom is the cemetery at Little Bighorn Battlefield National Monument named?
3. Baseball's "inventor," Abner Doubleday, fired the first shot defending what current national monument?
4. What two men, one named for the other, both have national monuments at their birthplaces, in Virginia and Missouri, respectively?
5. What national monument lies entirely within a missile-testing range?
6. Central Park, Battery Park, or Bryant Park—what Manhattan park is home to Castle Clinton National Monument?
7. What national monument is named for the world's largest "natural bridge"?
8. By tradition, newly designed U.S. flags always fly first over what national monument?
9. What kind of tree has both a national park and national monument named for it?
10. Despite not being part of the U.S. proper, what territory has a national park and two national monuments?

• **1958** • WORLD WAR I FINALLY ENDS in the tiny Pyrenees nation of Andorra, as a ceremonial peace is signed with Germany. Apparently, Andorra wasn't invited to sign the Treaty of Versailles forty years ago.

BETTER LATE THAN NEVER

1. Who was finally convicted in 1994 for the 1963 murder of the civil rights leader Medger Evers?
2. What country was originally selected to host both the Summer and Winter Olympics of 1940 but due to World War II hosted neither until the 1960s?
3. In 2004, who finally released a new version of his unfinished 1966 album, *Smile*?
4. In 1984, blacklist victims Michael Wilson and Carl Foreman posthumously got screen credit—and Oscars—for writing *Bridge on the River Kwai*. Why was novelist Pierre Boulle's solo writing credit on *Kwai* particularly suspicious?
5. How many other people die as a result of Hamlet's actions before he finally kills his intended victim, his uncle Claudius?

Answers to the questions on this page can be found on page 396.

• **1790** • THE CHINESE EMPEROR Qianlong summons opera troupes from the provinces to perform at his lavish eightieth birthday party. This leads to the formation of the Beijing Opera, still the most famous presenters of Chinese theater worldwide.

CONCRETE GALOSHES

Speaking of Chinese theater, who's the only star to leave these unusual imprints outside the famous Grauman's Chinese Theatre in Hollywood?

1. Ice skates	**5.** Wheels	**9.** Cigar (two answers)
2. Eyeglasses	**6.** Mouth	**10.** Hooves (three answers)
3. Braids	**7.** Fist	
4. Legs	**8.** Knees	

• **1971** • BRIAN DUNKLEMAN—aka "that genius who bailed on *American Idol* because he thought it would kill his stand-up career"—is born in Ellicottville, New York.

PITCHY KEEN

Give the full name of the Idol *contestant cheered on by these fan clubs.*

1. Blaker Girls	**3.** Care Bears	**5.** Sparklers
2. Clay-mates	**4.** The Soul Patrol	**6.** McPhans

• **1988** • FLORENCE GRIFFITH-JOYNER sets a new Olympic record in the 100-meter sprint. Yesterday, her sister-in-law Jackie Joyner-Kersee set a new world record in the heptathlon.

RELATIVELY RELATED

Test your knowledge on these famous in-laws.

1. Denny McLain, Bob Gibson, or Sandy Koufax—what Hall of Fame pitcher was actor Richard Widmark's son-in-law?

2. What two *West Wing* cast members were real-life brothers-in-law?

3. Who named his "Coffee Talk" character, Linda Richman, after his mother-in-law?

4. The wives of George Washington and Robert E. Lee were grandmother and granddaughter. What last name did they share?

5. Which two *Dukes of Hazzard* characters are actually brothers-in-law?

Answers to the questions on this page can be found on page 397.

• **1914** • THE FEDERAL TRADE COMMISSION is created as part of Woodrow Wilson's war against trusts.

TRADE COMMISSION

1. Who was traded for spy Rudolf Abel on February 10, 1962?
2. What was unusual about the 1960 trade of the Tigers' Jimmy Dykes for the Indians' Joe Gordon?

3. Martha Stewart was jailed for insider trading of what pharmaceutical stock?
4. Whom did Sixers owner F. Eugene Dixon call "the Babe Ruth of basketball" after the cash-

strapped Nets sold him for $3 million?
5. What Fox reality show is a clone of ABC's *Wife Swap*?

• **1985** • SHAMU, THE FIRST KILLER WHALE calf ever to thrive in captivity, is born at Sea World. Actually, "Shamu" is like "Lassie"—just a stage name shared by a lot of animals. This first Baby Shamu's real name is Kalina.

WHALE KNOWN FACTS

1. What rock band took its name from the answer to the goofy 1960s riddle "What's purple and lives at the bottom of the sea?"
2. What tiny crustaceans are the main food source for all baleen whales?

3. Other than a small population of blue whales off the coast of Sri Lanka, what's the only species known to communicate with "whale song"?
4. The film *Whale Rider* is about the traditions of what Pacific

people?
5. What mammals are the whales' closest living relatives on land?

• **2004** • THE CITY OF DENVER renames West Mile High Stadium Circle "John Elway Drive," to honor the Hall of Fame quarterback. I'm guessing Denver residents will always just call it "The Drive."

STREET BALL
What cities renamed a street near a sporting venue . . .

Easy	*Harder*	*Yeah, Good Luck*
1. Hank Aaron Drive	**1.** Brett Hull Way	**1.** Cyclone Taylor Boulevard
2. Dan Marino Boulevard	**2.** Peyton Manning Pass	**2.** Richard Petty Boulevard
3. John Stockton Drive	**3.** Mazeroski Way	**3.** Tony Canadeo Run
4. Jesse-Owens-Allee	**4.** Nolan Ryan Expressway	**4.** Edwin Flack Drive

Answers to the questions on this page can be found on page 397.

• **1892** • PHILADELPHIA LAWYER JOSEPH PUSEY patents the book of matches. But you couldn't "Close Cover Before Striking" on Pusey's flawed design—he'd put the friction strip on the *inside*.

MATCH BOOKS

Can you match these well-known novels to their lesser-known sequels?

1. *Advise and Consent*	**A.** *American Hunger*
2. *All Quiet on the Western Front*	**B.** *Closing Time*
3. *Black Boy*	**C.** *Jo's Boys*
4. *Cannery Row*	**D.** *The Mysterious Island*
5. *Catch-22*	**E.** *No Longer at Ease*
6. *Little Women*	**F.** *The Road Back*
7. *Things Fall Apart*	**G.** *A Shade of Difference*
8. *The Three Musketeers*	**H.** *Sweet Thursday*
9. *Twenty Thousand Leagues Under the Sea*	**I.** *Twenty Years After*
10. *A Wrinkle in Time*	**J.** *A Wind in the Door*

• **1964** • THE WARREN COMMISSION REPORT finds that Lee Harvey Oswald acted alone.

ACTING ALONE

Who made up the entire cast of these one-person shows?

Easy	*Harder*	*Yeah, Good Luck*
1. *Mark Twain Tonight!*	**1.** *700 Sundays*	**1.** *Sex, Drugs, Rock & Roll*
2. *Jesus Is Magic*	**2.** *I'm the One That I Want*	**2.** *Tru*
3. *Swimming to Cambodia*	**3.** *God Said "Ha!"*	**3.** *Comedy in Music*
4. *The Search for Signs of Intelligent Life in the Universe*	**4.** *A Knight Out*	**4.** *Give 'em Hell, Harry!*

• **1990** • THE MPAA RETIRES the X rating for movies, replacing it with the hopefully less stigmatized NC-17. The first NC-17 film, *Henry & June*, is released just a week later . . . but many theaters still refuse to exhibit films using the new rating.

X TERMINATIONS

1. What currently run on OS X?
2. Whose two brothers are Sprite and Racer X?
3. Who became the first wide receiver ever named the game's MVP, after Super Bowl X?
4. In Marvel Comics, who was the only female mutant in the original X-Men assembled by Professor X?
5. What American painter caused a scandal in Paris in 1884 with his sexually suggestive *Portrait of Madame X*?
6. Who discovered Pluto in 1930 while searching for Percival Lowell's hypothetical "Planet X"?
7. What was the birth surname of Malcolm X?
8. Who gave a name to a generation of slackers with his 1991 debut novel *Generation X*?
9. Félix Dupanloup, bishop of Orléans, led the long campaign that finally saw what person beatified in 1909 by Pope Pius X?
10. Clashes with what star led director Tony Kaye to try to remove his name from the film *American History X*?

Answers to the questions on this page can be found on page 397.

SEPTEMBER 28

• **551 B.C.** • THE CHINESE THINKER CONFUCIUS is born, as calculated by the government of Taiwan, which still celebrates the day as Teachers' Day.

WISE CRACKS

Here are some sagelike proverbs from another source: the theme songs of 1980s sitcoms. What shows gave us these immortal bits of wisdom?

1. There's a path you take, and a path untaken.
   The choice is up to you, my friend.

2. There ain't no nothing
   We can't love each other through.

3. Maybe the world is blind,
   Or just a little unkind.
   Don't know.

4. You take the good, you take the bad.
   You take them both.

5. We're nowhere near the end.
   The best is ready to begin.

6. Together, taking the time each day
   To learn all about
   Those things you just can't buy.

7. Any time you're out from under.
   Not getting hassled, not getting hustled.
   Keepin' your head above water,

Making a wave when you can.

8. Life is more than mere survival.

9. This flame in my heart
   And a long-lost friend
   Gives every dark street a light at the end.

10. Everywhere you look
    Everywhere you go
    There's a face of somebody who needs you.

• **1967** • FRANK ZAPPA NAMES HIS firstborn daughter "Moon Unit," anticipating the modern trend for self-indulgent celebrity baby names by almost thirty years.

POOR BABY

Name the celebrity parent(s) of these unfortunate tykes.

Easy
1. Apple Blythe
2. Hazel Patricia and Phinnaeus Walter
3. Shiloh Nouvel
4. Suri
5. Rumer Glenn, Scout LaRue, and Tallulah Belle

Harder
1. Kal-El Coppola
2. Frances Bean
3. Sage Moon Blood
4. Duncan Zowie
5. Jermajesty

Yeah, Good Luck
1. Denim Cole and Diezel Ky
2. Tryumph and Whizdom
3. Speck Wildhorse
4. Pilot Inspektor
5. Moxie CrimeFighter

Answers to the questions on this page can be found on page 398.

• **1963** • *My Favorite Martian* crash-lands on Earth.

LOST IN SPACE
What TV regulars hailed from these planets?

Easy	Harder	Yeah, Good Luck
1. Ork	1. Gallifrey	1. Quadris
2. Krypton	2. Melmac	2. Zetox
3. Vulcan	3. Remulak	3. Decapod 10

• **1967** • THE BBC AIRS a radio play of *King Lear*. Part of Act IV, Scene VI, will go out to an unexpectedly large audience when the Beatles, recording at Abbey Road, overdub four lines of the Bard's dialogue onto the end of "I Am the Walrus."

SHUT UP AND SING
Which songs feature these snatches of spoken-word chatter?

1. "Hal and his famous ashtray!"
2. "This ain't no disco. It ain't no country club either. This is L.A.!"
3. "This ain't rock 'n' roll. This is genocide!"
4. "*Señores y señoras, nosotros tenemos más influencia con sus hijos que tu tiene.*"
5. "I've got blisters on my fingers!"
6. "Do I what? Will I what? Oh, baby, you knooow what I like!"
7. "Weddings, parties, anything. With bongo jazz a speciality!"
8. "Come on, girls, do you believe in love? 'Cause I got something to say about it, and it goes something like this."
9. "You was definitely in the right. That geezer was cruising for a bruising!"
10. "Yeah, this album is dedicated to all the teachers that told me I'd never amount to nothin'. "

• **1981** • THE U.S. NATIONAL DEBT passes $1 trillion for the first time. Congress, unaccountably, elects to raise the debt ceiling rather than print a single trillion-dollar bill.

TIDY SUMS

1. What movie was originally titled *$3,000*, for the size of Vivian Ward's paycheck?
2. Who was at first reluctant to put his hometown into his stage name, for fear he'd be mistaken for *The Six Million Dollar Man*?
3. On what TV show did Michael Larson win $110,237 in a single taping in 1984?
4. Whose net worth is five multiplujillion, nine impossibidillion, seven fantasticatrillion dollars, and sixteen cents?
5. What pitcher's 1998 contract with the Dodgers made him baseball's first $100 million man?

Answers to the questions on this page can be found on page 398.

SEPTEMBER 30

• **1955** • THE IMPROBABLY NAMED COLLEGE student Donald Turnupseed makes the fateful left turn onto California State Route 41 that kills actor James Dean.

CRASH COURSE

Name these people who died in traffic accidents.

1. In 1895, who married Maria Skłodowska, a fellow instructor at the Sorbonne?
2. Who has appeared on more *People* magazine covers than any other person?
3. What future military great was General Pershing's aide during his 1916 campaign against Pancho Villa?
4. What western star was a pallbearer at Wyatt Earp's funeral?

5. In 1986, the Supreme Court ordered the Kerr-McGee energy company to pay $10 million to the estate of whom?
6. Whose famous flowing scarves led Gertrude Stein to observe, "Affectations can be dangerous"?
7. Who died in 1996 in a Jeep Cherokee that had been designed by his own namesake supercomputer?
8. What right fielder was called

"Master Melvin"?
9. In April 1956, who became the first movie actress to appear on a stamp?
10. Who had to rewrite his classic *The Seven Pillars of Wisdom* from scratch after leaving the manuscript in Reading train station?

• **1983** • BY THE POWER OF GREYSKULL, but also by the power of Mattel's marketing department, *He-Man* makes his TV cartoon debut.

MALE CALL

1. What Rudyard Kipling poem ends, "You'll be a Man, my son"?
2. In the AFI list of the fifty greatest movie villains, what movie was named number twenty for its villain "Man"?

3. Cats from the Isle of Man are often missing what anatomical feature?
4. What American divorcée was *Time*'s first female "Man of the Year" in 1936?

5. Who played "the Man" on *Chico and the Man*?

• **1990** • THE BRITISH SITCOM *Heil Honey I'm Home!*, in which Adolf Hitler and Eva Braun annoy their Jewish next-door neighbors, airs its first episode. After a storm of complaints, the first episode turns out to be the last episode as well.

TEST PILOT

Can you name these TV shows from the title of their first episodes?

Easy
1. "The Clampetts Strike Oil"
2. "I, Darrin, Take This Witch, Samantha"
3. "Meet the Bunkers"
4. "12:00 A.M.–1:00 A.M."
5. "Rosie the Robot"

Harder
1. "Two on a Raft"
2. "Welcome to the Hellmouth"
3. "MIA/NYC—Nonstop"
4. "Love Is All Around"
5. "The Case of the Restless Redhead"

Yeah, Good Luck
1. "Hi Diddle Riddle"
2. "The Pants Tent"
3. "Spur Line to Shady Rest"
4. "The Reluctant Stowaway"
5. "Matt Gets It"

Answers to the questions on this page can be found on page 398.

September Answers

SEPTEMBER 1	SEPTEMBER 2	SEPTEMBER 3

SEPTEMBER 1

HELP WANTED
1. Pony Express riders
2. *School of Rock*
3. John Tyler
4. Casting *The Monkees*
5. Douglas MacArthur

BETTER PLATE THAN NEVER

Easy
1. Minnesota
2. Wisconsin
3. Idaho
4. Delaware
5. Montana

Harder
1. Pennsylvania
2. Virginia
3. Indiana
4. Louisiana
5. New Hampshire

Yeah, Good Luck
1. West Virginia
2. South Carolina
3. Maine
4. Mississippi
5. North Dakota

NET GAIN
1. Roger Federer
2. "Philadelphia Freedom"
3. Martina Hingis (for Martina Navratilova)
4. Arthur Ashe
5. Maria Sharapova
6. Rod Laver
7. Evonne Goolagong
8. A let
9. Bill Tilden
10. Melbourne

SEPTEMBER 2

DAYS OF OUR LIVES
1. Aries (April)
2. A menorah
3. Baseball's All-Star break
4. Baskin-Robbins
5. Chile
6. Purim
7. *Playboy*'s Playmate of the Month
8. The Seven Virtues of Kwanzaa
9. June (the pearl)
10. Arizona and Hawaii
11. Hegira
12. Father's Day
13. Inauguration Day
14. Christmas Eve and New Year's Eve
15. Saturday

JUST DESERTS
1. Antarctica (low precipitation, no vegetation)
2. Dune
3. Philip Roth
4. The Takla Makan
5. King Hussein of Jordan
6. Dromedary (or Arabian; number of humps on a camel)
7. Australia
8. Death Valley
9. The Kalahari
10. Salt Lake City

SEPTEMBER 3

ACCESS OF EVIL
1. Martin Luther King, Jr.,'s assassination
2. Sigmund Freud
3. Oklahoma
4. Anteaters
5. Augustus Gloop
6. ~~Michelangelo~~ Van Gogh
7. Ivan Boesky

CLUBLAND

Easy
1. Chicago Bears
2. University of Houston
3. Pittsburgh Steelers
4. New York Yankees
5. Los Angeles Lakers

Harder
1. Golden State Warriors
2. Denver Broncos
3. Miami Dolphins
4. Philadelphia Flyers
5. University of Michigan

Yeah, Good Luck
1. Buffalo Bills
2. Milwaukee Brewers
3. Chicago White Sox
4. Washington Redskins
5. Buffalo Sabres

NINE OF SEVEN
1. Abbie Hoffman
2. Mickey Mantle
3. Piss
4. Three
5. Lance Armstrong (winning the Tour de France)
6. Samson
7. Sherlock Holmes
8. Isaac Newton
9. Whitney Houston

SEPTEMBER 4

REVERSE ENGINEERING
1. *Fantasia* ("Yen Sid" is "Disney" spelled backward)
2. Dick Fosbury
3. Polish
4. Daddy Mac and Mac Daddy
5. R

SO UNPRETTY
1. The Eiffel Tower
2. Britney Spears
3. A grapefruit
4. Tony Blair
5. Abraham Lincoln
6. The Troll doll
7. Salma Hayek
8. The Elephant Man
9. Anne of Cleves
10. A swan

"PRIME" DIRECTIVE
1. Jane Tennison
2. Jimmy Carter
3. Megatron
4. The Supremes
5. France and Spain
6. 23
7. Aristotle
8. Maggie Smith
9. Choice
10. They aired twice a week

SEPTEMBER 5

ALL THE MEN AND WOMEN MERELY PLAYERS
1. *Much Ado about Nothing*'s (Benedick and Beatrice)
2. Puck
3. Antonio (*The Merchant of Venice*)
4. *The Tempest*
5. Iago

SIZE MATTERS
1. Olives
2. Grand pianos
3. Champagne bottles
4. Hailstones
5. Starbucks cups

FUTURE SHOCK
1. Easter
2. The New York World's Fair
3. 2016
4. Orion
5. 6009
6. *Brave New World*
7. The Age of Aquarius
8. Ayers Rock
9. London
10. Buck Rogers

SEPTEMBER 6

NORTHERN EXPOSURE
Easy
1. Michael J. Fox
2. Evangeline Lilly
3. Jim Carrey
4. Raymond Burr
5. Martin Short
Harder
1. Victor Garber
2. Kim Cattrall
3. Lorne Greene
4. Jill Hennessy
5. Sandra Oh
Yeah, Good Luck (two answers each)
1. Dave Foley, Phil Hartman
2. Neve Campbell, Paula Devicq
3. William Shatner, James Doohan
4. Howie Mandel, Bruce Greenwood
5. Jason Priestley, Kathleen Robertson

SOMETHING'S FISHY
1. Bass
2. Marlin Perkins
3. Laura Harring
4. Salmon P. Chase
5. Tintin
6. Kurt Vonnegut's
7. Zebulon Pike (Pikes Peak)
8. A "vast wasteland"
9. EVOO (for extra-virgin olive oil)
10. Jackson Pollock's

ISTANBUL, NOT CONSTANTINOPLE
Easy
1. Ho Chi Minh City
2. New York
3. Tokyo
4. Mumbai
5. Beijing
Harder
1. Jakarta
2. Gdansk
3. Toronto
4. Kinshasa
5. Oslo
Yeah, Good Luck
1. Harare (Zimbabwe)
2. Sleepy Hollow
3. Nizhny Novgorod
4. Maputo (~~Tanzania~~) Mozambique
5. Kota Kinabalu (Malaysia)

SEPTEMBER 7	SEPTEMBER 8	SEPTEMBER 9

TURTLE POWER
1. Michelangelo and Donatello
2. Pecans
3. Dieter (*Sprockets*)
4. Elenore
5. A calf's (mock turtle soup is made from veal)
6. *Entourage*
7. The Galápagos Islands
8. Rocky Balboa's
9. Logo
10. Turtle Wax
11. Break dancing
12. Dr. Seuss
13. In Super Mario video games
14. Maryland
15. A (turtle) dove

GRANDCHILDREN OF MEN
1. Sue Grafton (for Kinsey Millhone)
2. Adlai Stevenson
3. They're seventh sons of seventh sons
4. Max Born
5. Orville Redenbacher

B.F.F.!!!
1. "The court"
2. Wrigley Field
3. Pennsylvania
4. Commodore
5. Gumby
6. Chancellorsville
7. His mother
8. 14
9. *Two Gentlemen of Verona*
10. "The One . . ."

SIBLING RIVALRY
1. Farmer and shepherd
2. Oasis
3. *Suspicion*
4. Attila the Hun
5. Dear Abby and Ann Landers
6. Lake Tahoe
7. The Indianapolis Colts and New York Giants (Peyton and Eli Manning)
8. The Doobie Brothers
9. Jan Brady
10. *Sense and Sensibility*

PRE-OCCUPATIONS
Easy
1. Woodrow Wilson
2. George W. Bush
3. Jimmy Carter
4. Thomas Jefferson
5. Ronald Reagan
Harder
1. Harry Truman
2. Theodore Roosevelt
3. Herbert Hoover
4. Dwight Eisenhower
5. Grover Cleveland
Yeah, Good Luck
1. James Garfield
2. Gerald Ford
3. Andrew Johnson
4. William Taft
5. Warren Harding

BUGGY RIDE
1. The boll weevil
2. Dragonflies
3. "Grasshopper"
4. The speed at which crickets chirp
5. The New Orleans Hornets (the Columbus Blue Jackets are now branded with Civil War–, not insect-related, imagery)
6. Egypt
7. Ants
8. Breathing
9. The honeybee
10. A mosquito

BORN TO RUNNER-UP
1. Haiti
2. Oxygen
3. Ted Kennedy
4. The Kansas City Chiefs
5. The Yukon

September Answers

SEPTEMBER 10	SEPTEMBER 11	SEPTEMBER 12

OLD SITCOMS NEVER DIE
Easy
1. *Bonanza*
2. *Lassie*
3. *The Andy Griffith Show*
4. *The Phil Silvers Show*
5. *Marcus Welby, M.D.*
Harder
1. *The Bob Cummings Show*
2. *Too Close for Comfort*
3. *Dragnet*
4. *Wagon Train*
5. *Ironside*
Yeah, Good Luck
1. *Treasury Men in Action*
2. *Fury*
3. *Richard Diamond, Private Detective*
4. *The Lineup*
5. *Captain Midnight*

DEAD HEADS
1. Vasco Nuñez de Balboa
2. Cool Hand Luke (Jackson)
3. The Queen of Hearts
4. The *v*
5. Two
6. They were already dead
7. Geek
8. John the Baptist
9. "In topless bar"
10. Ichabod Crane

GEORGE AND MARTHA
1. None
2. Dennis the Menace
3. Hippos
4. *Who's Afraid of Virginia Woolf?*
5. Little Lulu

ONE BRIEF ENSHRINING MOMENT
Easy
1. Rock and Roll
2. Baseball
3. Country Music
4. Swimming
5. Space
Harder
1. Clown
2. Chess
3. Basketball
4. Television
5. Bowling
Yeah, Good Luck
1. Stuntmen's
2. Nursing
3. Tennis
4. Professional Wrestling
5. Pro Football

SPY VS. SPY
1. East Germany
2. Israel
3. Iran
4. Great Britain
5. The Soviet Union

MAYBE I'M A MAZE
1. The cherry
2. The ear
3. The Spanish Civil War
4. *The Shining*
5. Daedalus

ANY WAY YOU SAY IT
1. "Freebird"
2. Pierre, South Dakota ("peer")
3. Joe Theismann (previously "theez-man")
4. "Either"
5. Arkansas

ME, A PHARAOH?
1. Nefertiti
2. Ptolemy
3. The death of all firstborn males
4. Anwar Sadat
5. An asp

DIRECT ORDERS
Easy
1. Monkeys and apes
2. Rabbits
3. Whales and dolphins
4. Elephants
Harder
1. Bats
2. Manatees and dugongs
3. Butterflies and moths
4. Tortoises
Yeah, Good Luck
1. Cockroaches
2. Parrots
3. Aardvarks
4. Frogs and toads

SEPTEMBER 13

TIMES NEW ROMAN
1. Don Novello (as Father Guido Sarducci)
2. El Salvador ("the Savior")
3. *Ben-Hur* or *A Man for All Seasons*
4. Baptism
5. Alfred Smith

THE CRATER GOOD
1. Mare or maria
2. A rabbit
3. United Press International (UPI)
4. Chappaquiddick
5. It's the tiny crescent at the base of each nail
6. Idaho
7. The Blue Moon Detective Agency
8. Around Pluto
9. Cats
10. Ohio (Neil Armstrong)
11. J. C. Watts
12. Jupiter and Mars
13. *Moonstruck*
14. *Cold Mountain*
15. "Contact"

SEPTEMBER 14

PAST BIBLE HEROES
Easy
1. Moses
2. Daniel
3. Jesus
4. Joshua
Harder
1. Samson
2. Joseph
3. Elijah
4. Shadrach, Meshach, and Abednego
Yeah, Good Luck
1. Elisha
2. Peter
3. Gideon
4. Paul

TALES FROM THE CRYPT
1. Mary Alice Young
2. *The Lovely Bones*
3. Facedown in a swimming pool
4. Edgar Allan Poe
5. *American Beauty*

BREAST IN SHOW
1. Jean-Paul Gaultier
2. Pink
3. Manatee
4. Liberty
5. *Thelma and Louise*

SEPTEMBER 15

CAN'T STOP THE MUSIC
1. Ukulele
2. *Twelfth Night*
3. The guitar
4. Louisiana and Tennessee
5. "Chopsticks" and "Heart and Soul"
6. The iPod
7. An electric organ
8. The violin
9. Rachel Griffiths
10. The harmonica

TWO-TIMERS
1. Grover Cleveland (once for each term)
2. New York City
3. The Booker Prize
4. Adlai Stevenson
5. Jack Nicklaus (who has three)
6. Richard Gere
7. A. J. Foyt
8. Che Guevara
9. Andrés Galarraga
10. "Blue Suede Shoes," "Mr. Tambourine Man," and "Walk This Way"

September Answers

SEPTEMBER 16	SEPTEMBER 17	SEPTEMBER 18

SEPTEMBER 16

AUTO MOTIVE
1. Hertz
2. Alamo
3. Dollar
4. Advantage
5. *Enterprise*

GREECE IS THE WORD
1. Hiccups
2. Hemlock
3. Christopher Plummer
4. Motion
5. Pythagoras

I WANNA BE FREE
Easy
1. Portugal
2. Italy
3. Japan
4. The United States
5. Great Britain
Harder
1. Russia
2. Denmark
3. Great Britain
4. Pakistan
5. Indonesia
Yeah, Good Luck
1. Haiti
2. France
3. Belgium
4. The Netherlands
5. Ethiopia

SEPTEMBER 17

ALLITERATURE
1. *The Scarlet Letter*
2. *The Prince and the Pauper*
3. *Pride and Prejudice*
4. *The Plague*
5. *Gulliver's Travels*
6. *Hamlet*
7. *The Sun Also Rises*
8. *Catch-22*
9. *To Kill a Mockingbird*
10. *Lord of the Flies*
11. *Nineteen Eighty-Four*
12. *David Copperfield*
13. *Ethan Frome*
14. *The Glass Menagerie*
15. *Tender Is the Night*
16. *Pinocchio*
17. *Fahrenheit 451*
18. *Far from the Madding Crowd*
19. *Heart of Darkness*
20. *Great Expectations*

SEPTEMBER 18

HANDS ACROSS AMERICA
1. *The Odd Couple*
2. Binion's Horseshoe
3. A full house
4. To die in your sleep
5. Travis McGee

ORAL EXAM
1. *Shakespeare in Love*
2. "Eskimo kissing"
3. Gustav Klimt
4. Kirk and Uhura (it was TV's first dramatic kiss to "cross the color line")
5. To the right
6. Ace Frehley
7. Dante's *Inferno*
8. She's the nurse kissing an unknown sailor in the famous photo of Times Square on V-J Day
9. *Dynasty*
10. The bonobo
11. Isaac and Jacob
12. *Cinema Paradiso*
13. Mistletoe
14. The "gift of gab"
15. Conrad Birdie (*Bye Bye Birdie*)

SEPTEMBER 19

TURN TURN TURN
1. The *Andrea Doria*
2. *Mr. Smith Goes to Washington*
3. Uranus
4. Crab
5. A urinal

THE LATE SHOW
Easy
1. James Dean
2. Brandon Lee
3. John Candy
4. Bruce Lee
Harder
1. Aaliyah
2. John Ritter
3. Bela Lugosi
4. Vic Morrow
Yeah, Good Luck
1. Natalie Wood
2. Jim Varney
3. Chris Farley
4. Trinidad Silva

SHIVER ME TIMBERS
1. Hispaniola
2. Stephen Decatur
3. Mexico and Luxembourg
4. Julius Caesar
5. February 29
6. Fifteen
7. Sparrows (Jack) and swans (Elizabeth)
8. Honus Wagner
9. *Shakespeare in Love*
10. "Professor Booty"

SEPTEMBER 20

PLAY-GIARISM
1. F
2. I
3. E
4. B
5. J
6. A
7. H
8. C
9. D
10. G

SIX IS COMPANY
1. An oft-mentioned character is never seen
2. Spin-offs of spin-offs
3. Set in Chicago
4. Aired in both black and white and color
5. Cast member(s) sing the theme song
6. Actor Ted McGinley
7. Switched networks in midrun
8. A character has twin children
9. Feature a psychiatrist
10. Based on a British series

SEPTEMBER 21

QUIZ-LING
1. Guy Fawkes
2. Gavrilo Princip (who shot Archduke Franz Ferdinand)
3. Imre Nagy
4. John Brown
5. Marie Antoinette

HALO, I LOVE YOU
1. Jaclyn Smith
2. Malachi
3. Gene Autry
4. The Phantom of the Opera
5. Abraham Lincoln

AX NICELY
Easy
#1: Jimmy Page
#5: Jimi Hendrix
#6: Slash
#10: Eric Clapton
#12: Chuck Berry
Harder
#20: Brian May
#24: Kirk Hammet
#29: Steve Vai
#44: Mike McCready
#45: Robby Krieger
Yeah, Good Luck
#57: Dimebag Darrel
#73: Trey Anastasio
#83: Stevie Ray Vaughan
#87: Vernon Reid
#98: John Petrucci

SEPTEMBER 22	SEPTEMBER 23	SEPTEMBER 24

PUBLIC ADDRESS SYSTEM
1. Edd "Kookie" Byrnes
2. 123 Sesame Street
3. Mrs. Hudson
4. Wrigley Field
5. Doctor Dolittle's
6. The Treasury
7. Dom DeLuise
8. The Pittsburgh Steelers
9. 1313
10. Jim Morrison's

BAD CALLS
1. The Colorado Buffaloes
2. He miscalled the coin toss
3. Basketball (the Soviet win in 1972)
4. England
5. Yankee Stadium

TV NATION
Easy
1. North Carolina
2. Washington
3. Colorado
4. Colorado
Harder
1. Georgia
2. North Carolina
3. Indiana
4. Kansas
Yeah, Good Luck
1. Ohio
2. Oregon
3. New York
4. Nevada

THE RULING CLASS
1. *The Cider House Rules*
2. Robert's Rules of Order
3. *The Rules: Time-Tested Secrets for Capturing the Heart of Mr. Right*
4. *8 Simple Rules for Dating My Daughter*
5. Marquess of Queensberry rules (for boxing)

VEEP VEEP
Easy
1. Abraham Lincoln
2. Richard Nixon
3. Franklin Roosevelt
Harder
1. Thomas Jefferson
2. William McKinley
3. Andrew Jackson
Yeah, Good Luck
1. Ulysses Grant
2. James Madison
3. Grover Cleveland

BUSINESS SCENTS
1. G
2. H
3. J
4. B
5. I
6. D
7. A
8. E
9. C
10. F

PUNK-TUATION
1. Blue Öyster Cult
2. Hüsker Dü
3. Mötley Crüe
4. Motörhead
5. Queensrÿche
6. Spiñal Tap

MONUMENT VALLEY
1. Most of Ellis Island
2. George Armstrong Custer
3. Fort Sumter
4. George Washington and George Washington Carver
5. White Sands
6. Battery Park
7. Rainbow Bridge
8. Fort McHenry
9. The sequoia
10. The Virgin Islands

BETTER LATE THAN NEVER
1. Byron De La Beckwith
2. Japan
3. Brian Wilson
4. He spoke no English
5. Six (Polonius, Ophelia, Rosencrantz, Guildenstern, Gertrude, and Laertes)

SEPTEMBER 25	SEPTEMBER 26	SEPTEMBER 27

CONCRETE GALOSHES
1. Sonja Henie
2. Harold Lloyd
3. Whoopi Goldberg
4. Betty Grable
5. R2-D2
6. Joe E. Brown
7. John Wayne
8. Al Jolson
9. Groucho Marx and George Burns
10. Tony, Champion, and Trigger

PITCHY KEEN
1. Blake Lewis
2. Clay Aiken
3. Carrie Underwood
4. Taylor Hicks
5. Jordin Sparks
6. Katharine McPhee

RELATIVELY RELATED
1. Sandy Koufax
2. Joshua Malina and Timothy Busfield
3. Mike Myers
4. Custis
5. Boss Hogg and Roscoe P. Coltrane

TRADE COMMISSION
1. Francis Gary Powers
2. They were managers
3. ImClone Systems
4. Dr. J
5. *Trading Spouses*

WHALE KNOWN FACTS
1. Moby Grape
2. Krill
3. Humpback whales
4. The Maori
5. Hippos

STREET BALL
Easy
1. Atlanta
2. Miami
3. Salt Lake City
4. Berlin
Harder
1. St. Louis
2. Knoxville
3. Pittsburgh
4. Arlington, Texas
Yeah, Good Luck
1. Ottawa
2. Daytona Beach
3. Green Bay
4. Sydney

MATCH BOOKS
1. G
2. F
3. A
4. H
5. B
6. C
7. E
8. I
9. D
10. J

ACTING ALONE
Easy
1. Hal Holbrook
2. Sarah Silverman
3. Spalding Gray
4. Lily Tomlin
Harder
1. Billy Crystal
2. Margaret Cho
3. Julia Sweeney
4. Ian McKellen
Yeah, Good Luck
1. Eric Bogosian
2. Robert Morse
3. Victor Borge
4. James Whitmore

X TERMINATIONS
1. Macintosh computers
2. Speed Racer's
3. Lynn Swann
4. Jean Grey (Marvel Girl)
5. John Singer Sargent
6. Clyde Tombaugh
7. Little
8. Douglas Copland
9. Joan of Arc
10. Edward Norton

SEPTEMBER 28

WISE CRACKS
1. *Who's the Boss?*
2. *Family Ties*
3. *Punky Brewster*
4. *The Facts of Life*
5. *Growing Pains*
6. *Silver Spoons*
7. *Good Times*
8. *Mr. Belvedere*
9. *Perfect Strangers*
10. *Full House*

POOR BABY
Easy
1. Gwyneth Paltrow and Chris Martin
2. Julia Roberts
3. Brad Pitt and Angelina Jolie
4. Tom Cruise and Katie Holmes
5. Bruce Willis and Demi Moore
Harder
1. Nicolas Cage
2. Kurt Cobain and Courtney Love
3. Sylvester Stallone
4. David Bowie
5. Jermaine Jackson
Yeah, Good Luck
1. Toni Braxton
2. Jayson Williams
3. John Mellencamp
4. Jason Lee
5. Penn Jillette

SEPTEMBER 29

LOST IN SPACE
Easy
1. Mork
2. Superman
3. Spock (or Tuvok)
Harder
1. Dr. Who
2. ALF
3. The Coneheads
Yeah, Good Luck
1. (*The Powers of*) Matthew Star
2. Gazoo (*The Flintstones*)
3. Dr. Zoidberg (*Futurama*)

SHUT UP AND SING
1. "Barbara Ann" (The Beach Boys)
2. "All I Wanna Do" (Sheryl Crow)
3. "Diamond Dogs" (David Bowie)
4. "Stop!" (Jane's Addiction)
5. "Helter Skelter" (The Beatles)
6. "Chantilly Lace" (The Big Bopper)
7. "Revolution Rock" (The Clash)
8. "Express Yourself" (Madonna)
9. "Money" (Pink Floyd)
10. "Juicy" (The Notorious B.I.G.)

TIDY SUMS
1. *Pretty Woman*
2. Stone Cold Steve Austin
3. *Press Your Luck*
4. Scrooge McDuck
5. Kevin Brown

SEPTEMBER 30

CRASH COURSE
1. Pierre Curie
2. Princess Diana
3. George Patton
4. Tom Mix
5. Karen Silkwood
6. Isadora Duncan (killed by one such scarf)
7. Seymour Cray
8. Mel Ott
9. Grace Kelly
10. T. E. Lawrence (of Arabia)

MALE CALL
1. "If"
2. *Bambi*
3. A tail
4. Wallis Simpson
5. Jack Albertson

TEST PILOT
Easy
1. *The Beverly Hillbillies*
2. *Bewitched*
3. *All in the Family*
4. *24*
5. *The Jetsons*
Harder
1. *Gilligan's Island*
2. *Buffy the Vampire Slayer*
3. *CSI: NY*
4. *The Mary Tyler Moore Show*
5. *Perry Mason*
Yeah, Good Luck
1. *Batman*
2. *Curb Your Enthusiasm*
3. *Petticoat Junction*
4. *Lost in Space*
5. *Gunsmoke*

• 1788 • DEACON WILLIAM BRODIE, an Edinburgh cabinetmaker and city councillor, is hanged on the gallows he himself designed and funded. Brodie, a respectable businessman by day, was an archcriminal by night, a dichotomy that helped inspire Robert Louis Stevenson's *Dr. Jekyll and Mr. Hyde.*

IDENTITY CRISIS

Can you match these actors to their on-screen multiple-personality alter egos? Name the film or TV show for extra credit.

1. Jim Carrey	**A.** "Norma" Bates
2. Sally Field	**B.** Eve Black
3. Andy Kaufman	**C.** Killer Bob
4. Ali Larter	**D.** Tyler Durden
5. Eddie Murphy	**E.** Hank Evans
6. Edward Norton	**F.** Vic Ferrari
7. Anthony Perkins	**G.** Peggy Louisiana
8. Jaleel White	**H.** Buddy Love
9. Ray Wise	**I.** Jessica Sanders
10. Joanne Woodward	**J.** Stefan Urquelle

• 1978 • THE ISLAND NATION of Tuvalu gains independence, making it the world's second-least-populated country, after the Vatican. Tuvalu's capital is the atoll of Funafuti, so Freetown, Sierra Leone, is no longer the only world capital that begins with the letter *F*. . .

A CAPITAL QUIZ

. . . but what's the only country whose capital begins with these letters?

1. Q	2. U	3. I	4. Z

• 1979 • A TWENTY-FOUR-YEAR-OLD WATERBURY, Connecticut, traffic reporter named Chris Berman joins fledgling cable network ESPN, hosting the 3 A.M. edition of *SportsCenter.* He will remain one of the network's most visible anchors for decades.

YOU'RE WITH ME, LEATHER

Using his trademark "Bermanisms," what baseball player has Chris Berman nicknamed . . .

Easy	Harder	Yeah, Good Luck
1. "Corn on the"	1. "Can you see?"	1. "You sank my"
2. "Fields forever"	2. "Supercalifragilisticexpiali"	2. "Nova"
3. "Say it ain't"	3. "Have gun will"	3. "Abraxas"
4. "Eat drink and be"	4. "Supreme Court"	4. "Buy a vowel"
5. "Remember the"	5. "Taco"	5. "Be home"

Answers to the questions on this page can be found on page 433.

OCTOBER 2

• **1871** • MORMON LEADER BRIGHAM YOUNG surrenders to federal authorities on bigamy charges. Actually, he got off easy—with fifty-two wives, I guess there could have been as many as fifty-one (or would it be twenty-six?) bigamy charges.

I DO, I DO, I DO, I DO . . .
Which spouse did these much-married people have in common?

1. Mickey Rooney and Frank Sinatra
2. John Phillips and Dennis Hopper
3. Arlene Dahl and Lana Turner
4. John Huston and Artie Shaw
5. Zsa Zsa Gabor and Magda Gabor

• **1955** • ALFRED HITCHCOCK DIRECTS and introduces the first episode of his CBS anthology *Alfred Hitchcock Presents*. The star, Vera Miles, is at the time one of Hitch's favorites, but he will never quite forgive her for getting pregnant and dropping out of a film of his two years from now.

McGUFFIN READERS
Which Hitchcock movie has the famous set piece involving . . .

Easy	*Harder*	*Yeah, Good Luck*
1. A crop duster	1. A pair of scissors	1. The Statue of Liberty
2. The Golden Gate Bridge	2. A wine cellar key	2. A potato truck
3. A motel shower	3. A cymbal crash	3. Windmills
4. A jungle gym	4. A tennis match	4. A poisoned glass of milk

• **1996** • LANCE ARMSTRONG IS DIAGNOSED with late-stage testicular cancer. Doctors give him only a 3 percent chance of surviving, but he'll go on to beat the cancer with chemotherapy and win seven straight Tours de France.

GO, LANCE, GO

1. What's the only U.S. military branch with the rank of lance corporal?
2. Winston Churchill's World War II plane *Ascalon* was named for whose legendary lance?
3. What makes the Holy Lance, or Spear of Destiny, so holy?
4. What war saw the Light Brigade's infamous lance charge?
5. What U.S. state's official sport, in line with its heraldic-looking flag, is jousting?

Answers to the questions on this page can be found on page 433.

• **1357** • KING DAVID II is released from prison under the Treaty of Berwick, ending the Wars of Scottish Independence.

GREAT SCOTT!

1. What 1975 novel begins, appropriately, with a quote from Scott Joplin?

2. According to Scott Baio's memoir, he lost his virginity to what costar?

3. What band did Scott Weiland join after the breakup of Stone Temple Pilots?

4. The Sharks, the Kings, or the Ducks—longtime Devils defenseman Scott Niedermayer ended his career captaining what NHL team?

5. What Fox News pundit replaced Scott McLellan as White House press secretary?

• **1773** • CAPTAIN COOK IS WELCOMED so warmly upon his first visit to the islands of Tonga that he names them the Friendly Islands. A writer who will live in Tonga some decades later will discover that Cook's "friendly reception" was just part of a local festival and that the chiefs spent most of the feast discussing how they would kill him.

CAN YOU BE MORE PACIFIC?

1. What Pacific country is named after a region of Africa?

2. Which of the Solomon Islands was the site of the 1942–43 military campaign that became a turning point of World War II?

3. What root is the Polynesian staple poi made from?

4. On what South Pacific island would you find Bounty Bay?

5. Papeari, Tahiti, is home to a museum named for what painter?

6. The modern plight of what people was explored in the novel and movie *Once Were Warriors*?

7. New Caledonia is found in Melanesia. What is "old" Caledonia?

8. An award for the best special teams player in college football is named for what Samoan running back?

9. What South Pacific island is called Rapa Nui in its own language?

10. Who wrote the short stories upon which the musical *South Pacific* was based?

• **1951** • SONNY CORLEONE IS VICIOUSLY gunned down at a tollbooth in *The Godfather*. (We know the exact date because of the baseball pennant game on the radio.)

DIE ANOTHER WAY
Give the cause of these memorable movie deaths.

Easy
1. Leonardo DiCaprio, *Titanic*
2. Kirk Douglas, *Spartacus*
3. Margaret Hamilton, *The Wizard of Oz*
4. Debra Winger, *Terms of Endearment*
5. Slim Pickens, *Dr. Strangelove*

Harder
1. Wallace Shawn, *The Princess Bride*
2. Steve Buscemi, *Fargo*
3. Samuel Jackson, *Deep Blue Sea*
4. Graham Chapman, *Monty Python's The Meaning of Life*
5. Jack Nicholson, *One Flew Over the Cuckoo's Nest*

Yeah, Good Luck
1. Susan Hayward, *I Want to Live!*
2. David Warner, *The Omen*
3. Yaphet Kotto, *Live and Let Die*
4. Vera Clouzot, *Les Diaboliques*
5. Dan Hedaya, *Blood Simple*

Answers to the questions on this page can be found on page 433.

OCTOBER 4

• **1883** • The original Orient Express runs for the first time, from Paris to the Romanian city of Giurgiu. Ah, glamorous Giurgiu.

EXPRESS YOURSELF

1. What director's first theatrical film was *The Sugarland Express*?
2. What future showman was a rider for the Pony Express in 1860?
3. What unusual item do the cast members of Andrew Lloyd Webber's *Starlight Express* wear throughout the play?
4. What question from American Express ads was first asked by actor Norman Fell?
5. *Midnight Express* is set in a prison in what country?
6. What U.S. metropolis's daily paper is the *Express-News*?
7. In a nod to a Frank Sinatra film, what baseball pitcher was nicknamed "the Express"?
8. What experimental writer's "Cut-Up Trilogy" ended with 1964's *Nova Express*?
9. What tiny item does the protagonist of *The Polar Express* choose as a Christmas gift?
10. What quarterback signed what was then the largest contract in sports history in 1984 with the USFL's Los Angeles Express?

• **1959** • Allen Kaprow's performance art series *18 Happenings in 6 Parts* begins at New York's Reuben Gallery. This was the first "Happening" of 1960s pop art—and it freaks me out!

POP GOES THE EASEL
What pop artists made their names with these favorite subjects?

Easy	Harder	Yeah, Good Luck
1. Blown-up comic panels	1. Flags and bull's-eyes	1. The "Radiant Baby"
2. Campbell's soup cans	2. The word "LOVE"	2. Rows of diner baked goods
3. L.A. swimming pools	3. Giant soft sculpture	3. "Combines"

• **1986** • Dan Rather is attacked and beaten on Park Avenue by two assailants repeating the mysterious question "Kenneth, what is the frequency?"

WHAT'S THE FREQUENCY, KENNETH?
No, you tell me. Give the frequency of these events.

1. The U.S. Census	4. *The Economist* being published	7. High tide, most places
2. The changing of the guard at Buckingham Palace, for most of the year	5. *Pon farr*, the Vulcan mating urge	8. Presidential elections in Mexico
3. The Ryder Cup	6. Old Faithful erupting, on average	9. Muslims' *salah* prayers
		10. A solstice

Answers to the questions on this page can be found on page 434.

• **1916** • THE KARABOVSK BRIDGE over the Amur River opens, completing the 5,800-mile Trans-Siberian Railway from Moscow to the Sea of Japan, the world's longest rail route.

EYE OF THE TAIGA

1. What name did Alexander Solzhenitsyn coin for the Stalin-era prison camps dotted like islands across Siberia?

2. What lake, the world's deepest, is called the Blue Eye of Siberia?

3. What happened at Tunguska, Siberia, at 7:17 A.M. on June 30, 1908?

4. What movie's climax is the retrieval of the second half of the "Triangle of Light" from a ruined

Siberian city?

5. Who was Dima, discovered in northeastern Siberian permafrost in 1977?

• **1949** • AMERICAN HELENE HANFF sends her first letter to Frank Doel of London's antiquarian bookshop Marks & Co. This kicks off a twenty-year transatlantic friendship, immortalized in the book, play, and film *84 Charing Cross Road*. Sadly, Marks & Co. is gone today, and 84 Charing Cross Road is an ugly wine bar franchise.

FAKE BOOKS
Do you know your fictional bookshops as well as your real ones?

1. Meg Ryan's children's bookstore in *You've Got Mail* is named for the 1940 comedy on which *You've Got Mail* is based. What's the name of her bookstore?

2. What fictional hero does his

book shopping at Flourish & Blotts?

3. Who's the only actor ever to win an Oscar for portraying a bookseller?

4. What comedian played a bookstore owner in the sitcom *These*

Friends of Mine, before the show was renamed after her?

5. What kind of specialty bookshop did Hugh Grant own in the 1999 film *Notting Hill*?

• **2004** • RODNEY DANGERFIELD HAS TUGGED on his too-tight collar for the last time, passing away after heart surgery. His tombstone reads "RODNEY DANGERFIELD—THERE GOES THE NEIGHBORHOOD."

GENTLEMAN COLLARS

1. Which president has his full collar and lapels, and not just his face, carved into Mount Rushmore?

2. For what world leader is the sherwani jacket, with its charac-

teristic upturned collar, usually named?

3. According to ads, what product targeted "ring around the collar"?

4. Daniel Whitney is the real

name of what Blue Collar Comedy Tour star?

5. What Japanese maestro conducts in a turtleneck rather than a shirt and bow tie?

Answers to the questions on this page can be found on page 434.

• **1807** • SIR HUMPHRY DAVY discovers potassium, the first element to be isolated by electrolysis. Davy has coined the name from "potash," but a couple years from now a couple Germans will think the name "kalium" more dignified, which is why potassium's periodic table symbol is a *K*.

K MART

1. What anesthetic has been given the street name "Special K"?
2. Who was the only U.S. president to have *K* as a middle initial?
3. In the CMYK model used in color printing, what color does *K* represent?
4. Who called his debut solo album *AmeriKKKa's Most Wanted?*

5. Who are Koby, Kory, Kacy, and Kody?
6. Whose works are indexed with "K numbers," beginning with K 1a, which he wrote at age 5?
7. Who wrote *The Castle*, about a man called K., and *The Trial*, about Joseph K.?
8. What word did George Eastman coin because, he said, he found the letter *K* to be "a strong, incisive sort of letter"?

9. The world's second highest mountain, K2, was originally named for what Englishman who first surveyed it?
10. What movie featured the line "Strange things are afoot at the Circle K"?

• **1966** • LSD IS BANNED in the United States.

ACID TEST

1. What's the common household name of acetylsalicylic acid?
2. What two acids did alchemists mix to make the gold-dissolving reagent called *aqua regia*?

3. What acid, when taken by prospective mothers, can prevent spina bifida in their babies?
4. What color will acid turn litmus paper?

5. Onions cause crying because of what acid forming on the surface of the eye?

• **2000** • SYLVESTER STALLONE'S REMAKE of *Get Carter* hits theaters. An online poll will later name it the worst remake in movie history.

TAKE TWO
What movies were remade as . . .

Easy
1. *The Birdcage*
2. *The Preacher's Wife*
3. *An Affair to Remember*
4. *Flubber*
5. *The Departed*

Harder
1. *The Point of No Return*
2. *The Truth About Charlie*
3. *Heaven Can Wait*
4. *Sommersby*
5. *Meet Joe Black*

Yeah, Good Luck
1. *The Last House on the Left*
2. *Ali—Fear Eats the Soul*
3. *A Pocketful of Miracles*
4. *Down and Out in Beverly Hills*
5. *Walk, Don't Run*

Answers to the questions on this page can be found on page 434.

• 1916 • IN THE MOST LOPSIDED U.S. college football score ever, Georgia Tech beats the Cumberland Bulldogs 222–0. Tech scores only 42 in the fourth quarter—way to ease up there, coach. In fact, the victorious Engineer coach is none other than John Heisman, later of Trophy fame.

CUP WITH PEOPLE

Whom are these sports trophies named after?

1. Baseball's "Commissioner's Award" for good character and charitable service
2. The Super Bowl trophy
3. The NHL trophy for best regular-season defenseman

4. Major League Baseball's Outstanding Designated Hitter
5. ATP Humanitarian of the Year
6. The Daytona 500 winner
7. National Thoroughbred Racing Association awards

8. PGA Tour Player of the Year
9. Best offensive player in Division I-AA football
10. The U.S. Basketball Writers Association college Player of the Year

• 2003 • ARNOLD SCHWARZENEGGER, whose previous political experience amounted to rescuing Alyssa Milano from a South American dictator in *Commando*, is elected governor of California.

PUMPED UP

Here's some "muscular" trivia, in honor of the Governator.

1. What activity do you perform with the body's "strongest" muscle—the one that can generate the most force?
2. Whose father was named "Poopdeck Pappy"?
3. Muscles come in three varieties: skeletal, smooth, and a third specialized type found only in what body part?
4. The name for what medical condition may have originated with Baseball Hall of Famer Charles Radbourn?

5. What bizarre film cycle by media artist (and Björk boyfriend) Matthew Barney takes its name from the muscle that raises and lowers the testicles?
6. Though he was never called the "Muscles from Brussels," Brussels Observatory founder Adolphe Quételet is the inventor of what, also called the Quételet Index?
7. The "Monkeemobile," from the Monkees' TV show, was a modified version of what classic

muscle car?
8. What chemical (and yogurt ingredient) was recently discovered to be an important muscle fuel and not the cause of fatigue it was long believed to be?
9. What shoulder muscle gets its name from its triangular shape?
10. Who owned a boa constrictor named Muscles?

Answers to the questions on this page can be found on page 435.

OCTOBER 8

• 1600 • THE TINY NATION of San Marino adopts the world's first written constitution.

CONSTITUTION HALL

1. What was the first state to ratify the U.S. Constitution?

2. Which word in the Preamble to the Constitution was originally handwritten with the British spelling but is most often transcribed with the more modern American spelling?

3. What two kinds of judicial punishment are prohibited by the Eighth Amendment?

4. What Pennsylvanian refused to sign the Declaration of Independence but *did* sign the Constitution?

5. How many articles are there in the unamended Constitution?

6. Which constitutional clause requires states to enforce one another's judicial rulings?

7. What was accomplished by the only constitutional amendment ratified by a series of state conventions?

8. According to Article 2, what's the minimum age for a U.S. president?

9. The "establishment" clause refers to what establishment?

10. Which of the thirteen colonies didn't attend the Constitutional Convention and was the last to ratify?

• 1935 • BANDLEADER OZZIE NELSON marries his singer, Harriet Hilliard. The long-running sitcom based on Ozzie and Harriet's family life will begin airing in 1944, though their sons, David and Ricky, will be played by actors, not the real boys, until 1949.

PRICKLY PAIRS
Name the real-life married couple in the casts of these TV shows.

Easy
1. *Ink*
2. *Mission: Impossible*
3. *L.A. Law*
4. *One Tree Hill*
5. *Roseanne*

Harder
1. *24*
2. *Webster*
3. *Deep Space Nine*
4. *St. Elsewhere*
5. *Melrose Place*

Yeah, Good Luck
1. *He & She*
2. *Watch Over Me*
3. *Bridget Loves Bernie*
4. *Ben Casey*
5. *JAG*

• 1999 • MUHAMMAD ALI'S DAUGHTER Laila makes her boxing debut, knocking out April Fowler in the first round.

FORT KNOCKS

1. Who first appeared in Walter Lantz's 1940 cartoon "Knock Knock"?

2. What cable network does Katherine Heigl work for in the film *Knocked Up*?

3. Jay-Z's ghetto anthem "Hard-Knock Life" samples a song from what Broadway hit?

4. What Stephen King novel is named for a children's rhyme about strange creatures who come "knocking at the door" every night?

5. What abdominal nerve cluster paralyzes the diaphragm when someone has the wind knocked out of him?

Answers to the questions on this page can be found on page 435.

OCTOBER 9

• 1910 • WITH TY COBB and Nap Lajoie in a tight race for the American League batting title and Lajoie's Indians playing St. Louis in a doubleheader, the Browns decide to lie down and let Lajoie hit safely in every at-bat, so the hated Cobb will lose the batting title.

STRENGTH IN NUMBERS
What ballplayer is associated with these legendary numbers?

Easy	Harder	Yeah, Good Luck
1. 755	1. 1.12	1. .424
2. 56	2. 511	2. 1,406
3. 61*	3. 4,256	3. 262
4. 2,632	4. 5,714	4. 2,297

• 1974 • OSKAR SCHINDLER DIES in Frankfurt and is buried in Jerusalem's Mount Zion cemetery.

I HAVE A LITTLE LIST

1. What car-racing aficionado, who has also *portrayed* a race car on-screen, is the only household name on Nixon's original "enemies list"?
2. "Things that almost rhyme with 'peas,' " on September 18, 1985, was the very first what?
3. Who calls her reality show *Life on the D-List*?
4. Joseph McCarthy rocketed to fame by announcing he had a list of fifty-seven Communists currently employed where?
5. At a 1900 Paris conference, mathematician David Hilbert produced his famous list of twenty-three what?

• 1992 • RIDLEY SCOTT'S COLUMBUS biopic hits screens. It was originally titled *Christopher Columbus*, but another company had already registered that title—and four variants—for its competing Columbus project (starring Tom Selleck as King Ferdinand!). Scott is forced to rename his film *1492: Conquest of Paradise*.

TITLE INSURANCE
Can you match up these otherwise unrelated movies and give the title they shared?

1. Harold Lloyd, 1925
2. The Marx Brothers, 1931
3. Fred Astaire/Ginger Rogers, 1937
4. Gene Tierney/Don Ameche, 1943
5. Richard Widmark/Sidney Poitier, 1950
6. Jose Ferrer/Zsa Zsa Gabor, 1952
7. Burt Lancaster/Katharine Hepburn, 1956
8. Jacques Tati, 1971
9. Dustin Hoffman/Geena Davis, 1992
10. James Spader/Holly Hunter, 1996

A. Cary Grant/Ginger Rogers, 1952
B. Warren Beatty/Julie Christie, 1978
C. Gene Hackman/Kevin Costner, 1987
D. Marlon Brando/Matthew Broderick, 1990
E. Matt Damon/Danny DeVito, 1997
F. Benicio del Toro/Michael Douglas, 2000
G. Nicole Kidman/Ewan McGregor, 2001
H. Jet Li, 2002
I. Richard Gere/Jennifer Lopez, 2004
J. Matt Dillon/Terrence Howard, 2004

• **1939** • A WOMAN NAMED Eleanor Rigby dies in Liverpool at age 44. Her tombstone will be discovered decades later at Saint Peter's Parish in Woolton, just a few feet from the spot where John Lennon first meets Paul McCartney—but there's no evidence that this Eleanor actually inspired the song of the same name.

WHO ARE YOU? I REALLY WANNA KNOW

Answer these questions about people in songs.

1. What state did Chuck Berry's "Johnny B. Goode" hail from?

2. What title character do we meet down at the New Amsterdam striking up "a conversation with this black-haired flamenco dancer"?

3. Whom did Lou Reed find "sweet," Beck consider a "soldier," and Perry Farrell quote as saying, "I'm done with Sergio. He treats me like a rag doll"?

4. How old is ABBA's "Dancing Queen"?

5. What 1983 hit did Quincy Jones want to rename, fearing that everyone would assume the title character was the tennis superstar?

6. What swashbuckling rogue from a 1921 novel does Freddie Mercury ask to "do the fandango"?

7. What title character in a 1970 song is named for a moon princess in Persian poetry and based on George Harrison's wife, Pattie?

8. What's the name of the girl to whom Bruce Springsteen insists he's

"Born to Run"?

9. What title character of a 2000 hit has become hip-hop slang for an obsessive fanboy?

10. What do these songs have in common: "Behind the Wall of Sleep" by the Smithereens, "Slow Turning" by John Hiatt, and "Funky Cold Medina" by Tone-Loc?

• **1961** • THE FIRST EXPANSION DRAFT in National League history stocks the Houston and New York Mets rosters. Among the selections are future manager of the year Don Zimmer and one-vote-away-from-the-Hall-of-Fame first baseman Gil Hodges.

EXPANSION DRAFT

Name these pairs of sports teams. In each pair, one team name can be spelled out (in order) in the letters of the longer team name.

1. In 1988, Tom Chambers switched between what two teams as the first unrestricted free agent in NBA history?

2. What two teams met in the World

Series that featured Carlton Fisk's dramatic game six home run?

3. Grant Fuhr and Marc Denis, the top two goalies on the most-games-played-in-a-season list, set those

records while playing for what teams?

4. What two ABA teams applied to join the NBA in 1975 but were restrained from doing so by a court order?

• **1985** • HOOPS STAR DRAZEN PETROVIC scores a world record 112 points in a Yugoslavian League game against SMELT Olimpja.

INTERNATIONAL BASKETBALL ASSOCIATION

In what foreign country were these NBA stars born?

Easy	*Harder*	*Yeah, Good Luck*
1. Dirk Nowitzki	**1.** Steve Nash	**1.** Manute Bol
2. Yao Ming	**2.** Patrick Ewing	**2.** Sarunas Marciulionis
3. Manu Ginobili	**3.** Pau Gasol	**3.** Vitaly Potapenko
4. Hakeem Olajuwon	**4.** Rik Smits	**4.** Michael Olowokandi

Answers to the questions on this page can be found on page 436.

• 1932 • ARCHAEOLOGIST AMEDEO MAIURI announces that he's discovered the grotto of the famed Cumaean Sibyl, the prophetess who guided Aeneas to hell in Virgil's *Aeneid*.

SIBYL RITES

1. Augury, in ancient Rome, was the art of foretelling the future by studying what?
2. The Pythia was the priestess at what most famous Greek oracle?
3. What Trojan princess was cursed by Apollo so that no one would ever believe her prophecies?
4. What mythical ship could prophesy the future because its bow contained an oak timber taken from the oracle at Dodona?
5. What punishment did the blind prophet Tiresias receive for seven years because he clubbed two snakes he found having sex?

• 1992 • DEION SANDERS, hoping to become the first person ever to play in two different pro sports on the same day, flies from Atlanta to Pittsburgh after a Falcons game, arriving just in time for the Braves' championship series game against the Pirates . . . but Braves manager Bobby Cox keeps him on the bench.

JOCK OF ALL TRADES

1. What future Yankees Hall of Famer was drafted by the San Diego Padres, the Minnesota Vikings, *and* the Atlanta Hawks in 1973?
2. What first president of the NFL was also an outfielder who drove in the winning run in the Reds-Cubs "double no-hitter" of 1917?
3. What NFL legend and actor is also a member of the Lacrosse Hall of Fame?
4. Baseball is sometimes said to have been the "fifth-best sport" of what legend, the first UCLA Bruin ever to letter in four sports?
5. Who won two track golds at the 1932 Olympics before rattling off a record seventeen straight amateur golf victories?
6. Who injured his hip in a playoff game against the Bengals in 1991, only to hit a home run in his first at-bat back for the White Sox in 1993?
7. Who took a year off from the Dallas Cowboys in 1979 to rack up a 6–0 record as a boxer?
8. What two-time National League Cy Young winner in the 1990s had also been drafted by the NHL's L.A. Kings?
9. Who won a national basketball championship with the Tar Heels in 1994 before she ditched basketball for track?
10. Who's the only Heisman Trophy winner ever to play in the NBA Finals?

• 2005 • HURRICANE VINCE, already unusual for having developed off the Moroccan coast, makes landfall over Spain, becoming the only tropical storm ever to strike mainland Europe.

STORMY WEATHER

1. What became the world's third nuclear power with the Hurricane test of 1952?
2. What actress, an Oscar nominee for *Nashville*, sings backup on Bob Dylan's "Hurricane"?
3. What wading bird is the mascot of the Miami Hurricanes?
4. What tropical fruit provides the syrup in a "hurricane" rum cocktail?
5. What comedian was sharing the stage with Kanye West when he made his "George Bush doesn't care about black people" comment at the 2005 Concert for Hurricane Relief?

Answers to the questions on this page can be found on page 436.

OCTOBER 12

• **1492** • COLUMBUS *DOESN'T DISCOVER AMERICA*. Sure, he takes all the credit, but land is first sighted by Rodrigo de Triana, the sailor who happens to be up in the crow's nest of the *Pinta* at two in the morning.

EGGS MARKS THE SPOT
Go out on a limb with this quiz about other famous nests.

1. What TV comedy show calls its set "The Eagle's Nest"?
2. What kind of nest is a vespiary?
3. What Celtics legend got his nickname from a character in *One Flew over the Cuckoo's Nest*?
4. What bird is the symbol of The Hague, since it's considered good luck in the Netherlands to have one nest in your house's chimney?
5. The Boar's Nest is the oldest restaurant in what fictional county?

• **1810** • THE FIRST OKTOBERFEST IS HELD, as Bavaria's crown prince Ludwig I holds a massive horse race to celebrate his wedding to Princess Therese. (Back then, you apparently needed a real excuse for massive public drunkenness. Even in Bavaria.)

LIFE IN THE FEST LANE
Celebrate good times—come on!—with these festival questions.

1. What is followed by the Eid ul-Fitr festival?
2. What game takes its name from the Basque words for "merry festival"?
3. The Woodstock Festival was actually moved from the town of Woodstock to what town forty miles away?
4. Hemingway's *The Sun Also Rises* is titled *Fiesta* in the U.K. What city's famous festival does the title refer to?
5. What's the most prestigious prize given at the Cannes Film Festival?

• **1992** • THE NIKOPAKA FESTA COMMITTEE of Yoshii, Japan, sets a new record for the world's longest sushi roll. This *kappa maki* is exactly one kilometer long.

A RAW DEAL

1. What vegetable—which, ironically, is almost never eaten raw today—takes its name from the Narragansett for "a green thing eaten raw"?
2. How can you quickly tell a raw egg from a boiled one without cracking the shell?
3. What breakfast dish of uncooked oats and fruit was introduced by Dr. Bircher-Benner at his Swiss hospital in 1900?
4. According to the old belief, raw oysters should be eaten only in months that have what letter in their name?
5. What French name do we give to the dish that is, ironically, called raw *filet américain* in France?

Answers to the questions on this page can be found on page 436.

OCTOBER 13

• **1962** • *Who's Afraid of Virginia Woolf?* opens on Broadway. The Pulitzer committee will try to award it the Pulitzer Prize for Drama, only to have Columbia University's trustees veto the selection, cowed by the play's edgy content.

WHO'S AFRAID OF . . .
What are the fears of these things called?

Easy	Harder	Yeah, Good Luck
1. Heights	1. Sunlight	1. Cats
2. Enclosed spaces	2. Death	2. Nudity
3. Spiders	3. Blood	3. Pain
4. Foreigners	4. Fire	4. Clowns
5. Open or public places	5. Public speaking	5. Childbirth

• **1972** • Uruguayan Air Force Flight 571, flying a Montevideo rugby team to a match in Chile, crashes in the Andes. The survivors subsist for two months by eating the frozen corpses of their dead teammates.

EAT ME!

1. On what island did the practice of eating human brains and organs lead to the spread of a disease called kuru?
2. Who made the satirical *Modest Proposal* to fight poverty by eating Irish babies?
3. The Donner Party was trapped by a snowstorm in what mountain range?
4. What was the occupation of the man whose liver Hannibal Lecter ate with fava beans?
5. The word "cannibal" comes from the same root as what geographic feature?
6. Sweeney Todd was "the demon barber of" what London thoroughfare?
7. The University of Colorado food court is named for what first American ever to be jailed for cannibalism?
8. What's the only Shakespeare play to feature cannibalism?
9. What movie was adapted from the novel *Make Room! Make Room!* but had its title changed so it wouldn't be confused with *Make Room for Daddy?*
10. Which of the planets is named for the Roman god who ate all his children?

• **2006** • *Infamous*, the second film version of Truman Capote's *In Cold Blood* snooping, is finally released. It was held back a year to avoid a showdown with Philip Seymour Hoffman's Oscar-winning performance in *Capote*.

MULTIPLEXITY
Give the other similarly themed, easily confused films that were being developed at the same time as . . .

Easy	Harder	Yeah, Good Luck
1. *A Bug's Life*	1. *Madagascar*	1. *Prefontaine*
2. *Tombstone*	2. *The Prestige*	2. *Dangerous Liaisons*
3. *Deep Impact*	3. *The Truman Show*	3. *First Daughter*
4. *Dante's Peak*	4. *Mission to Mars*	4. *Dr. Strangelove*

Answers to the questions on this page can be found on page 437.

• **1066** • THE NORMANS WIN the Battle of Hastings; William the Wanna-Be-Conqueror gets to simplify his nickname. Harold II, king of the Saxons, dies in the battle—allegedly from an arrow through the eye. Ouch.

WAR BONDS

Match these famous battles to their winning and losing commanders.

1. Actium	A. Alexander the Great	a. Mark Antony
2. Bosworth Field	B. Ulysses S. Grant	b. Napoleon Bonaparte
3. El Alamein	C. George Meade	c. Darius III
4. Gettysburg	D. Bernard Montgomery	d. Erich von Falkenhayn
5. Issus	E. Chester Nimitz	e. A. S. Johnston
6. Midway	F. Octavian	f. Robert E. Lee
7. Shiloh	G. Philippe Pétain	g. Leonidas I
8. Thermopylae	H. Earl of Richmond	h. Richard III
9. Verdun	I. Duke of Wellington	i. Erwin Rommel
10. Waterloo	J. Xerxes the Great	j. Isoroku Yamamoto

• **1937** • SERGEI PROKOFIEV'S *Lieutenant Kije* Suite premieres in the U.S. Even if you don't know Prokofiev, you've probably heard part of this suite—it provided the melody for the chorus of Sting's song "Russians."

THE SUITES HEREAFTER

1. What's the only planet left out of Gustav Holst's suite *The Planets*?
2. Ferde Grofé's best-known suite is based on the 1916 trip he took to watch the sun rise at what landmark?
3. Edvard Grieg's *Peer Gynt* suites come from the music he wrote for what playwright in 1876?
4. The famous 1892 suite containing "Russian," "Arabian," and "Chinese" dances is abridged from what ballet?
5. What famous Aaron Copland suite borrows part of its melody from the Shaker hymn "Simple Gifts"?

• **2004** • *MARMADUKE*, AMERICA'S FAVORITE completely unfunny one-panel comic starring a Great Dane, celebrates its fiftieth anniversary.

DOG PATCH

In what newspaper comic strip would you find these canine characters?

Easy	*Harder*	*Yeah, Good Luck*
1. Sandy	1. Daisy	1. Snert
2. Ruff	2. Earl	2. Roscoe
3. Snoopy	3. Farley, Edgar, Dixie	3. Puddles
4. Odie	4. Barfy and Sam	4. Fuzz
5. Dogbert	5. Otto	5. Louie

Answers to the questions on this page can be found on page 437.

• **1754** • The song "God Save the Queen" is first published, in a British magazine. Today, it's the national anthem of the United Kingdom, the "royal anthem" of Commonwealth nations like Canada, and, oddly, the national anthem of Liechtenstein. (The Liechtensteinians gave it new lyrics and call it "High above the young Rhine.")

COUNTRY MUSIC
What nation's anthems are quoted here?

Easy

1. "You are the See of Peter, who in Rome shed his blood."
2. "How can one count the blessings of the Nile for mankind?"
3. "Like a rock the Khmer race is eternal."
4. "True patriot love in all our sons command."
5. "Let us build our new Great Wall!"

Harder

1. "Live eternally within the life and the glory of Italy."
2. "In the thunder dragon kingdom, adorned with sandal woods . . ."
3. "Immortality's symbol—the cedar—is her pride."
4. "United people from Rumova to Maputo!"
5. "Prince of Orange am I, free and fearless."

Yeah, Good Luck

1. "The worthy sons of the soil, which Pichincha on high is adorning . . ."
2. "Your flag is a splendor of sky crossed with a band of snow; and there can be seen, in its sacred depths, five pale blue stars."
3. "I was born a princess, a maiden neutral between two nations. I am the only remaining daughter of the Carolingian empire."
4. "Their blood has washed out their foul footstep's pollution."
5. "The land of our fathers bestowed upon us all, from Zambezi to Limpopo."

• **1952** • E. B. White publishes a simple "hymn to the barn" he calls *Charlotte's Web*. It will go on to become the bestselling children's paperback of all time—putting generations of kids off bacon forever.

LITERARY LEGS

1. Whose first pet was a giant talking spider named Aragog?
2. Who originated the title role in Broadway's *Kiss of the Spider Woman*?
3. What son of the sky god Nyame is the trickster spider of much African myth?
4. What James Patterson detective first appeared in his novel *Along Came a Spider*?
5. In Greek myth, what woman lost a tapestry-weaving contest to Athena and was turned into a spider for her conceit?

Answers to the questions on this page can be found on page 437.

OCTOBER 16

• **1814** • NINE PEOPLE ARE KILLED as thousands of barrels of beer from the Meux and Company Brewers flood central London.

BREWTOPIA

1. What musical instrument is the trademark of Guinness?

2. What city is home to Germany's annual Oktoberfest celebration?

3. Who made this endorsement? "I had this beer brewed just for me. I think it's the best I've ever tasted. And I've tasted a lot. I think you'll like it, too."

4. What "smells like a beer," according to Billy Joel's "Piano Man"?

5. What Mexican beer got its name because it was created to commemorate the dawn of the twentieth century?

6. Which team won only two "Bud Bowls" over the event's eight-year life?

7. What kind of grain is malted to make nearly all modern beer?

8. Who was sentenced to jail for treason for leading the Beer Hall Putsch?

9. According to its longtime slogan, what city did Schlitz beer make famous?

10. Which signer of the Declaration of Independence owned a successful brewery?

• **1991** • BOXER GEORGE FOREMAN names his second daughter "Freeda George." Though Freeda will be the only one of his five daughters to bear her father's name, she has a sister Georgetta and five brothers, all named George. George, Sr., likes to joke that he still forgets their names.

MISTAKEN IDENTITY

These pairs of people pronounce their names the same but spell them differently. What name is shared by . . .

1. The author of "The Outcasts of Poker Flats" and the pro wrestler called "the Hit Man"

2. The creator of *The X-Files* and a longtime Minnesota Vikings wide receiver

3. The lone American buried in Red Square and the Lone Ranger

4. The English king who cracked down on witches and the actor who fell for a witch in *Bell, Book and Candle*

5. The actress who created the stage role of Peter Pan and the actress who created the screen role of Octopussy

6. The novelty bandleader who wrote a "William Tell Overture" adaptation for kitchen utensils and the director of *Adaptation*

7. The playwright of *The Alchemist* and the Canadian sprinter whose gold medal turned to lead in 1988

8. The Cleveland point guard who still leads the NBA in all-time free-throw percentage and the actor who played Skippy on *Family Ties*

9. The onetime cohost of *The PTL Club* and the onetime cochair of the Iraq Study Group

10. The man who replaced Craig Kilborn in 1999 and the man who replaced Hal "Green Lantern" Jordan in 1984

Answers to the questions on this page can be found on page 438.

• **1956** • AFTER CHATTING ABOUT breast-feeding at a church picnic, seven suburban Chicago moms meet at Mary White's home to continue the conversation. Their little circle will grow into La Leche League International.

ACHTUNG BABY

1. Meconium makes up a baby's first what?

2. What denomination of money is the baby swimming toward on the cover of Nirvana's *Nevermind*?

3. What was theologically disavowed in a 2007 Vatican document called "The Hope of Salvation for Infants Who Die Without Being Baptized"?

4. What was the 1928 claim to fame of Ann Turner Cook, today a Tampa mystery novelist?

5. According to the credits of her series, what TV baby is worth $847.63?

6. Who was the first baby to be depicted in wax in Madame Tussaud's?

7. What Stevie Wonder song ends with the sounds of his daughter Aisha playing in the bath?

8. According to the Social Security Administration, what has been America's most popular baby girl name for the past ten years running?

9. What letter did the media use to identify the baby in the Mary Beth Whitehead surrogate case of 1987?

10. What 1915 Irish novel begins with "baby tuckoo" meeting a "moocow"?

• **1966** • ON THE VERY FIRST *Hollywood Squares*, Paul Lynde isn't in the center square. Instead, it's Ernest Borgnine . . . whom I've always considered to be the straight Paul Lynde.

STUCK IN THE MIDDLE WITH YOU

1. What kind of device works because it has a part called a "gnomon" at its center?

2. What is the seldom-used last name of *Malcolm in the Middle* and his family?

3. What two NBAers, who can both play center, shared *Sports Illustrated* Sportsmen of the Year honors in 2003?

4. Whose castle stands in the middle of Disneyland?

5. What two kinds of particles make up the nucleus of an atom?

6. The U.S.'s center of population was in eastern Maryland at the time of the first census, but it's since moved seven states westward. What state is it in today?

7. What's in the center of a Pay-Day bar?

8. What's the name for the infinitely dense region at the center of a black hole?

9. What does New York's Goat Island sit smack dab in the middle of?

10. In Dante's *Inferno*, what biblical character dangles from the middle of Lucifer's three mouths in the center of hell?

Answers to the questions on this page can be found on page 438.

OCTOBER 18

• **1964** • COMEDIAN JACKIE MASON is banned from *The Ed Sullivan Show* when Ed thinks he sees Jackie giving him the finger on air.

DIGITAL DOMAIN
Ten finger questions, one for each finger.

1. What author's only screenplay was 1953's *The 5,000 Fingers of Dr. T*?

2. What future Motown legend played drums on Stevie Wonder's hit "Fingertips"?

3. Who would perform the penance act *yubistume*, slicing off joints of the little finger?

4. What vegetable is sometimes called a "lady's finger"?

5. What's the only vowel on a typewriter keyboard's "home row," where the fingers rest?

6. Rollie Fingers was only the second relief pitcher in the Baseball Hall of Fame. Who was the first?

7. How many fingers did E.T. have on each hand?

8. What famous logo first appeared on 1972's *Sticky Fingers*?

9. What country is led by Luiz Inácio Lula da Silva, who lost his left pinky in a 1964 factory accident?

10. What comedian produces his own albums via SUperFInger Entertainment?

• **1985** • PLAYERS FIRST VIE to save Princess Toadstool, as the first *Super Mario Bros.* game is released in the United States. Sales are super as well—the game will go on to become the bestselling video game of all time.

"SUPER" FRIENDS

1. What team has appeared in a record eight Super Bowls?

2. What's the result of Morgan Spurlock's first McDonald's meal in his documentary *Super Size Me*?

3. Eyebrows, armpits, or toenails—the word "supercilious" is derived from a Latin word for what part of the body?

4. What was the United States' top-selling toy in 1991 and 1992?

5. What comedian is the brother of faux daredevil "Super Dave" Osbourne?

6. Under what condition does a metal like tin or aluminum become superconductive?

7. What does the *G* stand for in Super G alpine skiing?

8. What's the name on Fogell's fake ID in the movie *Superbad*?

9. Todd Haynes's banned film *Superstar* retells whose life story using Barbie dolls?

10. What colorful object in the constellation Taurus was left behind by the SN 1054 supernova?

11. What is the name of Superboy's pet dog?

12. What teammate did Jim Rice once call "Chicken Man" for his superstitiously eating chicken before every game?

13. Because of its "Super Freak" sample, what 1990 hit credited Rick James as a cowriter?

14. What two TV series did Jared Padalecki and Jensen Ackles, respectively, leave in order to star in *Supernatural*?

15. Which day of the week is called "Super" in election years, when a large number of states all hold presidential primaries on the same day?

Answers to the questions on this page can be found on page 438.

• **1660** • Soldiers Daniel Axtel and Francis Hacker are hanged for their roles in the execution of King Charles I, making them the only Britons ever executed for regicide. What about the guy who hanged *them*? Is he a regicidicide?

MONARCHY IN THE U.K.

1. What's the only regnal name used by a British king since 1700 that wasn't George or Edward?
2. Queen Elizabeth owns more than a dozen dogs of what Pembrokeshire breed?
3. What nickname did Edward I receive for his then-freakishly tall height of 6 feet, 2 inches?
4. What's the only movie role that's gotten three different performers Oscar nominations?

5. What executed American shares his name with the Scottish manservant with whom Queen Victoria was rumored to have had an affair?
6. The red-and-white-rose emblem seen on British seals and coins was the emblem of which royal house?
7. Which monarch was called "Lackland," for having inherited no estate?

8. Who's the only monarch since the Norman Conquest to have three children inherit the throne?
9. For which New Testament saint is the British royal court popularly named?
10. The only two of Shakespeare's history plays whose titles label them as "Tragedies" are about kings with what name?

• **1999** • Martha Stewart Living Omnimedia goes public on the New York Stock Exchange and makes its founder and CEO a billionaire by the end of the trading day.

CEILING WHACKS
Answer these questions about women who broke the glass ceiling.

1. Who was both the first woman CEO of a Fortune 500 company and the only one ever to bring down a president?
2. America's wealthiest woman not named "Walton" is Abigail Johnson, who runs what Boston-based financial services company?
3. What was the last name of the founder and longtime chairman of Mary Kay Cosmetics?
4. Until Carly Fiorina's 2005 ouster, what was the largest company ever run by a woman?
5. In 2007, who overtook eBay CEO Meg Whitman to become America's wealthiest self-made woman?

• **2003** • Mother Teresa is beatified by Pope John Paul II.

FOUR SAINTS IN THREE ACTS
Who is the patron saint of . . .

Easy	*Harder*	*Yeah, Good Luck*
1. Animals	1. Children	1. Breast cancer
2. Scotland	2. Kings	2. Gibraltar
3. Lost causes	3. The East Indies	3. Astronomy
4. Lovers	4. Dancers	4. Firefighters

Answers to the questions on this page can be found on page 439.

OCTOBER 20

• **1942** • Actor Earl Hindman is born in Arizona. He will become best known for playing Wilson, the avuncular but always half-obscured neighbor on the Tim Allen sitcom *Home Improvement*.

FACE OFF
What live-action TV show regularly featured the voices of these unseen actors?

Easy	*Harder*	*Yeah, Good Luck*
1. William Daniels	1. Lorenzo Music	1. Ralph James
2. Bob Saget	2. Janeane Garofalo	2. Bob Johnson
3. John Forsythe	3. Mary Tyler Moore	3. Vic Perrin
4. Orson Welles	4. Kevin Pollak	4. Burt Reynolds
5. Daniel Stern	5. Ann Sothern	5. Paul Frees

• **1976** • Diego Maradona, perhaps the greatest soccer player of all time, makes his professional debut for the Argentino Juniors. He's only fifteen years old.

PAMPAS AND CIRCUMSTANCE

1. What one-word catchphrase did the Argentine-born Andrés Cantor make famous?
2. Martin Fierro is the greatest of what epic heroes of Argentine literature?

3. Whose first film, *¡Segundos Afuera!*, debuted in Buenos Aires in August 1937?
4. An Argentine would call them the Malvinas. What are they called in English?

5. What iconic Rita Hayworth title character is the wife of a Buenos Aires casino owner?

• **1992** • Kenny G releases *Breathless*, which will go on to sell 15 million copies, making it—sorry, jazz purists—the most successful instrumental album of all time. (The *G* is for "Gorelick," by the way.)

G WHIZ

1. Who was the credited author of the 1941 detective novel *The G-String Murders*?
2. What country joined the G7 in 1997, forming the G8?
3. What food item is the only common word in American English in which a *g* is pronounced as *j* though it precedes a vowel that's not *e, i,* or *y*?
4. What's the only Pixar film not to be rated G?

5. What company traded on the New York Stock Exchange with ticker symbol G before its 2005 merger with Procter & Gamble?

Answers to the questions on this page can be found on page 439.

• **1939** • THE BRIGGS ADVISORY COMMITTEE on Uranium meets for the first time, because President Roosevelt is alarmed by a letter he received from Albert Einstein and other physicists about the possibility of Nazi Germany developing an atomic bomb. It is the beginning of the Manhattan Project.

NUCLEAR FAMILY

1. What U.S. state is home to Three Mile Island?

2. What atomic bomb test got its name from J. Robert Oppenheimer's love for the religious poetry of John Donne?

3. Three of the last five U.S. presidents have pronounced nuclear "nucular." Which two got it right?

4. What password lets Matthew Broderick play Global Thermonuclear War in the film *WarGames*?

5. The Cuban Missile Crisis was defused by a U.S. offer to remove nuclear missiles from what country?

• **1954** • THE FIRST ADAPTATION of Ian Fleming's James Bond books hits TV screens. *Casino Royale* airs as an episode of CBS's anthology *Climax!*, with American (!) Barry Nelson playing Jimmy "Card Sense" Bond.

FOR YOUR ISLES ONLY

For an English icon, 007 sure hasn't been played by an Englishman very often. Match the first five Bonds to their ethnicity of birth.

1. Sean Connery
2. George Lazenby
3. Roger Moore
4. Timothy Dalton
5. Pierce Brosnan

A. Australian
B. English
C. Irish
D. Scottish
E. Welsh

• **1992** • MATTEL ANNOUNCES THAT Teen Talk Barbie will no longer say "Math class is tough!" after widespread public complaints that the sound bite is sexist.

HELLO, DOLLY

1. What kind of doll has Xavier Roberts's signature on its left buttock?

2. What traditional dolls represent the sacred spirits of Hopi religion?

3. What lounge singer persona did David Johansen adopt after leaving the New York Dolls?

4. The gender-confused title character in *Seed of Chucky* is named either Glen or Glenda in honor of what director?

5. Which dolls were friends with the Camel with the Wrinkled Knees?

6. What gambling game is the subject of the *Guys and Dolls* song "Luck Be a Lady"?

7. Though it was written in Italy, what country is the setting of the play *A Doll's House*?

8. On NBC's *The Office*, Angela gave Dwight a bobble-head doll version of whom?

9. What do *matryoshka* dolls famously do?

10. What film critic wrote the screenplay for Russ Meyer's *Beyond the Valley of the Dolls*?

Answers to the questions on this page can be found on page 439.

OCTOBER 22

• **1844** • PREACHER WILLIAM MILLER has announced to his followers that, based on his interpretation of Daniel 8:14, the world will end today. When Christ is a no-show, Miller is shattered, and his followers come to refer to the day as "the Great Disappointment."

GET USED TO DISAPPOINTMENT

1. What injury-plagued University of Kentucky center is best known for being drafted ahead of Michael Jordan in 1984?
2. What longest river in Canada was formerly called the Disappointment River?

3. Of what alien race is Jar Jar Binks, the controversial comic-relief character of the disappointing *Star Wars* prequels?
4. Who snapped on May 14, 1881, when Secretary of State James Blaine refused to appoint him

ambassador to France?
5. What company released 1983's Lisa, which turned out to be so sluggish and expensive that thousands of unsold units ended up buried in a Utah landfill?

• **1926** • A MONTREAL STUDENT sucker-punches an unprepared Harry Houdini in the gut, which will contribute to his death by peritonitis nine days later, on Halloween.

SUCKER!

1. What TV detective took up suckers as a vice after quitting smoking?
2. What comedian's last starring role was as himself in *Never Give a Sucker an Even Break*?

3. What mythical American animal takes its name from the Spanish for "goat-sucker"?
4. *I'm Gonna Git You Sucka* is the only film to star all five acting members of what family?

5. What's the more common name of the "suckerfish," often found attached to sharks and whales?

• **1976** • THE UNITED STATES BANS FD&C red dye No. 2, which has been linked to cancer in lab rats.

RED SCARE
Give the last name of the "Red" who did the following.

Easy
1. Created Clem Kadiddlehopper
2. Won an Oscar for *Sayonara*
3. Won nine titles coaching the Celtics

Harder
1. Formed the American Football League in 1926
2. Led the Oglala Sioux against U.S. forts on the Bozeman Trail
3. Married Kitty Sigurdson

Yeah, Good Luck
1. Sang the country hit "Teddy Bear"
2. Made duct-tape jokes on Canadian TV
3. Took prank calls at his New Jersey bar

Answers to the questions on this page can be found on page 440.

• **4004 B.C.** • GOD CREATES ADAM AND EVE, according to the calculations of seventeenth-century churchman John Lightfoot. According to Lightfoot, man was created at 9 A.M. This *was* sort of a late start to the day, but let's cut God some slack: he'd been up all night doing the firmament, waters, beasts of the earth, etc.

NOT AT ALL ABOUT EVE

These are questions about other first ladies.

1. Which president was married to a first lady whose first name was Eleanor?

2. What *Stalag 17* actor served as best man when Nancy Davis married Ronald Reagan?

3. Who received U.S. Secret Service protection longer than anyone else in history?

4. Where is the large reservoir that was renamed for Jacqueline Kennedy Onassis in 1994?

5. What name was shared by the second wives of two presidents, Theodore Roosevelt and Woodrow Wilson?

6. What was the name of Hillary Clinton's 2003 memoir, for which she received a record $8 million advance?

7. What president, while a career diplomat, married the only first lady born outside the U.S., London-born Louisa Johnson?

8. What opened its doors on October 4, 1982, in Rancho Mirage, California?

9. What future first lady also served occasionally as White House hostess for widower Thomas Jefferson?

10. Who lived longer than any other president or first lady, dying in 1982 at age 97?

• **1739** • ROBERT WALPOLE RELUCTANTLY declares war against Spain. The war fever has been stoked by a seaman named Richard Jenkins, who showed off his pickled ear to the House of Commons, claiming that the Spanish coast guard had severed it. Today, it's called the War of Jenkins' Ear.

WHOLE LOTTA LOBE

Do you know these ear facts, or did they go in one ear and out the other?

1. About what actor did Howard Hughes say "That man's ears make him look like a taxicab with both doors open"?

2. What's the more common name

for the stapes bone in the ear, the smallest bone in the human body?

3. What European country is home to the band Golden Earring, of "Radar Love" fame?

4. What ear condition comes from the Latin word for "ringing"?

5. To what three groups does Mark Antony say "Lend me your ears" in *Julius Caesar*?

• **2001** • APPLE INTRODUCES A DIGITAL music player it calls the iPod. MP3 players have been considered clunky and unsuccessful up to now, so analysts are not thrilled by the announcement.

BRANDED!

What company do we have to thank for these consumer items?

Easy	Harder	Yeah, Good Luck
1. Xbox	1. BlackBerry	1. Toughskins
2. Barbie	2. Fritos	2. Kleenex
3. Walkman	3. Victrola	3. ChapStick
4. Spam	4. Rogaine	4. Lunchables
5. Lexus	5. Frisbee	5. ThumbDrive

Answers to the questions on this page can be found on page 440.

OCTOBER 24

• **1831** • ARCHAEOLOGISTS UNCOVER THE celebrated "Alexander mosaic" in a Pompeii palace buried by the eruption of Mount Vesuvius. Made of one and a half million tiles, the huge floor mosaic shows Alexander the Great's victory over Darius III of Persia.

THE ELEMENTS OF TILE

1. What's the more common name for the "Word of Life" mosaic on the Hesburgh Library in South Bend, Indiana?
2. What Istanbul landmark was stripped of its famous golden mosaics in the 1204 Sack of Constantinople?
3. The first virus ever discovered, in 1930, was a "mosaic virus" infecting what cash crop?
4. What once-dominant software company began life in 1994 as the Mosaic Communications Corporation?
5. In what city would you find the famed *Moderniste* mosaics at Park Güell?

• **1901** • ANNIE EDSON TAYLOR, a 63-year-old widow in need of money, goes over Niagara Falls in a barrel of her own invention as a publicity gimmick, becoming the first person ever to try the stunt.

CASK ME ANOTHER

1. What's the name for the stopper used to seal a barrel?
2. What ascetic Greek philosopher lived in a barrel?
3. What Wisconsin senator invented the "Golden Fleece Award" for wasteful pork-barrel projects?
4. What's the correct name of the song whose chorus begins "Roll out the barrel"?
5. How big was the barrel of Dirty Harry's trademark gun?

• **2006** • HIP-HOP STAR SNOOP DOGG releases his first novel, *Love Don't Live Here No More*. Oddly, novelist Don DeLillo's rap debut, *White Noize*, hits the very same day (though DeLillo had guested the previous summer on Philip Roth's "All About the Zuckermans").

POP QUIZZLE
Give these answers not coined by Snoop.

1. What's the name of the aft mast on a ketch or yawl?
2. What last name is shared by Dustin Hoffman's character in *Midnight Cowboy* and Stockard Channing's character in *Grease*?
3. Who would have been known as the "Vancouver Mounties," had the Canadian government not complained?
4. What music term is the opposite of "arco," since it refers to plucking an instrument's strings rather than bowing them?
5. What cross-dressing comedian was born in Yemen in 1962?
6. What does the National Weather Service call raindrops that are less than half a millimeter in diameter?
7. What nickname did football star and future Supreme Court Justice Byron White receive in 1936 after the University of Colorado student paper rejected "Straight-A White," "Lord Byron," and "The Duke of Wellington"?
8. What's the appropriate first name of the 1923 Model T character in the animated film *Cars*?
9. According to slogans, what candy "Makes Mouths Happy" and is "Fun You Can Eat"?
10. What did Jay Sindler patent in 1934, after fishing an olive out of his martini glass one evening at the bar at Boston's Ritz-Carlton Hotel?

Answers to the questions on this page can be found on page 440.

OCTOBER 25

• **1870** • THE FIRST U.S. TRADEMARK is registered, to the Averill Chemical Paint Company.

I. P. FREELY
What company owns (or owned) these genericized trademarks?

Easy
1. Band-Aid
2. Touch-Tone
3. ZIP code
4. Aspirin
5. Bake-Off

Harder
1. Hula Hoop
2. Craisins
3. JumboTron
4. Ouija board
5. Jet-Ski

Yeah, Good Luck
1. Laundromat
2. Crock-Pot
3. Styrofoam
4. Onesie
5. Super Hero

• **1975** • *THE MARY TYLER MOORE SHOW*'s seldom-seen clown Chuckles is laid to rest in "Chuckles Bites the Dust," which *TV Guide* will later vote the best single TV episode of all time.

CHEERS, NOT JEERS
What series produced these entries on TV Guide's list?

Easy
1. "Richie Fights Back"
2. "Turkeys Away"
3. "Krusty Gets Kancelled"
4. "The One with the Prom Video"
5. "Latka the Playboy"

Harder
1. "The Germans"
2. "Getting Davy Jones"
3. "Love's Labor Lost"
4. "Password"
5. "Abyssinia Henry"

Yeah, Good Luck
1. "It May Look Like a Walnut"
2. "Tet '68"
3. "The Great Vegetable Rebellion"
4. "The Puppy Episode"
5. "Man from the South"

• **2001** • THE REPUBLIC OF RWANDA adopts its new flag, with three stripes and a golden sun. Until today, Rwanda had the world's only national flag to sport its own initial: a big black letter *R* in the middle, yellow stripe.

PENNANT RACE
What's the only national flag . . .

1. That's not rectangular
2. With a building on it
3. That's been continuously in use for more than six hundred years
4. With an AK-47 on it
5. That's monochromatic
6. Ever to fly over an entire continent
7. With a different design on its front and back
8. With six different colors (not counting seals)
9. To feature carpet designs
10. That displays a map of its country

A. Australia
B. Cambodia
C. Cyprus
D. Denmark
E. Libya
F. Mozambique
G. Nepal
H. Paraguay
I. South Africa
J. Turkmenistan

Answers to the questions on this page can be found on page 441.

OCTOBER 26

• **1676** • BACON'S REBELLION, THE FIRST frontiersmen's uprising in the American colonies, ends unexpectedly when dysentery fells ringleader Nathaniel Bacon.

ONE DEGREE
In what movie did these actors costar with the ubiquitous Kevin Bacon?

Easy	*Harder*	*Yeah, Good Luck*
1. Tom Hanks	1. Meryl Streep	1. Sharon Stone
2. Jack Nicholson	2. Robert De Niro	2. Jamie Lee Curtis
3. Sarah Jessica Parker	3. Reba McEntire	3. Wallace Shawn
4. Sean Penn	4. Steve Guttenberg	4. John Cleese
5. Neve Campbell	5. Walter Matthau	5. Keshia Knight Pulliam

• **1977** • SOMALI COOK ALI MAOW MAALIN is the last person in the world to be diagnosed with naturally occurring smallpox. (He got better.)

DOC TALK
What's the more colloquial name for these medical conditions?

Easy	*Harder*	*Yeah, Good Luck*
1. Rubella	1. Conjunctivitis	1. Hansen's disease
2. Tetanus	2. Trisomy 21	2. Epidemic parotitis
3. Bovine spongiform encephalopathy	3. Amyotrophic lateral sclerosis	3. Herpes zoster
4. Pertussis	4. Nocturnal enuresis	4. Pyrosis
5. Hypertension	5. Tinea pedis	5. Strabismus

• **2003** • WINDSOR, CALIFORNIA, BAKES the world's largest pumpkin pie. It weighs 300 pounds and measures 6¼ feet across.

EASY AS PIE
You shouldn't find these difficult at all.

1. What real-life couple played the intergalactic lovers in *Earth Girls Are Easy*?
2. "The Big Easy" sits on the southern shore of what lake?
3. What future movie star played "Easy Reader" on PBS's *The Electric Company*?
4. What DC Comics NCO led the men of Easy Company?
5. What are the Commodores and Faith No More "easy like"?

Answers to the questions on this page can be found on page 441.

• 1967 • RETIRED TENNIS PLAYER MARGARET SMITH marries a wool broker named Barry Court. When she comes out of retirement and wins the 1970 Grand Slam, she's therefore the most fittingly named player in tennis.

APTRONYMS

Name these other famous folks with appropriate names.

1. Who began singing with college friend Bobby Hatfield in 1962?

2. Who paid $39 to earn a seat at the 2003 World Series of Poker and went on to win the $2.5 million grand prize?

3. Who filled in as Ronald Reagan's press secretary for seven years after James Brady was wounded in the John Hinckley shooting?

4. Who coined the word "Cablinasian" to describe his unusual ethnic background?

5. What poet was inspired by the belt of daffodils he and his sister Dorothy saw during an 1802 walk around Lake Ullswater?

• 1971 • PRESIDENT MOBUTU SESE SEKO renames the Democratic Republic of the Congo "Zaire." The new name puts a crimp in a cool map oddity I've always liked: five neighboring nations (the two Congos, Chad, Cameroon, and the Central African Republic) whose names all start with the same letter.

IN ALPHABETICAL BORDER

What neighbor-beginning-with-the-same-letter is bordered by these countries?

Easy
1. Iran
2. Bolivia
3. Zambia
4. Latvia

Harder
1. Burma
2. Armenia
3. Ethiopia
4. Swaziland

Yeah, Good Luck
1. Burkina Faso
2. Mozambique
3. Kazakhstan
4. Guinea

• 2001 • TV INTERIOR-DECORATING CELEB Paige Davis (*Trading Spaces*) marries actor Patrick Page. For some reason, she elects to keep her maiden name.

AN INSIDE JOB

Answer these questions about other interior things.

1. What novel ends with a famous forty-page, eight-sentence interior monologue by Molly Bloom?

2. What Sean Connery movie shares its name with the trophy given annually to college football's best interior lineman?

3. What secretary of the interior resigned in 1983 after calling his staff "a black, a woman, two Jews, and a cripple"?

4. What material was used for the interior of the 1976 Chrysler Cordoba, according to the famous TV ads starring Ricardo Montal-

ban?

5. In what country's interior would you find the cleverly named Great Sandy Desert?

Answers to the questions on this page can be found on page 441.

OCTOBER 28

• **1533** • AT HER WEDDING to the Duke of Orléans, the fourteen-year-old Catherine de Medicis wears the first pair of high heels in recorded history.

FIRST DEGREE
Be the first to answer these questions about other famous firsts.

1. What was the first European nation to be led by a president?
2. Whose first line on the comics page, on October 12, 1931, was "Good evening, Mr. Trueheart—how's the delicatessen business this evening?"
3. What first was achieved in 2002, when a rerelease of "My Sweet Lord" replaced Aaliyah's "More than a Woman" atop the U.K. charts?
4. In 2005, who became the first professional golfer to win the same event—the Mizuno Classic—in five consecutive years?
5. Who was the pilot during history's first fatal plane crash, on September 17, 1908?
6. In 1811, what became the first modern city to surpass one million inhabitants?
7. What distinction is held by the broken laser pointer that Pierre Omidyar sold in 1995 for $14.83?
8. In addition to achieving another, more famous first, who became the first civilian in space, in June 1963?
9. What chemical element is named for the Greek word for "artificial," since it was the first synthetic element ever discovered?
10. What actress was the first *SNL* cast member ever to receive an Oscar nomination?

• **1995** • NEW ZEALAND TV airs a documentary called *Forgotten Silver,* about the making of a "recently rediscovered" 1908 biblical epic by director Colin McKenzie, the unheralded inventor of color and sound film. When McKenzie is acclaimed as a national hero, the startled filmmakers are forced to reveal that the whole movie was a comedic hoax.

MOVIE MOVIE
Match each film to the film-within-a-film being made within that film. Is that clear?

1. *All That Jazz*
2. *Barton Fink*
3. *Bowfinger*
4. *Day for Night*
5. *For Your Consideration*
6. *Mulholland Drive*
7. *The Player*
8. *Singin' in the Rain*
9. *The Stunt Man*
10. *Sullivan's Travels*

A. *The Burlyman*
B. *Chubby Rain*
C. *The Dancing Cavalier*
D. *Devil's Squadron*
E. *Habeas Corpus*
F. *Home for Purim*
G. *Meet Pamela*
H. *O Brother, Where Art Thou?*
I. *The Stand-Up*
J. *The Sylvia North Story*

Answers to the questions on this page can be found on page 442.

• **1941** • Actress Nanette Fabray makes her Broadway debut in *Let's Face It,* billed as "Nanette Fabares," her real name. She will change the spelling a few years later, the day after Ed Sullivan announces her on air as "Nanette Fab-bare-ass."

I NOW PRONOUNCE YOU . . .

How do (or did) these famous folks prefer to pronounce their names?

Easy	*Harder*	*Yeah, Good Luck*
1. Kim Basinger	1. Oscar Hammerstein	1. Diane Arbus
2. J. K. Rowling	2. Rachel Weisz	2. Liev Schreiber
3. Ralph Fiennes	3. Steve Buscemi	3. Robert Moog
4. D. L. Hughley	4. Kofi Annan	4. Dr. Seuss
5. Shia LaBeouf	5. Chloe Sevigny	5. Charlize Theron

• **1998** • Tom Cruise and Nicole Kidman win a libel lawsuit against Britain's *Express* newspaper, which alleged that Cruise is gay. It will be the first of several multimillion-dollar lawsuits aimed at defending the star's spotless heterosexuality.

DEAR CHURCH OF SCIENTOLOGY LAWYERS

To ward off any possible litigation, we'd like to honor Mr. Cruise with this quiz about . . . famous straits.
Name the strait between . . .

1. Alaska and Russia
2. Italy and Sicily
3. The Arabian Peninsula and Iran
4. South America and Tierra del Fuego
5. Spain and Morocco

• **1999** • Meryl Streep spent eight weeks learning to play the violin for her new film *Music of the Heart.* Streep is famous for her scrupulous preparation for roles, whether she's learning a Polish accent for *Sophie's Choice,* shutting down a plutonium plant for *Silkwood,* or traveling back in time to 1920s Kenya for *Out of Africa.*

ROLE PLAYING

Match these movie characters to their musical instrument of choice.

1. Woody Allen, *Sleeper*	A. Cello
2. Michael J. Fox, *Back to the Future*	B. Clarinet
3. Gene Hackman, *The Conversation*	C. Cornet
4. Tom Hanks, *The Man with One Red Shoe*	D. Drums
5. Alyson Hannigan, *American Pie*	E. Flute
6. Ron Howard, *The Music Man*	F. Guitar
7. Giuletta Masina, *La Strada*	G. Piano
8. Jack Nicholson, *Five Easy Pieces*	H. Saxophone
9. Tom Everett Scott, *That Thing You Do!*	I. Trumpet
10. Sigourney Weaver, *Ghostbusters*	J. Violin

Answers to the questions on this page can be found on page 442.

• **1938** • ORSON WELLES'S RADIO ADAPTATION of *The War of the Worlds* leads to nationwide panic when millions of listeners, switching over from Edgar Bergen on NBC, miss the disclaimers that no Martians are actually invading.

FEAR FACTOR

1. What terrifies Carrie White in the first scene of the film *Carrie*?

2. What playwright took the title *Who's Afraid of Virginia Woolf?* from graffiti he once saw written in soap on the mirror of a Greenwich Village bar?

3. What white object became a symbol of cowardice during World War I, when women were instructed to give them to men not in uniform?

4. What has the words "DON'T PANIC" written on it in large, friendly letters?

5. In what state is Cape Fear?

6. What are hexakosioihexekontahexaphobes afraid of?

7. The band Panic! at the Disco took its name from what band's 1986 song "Panic"?

8. What 1986 movie is the source of the line "Be afraid. Be very afraid"?

9. Billy, Danny, or Tommy—in the Kenny Rogers hit, what's the first name of the "Coward of the County"?

10. Whose presidency was doomed by the Panic of 1837?

• **1960** • MR. BLACKWELL ANNOUNCES his first "Ten Worst Dressed" list. His first "winner": Italian star Anna Magnani, whom he calls "the female counterpart of Emmett Kelly."

MR. JENNINGS'S TEN BEST DRESSED

1. What dressy item does Mr. Peanut wear on his feet?

2. What Mayfair street famous for its tailors was also the site of the Beatles' famous "rooftop concert" in *Let It Be*?

3. The record auction bid for a movie dress is the £410,000 paid in 2006 for the little black Givenchy worn in the famous first scene of what 1961 film?

4. What friend of George IV, whose famous name is now synonymous with fashionable dandies, fled England in 1816 due to his huge debts?

5. What color are the pinstripes on the Yankees' home uniforms, named by ESPN as the best sports garb of the twentieth century?

6. What husband of actress Gene Tierney designed Jackie Kennedy's state wardrobe?

7. What movie's sadistic villain, Frank Booth, confuses the protagonists by disguising himself as "the Well-Dressed Man"?

8. What fashion icon debuted in 1959 wearing a zebra-striped one-piece swimsuit?

9. Who designed wedding gowns for Mariah Carey, Jessica Simpson, and J. Lo, among many others?

10. What superhero switched to a stylish black costume in 1984, only to give it up when he discovered it was an alien symbiote?

Answers to the questions on this page can be found on page 442.

• **1945** • JIMMY DURANTE LEAVES an imprint of his famous "schnozzola" in the cement outside Grauman's Chinese Theatre.

NOSE CANDY

1. What was Frosty the Snowman's nose made out of?
2. What's the name for the bone-and-cartilage wall that divides the left and right airways of your nose?
3. What composer of fifteen symphonies also wrote *The Nose*, about a nose that leaves its owner's face and becomes a civil servant?
4. What leader of the Nez Percé Indians surrendered by saying "I will fight no more forever"?
5. In Carlo Collodi's novel, whom does Pinocchio angrily kill with a mallet at the beginning of the book?
6. What does "gesundheit" mean in German?
7. What Danish astronomer lost his nose in a 1566 duel and wore a metal prosthetic nose the rest of his life?
8. What does Toucan Sam encourage you to "follow your nose" to find?
9. What's the name of the woman silently loved by Cyrano de Bergerac?
10. A 2003 study of a Japanese minivan found that what phenomenon could be as harmful as glue sniffing?

• **1961** • JOSEF STALIN'S EMBALMED BODY is removed from Lenin's Tomb and buried outside the Kremlin.

INVASION OF THE BODY SNATCHERS

1. In 1973, the body of what Flying Burrito Brother was stolen from LAX by friends, who tried to cremate it at Joshua Tree?
2. After the 1955 coup that overthrew her husband, whose body was secretly shipped to Italy and buried in a Milan crypt under the name "Maria Maggi"?
3. What silent-film star has been buried under six feet of concrete since his body was stolen from a Swiss grave in a 1978 extortion plot?
4. The organs of what fifty-eight-year host of radio's *Letters from America* were illegally harvested before his 2004 cremation?
5. The body of what great actor (and grandfather of a modern star) was stolen in 1942 by director Raoul Walsh, who propped it up in a chair in Errol Flynn's home as a prank?

• **1981** • ACCORDING TO THE TIMELINE of the *Harry Potter* books, Voldemort kills young Harry's parents on this night . . . and leaves Harry himself with that fetching scar.

BEST(IARY) SELLERS

What kind of creatures are these nonhuman Harry Potter characters?

Easy	Harder	Yeah, Good Luck
1. Nagini	1. Norbert	1. Hermes
2. Crookshanks	2. Fang	2. Ronan
3. Buckbeak	3. Fawkes	3. Trevor
4. Dobby	4. Grawp	4. Tenebrus

Answers to the questions on this page can be found on page 443.

October Answers

OCTOBER 1

IDENTITY CRISIS
1. E (*Me, Myself & Irene*)
2. G (*Sybil*)
3. F (*Taxi*)
4. I (*Heroes*)
5. H (*The Nutty Professor*)
6. D (*Fight Club*)
7. A (*Psycho*)
8. J (*Family Matters*)
9. C (*Twin Peaks*)
10. B (*The Three Faces of Eve*)

A CAPITAL QUIZ
1. Ecuador (Quito)
2. Mongolia (Ulan Bator)
3. Pakistan (Islamabad)
4. Croatia (Zagreb)

YOU'RE WITH ME, LEATHER
Easy
1. Ty Cobb
2. Darryl Strawberry
3. Sammy Sosa
4. Eddie Murray
5. Roberto Alomar
Harder
1. Jose Canseco
2. Scott Brosius
3. Alan Trammel
4. Dave Justice
5. George Bell
Yeah, Good Luck
1. Lance Blankenship
2. Mike Scioscia
3. Rafael Santana
4. Kent Hrbek
5. Bert Blyleven

OCTOBER 2

I DO, I DO, I DO, I DO . . .
1. Ava Gardner
2. Michelle Phillips
3. Lex Barker
4. Evelyn Keyes
5. George Sanders

McGUFFIN READERS
Easy
1. *North by Northwest*
2. *Vertigo*
3. *Psycho*
4. *The Birds*
Harder
1. *Dial M for Murder*
2. *Notorious*
3. *The Man Who Knew Too Much*
4. *Strangers on a Train*
Yeah, Good Luck
1. *Saboteur*
2. *Frenzy*
3. *Foreign Correspondent*
4. *Suspicion*

GO, LANCE, GO
1. The Marines
2. St. George's
3. Traditionally, it pierced Jesus' side on the cross
4. The Crimean War
5. Maryland

OCTOBER 3

GREAT SCOTT!
1. *Ragtime*
2. Erin Moran
3. Velvet Revolver
4. The Anaheim Ducks
5. Tony Snow

CAN YOU BE MORE PACIFIC?
1. Papua New Guinea
2. Guadalcanal
3. Taro
4. Pitcairn Island
5. Paul Gauguin
6. The Maori
7. Scotland
8. Mosi Tatupu
9. Easter Island
10. James Michener

DIE ANOTHER WAY
Easy
1. Exposure (*not* drowning)
2. Crucifixion
3. Melted by water
4. Cancer
5. Atomic explosion
Harder
1. Poisoning (iocane powder)
2. Ax wounds
3. Eaten by mutant shark
4. Chased off cliff by topless women
5. Suffocated with pillow
Yeah, Good Luck
1. Gas chamber
2. Beheaded
3. Inflated and exploded using compressed air
4. Heart attack (from shock)
5. Buried alive

OCTOBER 4	OCTOBER 5	OCTOBER 6

OCTOBER 4

EXPRESS YOURSELF
1. Steven Spielberg's
2. Buffalo Bill Cody
3. Roller skates
4. "Do you know me?"
5. Turkey
6. San Antonio's
7. Nolan Ryan (*Von Ryan's Express*)
8. William Burroughs's
9. A sleigh bell
10. Steve Young

POP GOES THE EASEL
Easy
1. Roy Lichtenstein
2. Andy Warhol
3. David Hockney
Harder
1. Jasper Johns
2. Robert Indiana
3. Claes Oldenburg
Yeah, Good Luck
1. Keith Haring
2. Wayne Thiebaud
3. Robert Rauschenberg

WHAT'S THE FREQUENCY, KENNETH?
1. Every ten years
2. Every other day
3. Every other year
4. Weekly
5. Every seven years
6. Every ninety minutes
7. Twice a day
8. Every six years
9. Five times a day
10. Twice a year

OCTOBER 5

EYE OF THE TAIGA
1. *The Gulag Archipelago*
2. Lake Baikal
3. A giant explosion, probably a meteor strike
4. *Lara Croft: Tomb Raider*'s
5. A woolly mammoth

FAKE BOOKS
1. The Shop Around the Corner
2. Harry Potter
3. Roberto Benigni (*Life Is Beautiful*)
4. Ellen DeGeneres
5. A travel bookshop

GENTLEMAN COLLARS
1. George Washington
2. Jawaharlal Nehru
3. Wisk
4. Larry the Cable Guy
5. Seiji Ozawa

OCTOBER 6

K MART
1. Ketamine
2. James K. Polk
3. Black
4. Ice Cube
5. Roger Clemens's sons (the initial *K*s represent strikeouts)
6. Mozart's
7. Franz Kafka
8. Kodak
9. Henry Godwin-Austen
10. *Bill & Ted's Excellent Adventure*

ACID TEST
1. Aspirin
2. Hydrochloric acid and nitric acid
3. Folic acid
4. Red
5. Sulfuric acid

TAKE TWO
Easy
1. *La Cage aux Folles*
2. *The Bishop's Wife*
3. *Love Affair*
4. *The Absent-Minded Professor*
5. *Infernal Affairs*
Harder
1. *La Femme Nikita*
2. *Charade*
3. *Here Comes Mr. Jordan*
4. *The Return of Martin Guerre*
5. *Death Takes a Holiday*
Yeah, Good Luck
1. *The Virgin Spring*
2. *All That Heaven Allows*
3. *Lady for a Day*
4. *Boudu Saved from Drowning*
5. *The More the Merrier*

OCTOBER 7

CUP WITH PEOPLE
1. Roberto Clemente
2. Vince Lombardi
3. James Norris
4. Edgar Martinez
5. Arthur Ashe
6. Harley J. Earl
7. Eclipse
8. Jack Nicklaus
9. Walter Payton
10. Oscar Robertson

PUMPED UP
1. Biting or chewing (it's the masseter muscle of the jaw)
2. Popeye's
3. The heart
4. Charley horse
5. *The Cremaster Cycle*
6. BMI (body mass index)
7. A Pontiac GTO
8. Lactic acid
9. The deltoid
10. Michael Jackson

OCTOBER 8

CONSTITUTION HALL
1. Delaware
2. "Defence"
3. Cruel and unusual
4. John Dickinson
5. Seven
6. The "full faith and credit" clause
7. Prohibition was repealed
8. 35
9. Religion
10. Rhode Island

PRICKLY PAIRS
Easy
1. Ted Danson and Mary Steenburgen
2. Martin Landau and Barbara Bain
3. Michael Tucker and Jill Eikenberry
4. Chad Michael Murray and Sophia Bush
5. Roseanne Barr and Tom Arnold
Harder
1. Sarah Clarke and Xander Berkeley
2. Alex Karras and Susan Clark
3. Alexander Siddig and Nana Visitor
4. William Daniels and Bonnie Bartlett
5. Rob Estes and Josie Bissett
Yeah, Good Luck
1. Richard Benjamin and Paula Prentiss
2. Casper Van Dien and Catherine Oxenberg
3. Meredith Baxter and David Birney
4. Sam Jaffe and Bettye Ackerman
5. David James Elliott and Nanci Chambers

FORT KNOCKS
1. Woody Woodpecker
2. E!
3. *Annie*
4. *The Tommyknockers*
5. The solar plexus

OCTOBER 9

STRENGTH IN NUMBERS
Easy
1. Hank Aaron
2. Joe DiMaggio
3. Roger Maris
4. Cal Ripken, Jr.
Harder
1. Bob Gibson (ERA)
2. Cy Young (wins)
3. Pete Rose (hits)
4. Nolan Ryan (strikeouts)
Yeah, Good Luck
1. Rogers Hornsby
2. Rickey Henderson (steals)
3. Ichiro Suzuki (hits)
4. Hank Aaron (RBIs)

I HAVE A LITTLE LIST
1. Paul Newman
2. Top Ten List, on *Late Night with David Letterman*
3. Kathy Griffin
4. At the State Department
5. Unsolved math problems

TITLE INSURANCE
1. D, *The Freshman*
2. A, *Monkey Business*
3. I, *Shall We Dance?*
4. B, *Heaven Can Wait*
5. C, *No Way Out*
6. G, *Moulin Rouge*
7. E, *The Rainmaker*
8. F, *Traffic*
9. H, *Hero*
10. J, *Crash*

OCTOBER 10

WHO ARE YOU? I REALLY WANNA KNOW
1. Louisiana
2. "Mr. Jones" (Counting Crows)
3. Jane
4. Seventeen
5. "Billie Jean"
6. Scaramouche
7. Layla
8. Wendy
9. Stan
10. Each mentions a Rolling Stone: "like Bill Wyman," "like Charlie Watts," and "like Mick Jagger," respectively

EXPANSION DRAFT
1. The Suns and SuperSonics
2. The Reds and Red Sox
3. The Blues and Blue Jackets
4. The Nets and Nuggets

INTERNATIONAL BASKETBALL ASSOCIATION
Easy
1. (West) Germany
2. China
3. Argentina
4. Nigeria
Harder
1. South Africa
2. Jamaica
3. Spain
4. The Netherlands
Yeah, Good Luck
1. Sudan
2. Lithuania (then part of the USSR)
3. Ukraine (then part of the USSR)
4. Nigeria

OCTOBER 11

SIBYL RITES
1. The flight of birds
2. Delphi
3. Cassandra
4. The *Argo*
5. He was transformed into a woman

JOCK OF ALL TRADES
1. Dave Winfield
2. Jim Thorpe
3. Jim Brown
4. Jackie Robinson
5. "Babe" Didrikson Zaharias
6. Bo Jackson
7. Ed Jones
8. Tom Glavine
9. Marion Jones
10. Charlie Ward

STORMY WEATHER
1. The United Kingdom
2. Ronee Blakley
3. The ibis
4. Passion fruit
5. Mike Myers

OCTOBER 12

EGGS MARKS THE SPOT
1. *The Colbert Report*
2. A wasps' nest
3. Robert "Chief" Parish
4. The stork
5. Hazzard County (*The Dukes of Hazzard*)

LIFE IN THE FEST LANE
1. Ramadan
2. Jai alai
3. Bethel
4. Pamplona's
5. The Palme d'Or

A RAW DEAL
1. Squash
2. Spin it—a boiled egg spins faster and longer
3. Muesli
4. *R*
5. Steak tartare

OCTOBER 13

WHO'S AFRAID OF . . .
Easy
1. Acrophobia
2. Claustrophobia
3. Arachnophobia
4. Xenophobia
5. Agoraphobia

Harder
1. Heliophobia
2. Necrophobia
3. Hemophobia
4. Pyrophobia
5. Glossophobia

Yeah, Good Luck
1. Ailurophobia
2. Gymnophobia
3. Algophobia
4. Coulrophobia
5. Tokophobia

EAT ME!
1. New Guinea
2. Jonathan Swift
3. The Sierra Nevada
4. A census taker
5. The Caribbean Sea
6. Fleet Street
7. Alferd Packer
8. *Titus Andronicus*
9. *Soylent Green*
10. Saturn

MULTIPLEXITY
Easy
1. *Antz*
2. *Wyatt Earp*
3. *Armageddon*
4. *Volcano*

Harder
1. *The Wild*
2. *The Illusionist*
3. *EdTV*
4. *Red Planet*

Yeah, Good Luck
1. *Without Limits*
2. *Valmont*
3. *Chasing Liberty*
4. *Fail-Safe*

OCTOBER 14

WAR BONDS
1. F, a
2. H, h
3. D, i
4. C, f
5. A, c
6. E, j
7. B, e
8. J, g
9. G, d
10. I, b

THE SUITES HEREAFTER
1. Earth (though Pluto, then not yet discovered and now no longer a planet, isn't included either)
2. The Grand Canyon
3. Henrik Ibsen
4. *The Nutcracker*
5. *Appalachian Spring*

DOG PATCH
Easy
1. *Little Orphan Annie*
2. *Dennis the Menace*
3. *Peanuts*
4. *Garfield*
5. *Dilbert*

Harder
1. *Blondie*
2. *Mutts*
3. *For Better or For Worse*
4. *The Family Circus*
5. *Beetle Bailey*

Yeah, Good Luck
1. *Hagar the Horrible*
2. *Pickles*
3. *Luann*
4. *Ziggy*
5. *Overboard*

OCTOBER 15

COUNTRY MUSIC
Easy
1. Vatican City
2. Egypt
3. Cambodia
4. Canada
5. China

Harder
1. San Marino
2. Bhutan
3. Lebanon
4. Mozambique
5. The Netherlands

Yeah, Good Luck
1. Ecuador
2. Honduras
3. Andorra
4. The United States
5. Zimbabwe

LITERARY LEGS
1. Hagrid's (*Harry Potter*)
2. Chita Rivera
3. Anansi
4. Alex Cross
5. Arachne

October Answers

OCTOBER 16

BREWTOPIA
1. A harp
2. Munich
3. Billy Carter
4. The microphone
5. Dos Equis ("Two *X*s," or Roman numeral XX)
6. Bud Light
7. Barley
8. Adolf Hitler
9. Milwaukee
10. Samuel Adams

MISTAKEN IDENTITY
1. Bret Hart(e)
2. C(h)ris Carter
3. John Reed/Reid
4. James Stuart/Stewart
5. Maud(e) Adams
6. Spike Jones/Jonze
7. Ben Jo(h)nson
8. Mark/Marc Price
9. Jim Bak(k)er
10. Jo(h)n Stewart

OCTOBER 17

ACHTUNG BABY
1. Stool
2. A $1 bill
3. Limbo
4. She was the model for the Gerber baby
5. Maggie Simpson (according to the grocery checkout scan)
6. Shiloh Jolie-Pitt
7. "Isn't She Lovely"
8. Emily
9. *M*
10. *A Portrait of the Artist as a Young Man*

STUCK IN THE MIDDLE WITH YOU
1. A sundial
2. Wilkerson
3. David Robinson and Tim Duncan
4. Sleeping Beauty's
5. Protons and neutrons
6. Missouri
7. Caramel
8. A singularity
9. Niagara Falls
10. Judas Iscariot

OCTOBER 18

DIGITAL DOMAIN
1. Dr. Seuss's
2. Marvin Gaye
3. A *yakuza*
4. Okra
5. *A*
6. Hoyt Wilhelm
7. Four (well, three and a thumb)
8. The Rolling Stones' lips and tongue
9. Brazil
10. Dane Cook

"SUPER" FRIENDS
1. The Dallas Cowboys
2. He throws up
3. The eyebrows
4. The Super Soaker
5. Albert Brooks
6. Very low temperatures
7. Giant
8. McLovin
9. Karen Carpenter's
10. The Crab Nebula
11. Krypto
12. Wade Boggs
13. "U Can't Touch This"
14. *Gilmore Girls* and *Smallville*
15. Tuesday

OCTOBER 19

MONARCHY IN THE U.K.
1. William (IV)
2. Welsh corgi
3. "Longshanks"
4. Henry VIII (Charles Laughton, Richard Burton, and Robert Shaw)
5. John Brown
6. The Tudors
7. King John
8. Henry VIII
9. Saint James
10. Richard (II and III)

CEILING WHACKS
1. Katharine Graham (*The Washington Post*)
2. Fidelity Investments
3. Ash
4. Hewlett-Packard
5. Oprah Winfrey

FOUR SAINTS IN THREE ACTS
Easy
1. Saint Francis of Assisi
2. Saint Andrew
3. Saint Jude
4. Saint Valentine
Harder
1. Saint Nicholas
2. Edward the Confessor
3. Saint Frances Xavier
4. Saint Vitus
Yeah, Good Luck
1. Saint Agatha
2. Saint Bernard of Clairvaux
3. Saint Dominic
4. Saint Florian

OCTOBER 20

FACE OFF
Easy
1. *Knight Rider*
2. *How I Met Your Mother*
3. *Charlie's Angels*
4. *Magnum, P.I.*
5. *The Wonder Years*
Harder
1. *Rhoda*
2. *Felicity*
3. *Richard Diamond, Private Detective*
4. *The Drew Carey Show*
5. *My Mother the Car*
Yeah, Good Luck
1. *Mork & Mindy*
2. *Mission: Impossible*
3. *The Outer Limits*
4. *Out of This World*
5. *The Millionaire*

PAMPAS AND CIRCUMSTANCE
1. "¡GOOOOOOOOOOOOLLL!"
2. Gauchos
3. Eva Perón (then Duarte)
4. The Falklands
5. Gilda

G WHIZ
1. Gypsy Rose Lee
2. Russia
3. Margarine
4. *The Incredibles*
5. Gillette

OCTOBER 21

NUCLEAR FAMILY
1. Pennsylvania
2. Trinity
3. Ronald Reagan and George H. W. Bush
4. "Joshua"
5. Turkey

FOR YOUR ISLES ONLY
1. D
2. A
3. B
4. E
5. C

HELLO, DOLLY
1. Cabbage Patch Kids
2. Kachina dolls
3. Buster Poindexter
4. Ed Wood
5. Raggedy Ann and Andy
6. Craps
7. Norway
8. Himself
9. Nest inside one another (they're Russian stacking dolls)
10. Roger Ebert

OCTOBER 22

GET USED TO DISAPPOINT-MENT
1. Sam Bowie
2. The Mackenzie
3. The Gungans
4. Charles Guiteau (James Garfield's assassin)
5. Apple computer

SUCKER!
1. Kojak
2. W. C. Fields's
3. The chupacabra
4. The Wayans
5. The remora

RED SCARE
Easy
1. Red Skelton
2. Red Buttons
3. Red Auerbach
Harder
1. Red Grange
2. Red Cloud
3. Red Forman (*That '70s Show*)
Yeah, Good Luck
1. Red Sovine
2. Red Green
3. Red Deutsch

OCTOBER 23

NOT AT ALL ABOUT EVE
1. Jimmy Carter (Eleanor Rosalynn Carter; Eleanor Roosevelt's first name was Anna)
2. William Holden
3. Lady Bird Johnson
4. Central Park
5. Edith
6. *Living History*
7. John Quincy Adams
8. The Betty Ford Center
9. Dolley Madison
10. Bess Truman

WHOLE LOTTA LOBE
1. Clark Gable
2. The stirrup
3. The Netherlands
4. Tinnitus
5. Friends, Romans, countrymen

BRANDED!
Easy
1. Microsoft
2. Mattel
3. Sony
4. Hormel
5. Toyota
Harder
1. Research in Motion
2. PepsiCo
3. RCA Victor
4. Pfizer (originally Upjohn)
5. Wham-O
Yeah, Good Luck
1. Sears
2. Kimberly-Clark
3. Wyeth
4. Oscar Mayer (Kraft)
5. Trek

OCTOBER 24

THE ELEMENTS OF TILE
1. Touchdown Jesus
2. The Hagia Sophia
3. Tobacco
4. Netscape
5. Barcelona

CASK ME ANOTHER
1. A bung
2. Diogenes
3. William Proxmire
4. "Beer Barrel Polka"
5. .44 inch (a .44 Magnum)

POP QUIZZLE
1. The mizzenmast
2. Rizzo
3. The Grizzlies (of the NBA)
4. "Pizzicato"
5. Eddie Izzard
6. Drizzle
7. "Whizzer"
8. Lizzie
9. Twizzlers
10. The swizzle stick

OCTOBER 25

I. P. FREELY
Easy
1. Johnson & Johnson
2. AT&T
3. The U.S. Postal Service
4. Bayer
5. Pillsbury
Harder
1. Wham-O
2. Ocean Spray
3. Sony
4. Parker Brothers (Hasbro)
5. Kawasaki
Yeah, Good Luck
1. Westinghouse
2. Rival
3. Dow Chemical
4. Gerber
5. Marvel and DC Comics (Time Warner), jointly owned

CHEERS, NOT JEERS
Easy
1. *Happy Days*
2. *WKRP in Cincinnati*
3. *The Simpsons*
4. *Friends*
5. *Taxi*
Harder
1. *Fawlty Towers*
2. ~~The Munsters~~ The Brady Bunch
3. *ER*
4. *The Odd Couple*
5. *M*A*S*H*
Yeah, Good Luck
1. *The Dick Van Dyke Show*
2. *China Beach*
3. *Lost in Space*
4. *Ellen*
5. *Alfred Hitchcock Presents*

PENNANT RACE
1. G
2. B (Angkor Wat)
3. D
4. F
5. E (green)
6. A
7. H
8. I
9. J
10. C

OCTOBER 26

ONE DEGREE
Easy
1. *Apollo 13*
2. *A Few Good Men*
3. *Footloose*
4. *Mystic River*
5. *Wild Things*
Harder
1. *The River Wild*
2. *Sleepers*
3. *Tremors*
4. *Diner*
5. *JFK*
Yeah, Good Luck
1. *He Said, She Said*
2. *Queens Logic*
3. *Starting Over*
4. *The Big Picture*
5. *Beauty Shop*

DOC TALK
Easy
1. German measles
2. Lockjaw
3. Mad cow disease
4. Whooping cough
5. High blood pressure
Harder
1. Pinkeye
2. Down syndrome
3. Lou Gehrig's disease
4. Bed-wetting
5. Athlete's foot
Yeah, Good Luck
1. Leprosy
2. Mumps
3. Shingles
4. Heartburn
5. Crosseye or squint

EASY AS PIE
1. Geena Davis and Jeff Goldblum
2. Lake Pontchartrain
3. Morgan Freeman
4. Sergeant Rock
5. Sunday morning

OCTOBER 27

APTRONYMS
1. Bill Medley (the Righteous Brothers)
2. Chris Moneymaker
3. Larry Speakes
4. Tiger Woods
5. William Wordsworth

IN ALPHABETICAL BORDER
Easy
1. Iraq
2. Brazil
3. Zimbabwe
4. Lithuania
Harder
1. Bangladesh
2. Azerbaijan
3. Eritrea
4. South Africa
Yeah, Good Luck
1. Benin
2. Malawi
3. Kyrgyzstan
4. Guinea-Bissau

AN INSIDE JOB
1. *Ulysses*
2. *Outland*
3. James Watt
4. Rich "Corinthian" leather
5. Australia

October Answers

OCTOBER 28

FIRST DEGREE
1. France
2. Dick Tracy's
3. Two consecutive posthumous number ones
4. Annika Sorenstam
5. Orville Wright
6. London
7. It was the first item sold on eBay
8. Valentina Tereshkova (first woman in space)
9. Technetium
10. Joan Cusack (*Working Girl*)

MOVIE MOVIE
1. I
2. A
3. B
4. G
5. F
6. J
7. E
8. C
9. D
10. H

OCTOBER 29

I NOW PRONOUNCE YOU . . .
Easy
1. BAY-sing-er
2. ROH-ling
3. rayf fines
4. HYOO-glee
5. SHY-uh luh-BUFF
Harder
1. HAM-ur-styne
2. VICE
3. boo-SEM-ee
4. KOH-fee ANN-un
5. KLOH-ee SEV-uh-nee
Yeah, Good Luck
1. dee-AN AR-bus
2. lee-EV SHRY-burr
3. MOAG
4. SOYSS
5. shar-LEEZ THROWN

DEAR CHURCH OF SCIENTOL-OGY LAWYERS
1. The Bering Strait
2. The Strait of Messina
3. The Strait of Hormuz
4. The Strait of Magellan
5. The Strait of Gibraltar

ROLE PLAYING
1. B
2. F
3. H
4. J
5. E
6. C
7. I
8. G
9. D
10. A

OCTOBER 30

FEAR FACTOR
1. Her first period
2. Edward Albee
3. Feathers
4. The Hitchhiker's Guide to the Galaxy
5. North Carolina
6. The number 666
7. The Smiths'
8. *The Fly*
9. Tommy
10. Martin Van Buren's

MR. JENNINGS'S TEN BEST DRESSED
1. Spats
2. Savile Row
3. *Breakfast at Tiffany's*
4. Beau Brummell
5. Navy blue
6. Oleg Cassini
7. *Blue Velvet*
8. Barbie
9. Vera Wang
10. Spider-Man

OCTOBER 31

NOSE CANDY
1. A button
2. The septum
3. Dmitri Shostakovich
4. Chief Joseph
5. The cricket
6. "Health"
7. Tycho Brahe
8. Froot Loops
9. Roxane
10. "New car smell"

INVASION OF THE BODY SNATCHERS
1. Gram Parsons
2. Eva Perón's
3. Charlie Chaplin
4. Alistair Cooke
5. John Barrymore

BEST(IARY) SELLERS
Easy
1. Snake
2. Cat
3. Hippogriff
4. House elf
Harder
1. Dragon
2. Dog
3. Phoenix
4. Giant

Yeah, Good Luck
1. Owl
2. Centaur
3. Toad
4. Thestral

• 1911 • DURING A RECONNAISSANCE MISSION against Turkish forces in Libya, an Italian pilot named Giulio Gavotti invents the aerial bombing raid when he realizes he can toss grenades at targets from his small plane. I'm guessing he was the kind of guy who threw stuff off overpasses when he was a kid.

DA BOMB

1. What was the code name of the atomic bomb dropped on Hiroshima?

2. What famous B-17 was named for a Tennessee cotton entrepreneur's daughter named Margaret Polk?

3. What club, whose first chapter formed in San Bernardino in 1948, borrowed the World War II nickname for the 303rd Bombardment Group?

4. *Slaughterhouse-Five* was inspired by the firebombing of

what German city?

5. What 1989 song was named for the tin-roofed cabin where the B-52s wrote their hit song "Rock Lobster"?

• 1939 • HOLLYWOOD'S STRICT MORAL CONSCIENCE, the Production Code, passes an amendment allowing certain uses of the words "damn" and "hell" in historical or literary context. The rule is specifically designed to avoid censoring Clark Gable's last line in *Gone With the Wind*.

FRANKLY, MY DEAR . . .
On what rivers would you find these dams?

1. Aswan High Dam
2. Hoover Dam

3. Three Gorges Dam
4. Grand Coulee Dam

5. Fort Peck Dam

• 1944 • THE WORD "VEGAN" is coined when Donald Watson founds the United Kingdom's Vegan Society. Watson is fed up with ovolacto types co-opting the "vegetarian" label, so he wants a new concept that would be "the beginning and the end of vegetarianism"—hence, veganism.

SOCIETY PAGES

1. What turn-of-the-century event was provoked by the Society of Right and Harmonious Fists?

2. What rapper lost his role in *Menace II Society* when, he said, he made the mistake of beating up the directors?

3. What Baptist missionary is remembered today only because he was shot by Chinese Communists near Xi'an in 1945?

4. What British band released *The Village Green Preservation*

Society the same day the Beatles' "White Album" came out?

5. What's the largest of the Society Islands?

6. What author's words are read to open every meeting of the *Dead Poets Society*?

7. What famous inventor was a founder, and the second president, of the National Geographic Society?

8. The Crosby-Sinatra-Kelly film *High Society* was a musical remake of what classic film?

9. What's the more common name for Saint Ignatius of Loyola's Society of Jesus?

10. Who coined the phrase "conventional wisdom" in his book *The Affluent Society*?

Answers to the questions on this page can be found on page 477.

NOVEMBER 2

• 1949 • THE POPULAR PARLOR GAME "Twenty Questions" becomes a TV hit, debuting on New York's WWOR-TV station.

"20" QUESTIONS

1. In what mountain range did Rip van Winkle take his twenty-year nap?

2. What Matchbox 20 song was a number one hit in the U.S. but hit only number 79 in the U.K., where its title is a synonym for "gay"?

3. Who was the only twentieth-century president never to appoint a Supreme Court justice?

4. What TV drama will equal *Gunsmoke*'s twenty-season longevity record if it lasts through 2010?

5. *H2o* wasn't the twentieth *Halloween* film. What number in the title would have been more accurate?

6. Of the twenty possible first moves in chess, how many don't involve a pawn?

7. In the measurement for "20/20 vision"—twenty of what?

8. What was unusual about pitcher Bartolo Colón's twenty-win season in 2002?

9. What shape is each of the twenty faces on a regular icosahedron?

10. When a CB radio user asks "What's your 20?" what should you tell him?

11. What U.S. president broke the "Twenty-Year Curse"?

12. What two star Detroit Lions running backs both had the same initials, both won a Heisman, and both wore number 20?

13. What brand of cleaner was represented by a "20-Mule Team"?

14. What's the more modern word for a vicenarian?

15. What economist, on Britain's new £20 note, is the first Scotsman ever to appear on Bank of England currency?

16. The city of Paris is divided into twenty boroughs called what?

17. What TV show set each of its six seasons exactly twenty years in the past?

18. What two cities were connected by the 20th Century Limited?

19. Who wrote the twenty-novel series that stretched from 1969's *Master and Commander* to 1999's *Blue at the Mizzen*?

20. The Beatles had twenty U.S. number one hits, but what Beatles song has the word "twenty" in its first line?

• 1959 • CHARLES VAN DOREN admits to Congress that he was fed the answers on TV's *Twenty-One*.

TWENTY-ONE QUESTIONS

Without being given the answers, can you answer these questions from Van Doren's Twenty-One *streak?*

1. What Massachusetts statesman said, "Taxation without representation is tyranny"?

2. What synthetic fiber has replaced silk in women's stockings?

3. Who preceded Joe Louis as world heavyweight champion?

4. What two countries' armies faced each other at Lake Ladoga?

5. Who was the cruel wife of the biblical king Ahab?

Answers to the questions on this page can be found on page 477.

• **1948** • "DEWEY DEFEATS TRUMAN" trumpets the early edition of the *Chicago Daily Tribune*. When Dewey's lead starts to vanish overnight, the frantic *Tribune* sends out staff to recover as many of the papers as possible, but thousands have already been sold.

MASTHEAD HUNTING
What's the largest U.S. city whose largest paper is called . . .

Easy	Harder	Yeah, Good Luck
1. The *Globe*	1. The *Star-Ledger*	1. The *Mercury News*
2. The *Sun-Times*	2. The *Times-Picayune*	2. The *Sentinel*
3. The *Rocky Mountain News*	3. The *Free Press*	3. The *Beacon Journal*
4. The *Post*	4. The *Inquirer*	4. The *Courant*
5. The *Plain Dealer*	5. The *Star Tribune*	5. The *Observer*

• **1948** • A YOUNG DIPLOMAT'S WIFE, the former Julia McWilliams, arrives in Le Havre, France, with her husband. She has no particular interest in food, but the simple lunch they order at a Rouen restaurant—oysters, sole, salad, and wine—makes history, since it introduces Julia Child to French cuisine.

BROADCAST STEWS
What nom de cuisine *did these chefs use to title their TV programs?*

1. Ina Garten	3. Jamie Oliver	5. Jennifer Paterson and Clarissa
2. Jeff Smith	4. Graham Kerr	Dickson Wright

• **1983** • IN THE BASEMENT of the University of Vermont's Slade Hall, a quartet formerly called Blackwood Convention gives its first concert under its new name, Phish.

JAM BANDS

1. What former frontman of the Jam played lead guitar on Oasis's "Champagne Supernova"?
2. What Detroit rock band was dropped by Elektra Records during the controversy over its song "Kick Out the Jams"?
3. What NBA player was Pearl Jam originally named for?
4. What 1986 New Wave hit, written by Jimmy Jam and Terry Lewis, is the only *Billboard* number one ever in which the artist's name contains the title of the song?
5. Who became president of Def Jam Records in 2005?

Answers to the questions on this page can be found on page 477.

• **1899** • SIGMUND FREUD PUBLISHES his landmark *The Interpretation of Dreams.*

THESE DREAMS
What kinds of dreams are described by the names of . . .

1. Smashing Pumpkins' major-label debut
2. The winner of the 1994 Sundance Audience Award for Best Documentary
3. The play that ends with Theseus's wedding to the Amazon Hippolyta
4. The German band that provided the soundtracks to *Risky*
Business and *Legend*
5. The TV series on which Nick Lachey played Tom Jones and Usher played Marvin Gaye

• **1952** • DWIGHT EISENHOWER DEFEATS Adlai Stevenson in the baldest presidential election in U.S. history.

CUE-BALL LIBRE
Ten other famous men with no hair apparent.

1. Larry David's real-life wife was named Laurie, but what was her name on *Curb Your Enthusiasm*?
2. What politician's first wife, Regina Peruggi, was also his second cousin?
3. Michael Jordan is now a part owner of what NBA team?
4. Who was the only member of the Magnificent Seven to appear in the sequel *Return of the Seven*?
5. What prime minister did Nikita Khrushchev interrupt with his famous shoe-banging routine at the U.N.?
6. In what foreign country did Gandhi spend more than twenty years of his life?
7. What was the first name of TV's Kojak?
8. What austere phase in Pablo Picasso's painting was influenced by his friend Carlos Casagemas's suicide?
9. What Oscar-winning singer did Andre Agassi date before marrying Brooke Shields?
10. What does the *J* in "Homer J. Simpson" stand for?

• **1991** • THE RONALD REAGAN Presidential Library is dedicated in Simi Valley, California. For the first time in history, five U.S. presidents are present at the same event.

THE BOOKS STOP HERE
What president's library is located in each of these spots?

Easy
1. Atlanta, Georgia
2. Little Rock, Arkansas
3. Yorba Linda, California
4. Springfield, Illinois
5. Hyde Park, New York

Harder
1. Abilene, Kansas
2. West Branch, Iowa
3. Austin, Texas
4. Ann Arbor, Michigan
5. College Station, Texas

Yeah, Good Luck
1. Canton, Ohio
2. Biloxi, Mississippi
3. Fremont, Ohio
4. Northampton, Massachusetts
5. Staunton, Virginia

Answers to the questions on this page can be found on page 478.

• 1917 • WALTER BUTLER SENDS a postcard from the Flanders trenches to let his fiancée know he's still alive and well. Sadly, the postcard is lost on its way to Swindon and isn't delivered until February 2007. (Butler's now-86-year-old daughter Joyce will take delivery.) And that's what happens when you don't give the postman a Christmas present.

MAIL BONDING

1. Canadian postal codes use both letters and numbers: the prime minister's code, for example, is K1A 0A2. What postal code is reserved for the one million letters to Santa that Canada receives every year?

2. In the New Testament, what two Greek congregations received two letters each from the apostle Paul?

3. What's the updated name for the USPS mail class once known as "Book Rate"?

4. What notorious figure was well known for his consistent use of $1 Eugene O'Neill postage stamps?

5. What Missouri city was the eastern terminus of the Pony Express?

6. C. S. Lewis's *The Screwtape Letters* are written to what junior devil, Screwtape's nephew?

7. What was Fred Rogers's middle name, which he gave to the "Speedy Delivery" mailman on *Mister Rogers' Neighborhood*?

8. Who is pictured on the penny black, the world's first adhesive postage stamp?

9. Who replaced the U.S. Postal Service as sponsor of its champion cycling team in 2004?

10. The postman in the film *Il Postino* delivers the mail to what exiled poet?

• 1935 • PARKER BROTHERS RELEASES the board game Monopoly. Though it was patented by Philadelphia salesman Charles Darrow, he'd actually ripped off the design from an older board game called The Landlord's Game.

COMMUNITY CHEST

Ten U.S. states have Monopoly properties named for them. Can you match them up?

1. The last U.S. state to get a Wal-Mart

2. The birthplace of more vice presidents than any other: eight

3. The only state with an automobile on its state quarter

4. The state whose state university has the winningest basketball program in NCAA history

5. The first state readmitted to the Union after the Civil War

6. The state with the highest per capita income in the country

7. The state in which the New World's first English baby was born

8. The first state to have two different major-league teams win consecutive World Series

9. The state that shared a border with Pennsylvania and Ohio until 1863

10. The first state to name an official state toy, the Slinky

A. Connecticut
B. Illinois
C. Indiana
D. Kentucky
E. New York
F. North Carolina
G. Pennsylvania
H. Tennessee
I. Vermont
J. Virginia

Answers to the questions on this page can be found on page 478.

NOVEMBER 6

• **1962** • RICHARD NIXON LOSES his race for governor of California, leading to his sadly empty promise "You won't have Nixon to kick around anymore."

JUST FOR KICKS

1. How far must an untouched onside kick in football travel to be recovered by the kicking team?
2. In the movie *They Live*, Roddy Piper says he's come to "kick ass" and enjoy what other activity?
3. What's the only Olympic martial art in which kicking is allowed?
4. Who "tested" and "approved" Kix cereal?
5. According to Cole Porter's "I Get a Kick out of You," what two rhyming substances provide him "no kick"?

• **1990** • RICHMOND COUNTY, NEW YORK, aka Staten Island, votes to begin the process of seceding from New York City. The movement will later be defused by the election of Rudolph Giuliani, who will win the mayor's office on the strength of his Staten Island support.

TOWN AND COUNTY
What major American city is the seat of each of these counties?

Easy	Harder	Yeah, Good Luck
1. Cook County	1. Harris County	1. Bexar County
2. Dade County	2. King County	2. Clark County
3. Cuyahoga County	3. Maricopa County	3. Hennepin County
4. Fulton County	4. Allegheny County	4. Multnomah County
5. Wayne County	5. Broward County	5. Marion County

• **2001** • AMERICA MEETS JACK BAUER, as *24* debuts on Fox. The pilot's final scene, in which a terrorist blows up a Boeing 747, is heavily edited, airing as it does just two months after the 9/11 attacks.

NUMB3RS
What numbers complete these TV series' titles?

Easy	Harder	Yeah, Good Luck
1. *Adam* ____	1. *Room* ____	1. *Jake* ____
2. *Beverly Hills* ____	2. *Cleopatra* ____	2. *Level* ____
3. *Route* ____	3. *Blake's* ____	3. *Code* ____
4. *Reno* ____	4. *Mystery Science Theater* ____	4. *Number* ____
5. *Babylon* ____	5. *Sealab* ____	5. *James at* ____

Answers to the questions on this page can be found on page 478.

NOVEMBER 7

• **1628** • PHILIP STANHOPE IS CREATED the first earl of Chesterfield. His descendants will receive an even greater honor in the 1850s, when a type of straight-armed sofa is named for the family.

SOFA SO GOOD

1. What movie was Tom Cruise promoting when he indulged in his couch-jumping episode on *Oprah*?
2. Whose famous couch was a gift from the grateful Madame Benvisti in 1890?
3. What's pictured in the painting that hangs above *The Simpsons'* couch?
4. What's the largest of the Midwest's "Quad Cities"?
5. In what anthem is Cheap Trick shocked to discover "Mom and Dad . . . rolling on the couch"?

• **1949** • IN ARTICLE 12 of its new constitution, the nation of Costa Rica abolishes its army.

YOU AND WHAT ARMY?

1. What country is a member of NATO despite having no standing army?
2. What landlocked nation still has a naval ensign despite having lost its access to the sea in 1884's War of the Pacific?
3. Members of what nation's security force must, by law, be citizens of Switzerland?
4. What island nation's 1,200-man army was disbanded after a 1983 invasion?
5. What country, by law, refers to its military as "Self-Defense Forces"?

• **2000** • ALABAMA BECOMES THE last state in the Union to vote its antimiscegenation law off the books. Shockingly, 40 percent of voters opposed the repeal.

BLACK AND WHITE AND WED ALL OVER
Give the other half of these famous interracial marriages.

Easy
1. Lisa Marie Presley
2. Iman
3. Connie Chung
4. John Rolfe
5. Heidi Klum

Harder
1. Ben Harper
2. Idina Menzel
3. Les Moonves
4. Mariah Carey
5. Dennis Rodman

Yeah, Good Luck
1. Peggy Lipton
2. Georg Stanford Brown
3. Vic Damone
4. Elin Nordegren
5. Alexander Payne

• **1971** • "STAIRWAY TO HEAVEN" is released on that Led Zeppelin album with the funky runes that I can't type here. But the iconic song is never released as a single, because Zeppelin refuses to cut down its eight-minute running time.

HOW LONG? HOW LONG MUST WE SING THIS SONG?

Name the artists who tried our patience with these ten-minute-plus epics.

Easy	*Harder*	*Yeah, Good Luck*
1. "The End"	1. "Marquee Moon"	1. "Telegraph Road"
2. "Shine On, You Crazy Dia-	2. "Sister Ray"	2. "Pass the Hatchet, I Think I'm
mond"	3. "Three Days"	Goodkind"
3. "Rapper's Delight"	4. "Voodoo Chile"	3. "Brownsville Girl"
4. "I'd Do Anything for Love"	5. "2112"	4. "The Diamond Sea"
5. "In-A-Gadda-Da-Vida"		5. "Third Eye"

• **1975** • DANIEL RUETTIGER, of *Rudy* fame, makes his one-play appearance in a Notre Dame football game—and records a sack against Georgia Tech.

VARSITY BLUES

Which college sport is central to these movies?

1. *Flubber*	3. *We Are Marshall*	5. *Without Limits*
2. *Back to School*	4. *Love Story*	

• **1975** • THE LAND SHARK, cleverest of all sharks, makes his *Saturday Night Live* debut. "Plumber, ma'am." (Pause.) "Candygram."

SKIT AIN'T OVER TILL IT'S OVER

Name the SNL characters—not cast members—behind these catchphrases.

Easy	*Harder*	*Yeah, Good Luck*
1. "Schwing!"	1. "Never mind!"	1. "We are two wild and crazy
2. "Superstar!"	2. "You look like a rabbit."	guys!"
3. "You look mahvelous."	3. "I'm jus' keeeding!"	2. "I must say."
4. "Could it be . . . Satan?!"	4. "Touch him! Touch my mon-	3. "Oh no!"
5. "We're going to pump . . . you	key!"	4. "A van down by the river!"
up!"	5. "Yeah, that's the ticket."	5. "Bum lookers!"

Answers to the questions on this page can be found on page 479.

• **1967** • THE FIRST ISSUE OF *Rolling Stone* magazine is published, using a mailing list that Jann Wenner stole from a Bay Area radio station.

(LIKE A) ROLLING STONE

These are fifteen songs from Rolling Stone's list of the "500 Greatest Songs of All Time," with only the parenthesized parts of the song title shown. Can you restore the rest of the title?

Easy	Harder	Yeah, Good Luck
1. (I Can't Get No)	**1.** (Slight Return)	**1.** (We're Gonna)
2. (When He Walked Me Home)	**2.** (Walkin' in the Sand)	**2.** (To Stop Now)
3. (Don't Fear)	**3.** (This Bird Has Flown)	**3.** (The Way I Love You)
4. (That's What I Want)	**4.** (What's So Funny 'Bout)	**4.** (Your Love Keeps Lifting Me)
5. (Are Made of These)	**5.** (Falletinme Be Mice Elf Again)	**5.** (I Feel Like Being a)

• **1992** • CHARLES FRASER-SMITH, the British gadgeteer upon whom Ian Fleming based his quartermaster character, Q, dies.

RIGHT ON Q

1. What former child star is the superintendent of Broadway's *Avenue Q*?
2. Whose sayings may have been collected in the hypothetical "Q Document"?
3. Hissy, Slimy, or Coily—what's the name of the snake who bedevils video game character Q*Bert?
4. What does it mean when a *Q* is appended to the end of a company's stock ticker symbol?
5. What does the *Q* stand for in the 1982 film *Q: The Winged Serpent*?
6. What playing card appears in the title of Stacey Q's biggest pop hit?
7. What NBA team plays at "the Q"—Quicken Loans Arena?
8. What were called "Baby Gays" when they were invented in 1928?
9. What movie title character never says a word, leaving the talking to his sidekick, Timothy Q. Mouse?
10. Two Arab nations, Iraq and Qatar, have the letter *Q* in their names. What two African nations do as well?

• **1993** • CRAYOLA UNVEILS SIXTEEN new crayons, with colors chosen in a nationwide contest. Winners include asparagus, timberwolf, and macaroni and cheese.

HARD PALETTE

What color of the rainbow is closest to these shades?

Easy	Harder	Yeah, Good Luck
1. Crimson	**1.** Mauve	**1.** Cerulean
2. Azure	**2.** Viridian	**2.** Cerise
3. Lilac	**3.** Fuchsia	**3.** Malachite
4. Teal	**4.** Cyan	**4.** Heliotrope
5. Saffron	**5.** Chartreuse	**5.** Titian

Answers to the questions on this page can be found on page 479.

• **1871** • SENT TO AFRICA by *The New York Herald,* Henry Stanley finally finds his missionary quarry in a tiny village on the shores of Lake Tanganyika. "Dr. Livingstone, I presume?" he asks.

COME-ON PILGRIM
Try to get lucky with these questions about great pickup lines.

1. What famous disco refrain of 1974 is drawn, word for word, from scene six of *A Streetcar Named Desire,* where Blanche DuBois uses it as a come-on to Mitch?
2. What was Joey Tribbiani's three-word pickup catchphrase on *Friends?*

3. In 1936, who asked a police officer at L.A.'s train station, "Is that a gun in your pocket, or are you just happy to see me?"
4. What Cleveland power-pop quartet specialized in songs about talking women into bed, such as "I Wanna Be with You," "Tonight," and "Go All the

Way"?
5. Who, upon first meeting Ted Hughes at a party, recited one of his poems to him, then led him to a closet, where she bit his cheek so hard he bled?

• **1928** • KNUTE ROCKNE RALLIES his underdog Notre Dame team to victory over Army with his famous "Win One for the Gipper" speech. The speech will go on to become one of the most-quoted lines in movie history, whether or not the late George Gipp ever said anything of the kind.

LOOK WHO'S TALKING NOW
Can you identify iconic movie lines when given the line that immediately follows *them?*

Easy
1. "Well, I'm the only one here."
2. "He wants to call somebody."
3. "Son, we live in a world with walls that must be guarded. Who's gonna do it? You? You, Lieutenant Weinberg?"
4. "I could've been somebody, instead of a bum, which is what I am."
5. "We have a main bus B undervolt."

Harder
1. "I gots to know."
2. "Then we'll figure out what to do about the depression and the inflation and the oil crisis."
3. "I work and work until I'm half dead, and I hear people saying 'She's getting old,' and what do I get? A daughter who cares as much about the beautiful dresses I give her as she cares about me!"
4. "Hey, Annie! Annie, what was that?"
5. "I can't let him go. I can't. There must be some way to bring him back!"

Yeah, Good Luck
1. "In your dreams? While you're awake?"
2. "I knew there was something wrong with them."
3. *"Oui, mon capitaine."*
4. "You know, one time we had a hill bombed for twelve hours."
5. "Now, you just go outside and enjoy yourself, and, ah, forget about all this nonsense. I want you to leave it all to me."

Answers to the questions on this page can be found on page 480.

• 1839 • AFTER EIGHT SUCCESSIVE LOSSES, Marcus Morton wins the governorship of Massachusetts—by the narrowest of margins. He receives 51,034 of 102,066 votes, a one-vote majority.

COUNT AND RECOUNT

Can you match up these quantities by giving the number they have in common?

1. Ali Baba's thieves
2. Dalai Lamas
3. Hearts of an octopus
4. Maximum tracks on a CD
5. Permanent Security Council members
6. Playing cards in a standard deck
7. Positions in the *Kama Sutra*
8. Spots on a six-sided die
9. States bordering the Great Lakes
10. Words in the Pledge of Allegiance

A. Days of Noah's flood
B. Huxtable children
C. Ivy League universities
D. "Luftballoons"
E. Rounds in a presidential salute
F. Spaces on a chessboard
G. Stocks in the Dow Jones
H. Teams in the American League
I. Teaspoons in a tablespoon
J. White keys on a piano

• 1975 • ARNOLD SCHWARZENEGGER WINS his sixth Mr. Olympia competition and retires from bodybuilding. This contest will be the subject of the 1977 documentary *Pumping Iron.*

GONE WITH THE WIN

What kind of contest is featured in these movies?

1. *Urban Cowboy*
2. *They Shoot Horses, Don't They?*
3. *Stand by Me*

4. *Drop Dead Gorgeous*
5. *Christmas in July*

• 2005 • THE NATIONAL TOY HALL of Fame, in Rochester, New York, finally admits into its hallowed halls childhood's most captivating toy: the empty cardboard box.

"BOX" OFFICE

1. In 1984, who became the first woman to appear on the front of a Wheaties box?
2. Which song from Big Boi's *Speakerboxxx* replaced his Out-Kast bandmate's hit "Hey Ya!" at number one in 2004?
3. In reality, what color are the airplane voice recorders called "black boxes"?
4. What's the all-time bestselling game in Xbox history?
5. Who warned his wife, Pandora, not to open her famous box?
6. What day of the year is Boxing Day celebrated?
7. What TV title character owned and managed the Lanford Lunch Box?
8. According to the annual
Quigley poll, who was the top box-office draw of 1973, 1983, and also of 1993?
9. Who or what occupied the very first "Skinner box"?
10. What German immigrant founded the company that later produced the famous "850 Peacock" jukebox?

Answers to the questions on this page can be found on page 480.

NOVEMBER 12

• **1955** • WASHINGTON STATE TAKES ON San Jose State despite windy, freezing weather in Pullman, Washington. The football game produces perhaps the smallest paid attendance in sports history: one.

WEE THE PEOPLE
Just a few small questions.

1. What TV show does HBO bill as "the story of a man with small parts"?
2. What miniature items come in sizes from *mame* to *shito* to *shohin*?
3. In Munchkinland, what's the male counterpart of the "Lullaby League"?
4. What's the more familiar name for Mozart's *Serenade for Strings in G Major*?
5. What island is also, by area, America's smallest county?
6. What's the only near-actual-size item used as a token in Monopoly?
7. Which two moons of the solar system are actually larger than Mercury, the smallest planet?
8. What was founded in 1939 in Williamsport, Pennsylvania?
9. What single-celled creature, commonly seen under microscopes, takes its name from the Greek for "oblong"?
10. Who removed the "Lil'" from his stage name when he released his album *Doggy Bag*?

• **1955** • LIGHTNING STRIKES the Hill Valley clock tower at 10:04 P.M., stopping the hands of the clock in that position for decades. (The same bolt of lightning also sends Marty McFly *Back to the Future*.)

TELLING TIME

1. Why isn't it correct to point out the time on London's iconic Big Ben?
2. What are the only two Major League Baseball teams that play their home games in Mountain Time?
3. What famous event happened "on the eleventh hour of the eleventh day of the eleventh month"?
4. What Dutchman invented the pendulum clock in 1656?
5. At what time of night does daylight saving time begin and end?

• **1970** • THE OREGON HIGHWAY DIVISION tries to dispose of a stinky beached whale carcass with explosives, but it uses too much dynamite: blubber flies a quarter mile into the air and smashes cars in a distant parking lot.

ONCE MORE UNTO THE BEACH

1. What volcanic peak rises above the eastern end of Waikiki Beach?
2. What 1980s slang word for "awesome" was originally a surfer term for a wave with a rideable barrel?
3. What two adjacent Rio de Janeiro beaches were immortalized in the names of pop songs, in 1964 and 1978, respectively?
4. In what country is the beach from Alex Garland's 1996 novel *The Beach*?
5. What movie begins with Joel and Clementine taking the train to snowy Montauk Beach on Valentine's Day, though they don't know why?
6. How many arms do most starfish have?
7. Who wasn't allowed to use his own first name in 1987's *Back to the Beach*, because of copyright issues with the *Beach Party* movies?
8. What breed is the black dog depantsing the Coppertone girl in the original ad?
9. Who was the only original Beach Boy not related to the other four?
10. On which of the five landing beaches was the bloodiest battle of D-day?

Answers to the questions on this page can be found on page 480.

• **1797** • DURING A WALK in the Quantock Hills, poet William Wordsworth tells his friend Samuel Taylor Coleridge about a book he's reading, about George Shelvocke's voyages as a privateer. One episode, about the shooting of a black albatross, sparks in Coleridge the idea for the poem that will become his masterpiece, *The Rime of the Ancient Mariner.*

LIGHTBULBS
Inspiration can strike in the oddest places.

1. What fifty-five-year-old TV logo was based on hex symbols painted on Shaker barns to ward off evil spirits?

2. What Coldplay song was inspired by the phone book sitting next to Chris Martin as he wrote its lyrics?

3. What product was the result of Minnesota researcher Arthur Fry sitting in church, wishing he had a better way to mark the pages of his choir hymnal?

4. What TV show was inspired by James L. Brooks reading an article called "Hip-Shifting for the Night Fleet" in *New York* magazine?

5. According to legend, what did Galileo invent after watching a bronze chandelier being lit in a Pisan cathedral?

6. Who devised the famous "Notre Dame shift" while watching an intricately choreographed chorus line at a dance hall?

7. What did 11-year-old Frank Epperson invent in 1905 when he left a glass of homemade soda he was stirring out on his back porch overnight?

8. What 1977 bestseller was inspired by the author's stay in room 217 of the Stanley Hotel in Estes Park, Colorado?

9. What song did John Lennon write after reading two newspaper stories—one about the death of Guinness heir Tara Browne and one about a pothole problem?

10. What invention occurred to Swiss electrical engineer Georges de Mestral while he was pulling burrs off his wool hunting pants during a weekend hiking trip?

• **1942** • THE FIRST CABLE TV PROGRAM is telecast: from Tuckerman, Arkansas, the Tennessee and Mississippi football teams square off live.

CABLE GUYS

1. What did the *H* in VH-1 originally stand for?

2. Who's the only original CNN Headline News anchor still with the network?

3. In an unprecedented feat, the top seventeen cable broadcasts of 2006 were *all* episodes of what program?

4. What rock star faced off against what serial killer in the very first *Celebrity Deathmatch* bout on MTV?

5. What phrase did Fox News sue to remove from the subtitle of a 2003 Al Franken book?

6. What audience is targeted by the cable networks Here! and Logo?

7. What two HBO series removed shots of the World Trade Center from their credits following the 9/11 attacks?

8. What cable channel's French Canadian version is called MétéoMédia?

9. Handball, volleyball, or softball—what sport's "World Series" was the first sporting event ever aired on ESPN?

10. What director sued in 2003 over the new on-screen name of the former Nashville Network?

Answers to the questions on this page can be found on page 481.

NOVEMBER 14

• **1922** • FUTURE U.N. SECRETARY-GENERAL Boutros Boutros-Ghali, the grandson of former Egyptian prime minister Boutros Ghali, is born in Cairo.

NAME DISENTANGLEMENT

In each correct answer, the subject's last name will contain the letters, in order, of his or her first name (though not necessarily consecutively).

1. Because her father is a friend of the Dalai Lama's and a leading American scholar of Buddhism, what actress is named for an Indian goddess?
2. What newsman did George Clooney play in 2005's *Good Night and Good Luck*?
3. What sportscaster was "traded" from Disney to NBC in 2006 in exchange for the rights to 1920s cartoon character Oswald the Lucky Rabbit?

4. What writer said, during her public feud with Lillian Hellman, "Every word she writes is a lie, including 'and' and 'the' "?
5. What secretary of commerce was killed in a 1996 plane crash over Croatia?
6. What actor's speech from *Brassed Off* is sampled at the beginning of the Chumbawumba hit "Tubthumping"?
7. The "Dandelion" crater on the moon is named in honor of what

author?
8. Who wrote the Janis Joplin hit "Me and Bobby McGee"?
9. What title character's story demonstrates that "every happy family is unhappy in its own way"?
10. Who plays Angel Eyes, the "Bad" in *The Good, the Bad, and the Ugly*?

• **1972** • THE DOW JONES closes above 1,000 for the first time.

POWERS OF TEN

1. In 1980, who was fired from the set of *One Day at a Time* for drug problems?
2. What two Jewish holidays are spanned by the Ten Days of Repentance?

3. Who briefly returned to power in the 1815 campaign called the Hundred Days?
4. What historical figure is the subject of *Anne of the Thousand Days*?

5. Someone who is ten thousand days old is what age, also the age at which Brian Jones, Jimi Hendrix, Janis Joplin, Jim Morrison, and Kurt Cobain all died?

• **2005** • LEEUWARDEN, IN THE NETHERLANDS, is preparing for its annual Domino Day, in which millions of domino bricks are toppled, when a sparrow flies into the event building and knocks over 23,000 dominoes. The distraught organizers call in a hunter to shoot the sparrow, leading to an international animal rights controversy.

DOMINO EFFECT

1. Domino's ads urged viewers to avoid what red-suited, pizza-ruining villain?
2. What stage name did Ernest Evans adopt in tribute to Fats Domino?

3. Dwight Eisenhower's famous 1954 "domino theory" news conference referenced what part of the world?
4. What's the maximum number of pips on a domino from a stan-

dard set?
5. What British actor was the father of the bounty hunter Domino, played on-screen by Keira Knightley?

Answers to the questions on this page can be found on page 481.

• 1505 • BLOWN OFF COURSE by a storm, Portuguese missionary Lourenço de Almeida arrives in Sri Lanka, founding the first European settlement there and naming the island Ceylon.

THE MYSTERIOUS ISLANDS
Can you I.D. these islands from their outlines?

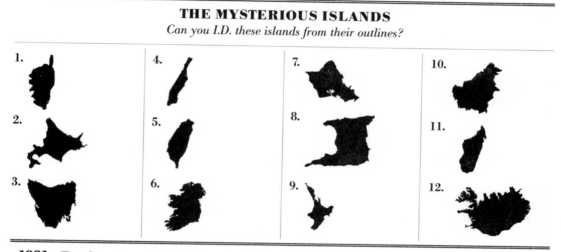

• 1981 • *THE STEELER AND THE PITTSBURGH KID,* perhaps the only movie ever based on a TV ad, airs on NBC. "Mean" Joe Greene reprises his role as the jersey-throwing Steeler; a pre-*E.T.* Henry Thomas makes his TV debut as the Coke-offering kid.

MEAN STREAK

1. What *SNL* alum plays the high school principal in the movie *Mean Girls*?
2. Apart from the British Isles, what are the only two European countries on Greenwich Mean Time?
3. Who is the archenemy of Bugs Meany and his gang, the Tigers?
4. What Greek letter is used to represent the number 1.618 . . . , the "golden mean"?
5. What Beatles title character is Mean Mr. Mustard's sister?

• 1994 • BRIT JOURNALIST MARK SIMPSON coins the word "metrosexual" in an article titled "Here Come the Mirror Men" in *The Independent*.

TRANSMETROPOLITAN
Match these crime fighters to the cities they protect.

1. Darkwing Duck
2. The Flash
3. Green Lantern
4. The Incredibles
5. The Mighty Heroes
6. Mighty Mouse
7. Mystery Men
8. The Powerpuff Girls
9. The Tick
10. Underdog

A. Capitol City
B. Central City
C. Champion City
D. The City
E. Coast City
F. Good Haven
G. Metroville
H. Mouseville
I. St. Canard
J. Townsville

Answers to the questions on this page can be found on page 481.

NOVEMBER 16

• **1906** • WHILE TEDDY ROOSEVELT is visiting the Panama Canal (the first foreign trip by a sitting president, by the way), a photograph is taken of the president in a black-banded straw hat. This helps cement in the public mind the idea that this type of Ecuadorian-made hat is, in fact, a "Panama hat."

OFF THE TOP OF YOUR HEAD

1. Whose hat bears a slip of paper reading "In this style 10/6"?

2. What signature salad was invented at Hollywood's Brown Derby restaurant in 1937?

3. In 2002, what city dedicated a bronze statue of a young woman tossing a tam-o'-shanter into the air at the corner of Seventh Street and Nicollet Mall?

4. What type of paper got its name from a seventeenth-century watermark of a belled jester's hat?

5. In addition to being a hat, "Fez" is also the third largest city of what country?

6. How many rays are there on the Statue of Liberty's crown?

7. What are the only two NFL teams with football helmets pic-tured on their helmet logos?

8. Who wears a red *zucchetto* hat?

9. From what sport did hockey borrow the term "hat trick," for a trio of goals?

10. In a 1985 hit song, what does a girl wear into Mr. McGee's five-and-dime store?

• **1959** • *THE SOUND OF MUSIC* opens on Broadway. Jon Voight is an understudy for the part of Nazi bicycle messenger Rolf, and he ends up marrying Lauri Peters, his Liesl.

THE HILLS ARE ALIVE

1. What hill in Somerset, England, was immortalized in 1977 by Peter Gabriel, who used to jog there?

2. What nickname did Dong Ap Bia receive in 1969 from all the U.S. soldiers who were "chewed up" there?

3. What Caribbean island was largely evacuated in 1995 when the Soufrière Hills volcano erupted?

4. What's the mascot of the basketball team on TV's *One Tree Hill*?

5. What historical event actually happened, for the most part, on nearby Breed's Hill?

• **1981** • GUEST STAR ELIZABETH TAYLOR is on hand when Luke and Laura get married on *General Hospital*, still the highest-rated hour of daytime television ever.

VERY SPECIAL EPISODES
What TV characters married these characters on-screen?

Easy
1. Mindy McConnell
2. Daphne Moon
3. Chandler Bing
4. Agent 99
5. Simka Dahblitz

Harder
1. Joe Gerard
2. Byron Sully
3. Carol Martin
4. Luka Kovac
5. Brenda Chenoweth

Yeah, Good Luck
1. Steve Brady
2. Connie McDowell
3. Joy Darville
4. Lee Stetson
5. Martha Hale

Answers to the questions on this page can be found on page 482.

• **1933** • ZEPPO MARX GETS his last hurrah, as the Marx Brothers movie *Duck Soup* is released. Zeppo decides to quit performing to become a Hollywood agent, and the remainder of the Marx Brothers' oeuvre will feature only his three brothers Groucho, Harpo, and Chico.

A GOOD CAST IS WORTH REPEATING

What three stars appear in both these movies?

1. *The Conversation* and *Apocalypse Now*
2. *The Adventures of Robin Hood* and *Captain Blood*
3. *Sense and Sensibility* and *Love Actually*
4. *Romancing the Stone* and *The War of the Roses*

5. *Starsky & Hutch* and *Anchorman*
6. *Titanic* and *Revolutionary Road*
7. *Casablanca* and *The Maltese Falcon*
8. *A League of Their Own* and *Sleepless in Seattle*

9. *The Breakfast Club* and *St. Elmo's Fire*
10. *Pillow Talk* and *Lover Come Back*

• **1978** • THE INFAMOUS *Star Wars Holiday Special* is broadcast for the only time. The *Star Wars* cast helps Chewbacca celebrate "Life Day" with the help of special guests like Bea Arthur, Art Carney, and (making his very first appearance) Boba Fett.

THE PICTURES GOT SMALL!

Name the only actor to reprise his or her role as a regular in these movie-to-TV transitions.

Easy
1. *M*A*S*H*
2. *The Paper Chase*
3. *Shaft*

Harder
1. *The Love Bug*
2. *Tremors*
3. *Alice*

Yeah, Good Luck
1. *The Client*
2. *Harry and the Hendersons*
3. *Police Academy*

• **1981** • C. EVERETT KOOP is sworn in as surgeon general of the United States—presumably wearing epaulets.

C HUNT

1. What crooner's albums include *Saturday Night with Mr. C* and *Sing to Me Mr. C*?
2. What Nobel laureate wrote "Vitamin C and the Common Cold" in 1970, when he was taking as much as 18,000 mg of the stuff a day?
3. What does the *C* stand for in military C rations?
4. What's the name for the "tail" added to the letter *c* in French to indicate a soft /s/ sound?
5. What was the real name of the C+C Music Factory hit often called "Everybody Dance Now"?

Answers to the questions on this page can be found on page 482.

• **1836** • *The Posthumous Papers of the Pickwick Club,* the first novel by the young Charles Dickens, hits bookstores.

WELCOME TO THE CLUB

1. What club did John Muir found in San Francisco in 1892?
2. What famous nightclub was, as its name implies, the building where TV hits like *The $64,000 Question* and *Jack Benny* were once taped?
3. What's the only warehouse club store that outsells Wal-Mart's Sam's Club?
4. The last of what clubs closed in Manila in 1991?

5. How many contributors did struggling Christian-themed TV station WYAH recruit in a 1962 telethon?
6. What "red hot mama" was the first woman ever roasted by the Friars Club?
7. Name either of the two Nobel laureates on the cover of *Sgt. Pepper's Lonely Hearts Club Band.*
8. What is the first rule of Fight

Club?
9. What kind of club opened for the first time in 1950 on Mallorca?
10. Who thanked L.A.'s "Tuesday Night Music Club" when she won her first Grammys?

• **1947** • On the early DuMont network sitcom *Mary Kay and Johnny,* the title characters (married in real life) become the first sitcom couple to share a double bed.

BED-AZZLED

1. What's unusual about inventor William Murphy's namesake Murphy bed?
2. Who held two "Bed-ins for Peace" in 1969?
3. What section of Bed Bath &

Beyond holds the universal remote in Adam Sandler's *Click*?
4. Inventor Charles Hall was unable to patent the water bed in 1968 because what author had already described one in his

novel *Stranger in a Strange Land*?
5. Who does Bob Newhart find himself in bed with in the final *Newhart*?

• **1992** • The death of Superman, at the hands of an alien bruiser called Doomsday, sells a gajillion comic books. (The Man of Steel "gets better" by the following August.)

REVIVAL MEETING

1. What crime were "resurrectionists" guilty of?
2. In 2005, what TV show became the first canceled series ever to be revived due to strong DVD sales?

3. What villain was placed in cryonic freeze aboard the SS *Botany Bay*?
4. On April 24, 1976, for what service did Lorne Michaels make an on-air offer of $3,000?

5. What brand, Coke's first diet soft drink, was relaunched as an energy drink in 2006?

Answers to the questions on this page can be found on page 482.

• **1863** • AFTER EDWARD EVERETT, the main speaker, delivers a two-hour oration, Abraham Lincoln reads ten sentences, dedicating a soldiers' cemetery at Gettysburg. Lincoln's prophecy that "the world will little note nor long remember what we say here" turns out to be true only of Everett's speech.

BULLY PULPITS
What U.S. presidents gave these famous speeches?

Easy	Harder	Yeah, Good Luck
1. *"Ich Bin ein Berliner"*	1. "The Silent Majority"	1. "Atoms for Peace"
2. "A House Divided"	2. "The Evil Empire"	2. "The Great Arsenal of Democracy"
3. "A Place Called Hope"	3. "National Malaise"	3. "The Man with the Muck Rake"

• **1954** • SAMMY DAVIS, JR., loses his left eye in a San Bernardino car accident, when a 72-year-old woman backs her car out of a driveway into his path. Humphrey Bogart persuades him to get a glass eye, and he's back performing just two months later.

I CAN SEE RIGHT THROUGH YOU
Raise a glass to these ten questions about glass.

1. What city's famous glass is made principally on the island of Murano?

2. What novel's sequel took place inside a "great glass elevator"?

3. The tallest variety of champagne glass shares its name with what musical instrument?

4. What dark volcanic glass is used today to make scalpel blades for cardiac surgery?

5. Who designed the glass pyramid at the entrance to the Louvre?

6. What movie's villain gives the famous command *"Schiess dem Fenster!"* meaning "Shoot the glass"?

7. What toy works because the aluminum dust and plastic beads inside it stick to a sheet of glass?

8. Where was the glass bridge called the Skywalk opened in 2007?

9. Who gave nicknames like "In Your Face Disgrace," "Dunk You Very Much," and "Rim Wrecker" to his trademark backboard-shattering slam dunks?

10. Which crystal animal breaks at the end of Tennessee Williams's *The Glass Menagerie*?

• **1990** • MILLI VANILLI IS STRIPPED of its Best New Artist Grammy when it's revealed that the duo lip-synched all its hits.

LIP SINK

1. Former *Playboy* model Lorelei Shark owns the iconic lips on the poster of what 1975 movie?

2. In the Flaming Lips song "She Don't Use Jelly," what *does* she put on toast?

3. What outspoken Dodgers manager with ninety-five career ejections was called "the Lip"?

4. According to a World War II propaganda campaign, what do loose lips do?

5. Scarlet, crimson, or vermilion—which shade of red is also the medical term for the red tissue of the lips?

Answers to the questions on this page can be found on page 483.

NOVEMBER 20

• **1831** • HANSON GREGORY IS BORN in Rockport, Maine. In 1847, as a young sailor in the lime trade, Gregory will tire of the soggy fried cakes served aboard ship and use the ship's tin pepper box to stamp out the middle of the frying dough, thus accidentally inventing the modern doughnut.

THE ACCIDENTAL TORUS

1. Which nation can boast the most doughnut shops per capita?
2. Who said, "Doughnuts . . . is there anything they can't do?" when they helped him stop a runaway monorail?

3. What word from a 1900 children's book does Dunkin' Donuts use to name its doughnut holes?
4. Louisiana and Massachusetts are the only states with official state

doughnuts. What are the two pastries in question?
5. What doughnut maker blamed its 2004 stock plunge on the low-carb diet craze?

• **1965** • SPORTSCASTER CHICK HEARN calls a college football game in Fayetteville, Arkansas. This becomes notable only the next day, when bad weather strands him in Arkansas and he misses the Lakers game he was scheduled to call. After that missed game, Hearn will broadcast 3,338 consecutive games for the Lakers, a streak that won't end until 2001.

THE PLAY-BY-PLAY'S THE THING

Can you match these famous calls to the sportscasters who made them, as well as the subject of the call?

1. "_____ stole the ball! _____ stole the ball!"
2. "He is moving like a tremendous machine!"
3. "Do you believe in miracles?"
4. "The Giants win the pennant!"
5. "Maybe . . . yes, *sir*!"
6. "Down goes _____! Down goes _____!"
7. "I don't believe what I just saw."
8. "They're all gone."
9. "Oh, the band is out on the field! He's gonna go into the end zone!"
10. "Two and two to Harvey Kuenn, one strike away."

A. Chic Anderson
B. Jack Buck
C. Howard Cosell
D. Russ Hodges
E. Verne Lundquist
F. Jim McKay
G. Al Michaels
H. Johnny Most
I. Vin Scully
J. Joe Starkey

a. Joe Frazier
b. Kirk Gibson
c. John Havlicek
d. Israeli Olympians
e. Sandy Koufax
f. Kevin Moen
g. Jack Nicklaus
h. Secretariat
i. Bobby Thomson
j. U.S. men's hockey

• **1974** • PERFORMANCE ARTIST VINCENT TRASOV loses his bid for mayor of Vancouver, British Columbia, in which he ran dressed as Mr. Peanut, doing a dapper tap dance whenever cameras were on.

BREAK A LEGUME

1. In 1916, who wrote *How to Grow the Peanut and 105 Ways of Preparing It for Human Consumption*?
2. Which *Peanuts* character's last name was Reichardt?

3. The dark blue Peanut the elephant was the rarest and most valuable regular-edition what?
4. What Disney fixture pitched Skippy peanut butter on TV ads dur-

ing the 1980s?
5. What word do we get from the Bantu word *"nguba,"* meaning "peanut"?

Answers to the questions on this page can be found on page 483.

• 1846 • Sweeney Todd, the famed barber/serial killer, makes his debut in a penny-dreadful story titled "The String of Pearls."

A LITTLE OFF THE TOP

1. Who hires a barber in Judges 16:19?
2. What Mozart opera functions as a sequel to Rossini's *The Barber of Seville*, though it was written thirty years earlier?
3. What two award-winning directors, who share the same last name, both worked on the 1982 student film *Joe's Bed-Stuy Barbershop: We Cut Heads?*
4. What cartoonist was raised a barber's son, just like his most famous creation?
5. What band sang the 1994 indie anthem "Cut Your Hair"?

• 1916 • A German mine sinks the British hospital ship *Britannic*. The *Britannic* was originally slated to be named *Gigantic,* but the 1912 sinking of its similarly named sister ship, RMS *Titanic,* changed that idea.

WHICH CRAFT?

1. Who was killed in his sleep when his own rotting ship, the *Argo,* collapsed on top of him?
2. What modern-day nation is the "Lusitania" after which the ship was named?
3. By the word's original definition, who, specifically, would sing a barcarole?
4. The *Argus* is the ship visible at the upper right of what Théodore Géricault painting commemorating a famous shipwreck?
5. On its most famous voyage, what ship lost its companion ship, the *Speedwell,* to a leak?
6. Why did Joseph Hazelwood spend three years working at Bean's Café, an Anchorage, Alaska, soup kitchen?
7. What Oscar winner was present the night Natalie Wood drowned on Robert Wagner's yacht?
8. In what Richard Wagner opera does the Norwegian sea captain's daughter Senta fall in love with the title ship's captain?
9. The name of Bill Murray's ship in *The Life Aquatic* is the *Belafonte,* a musical joke on what real-life ship's name?
10. What famous diamond is Bill Paxton hunting for in the film *Titanic?*

• 1980 • In the worst disaster in Nevada history, fire strikes the MGM Grand in Las Vegas. When flames reach the casino floor, many gamblers actually refuse to leave their tables. "No, don't you see? I'm hot here! I'm *on fire!*"

AND I AM TELLING YOU I'M NOT GOING

1. On what TV show did Thom McKee last a record eighty-eight consecutive games in 1980?
2. What fad did Alvin "Shipwreck" Kelly begin in 1924?
3. Whose tenure as U.S. chief justice was a record thirty-four years?
4. What's the name of the recluse in *To Kill a Mockingbird* who, according to town rumor, hasn't left home in daylight for decades?
5. What place mentioned in Joshua 5 is believed to be the world's oldest surviving city, having been located on the Jordan's west bank for 11,000 years?

Answers to the questions on this page can be found on page 483.

• **1183** • DURING THE CRUSADES, Saladin besieges the Kingdom of Jerusalem at Kerak Castle. When informed that Humphrey IV of Toron is marrying Princess Isabella within the castle walls, Saladin agrees not to target the wedding pavilion and is even sent some of the wedding feast by the groom's mother.

A GROOM OF ONE'S OWN

1. What novel opens with the traditional Lithuanian wedding feast of the Rudkus family?
2. Prince Charles and Diana Spencer bucked royal tradition by getting married in what building?
3. The familiar "Wedding March" was written by Felix Mendelssohn to accompany the wedding in what Shakespeare play?
4. What slang term for marriage comes from the Celtic practice of "handfasting"?

5. The would-be groom from Britney Spears's fifty-four-hour quickie Vegas wedding was a childhood friend who shared his name with what sitcom star?
6. Who took time out at his wedding feast to ask all his groomsmen a weird riddle about a beehive nested inside the carcass of a lion?
7. What musical begins with Sophie planning to marry Sky but ends with her mother, Donna, marrying Sam instead?

8. At the end of the Adam Sandler film, what 1983 hit is sung at *The Wedding Singer*'s own wedding?
9. Traditionally, what's the only event in a marriage celebration paid for by the groom's family, not the bride's?
10. Peter Boyle was the best man at the wedding of what rock couple?

• **1950** • THE LOWEST-SCORING GAME in NBA history sees the Fort Wayne Pistons defeat the Minneapolis Lakers 19–17. Four years later, the twenty-four-second shot clock will save basketball.

SUITE IN LOW

1. What's the lowest card of each suit in a pinochle deck?
2. The sacral and coccygeal are the two lowest types of what?

3. Why did rocker Nick Lowe name his debut EP *Bowi*?
4. What novelist cowrote the U2 song "The Ground Beneath Her

Feet"?
5. What two nations share the world's lowest point on land?

• **1967** • THE ROBOT ON *Lost in Space* utters the phrase "Danger, Will Robinson!" for—believe it or not—the one and only time in the series' run.

METALHEADS
On what TV series would you meet these robots?

Easy
1. Cylons
2. Data
3. Rosie the Maid

Harder
1. Tom Servo
2. Megatron
3. Twiki

Yeah, Good Luck
1. H.E.L.P.eR.
2. Conky 2000
3. Hymie

Answers to the questions on this page can be found on page 484.

NOVEMBER 23

• **1867** • AT A NEW YORK BAR, British singer Charles Vivian founds the Jolly Corks, a fraternal organization that will soon become the Benevolent and Protective Order of Elks.

CORKS CREW

1. What Chicago quartet's major-label debut was 2005's *From Under the Cork Tree*?
2. On what TV series did Down syndrome actor Chris Burke play Corky Thatcher?

3. Who's the only major-league player in the last decade to be suspended for using a corked bat?
4. On August 22, 1922, who was killed in an ambush outside the

County Cork town of Béal na mBláth?
5. What Benedictine monk invented the method of keeping a champagne bottle corked during fermentation?

• **1903** • COLORADO GOVERNOR JAMES PEABODY sends troops into Cripple Creek, Colorado, to quell a miners' strike, beginning the Colorado Labor Wars.

IT'S ALL CREEK TO ME

1. What two competing American food companies are both head-quartered in Battle Creek, Michigan?
2. What 1996 hit was the theme song of TV's *Dawson's Creek*?

3. Spuyten Duyvil Creek, meaning "Devil's Spout," forms the northern boundary of what American island?
4. What's the unusual title event in the film *The Miracle of Mor-*

gan's Creek?
5. What world metropolis is built on the banks of Suzhou Creek?

• **1970** • HOWARD COSELL IS SO DRUNK at a *Monday Night Football* game in Philadelphia that he throws up on "Dandy" Don Meredith's cowboy boots during the second quarter. According to John Madden, Cosell took a cab all the way home from Philadelphia to New York at halftime.

TAXICAB CONFESSIONS

1. Whose narration for Michael Jackson's "Thriller" had been written in the taxi on the way to the studio that morning?
2. What are the names of the cop and taxi driver in *It's a Wonderful Life*?

3. What model Ford are most New York cabs?
4. Judd Hirsch, Jeff Conaway, or Tony Danza—which *Taxi* regular is actually driving across the Queensboro Bridge during the show's credits?

5. What author of *A Death in the Family* himself died in a New York taxi in 1955?

Answers to the questions on this page can be found on page 484.

• **1958** • A ROD SERLING TIME TRAVEL script called "The Time Element" airs as part of *Desilu Playhouse*. The broadcast is such a hit that CBS picks up Serling's idea for a genre anthology series called *The Twilight Zone.*

PRESENTED FOR YOUR APPROVAL

Can you spoil the endings of these classic Twilight Zone *episodes?*

1. "To Serve Man." Benevolent aliens appear on Earth, bearing the title book and promising great technological advances. But when U.N. code breakers finally manage to translate the book . . .

2. "Time Enough at Last." A bookworm reading in a bank vault survives a nuclear holocaust and is thrilled that he finally has ample time to read. Just then . . .

3. "The Eye of the Beholder." A woman with a bandaged face is recovering in a hospital room from one last attempt to cure her disfiguring ugliness. But when the bandages come off . . .

4. "The Invaders." An old woman in a remote cabin is menaced by a flying saucer full of tiny aliens. After destroying the ship with an ax . . .

5. "Five Characters in Search of an Exit." A soldier, a clown, a hobo, a ballerina, and a bagpiper find themselves trapped in a mysterious dark cylinder with no memory of how they got there. The major manages to escape, but . . .

• **1976** • AT SAN FRANCISCO's Winterland Ballroom, the Band gives its famous farewell concert, *The Last Waltz.* Since it's Thanksgiving Day, the crowd enjoys a turkey dinner before the Band takes the stage.

ALL I GOTTA DO IS ACT NATURALLY

What artists were featured in these documentaries/concert films?

Easy
1. *Stop Making Sense*
2. *Gimme Shelter*
3. *Let It Be*
4. *The Song Remains the Same*
5. *The Kids Are Alright*

Harder
1. *Don't Look Back*
2. *Some Kind of Monster*
3. *Shut Up and Sing*
4. *The Filth and the Fury*
5. *Heart of Gold*

Yeah, Good Luck
1. *I Am Trying to Break Your Heart*
2. *Wild Man Blues*
3. *Gigantic*
4. *Lord Don't Slow Me Down*
5. *Bring on the Night*

• **1983** • BIG BIRD's *SESAME STREET* friends have to break it to him that Mr. Hooper, his storekeeper friend, has died.

BIG BIRDS

What's the tallest bird native to each of these continents?

1. Africa
2. South America
3. North America
4. Australia
5. Antarctica

Answers to the questions on this page can be found on page 484.

• **1851** • ATTORNEY HENRY WELLES SMITH, feeling that there are already too many "Smiths" practicing law in the city of Boston, has the Massachusetts legislature change his name to "Henry Fowle Durant." Using his sexy new name, the former Mr. Smith will go on to found Wellesley College.

JOB DESCRIPTION

Those Smiths probably all had ancestors who were blacksmiths, but what would each of these famous people make if their surnames still reflected their occupations?

1. Anderson Cooper	**3.** Raymond Chandler	**5.** Noah Webster
2. Rufus Wainwright	**4.** Louise Fletcher	

• **1851** • IT'S FUN TO STAY at the YMC, eh? The first Young Men's Christian Association in North America opens in Montreal.

ASSOCIATIVE MEMORY

How much do you know about these associations?

1. What former U.S. president was elected to head the National Rifle Association in 1883?
2. What sport gets its name from a contraction of the word "association"?
3. What hit by the Association was, according to BMI, the second-most-aired pop song of the twentieth century?
4. What disease was the American Lung Association originally founded to fight?
5. What fraternal association, named for a part of a sea-based aircraft, made headlines for its 1991 Las Vegas symposium?
6. What legendary NBA center was the first commissioner of the American Basketball Association?
7. What association awards the yearly Spingarn Medal?
8. What Steven Spielberg movie inspired the Motion Picture Association of America to create the PG-13 rating?
9. Who invented the "free association" technique in 1896?
10. What Fort Payne quartet is the only band ever named Entertainer of the Year at the Country Music Association awards?

• **1956** • HUNGARY'S NATIONAL CARRIER, Malév Hungarian Airlines, is born. Dear Hungary: Maybe *"Malév"* means "awesome airline" in Hungarian, I don't know, but in English it sounds a *little* too much like "malevolent."

FLIGHT TESTING

Name the home country of these airlines.

Easy	*Harder*	*Yeah, Good Luck*
1. Qantas	**1.** Aer Lingus	**1.** Asiana
2. KLM	**2.** Varig	**2.** Copa
3. Aeroflot	**3.** ANA	**3.** Avianca
4. Lufthansa	**4.** Sabena (until 2001)	**4.** Garuda
5. El Al	**5.** Air Astana	**5.** Druk Air

Answers to the questions on this page can be found on page 485.

NOVEMBER 26

• **43 B.C.** • THE SECOND TRIUMVIRATE forms and takes over Rome. The triumvirs mostly hate each other, despite their complicated family relationships: Mark Antony was married to Octavian's sister, while Octavian was married to Antony's stepdaughter.

SECOND TIME AROUND

You're just seconds away from a quiz about "second" things.

1. Back when developing nations were still called "the Third World," what was the Second World?
2. What large religious denomination believes that Christ's Second Coming *already happened*, back in 1914?
3. Which two original *SNL* Not Ready for Prime Time Players got their start with Chicago's Second City comedy troupe?
4. What active slugger has more homers than any other second base-man in major-league history?
5. What novel's narrator is referred to only as "the second Mrs. de Winter"?

• **1927** • NOVICE NUN MARIA KUTSCHERA marries Austrian naval hero Georg von Trapp, a story that will later inspire a little musical you may have heard of. Just two months later, according to official records, Maria's first daughter with the captain will be born, so it looks as though someone might have been playing "hide the lonely goatherd" a little early.

NUN OF THE ABOVE

In what film did these people portray nuns?

Easy
1. Ingrid Bergman
2. Debbie Reynolds
3. Whoopi Goldberg
4. Eric Idle
5. Susan Sarandon

Harder
1. Audrey Hepburn
2. Meg Tilly
3. Deborah Kerr (two options)
4. Rosalind Russell (two options)
5. Shirley MacLaine

Yeah, Good Luck
1. Loretta Young
2. Betty Aberlin
3. Gladys Cooper
4. Kathleen Freeman
5. Mary Tyler Moore

• **1991** • WITH THE END of the Cold War, the *Bulletin of the Atomic Scientists* magazine resets the symbolic "Doomsday Clock," which has been ticking down to nuclear midnight since 1947, back to 11:43 P.M. It's the clock's biggest move ever and its all-time low.

BEAT THE CLOCK

1. Which Coldplay album features the band's Grammy-winning song "Clocks"?
2. How much longer is the NFL play clock than the NBA shot clock?
3. On most clock faces, the number four is displayed in what nonstandard Roman-numeral fashion?
4. What chemical element is most often used in atomic clocks, since the frequency of radiation it emits is used to officially define the length of one second?
5. What TV series used "Rock Around the Clock" as its original theme?
6. Which three digits, on a standard seven-segment clock radio display, are made up of the same number of dashed line segments as the numbers they express?
7. What song does Bill Murray's alarm clock play every morning in *Groundhog Day?*
8. What's the modern word that means the same thing as "widder-shins"?
9. What silent comic hangs from the hands of a clock in his movie *Safety Last!?*
10. Whose first case involved discovering *The Secret of the Old Clock?*

Answers to the questions on this page can be found on page 485.

• **1928** • THE CUSTOMS COURT decides in favor of Romanian sculptor Constantin Brancusi, who was assessed a $4,000 import duty when customs officials decided his modernist masterpiece *Bird in Space* didn't qualify as art, merely as "a manufacture of metal."

GENTLEMEN PREFER BRONZE

1. What appropriate sculpture appeared on the cover of the first issue of the puzzle magazine *Games*?
2. What name did Marcel Duchamp suggest for the distinc-tive hanging sculpture of Alexander Calder?
3. What is the naked man doing in the most famous bronze by the Greek sculptor Myron?
4. What play is named for a mythical sculptor who fell in love with his ivory statue?
5. What city is overlooked by the statue of Christ the Redeemer atop Corcovado?

• **1941** • THE "STATE OF JEFFERSON," a big chunk of southern Oregon and Northern California with its "capital" at Yreka, proclaims its independence from the U.S., even setting up an armed road-block on Highway 99. But the secession movement will peter out the following month with the death of its founder and then the attack on Pearl Harbor.

WE GOTTA GET OUT OF THIS PLACE
From what country have these proposed states hoped to secede?

Easy	Harder	Yeah, Good Luck
1. Chechnya	1. Biafra	1. Cabinda
2. Kosovo	2. Tamil Eelam	2. Chittagong
3. Chiapas	3. Waziristan	3. Nagorno-Karabakh
4. Tibet	4. Aceh	4. Euskal Herria
5. Darfur	5. Zanzibar	5. Caprivi

• **1971** • THE SOVIET PROBE *Mars 2* crashes on the Martian surface, becoming the first man-made object to land on the red planet.

MARTIAN CHRONICLES

1. *Veronica Mars* takes place in a California town with what plane-tary name?
2. What Mars product was origi-nally sold as three separate pieces of candy: one chocolate, one vanilla, and one strawberry?
3. What is Laura's occupation in *The Eyes of Laura Mars*?
4. The last surviving veteran of the American Revolution shared his name with what author of *Men Are from Mars, Women Are from Venus*?
5. What band named the disks of its double album *Stadium Arcadium* "Jupiter" and "Mars"?

Answers to the questions on this page can be found on page 485.

• **1888** • NINA WILCOX IS BORN in Connecticut. Later in life, as Nina Wilcox Putnam, she will draft the first 1040 form for the IRS in 1913 *and* write the story for Universal's *The Mummy* in 1932.

THEORY OF FORMS

1. What movie introduced "TPS reports" as shorthand for "pointless paperwork"?
2. What band is named for a British government form for claiming unemployment benefits?

3. What color was 1945's I-151 form, the "Alien Registration Receipt Card"?
4. What letter is used for the series of IRS forms covering relationships between employers and taxpayers?

5. What movie "religion" did 390,000 Britons put on their 2001 census form, causing the government to assign an official code to this new faith?

• **1951** • JOHN VAN DRUTEN'S PLAY *I Am a Camera* opens on Broadway, leading Walter Kerr to write perhaps the most famous bad review in history: the three-word "Me no Leica."

THUMB WAR

They say that living well is the best revenge, but sometimes slamming your critics by name is just more fun. Match each movie with the film critic it names a nasty character for.

1. *Galaxy Quest*
2. *Godzilla* (1998)
3. *Lady in the Water*
4. *The Ref*
5. *Willow*

A. Roger Ebert
B. Manny Farber
C. Pauline Kael
D. Andrew Sarris
E. Gene Siskel

• **1985** • NBC SPORTCASTER AHMAD RASHAD proposes to network-mate Phylicia Ayers-Allen on live TV during halftime at a Jets-Lions game. They will divorce in 2001, though not on live TV.

JOCK HITCH

What athlete was or is married to . . .

Easy
1. Nomar Garciaparra
2. Bridgette Wilson
3. Andre Agassi
4. Posh Spice
5. Halle Berry

Harder
1. Brigitte Nielsen
2. Janet Jones
3. Andy Mill
4. Ashley Judd
5. Vanessa Williams

Yeah, Good Luck
1. Ray Knight
2. Jane Russell
3. Terry Bradshaw
4. Colleen Kay Hutchins
5. Carol Alt

Answers to the questions on this page can be found on page 486.

• **1907** • CRIMEAN WAR NURSE Florence Nightingale becomes the first woman ever awarded the Order of Merit by the British Crown. An accomplished statistician, she was also the first woman elected to the Royal Statistical Society in 1858.

COT BEHIND ENEMY LINES

1. Walter Reed, of V.A. hospital fame, was the surgeon who first discovered the transmission vector of what disease?

2. Who was, ironically, laid up in a Germany military hospital with a leg wound when his 1968 dance hit boasted, "We dance just as good as we walk"?

3. What 1942 invention of Dr. Harry Coover was used to close battle wounds in Vietnam?

4. Stories of what controversial comic's Navy cross-dressing inspired Klinger's antics on *M*A*S*H*?

5. Before they became writers, what did Ernest Hemingway,

John Dos Passos, E. E. Cummings, Somerset Maugham, and Dashiell Hammett have in common?

• **1920** • TWO BRITISH SILENT FILMS, *The Great Day* and *The Call of Youth*, hit London theaters. The movies are lousy, but their title cards are the first screen work of a young artist named Alfred Hitchcock.

TITLE CARDS

What movie titles are "illustrated," using letters and symbols, in the cards below?
For example, the first one is Big Trouble in Little China.

chTROUBLEina	i v e t (r i / v e r)	monsters	m i l l e r / m i l e r
y b a b	Pac1f1c	Batm	prisionero
H A W K	the shop	2. boogaloo	act o
anger	J O M I A W	alevel	story

Answers to the questions on this page can be found on page 486.

NOVEMBER 30

• **1930** • CAT BURGLAR TURNED RADIO HOST G. Gordon Liddy is born in Hoboken, New Jersey.

INITIAL CONTACT

Give the missing first initial of these folks who went by their middle names.

Easy	*Harder*	*Yeah, Good Luck*
1. _. Ross Perot	1. _. Epatha Merkerson	1. _. Whitney Brown
2. _. Night Shymalan	2. _. Frank Baum	2. _. Beam Piper
3. _. Scott Fitzgerald	3. _. Buckminster Fuller	3. _. Gary Gray
4. _. Ron Hubbard	4. _. Emmett Walsh	4. _. King Jordan
5. _. Edgar Hoover	5. _. Thomas Howell	5. _. Gary Gygax

• **1954** • A NINE-POUND METEORITE crashes through the roof of an Alabama house, badly bruising a napping housewife named Ann Hodges. She is the only person ever to have been injured by a falling meteorite.

IT CAME FROM OUTER SPACE!

1. A 1996 study of meteorite ALH84001 led scientists to announce that the stone might contain evidence of life where?

2. How many rows of aliens are there in the original Space Invaders?

3. Denver, Kansas City, or Houston—what U.S. city does Bill Pullman nuke in the hope of defeating the aliens in *Independence Day*?

4. What was the name of Ziggy Stardust's backing band?

5. Who's the only actor to appear in both film versions of *Invasion of the Body Snatchers*?

• **1974** • TWO ANTHROPOLOGISTS AT HADAR, Ethiopia, discover an amazingly complete fossilized skeleton of a female *Australopithecus afarensis*. Celebrating in camp that night with the Beatles on the tape player, the pair decide to name their specimen "Lucy."

MISSING LINKS

1. *Link's Awakening* is the only video game in its series not to feature what title character?

2. The *Collision Course* EP is a mashup of Linkin Park songs with tracks by what rapper?

3. What famed golf links were the first public course ever to be selected by *Golf Digest* as America's best?

4. Who started out gutting chickens in her mum's Liverpool market stall before becoming the host of the BBC and NBC quiz show *The Weakest Link*?

5. *A, B,* or *C*—which letter of the alphabet is the element used to create hyperlinks in HTML Web documents?

Answers to the questions on this page can be found on page 486.

November Answers

NOVEMBER 1

DA BOMB
1. Little Boy
2. *Memphis Belle*
3. The Hell's Angels
4. Dresden
5. "Love Shack"

FRANKLY, MY DEAR . . .
1. The Nile
2. The Colorado
3. The Yangtze
4. The Columbia
5. The Missouri

SOCIETY PAGES
1. The Boxer Rebellion
2. Tupac Shakur
3. John Birch
4. The Kinks
5. Tahiti
6. Henry David Thoreau
7. Alexander Graham Bell
8. *The Philadelphia Story*
9. The Jesuits
10. John Kenneth Galbraith

NOVEMBER 2

"20" QUESTIONS
1. The Catskills
2. "Bent"
3. Jimmy Carter
4. *Law & Order*
5. 7
6. Four
7. Feet
8. He got ten wins for two different teams
9. An (equilateral) triangle
10. Your location
11. Ronald Reagan (by being elected in a year ending with "o" and surviving his term)
12. Billy Sims and Barry Sanders
13. Borax
14. "Twentysomething"
15. Adam Smith
16. Arrondissements
17. *The Wonder Years*
18. Chicago and New York
19. Patrick O'Brian
20. "Sgt. Pepper's Lonely Hearts Club Band"

TWENTY-ONE QUESTIONS
1. James Otis
2. Nylon
3. James J. Braddock
4. Finland and the Soviet Union
5. Jezebel

NOVEMBER 3

MASTHEAD HUNTING
Easy
1. Boston
2. Chicago
3. Denver
4. Washington, D.C.
5. Cleveland
Harder
1. Newark
2. New Orleans
3. Detroit
4. Philadelphia
5. Minneapolis
Yeah, Good Luck
1. San Jose
2. Orlando
3. Akron
4. Hartford
5. Charlotte

BROADCAST STEWS
1. The Barefoot Contessa
2. The Frugal Gourmet
3. The Naked Chef
4. The Galloping Gourmet
5. Two Fat Ladies

JAM BANDS
1. Paul Weller
2. MC5
3. Mookie Blaylock
4. "Human," by the Human League
5. Jay-Z

NOVEMBER 4

THESE DREAMS
1. Siamese
2. Hoop
3. A Midsummer Night's
4. Tangerine
5. American

CUE-BALL LIBRE
1. Cheryl
2. Rudolph Giuliani
3. The Charlotte Bobcats
4. Yul Brynner
5. Harold Macmillan
6. South Africa
7. Theo
8. The Blue Period
9. Barbra Streisand
10. Jay

THE BOOKS STOP HERE
Easy
1. Jimmy Carter
2. Bill Clinton
3. Richard Nixon
4. Abraham Lincoln
5. Franklin Roosevelt

Harder
1. Dwight Eisenhower
2. Herbert Hoover
3. Lyndon Johnson
4. Gerald Ford
5. George H. W. Bush

Yeah, Good Luck
1. William McKinley
2. Jefferson Davis
3. Rutherford Hayes
4. Calvin Coolidge
5. Woodrow Wilson

NOVEMBER 5

MAIL BONDING
1. HoH oHo
2. The Corinthians and the Thessalonians
3. Media Mail
4. The Unabomber, Ted Kaczynski
5. St. Joseph
6. Wormwood
7. McFeely
8. Queen Victoria
9. The Discovery Channel
10. Pablo Neruda

COMMUNITY CHEST
1. I
2. E
3. C (an Indy 500 car)
4. D
5. H
6. A
7. F
8. B (the Cubs and White Sox)
9. J (until West Virginia was created)
10. G

NOVEMBER 6

JUST FOR KICKS
1. 10 yards
2. "Chew bubble gum"
3. Tae kwon do
4. Kid-tested, mom-approved
5. Champagne and cocaine

TOWN AND COUNTY
Easy
1. Chicago
2. Miami (now renamed Miami–Dade County)
3. Cleveland
4. Atlanta
5. Detroit
Harder
1. Houston
2. Seattle
3. Phoenix
4. Pittsburgh
5. Fort Lauderdale
Yeah, Good Luck
1. San Antonio
2. Las Vegas
3. Minneapolis
4. Portland, Oregon
5. Indianapolis

NUMB3RS
Easy
1. 12
2. 90210
3. 66
4. 911!
5. 5
Harder
1. 222
2. 2525
3. 7
4. 3000
5. 2021 (or 2020)
Yeah, Good Luck
1. 2.0
2. 9
3. 3
4. 96
5. 15 (later 16)

NOVEMBER 7

SOFA SO GOOD
1. War of the Worlds
2. Sigmund Freud's
3. A sailboat
4. Davenport, Iowa
5. "Surrender"

YOU AND WHAT ARMY?
1. Iceland
2. Bolivia
3. Vatican City
4. Grenada's
5. Japan

BLACK AND WHITE AND WED ALL OVER
Easy
1. Michael Jackson
2. David Bowie
3. Maury Povich
4. Pocahontas
5. Seal
Harder
1. Laura Dern
2. Taye Diggs
3. Julie Chen
4. ~~Tommy Mottola~~ Nick Cannon
5. Carmen Electra
Yeah, Good Luck
1. Quincy Jones
2. Tyne Daly
3. Diahann Carroll
4. Tiger Woods
5. Sandra Oh

NOVEMBER 8

HOW LONG? HOW LONG MUST WE SING THIS SONG?
Easy
1. The Doors
2. Pink Floyd
3. The Sugarhill Gang
4. Meat Loaf
5. Iron Butterfly

Harder
1. Television
2. The Velvet Underground
3. Jane's Addiction
4. The Jimi Hendrix Experience
5. Rush
Yeah, Good Luck
1. Dire Straits
2. Yo La Tengo
3. Bob Dylan
4. Sonic Youth
5. Tool

VARSITY BLUES
1. Basketball
2. Diving
3. Football
4. Hockey
5. Track

SKIT AIN'T OVER TILL IT'S OVER
Easy
1. Wayne Campbell
2. Mary Katherine Gallagher
3. Fernando
4. The Church Lady
5. Hans and Franz
Harder
1. Emily Litella
2. The two a-holes
3. Fericito
4. Dieter
5. The Pathological Liar, Tommy Flanagan
Yeah, Good Luck
1. The Festrunk Brothers
2. Ed Grimley
3. Mr. Bill
4. Matt Foley, Motivational Speaker
5. Simon

NOVEMBER 9

(LIKE A) ROLLING STONE
Easy
1. "Satisfaction"
2. "Da Doo Ron Ron"

3. "The Reaper"
4. "Money"
5. "Sweet Dreams"
Harder
1. "Voodoo Child"
2. "Remember"
3. "Norwegian Wood"
4. "Peace, Love, and Understanding"
5. "Thank You"
Yeah, Good Luck
1. "Rock Around the Clock"
2. "I've Been Loving You Too Long"
3. "I Never Loved a Man"
4. "Higher and Higher"
5. "Get Up (I Feel Like Being a) Sex Machine"

RIGHT ON Q
1. Gary Coleman
2. Jesus'
3. Coily
4. The company is in bankruptcy.
5. Quetzalcoatl
6. The two of hearts
7. The Cleveland Cavaliers
8. Q-tips
9. Dumbo
10. Equatorial Guinea and Mozambique

HARD PALETTE
Easy
1. Red
2. Blue
3. Violet
4. Blue
5. Yellow
Harder
1. Violet
2. Green
3. Violet
4. Blue
5. (Yellow-)green
Yeah, Good Luck
1. Blue
2. Red
3. Green
4. Violet
5. Orange

NOVEMBER 10

COME-ON PILGRIM
1. *"Voulez-vous coucher avec moi ce soir?"*
2. "How *you* doin'?"
3. Mae West
4. The Raspberries
5. Sylvia Plath

LOOK WHO'S TALKING NOW
Easy
1. "You talkin' to me?" (*Taxi Driver*)
2. "E.T. phone home." (*E.T.: The Extra-Terrestrial*)
3. "You can't handle the truth!" (*A Few Good Men*)
4. "I coulda been a contender." (*On the Waterfront*)
5. "Houston, we have a problem." (*Apollo 13*)
Harder
1. "Do you feel lucky? Well, do ya, punk?" (*Dirty Harry*)
2. "I'm as mad as hell and I'm not going to take this anymore!" (*Network*)
3. "No wire hangers, ever!" (*Mommie Dearest*)
4. "Build it, and he will come." (*Field of Dreams*)
5. "Frankly, my dear, I don't give a damn." (*Gone With the Wind*)
Yeah, Good Luck
1. "I see dead people." (*The Sixth Sense*)
2. "I am big! It's the pictures that got small." (*Sunset Boulevard*)
3. "Round up the usual suspects." (*Casablanca*)
4. "I love the smell of napalm in the morning." (*Apocalypse Now*)
5. "I'm going to make him an offer he can't refuse." (*The Godfather*)

NOVEMBER 11

COUNT AND RECOUNT
1. A (40)
2. H (14)
3. I (3)
4. D (99)
5. B (5)
6. J (52)
7. F (64)
8. E (21)
9. C (8)
10. G (30)

GONE WITH THE WIN
1. Mechanical bull riding
2. A dance marathon
3. Pie eating
4. A beauty pageant
5. Slogan writing

"BOX" OFFICE
1. Mary Lou Retton
2. "The Way You Move"
3. Orange
4. *Halo*
5. Epimetheus
6. December 26
7. Roseanne Conner
8. Clint Eastwood
9. A lab rat
10. Rudolph Wurlitzer

NOVEMBER 12

WEE THE PEOPLE
1. *Extras*
2. Bonsai trees
3. The Lollipop Guild
4. *A Little Night Music (Eine kleine Nachtmusik)*
5. Manhattan
6. The thimble
7. Ganymede and Titan
8. The Little League
9. The paramecium
10. Bow Wow

TELLING TIME
1. Big Ben is technically the bell, not the clock
2. The Colorado Rockies and Arizona Diamondbacks
3. World War I ended
4. Christiaan Huygens
5. 2 A.M.

ONCE MORE UNTO THE BEACH
1. Diamond Head
2. "Tubular"
3. ("The Girl from") Ipanema and Copacabana
4. Thailand
5. *Eternal Sunshine of the Spotless Mind*
6. Five
7. Frankie Avalon
8. A cocker spaniel
9. Al Jardine
10. Omaha Beach

NOVEMBER 13	NOVEMBER 14	NOVEMBER 15

LIGHTBULBS
1. The CBS eye
2. "Yellow"
3. Post-its
4. *Taxi*
5. The pendulum
6. Knute Rockne
7. The Popsicle
8. *The Shining*
9. "A Day in the Life"
10. Velcro

CABLE GUYS
1. Hits
2. Chuck Roberts
3. *Monday Night Football*
4. Marilyn Manson and Charles Manson
5. "Fair and Balanced"
6. Gays and lesbians
7. *Sex and the City* and *The Sopranos*
8. The Weather Channel
9. Softball
10. Spike Lee ("Spike")

NAME DISENTANGLEMENT
1. Uma Thurman
2. Fred Friendly
3. Al Michaels
4. Mary McCarthy
5. Ron Brown
6. Pete Postlethwaite
7. Ray Bradbury (*Dandelion Wine*)
8. Kris Kristofferson
9. Anna Karenina's
10. Lee Van Cleef

POWERS OF TEN
1. Mackenzie Phillips
2. Rosh Hashanah and Yom Kippur
3. Napoleon
4. Anne Boleyn
5. 27

DOMINO EFFECT
1. The Noid
2. Chubby Checker
3. Southeast Asia
4. Twelve
5. Laurence Harvey

THE MYSTERIOUS ISLANDS
1. Corsica
2. Hokkaido
3. Tasmania
4. Manhattan
5. Taiwan
6. Ireland
7. Oahu
8. Trinidad
9. North Island (of New Zealand)
10. Borneo
11. Madagascar
12. Iceland

MEAN STREAK
1. Tim Meadows
2. Iceland and Portugal
3. Encyclopedia Brown
4. Φ (phi)
5. Polythene Pam

TRANSMETROPOLITAN
1. I
2. B
3. E
4. G
5. F
6. H
7. C
8. J
9. D
10. A

NOVEMBER 16

OFF THE TOP OF YOUR HEAD
1. The Mad Hatter's
2. The Cobb salad
3. Minneapolis (the statue depicts *The Mary Tyler Moore Show*'s Mary Richards)
4. Foolscap
5. Morocco
6. Seven
7. The Oakland Raiders and Miami Dolphins
8. A Catholic cardinal
9. Cricket
10. A raspberry beret

THE HILLS ARE ALIVE
1. Solsbury Hill
2. Hamburger Hill
3. Montserrat
4. The Ravens
5. The battle of Bunker Hill

VERY SPECIAL EPISODES
Easy
1. Mork
2. Niles Crane (*Frasier*)
3. Monica Geller (*Friends*)
4. Maxwell Smart
5. Latka Gravas
Harder
1. Rhoda Morgenstern
2. Dr. Michaela Quinn
3. Mike Brady
4. Abby Lockhart (*ER*)
5. Nate Fisher (*Six Feet Under*)
Yeah, Good Luck
1. Miranda Hobbes (*Sex and the City*)
2. Andy Sipowicz (*NYPD Blue*)
3. Darnell Turner (*My Name is Earl*)
4. (*The Scarecrow and*) Mrs. King
5. (Lieutenant Charles) *Hennesey*

NOVEMBER 17

A GOOD CAST IS WORTH RE-PEATING
1. Frederick Forrest, Robert Duvall, Harrison Ford
2. Errol Flynn, Olivia de Havilland, Basil Rathbone
3. Hugh Grant, Emma Thompson, Alan Rickman
4. Michael Douglas, Kathleen Turner, Danny DeVito
5. Ben Stiller, Vince Vaughn, Will Ferrell
6. Leonardo DiCaprio, Kate Winslet, Kathy Bates
7. Humphrey Bogart, Peter Lorre, Sydney Greenstreet
8. Tom Hanks, Bill Pullman, Rosie O'Donnell
9. Emilio Estevez, Judd Nelson, Ally Sheedy
10. Rock Hudson, Doris Day, Tony Randall

THE PICTURES GOT SMALL!
Easy
1. Gary Burghoff
2. John Houseman
3. Richard Roundtree
Harder
1. Dean Jones
2. Michael Gross
3. Vic Tayback
Yeah, Good Luck
1. Ossie Davis
2. Kevin Peter Hall
3. Michael Winslow

C HUNT
1. Perry Como
2. Linus Pauling
3. Combat
4. A cedilla (or *cedille*)
5. "Gonna Make You Sweat"

NOVEMBER 18

WELCOME TO THE CLUB
1. The Sierra Club
2. Studio 54
3. Costco
4. Playboy Clubs
5. Seven hundred (hence, *The 700 Club*)
6. Sophie Tucker
7. Albert Einstein or George Bernard Shaw
8. "You do not talk about Fight Club"
9. Club Med
10. Sheryl Crow

BED-AZZLED
1. It flips up into a cabinet when not in use
2. John Lennon and Yoko Ono
3. Way Beyond
4. Robert Heinlein
5. His previous TV wife, Suzanne Pleshette

REVIVAL MEETING
1. Grave robbing (stealing corpses)
2. *Family Guy*
3. Khan Noonian Singh (*Star Trek II*)
4. A Beatles reunion
5. Tab

NOVEMBER 19	NOVEMBER 20	NOVEMBER 21

NOVEMBER 19

BULLY PULPITS
Easy
1. John Kennedy
2. Abraham Lincoln
3. Bill Clinton
Harder
1. Richard Nixon
2. Ronald Reagan
3. Jimmy Carter
Yeah, Good Luck
1. Dwight Eisenhower
2. Franklin Roosevelt
3. Theodore Roosevelt

I CAN SEE RIGHT THROUGH YOU
1. Venice's
2. *Charlie and the Chocolate Factory*'s
3. The flute
4. Obsidian
5. I. M. Pei
6. *Die Hard*
7. An Etch-a-Sketch
8. The Grand Canyon
9. Darryl Dawkins
10. A unicorn

LIP SINK
1. *The Rocky Horror Picture Show*
2. Vaseline
3. Leo Durocher
4. Sink ships
5. Vermilion

NOVEMBER 20

THE ACCIDENTAL TORUS
1. Canada
2. Homer Simpson
3. "Munchkins"
4. The beignet and the Boston cream
5. Krispy Kreme

THE PLAY-BY-PLAY'S THE THING
1. H, c
2. A, h
3. G, j
4. D, i
5. E, g
6. C, a
7. B, b
8. F, d
9. J, f
10. I, e

BREAK A LEGUME
1. George Washington Carver
2. Peppermint Patty's
3. Beanie Baby
4. Annette Funicello
5. "Goober"

NOVEMBER 21

A LITTLE OFF THE TOP
1. Delilah
2. *The Marriage of Figaro*
3. Spike and Ang Lee
4. Charles Schulz
5. Pavement

WHICH CRAFT?
1. Jason
2. Portugal
3. A Venetian gondolier
4. *The Raft of the Medusa*
5. The *Mayflower*
6. He captained the *Exxon Valdez* into its famous oil spill
7. Christopher Walken
8. *The Flying Dutchman*
9. Jacques Cousteau's *Calypso*
10. "The Heart of the Ocean"

AND I AM TELLING YOU I'M NOT GOING
1. *Tic Tac Dough*
2. Flagpole sitting
3. John Marshall's
4. Boo Radley
5. Jericho

NOVEMBER 22	NOVEMBER 23	NOVEMBER 24

A GROOM OF ONE'S OWN
1. *The Jungle*
2. Saint Paul's Cathedral (rather than Westminster Abbey)
3. *A Midsummer Night's Dream*
4. "Tying the knot"
5. Jason Alexander
6. Samson
7. *Mamma Mia!*
8. "True"
9. The rehearsal dinner
10. John Lennon and Yoko Ono

SUITE IN LOW
1. Nine
2. Vertebrae
3. As joking reference to Bowie's album *Low*
4. Salman Rushdie
5. Israel and Jordan (the Dead Sea)

METALHEADS
Easy
1. *Battlestar Galactica*
2. *Star Trek: The Next Generation*
3. *The Jetsons*
Harder
1. *Mystery Science Theater 3000*
2. *Transformers*
3. *Buck Rogers in the 25th Century*
Yeah, Good Luck
1. *The Venture Bros.*
2. *Pee-Wee's Playhouse*
3. *Get Smart*

CORKS CREW
1. Fall Out Boy's
2. *Life Goes On*
3. Sammy Sosa
4. Michael Collins
5. Dom Pérignon

IT'S ALL CREEK TO ME
1. Kellogg's and Post
2. "I Don't Want to Wait"
3. Manhattan
4. The birth of sextuplets
5. Shanghai

TAXICAB CONFESSIONS
1. Vincent Price
2. Bert and Ernie
3. Crown Victoria
4. Tony Danza
5. James Agee

PRESENTED FOR YOUR APPROVAL
1. It's a cookbook—the aliens eat people!
2. His glasses break!
3. She's beautiful . . . but all the disappointed doctors are hideously ugly!
4. We learn it's a U.S. Air Force spaceship—the woman is a giant!
5. He falls onto a snowy sidewalk—they are all dolls in a charity drive barrel!

ALL I GOTTA DO IS ACT NATURALLY
Easy
1. Talking Heads
2. The Rolling Stones
3. The Beatles
4. Led Zeppelin
5. The Who
Harder
1. Bob Dylan
2. Metallica
3. The Dixie Chicks
4. Sex Pistols
5. Neil Young
Yeah, Good Luck
1. Wilco
2. Woody Allen and his New Orleans Jazz Band
3. They Might Be Giants
4. Oasis
5. Sting

BIG BIRDS
1. The ostrich
2. The rhea
3. The whooping crane
4. The emu
5. The emperor penguin

NOVEMBER 25

JOB DESCRIPTION
1. Barrels
2. Wagons
3. Candles
4. Arrows
5. Cloth

ASSOCIATIVE MEMORY
1. Ulysses Grant
2. Soccer
3. "Never My Love"
4. Tuberculosis
5. Tailhook Association
6. George Mikan
7. The NAACP
8. *Indiana Jones and the Temple of Doom*
9. Sigmund Freud
10. Alabama

FLIGHT TESTING
Easy
1. Australia
2. The Netherlands
3. Russia (formerly the USSR)
4. Germany
5. Israel
Harder
1. Ireland
2. Brazil
3. Japan
4. Belgium
5. Kazakhstan
Yeah, Good Luck
1. South Korea
2. Panama
3. Colombia
4. Indonesia
5. Bhutan

NOVEMBER 26

SECOND TIME AROUND
1. The Communist bloc
2. Jehovah's Witnesses
3. John Belushi and Dan Aykroyd
4. Jeff Kent
5. *Rebecca*

NUN OF THE ABOVE
Easy
1. *The Bells of St. Mary's*
2. *The Singing Nun*
3. *Sister Act* (1 and 2)
4. *Nuns on the Run*
5. *Dead Man Walking*
Harder
1. *The Nun's Story*
2. *Agnes of God*
3. *Black Narcissus* or *Heaven Knows, Mr. Allison*
4. *Sister Kenny* or *The Trouble with Angels*
5. *Two Mules for Sister Sara*
Yeah, Good Luck
1. *Come to the Stable*
2. *Dogma*
3. *The Song of Bernadette*
4. *The Blues Brothers*
5. *A Change of Habit*

BEAT THE CLOCK
1. *A Rush of Blood to the Head*
2. Sixteen seconds (forty versus twenty-four)
3. IIII (not IV)
4. Cesium
5. *Happy Days*
6. 4, 5, and 6
7. "I Got You Babe" (Sonny and Cher)
8. "Counterclockwise"
9. Harold Lloyd
10. Nancy Drew's

NOVEMBER 27

GENTLEMEN PREFER BRONZE
1. Rodin's *The Thinker*
2. *Mobiles*
3. Throwing a discus
4. *Pygmalion*
5. Rio de Janeiro

WE GOTTA GET OUT OF THIS PLACE
Easy
1. Russia
2. Serbia
3. Mexico
4. China
5. Sudan
Harder
1. Nigeria
2. Sri Lanka
3. Pakistan
4. Indonesia
5. Tanzania
Yeah, Good Luck
1. Angola
2. Bangladesh
3. Azerbaijan
4. Spain (the Basques)
5. Namibia

MARTIAN CHRONICLES
1. Neptune
2. 3 Musketeers
3. Fashion photographer
4. John Gray
5. Red Hot Chili Peppers'

NOVEMBER 28

THEORY OF FORMS
1. *Office Space*
2. UB40
3. Green
4. *W*
5. Jedi

THUMB WAR
1. D
2. A
3. B
4. E
5. C

JOCK HITCH
Easy
1. Mia Hamm
2. Pete Sampras
3. Steffi Graf
4. David Beckham
5. David Justice
Harder
1. Mark Gastineau
2. Wayne Gretzky
3. Chris Evert
4. Dario Franchitti
5. Rick Fox
Yeah, Good Luck
1. Nancy Lopez
2. Bob Waterfield
3. JoJo Starbuck
4. Ernie Vandeweghe
5. Ron Greschner

NOVEMBER 29

COT BEHIND ENEMY LINES
1. ~~██████~~ Yellow fever
2. Archie Bell ("Tighten Up")
3. Superglue (cyanoacrylate)
4. Lenny Bruce
5. They drove ambulances during World War I

TITLE CARDS
Answers run from left to right, top to bottom.
Big Trouble in Little China
A River Runs Through It
Monsters Inc.
Miller's Crossing
Bringing Up Baby
Ocean's Eleven
Batman Begins
The Spanish Prisoner
Black Hawk Down
The Shop Around the Corner
Breakin' 2: Electric Boogaloo
Missing in Action
The Upside of Anger
Letters from Iwo Jima
All About Eve
West Side Story

NOVEMBER 30

INITIAL CONTACT
Easy
1. H
2. M
3. F
4. L
5. J
Harder
1. S
2. L
3. R
4. M
5. C
Yeah, Good Luck
1. A
2. H
3. F
4. I
5. E

IT CAME FROM OUTER SPACE!
1. Mars
2. Five
3. Houston
4. The Spiders from Mars
5. Kevin McCarthy

MISSING LINKS
1. Zelda
2. Jay-Z
3. Pebble Beach
4. Anne Robinson
5. *A*

• **1885** • At Morrison's Old Corner Drug Store in Waco, Texas, the first Dr Pepper is served.

BAD MEDICINE

Match these luminaries to their doctorate programs.

1. Dr. Jane Goodall	**A.** Clinical psychology
2. Doc Holliday	**B.** Dental surgery
3. Dr. J	**C.** Education
4. Dr. Henry Kissinger	**D.** Ethology
5. Dr. Laura	**E.** International relations
6. Dr. Octopus	**F.** Medicine
7. Dr. Phil	**G.** Nuclear physics
8. Dr. Ruth	**H.** Philosophy
9. Dr. Scholl	**I.** Physiology
10. Dr. Albert Schweitzer	**J.** None

• **1927** • Norway annexes Bouvet Island, a tiny volcanic dot in the South Atlantic. Bouvet, later seen as the setting for 2004's *Alien vs. Predator,* is the most remote island in the world, since the nearest inhabited land is Antarctica, a thousand miles south.

FAR AND AWAY

Answer these questions about remote destinations.

1. What U.S. territory is the closest island to the Mariana Trench, the deepest point in the oceans?
2. What is NASA's *New Horizons* probe scheduled to take the first fly-by photos of in July 2015?
3. What was the first city outside the U.S. to host a season of MTV's *The Real World?*
4. The point in the South Pacific farther from land than any other point on Earth is named for what literary character?
5. What two better-known names accompanied Ootah, Ooqueah, Seegloo, and Egigingwah in April 1909?
6. On TV's *Lost,* Oceanic Airlines 815 crashed while flying between what two cities?
7. Aboard what ship did Columbus first sight America (well, the Bahamas) in 1492?
8. To what country did Dave Chappelle head after abruptly shutting down production of *Chappelle's Show* in 2005?
9. What capital of Western Australia is the most isolated city on Earth, more than 1,300 miles from its closest neighbor, Adelaide?
10. Where do Wallace and Gromit go on their day trip in their very first appearance, *A Grand Day Out?*

Answers to the questions on this page can be found on page 521.

DECEMBER 2

• **1859** • ABOLITIONIST JOHN BROWN is hanged in Charles Town, Virginia. Future Civil War hero Thomas (soon to be "Stonewall") Jackson heads up the security detail, and in the ranks of militia officers standing guard is no less than John Wilkes Booth.

A HASH OF BROWNS

1. Father-and-son California governors Pat Brown and Jerry Brown actually shared what first name?

2. Omaha, Topeka, or Indianapolis—the famous *Brown v. Board of Education* case took on the Board of Education of what U.S. city?

3. What Dan Brown novel features the first appearance of his protagonist Robert Langdon?

4. Which James Brown song's famous call-and-response chorus is actually performed by white and Asian-American kids?

5. Alton Brown serves as the commentator on the transplanted American version of what cult series?

6. In 2006, who broke Jim Brown's forty-year-old NFL record by scoring 100 touchdowns in only 89 games?

7. In 2005, what odd medical occurrence delayed *Black Roses*, the new album by Brooklyn rapper Foxy Brown?

8. Why did Bristol postal worker Louise Brown make headlines in 1978 by doing nothing more than being born?

9. Who is Charlie Brown's favorite baseball player?

10. An easy question for Jim Croce fans: what is Encyclopedia Brown's real first name?

11. What is Joe E. Brown's famous last line in *Some Like It Hot*, after Jack Lemmon confesses to him that he's not a woman at all?

12. What magazine did Helen Gurley Brown edit from 1966 to 1998?

13. Why did young Avery Brown become a political cause célèbre in 1992?

14. What is Jackie Brown's occupation in Quentin Tarantino's 1997 film?

15. What distinctive physical feature gave Hall of Fame pitcher Mordecai Brown his famous nickname?

• **1969** • BARBARA EDEN FINALLY marries her "master," Major Tony Nelson, on TV's *I Dream of Jeannie*. As is typical with this kind of last-ditch resolution of sitcom sexual tension, the show will be canceled just months later.

ALL WISHED UP

1. What kind of movies compete in the annual Genie Awards?

2. Complete this analogy. Aladdin's genie : lamp :: Kazaam : _____.

3. Christina Aguilera's "Genie in a Bottle" was the second debut single by a female artist to top the charts in 1999. What was the first?

4. According to the Qur'an, what famous king had the power to control the *djinn*?

5. What enterprising TV star is married to Genie Francis, *General Hospital*'s Laura Spencer?

Answers to the questions on this page can be found on page 521.

• **1976** • A HELIUM PIG is flown over London's Battersea Power Station, for the shooting of the photo on the cover of Pink Floyd's *Animals*. High winds snap the pig loose (an on-hand marksman having been sent home as an insurance risk) and the out-of-control balloon leads to grounded flights at Heathrow Airport and a lengthy pursuit in a police helicopter.

ZOOROPA
What animal is pictured on the covers of these pop albums?

1. *Pet Sounds*, the Beach Boys
2. *Dolittle*, the Pixies
3. *Tapestry*, Carole King
4. *The College Dropout*, Kanye West

5. *Armed Forces*, Elvis Costello and the Attractions
6. *Graceland*, Paul Simon
7. *Vs.*, Pearl Jam
8. *For Your Pleasure*, Roxy Music

9. *American Recordings*, Johnny Cash
10. *Enema of the State*, Blink-182

• **1984** • 103-YEAR-OLD HARRY STEVENS becomes the world's oldest groom, marrying Thelma Lucas (84 years old—robbing the cradle!) in a Wisconsin retirement home.

LOVE THROUGH THE AGES
Name the other half of these May-December marriages.

Easy
1. Heather Mills
2. Lauren Bacall
3. Ashton Kutcher
4. Larry Fortensky
5. Michael Douglas

Harder
1. Edie Brickell
2. Jessica Sklar
3. Peter Sellers
4. Carlo Ponti
5. Dyan Cannon

Yeah, Good Luck
1. Heather Harlan
2. J. Howard Marshall
3. Dina Ruiz
4. Wendy Deng
5. René Angélil

• **1992** • ELIZABETH TAYLOR MAKES her *Simpsons* debut, playing young Maggie Simpson on the episode "Maggie's First Word." (Maggie's first word is "Daddy.")

TELL ME, BABY
Match these TV characters to their first words as infants.

1. "Abba gabba goo"
2. "Ay carumba!"
3. "Boat"
4. "Cookie"
5. "Gleeba"
6. "Hardware"
7. "JFK"
8. "No!"
9. "Norm"
10. "Schmuck"

A. Mabel Buchman, *Mad About You*
B. Frederick Crane, *Frasier*
C. Joanie Cunningham, *Happy Days*
D. Chuckie Finster, *Rugrats*
E. Pebbles Flintstone, *The Flintstones*
F. Maya Gallo, *Just Shoot Me*
G. Emma Green-Gellar, *Friends*
H. Fox Mulder, *The X-Files*
I. Bart Simpson, *The Simpsons*
J. Michelle Tanner, *Full House*

Answers to the questions on this page can be found on page 521.

DECEMBER 4

• **1961** • AFTER A WALL STREET stockbroker tips off *The New York Times,* the Museum of Modern Art finally takes another look at *Le Bateau,* a Matisse painting that has been hanging there for forty-seven days and seen by 118,000 people. For the entire exhibition, nobody has noticed that it was hanging upside down.

BOTTOM TO TOP
Upside-down trivia you'll flip for.

1. What was 1918's famed "inverted Jenny"?

2. What Dutch artist is well known for lithographs like 1953's *Relativity,* with its gravity-defying upside-down staircases?

3. If, from anywhere in the contiguous U.S., you were to tunnel through the center of the earth and come out the other side, in what body of water would you emerge?

4. In what movie does Fred Astaire do his famous dancing-on-the-ceiling number to "You're All the World to Me"?

5. What lowercase letter is turned upside down to denote the neutral vowel "schwa"?

6. What band's hit "Head over Heels" anchored the soundtrack of the 2001 movie *Donnie Darko*?

7. If you turned the Indonesian flag upside down—as a distress signal, say—you would actually be flying the flag of what other nation?

8. Mike Leigh's 1999 movie *Topsy Turvy* is a behind-the-scenes look at what famous partnership?

9. What company chose to call a spun-off division "Dynec" so that its own corporate logo could be turned upside down to make the new company's "dy" logo?

10. Traditionally, which of Jesus' disciples asked the Romans to crucify him upside down?

• **1998** • HASBRO CLOSES the Milton Bradley Wood Products Company in Fairfax, Vermont, which has, for twenty years, produced North America's entire supply of Scrabble tiles: a million a day.

INTO THE WOODS
Never fear: Scrabble tiles are still made of Vermont maple, but now the logs are shipped to China and then shipped back in tile form. What kind of wood are (or were) these items made from?

1. The "Spruce Goose"	**A.** Ash
2. Dixon Ticonderoga pencils	**B.** Balsa
3. Walt Disney's Pinocchio	**C.** Birch
4. Most electric chairs	**D.** Cedar
5. Harry Potter's wand	**E.** Gopher wood
6. *Kon-Tiki*	**F.** Holly
7. Noah's ark	**G.** Maple
8. The *Mona Lisa*	**H.** Oak
9. Most Louisville Sluggers	**I.** Pine
10. B. B. King's "Lucille"	**J.** Poplar

Answers to the questions on this page can be found on page 522.

• **1945** • FLIGHT 19, made up of five U.S. Navy bombers, disappears on a training mission off the coast of Florida. In the 1950s, this incident will become one of the founding myths of the "Bermuda Triangle" legend.

BIZARRE QUIZ TRIANGLE

1. What state's three most prestigious universities form its Research Triangle?

2. In what novel would you find the love triangle of Charles Darnay, Lucie Manette, and Sydney Carton?

3. What word, from the Greek for "uneven," refers to a triangle whose sides all have different lengths?

4. Goya's controversial 1798 painting *The Naked Maja* includes the first depiction of what in Western art?

5. A Citgo Petroleum sign in Kenmore Square is the iconic red triangle that can be seen above left field in what major-league ballpark?

6. What nerdy Martin Short character played the triangle?

7. What is shipped along Indochina's "Golden Triangle"?

8. A red and blue triangle is, appropriately, the logo of what major airline?

9. What industry-changing event happened at New York's Triangle Shirtwaist Factory on March 25, 1911?

10. "Triangle Man" is the only combatant who goes 2–0 in what They Might Be Giants song?

11. What NBA head coach won nine championship rings using the "triangle offense"?

12. What's the only European country with a single triangle on its flag?

13. Why did the pink triangle, as a gay pride symbol, originate?

14. What's the longest side of a right triangle called?

15. What game uses twenty-two balls, including fifteen red ones arranged in a triangle?

• **1952** • LONDON'S QUAINT "pea-soup fog" becomes a little less charming as "the Big Smoke" descends on the city. The lethal sulfur-coal smog will kill thousands by the time it lifts four days later, resulting in new clean air legislation in the U.K.

GIVE PEAS A CHANCE

1. Whose landmark 1865 paper recorded seven characteristics of peas, including "color, form, and size of the pods"?

2. What 1959 musical ends with the happy refrain "It wasn't the pea at all"?

3. What breakfast cereal becomes a disturbing sexual metaphor in the Black-Eyed Peas hit "My Humps"?

4. What Roman orator was named for the chickpea?

5. How long has "pease-porridge" been in the pot, according to the nursery rhyme?

Answers to the questions on this page can be found on page 522.

DECEMBER 6

• **1884** • THE CAPSTONE IS PLACED atop the Washington Monument during its dedication ceremony. The pyramidal cap is made of a rare element as precious, at the time, as silver: aluminum!

LANDMARK DECISIONS

1. Inside what world landmark can you see a plaque bearing the equation "$y = -127.7 \text{ ft} \times \cosh(x/127.7 \text{ ft}) + 757.7 \text{ ft}$"?

2. What Indian city is home to the Taj Mahal?

3. What lies broken at the feet of the Statue of Liberty?

4. What's the more common name for the Duomo's campanile at the Campo dei Miracoli?

5. What was originally painted Galaxy Gold, Orbital Olive, and Re-entry Red for its 1962 opening?

6. What did Danish architect Jørn Utzon design to be built on Bennelong Point in 1957?

7. What landmark's history did Spinal Tap describe by saying "No one knows who they were or what they were doing"?

8. What nation is missing from this list? Greece, Greece, Egypt, Egypt, Turkey, Turkey, _____.

9. In 1969's *The Love Bug*, Herbie tries to kill himself at what landmark?

10. For what saint is the famous onion-domed cathedral in Moscow's Red Square named?

• **1964** • *RUDOLPH THE RED-NOSED REINDEER* debuts in glorious stop-motion on NBC. Since then, no TV special has been aired in more consecutive years.

OH CAROL, I'M SO IN LOVE WITH YOU

1. In what modern-day country is Good King Wenceslas's feast day a public holiday?

2. Where should the comma go in "God Rest You Merry Gentlemen"?

3. What's the last Christmas carol sung in both *A Charlie Brown Christmas* and *It's a Wonderful Life*?

4. On how many of "The Twelve Days of Christmas" are birds given as the new gift?

5. What does Alvin want for Christmas, according to "The Chipmunk Song"?

6. In Irving Berlin's original "White Christmas," the song is set in what city?

7. What name is given to the snowman in "Winter Wonderland"?

8. "Silent Night," "Santa Claus Is Coming to Town," or "Jingle Bells"—what was the first song ever broadcast to Earth from space?

9. What jazz singer cowrote "The Christmas Song," though he didn't record it until decades later?

10. "What Child Is This?" is sung to the tune of what old standard?

Answers to the questions on this page can be found on page 522.

• **1905** • THE FIRST SUCCESSFUL human organ transplant is performed by Austrian ophthalmologist Eduard Zirm. Laborer Alois Grogar, who was blinded in an accident, gets a new set of corneas.

DOCTOR, MY EYES

1. What country is led today by London-trained ophthalmologist Bashar al-Assad?
2. What eye doctor, along with neurologist Bernard Sachs, first discovered a namesake disease among Ashkenazi Jewish patients?
3. What language was invented by Polish ophthalmologist L. L. Zamenhof?
4. Who was working as an eye doctor when he unsuccessfully killed off his most famous character in the short story "The Final Problem"?
5. In what sci-fi movie does Peter Stormare play shady eye doctor Solomon Eddie?

• **1941** • AN ANONYMOUS CHAPLAIN (often credited as Howell M. Forgy aboard the USS *New Orleans*) steps into military history with his seven-word Sunday-morning sermon at the Pearl Harbor gun turrets: "Praise the Lord and pass the ammunition."

MESSAGE IN A BATTLE
Who spoke these famous quotes from American military lore?

Easy
1. "I have not yet begun to fight."
2. "Damn the torpedoes!"
3. "I shall return."

Harder
1. "War is hell."
2. "You may fire when ready, Gridley."
3. "We have met the enemy and they are ours."

Yeah, Good Luck
1. "Nuts!"
2. "Don't give up the ship!"
3. "Lafayette, we are here."

• **1963** • CBS TRIES OUT instant replay during its telecast of the Army-Navy football game. "This is not live!" announcer Lindsey Nelson tells confused viewers. "Ladies and gentlemen, Army has not scored again."

FOR INSTANTS
How fast can you answer these questions about other "instant" things?

1. What company produced the first commercial instant camera, in 1947?
2. What movie features the line "Howard Beale is processed instant God, and right now, it looks like he may just go over bigger than Mary Tyler Moore"?
3. "Let's see if they notice!" What brand of instant coffee secretly replaced restaurant coffee in 1980s TV ads?
4. What Stephen King novel takes its title from the chorus of John Lennon's "Instant Karma!"?
5. What does the instant-messaging acronym "A/S/L" request?

Answers to the questions on this page can be found on page 523.

DECEMBER 8

• **65 B.C.** • THE ROMAN POET Horace is born. He will pen some of the best-remembered Latin phrases of the classical era, including "*Carpe diem*" and "*Dulce et decorum est.*"

LATIN LOVERS
Give the common Latin phrase that literally translates as . . .

Easy	Harder	Yeah, Good Luck
1. Stiffness of death	1. Something for something	1. After this, therefore because of this
2. And the rest	2. Let the buyer beware	2. Without which not
3. It does not follow	3. Blank slate	3. Wonderful to say
4. Voice of the people	4. A not-pleasing person	4. With great praise
5. My fault	5. To the point of disgust	5. Under penalty

• **1938** • THE LESLIE HOWARD–Wendy Hiller film adaptation of George Bernard Shaw's *Pygmalion* premieres in New York. Shaw himself helped adapt the play for the screen, and as a result he will become the only person ever to win both a Nobel Prize and an Oscar.

DOUBLE THREATS

1. Who's the only scientist to have won Nobel Prizes in both physics and chemistry?
2. In 2001, who became the first person ever to have America's number one album and number one movie in the same week?
3. Who's the only person to have played in both a World Series and a Super Bowl?
4. Who received a Congressional Medal of Honor, for war, as well as a Nobel Prize for Peace?
5. What longtime ABC analyst is the only winner of both of an Emmy and an Olympic gold medal?

• **1981** • NBA STAR LLOYD B. FREE makes his old playground nickname official, legally changing his name to World B. Free.

SEE YOU IN COURT
Name these basketball players from their nicknames.

Easy	Harder	Yeah, Good Luck
1. The Answer	1. The Iceman	1. Plastic Man
2. Pistol Pete	2. The Round Mound of Rebound	2. Dr. Dunkenstein
3. T-Mac	3. The Big Dipper	3. The Human Eraser
4. Dr. J	4. The Glove	4. Hot Plate
5. Larry Legend	5. The Big Ticket	5. The Owl Without a Vowel

Answers to the questions on this page can be found on page 523.

• **1898** • LIEUTENANT COLONEL John Henry Patterson kills the first of the two lions that have eaten almost 140 workers building the Uganda Railway in Tsavo, Kenya. The attacks inspired Patterson's book *The Man-Eaters of Tsavo* and the movie *The Ghost and the Darkness*.

LET US PREY

1. What's the "predator" in the Nashville Predators' NHL logo?
2. According to the World Health Organization, what's the world's deadliest animal, killing more than two million people every year?
3. What's the only animal on the American Film Institute's list of the fifty greatest villains in movie history?
4. "Nanook," of "of the North" fame, is named for the Inuit word for what predator?
5. What Caribbean island chain did Frances Drake name for the ten-foot crocodiles that lived there?

• **1970** • JERRY LEE LEWIS is divorced from his third wife and second cousin, Myra Gale Brown. Or was it second wife and third cousin? Anyway, the thirteen-year-old.

ALL KILLER, NO FILLER

1. Who wrote the slogan "This machine kills fascists" on his guitar?
2. A concert by what 1970s singer-songwriter was the inspiration for "Killing Me Softly with His Song"?
3. Arthur "Killer" Kane played bass for what seminal punk band?
4. What Bruce Springsteen title track is narrated by a serial killer?
5. What celebrity sibling appears in the video to the Killers' "Mr. Brightside"?

• **1990** • AIR FORCE'S CHRIS HOWARD becomes the inaugural winner of the Vincent de Paul Draddy Award for scholar-athletes, often called the "Academic Heisman." Former Manhattan College QB Vin Draddy was best known, later in life, for introducing Izod and Lacoste shirts to America.

BEST IN THEIR FIELD
Match the college football awards to their position.

1. Dave Rimington Trophy
2. Davey O'Brien Award
3. Dick Butkus Award
4. Doak Walker Award
5. Fred Biletnikoff Award
6. Jim Thorpe Award
7. John Mackey Award
8. Lou Groza Award
9. Ray Guy Award
10. Ted Hendricks Award

A. Center
B. Defensive back
C. Defensive end
D. Linebacker
E. Placekicker
F. Punter
G. Quarterback
H. Running back
I. Tight end
J. Wide receiver

Answers to the questions on this page can be found on page 523.

DECEMBER 10

• 1972 • THE AMERICAN LEAGUE votes to adopt the controversial designated hitter rule.

AND OTHER REALLY BAD IDEAS

1. Because vending machine operators rejected the original eleven-sided design, what unpopular 1979 coin was too easily mistaken for a quarter?

2. Who starred in *Jade* and *Kiss of Death* after the ill-advised decision to leave his hit TV show?

3. What lake, once the world's fourth largest, is now a quarter of its previous size due to Soviet-era irrigation projects?

4. What blunder led President Kennedy to say "Victory has a hundred fathers and defeat is an orphan"?

5. A red boomerang is the logo for what Australian swimwear brand?

6. What did Pepsi call its disastrous "clear alternative" to cola in 1992?

7. What French minister of defense championed a line of concrete forts on the German border, to protect France from invasion?

8. What Japanese weed took over the American South after being introduced at the 1876 Philadelphia Centennial Exposition?

9. What car company produced only one model, the DMC-12?

10. If Biosphere 2 was the failed 1991 ecological experiment, what was Biosphere 1?

11. During the O. J. Simpson trial, what Johnny Cochran couplet was the result of the prosecution's ill-advised decision to have Simpson try on the "bloody glove"?

12. What major-league team signed Michael Jordan during his bizarre flirtation with baseball?

13. What nation did Hitler attack in the disastrous Operation Barbarossa?

14. What movie innovation was used for only a single feature, 1960's *Scent of Mystery*?

15. What TV character cut her hair after a rough breakup with Ben Covington?

• 1984 • ANTI-APARTHEID ACTIVIST Archbishop Desmond Tutu receives the Nobel Peace Prize.

TUTU FUNNY
Ballet trivia to keep you on your toes.

1. How many basic positions are there in classical ballet?

2. What ballet film scored a record eleven Oscar nominations without winning a single one?

3. What one-legged ballet stance was so named because it was borrowed from Middle Eastern dance?

4. What Stravinsky ballet was the only work by a living composer included in Disney's *Fantasia*?

5. Which of the animals from Saint-Saëns's *Carnival of the Animals* became the most famous showpiece of ballerina Anna Pavlova?

Answers to the questions on this page can be found on page 524.

DECEMBER 11

• **1967** • AFTER HE PAYS the eleven-guinea fee, Oliver Greenhalgh is accepted as a member of the English Association of Estate Agents and Valuers. Unfortunately for the association, it's been taken in by a headline-making TV news sting investigating phony professional associations. Oliver Greenhalgh is a housecat.

PUSSY GALORE

1. What musical takes place at the Kit Kat Klub?
2. What has been America's most popular pedigreed cat breed since 1871?
3. Besides his famous red and white chapeau, what other red article of clothing does the Cat in the Hat wear?
4. Of what quarterback did Thomas "Hollywood" Henderson say "He couldn't spell 'cat' if you spotted him the *c* and the *t*"?
5. What is supposedly noteworthy about the $3,950 cats that Allerca, a San Diego biotech company, announced for sale in 2006?
6. What's the name of Audrey Hepburn's cat in *Breakfast at Tiffany's*?
7. What parasitic disease, a cause of birth defects and schizophrenia, is often transmitted by cat feces?
8. What cat pretended to belong to the Marquis of Carabas?
9. What are a cat's vibrissae?
10. Whenever Felix the Cat gets into a fix, what does he reach into?

• **2001** • THE LAST EPISODE of Emeril Lagasse's short-lived sitcom airs, ending the remarkable TV career of Robert Urich. Urich was a regular in thirteen different series, more than any other actor in TV history.

GET READY TO MATCH THE STARS

Match the roles in hit TV series that were played by the same actor, and name the actor. (For extra credit, name the shows involved.)

1. Peg Bundy
2. Joe Cartwright
3. Sabrina Duncan
4. Bill Gannon
5. Alex P. Keaton
6. John Kelly
7. Ilya Kuryakin
8. Mary Beth Lacey
9. Paige Matheson
10. Samantha Micelli
11. Tony Nelson
12. Laura Petrie
13. Alexander Scott
14. Kelly Taylor
15. Opie Taylor

A. Edie Britt
B. Horatio ~~Caine~~ Caine
C. Richie Cunningham
D. J. R. Ewing
E. Mike Flaherty
F. Maxine Gray
G. Phoebe Halliwell
H. Cate Hennessy
I. Cliff Huxtable
J. Charles Ingalls
K. Amanda King
L. Ducky Mallard
M. Sherman Potter
N. Mary Richards
O. Valerie Tyler

DECEMBER 12

• **1792** • BEETHOVEN BEGINS STUDYING with his most famous tutor, Austrian composer Joseph Haydn.

HOT FOR TEACHER
What general subject was taught by these film and TV teachers?

Easy	*Harder*	*Yeah, Good Luck*
1. John Houseman, *The Paper Chase*	1. Howard Hesseman, *Head of the Class*	1. Robert Donat, *Goodbye, Mr. Chips*
2. Richard Dreyfuss, *Mr. Holland's Opus*	2. Edward James Olmos, *Stand and Deliver*	2. Stephen Colbert, the *Strangers with Candy* movie
3. Robin Williams, *Dead Poets Society*	3. Glenn Ford, *Blackboard Jungle*	3. Hayley Mills, *Good Morning, Miss Bliss*
4. Rex Harrison, *My Fair Lady*	4. Cate Blanchett, *Notes on a Scandal*	4. Dennis Quaid, *The Rookie*
5. Julie Walters, *Billy Elliot*	5. Tina Fey, *Mean Girls*	5. George Segal, *Who's Afraid of Virginia Woolf?*

• **1917** • FATHER FLANAGAN founds Boys Town, Nebraska.

BOY BANDS
What "Boys" recorded these albums?

Easy	*Harder*	*Yeah, Good Luck*
1. *Licensed to Ill*	1. *Please*	1. *Stop Staring at Me!*
2. *Cooleyhighharmony*	2. *Sacred*	2. *Young, Loud and Snotty*
3. *Surf's Up*	3. *Till Death Do Us Part*	3. *Crushin'*
4. *Millennium*	4. *Step On Out*	4. *Fisherman's Blues*

• **1925** • A NEW WORD and a new industry are born when Pasadena architect Arthur Heineman opens the Motel Inn in San Luis Obispo, California.

MOTEL SIX

1. What motel was reopened as the National Civil Rights Museum in 1991?
2. What bug control company manufactures the Roach Motel?
3. In *Psycho*, what pastime of Norman Bates's does Marion Crane call a "strange hobby"?
4. "A House Is Not a Motel" is the B-side of what 1967 single by Love?
5. In 1988, who was photographed leaving the Travel Inn in Lake Charles, Louisiana, with a prostitute named Debra Murphree?
6. What Richard Linklater film is set, in real time, entirely inside a Lansing, Michigan, motel room?

Answers to the questions on this page can be found on page 524.

• **1977** • THE BEE GEES RELEASE their disco hit "Stayin' Alive." The drummer listed on the track is the fictitious "Bernard Lupe," as the song's drum part is actually a sample from the already recorded "Night Fever."

A G THANG

What number one song by each of these artists leaves a final g off an "-ing" word of the title, just like "Stayin' Alive"?

Easy	Harder	Yeah, Good Luck
1. Ricky Martin	1. Ricky Nelson	1. Bobby Lewis
2. Alicia Keys	2. The Temptations	2. Lou Christie
3. Bon Jovi	3. Neil Diamond	3. Eddie Kendricks
4. B. J. Thomas	4. Roberta Flack	4. Stevie Wonder
5. Will Smith	5. New Kids on the Block	5. Minnie Riperton

• **1982** • VANNA WHITE MAKES her *Wheel of Fortune* debut, replacing former letter turner Susan Stafford.

YOU SPIN ME RIGHT ROUND

An examination on rotation.

1. What do we more commonly call Turkey's Mevlevi order of Sufi mystics, for their famous spinning dance?

2. What's the highest number on a standard roulette wheel?

3. The gyroscope was named and invented by what Frenchman, the year after he hung his famous pendulum?

4. What name was coined by Mussolini on November 1, 1936, when he claimed in a speech that all Europe would soon "revolve" around Italy and Germany?

5. What ballet's Act III ends with Odile doing thirty-two *fouettés en tournant* in a row?

6. In "Rumpelstiltskin," what does the miller's daughter promise the dwarf the last time he spins straw into gold for her?

7. What word do Americans use for the billiards term that's called "side" in Britain?

8. What exhibits "Chandler wobble" as it revolves?

9. What song—one of the most famous B-sides in pop history—plays during the pottery wheel scene in the movie *Ghost*?

10. Warner Bros. has partnered with the Australian government to try to save what mammal, which is being driven extinct by cancerous facial tumors?

11. What's the only TV show ever to spawn five prime-time spin-offs?

12. What was the first name of the Norwegian figure skater Paulsen, who invented his trademark maneuver in 1882?

13. What hit Broadway musical was based on *Liliom*, a Hungarian play about a carnival barker who kills himself after a botched robbery?

14. What book of the Bible provides the lyrics to the song "Turn! Turn! Turn!"?

15. The Fujita Scale is used to measure the power of what?

Answers to the questions on this page can be found on page 525.

DECEMBER 14

• **1721** • ALEXANDER SELKIRK, once the marooned model for Defoe's *Robinson Crusoe*, is buried at sea off West Africa after a yellow fever epidemic sweeps his navy ship.

PASSING AWEIGH
Name these other bodies buried at sea.

1. The annual National Spelling Bee is still named for what founder of UPI?
2. What Polish soldier, killed at the Battle of Savannah, was called "the father of American cavalry"?
3. Who was sent to sleep with the fishes in *The Sopranos'* season-two finale?
4. Whom did Spanish sailors call "el Dragón," playing on his name?
5. What late drummer hosted Charles Manson's "Family" at his Pacific Palisades house for much of 1968?

• **1836** • THE "TOLEDO WAR," a boundary dispute between Ohio and Michigan, ends when a convention in Ann Arbor agrees to cede "the Toledo Strip" to Ohio, receiving in return the entire Upper Peninsula. Tensions between Ohio and Michigan are today played out on Big Ten football fields, not by state militias.

BAD BLOOD
Feuds for thought.

1. The Hatfields and the McCoys lived across what Appalachian state line from each other?
2. The twenty top-TV-rated U.S. sports events of all time are all Super Bowls, except for one. What 1994 showdown was the third-most-watched sports event ever?
3. Pepsi lost the cola wars to Coke but is winning the water war. What Pepsi water brand outsells Coke's Dasani?
4. In what city did Joe Frazier and Muhammad Ali's third and final fight take place?
5. What high-definition disk technology is Sony's rival to HD DVD?
6. What famous rivalry ended in Weehawken, New Jersey, in 1804?
7. What industrial-sounding name is given to the annual Auburn-Alabama football game?
8. Who defended his book *A Man in Full* by feuding with critics John Updike, Norman Mailer, and John Irving, whom he called "My Three Stooges"?
9. What famous pair of rivals are surnamed Cooper and Lodge, respectively?
10. What island has since 1983 been racked by civil war between the government and the rebel Tamil Tigers?

• **1966** • LESTER FLATT AND EARL SCRUGGS guest on *The Beverly Hillbillies*, recording a jingle for the "Foggy Mountain Soap" commercial in which Jed and Granny are starring.

CONSUME MASS QUANTITIES!
What TV shows created these fictional products?

Easy	*Harder*	*Yeah, Good Luck*
1. Vitameatavegamin	**1.** Talky Tina	**1.** The Cornballer
2. Krusty-O cereal	**2.** Blue Moon shampoo	**2.** Miracle Salve
3. Happy Fun Ball	**3.** Alamo beer	**3.** Ori-dent electric toothbrush

Answers to the questions on this page can be found on page 525.

• **1964** • THE CANADIAN HOUSE OF COMMONS votes to adopt the new maple leaf flag, replacing the Union Jack.

IF YOU LEAF ME NOW
What type of leaf . . .

1. Was given to winners at the ancient Olympics
2. Makes up the entire diet of koalas
3. Did the gang paint on the Point Place water tower on *That '70s Show*

4. Did Adam and Eve use to make aprons
5. Is stuffed to make yaprak dolmades
6. Indicates multiple decorations on U.S. military award
7. Was O. Henry's "The Last

Leaf"
8. Is read by tasseomancers
9. Is the preferred food of giraffes
10. Appears on the cover of Bing Crosby's album *Merry Christmas*

• **1966** • CHAIN SMOKER WALT DISNEY dies of lung cancer—and is cremated and buried at Forest Lawn, despite what you've heard.

ICY DEAD PEOPLE—ALL THE TIME!

1. Whose is the most famous frozen head awaiting thawing at the Alcor Life Extension Foundation in Scottsdale, Arizona?
2. What counterculture icon had long planned to freeze his corpse

but ended up having his ashes shot into space in the same rocket with Gene Roddenberry's?
3. What movie predicts that the future will hold Intoxication orbs and Orgasmatron booths?

4. What TV show's pilot takes place on December 31, 1999, and December 31, 2999?
5. What's the name of Dr. Evil's cat, frozen with him in 1967?

• **1979** • OVER A BORING SCRABBLE GAME, two Montreal journalists try to come up with their own get-rich-quick idea for a board game, and the billion-dollar phenomenon Trivial Pursuit is born.

BOARD SILLY

1. Who is called "Dr. Black" in England and "Mr. Boddy" in North America?
2. What game, cocreated by former Microsoft employee of the year Richard Tait, first launched in Starbucks outlets, not toy stores?
3. Which of the railroads in Monopoly isn't named after an actual railroad?
4. It's neither Chinese nor checkers. In what country was "Chinese checkers" *really* born—

India, Germany, or the U.S.?
5. The word "ONE" is worth three points in Scrabble, if you add up the face value of the three tiles. What's the only number that's worth its own number of points?
6. Which of the four Hungry Hungry Hippos shares his name with one of the Seven Dwarfs?
7. Elasund is the "first city" of what fictional island?
8. What's the only chess piece that changes the color of its square every time it moves?

9. Presumably because he's a bad role model for today's children, what character was replaced by "Mama Ginger Tree" in the latest version of Candy Land?
10. Who started out as a lithographer, made a fortune on a print of a young, clean-shaven Abe Lincoln, but saw his sales collapse after Lincoln grew a beard?

Answers to the questions on this page can be found on page 525.

DECEMBER 16

• **1959** • Chicago's Second City Theatre opens, home to the improv troupe that will give the world legendary comics, from Fred Willard to Bill Murray to Stephen Colbert.

WE'RE NUMBER TWO!
What nation is home to these "second cities"?

Easy	*Harder*	*Yeah, Good Luck*
1. Antwerp	1. Guayaquil	1. Oran
2. Medellín	2. Mandalay	2. Split
3. Mumbai	3. Bergen	3. Plovdiv
4. Cape Town	4. Surabaya	4. Santa Cruz de la Sierra
5. Tel Aviv	5. Mombasa	5. Samarkand

• **1970** • *Love Story* is released, trumpeted by one of Hollywood's most famous taglines: "Love means never having to say you're sorry."

TAG! YOU'RE IT
What movies used these memorable taglines?

1. You won't believe your eye.
2. This is Benjamin. He's a little worried about his future.
3. The Monster demands a Mate!
4. Does for rock and roll what *The Sound of Music* did for hills.
5. It's 4 A.M.—do you know where your car is?
6. For anyone who has ever wished upon a star.
7. Before you die, you see . . .
8. It's scrumdiddlyumptious!
9. An adventure sixty-five million years in the making.
10. They'll never get caught. They're on a mission from God.
11. Garbo *laughs*!
12. This is the weekend they didn't play golf.
13. Where were you in '62?
14. She was marked with the curse of those who slink and court and kill by night!
15. Check in. Relax. Take a shower.
16. Just when you thought it was safe to go back in the water.
17. Jim Stark—a kid from a "good" family—what makes him tick . . . like a bomb?
18. For three men, the Civil War wasn't hell. It was practice!
19. Escape or die frying.
20. They're young . . . they're in love . . . and they kill people.
21. Being the adventures of a young man whose principal interests are rape, ultraviolence, and Beethoven.
22. Five criminals. One lineup. No coincidences.
23. The chauffeur's daughter who learned her stuff in Paris!
24. The fiery cross of the Ku Klux Klan.
25. Look closer.

Answers to the questions on this page can be found on page 526.

• **1865** • THE LATE FRANZ SCHUBERT's "Unfinished Symphony" is first performed, in Vienna. The last movement of his third symphony is tacked on so listeners don't experience *Schubertus interruptus*. More than a hundred years later, the symphony will become Gargamel's theme music on *The Smurfs*.

I HEAR A SYMPHONY
Who composed symphonies nicknamed . . .

1. "Tragic," "Resurrection," and ". . . of a Thousand"
2. "Eroica," "Pastoral," and "Choral"

3. "The Farewell," "The Clock," and "The Surprise"
4. "Winter Daydreams," "Little Russian," and "Pathétique"

5. "Reformation," "Scottish," and "Italian"

• **1892** • *VOGUE* MAGAZINE IS launched in New York. Back then, I think the devil wore Prada stays and bloomers.

CHIC-ER BY THE DOZEN
Match these down-market retailers to the designers slumming there.

1. Oscar de la Renta
2. Norma Kamali
3. Stella McCartney
4. Nicole Miller
5. Isaac Mizrahi
6. Kate Moss
7. Roland Mouret
8. Laura Poretzky
9. Vera Wang
10. Vivienne Westwood

A. Dillard's
B. Gap
C. H&M
D. JCPenney
E. Kohl's
F. Nine West
G. Payless
H. Spiegel
I. Target
J. Top Shop

• **2004** • ARCHAEOLOGISTS ANNOUNCE that they've discovered the world's oldest musical instrument in a cave in the Swabian Alps. It's a three-hole ivory flute, carved from a mammoth's tusk around 35,000 years ago. (Other instruments made from swan bones have already been found at the same site, so maybe this cave was also the world's oldest band camp.)

FLUTE-Y FLAKES

1. What band, after winning the first hard rock/metal Grammy in 1989, took out an ad reading "The flute is a (heavy) metal instrument"?
2. What movie director's father was Arturo Toscanini's first flautist in the NBC Symphony Orchestra?
3. Which character reaches an F an astonishing two and a half octaves above middle C in her famous aria from Mozart's *The Magic Flute*?
4. What title character of the 2004 film *Anchorman* plays the jazz flute?
5. After what Greek god is the flute sometimes called a "syrinx" usually named?

Answers to the questions on this page can be found on page 526.

DECEMBER 18

• **1912** • THE DISCOVERY OF the "Piltdown Man" fossils in Sussex is announced to the Geological Society of London. Not until 1953 will the remains (a mixture of human and ape bones, actually) be discredited as a hoax.

UNEARTHED

1. What was the brontosaurus renamed in 1903, when it was discovered that the original fossils of that dinosaur had been given an earlier name?
2. Thanks to DNA testing, from where was the body of Vietnam vet Michael Blassie disinterred in 1998 and returned to his family?
3. What ancient city did Heinrich Schliemann discover under the Turkish hill of Hisarlik?
4. What is the "big W" under which $350,000 is buried in *It's a Mad, Mad, Mad, Mad World?*
5. Taylor, Tyler, or Taft—what U.S. president was exhumed in 1991 to look for signs of arsenic poisoning?

• **1952** • PATTI PAGE ASKS the immortal musical question "(How Much Is) That Doggie in the Window?"

NO REST FOR THE QUERY

1. What does New Mexico's official state question, "Red or green?" refer to?
2. What clothing line uses a question mark as its emblem?
3. Who was the target of Joseph Welch's 1954 question "Have you no sense of decency, sir?"
4. What question was popularized when it was used as the subtitle of Charles Sheldon's 1896 religious novel *In His Steps?*
5. When is the Ma Nishtana—"Why is this night different from all other nights?"—recited?
6. What 1982 musical question prompts the line "This indecision's bugging me; *esta indecisión me molesta*"?
7. What not-yet-famous actor was the first target of Mae West's question "Why don't you come up sometime and see me?"
8. What's the only TV show with a question for a title ever to lead the Nielsen ratings for a season?
9. What question did Alfred E. Neuman first ask on a July 1955 magazine cover?
10. About what Baroness Orczy title character is the question asked "Is he in heaven? Is he in hell?"

• **1983** • THE TALKING HEADS are in the middle of a three-night set of concerts at Hollywood's Pantages Theater, which Jonathan Demme films for his hit Talking Heads concert film.

TALKING HEADS
Answer these questions on TV pundits.

1. What *McLaughlin Group* regular once had the star of *From Here to Eternity* as a brother-in-law?
2. What pundit had an executive producer credit on *All the King's Men*, a film based on a former governor of his home state?
3. What controversial commentator once briefly dated *Politically Incorrect* host Bill Maher?
4. What pundit does Bill O'Reilly regularly refer to as "Stuart Smalley"?
5. Who announced in 2006 that he would no longer wear bow ties on air, saying, "I wanted to give my neck a break"?

Answers to the questions on this page can be found on page 526.

• 1942 • ROBERT STROUD BECOMES prisoner 594-AZ, as he's transferred to Alcatraz Prison. The famed "Birdman" actually raises no birds at Alcatraz—he gained his ornithological fame during his earlier years at Leavenworth.

I AM NOT A NUMBER!

1. What literary character's prison number, 24601, is sometimes said to refer to the date of Victor Hugo's conception?

2. Who was known as "466/64" during his eighteen years breaking rock on Robben Island?

3. What Scrooge McDuck nemeses typically wear numbers 176-167, 176-671, and 176-761, even when they're out of jail?

4. What French novel's title character is prisoner 34 in Château d'If?

5. What was Patrick McGoohan's number on *The Prisoner*?

6. Who was addressed for decades only as "prisoner number seven" in Berlin's Spandau Prison?

7. What Alexander Solzhenitsyn title character was prisoner S-854?

8. In what film does the prison guard always call Alex De Large "six-double-five-three-two-one"?

9. Who played prisoner #95H522, the narrator of HBO's *Oz*?

10. Name one of the two movies in which Dan Aykroyd wears prisoner number 7474505B, a tribute to John Belushi's Joliet number in *The Blues Brothers*.

• 1980 • JERRY SEINFELD MAKES his final appearance as "Frankie, the mail boy" on the sitcom *Benson*. After being abruptly fired, he vows never again to return to sitcoms unless he can have creative control.

A QUIZ ABOUT NOTHING

1. According to "Me and Bobby McGee," what's "just another word for nothing left to lose"?

2. What two American scientists proved, in an 1887 experiment, that the vacuum of space *wasn't* filled with a mysterious "ether" that allowed light to propagate?

3. What ex–chief executive ran again for the presidency as the anti-immigrant "Know-Nothing" candidate in 1856?

4. How many blank tiles are there in a game of Scrabble?

5. Who began to formulate his trademark philosophy in the essay *Being and Nothingness*?

6. Whose lead role as a black-listed comedian in the Woody Allen film *The Front* mirrored his own experience during the McCarthy era?

7. Who sings the "I want my MTV" falsetto on the Dire Straits hit "Money for Nothing"?

8. What Judy Blume title character first appeared as the bratty younger brother in *Tales of a Fourth Grade Nothing*?

9. In British sport, it's a "clean sheet." What would an American sports fan call it?

10. On what day of the year do anticonsumerism activists celebrate "Buy Nothing Day"?

11. What 1988 action movie was based on Roderick Thorp's novel *Nothing Lasts Forever*?

12. What word did Buddha define as "where is no-thing, where naught is grasped, the isle of No-beyond"?

13. Who wrote Sinéad O'Connor's number one hit "Nothing Compares 2 U"?

14. What symbol did Andre Weil adopt from Norwegian to represent the "empty set" in mathematics?

15. What U.S. Steel tycoon is famous for the sentiment "I owe the public nothing!"?

Answers to the questions on this page can be found on page 527.

DECEMBER 20

• **1932** • THE AP REPORTS that the alumni of Chicago's Norton College finally decided to smoke a cigar given to the school's founder by Ulysses S. Grant more than fifty years ago. Horace Norton's grandson Winstead ceremonially lights the cigar . . . only to have it explode on the second puff. That Ulysses Grant—quite the prankster.

GIVE THAT MAN A CIGAR

1. In what famous American painting can you see an ad for Phillies cigars?
2. Hey, kids, smoking is cool! What comedian chews on a cigar in the very first episode of PBS's children's show *The Electric* *Company*?
3. When Cigar won sixteen races in a row in 1996, he tied the record of what 1948 Triple Crown winner?
4. A teenage Samuel Beckett's cigar smoking during an inter- view led to the 1922 asthma and pneumonia attack that killed off what French author?
5. What popular Cuban cigar is named in honor of the Alexandre Dumas novels supposedly beloved of its rollers?

• **1971** • RADIO HOST LARRY KING is arrested for grand larceny, after getting entangled with in- dicted financier Louis Wolfson. King does no jail time but is off the air for three years.

A FACE FOR RADIO

1. New York DJ "Murray the K" was the first person ever to re- ceive what nickname, later ap- plied to people like Derek Taylor and George Martin?
2. What radio star was the first man ever to top Mr. Blackwell's "Worst Dressed" list?
3. What are "all the children" in Lake Wobegon, according to Gar- rison Keillor?
4. In what state did the Martians land in Orson Welles's famous *War of the Worlds* broadcast?
5. Don Imus was fired in 2007 for insulting what school's bas- ketball team?
6. In what movie did Wolfman Jack make his film debut?
7. What quarterback famously knocked down Jim Rome for comparing him to a similarly named female tennis player?
8. Whose 1994 wedding to Marta Fitzgerald was hosted and offici- ated by Supreme Court Justice Clarence Thomas?
9. What radio legend returned to broadcasting to narrate TV's *The Untouchables*?
10. What avant-garde composer is the first cousin, once removed, of the host of NPR's *This Ameri- can Life*?

• **2002** • NBC AIRS THE "winter finale" of its drama *Providence*—but when much of the cast elects not to return, this ends up being the show's farewell.

THE CAPITAL GANG
Providence was set in, um, Providence. What state capitals were the setting for . . .

Easy	*Harder*	*Yeah, Good Luck*
1. *Hawaii Five-O*	**1.** *Medium*	**1.** *Judging Amy*
2. *Dynasty*	**2.** *Matlock*	**2.** *Men Behaving Badly*
3. *Ally McBeal*	**3.** *Family Ties*	**3.** *Eight Is Enough*

Answers to the questions on this page can be found on page 527.

• **841 B.C.** • THE FIRST CHINESE NEW YEAR (as far as we can date it definitively) takes place around the winter solstice. Since seven-inch copper knives were the common currency of the Zhou dynasty, those little red New Year's cash envelopes must have been a *lot* bigger back then.

THE BEAST IN ME

Under which Chinese "Year of the . . ." animal were these famous folks, each rather appropriately, born?

Easy	Harder	Yeah, Good Luck
1. E. B. White	1. Thomas Harris	1. Magglio Ordóñez
2. Charles Schulz	2. William Jennings Bryan	2. James Clavell
3. Bruce Lee	3. "Buffalo Bill" Cody	3. Lasse Hallström
4. Lewis Carroll	4. Naomi Watts	4. Thurl Ravenscroft

• **2012** • ACCORDING TO THE MOST popular reading of the Mayan Long Count calendar, the end of the world is scheduled for today. Dress warmly if you're going out.

THE GRAND "FINALLY"

Some more trivia about endings, while you're waiting for the end of the world.

1. What play ends with the stage direction "Nothing is heard but the thud of the ax on a tree far away"?

2. Unlike in the NFL, how deep is the end zone in Canadian football?

3. Who was Kurt Cobain quoting when he ended his suicide note "I don't have the passion anymore, and so remember, it's better to burn out than to fade away"?

4. What ended the Crimean War, the Spanish-American War, the Seven Years' War, the Albigensian Crusade, and the American Revolution?

5. What classic 1968 movie has no dialogue for the first twenty-five minutes or the final twenty-three minutes?

6. Who was the last U.S. president to sport facial hair in office?

7. R.E.M.'s "It's the End of the World as We Know It" was based on a dream singer Michael Stipe had about being at a party attended only by people with what initials?

8. What musical's finale is called "John 19:41"?

9. In what peninsular British county is Land's End?

10. What video-game franchise invented creatures like Moogles, Chocobos, Tonberries, and Cactuars?

11. What has an axon on one end and dendrites on the other?

12. In the title of a 1980 sci-fi novel, what's another name for Milliways?

13. Until "Who shot J.R.?" in 1980, what show's finale was the top-rated series TV show in TV history?

14. What two cities were the endpoints of Route 66?

15. Who hit a home run (number 521) in the final at-bat of his career, on September 28, 1960?

Answers to the questions on this page can be found on page 527.

DECEMBER 22

• **1872** • PHILEAS FOGG ARRIVES at London's Reform Club in time to win his £20,000 wager with the surprised gentlemen of the club—he has traveled *Around the World in Eighty Days.*

IN DA CLUB
What clubs had these members on their rolls?

1. Tyler Durden, Robert Paulson, Angel Face
2. Duke Ellington, Lena Horne, Cab Calloway, Dorothy Dandridge
3. June Woo, An-mei Hsu, Lindo Jong, Ying-Ying St. Clair
4. Darlene Gillespie, Doreen Tracy, Cubby O'Brien, Bobby Burgess
5. Boy George, Mikey Craig, Roy Hay, Jon Moss
6. Pat Robertson, Terry Meeuwsen, Lee Webb
7. Ibrahim Ferrer, Compay Segundo, Pío Leyva, Rubén González
8. Kristy Thomas, Claudia Kishi, Mary Anne Spier, Stacey McGill
9. Eddie Murray, Harmon Killebrew, Willie Mays, Mel Ott
10. Claire Standish, Brian Johnson, John Bender, Andrew Clark, Allison Reynolds

---

• **1941** • ARCHIE ANDREWS AND PALS make their first appearance in Bob Montana's *Pep Comics* No. 22.

SHALL WE GATHER AT THE RIVER(DALE)?
Who played these title characters of TV comedies?

1. Archie Bunker
2. Reggie Potter
3. Betty Suarez
4. Veronica Chase

• **1998** • OWNER BUD ADAMS announces that, since his team's name no longer makes sense, the Tennessee Oilers will become the Tennessee Titans. If only the Utah Jazz and L.A. Lakers owners were so sensible.

GRIDIRONY
Gregg Easterbrook's "Tuesday Morning Quarterback" column is well known for the unusual nicknames he gives NFL teams. Which team does he call . . .

Easy	*Harder*	*Yeah, Good Luck*
1. The Marine Mammals	1. Blue Men Group	1. The Hyperboreans
2. Jersey/A and Jersey/B	2. The Flaming Thumbtacks	2. The Lucky Charms
3. Potomac Drainage Basin Indigenous Persons	3. Les Mouflons	3. CAUTION: MAY CONTAIN FOOTBALL-LIKE SUBSTANCE
4. Squared Sevens	4. The Boy Scouts	4. The Flying Elvii
5. The Nevermores	5. The Moo Cows	5. The Hypocycloids

Answers to the questions on this page can be found on page 528.

• **1823** • "A Visit from St. Nicholas," aka "The Night Before Christmas," debuts anonymously in the Troy, New York, *Sentinel*. It will be twenty years before the author, Bible professor Clement Moore, steps forward.

SANTA BABY
What does the poem compare each of these parts of Santa to?

1. His cheeks	**3.** His mouth	**5.** His pipe smoke
2. His nose	**4.** His beard	**6.** His belly

• **1888** • VINCENT VAN GOGH cuts off his left earlobe with a razor, wraps it in newspaper, and delivers it to a teenage prostitute of his acquaintance, with instructions to "keep this object carefully."

BEARD = WEIRD
Van Gogh isn't the only bewhiskered oddball in history.

1. What onetime *Sports Illustrated* cover boy, now living in exile in Iceland, sat next to Barbra Streisand in his high school Spanish class?

2. In what state was Ted Kaczynski's "Unabomber" cabin located?

3. What Russian was the most famous member of the Khlysty sect, which tried to overcome sin via self-flagellation and wild orgies?

4. What Rock Hudson movie did a reclusive Howard Hughes watch repeatedly?

5. In the trailer for what Mel Gibson–directed film does the outrageously bearded director make a one-frame subliminal cameo, grinning maniacally at the camera?

6. What nutty Bavarian "swan king" once banned both sneezing and coughing?

7. What author of absurdist plays like *Ubu Roi* practiced eccentric habits like eating all his meals backward, from dessert to appetizer?

8. Which ambidextrous U.S. president could write simultaneously in Greek with one hand and Latin with the other?

9. What French composer of the *Gymnopédies* liked to sprinkle his music with goofy performance directions such as "Light as an egg" or "Like a nightingale with a toothache"?

10. What unusual title did San Francisco's Joshua Norton grant himself in 1859?

• **1975** • CONGRESS PASSES THE Metric Conversion Act. Its well-meaning attempt at "metrication" won't last, but hey, it's not as if we're the *only* country still using drams and gills and furlongs. There's also Liberia. And, um, Burma.

A GAME OF INCHES
Metric? What is this, Russia? Convert these metric measurements back to good old-fashioned American *units!*

1. 4.8 Kilometer Island
2. 22.9 Centimeter Nails
3. 233°C
4. "3.52 Dekaliters and 8.8 Liters"

5. 37.8-liter hat
6. The whole 8.2 meters
7. *Four Hundred and Four Point Seven Hectares*
8. Just 4.18 Kilojoules!

9. "Fourteen and a Half Tonnes"
10. *111,191 Kilometers Under the Sea*

Answers to the questions on this page can be found on page 528.

DECEMBER 24

• **1777** • Captain James Cook discovers the Pacific island today called Kiritimati—the local spelling for "Christmas." Its proximity to the International Date Line makes it the first inhabited place in the word to experience the new year each January 1.

ISLAND-HOPPING
In what body of water would you find these islands?

Easy	Harder	Yeah, Good Luck
1. Aruba	1. Isle Royale	1. Ukerewe
2. Tonga	2. Mauritius	2. Gotland
3. Cyprus	3. Lesbos	3. Wizard Island
4. Guernsey	4. Tristan de Cunha	4. Krakatoa
5. Bahrain	5. The Isle of Man	5. Three Mile Island

• **1818** • The organ at Oberndorf, Austria's, Church of Saint Nicholas isn't working, so Father Joseph Mohr brings his organist, Franz Gruber, some lyrics he's been working on and asks Gruber to compose a guitar arrangement. Gruber spends the day working on the tune, finishing just in time for midnight Mass, when "Silent Night" makes its debut.

SHHHH!
An unusually quiet quiz for a silent night.

1. John Cage's famous piece *4′33″*, 273 seconds of utter silence, was first "performed" on what instrument?
2. During what war is *All Quiet on the Western Front* set?
3. Upon pain of death, Mafia members must maintain what Sicilian code of silence?
4. At the 1998 Oscars, who asked for a moment of silence for "1,500 men, women, and children" who had died in 1912, then grinned and yelled, "Now let's party till dawn!"?
5. What group's worship services include, between the "vocal ministry," long periods of "expectant waiting," in which the congregation sits in complete silence?
6. What's the last word spoken in both Jean-Luc Godard's film *Contempt* and David Lynch's *Mulholland Drive*?
7. Harpo Marx was a member of what literary circle, which also included Dorothy Parker and Robert Benchley?
8. On TV's *The Electric Company*, what superhero was "stronger than silent *E*"?
9. Plutarch claimed that it was Julius Caesar setting his own boats afire that led to what institution's destruction?
10. Three aliens in *Return of the Jedi* are named Klaatu, Barada, and Nikto, in a nod to what classic sci-fi film?

• **1966** • WPIX-TV in New York begins an annual tradition by airing "The Yule Log," a three-hour film loop of a roaring Christmas fireplace. The film was shot at Gracie Mansion, where sparks from the fire destroyed a $4,000 antique rug.

MY HEARTH WILL GO ON

1. What is emerging from a dining room fireplace in René Magritte's surrealist painting *Time Transfixed*?
2. After whom was the "circulating stove," invented in 1742, named?
3. Nineteen thirty-three's "On the Bank Crisis" was the first of what programs?
4. Until 1975, what daytime soap began with a roaring fireplace, suggesting its working title, *Between Heaven and Hell*?
5. What actor was arrested in 2007 for firing a pistol at his son Griffin, who was swinging a fireplace poker at him?

Answers to the questions on this page can be found on page 528.

• **1734** • THE FIRST PART OF Bach's *Christmas Oratorio* was first performed in Leipzig. Bach originally divided the piece into six cantatas, to be performed on six of the twelve days of Christmas.

ROCKIN' AROUND THE CHRISTMAS TREE
Who originally recorded these latter-day holiday favorites?

Easy	*Harder*	*Yeah, Good Luck*
1. "Feliz Navidad"	1. "Santa Baby"	1. "A Holly Jolly Christmas"
2. "The Christmas Song"	2. "Have Yourself a Merry Little Christmas"	2. "Merry Christmas Darling"
3. "The Hanukkah Song"	3. "Frosty the Snowman"	3. "Christmas (Baby Please Come Home)"
4. "Do They Know It's Christmas?"	4. "Mary's Boy Child"	4. "Jingle Bell Rock"
5. "All I Want for Christmas Is You"	5. "Silver Bells"	5. "It's the Most Wonderful Time of the Year"

• **1821** • CLARA BARTON, FOUNDER OF the American Red Cross, is born on Christmas Day in Massachusetts. In 1973, she'll be named a charter member of the National Women's Hall of Fame.

GIRL, YULE BE A WOMAN SOON

1. How old is the Grinch's nemesis, little Cindy-Lou Who?
2. What's the first human gift given in the song "The Twelve Days of Christmas"?
3. What woman from the Bible is the cousin of Mary, the mother of Jesus?
4. What was the first name of eight-year-old Miss O'Hanlon, who wrote a famous letter to *The New York Sun* in 1897?
5. Whose secret decoder pin does Ralphie send away for in *A Christmas Story*?

• **1914** • AN UNOFFICIAL TRUCE begins between the German and British troops on the western front of World War I, with carols and gifts exchanged across no-man's-land.

PEACE ON EARTH
Where would you find these True Meanings of Christmas™?

1. "Remember, no man is a failure who has friends."
2. "Maybe Christmas doesn't come from a store. Maybe Christmas . . . perhaps . . . means a little bit more."
3. "I will honour Christmas in my heart, and try to keep it all the year. I will live in the Past, the Present, and the Future."
4. "Glory to God in the highest, and on Earth, peace, goodwill towards men. That's what Christmas is all about."
5. "Of all who give and receive gifts, such as they are wisest. Everywhere they are wisest."

Answers to the questions on this page can be found on page 529.

DECEMBER 26

• **1865** • INVENTOR JAMES MASON patents the coffee percolator.

AVERAGE JOE

1. What Italian drink is made by dropping a dollop of foamed milk atop an espresso?

2. What 2004 video game could be sexed up by the infamous "Hot Coffee" mod?

3. After Stella Liebeck burned herself with hot coffee in 1992, a jury ruled that what company should pay her $2.9 million in damages?

4. What's the name of the coffee shop gathering place on TV's *Friends*?

5. In 1817, Reverend Samuel Ruggles planted the first coffee in what district of Hawaii's Big Island?

6. What TV show's Double R Diner served a "damn fine cup of coffee"?

7. What was the first species of coffee bean to be cultivated—in the Middle East, as its name suggests?

8. According to the ad jingle, what's "the best part of waking up"?

9. What's paired with coffee in the title of an Otis Redding song and a Jim Jarmusch movie?

10. Starbucks Coffee was named for the first mate in what novel?

• **1928** • JOHNNY WEISSMULLER RETIRES undefeated from amateur swimming, though he will go on to model swimwear as a BVD spokesman and a loincloth as the movies' Tarzan.

CHEST THE FACTS

1. Whose bare chest in 1934's *It Happened One Night* has been described as an economic disaster for the undershirt industry?

2. What 1987 children's book is frequently challenged in libraries because of the picture of the top-less woman at the upper right of the "On the Beach" pages?

3. What two words were written on performance artist Michael Portnoy's torso when he ripped off his shirt to join Bob Dylan onstage at the 1998 Grammys?

4. The Descamisados, or "Shirt-less Ones," were supporters of what world leader, president of his nation from 1946 to 1955?

5. Whose book title *It's Not About the Bra* refers to her famous 1999 shirt removal?

• **1966** • ACTIVIST RON KARENGA and his family and friends celebrate the first Kwanzaa, a seven-day holiday he has invented to remind American blacks of their African roots.

ROUTE OF AFRICA

1. What organization was headed by Albert Lutuli, the first African ever to win the Nobel Peace Prize?

2. What not-really-a-singer was the only Canadian member of USA for Africa?

3. What two African countries each border nine other nations, including each other?

4. What can be "Africanized" by the *Mellifera scutellata* species?

5. What 1973 movie's tagline was "The brother man in the mother-land!"

6. What second-highest mountain in Africa was Elizabeth II visiting in 1952 when she acceded to the throne?

7. In what modern-day nation is the city of Timbuktu?

8. What kind of African antelope was named for Scottish explorer Joseph Thomson?

9. As Disney fans might know, what's the Swahili word for "lion"?

10. In what African nation does Alex Haley's *Roots* begin?

Answers to the questions on this page can be found on page 529.

• **1900** • Carry Nation smashes up the saloon in Wichita's Carey Hotel, the first protest in her legendary campaign of "hatchetation."

EVE OF DESTRUCTION

1. Whose famous guitar-smashing habits began when he accidentally broke his guitar neck on the low ceiling of a London tavern in September 1964?
2. What was destroyed by the Babylonians in 586 B.C. and by the Romans in A.D. 70?
3. American student Michael Fay was caned in 1994 for vandalizing cars in what country?
4. What title object of a 1957 movie was built, and then blown up, by Colonel Nicholson?
5. What iconic object from American history broke in two when Theophilus Cotton tried to move it from the waterfront to the town square in 1774?

• **1945** • The World Bank and the International Monetary Fund are created by the signing of the Bretton Woods Agreement.

INTERNATIONAL MONETARY FUN

What countries use these currencies?

Easy	*Harder*	*Yeah, Good Luck*
1. Yen	**1.** Quetzal	**1.** Lek
2. Rand	**2.** Baht	**2.** Bolívar
3. Pound sterling	**3.** Real	**3.** Hryvnia
4. Yuan	**4.** Rupiah	**4.** Kwanza
5. Shekel	**5.** Balboa	**5.** Ngultrum

• **2006** • Liechtenstein gets a little bigger, as a new survey reveals that the tiny Alpine nation is half a square kilometer bigger than previously thought. Liechtenstein is, along with Uzbekistan, one of the world's only two doubly landlocked countries—landlocked countries that border only *other* landlocked countries.

NO-SEA-UMS

1. What landlocked country has nevertheless won two America's Cups?
2. Which U.S. state capital is "landlocked" in that it's not accessible by land—only by sea or air?
3. The creations of two of the world's newest countries—Eritrea and Montenegro—left two other nations landlocked. Name them.
4. What two landlocked nations are the world's least populated and least densely populated, respectively?
5. Which of the original thirteen American colonies was the only landlocked one?

Answers to the questions on this page can be found on page 529.

DECEMBER 28

• **1869** • WILLIAM SEMPLE RECEIVES the first patent for chewing gum.

ON THE BUBBLE

1. What kind of bubbles in the bloodstream can cause "the bends"?
2. What color is Mr. Bubble?
3. What kind of animal is Michael Jackson's beloved Bubbles?
4. What's the answer to the disputed Trivial Pursuit question in the *Seinfeld* episode "The Bubble Boy"?
5. In parts of New England and Wisconsin, what do residents call a "bubbler"?
6. Who are Bubbles, Blossom, and Buttercup?
7. What material's name is actually a registered trademark of the Sealed Air Corporation?
8. The first of whose famous bubble machines was improvised using a bread pan, a clock motor, and a fan?
9. What famous seventeenth-century economic bubble saw a prized "Semper Augustus" bulb being sold for 6,000 florins?
10. The Model 1015, or "Bubbler," from 1946, is still the most iconic design of what object?

• **1917** • H. L. MENCKEN publishes his famous hoax "A Neglected Anniversary," a fictional history of the bathtub. Many still believe Mencken's (made-up) claim that Americans were vehemently antibathtub until Millard Fillmore installed one in the White House in 1850.

SPLISH SPLASH

1. The Trevi Fountain in Rome was wrapped in black crepe in 1996 to mourn the death of what actor?
2. Who beat the USSR in the violent "Blood in the Water" Olympic water polo showdown of 1956?
3. According to Mikmaq Indian legend, what bay's powerful tides are the result of a giant whale splashing its tail?
4. Who likes to go swimming with his friends at Goo Lagoon?
5. Who named his Gemini capsule *Molly Brown*, in response to the 1961 sinking of his *Liberty Bell* capsule at splashdown?

• **1985** • EDDIE MURPHY'S RICK JAMES–produced single "Party All the Time," later judged by *Blender* magazine to be the eighth "Worst Song Ever," peaks at number two on the *Billboard* charts. Only the tyranny of Lionel Richie's "Say You, Say Me" in the top spot saves America from the ignominy of an Eddie Murphy number one.

TOWER OF DABBLE

Match these actors to their ill-conceived vanity bands. (Kidding, Russell—put the phone down . . .)

1. The Accelerators
2. Dogstar
3. The Honey Brothers
4. The Licks
5. The Ordinary Fear of God
6. Phantom Planet
7. Ringside
8. The Sharks
9. 30 Seconds to Mars
10. Wicked Wisdom

A. Russell Crowe
B. Balthazar Getty
C. Adrian Grenier
D. Jared Leto
E. Juliette Lewis
F. Jada Pinkett Smith
G. Dennis Quaid
H. Keanu Reeves
I. Jason Schwartzman
J. Bruce Willis

Answers to the questions on this page can be found on page 530.

• **1721** • MADAME DE POMPADOUR is born in Paris. She will grow up to become King Louis XV's favorite mistress despite—I can only assume—a namesake haircut that makes her look like Little Richard.

LEGENDS OF THE FOLLICLES

Match these famous names with their characteristic haircuts.

1. Jennifer Aniston	**A.** The beehive
2. Travis Bickle	**B.** The bob
3. Louise Brooks	**C.** The bouffant
4. Drew Carey	**D.** The bowl cut
5. George Clooney	**E.** The Caesar
6. Farrah Fawcett	**F.** Cornrows
7. Allen Iverson	**G.** The flattop
8. Rick James	**H.** The flip
9. Moe Howard	**I.** The Jewfro
10. Gabe Kaplan	**J.** The Jheri Curl
11. MacGyver	**K.** The mohawk
12. Kate Pierson	**L.** The mullet
13. Margaret Thatcher	**M.** The pageboy
14. Friar Tuck	**N.** The Rachel
15. Prince Valiant	**O.** Tonsure

• **1806** • PANTOMIME CLOWN JOSEPH GRIMALDI, the "father of modern clowning," makes his Covent Garden debut. Grimaldi is so innovative and celebrated a performer that clowns are called "joeys" for decades.

BOY, IS MY NOSE RED

1. For what musical did Stephen Sondheim write "Send in the Clowns"?

2. Clownfish can survive in coral reefs because they're immune to what predator?

3. What future weatherman was also, in 1963, TV's first Ronald McDonald?

4. What kind of clown is a "barrel man"?

5. What opera is mentioned in Smokey Robinson's "Tears of a Clown"?

6. What comedian made his directorial debut with *Shakes the Clown*?

7. What two Disney dogs were voiced by Pinto Colvig, the original Bozo the Clown?

8. What TV clown once boasted that he made $2.5 million a year from lithographs of his clown paintings?

9. What face-painted group are "Juggalos" devoted fans of?

10. What novel features Pennywise the Dancing Clown?

Answers to the questions on this page can be found on page 530.

DECEMBER 30

• **1853** • FOR $10 MILLION, the United States buys from Mexico what is now southern Arizona and New Mexico, in the Gadsden Purchase.

BUY ANY MEANS NECESSARY

1. The first newspaper William Randolph Hearst ever bought was what city's *Examiner*?
2. The Yankees bought Babe Ruth for $100,000 in 1919, but only after the Red Sox had turned down the White Sox's offer to trade what player for him?
3. In 1987, whose skeleton did Michael Jackson offer to buy for $1 million?
4. Why did an Internet casino spend $28,000 for a grilled cheese sandwich auctioned on eBay in 2004?
5. What did a Dallas clothing manufacturer sell to *Life* magazine for $150,000 in 1963?

• **1956** • A YOUNG BOLIVIAN MAN throws a rock at the *Mona Lisa*, damaging the lower right corner. As a result, the famous painting is placed behind bulletproof glass.

GRIN REAPERS
Trivia that will bring a smile to your face.

1. What country joined the world's nuclear powers by detonating "Smiling Buddha" in 1974?
2. Who can turn the world on with her smile?
3. What four-word slogan appeared below the ubiquitous yellow smiley face of the 1970s craze?
4. What actress had her smile insured with Lloyds of London for $10 million despite always wearing braces in her most famous role?
5. What did she say when "She Smiled Sweetly," according to the Rolling Stones?

• **1975** • THE MALAGASY REPUBLIC is renamed the Democratic Republic of Madagascar after a not-so-democratic military coup puts socialist president Didier Ratsiraka in office.

A CONSPIRACY OF CARTOGRAPHERS
What's the current name of the country that was once called . . .

Easy	*Harder*	*Yeah, Good Luck*
1. Siam	1. Upper Volta	1. Trucial States
2. Persia	2. British Honduras	2. Dahomey
3. Rhodesia	3. Bechuanaland	3. The Gilbert Islands
4. Ceylon	4. Dutch Guiana	4. Basutoland
5. Zaire	5. Kampuchea	5. New Hebrides

Answers to the questions on this page can be found on page 530.

• **1946** • BETTER LATE THAN NEVER! President Truman signs a document officially proclaiming "the cessation of hostilities of World War II."

AND IN THE END . . .

1. What recurring James Fenimore Cooper character is called "Hawkeye" in *The Last of the Mohicans*?

2. Until his 1997 retirement, who was the last NHLer to be playing without a helmet?

3. What movie's last line is "Mein führer, I can walk!"?

4. Despite his claim to have a "truly marvelous proof," what French mathematician's "Last Theorem" went unproven for 350 years?

5. Which character writes the final message "Good-bye" at the end of the last *M*A*S*H* episode?

6. Who was the last surviving member of the Warren Commission?

7. What musician played Pontius Pilate in *The Last Temptation of Christ*?

8. What showman's last words were "How were the receipts today in Madison Square Garden?"

9. What's the last letter of the Greek alphabet?

10. The "Juneteenth" holiday celebrates the last state to, in effect, abolish slavery. Which state?

11. What was the last major-league team to add lights for night games at its home field?

12. On January 27, 2006, what communications company sent its last message, having long since switched over to financial services?

13. Who was the last king of England to die in combat?

14. What John Wayne film is the last picture show in *The Last Picture Show*?

15. Who sang "One for My Baby" as Johnny Carson's last guest?

• **1982** • NBC CANCELS ITS daytime soap *The Doctors* after a twenty-year run, throwing a young Alec Baldwin out of work. (It's weird to see the phrase "Baldwin out of work" without the words "Billy" or "Stephen," huh?)

HAPPY TRAILS
Who made these TV sign-offs famous?

1. "Good night and good luck."

2. "Good night and may God bless."

3. "Go home!"

4. "Say good night, Gracie."

5. "And that's the way it is."

6. "Grease for peace."

7. "And so it goes."

8. "Good night, Mrs. Calabash, wherever you are."

9. "That's the news and I am outta here!"

10. "Courage!"

Answers to the questions on this page can be found on page 531.

December Answers

DECEMBER 1

BAD MEDICINE
1. D
2. B
3. J
4. E
5. I
6. G
7. A
8. C
9. F
10. H

FAR AND AWAY
1. Guam
2. Pluto
3. London
4. Captain Nemo
5. Robert Peary and Matthew Henson (to the North Pole)
6. Sydney and Los Angeles
7. The *Santa María*
8. South Africa
9. Perth
10. The moon

DECEMBER 2

A HASH OF BROWNS
1. Edmund
2. Topeka
3. *Angels and Demons*
4. "Say It Loud—I'm Black and I'm Proud"
5. *Iron Chef*
6. LaDainian Tomlinson
7. Sudden deafness
8. She was the first test-tube baby
9. Joe Shlabotnik
10. Leroy
11. "Well, nobody's perfect."
12. *Cosmopolitan*
13. Dan Quayle criticized his single mom, Murphy Brown
14. Flight attendant
15. Two missing fingers on his right hand ("Three Finger")

ALL WISHED UP
1. Canadian films
2. Boom box
3. ". . . Baby One More Time"
4. Solomon
5. Jonathan Frakes

DECEMBER 3

ZOOROPA
1. Goats
2. A monkey
3. A cat
4. A bear (suit)
5. An elephant
6. A horse
7. A sheep
8. A panther
9. A dog
10. A butterfly (tattoo)

LOVE THROUGH THE AGES
Easy
1. Paul McCartney
2. Humphrey Bogart
3. Demi Moore
4. Elizabeth Taylor
5. Catherine Zeta-Jones
Harder
1. Paul Simon
2. Jerry Seinfeld
3. Britt Ekland
4. Sophia Loren
5. Cary Grant
Yeah, Good Luck
1. Tony Randall
2. Anna Nicole Smith
3. Clint Eastwood
4. Rupert Murdoch
5. Céline Dion

TELL ME, BABY
1. E
2. I
3. F
4. J
5. G
6. C
7. H
8. D
9. B
10. A

December Answers

DECEMBER 4

BOTTOM TO TOP
1. A prized postage stamp (the airplane was printed upside down)
2. M. C. Escher
3. The Indian Ocean
4. *Royal Wedding*
5. *e*
6. Tears for Fears
7. Poland
8. Gilbert and Sullivan
9. Hewlett-Packard ("hp" upside down looks like "dy")
10. Peter

INTO THE WOODS
1. C
2. D
3. I
4. H
5. F
6. B
7. E
8. J
9. A
10. G

DECEMBER 5

BIZARRE QUIZ TRIANGLE
1. North Carolina's
2. *A Tale of Two Cities*
3. "Scalene"
4. Female pubic hair
5. Fenway Park
6. Ed Grimley
7. Opium
8. Delta
9. A fire
10. "Particle Man"
11. Phil Jackson
12. The Czech Republic
13. The Nazis forced homosexuals to wear one
14. The hypotenuse
15. Snooker

GIVE PEAS A CHANCE
1. Gregor Mendel's
2. *Once Upon a Mattress*
3. Cocoa Puffs
4. Cicero (from the Latin *ceci*, meaning chick peas)
5. Nine days

DECEMBER 6

LANDMARK DECISIONS
1. St. Louis's Gateway Arch
2. Agra
3. Shackles
4. The Leaning Tower of Pisa
5. The Space Needle
6. The Sydney Opera House
7. Stonehenge
8. Iraq (modern-day sites of the Seven Wonders of the Ancient World)
9. The Golden Gate Bridge
10. Basil

OH CAROL, I'M SO IN LOVE WITH YOU
1. The Czech Republic
2. After "Merry"
3. "Hark! The Herald Angels Sing"
4. Six (partridge, doves, hens, calling birds, geese, swans)
5. A hula hoop
6. "In Beverly Hills, L.A."
7. Parson Brown
8. "Jingle Bells" (by a harmonica-playing Wally Schirra aboard *Gemini 6*)
9. Mel Tormé
10. "Greensleeves"

DECEMBER 7

DOCTOR, MY EYES
1. Syria
2. Warren Tay (Tay-Sachs disease)
3. Esperanto
4. Arthur Conan Doyle
5. *Minority Report*

MESSAGE IN A BATTLE
Easy
1. John Paul Jones
2. David Farragut
3. Douglas MacArthur
Harder
1. William Tecumseh Sherman
2. George Dewey
3. Oliver Hazard Perry
Yeah, Good Luck
1. Anthony McAuliffe
2. James Lawrence
3. Charles E. Stanton

FOR INSTANTS
1. Polaroid
2. *Network*
3. Folgers Crystals
4. *The Shining* ("We all shine on")
5. Age/sex/location

DECEMBER 8

LATIN LOVERS
Easy
1. Rigor mortis
2. Et cetera
3. Non sequitur
4. Vox populi
5. Mea culpa
Harder
1. Quid pro quo
2. Caveat emptor
3. Tabula rasa
4. Persona non grata
5. Ad nauseam
Yeah, Good Luck
1. Post hoc ergo propter hoc
2. Sine qua non
3. Mirabile dictu
4. Magna cum laude
5. Sub poena

DOUBLE THREATS
1. Marie Curie
2. Jennifer Lopez (*J. Lo* and *The Wedding Planner*)
3. Deion Sanders
4. Theodore Roosevelt
5. Dick Button

SEE YOU IN COURT
Easy
1. Allen Iverson
2. Pete Maravich
3. Tracy McGrady
4. Julius Erving
5. Larry Bird
Harder
1. George Gervin
2. Charles Barkley
3. Wilt Chamberlain
4. Gary Payton
5. Kevin Garnett
Yeah, Good Luck
1. Stacey Augmon
2. Darrell Griffith
3. Marvin Webster
4. John Williams
5. Bill Mlkvy

DECEMBER 9

LET US PREY
1. A saber-toothed tiger, or smilodon
2. The mosquito
3. The shark (in *Jaws*)
4. The polar bear
5. The Cayman Islands

ALL KILLER, NO FILLER
1. Woody Guthrie
2. Don McLean
3. The New York Dolls
4. "Nebraska"
5. Eric Roberts

BEST IN THEIR FIELD
1. A
2. G
3. D
4. H
5. J
6. B
7. I
8. E
9. F
10. C

DECEMBER 10

AND OTHER REALLY BAD IDEAS
1. The Susan B. Anthony dollar
2. David Caruso (*NYPD Blue*)
3. The Aral Sea
4. The Bay of Pigs invasion
5. Speedo
6. Crystal Pepsi
7. André Maginot
8. Kudzu
9. DeLorean
10. Life on Earth—the natural biosphere
11. "If it doesn't fit, you must acquit."
12. The Chicago White Sox
13. The Soviet Union
14. Smell-O-Vision
15. Felicity Porter

TUTU FUNNY
1. Five
2. *The Turning Point*
3. Arabesque
4. *The Rite of Spring*
5. A swan ("The Dying Swan")

DECEMBER 11

PUSSY GALORE
1. *Cabaret*
2. Siamese
3. His bow tie
4. Terry Bradshaw
5. They're hypoallergenic
6. Cat
7. Toxoplasmosis
8. Puss-in-Boots
9. Its whiskers
10. His Bag of Tricks

GET READY TO MATCH THE STARS
1. H (Katey Sagal in *Married . . . with Children* and *8 Simple Rules*)
2. J (Michael Landon in *Bonanza* and *Little House on the Prairie*)
3. K (Kate Jackson in *Charlie's Angels* and *The Scarecrow and Mrs. King*)
4. M (Harry Morgan in *Dragnet* and *M*A*S*H*)
5. E (Michael J. Fox in *Family Ties* and *Spin City*)
6. B (David Caruso in *NYPD Blue* and *CSI: Miami*)
7. L (David McCallum in *The Man from U.N.C.L.E.* and *NCIS*)
8. F (Tyne Daly in *Cagney and Lacey* and *Judging Amy*)
9. A (Nicollette Sheridan in *Knots Landing* and *Desperate Housewives*)
10. G (Alyssa Milano in *Who's the Boss?* and *Charmed*)
11. D (Larry Hagman in *I Dream of Jeannie* and *Dallas*)
12. N (Mary Tyler Moore in *The Dick Van Dyke Show* and *The Mary Tyler Moore Show*)
13. I (Bill Cosby in *I Spy* and *The Cosby Show*)
14. O (Jennie Garth in *Beverly Hills 90210* and *What I Like About You*)
15. C (Ron Howard in *The Andy Griffith Show* and *Happy Days*)

DECEMBER 12

HOT FOR TEACHER
Easy
1. Law (contracts)
2. Music
3. Poetry
4. Phonetics
5. Dance
Harder
1. (U.S.) history
2. Math (A.P. Calculus)
3. English
4. Art (pottery)
5. Math
Yeah, Good Luck
1. Classics
2. Science
3. History
4. Chemistry
5. Biology

BOY BANDS
Easy
1. The Beastie Boys
2. Boyz II Men
3. The Beach Boys
4. The Backstreet Boys
Harder
1. Pet Shop Boys
2. Los Lonely Boys
3. The Geto Boys
4. The Oak Ridge Boys
Yeah, Good Luck
1. The Jerky Boys
2. The Dead Boys
3. The Fat Boys
4. The Waterboys

MOTEL SIX
1. The Lorraine Motel (where Dr. King was shot)
2. Black Flag
3. Taxidermy
4. "Alone Again Or"
5. Jimmy Swaggart
6. *Tape*

DECEMBER 13

A G THANG
Easy
1. "Livin' La Vida Loca"
2. "Fallin' "
3. "Livin' on a Prayer"
4. "Raindrops Keep Fallin' on My Head"
5. "Gettin' Jiggy Wit It"
Harder
1. "Travelin' Man"
2. "Papa Was a Rollin' Stone"
3. "Cracklin' Rosie"
4. "Feel Like Makin' Love"
5. "Hangin' Tough"
Yeah, Good Luck
1. "Tossin' and Turnin' "
2. "Lightnin' Strikes"
3. "Keep on Truckin' "
4. "You Haven't Done Nothin' "
5. "Lovin' You"

YOU SPIN ME RIGHT ROUND
1. (Whirling) dervishes
2. 36
3. Jean-Bernard-Léon Foucault
4. The Axis
5. *Swan Lake*
6. Her firstborn child
7. "English"
8. The earth
9. "Unchained Melody"
10. The Tasmanian devil
11. *All in the Family* (if you count *Archie Bunker's Place* and *704 Hauser*)
12. Axel
13. *Carousel*
14. Ecclesiastes
15. Tornadoes

DECEMBER 14

PASSING AWEIGH
1. E. W. Scripps
2. Casimir Pulaski
3. "Big Pussey" Bonpensiero
4. Sir Francis Drake
5. Dennis Wilson

BAD BLOOD
1. West Virginia–Kentucky
2. Women's figure skating at the Lillehammer Olympics (Nancy Kerrigan and Tonya Harding)
3. Aquafina
4. ("The Thrilla in") Manila
5. Blu-Ray
6. Alexander Hamilton versus Aaron Burr
7. The Iron Bowl
8. Tom Wolfe
9. Betty and Veronica
10. Sri Lanka

CONSUME MASS QUANTITIES!
Easy
1. *I Love Lucy*
2. *The Simpsons*
3. *Saturday Night Live*
Harder
1. *The Twilight Zone*
2. *Moonlighting*
3. *King of the Hill*
Yeah, Good Luck
1. *Arrested Development*
2. *The Andy Griffith Show*
3. *Seinfeld*

DECEMBER 15

IF YOU LEAF ME NOW
1. (Bay) laurel
2. Eucalyptus
3. Marijuana
4. Fig
5. Grape
6. Oak
7. Ivy
8. Tea
9. Acacia
10. Holly

ICY DEAD PEOPLE—ALL THE TIME!
1. Ted Williams's
2. Timothy Leary
3. *Sleeper*
4. *Futurama*'s
5. Mr. Bigglesworth

BOARD SILLY
1. The murder victim in Clue
2. Cranium
3. Short Line
4. Germany
5. "TWELVE"
6. Happy
7. (Settlers of) Catan
8. The knight
9. Plumpy
10. Milton Bradley

DECEMBER 16

WE'RE NUMBER TWO!

Easy
1. Belgium
2. Colombia
3. India
4. South Africa
5. Israel

Harder
1. Ecuador
2. Burma
3. Norway
4. Indonesia
5. Kenya

Yeah, Good Luck
1. Algeria
2. Croatia
3. Bulgaria
4. Bolivia
5. Uzbekistan

TAG! YOU'RE IT

1. *Monsters, Inc.*
2. *The Graduate*
3. *Bride of Frankenstein*
4. *This Is Spinal Tap*
5. *Repo Man*
6. *Pinocchio*
7. *The Ring*
8. *Willy Wonka and the Chocolate Factory*
9. *Jurassic Park*
10. *The Blues Brothers*
11. *Ninotchka*
12. *Deliverance*
13. *American Graffiti*
14. *Cat People*
15. *Psycho*
16. *Jaws 2*
17. *Rebel Without a Cause*
18. *The Good, the Bad, and the Ugly*
19. *Chicken Run*
20. *Bonnie and Clyde*
21. *A Clockwork Orange*
22. *The Usual Suspects*
23. *Sabrina*
24. *The Birth of a Nation*
25. *American Beauty*

DECEMBER 17

I HEAR A SYMPHONY

1. Gustav Mahler
2. Ludwig van Beethoven
3. Joseph Haydn
4. Peter Ilyich Tchaikovsky
5. Felix Mendelssohn

CHIC-ER BY THE DOZEN

1. A
2. H
3. C
4. D
5. I
6. J
7. B
8. G
9. E
10. F

FLUTE-Y FLAKES

1. Jethro Tull
2. Francis Ford Coppola's
3. The Queen of the Night
4. Ron Burgundy
5. Pan (the panpipes)

DECEMBER 18

UNEARTHED

1. Apatosaurus
2. The Tomb of the Unknowns at Arlington
3. Troy
4. Four palm trees
5. Zachary Taylor

NO REST FOR THE QUERY

1. The two types of chili sauce
2. Guess?
3. Joseph McCarthy
4. "What would Jesus do?"
5. During the Passover seder
6. "Should I Stay or Should I Go?"
7. Cary Grant
8. *Who Wants to Be a Millionaire*
9. "What, me worry?"
10. The Scarlet Pimpernel

TALKING HEADS

1. Eleanor Clift (married to Montgomery Clift's brother)
2. James Carville
3. Ann Coulter
4. Al Franken
5. Tucker Carlson

DECEMBER 19

I AM NOT A NUMBER!
1. Jean Valjean
2. Nelson Mandela
3. The Beagle Boys
4. *The Count of Monte Cristo*'s
5. Number Six
6. Rudolf Hess
7. (*One Day in the Life of*) Ivan Denisovich
8. *A Clockwork Orange*
9. Harold Perrineau
10. *Trading Places* or *The Couch Trip*

A QUIZ ABOUT NOTHING
1. "Freedom"
2. Albert Michelson and Edward Morley
3. Millard Fillmore
4. Two
5. Jean-Paul Sartre
6. Zero Mostel's
7. Sting
8. Fudge (Hatcher)
9. A shut-out
10. "Black Friday," the day after Thanksgiving
11. *Die Hard*
12. "Nirvana"
13. Prince
14. ø
15. J. P. Morgan

DECEMBER 20

GIVE THAT MAN A CIGAR
1. *Nighthawks* (Edward Hopper)
2. Bill Cosby
3. Citation
4. Marcel Proust
5. Montecristo

A FACE FOR RADIO
1. The "Fifth Beatle"
2. Howard Stern
3. Above average
4. New Jersey
5. Rutgers
6. *American Graffiti*
7. Jim Everett (Chris Evert)
8. Rush Limbaugh's
9. Walter Winchell
10. Philip Glass (Ira Glass's cousin)

THE CAPITAL GANG
Easy
1. Honolulu
2. Denver
3. Boston
Harder
1. Phoenix
2. Atlanta
3. Columbus
Yeah, Good Luck
1. Hartford
2. Indianapolis
3. Sacramento

DECEMBER 21

THE BEAST IN ME
Easy
1. Pig
2. Dog
3. Dragon
4. Rabbit
Harder
1. Dragon
2. Monkey
3. Horse
4. Monkey
Yeah, Good Luck
1. Tiger (Detroit Tigers)
2. Rat (*King Rat*)
3. Dog (*My Life as a Dog*)
4. Tiger (Tony the Tiger)

THE GRAND "FINALLY"
1. *The Cherry Orchard*
2. Twenty yards
3. Neil Young
4. A Treaty of Paris
5. *2001: A Space Odyssey*
6. William Howard Taft
7. L.B. ("Leonard Bernstein, Leonid Brezhnev, Lenny Bruce, and Lester Bangs")
8. *Jesus Christ Superstar*'s
9. Cornwall
10. *Final Fantasy*
11. A neuron (or nerve cell)
12. The Restaurant at the End of the Universe
13. *The Fugitive*'s
14. Chicago and Los Angeles
15. Ted Williams

DECEMBER 22	DECEMBER 23	DECEMBER 24

IN DA CLUB
1. Fight Club
2. The Cotton Club
3. The Joy Luck Club
4. The Mickey Mouse Club
5. Culture Club
6. The 700 Club
7. The Buena Vista Social Club
8. The Baby-Sitters Club
9. The 500 Home Run Club
10. The Breakfast Club

SHALL WE GATHER AT THE RIVER(DALE)?
1. Carroll O'Connor
2. Richard Mulligan
3. America Ferrera
4. Kirstie Alley

GRIDIRONY
Easy
1. Miami Dolphins
2. New York Giants and Jets
3. Washington Redskins
4. San Francisco 49ers
5. Baltimore Ravens
Harder
1. Seattle Seahawks
2. Tennessee Titans
3. St. Louis Rams
4. New Orleans Saints
5. Houston Texans
Yeah, Good Luck
1. Minnesota Vikings
2. Indianapolis Colts
3. Arizona Cardinals
4. New England Patriots
5. Pittsburgh Steelers

SANTA BABY
1. Roses
2. A cherry
3. A bow
4. The snow
5. A wreath
6. A bowlful of jelly

BEARD = WEIRD
1. Bobby Fischer
2. Montana
3. Rasputin
4. *Ice Station Zebra*
5. *Apocalypto*
6. (Mad King) Ludwig II
7. Alfred Jarry
8. James Garfield
9. Erik Satie
10. Emperor of the United States

A GAME OF INCHES
1. Three Mile Island
2. Nine Inch Nails
3. *Fahrenheit 451*
4. "A Bushel and a Peck" (*Guys and Dolls*)
5. Ten-gallon hat
6. The whole nine yards
7. *A Thousand Acres*
8. Just one calorie!
9. "Sixteen Tons"
10. *Twenty Thousand Leagues Under the Sea*

ISLAND-HOPPING
Easy
1. The Caribbean Sea
2. The Pacific Ocean
3. The Mediterranean Sea
4. The English Channel
5. The Persian Gulf
Harder
1. Lake Superior
2. The Indian Ocean
3. The Aegean Sea
4. The Atlantic Ocean
5. The Irish Sea
Yeah, Good Luck
1. Lake Victoria
2. The Baltic Sea
3. Crater Lake
4. The Sunda Strait
5. The Susquehanna River

SHHHH!
1. The piano
2. World War I
3. *Omertà*
4. James Cameron
5. The Quakers'
6. *"Silencio"*
7. The Algonquin Round Table
8. Letterman
9. The library at Alexandria's
10. *The Day the Earth Stood Still*

MY HEARTH WILL GO ON
1. A steam locomotive
2. Benjamin Franklin
3. FDR's "Fireside Chats"
4. *One Life to Live*
5. Ryan O'Neal

December Answers

DECEMBER 25

**ROCKIN' AROUND THE CHRIST-
MAS TREE**
Easy
1. José Feliciano
2. Nat King Cole
3. Adam Sandler
4. Band Aid
5. Mariah Carey
Harder
1. Eartha Kitt
2. Judy Garland
3. Gene Autry
4. Harry Belafonte
5. Bing Crosby
Yeah, Good Luck
1. The Quinto Sisters
2. The Carpenters
3. Darlene Love
4. Bobby Helms
5. Andy Williams

GIRL, YULE BE A WOMAN SOON
1. "Not more than two"
2. Eight maids a-milking
3. Elizabeth
4. Virginia ("Yes, Virginia, there
is a Santa Claus.")
5. Little Orphan Annie's

PEACE ON EARTH
1. *It's a Wonderful Life*
2. *How the Grinch Stole
Christmas*
3. *A Christmas Carol*
4. *A Charlie Brown Christmas*
5. "The Gift of the Magi"

DECEMBER 26

AVERAGE JOE
1. A macchiato
2. *Grand Theft Auto: San Andreas*
3. McDonald's
4. Central Perk
5. Kona
6. *Twin Peaks*
7. Arabica
8. "Folgers in your cup"
9. Cigarettes
10. *Moby-Dick*

CHEST THE FACTS
1. Clark Gable's
2. *Where's Waldo?*
3. "Soy Bomb"
4. Juan Perón
5. Brandi Chastain's

ROUTE OF AFRICA
1. The African National Congress
2. Dan Aykroyd
3. Sudan and the Democratic Republic of the Congo
4. Honeybees
5. *Shaft in Africa*'s
6. Mount Kenya
7. Mali
8. A gazelle
9. "Simba"
10. The Gambia

DECEMBER 27

EVE OF DESTRUCTION
1. Pete Townshend's
2. The temple in Jerusalem
3. Singapore
4. The bridge on the river Kwai
5. Plymouth Rock

**INTERNATIONAL
MONETARY FUN**
Easy
1. Japan
2. South Africa
3. Great Britain
4. China
5. Israel
Harder
1. Guatemala
2. Thailand
3. Brazil
4. Indonesia
5. Panama
Yeah, Good Luck
1. Albania
2. Venezuela
3. Ukraine
4. Angola
5. Bhutan

NO-SEA-UMS
1. Switzerland
2. Juneau
3. Ethiopia and Serbia
4. Vatican City and Mongolia
5. Pennsylvania (which had a
short Great Lakes border but no
Atlantic coast)

DECEMBER 28

ON THE BUBBLE
1. Nitrogen
2. Pink
3. A chimpanzee
4. The Moops (or Moors)
5. A drinking fountain
6. The Powerpuff Girls
7. Bubble Wrap
8. Lawrence Welk's
9. Tulip mania
10. The jukebox

SPLISH SPLASH
1. Marcello Mastroianni (who splashed there in *La Dolce Vita*)
2. Hungary
3. The Bay of Fundy
4. SpongeBob SquarePants
5. Gus Grissom

TOWER OF DABBLE
1. J
2. H
3. C
4. E
5. A
6. I
7. B
8. G
9. D
10. F

DECEMBER 29

LEGENDS OF THE FOLLICLES
1. N
2. K
3. B
4. G
5. E
6. H
7. F
8. J
9. D
10. I
11. L
12. A
13. C
14. O
15. M

BOY, IS MY NOSE RED
1. *A Little Night Music*
2. Sea anemones
3. Willard Scott
4. A rodeo clown
5. *Pagliacci*
6. Bobcat Goldthwait
7. Goofy and Pluto
8. Red Skelton
9. Insane Clown Posse
10. *It*

DECEMBER 30

BUY ANY MEANS NECESSARY
1. San Francisco
2. "Shoeless Joe" Jackson
3. The Elephant Man's
4. It had the Virgin Mary's face on it
5. The Zapruder film (of the Kennedy assassination)

GRIN REAPERS
1. India
2. You, girl, and you should know it (Mary Richards)
3. Have a nice day!
4. America Ferrera
5. "Don't worry"

A CONSPIRACY OF CARTOGRAPHERS
Easy
1. Thailand
2. Iran
3. Zimbabwe
4. Sri Lanka
5. The Democratic Republic of the Congo
Harder
1. Burkina Faso
2. Belize
3. Botswana
4. Suriname
5. Cambodia
Yeah, Good Luck
1. The United Arab Emirates
2. Benin
3. Kiribati
4. Lesotho
5. Vanuatu

DECEMBER 31

AND IN THE END . . .

1. Natty Bumppo
2. Craig MacTavish
3. *Dr. Strangelove or: How I Learned to Stop Worrying and Love the Bomb*
4. Pierre de Fermat's
5. B. J. Hunnicutt
6. Gerald Ford
7. David Bowie
8. P. T. Barnum
9. Omega
10. Texas
11. The Chicago Cubs
12. Western Union
13. Richard III
14. *Red River*
15. Bette Midler

HAPPY TRAILS

1. Edward R. Murrow
2. Red Skelton
3. Tracey Ullman
4. George Burns
5. Walter Cronkite
6. Jon "Bowzer" Bauman (of Sha Na Na)
7. Linda Ellerbee
8. Jimmy Durante
9. Dennis Miller
10. Dan Rather

Acknowledgments

The big *Ken Jennings* above the title of this book is a big lie. Sure, it helps sales within the coveted People Who Watched *Jeopardy!* Back in 2004 demographic, but getting a book this size together is a collaborative affair. I had a lot of help.

The trivia gods of my childhood—Fred L. Worth, the staff of *Games* magazine, and especially the *Jeopardy!* writers—inspired it.

My agent, Jud Laghi—one of the best-looking straight men in publishing—sold it.

Bruce Tracy, ably assisted by Ryan Doherty, edited it.

Simon Sullivan designed it.

Eight thousand Tuesday Trivia subscribers on Ken-Jennings.com unknowingly play-tested parts of it.

Some of the best trivia players and writers I know—Cannon Alsobrook, Steve Butler, Joshua Davey, Raj Dhuwalia, Ray Hamel, Robert Jen, Mitchell Kaufman, Ed Toutant, and Brad and Eric Williams—helped review and fact-check it.

Aileen Lau of StimulEye designed the "Electric Boogaloo" font for it.

My family—Mindy, Dylan, and Caitlin—put up with it.

You bought it.

So, really, the cover should more accurately say *Ken Jennings's and Fred L. Worth's and* Games *magazine's and* Jeopardy!*'s and Jud Laghi's and Bruce Tracy's and Ryan Doherty's and Simon Sullivan's and Tuesday Trivia's and Cannon Alsobrook's and Steve Butler's and Joshua Davey's and Raj Dhuwalia's and Ray Hamel's and Robert Jen's and Mitchell Kaufman's and Ed Toutant's and Brad and Eric Williams's and Aileen Lau's and Mindy, Dylan, and Caitlin's and Your Trivia Almanac.*

Please take a *very* fine-tip marker and edit your cover accordingly. Unless it's a library book.

KEN JENNINGS
Seattle, August 2007

About the Author

Ken Jennings spent much of his childhood in Seoul, South Korea. A graduate of Brigham Young University, he worked as a computer programmer until becoming an unlikely celebrity due to his unprecedented record-breaking streak on the television quiz show *Jeopardy!* He lives outside Seattle with his wife and two children. For more information, visit www.ken-jennings.com.